A HISTORY OF
THE UNITED STATES

THE MACMILLAN COMPANY
NEW YORK · BOSTON · CHICAGO
DALLAS · SAN FRANCISCO

MACMILLAN & CO., Limited
LONDON · BOMBAY · CALCUTTA
MELBOURNE

THE MACMILLAN CO. OF CANADA, Ltd.
TORONTO

A HISTORY

OF

THE UNITED STATES

BY

EDWARD CHANNING

VOLUME III

THE AMERICAN REVOLUTION

1761–1789

New York

THE MACMILLAN COMPANY

1927

16669

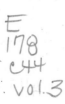

Norwood Press
J. S. Cushing Co. — Berwick & Smith Co.
Norwood, Mass., U.S.A.

CONTENTS

MAPS

A HISTORY OF THE UNITED STATES

CHAPTER I

THE BEGINNINGS OF AN ERA, 1760–1763

"Government is a conditional compact between king and people. . . . A violation of the covenant by either party discharges the other from its obligation." "An Act [of Parliament] against the Constitution is void." In these thirty words Patrick Henry and James Otis denied the divine origin of the British kingship and the legislative supremacy of the British Parliament, and substituted therefor the Common Law and the eternal rights of man. Moreover, these phrases shadow forth the reason for the secession of the old English North American colonies from the British Empire and the principles which underlie our own system of government to this day. There was nothing new or strange in them. They had been held in England for centuries, but no one, since the days of Cromwell and his Ironsides, had thought of applying them to the settlement of ordinary everyday affairs of political life.

Commercialism, the desire for advantage and profit in trade and industry, was at the bottom of the struggle between England and America; the immutable principles of human association were brought forward to justify colonial resistance to British selfishness. The governing classes of the old country wished to exploit the American colonists for their own use and behoof; the Americans desired to work their lands and carry on their trade for themselves. Acts of Parliament restraining colonial navigation and taxing the colonists of the continent for the benefit of the West Indian sugar planters had been on the statute book for years. The Northerners had observed whatever of them they liked and had attended little to the rest, except now and then to bribe an inquisitive governor or an overcurious customs collector. In 1760 William Pitt, finding that the continental colonists were trading with the French and Spanish Islands in the West Indies, cast about for the best means to put a stop to this traffic with the enemy. His advisers told him that if the Sugar Act of 1733 [1] were enforced, this trade must come to an end. This was true because this law provided a prohibitive duty of sixpence per gallon on all molasses brought into the northern colonies, except that which came from British plantations. To enforce the act would deprive the French and Spanish planters of the means of paying for the lumber, fish, and flour which they needed for their slaves and for themselves. Thereupon, Pitt ordered the provisions of the act to be enforced to the letter.

The Sugar Act had never been executed for two reasons. In the first place, as soon as it was passed the British sugar planters discovered that what they really wanted was the right to export sugar directly from the islands to continental Europe. Obtaining this favor, they no longer needed the northern American market. In the second place, in the existing conditions of trade, an adequate supply of molasses for distillation into rum was absolutely necessary for the prosperity of New England

---

[1] George II, Cap. 13 (Ruffhead's *Statutes at Large*, vi, 11C). For the passage of this act and some account of it see the present work, ii, 515–521.

and the Middle Colonies. Rum was the currency used in the African trade and in the fur trade, and enormous quantities of it were consumed at home and in other English colonies. Not one quarter enough molasses was produced in the English islands to satisfy the needs of the northern distillers — they must have foreign molasses or go out of business. In the absence of any efficient customs service it was not difficult to evade this law or any other. A false clearance might be obtained at Anguilla, or some other British island, or collectors, governors, and judges might be bribed by the payment of a small percentage of the duty that should have been levied under the act. Even when the officials wished to collect the duty, they found it very difficult to do so where the whole population was against them. Ordinary search warrants were of little use because these were issued only upon information and applied only to certain specified goods in specified places. A writ of assistance was more efficacious because it enabled the holder to search any house or ship, to break down doors, open trunks and boxes, and seize goods at will. In case of opposition, he might call upon the civil authorities for aid. These general writs had been used in England for a long time,[1] and a few of them had been issued in the colonies. The announcement that the Sugar Act was to be enforced caused more alarm at Boston than the taking of Fort William Henry had, three years earlier. There was doubt as to the legality of the existing writs, and the death of the old king put an end to whatever virtue there was in them. The collectors applied for new writs, and the merchants determined to oppose their being granted.

---

[1] On March 26, 1621, we find that "Mr. *Alford* . . . desireth, that there may be a Consideration, that Writs of Assistance be not so frequently granted to Sheriffs." *Proceedings and Debates of the House of Commons, In 1620 and 1621,* p. 225.

It happened that in Massachusetts, the year 1760 saw an extensive change in the higher offices. There was a new governor, Francis Bernard, an English gentleman of third-rate abilities, whom the pressure of a large and grow- ing family sent to the colonies. A predecessor, Governor Shirley, had promised Colonel Otis the chief justiceship whenever it became vacant; but now, on the death of Chief Justice Sewall, Bernard gave the office to Thomas Hutchinson. He was a man of fortune, of considerable abilities, a native of the colony of an old family; but he was a merchant, not a lawyer, and had gained unpopularity by striving for honest money.[1] Under these circumstances, the appearance of Colonel Otis's son, James Otis, Jr., in opposition to the granting of the writs aroused remark. Hutchinson felt sure that it was due to pique and to a wish to cast further odium upon himself.

The king's advocate, Jeremiah Gridley, set forth the law applicable to the question in issue (February, 1761). This was simply whether the Superior Court of Massa- chusetts was entitled to exercise the functions of the Court of Exchequer in England. To the latter, Parliament had given the right to grant writs of assistance. It made no difference whether these writs were compatible with the rights of the subject, said Gridley, — that was for Parlia- ment to judge. Parliament having so determined, it was not for subjects to resist. From a technical, legal point of view, there was little to be said in reply. What little there was to say was well said by Oxenbridge Thacher. It was then Otis's turn. Abandoning all attempt to

---

[1] J. K. Hosmer, in his *Life of Thomas Hutchinson* (Boston, 1896), has endeav- ored to do justice to an unpopular man; but the best way to gain an insight into Hutchinson's character and to appreciate his good qualities and his shortcomings is to read a couple of hundred pages in his *Diary and Letters*, acrimoniously edited by P. O. Hutchinson (Boston, 1884- 86).

argue the question of law, he applied himself to the rights of the colonists as men and as Englishmen.[1] Thacher and Otis made so great an impression on the popular mind that Hutchinson hesitated to act. He referred the question to England, and the law authorities there, deciding that the colonial court had the power to grant the writs, Hutchinson ordered them to be issued.[2] From that time until the outbreak of the war, they were regularly used[3] in Massachusetts, and in other colonies as well.

As a plentiful supply of cheap molasses made for prosperity in New England, so the production and sale of tobacco was the key to the economic existence of Virginia. Corn and wheat, lumber and fruit were produced there and exported to the West Indies; but tobacco was the staple of the Old Dominion[4] and, in a lesser degree, of her neighbors. The marketing of this crop had fallen into the hands of merchants of London, Bristol, and Glasgow.

---

[1] Our knowledge of what Otis said on this occasion is derived entirely from the rough notes taken by John Adams, *Works of John Adams*, ii, 125; Quincy's *Massachusetts Reports*, 469; and *American History Leaflets*, No. 33. Adams's notes formed the basis of the first printed account of the speech that was published in the *Massachusetts Spy* for April 29, 1773; in G. R. Minot's *History of Massachusetts Bay*, ii, 89; and with corrections by Adams fifty years after the event in William Tudor's *Life of James Otis*, chs. v–vii. For bibliographical details, see Dr. S. A. Green's article in Massachusetts Historical Society's *Proceedings*, Second Series, vi, 190.

[2] "The Writs of Assistance prayed for, though contrary to the spirit of the English constitution, could hardly be refused by a Provincial Court, before general warrants had been condemned in England, and before the Revolution had actually begun in America." Horace Gray in the Appendix to Josiah Quincy's *Reports of Cases . . . in the Superior Court of Massachusetts Bay between 1761 and 1772* (Boston, 1865), p. 540. Mr. Gray was later chief justice of Massachusetts and later still one of the justices of the Supreme Court of the United States.

[3] Several instances are noted in the present volume (pp. 93, 95 n.). No writs were issued in Rhode Island or Connecticut, for there the judges were controlled by public opinion. In Georgia the three assistant judges outvoted Chief Justice Anthony Stokes, much to that gentleman's dismay. See *A Narrative of the Official Conduct of Anthony Stokes* (London, 1784), pp. 3–6; see also Essex Institute's *Collections*, ii, 169.

[4] Exports of Virginia for six months in 1763: 22,384 hhds. tobacco valued at £223,840; pitch, turpentine, wheat, corn, pork, beef, bread, flour, lumber, shingles, iron valued at £44,804. Governor Fauquier to the Lords of Trade, "Sparks Manuscripts," No. 43, vol. iv, 67.

These also bought goods of every description and sent them to their American correspondents. The whole business was carried on on credit, the planters usually being in debt to their agents. Naturally, every act of the Virginia Assembly was closely scanned in Britain to make sure that the planters had passed nothing to favor themselves at the expense of their agents. As one means of checking such legislation, the governors of Virginia and the other royal provinces were strictly charged to give their assent to no act whatever, unless it contained a clause suspending its operation until the royal will were ascertained.[1] As tobacco was the medium of exchange between Virginia and Britain, so it was the money of account in the colony. There all the utilities of life from the cradle to the grave were estimated in pounds of tobacco. Every minister of the Established Church was entitled in each year to receive seventeen thousand two hundred and eighty pounds of tobacco, whether his parish were large or small, his fame and abilities great or little, or tobacco high or low in price, — and it varied from one penny to sixpence per

[1] The royal veto was rigorously used to enforce this policy, even as to private acts; as, for example, one authorizing the executors of Governor Spotswood to pay the debts of the deceased. Nearly every law for ameliorating the condition of debtors in Virginia was repealed in England, although it had previously received the governor's consent. Possibly the most glaring example of the misuse of the royal veto in this period had to do with the neighboring colony of North Carolina; a law of that colony giving Presbyterian ministers the right to perform the marriage ceremony was disallowed in England, because it would deprive the clergy of the Established Church of their fees, although there were not then half a dozen such clergymen in the whole colony. Another law, also of North Carolina, was repealed on the ground that it would lead to emigration from England to the prejudice of the landed interests and the manufacturers. Sometimes important laws were overlooked in England. In 1774 Governor Martin requested definite action on a law that had been passed in 1754 but had never been confirmed or annulled. For this and other matter relating to the exercise of the royal veto, see " Board of Trade Journals " (Ms.): lxviii, 125, 156; lxxvi, 148; lxxviii, 194, 218; lxxxi, 46; "Colonial Office Papers," v, 1369, Virginia, pp. 367, 369; *Colonial Records of North Carolina*, vi, 1036; ix, 7, 249, 251, 991. This subject is well treated by O. M. Dickerson in ch. v of his *American Colonial Government* (Cleveland, 1912).

pound.[1] In 1755 a partial failure of the crop in a few
counties induced the Assembly to give the people of those
counties the right to redeem their tobacco debts in money
at the rate of twopence for each pound of tobacco. A
probable failure of the crop throughout the province in 1758
led to the passage of another Two Penny Act.[2] This time,
the privilege of redemption was extended to the whole province and to all debts, fees, and salaries. The operation of
the act was limited to one year. The governor assented to
it although it had no suspending clause, so urgent seemed
the need. Many of the burgesses who voted for the
measure were themselves creditors and were heavy losers
by the law; but the ministers, whose entire income was derived from tobacco, suffered more severely than any other
class in the community. When tobacco had been low in
price, they had received no more of it, and now that their
seventeen thousand pounds of tobacco would sell for about
four hundred pounds of Virginia money, they felt that
they were entitled to receive it, instead of the one hundred
and forty-four pounds that they would get under the Two
Penny Act.[3] The ministers appealed to the crown. The

[1] Commissary Blair informed the
Lords of Trade, in 1697, that he had
recently sold "tithe tobacco" at ten
shillings per hundredweight, and that
sometimes it had fallen as low as five
shillings, or from one and two-tenths to
six-tenths of a penny per pound. The
inference from this is that the assembly
intended to provide a lower scale of
compensation for the clergy than has
usually been stated. "Board of Trade
Journals" (Ms.), August 25, 1697. See
also *Virginia Magazine of History*, x, 347.

[2] Hening's *Statutes of Virginia*, vi,
568.

[3] Their case is graphically set forth
in the brief which John Camm, rector of
Yorkhampton parish, presented to the
Judicial Committee of the Privy Council.

He says: "The injustice of it [act of
1758] is at first sight so glaring that it
needs no comment; what can be more
cruel upon the Clergy, or substantially
unjust, than to leave it in the Election
of the Debtor to pay in Tobacco or Money
at his Pleasure? If the Tobacco was
not worth 16^s 8^d per 100 Pounds, the
clergy were to take their Dues in
Tobacco; if, as in the present year, it
was $2£$ 10^s per 100 Pounds, they were to
take 16^s 8^d." "Hardwick Papers"
(transcripts) in Library of Congress.
The Virginia side of the case was stated
in a letter from the Committee of Correspondence to the agent in London, dated
December 12, 1759. *Virginia Magazine of
History*, x, 347.

law was disallowed, but the governor was not informed of it until the summer of 1760.

Meantime, the vestries had taken advantage of the law to commute their tobacco payments into money. Then, when the transaction was apparently closed, came the announcement that the act had been annulled. Deciding that the law had been void from the outset, the colonial judges declared the clergymen were legally entitled to every ounce of their tobacco, or to the full value in money. The vestrymen were indignant. It seemed to them that the parsons " wanted an Opportunity of feasting as largely as they could on all, both rich and poor."[1] They determined to fight, and so did the ministers. Suit after suit was brought. One of them rose into supreme importance, because it furnished the occasion for the entrance of Patrick Henry into political life. This remarkable man belonged to a respectable Virginia family of the middle group. He had received a good education as the times went, and was now, although still young, earning his living at the law. James Maury, the settled clergyman of Fredericksville, was one of those to appeal to the courts to enforce his claim. The fact that Patrick Henry's father was the presiding justice of the county court may have influenced the vestry in employing the son, when the case seemed to be going against them.[2] The law was so plainly on Maury's side that Patrick Henry said very

---

[1] *Virginia Magazine of History*, x, 352.

[2] The fullest account of the Parson's Cause is in William Wirt Henry's *Patrick Henry, Life, Correspondence, and Speeches* (New York, 1891), vol. i, pp. 30–46. The only original source of Henry's speech in the Maury trial is Maury's own account of it in a letter to the Rev. John Camm, written on December 12, 1763, ten days after the trial, Ann Maury's

Memoirs of a Huguenot Family (New York, 1872), pp. 418–423. The act of 1758 is in Hening's *Statutes of Virginia*, vii, 240. William Wirt's *Life of Patrick Henry* is now hopelessly out of date; but Moses Coit Tyler's *Patrick Henry*, in " American Statesmen " series, although written before the publication of Henry's *Henry*, is still a stimulating and useful book.

little as to that. He went at once to the basis of government, and so excited the prejudices of the jurymen that instead of awarding the parson several hundred pounds, they
gave him only one penny.[1]

In Otis and Henry we see two Americans representing
two very different types of colonial life, looking upon their
countrymen as entitled to the inalienable rights of men and
Englishmen.[2] Otis based his denial of the supremacy of
the British Parliament upon Sir Edward Coke's declaration
that the Common Law in many cases controlled acts of
Parliament; for when a law is against common right and
reason, it may be adjudged null and void. In later printed
papers, Otis reiterated and amplified his early statements.[3] According to him, men are naturally equal.
Government is founded upon the necessities of our natures;
it is originally in the people, who can never absolutely
renounce their divine right; it is a trust to be administered
for the good of the whole — if the trustee is unfaithful,
he must be opposed. Henry followed in a similar train
of thought: government is a conditional compact; the
violation of the agreement by either party discharges the
other from its obligation. The disallowance of the Two

---

[1] The clergymen's compensations were arranged on a permanent basis in 1769 by an act of the General Assembly which was not disallowed in England. Accord-ing to this law, all county and parish levies were to be made in money at the rate of twopence per pound of tobacco — to be paid in either tobacco or money. Hening's *Statutes of Virginia*, viii, 381–385.

[2] In South Carolina, also, Christopher Gadsden claimed for the colonists the full rights of British subjects. *South Carolina Gazette*, June 29, 1763.

[3] In his *Vindication of the Conduct of the House of Representatives of the Province of the Massachusetts Bay* (Boston, 1762), James Otis sets forth his ideas as follows: (1) God made all men naturally equal; (2) Ideas of earthly superiority are educational, not innate; (3) Kings were made for the good of the people, and not the people for them; (4) No government has a right to make slaves of the subjects; (5) Though most governments are, *de facto*, arbitrary, and consequently the curse and scandal of human nature, yet none are, *de jure*, arbitrary. Tudor's *Life of James Otis*, p. 125. See also a more detailed discus-sion in Otis's *Rights of the British Colonies Asserted and proved* (Boston, 1765).

Penny Act was so gross an instance of misrule that the people of Virginia must provide for their own safety.

The conception of government resting upon the consent of the governed takes one back to the feudal centuries, and the thought of a fundamental law overriding legislative enactments is found in the theoretical writings of the Stuart time. Thomas Edwards, in his "Gangræna,"[1] which was published in 1646, credits the Puritan sectaries with asserting that by "naturall birth all men are equally and alike born to like propriety, liberty, and freedom." And, again, that notwithstanding whatever agreements may have been made in times past, men of the present age ought to be absolutely free from what their forefathers yielded unto and be "estated in their natural and just liberties agreeable to right reason." Following these earlier writers, John Locke, in the second of his "Two Treatises of Government," set forth the glittering generalities that became the political gospel of the American revolutionists.[2] To him and to them, men in a state of nature were essentially good, and government was

---

[1] Thomas Edwards's *The Third Part of Gangræna, or, A new and higher Discovery of the Errors, . . . of the Sectaries* (London, 1646), pp. 16, 17.

[2] John Locke's writings dealing with the principles of government are his *Two Treatises of Government, Essay concerning the Humane Understanding,* and *Letters Concerning Toleration.* These were all published at the epoch of the Revolution of 1688–1689. The first treatise of government is an analysis of Sir Robert Filmer's *Patriarcha;* the second treatise is declaratory of the true theory of the state. This treatise should be read thoroughly by every student of American history and politics; a convenient summary is in William A. Dunning's *Political Theories from Luther to Montesquieu,* ch. x. Dean

Tucker calls attention to "the evil Consequences arising from the Propagation of Mr. Locke's democratical Principles" (*Four Letters on Important National Subjects,* p. 89). On the other hand, the author of *Plain English. A Letter to the King* (October, 1775), p. 12, asserts that "The love of liberty is a principle implanted in all animals; a principle inextinguishable. Nations and individuals, and even the lowest of the brute creation, are herein alike."

Not only Otis and the other leaders of the American Revolution were greatly indebted to Locke for his clear statement of political theory, but Rousseau, whose *Contrat Social* was published in Amsterdam in 1762, also drew largely from the same source, as may be seen from a comparison of their writings.

formed to protect men in their right to life, liberty, and property. Men, being "by Nature, all free, equal and independent," agree among themselves to form a community for their peaceable living. Government being for the good of the whole, whenever the governor acts contrary to the general good, the original compact is broken, and the government itself is dissolved. True it is, says Locke, that many wrong and inconvenient acts will be borne without a murmur; "but if a long train of Abuses, Prevarications and Artifices, all tending the same way, make the design [of tyranny] visible to the People . . . 'tis not to be wonder'd that they should then rouze themselves, and endeavour to put the rule into such hands which may secure to them the ends for which Government was at first erected."[1] American statesmen, Otis, Henry, Gadsden, the Adamses, Dickinson, Jefferson, George Mason, and the rest combined these ideas with the practical knowledge which they had gained in their political careers and enunciated a theory that was incompatible with the ideas of empire as they were then held by Englishmen. These found their highest expression in the "Commentaries" of William Blackstone. He tells us that, however just Locke's theories may be, they cannot possibly apply to the existing government, for "if the parliament will positively enact a thing to be done which is unreasonable, I know of no power that can control it"; and again, "what the parliament doth, no authority upon earth can undo."[2]

[1] Locke's *Two Treatises of Government* (London, 1698), p. 341, Bk. ii, § 225.

[2] William Blackstone's *Commentaries on the Laws of England* (Oxford, 1768), i, 91, 161. On a preceding page (160) he says: "It [Parliament] hath sovereign and uncontrollable authority in the making, confirming, enlarging, restraining, abrogating, repealing, reviving, and expounding of laws, concerning matters of all possible denominations, ecclesiastical, or temporal, civil, maritime, or criminal." Brinton Coxe in his *Judicial Power* (p. 165) says: "Since

Technically speaking, all the subjects of the British crown lived under one government, the Parliament of Great Britain being the supreme governor. Actually, administrative ideas prevailing in England and in America were different. In the mother country, the system of responsible government was thoroughly established, — successive ministries representing the party, or the combination of factions, that was momentarily supreme in the House of Commons. In America the idea of a separation of powers had become firmly fixed, — there was nothing approaching the cabinet system in any colony. In England the House of Commons was elected by a system that had been archaic and illogical for centuries, accidents and the memories of the oldest inhabitants taking the place of known published laws. In America the assemblies were chosen according to general regulations and, in a measure, represented all portions of the community. At the first glance, government in England by king, Lords, and Commons seems to be similar to government in America by the governor, the council, which was composed of leading inhabitants, and the representative assembly. In reality the two systems had little in common, and colonial recognition of the supremacy of the British Parliament as an imperial legislature had already passed into the realm of impossibilities.

In other ways, the North American colonists had drifted far apart from the dwellers in Britain. The Americans were no longer, for the most part, of English stock. The great influx of Germans had introduced new

the Revolution of 1688 an English court would never think of holding an Act of Parliament to be void because it conflicted with the royal prerogative.''

For a masterly treatment of parliamentary supremacy, see Charles H. McIlwain's *The High Court of Parliament and its Supremacy*, especially chs. iv and v. Abundant references to the sources and to secondary works will be found in the footnotes to this volume.

and aggressive elements, and the descendants of French Huguenots were numerous. Moreover, the early English stock itself had lost many of the characteristics which one associates with the Anglo-Saxon. The presence of negroes, slave and free, had also wrought changes in the attitude of the white race toward the laboring classes in many colonies. Industrially, too, America and England were rapidly diverging. The former was still an agricultural country, while England was even then halting on the threshold of that great industrial revolution which accompanied the establishment of the factory system. In religion, too, the outlook was unlike. Since the time of the Great Awakening, there had been a constant loosening of religious bonds, until a goodly number of colonists had ceased attending any religious services whatever. The Church of England was established by law in nearly half the colonies, and was making a vigorous effort to gain a foothold in the rest. At every turn, the churchmen invited the royal government to advance their interests or to protect them from attack. The more zealous among them desired the appointment of an American bishop, and the fear of having such an establishment forced upon them turned many a man away from his natural loyalty to the Britisn crown.[1] Political discussion was fast replacing religious controversy. The newspapers of Charleston, Philadelphia, New York, and New England teemed with essays attacking Church and State. To us they seem dull and unattractive, but there was a demand for them at the time, or editors and publishers would not have given them so great a space. It is, however, in the

[1] The thesis that "ecclesiasticism" was a potent cause in bringing about disunion is stated by Mellen Chamber-lain in his *John Adams, the Statesman of the American Revolution,* 17-45.

spread of elementary education throughout the American continent and the confinement of culture to the governing classes in England that one sees the greatest possibilities of estrangement.

Lord George Germain, whose name will be frequently met with in this volume, declared it absurd for "men of a mercantile cast [to be] every day collecting themselves together, and debating about political matters" in meetings in Boston and elsewhere in the colonies, — they would better be about their businesses, buying and selling. Many people in England had already come to think that the colonists were no longer "an assemblage of needy vagrants";[1] but there was a general concensus of opinion that the king could have no subjects who were not under the control of the Parliament. Indeed, the colonists were commonly regarded in the mother country as "subjects of Great Britain"; the interests of the latter were all-important. The colonists, on the other hand, were ambitious for power and place. They wished to enjoy the consideration and emoluments that belonged to positions which were habitually given to British placemen.[2] They already had a large measure of self-government and were determined not to part with one jot or tittle of it. At the close of the French and Indian War there were no more loyal subjects than the Americans; but they felt their own importance and strength. They resented the constantly reiterated assertions of despotic power on the part of

---

[1] Alexander Elmsley, a keen-witted Englishman, in a letter to Samuel Johnston of North Carolina, stated the matter very clearly. "Most think," he said, " the K as king can have no subjects that are not under the control of the Parliament of Great Britain. But . . . . 19 in 20 of all sensible people think that as the colonists are no longer an assemblage of needy vagrants . . . the Ministry ought either to give up taxing the colonists or to admit a reasonable number to Parliament." Even so liberal a minded man as Adam Smith likened the colonial assemblies to parish vestries. *Wealth of Nations* (second edition), ii, 229

[2] McCrady's *South Carolina in the Revolution*, ii, 796.

unreformed parliamentarians and an unreformable king. They dreaded the ever tightening grasp of the custom-house upon their trade and their means of livelihood. They felt that the government was careless of their rights and unfriendly to their further growth toward the west.[1]

The Iroquois and the Indians may be roughly divided into two classes, those under British influence and those favorable to the French. The conquest of New France brought the French tribes within the sweep of British policy, — greatly to their disgust and dismay. For years Sir William Johnson had been superintendent of Indian affairs in New York. He had ably cared for the natives, and, had it been possible to place the sole management of all Indian affairs in his hands at this critical moment, all might have gone well. As matters stood, it was the soldiers and not the civilians that had control beyond the borders.

Jeffrey Amherst, the English commander-in-chief, was a general of proved ability. At the moment, he was actuated by military necessity, by the need of economy, and by a professional soldier's contempt of savages. Amherst thought it absurd to bribe the natives to keep quiet. He cut off their annual presents, stopped their supply of powder and lead, and directed that no rum should pass the outposts into their country. The dangers of this policy were pointed out to him by those who were familiar with the needs and feelings of the natives; but he seems never to have asked himself how the Indians were to live without their regular supply of ammunition and goods. To him they were "pernicious vermin" and an "execrable race," who might well be hunted with dogs or put out of

---

[1] See on this point the *Report of the Lords of Trade* in 1772 on the Walpole grant, calling attention to the principle of confining the western settlements to within reach of British commerce, which had been adopted by the Board and confirmed by the king.

the way by presents of blankets innoculated with the smallpox.[1] Deprived of their means of hunting and of defending themselves, and seeing English outposts replacing those of the French, a general unrest came over them, which spread even to the Iroquois. Ignorant of the completeness of British successes, French traders and settlers fanned the flame of Indian discontent and assured the natives that the English occupation was only temporary. Pontiac, a sachem of the Pottawattamies, and an exceedingly able aboriginal ruler, placed himself at the head of a movement to throw off the English yoke.

On May 7, 1763, sixty Indians, with Pontiac at their head, came to the fort at Detroit and asked for a conference with Major Gladwin, the British commander of that post. Outwardly their demeanor was peaceful, but under their garments they carried sawed-off muskets with the intention of killing the British officers when Pontiac should give the signal.[2] Gladwin had been forewarned, and the Indians found the garrison under arms. The signal was not given, and the natives retired. For the next six months, the Indians blockaded Detroit, but at no time laid siege to the fort. Elsewhere they were more successful,[3] and captured and massacred all the other garrisons west of Niagara.

---

[1] See Note II at end of Chapter.

[2] In studying the Indian troubles of 1763, reliance has been placed on the "Pontiac Manuscript" (Michigan Pioneer and Historical Society's *Collections*, viii, 266); the "Gladwin Manuscripts," edited by Charles Moore (*ibid.*, xxvii, 605); and a "Diary of the Siege of Detroit" which was apparently written by one of the beleaguered officers and forms, with other documents, No. iv of Munsell's *Historical Series*. See also Charles Moore's *The Northwest under Three Flags*.

[3] Following is a chronology of the Indian troubles: 1760, November 29, the English take possession of Detroit; 1763, February 10, Peace of Paris ; May, attempted treachery at Detroit, capture of Sandusky, capture of Fort St. Joseph, Indian traders in the Ohio country murdered ; June, capture of Michilli-mackinac, Report of Board of Trade as to Indian policy, capture of Presque Isle, LeBœuf captured, Venango captured; July, Fort Pitt attacked; August 5, 6, battle of Bushy Run; September 14, massacre of Devil's Hole; October 7, proclamation issued; October 12, Indians besieging Detroit ask for peace

Even in September, a party of them drew a portion of the garrison of that post into ambush at Devil's Hole and killed many of them. As long as Detroit held out, Indian success was only partial. In the first months of the blockade, the French inhabitants of the neighborhood kept on living in their houses. They supplied the Indians with food and also gave information to the English. Throughout the whole time, Gladwin was able to communicate with Niagara and to bring ammunition, supplies, and reën-forcements from that place. Only one disaster was experienced by the defenders and this was due to a night sally that was made by Gladwin's subordinate or colleague, Captain Dalzell, against the wishes of the commander. By September, the English were strong enough to establish posts at some distance from the fort, and thus to enjoy a greater measure of security. The greatest blow to the Indian cause came in the shape of a letter from the French commander in the Illinois country, stating that the French and English were no longer at war and refusing to aid the enemies of the latter. On October 12 Pontiac asked for terms, but was told that arrangements must be made with General Amherst.[1] In the following spring Sir William Johnson came to Detroit and arranged all matters with the northwestern tribes.

---

[1] Major Gladwin wrote to Amherst as to the result of the campaign, the Indians " have lost between eighty and ninety of their best warriors, but if your Excellency still intends to punish them further for their barbarities, it may be easily done, without any expense to the Crown, by permitting a free sale of rum, which will destroy them more effectually than fire and sword, but on the contrary, if you intend to accomodate matters in Spring, which I hope you will for the above reasons, it may be necessary to send up Sir William Johnson." Owing, doubtless, to his inability to read manuscripts with his own eyes, Parkman omitted to print the latter part of this sentence after the words " fire and sword," — and thereby gave an incomplete impression of Gladwin's intentions. See the " Gladwin Manuscripts " in Michigan Pioneer and Historical Society's *Collections*, xxvii, 676; Parkman's *Pontiac* (ninth edition), i, 109 note; and Charles Moore's *The Northwest under Three Flags*, 137.

c

A spirit of restlessness also ran through the Indian tribes of the Ohio Valley. They murdered one hundred English traders and more, captured Forts LeBœuf and Venango, gathered about Fort Pitt, and even threatened Fort Ligonier in what is now central Pennsylvania. The garrison of LeBœuf retreated safely to Fort Pitt, and the security of Ligonier was assured by the arrival of a small force of soldiers which Colonel Henry Bouquet had dispatched for that purpose. This enterprising officer was a Swiss by birth, and at the moment was in command of the Royal American regiment, one of the battalions of which had recently come to Pennsylvania from the West Indies to restore the health of the soldiers and fill the depleted ranks with recruits. Gathering whatever forces he could, Bouquet, with necessary supplies, set out for the succor of Fort Pitt. He marched with all possible care, but was nevertheless attacked with great suddenness by an Indian war party at a most inconvenient spot, where it was utterly impossible to procure water. This was on August 5, 1763. Throughout the afternoon of that day and again the next morning the conflict continued, the Indians surrounding the whites at a distance of about five hundred yards. The soldiers were now frantic with thirst and disposed to break ranks and make for the water, no matter at what cost. Bouquet then had recourse to a desperate stratagem. Retiring a part of his men, he stationed them behind the bags of provision that were intended for the beleaguered garrison. The Indians, thinking that the whites were retreating, rushed forward to massacre them, but were met by a murderous fire from either side as well as in front. Staggered by this unexpected blow, they made off at full speed, leaving the weary and thirsting soldiers free to make their way to Bushy Run, which was not far from

the scene of conflict.[1]   There were isolated murders after
this, and a formidable expedition had to be made into
the Ohio country, but Bushy Run and Gladwin's defense
of Detroit were the turning points in this widespread
Indian uprising.

The capitulation of Montreal, 1760, had surrendered to
the British New France and its dependencies, but had not
included the Illinois country. This region, with all of the
French possessions east of the Mississippi and of the River
Iberville, were handed over to the British by the treaty
which was signed at Paris on February 10, 1763. As a
part of the same great settlement Spain relinquished to
England all of her domains in North America. France,
to recompense Spain for this loss, turned over to his Most
Catholic Majesty all that part of Louisiana which lay
westward of the Mississippi and the River Iberville. In
this way, the French withdrew from the North American
continent, and England and Spain became the undisputed
possessors of great territories that were as yet scarcely
touched by the pioneer. The acquisition of New France
and Florida necessitated new arrangements as to colonial
government in America, and the uneasiness of the tribes in
the interior demanded the formulation of a new Indian
policy. These matters were taken up by the home government at an early date, but sudden and numerous
changes in the higher offices, incidental to the royal on-
slaught on the Whig supremacy, put off the settlement of

---

[1] On the battle of Bushy Run, or
more properly of Edgehill, see two
letters from Bouquet to Amherst, dated
on the field of battle, in Michigan Pioneer
Society's *Collections*, xix, 219–222 (also
printed in Parkman's *Conspiracy of
Pontiac*, Appendix D). See also Penn-
sylvania-German Society's *Proceedings*,
xv, ch. xxxiii; [William Smith's] *An
Historical Account of the Expedition . . .
under the command of Henry Bouquet*,
Philadelphia, 1766; reprinted at Cincinnati, 1868; *Canadian Archives*, 1889,
Archivist's Report, Note D and Calendar
of Bouquet Collection.

these questions as it did that of many others. At length in June, 1763, the Lords of Trade made a report which be-came the basis of the proclamation that was issued in the following October.[1]

The Proclamation of 1763 provided for the government of three new provinces, and also contained regulations for administering Indian affairs in the immediate future. The three new provinces were Quebec, East Florida, and West Florida. Their boundaries were confined within modest limits that in no way trenched upon the old thirteen colonies. The forty-fifth parallel, which had been given as the northern limit of New England in the charter of 1620 and had later been agreed to as the boundary between New York and New France, was used as the southern boundary of Quebec from the St. Lawrence to the Connecticut. Eastwardly, from the Connecticut it followed the height of land that separated the rivers which empty themselves into the St. Lawrence from those that fall into the sea. Northwestwardly, from the St. Lawrence the province of Quebec was terminated by a straight line that ran from the point where the forty-fifth parallel crossed the river to Lake Nipissing, thus giving Quebec a definite western boundary. The northern limit of the Floridas was the thirty-first parallel from the Mississippi

---

[1] Clarence W. Alvord of the University of Illinois read a paper on the "Genesis of the Proclamation of 1763" before the Michigan Pioneer and Historical Society on December 13, 1907. This, with the papers printed by Shortt and Doughty with the title of "Documents Relating to the Constitutional History of Canada" in the *Report on Canadian Archives for 1906*, p. 119, state the essential facts. The Proclamation was printed at the time in the *Annual Register*, vi, 208, and has been reprinted in the *Canadian Archives*, and with Professor Alvord's article, and also in *American History Leaflets*, No. 5. On the later history of the Indian reservations, see Alvord's "Treaty of Fort Stanwix" in the State Historical Society of Wisconsin's *Proceedings* for 1908, and Max Farrand's article on "The Indian Boundary Line" in the *American Historical Review*, x, 782. A map of the British Dominions as fixed by the Treaty and Proclamation of 1763 is in the *Annual Register*.

to the Chattahoochee. Eastwardly from that river, or
rather from its continuation, the Appalachicola, a straight
line from the mouth of the Flint to the source of the St.
Mary's marked the northern limit of East Florida. The
land between the St. Mary's and the Altamaha, the old
southern boundary of Georgia, was added to that province.
It was soon found that the boundaries of West Florida
were too restricted and the northern limit was pushed
upward to the confluence of the Yazoo and the Mississippi,
or to 32° 30' of northerly latitude.

As to the government of the three new provinces on the
mainland, they were to be of the ordinary type of royal
provinces as soon as circumstances should permit the summoning of assemblies. Until that time, the governors
were to exercise complete powers, but the inhabitants
were to enjoy the benefit of " the laws of our realm of
England." It was the evident intention of Lord Shelburne, or whoever framed this proclamation, that the
inhabitants of the new governments should have the same
privileges that were enjoyed by the people of the older
settlements. It proved to be impossible to summon assemblies in them, because for years Frenchmen and Spaniards remained much more numerous than the English
settlers.

The regulation of the Indian trade was taken over by
the imperial government. In the future every trader
must give security for the observance of whatever rules
might be made. No governor of any of the three new provinces could grant any lands beyond the boundaries of his
government, and " for the present, and until our further
pleasure be known," no governor of the older colonies
could grant any land " beyond the Heads or Sources of
any of the Rivers which fall into the Atlantic Ocean from

the West and North West,[1] or upon any Lands whatever, which, not having been ceded to or purchased by Us as aforesaid, are reserved to the said Indians, or any of them." No one could purchase any of the reserved lands or settle on them without first obtaining permission, and those who had already inadvertently done so must remove forthwith.   The intention was to reserve to the Indians, for the time being, the lands lying within the rectangle between the Floridas on the south, the Hudson Bay Company's territories on the north, the Alleghanies and the Mississippi.   The fact that the reserved territory for the most part lay within the chartered limits of the older colonies does not seem to have occurred to those who drew up this proclamation.   Neither do they appear to have counted upon the alertness and pertinacity of the western pioneers.   The plan, although it was not expressed in the Proclamation, was to secure cessions from the Indians from time to time, and thus open to settlement one tract after another, without the danger of arousing the natives.   Within the limits of the colonies, omitting the reserved tract, lands might be granted to officers and soldiers who had served in the late war, who were actually residing in America and should personally apply for grants.   It was doubtless the expectation that many of those who were displaced or " reformed " by the reduction of the army might be thus cared for, — to the relief of the royal treasury.

Officers and soldiers who had served in America returned home with their minds filled with visions of the prosperity that they had seen and the easy successes to be won in the New World.   Many of them came back to

---

[1] The *Annual Register* for 1763 (vol.   north west."
vi, p. 211) prints this phrase " west or

the colonies. Among them were Horatio Gates and Charles Lee, who settled in the Valley of Virginia, Arthur St. Clair, who obtained land in Pennsylvania, and Richard Montgomery, who took up his abode in New York and married the sister of Robert R. Livingston. Others came to America in these years who were not veterans of the recent conflict. Among them were some of the greatest figures of Revolutionary annals, Alexander Hamilton, James Wilson, and John Paul Jones. Migration from the older parts of the colonies to the newer settlements redoubled in vigor and soon began to take a distinctly westward direction, — more than one thousand emigrant wagons passing through Salisbury, North Carolina, in the year 1765.[1]

The greed of Englishmen for wild lands and for lands already partly adapted to the uses of civilization was not confined to military men or to those who actually emigrated. Noblemen and speculators were constantly applying to the royal government for western lands and for valuable tracts east of the Alleghanies.[2] One of these, Lord Rochford, fixed his eyes on islands in Delaware Bay which he alleged were not included in any of the earlier charters. Lord Holland and his associates asked for lands in New York that had been claimed by the Van Rensellaers for generations. A syndicate of Englishmen and Americans applied for an enormous tract which lies

---

[1] This is Governor Tryon's estimate (*Colonial Records of North Carolina*, vii, 248).

[2] The manuscript journals of the Lords of Trade (vols. lxx–lxxxi) contain much information as to these applications for grants, and the last three of these volumes have many entries concerning the proposed "Walpole Patent." For the names of the associates in this business, I am indebted to Mr. Worthington C. Ford, who placed at my disposal many manuscripts and transcripts which he and his brother, Paul Leicester Ford, collected years ago. Details of the Walpole scheme and of other western enterprises are given with bibliography in George H. Alden's "New Governments West of the Alleghanies before 1780" in *Bulletin of the University of Wisconsin*, Historical Series, ii, No. 1.

partly in West Virginia and partly in eastern Kentucky. There they proposed to establish a new colony, Vandalia, with a government separate from that of Virginia. Among the Americans interested in this venture were Benjamin Franklin and Joseph Galloway, of Philadelphia, and Sir William Johnson, the Indian superintendent. The English promoter of the enterprise was Thomas Walpole, a man of influence in political and financial circles. Interested with him were some of the best known men in the kingdom, Earl Temple, Lord Camden, and Thomas Pitt; and the two secretaries of the Lords of the Treasury, John Robinson and Grey Cooper, — the former being the expertest wire-puller of the day. Had not the troubles in America interrupted this project, the establishment of a new series of colonies westward of the Alleghany water parting might well have been begun. It was fortunate that slight success attended any of these western ventures before the separation from England and the establishment of republican governments in the older colonies on the seaboard because the political and commercial interests of the westerners were necessarily often unlike those of the Atlantic colonies. In all these ways the years 1760-1763 were epochal, for in them may be discovered the beginnings of the movement which was to make the next ten years so memorable.

NOTES

I. General Bibliographical Note. — The material, in print and manuscript, relating to the Revolutionary period is vast in extent and still unsatisfying. In the Record Office, in the British Museum, in the Royal Institution, and in countless muniment rooms and boxes in private houses and corporations in England are masses of manuscripts, while the storehouses in American libraries and public depositories are even greater in extent. Much of this material has been printed, but more of it has not seen the book form. It is impossible for any man within the scope of a single lifetime to master even a tithe of this material, and yet, some of the most important papers are still almost inaccessible. In the footnotes to the present volume, references will be found to many unprinted papers; but the author has read many others, which have afforded each its little bit of information. The printed collections, from the incompleted *American Archives* [1] associated with the name of Peter Force, to the innumerable volumes of letters, diaries, and journals, each contributing its portion of illustrative matter, are almost beyond enumeration. Citations to such of these only as were useful in clearing up particular points are given in the footnotes to the following pages, but in the notes at the end of the chapters enumerations of the more important of them are appended. Volumes VI and VII of Winsor's *Narrative and Critical History* contain a minute bibliography of nearly all known material up to the year 1886, when it was printed, but great quantities of matter have been brought to light since that time, and no revision of that work has yet been attempted. The narrative portions of this part of the book are more uneven than were those of the earlier volumes. Moreover, in dealing with the causes and course of the Revolution, slight attention was paid to the industrial side of the problem. This is the prevailing defect of all works on this period.

Among the printed works bearing on the general theme, the third

---

[1] [Peter Force compiler], *American Archives: Fourth Series, containing A Documentary History of the English Colonies in North America from the King's Message to Parliament, of March 7, 1774, to the Declaration of Independence* (6 vols.) and *American Archives: Fifth Series, containing A Documentary History of the United States of America, from the Declaration of Independence, July 4, 1776* (3 vols. to end of 1776; the intention was to go to the Treaty of Peace, 1783; but the set was never completed).

and fourth volumes of W. E. H. Lecky's *History of England in the Eighteenth Century*[1] and Sir George Otto Trevelyan's *American Revolution*[2] stand preëminent for their point of view, their general fairness toward America, and the historical insight of their authors; but both are unfair to the men who mismanaged British affairs in that epoch in requiring of them the standards of our day and not of their own time. George Bancroft's volumes[3] are so clouded by the author's democratic prejudices that one hesitates to accept his judgments. He did a vast amount of work in collecting manuscripts and correlating them; but oftentimes seemed unable to understand the lessons which they should have taught. John Fiske's charmingly written volumes on the American Revolution have done much to popularize the subject, as have the two volumes of Henry Cabot Lodge. Of the smaller and more recent books, Professor C. H. Van Tyne's *American Revolution,* in Albert Bushnell Hart's *American Nation* series, and Sydney George Fisher's *Struggle for American Independence* are especially noteworthy. The latter, indeed, notwithstanding the language in which the author sometimes clothes his thought and also numerous slips in details is certainly a remarkable book. Mary A. M. Marks's work[4] contains the results of a study of otherwise unused material, but her knowledge of American conditions and books is limited. The works dealing with the strictly military side and with the formation of the Constitution will be taken up on later pages.

The yearly volumes of the *Annual Register, or a View of the History, Politics, and Literature for the Year,* contain, among other things a "Chronicle" and a collection of "State Papers." The former, during the period of the American Revolution, was compiled by Edmund Burke. It forms one of the best histories of that movement, and was the basis of many later works — often without acknowledgment.[5]

---

[1] Eight volumes; reprinted in America with a different pagination. The chapters relating to America have been published in a single volume, under the editorship of Professor Woodburn.

[2] G. O. Trevelyan's *American Revolution* (Part i, 1766-76; Part ii, 2 vols.). Two other volumes entitled *George the Third and Charles Fox, the Concluding Part of the American Revolution* will complete this work. Of these vol. i was published in 1912.

[3] George Bancroft's *History of the United States from the Discovery of the American Continent* (vols. v to x cover the years 1763-82).

[4] *England and America, 1763 to 1783* (2 vols., London, 1907).

[5] See Orin G. Libby in American Historical Association's *Reports,* 1899, i, 365-388, and *Some Pseudo-Histories of the American Revolution;* it is greatly to be hoped that Dr. Libby will publish his study of the *Annual Register* itself.

The London publisher, John Almon, himself compiled, or had col
lected for him, many useful works. Among them are the *Collection
of Interesting, Authentic Papers relative to the Dispute between Great
Britain and America, 1764–1775* (London, 1777), that is always referred to as the " Prior Documents " from the running headline ;
Biographical Anecdotes; [1] the *Remembrancer;* [2] the *Parliamentary
Register;* [3] and innumerable tracts.[4] It is also interesting to follow
the course of the disputations and campaigns in the *Gentleman's
Magazine,*[5] the *Political Magazine,*[6] or best of all in the charming and
wildly prejudiced letters and journals of Horace Walpole, the lord of
Strawberry Hill.[7]

An excellent collection of speeches, and " neglected pieces " of one
kind or another was compiled by Hezekiah Niles and published at
Baltimore in 1822 (reprinted, 1876) under the title of *Principles and
Acts of the Revolution in America.*

II. Amherst's Indian Policy. — See memorandum signed " J. A." to
Croghan's letter of April 30, 1763, from Fort Pitt : —

" You will do well to try to inoculate the Indians by means of
blankets, as well as to try every other method that can serve to ex-
tirpate this execrable race. I should be very glad your scheme for
hunting them down by dogs could take effect." The date of this
memorandum is uncertain ; it may have been made in 1764. A post-
script in a letter of Bouquet to Amherst, dated Carlisle, July 13,
1763, appears to be in answer to a suggestion made by Amherst in an
earlier note : " I will try to inoculate the —— with some blankets
that may fall into their hands, would like to use the Spanish method

---

[1] *Biographical, Literary, and Political Anecdotes of several of the Most
Eminent Persons* . . . . *with an Appendix* (London, 1797, 3 vols., the last
one forming the Appendix).

[2] *The Remembrancer; or Impartial
Repository of Public Events* (17 vols.,
London, 1775–83).

[3] *Parliamentary Register; or, History of the Proceedings and Debates of
the House of Commons,* 1774–82 (25 vols.,
London, 1775–82).

[4] *A Collection of the most Interesting
Tracts, lately published in England and
America, on the Subjects of Taxing the
American Colonies, and Regulating their
Trade* (6 vols., London, 1766–79).

[5] *The Gentleman's Magazine : or

Monthly Intelligencer* (vols. 33–53,
London, 1763–83).

[6] *Political Magazine and Parliamentary, Naval, Military, and Literary
Journal* (9 vols. London, 1780–85).

[7] Of the numerous editions of Walpole's *Letters,* that by Peter Cunningham
in nine volumes is most frequently
referred to; but Mrs. Paget Toynbee's
Letters of Horace Walpole (16 vols.,
Oxford, 1905) contains matter that
students value nowadays, which did not
appeal to the earlier editors.

*Last Journals of Horace Walpole
during the Reign of George III from
1771–1783, with Notes by Dr. Doran,*
edited by A. Francis Steuart, 2 vols.
(London, 1910).

to hunt them with dogs." Earlier, in January, 1763, Bouquet had informed the commander-in-chief that it had been "customary to give powder, lead, vermilion, and knives to the Indians . . . . since those presents have been surpressed, those Indians have become very troublesome at Fort Pitt, and more so at the out posts."[1] Amherst's reply denies the necessity.

[1] See "Pontiac Papers" in the Parkman Manuscripts in the cabinet of the Massachusetts Historical Society, under the dates given above. Mr. Parkman seems never to have used this material, possibly because he acquired it after the completion of his *Conspiracy of Pontiac.*

CHAPTER II

THE NEW COLONIAL POLICY, 1764–1765

THE end of the French war found England in a serious mood. Her debt had almost doubled since the day when Braddock began his ill-fated march toward Fort Duquesne,[1] and her yearly expenditure had increased threefold. The land tax was constantly rising, and the means for its payment were not growing commensurately. For years, the Lords of Trade and Plantations had regarded with jealous eyes colonial indifference to their behests. An army would be required in America to overawe the Canadians and to look after the Indians. Why not retain a considerable force in the colonies and make the settlers contribute largely towards its support?[2] The troops would be at hand

[1] In his *Estimate of the Strength of Great Britain* (London, 1802), p. 139, Chalmers gives "the whole debt, which was incurred, by the hostilities of 1756" at £72,111,000. A table in the *Commons Journals* (xxix, 760) gives the total funded debt as £129,586,789 and the interest charge as £4,688,117. See also the figures in *The Regulations lately made Concerning the Colonies and the Taxes imposed upon them Considered* (1765 ed., p. 56). This is generally attributed to George Grenville, and his name is printed on the title page of the third edition which was published in 1775, five years after his death. In 1766, while Grenville was still living, Thomas Whately informed John Temple that he himself had written it. As he was joint secretary of the treasury with Charles Jenkinson in Grenville's administration, a fair surmise might be that he collabo-

rated with his chief in its production. See *Bowdoin and Temple Papers*, Pt. i, 77.

[2] See Richard Rigby to the Duke of Bedford, February 23, 1763. "I understand part of the plan of the army is, and which I very much approve, to make North America pay its own army." *Bedford Correspondence*, iii, 210. A few days later, March 1, Charles Calvert, writing from London to Governor Sharpe in Maryland, says that he is "by Authority informed, that a scheme is forming for establishing 10,000 men to be British Americans standing force there, and paid by the Colonies. 'Tis said to be levied by Poll tax throughout the Colonies." "Bancroft Mss." in the Lenox Library. Mr. Wilberforce Eames very kindly had a copy of this letter made for me. These extracts are printed in Bancroft's *United States* (original ed.), v, 86 note.

in case of resistance to the enforcement of the customs laws. Moreover, the retention of ten thousand soldiers would keep many officers in the service who otherwise would be retired on half-pay, and new places that might be established in an enlarged colonial civil service would provide comfortable salaries for younger sons and for the poor relations of the ruling families.[1]

In 1760 the wise and unlovely George the Second had given place to a young and inexperienced king, the ever memorable George the Third.   He was now in his twenty-third year and had all the instincts of a middle-class Englishman.   " Born and educated in this country, I glory in the name of Briton," he declared.   He was determined to be no mere figurehead in the hands of the Whig oligarchy, no mere " roi faineant," no " King of the Mahrattas."   He was a politician, shrewd and unpitying, whose whole ambition was to place the kingship back where it had been in the days of the early Stuarts.   Lord Waldegrave, his tutor, had written that he would seldom do wrong, " except when he mistakes wrong for right ; but as often as this shall happen, it will be difficult to undeceive him." [2] The misfortunes of his armies in America, the splitting asunder of his empire, not even the French Revolution itself undeceived him.   Permanent mental incapacity found him still firm in the belief that he was right and always had been, and all the rest of the world was wrong. The modern American student sees in the third George no mere tyrant, no misguided monarch, but an instrument of

---

[1] In this connection it is well to remember that Parliament had been so well satisfied with the zeal displayed by the provincials, that it had voted them nearly one million pounds sterling as " compensation " for their extraordinary expenditures. See the present work, vol. ii, p. 578, note 3. On the other hand, the colonists had not generally complied with the requisitions that had been made on them in the closing months of the Indian campaigns.

[2] Waldegrave's *Memoirs from 1754 to 1758*, p. 9.

a benign providence bringing, through pain and misery, benefit to the human race. To destroy the power of the Whig domination, he drove William Pitt from office and made peace with France and Spain. He purchased the balance of power in the House of Commons with the nation's money, and thus converted government responsible to the great families of England into government responsible to himself. He permitted his ministers to establish a new colonial policy that could have but one termination. Looking backward, it is clear that the interests of Great Britain would have been best served by the abandonment of all petty restrictions in colonial government[1] and trade and by building up American commerce and industry. Seldom is a nation endowed with rulers of such certain judgment, of so prophetic imaginations, and courages commensurate to the inauguration and prosecution of so broad a policy as this. Meeting the demands of the hour as they arise is the ordinary life of a nation, nor ought the historian to expect otherwise.

Presiding at a meeting of the inhabitants of Boston, which had been called to celebrate the signing of the Treaty of Paris of 1763, James Otis declared that the colonists had abundant reasons for rejoicing in the conquest of Canada, and asserted that the constitution of the British empire was admirably adapted for the extension of civil and religious liberty over the whole continent. " Every British subject in America," he exclaimed, " is of common right, by acts of Parliament, and by the laws of God and

---

[1] In his preface to Chalmers's *Introduction to the Revolt* (p. v) Jared Sparks truly says that the questions which arose as to America were not " to be settled by technical constructions of laws. . . . There were deeper principles in the British constitution," — but Chalmers, like the king and his ministers, knew them not. George Louis Beer's *British Colonial Policy, 1754–1765*, is the only thorough study of the economic aspects of the early years of the Revolutionary movement that has yet been made.

nature, entitled to all the essential privileges of Britons."
Some jealousies had already arisen, but the true interests
of Great Britain and her plantations were mutual, "and
what God in his Providence has united let no man dare
attempt to pull asunder."[1]   Never had the colonists felt a
greater pride in their connection with the British empire.
But, in truth, the colonial condition was not compatible
with prosperity and power,[2] and life on the fringe of the
New World wilderness, far removed from control in
Church, State, and society, made for freedom from Old
World restraints, aroused a spirit of self-dependence, and
invited to liberty of utterance and of action.[3] No sooner was
it noised about that new taxes were to be laid and old
ones strictly collected than vigorous protests were uttered,
and mobs reckoned with those who had the temerity to
try to enforce obnoxious enactments.

The Americans felt that they were already overburdened
with taxations.   They had borne their full share and more
in the conquest of Canada.   Parliament had repaid some of
their extraordinary expenses, but in 1765, two years after
the peace, they still owed three quarters of a million
pounds sterling.[4]   Even in that year, when it was proposed
to extort money by new duties levied by parliamentary fiat,
Massachusetts was raising £37,500 annually for the purpose

---

[1] *Boston Post Boy and Advertiser*,
March 21, 1763.

[2] David Hume, in his *History of England* (vol. v, London, ed. 1763, p. 127),
referring to the objections of speculative
reasoners to the planting of the American
colonies because they would shake off the
yoke of the mother country, after drain-
ing her of inhabitants, concludes by
declaring that time has shown "the
views, entertained by those who encouraged such generous undertakings,
were more just and solid" than those of
the objectors. Hume lived to see the

American Declaration of Independence ;
the statement is an interesting indication
of the failure of one historian to be a true
prophet.

[3] Professor F. J. Turner has set forth
the influence of the frontier on American
development in his article " The Significance of the Frontier in American
History " in the American Historical
Association's *Report* for 1893, p. 197.

[4] " A State of the Debts incurred by
the British Colonies in North America
for the extraordinary expenses of the
late war, distinguishing what part of

of paying off her war debt.[1]   How one colonist felt is seen
in John Hancock's statement that not a man in England
was so heavily taxed in proportion to his estate as himself.[2]
He was writing under great provocation and may have
exaggerated somewhat; but the "Boston Town Records"
certainly go far toward justifying him, for it appears that
the town was then raising about £18,000 in each year, of
which nearly one half was being used for the expenses of
the province, including the discharge of the public debt, a
sum that was equivalent to about one-half of the per capita
tax of that town in the year 1910.   It was a favorite idea
in England that the colonies were doing very little for the
support of their governments and might easily bear the
burden of considerable taxation.   One of the permanent
officials of the treasury, Thomas Whately, stated in 1766
that the establishments of all the colonies put together
did not amount to £160,000 a year.[3]   Yet at that very
moment an inspection of the laws would have shown him
that three colonies, Massachusetts, Virginia, and South

---

said debt remains undischarged and the means for discharging it."

COLONY	SUM £	UNDIS-CHARGED £	PROVISION FOR DISCHARGING
N.H.	. . .	18,000	Taxes,1766–67
Mass.	818,000	160,000	Taxes in five years
R.I.	80,000	13,000	Taxes in 1767
Conn.	259,000	. . .	. . . .
N.Y.	291,000	115,000	Taxes, 1766–68
N.J.	204,000	181,000	Taxes in 17 years
Pa.	313,000	121,000	Taxes, 1767–79
Md.	39,000	. . .	. . . . . .
Va.	385,000	143,000	Taxes, 1766–69
N.C.	30,000	6,968	Taxes
S.C.	90,000	. . .	. . . .
Ga.	1,000	827	. . . .

Board of Trade Papers, Plantations General, xxi, 27.

On January 22, 1766, the House of Commons voted an address to the king, asking that the Board of Trade prepare a return showing the precise things that are contained in the above statement. *Commons Journals*, xxx, 484, 504.

[1] November 23, 1765. Bernard's *Select Letters*, 31.

[2] A. E. Brown's *John Hancock*, 98.

[3] Thomas Whately's *Considerations on the Trade and Finances of the Kingdom, and on the Measures of Administration* (London, 1766), p. 72. Whately's frame of mind may be gathered from an earlier page in the same volume (65). There he says that the illicit trade between the colonies and foreign nations "was all stolen from the commerce, and part of it from the manufactures of Great Britain, contrary to the fundamental principle of colonization, to every maxim of policy, and to the express provision of the law."

D

Carolina, were even then appropriating more than that sum,[1] notwithstanding the fact that salaries in Virginia were paid out of permanent revenue, and were, therefore, not included in the appropriations made by the assembly.[2]

Beside what the colonists paid in direct taxation by vote of their own assemblies, they were contributing indirectly several hundred thousand pounds to the royal exchequer in each year. This was owing to the operation of the colonial system that gave to British merchants, manufacturers, and shipowners a practical monopoly of many branches of colonial trade. It was estimated that the obligation of sending Chesapeake tobacco to Great Britain cost about one hundred thousand pounds yearly in the way of commissions,[3] and it was said that one-third of the cost of British manufactured goods that were sold in the colonies was due to the heavy taxes that were paid in England. Including wages and profits to operatives and manufacturers, America contributed nearly two million pounds sterling yearly to the income of the home land.[4]   On

---

[1] The total amount was £ 224,998 lawful money. See *Massachusetts Province Laws*, iv, 716; Ripley's *Financial History of Virginia* (p. 41), from "Journals of the Assembly"; and Cooper's *Statutes of South Carolina*, iv, 214. On this general subject, see *Boston Town Records*, 1758–69, p. 73, *Massachusetts Province Laws*, iii, iv, especially iv, p. 585; Hening's *Statutes of Virginia*, vii, viii; *Colonial Laws of New York* (ed. 1894), iii, iv. In using these books, the matter will be found listed under "French and Indian War," "Debts," "Frontier," "Appropriations," and "War." See also *Colonial Records of North Carolina*, vii, 447.

[2] From notes taken by Jared Sparks in London ("Manuscripts," No. 43, vol. iii, 214) it appears that the duty of two shillings per hogshead of tobacco exported from Virginia produced in the

twelve months from April 25, 1769, to April 24, 1770, £ 6491, which was used to pay the salaries of the governor, the councilors, the judges, attorney-general, and some other officials. In 1767 the quitrents, including arrears, produced £ 5738. Of this £ 2352 were used to pay salaries.

[3] *An Appeal to the Justice and Interests of the People of Great Britain* (fourth edition, London, 1776), p. 35.

[4] Sir Robert Walpole had passed over "some irregularities," for he was convinced that if the colonists gained five hundred thousand pounds by foreign commerce, full half of it within two years " will be in his majesty's exchequer, by the labour and product of this kingdom. . . . This is taxing them more agreeably to their constitution and to ours." Bisset's *Reign of George III*, i, 403 note.   Mr. Pitt declared that

the other hand the royal government paid bounties on certain colonial productions,[1] but these did not amount to more than a small percentage of the profit that the mother country derived from her colonies.

When William Pitt was driven from office, Lord Bute undertook to direct the affairs of the kingdom. His leading supporters were George Grenville, Chancellor of the Exchequer, Lord Halifax, Secretary of State, and Charles Townshend, First Lord of Trade. To the two last named, with a group of army men and Thomas Whately, the inception of the new policy was due. Halifax had long been at the Board of Trade, and had greatly disliked the inability of the government to secure obedience to its commands in America.[2] Up to the year 1763, owing to the French war, he had been unable to carry his plans into effect, but now that England was at peace with the world, and was likely to remain so for some time to come, the way seemed clear for a reckoning. Grenville also was interested

colonial commerce brought in a profit of two million pounds to British merchants in each year (*The Speech of Mr. P . . . And several others, In a certain august Assembly On a late important Debate*, p. 28). What Pitt had in mind, probably, was that the amounts paid in wages, etc., in working up the raw material that was sold to the colonists amounted to about that sum. Daniel Dulaney (*Considerations on Imposing Taxes in the British Colonies* (Annapolis, 1765), p. 43) states that a bale of English cloth has an artificial value of 51 per cent. Rating this artificial value at only one-third of the total, he computes that what with extra freight, profits to English merchants for commission, and the monopoly conferred by the " enumeration " that out of every £2,000,000 worth of goods imported into the colonies £1,636,666 represented taxes, profits, etc., and only £363,334 real value. Adam Smith in his *Wealth of Nations* (second edition, ii, 212) states that some moderate and gradual relaxation of the laws of trade till colonial commerce should be " in a great measure free " was necessary to relieve Great Britain from overgrown employments; in other words that the building up British manufactures at the expense of the colonists was bad economy.

[1] See James Macpherson's *The Rights of Great Britain Asserted* (London, 1776, p. 15 note): —

Indigo,	1749–73 . . .	£145,022
Hemp and flax, 1766–72 . . .		5,560
Naval stores { 1706–29 . . .		430,178
1729–74 . . .		1,028,584
		1,609,344

In addition there were bounties on raw silk and on a few other commodities.

[2] The determination to make effective the imperial control comes out clearly in O. M. Dickerson's *American Colonial Government* (Cleveland, 1912), which is based on a careful and prolonged study of the " Colonial Papers " in London.

because he found that the colonial customs were producing
less than two thousand pounds in each year at a cost of
collection of more than four times that amount.[1] The new
plans contemplated, therefore, a stiffening of the customs
service to enforce the existing laws and acts of trade and
to make the Sugar Act productive by reducing the rates,
thereby doing away with some of the temptation to smuggle ;
to change it, in other words, from a regulation of trade to
a revenue-producing measure.   At that time, as for years,
a drawback had been allowed on European manufactures
exported to the plantations.   This was now to be ended.
Additional imposts were to be collected on some of these
goods in America, and the wines of Madeira and the Azores
were to be assessed at a very high rate on importation into
the colonies in comparison with the rates on wines that
were imported through Great Britain.   In the future the
colonists were to shoulder a large part of the expense of
maintaining the soldiers who were stationed among them.
Finally, the stamp duties were to be extended to America.
In all, what with the amount to be saved by compelling
the colonists to feed and house the troops, and what would
be collected indirectly through the custom houses, or directly through the stamp offices, the whole expense of maintaining ten thousand troops might be recouped [2] and there

---

[1] October 11, 1763, the Lords of Trade
wrote to Governor Bernard that the
American customs revenue was "not
yet sufficient to defray a fourth part of
the expence necessary for collecting it;
and that through neglect, connivance
& fraud, not only the Revenue is im-
paired, but the Commerce of the Colonies
is diverted from it's natural course."
" Bernard Papers " (Ms.), x, 131. Grenville made a similar statement in a
letter to Horace Walpole (*Grenville
Papers*, ii, 114). The same idea is given
in a pamphlet entitled *Regulations*

Lately Made concerning the Colonies
(third edition, London, 1775, p. 55). The
words are as follows: "Remittance
from all the Colonies, at an Average of
thirty Years has not amounted to 1900 £
a year and to make it still more ridic-
ulous, the Establishment of Officers
necessary to collect this 1900 £ amounts
to 7600 £ *per Annum*."

[2] In the *Commons Journals* (xxix, 681)
is an estimate of the charge of the forces
serving in the Plantations, Minorca, and
Gibraltar for the year December 25, 1763,
to December 24, 1764, which was pre-

might even be something left over for the support of the civil establishment. As parts of the general scheme, colonial manufacturing was still further restrained, more colonial staples were placed on the enumerated list,[1] and trade was to be made safer by extending the prohibition against issuing paper money to all the colonies.[2] The only boon given in return for all this restriction and taxation was to permit the New England whalemen to take whales in the Gulf of St. Lawrence and to export their oil to Great Britain.[3] It was a far-reaching plan, and had it been carried out in its entirety would have wrought an important change in the working of the imperial constitution.

Before anything was done to carry into effect the scheme that has just been outlined Lord Bute, frightened by public clamor, resigned his high office and retired behind the throne, from which vantage point he was generally supposed to have dictated to successive ministries. Grenville became First Lord of the Treasury as well as Chancellor of the Exchequer. Halifax continued as Sec-

---

sented on November 29, 1763. The total charge is £ 372,774. Deducting from this the cost of the garrisons at Minorca and Gibraltar, leaves £ 252,096. Adding to this sum the amount voted for ordnance in the Plantations (*ibid.*, xxix, 686) gives a total in round numbers of £ 276,000. G. L. Beer's *British Colonial Policy, 1754-1765*, p. 267 note, says that the total cost of the American army was about £ 320,000 yearly. Macpherson (*Rights of Great Britain*, 99) gives the following figures for money voted for forces employed in the defence of America: —

1755	£ 81,059 yearly
1756	142,813
1757	249,854
1762	615,845
1763	310,317
1764	252,093
1765–68	268,054–279,668
1774	247,324

His figures for 1764 are substantially the same as those given in the *Commons Journals*. Probably the discrepancy between the estimates given in this note arises from different treatment of the ordnance charges. None of these estimates include the charges for the navy or for fortifications and extras, such as presents for the Indians. The total cost was well over £ 300,000 in 1764.

[1] 4 George III, Cap. 15, "enumerates" hides and skins.

[2] See note I on p. 52.

[3] 4 George III, Cap. 29 (Ruffhead's *Statutes at Large*, ix, 190). According to a table in the Massachusetts Historical Society's *Collections*, First Series, iii, 161, the value of the Nantucket whale-catch increased fourfold between 1756 and 1770; but exactly how much of this was due to the opening of the St. Lawrence is unknown.

retary of State ; but Charles Townshend declined the offers that were made to him, and for a few months was out of employment for the only time during his political career. George Grenville's name is one of the blackest in American history; but his contemporaries thought well of him. He possessed fair abilities, but was unable to see far beyond the letter of the law books. He refused to adopt that part of the plan which provided for the establishment of an American civil list by parliamentary enactment. He accepted the rest, and the responsibility for taking the first steps in carrying out the policy that led to American resistance and separation must rest on his shoulders.[1] It was suggested at the time that American members should be admitted to the House of Commons, but as no one took much interest in the matter, Grenville did not think it worth while to act on this proposal.

Grenville's first step was to apply to the Commissioners of the Customs and the Lords of Trade for advice as to the best means to invigorate the customs service.[2] The latter made no useful suggestions, but the Commissioners called attention to the fact that many American customs officials lived in England and administered their duties by deputy to the injury of the revenue. Thereupon, Grenville revoked leaves of absence with a vigorous hand and

---

[1] Charles Jenkinson, who was one of the joint secretaries of the treasury in 1763, years afterwards declared that "Mr. Grenville had no concern whatever in the first causes of the disquietudes there [in America]. They originated in the projects which were formed while Lord Bute was in office." Almon's *Biographical Anecdotes*, ii, 81. On p. 84 of the same volume, the following statement is also attributed to Jenkinson: "The measure of the Stamp Act was not Mr. Grenville's; if the act was a good one, the merit was not due to Mr.

Grenville; if it was a bad one, the errors or the ill policy of it did not belong to him." This work was published some years after Grenville's death. While he was still living, Colonel Onslow asserted in the House of Commons that Grenville in "starting the idea of taxing America" had been actuated by the best intentions. See Cavendish's *Debates*, ii, 25, 33 note.

[2] Beer's *British Colonial Policy, 1754–1765*, p. 275, citing "Board of Trade Papers." See also Halifax to Bernard, August 11, 1764, asking for information as to illicit trade. "Bernard Papers," x, 183.

prepared a circular letter to the colonial governors directing them to be diligent in the performance of their duties
as to trade and customs.[1] He also caused deputations to
be issued to the commanders of some of the smaller
ships on the American station, giving them authority to
seize vessels carrying on illicit trade. They certainly
did effective work in putting an end to evasions of the
laws.[2] In March, 1764, he introduced into the House of
Commons twenty-two resolutions. These were speedily
adopted by the Committee of Ways and Means and upon
them the Stamp Act and the American Revenue Act of
1764 were based.[3] So many novel questions arose in
connection with the extension of the stamp duties to the
colonies that Grenville postponed final action on that
part of the scheme to give the American assemblies an
opportunity to suggest more agreeable methods of rais-

---

[1] " Journal of the Board of Trade "
(Ms.), lxxi, 241.

[2] " Sparks Manuscripts," No. 43,
vol. i, p. 202 ; iv, 77. The naval officers
claimed one-half of the proceeds of
seizures under an Order in Council of
June 1, 1763, which was based on the
act of 3 George III., Cap. 22, § iv, entitled
" An Act for the further Improvement
of his Majesty's Revenue of Customs,
and for the Encouragement of Officers
making Seizures." Ruffhead's *Statutes
at Large*, ix, 54.

[3] *Parliamentary History*, xv, 1426.
At this time, William Knox
began his intimacy with Mr. Grenville
which continued until that gentleman's
death in 1770. He then attached himself
to Lord George Germain, with whom he
served as under secretary. Knox had
held a minor office in Georgia and had
acquired some property there. He
had a keen mind and clear ideas as to
colonial policy which commended him to
those who had charge of American
affairs. In 1764 he laid a plan before
Grenville for a redistribution of imperial
burdens. This is nowhere printed in

his published writings; but from
scattered hints as to its contents, it may
be the paper that is calendered in the
Royal Historical Manuscripts Commission's *Reports* (*Various Collections*, vi,
89, 286) as " Hints relative to our Commerce " ; or the one printed in Knox's
Extra Official State Papers (ii, 29 and
Appendix No. xi). These two documents
seem to belong together and it is quite
possible that the latter, which refers to
years just preceding the Revolutionary
outbreak, repeats the details of the plan
which was laid before Grenville in 1764.
Knox computes the just proportion of
the imperial expenses which the colonists
may properly bear as one and one-quarter
million pounds; but in view of the
benefits which England derives from the
monopoly of colonial commerce, he suggests that only three hundred thousand
pounds should be raised annually by
duties and taxes imposed by Parliament.
Whenever any colony should place at
the disposal of the imperial government
a sum equal to eight per cent of its
exports in 1763, parliamentary taxation
should cease as to that colony.

ing the necessary funds.   The revenue law was pushed through at once.

The preamble of this celebrated enactment[1] recites the expediency of establishing new provisions for improving the revenue of " this kingdom," and for extending and securing commerce between it and the colonies.   It closed with the assertion that it is just and necessary to raise a revenue in the plantations " for defraying the Expences of defending, protecting, and securing the same."   For these reasons " We, Your Majesty's most dutiful and loyal Subjects, the Commons of Great Britain in Parliament assembled, being desirous to make some Provision . . . towards raising the said revenue in America, have resolved to give and grant unto Your Majesty " the pre- scribed duties.   These were to be levied in the colonies upon silks and other stuffs from the East, and upon fine fabrics from Europe.   The wines of Madeira and the other Atlan- tic islands imported directly into the colonies were to pay · seven pounds, or one hundred and forty shillings, per ton of two hundred and fifty-two gallons, while the wines of Portugal and Spain and other countries, except France, imported through Great Britain were to pay only ten shillings per ton.   French wines could not be imported at all.[2]   In the future no drawbacks were to be allowed with the exception of those on a few specified com- modities.   The operation of the act, therefore, would greatly increase the price of many articles in America,[3] for the failure to pay back any part of the duties lev- ied on European goods upon importation into Great Britain

---

[1] 4 George III, Cap. 15 (*Statutes at Large*, ed. 1786, vol. vii, p. 457).

[2] At this time, the importation of French wines into England was pro- hibited.

[3] Before this change was made, many foreign goods could be bought cheaper in the plantations than in Eng- land: Adam Smith's *Wealth of Nations*, ii, 181, 182 (London, 1776).

would compel merchants to charge more for those fabrics, and this in turn would enable British manufacturers to obtain higher prices for their productions. Add to this the imposts to be levied in America and the ultimate consumer was likely to pay a good deal more than he had been paying for many articles, — unless he took to making them himself.

As soon as it was known in America that the government was intending to renew the Sugar Act of 1733, the merchants of Boston, Newport, New York, and other places sent memorials to England, stating that the vigorous execution of the old law was the primal cause of the declining commerce of the North. The Rhode Islanders asserted that of the fourteen thousand hogsheads of molasses that were imported into that colony in one year, only twenty-five hundred were of English production, — all the English sugar plantations put together could not satisfy the needs of the distillers of that one colony. The Boston men said that the business could not be carried on if the duty on molasses was more than one penny per gallon. A higher duty would be prejudicial to trade, destroy the fishing industry, and force the colonists from commerce into manufacturing. Grenville was deaf to all these representations and decided to tax foreign molasses imported into the northern colonies at the rate of threepence per gallon. At the same time, the importation of foreign rum was absolutely prohibited; but rum of British distillation could be imported free from any duty. There were other provisions as to sugar, coffee, and pimento, but these need not detain us here.

Important as were these parts of the law, they were as nothing in comparison with the regulations that were devised for their enforcement and for the enforcement of

all the laws relating to commerce and navigation, old as
well as new. The rates were changed before long, but the
administrative part of the law was reënacted again and
again. For more than three-quarters of a century the law
had required all ship masters, loading goods in colonial
ports, to give bonds to land all enumerated commodities
in Great Britain or in some British plantation. In the
future, they were likewise to give bonds to land no non-
enumerated goods on any part of the European continent
north of Cape Finisterre. Furthermore, every captain
must obtain and have in his possession certificates from the
collector of customs at the port where the goods had been
shipped stating that these bonds and some of lesser moment
had been given. Certificates, also, were to be obtained by
vessels taking on West India produce giving details as to
the origin of the cargo, and all portions of it not certified
to were to be treated as of foreign origin. In the preced
ing year, the provisions of the " Hovering Act " of George I
had been extended to cover all vessels found near the coast
of Ireland or the plantations.[1] According to the new law,
the master of any British vessel found within two leagues of
any colony must produce the required certificate, whether
he was stopped while sailing to Europe, or from one colony
to another, as from Pennsylvania across the Delaware to
New Jersey, or from New York to Jamaica. Then there
was the further requirement that no vessel should be
cleared from any British port unless the whole cargo had
been shipped in Great Britain. The only important exceptions to this general rule were salt and Irish linens. Colonial
navigation and trade were now in a strait-jacket.

The penalties for disobedience of this law were many
and severe, and counterfeiting of certificates was to be

---

[1] 3 George III, Cap. 22, § 9. The original act is 5 George I, Cap. 11.

punished by a fine of five hundred pounds. Suits for
forfeitures might be brought in any colonial court or in any
admiralty court at the election of the informer or prosecutor. A court of Vice-Admiralty had been established at
Halifax to which informers and prosecutors naturally
turned. In June, 1765, to do away with the hardships
that this involved, the Lords of the Treasury, while Mr.
Grenville was still in office, recommended the removal of
this court from Halifax to Boston, and the establishment
of two others at Philadelphia and Charleston ; but nothing
was done at that time.[1] The net proceeds of the seizures
were to be divided in the usual manner, one-third to the
king, one-third to the governor, and one-third to the prosecutors; but where the seizures were made at sea by the
king's ships one-half went to the king, the other to the
prosecutor. Every opportunity was taken to encourage
seizures and prosecutions. If, for example, the produce of
any one seizure was not sufficient to pay the expenses, the
charges might be defrayed out of the customs — even when
no suit was brought. Finally, the burden of proof as to
whether duties had been paid or the goods were of British
or foreign origin was laid upon the owner or claimant.

One other clause of this act and of the Stamp Act demands attention. This required the net proceeds of the
duties collected under them to be paid into the " Receipt
of his Majesty's Exchequer." The radical leaders in
America at once laid hold of this provision and declared
that these laws would drain the colonies of all their gold
and silver. The government in England denied that it had
any intention of drawing specie from America. These
statements were not believed in the colonies ; but they were
'true. The payment of money into the Receipt of his

----

[1] Board of Trade Papers, " Plantations General," xx, 285.

Majesty's Exchequer did not necessarily mean the paying over the counter of so many pounds in gold and silver, — the payment might be made in drafts from the office of the paymaster of the forces in exchange for supplies bought in America with funds contributed by the customs collectors there. This was the mode actually prescribed by the Lords of the Treasury in 1764. The net proceeds of the duties and taxes were to be handed over to the deputy paymaster of the forces at New York and by him expended in America in the purchase of supplies for the army. The accounting between the two services would be done in London and would thus satisfy the requirements of the law.[1] Although this was true in 1764 and 1765, the American radicals were quite justified in their outcry in the absence of any explicit statement to the contrary. Moreover, by a stroke of the pen, the Treasury Board might order the actual money to be sent across the Atlantic, and this, as a matter of fact, was done after 1767.

It was hoped that the funds arising under these laws would go far towards providing for the support of the soldiers that were to be kept in the colonies. The rest

[1] The protest of sundry lords against the repeal of the Stamp Act (*Parliamentary History*, xvi, 188) notes a minute of the Treasury Board of July 9, 1765, directing the funds raised under the Stamp Act to be paid to the deputy paymaster of the forces in America, and used to defray military expenses there. October 21, 1765, John Temple, then surveyor general in the northern district, informed the paymaster at New York that the Lords of the Treasury had instructed him to pay over the produce of the American duties to the deputy paymaster at New York to be immediately expended by him in defraying the subsistence of the troops. "Temple Papers" (Ms.) under date. Moreover, Thomas Whately, who was then one of the secretaries of the Treasury Board, wrote to Temple that the "whole money" to be raised by the stamp duties would "never be drawn out" of the colonies; the "Paymaster General wanting to remit money for subsistence, &c, will apply to the Commissioners of Customs or Stamps for bills or orders upon their officers in the Colonies. These officers will in consequence thereof pay over the money in their hands to the deputy paymasters, & whatever sums shall be thus advanced in America will be paid here by the Paymaster General to the Commissioners of Customs or Stamps, who will pay the same into the Exchequer as American revenue in conformity to the act." *Bowdoin and Temple Papers*, i, 51, 59.

of the expense of maintaining them, or a large part of it, would be met by the colonists themselves under the terms of the Quartering Act. This law had been passed at the express desire of General Gage, who was now commander-in-chief of the British forces in America.[1] It required the several provinces to provide barracks for the troops that might be stationed therein, to supply them with certain necessary utensils, with vinegar and salt, with rum or beer, and to pay for their transportation within the province over and above a specified amount per mile which would be provided by the British exchequer. Granting that it was necessary to keep a force of ten thousand men in America and to oblige the colonists to pay for them, the working of this particular law was unjust. New York was the strategic center of America[2] with its lines of transportation to Canada, to the frontier, and to the West Indies. Gage established his headquarters there and kept several regiments within the limits of the province, not because they were needed there to preserve order or to overawe the Canadians or the Indians, but simply because that was the most convenient place for them. The New Yorkers were quite unwilling to bear so disproportionate a part of the total charge. The assembly refused to comply with all of the provisions of the law, and Parliament directed the governor of the province to give his assent to no legislative act of the assembly until its provisions were fully met.[3] In this way there developed

---

[1] *Calendar of Home Office Papers,* 1760-65, p. 529. The act is 5 George III, Cap. 33 (Pickering's *Statutes at Large,* xxvi, 305). The act of 6 George III, Cap. 18, differs in some particulars from this one. It is not given in the compilations, but has been examined in one of the original printed copies, see below, p. 52.

[2] From 1716 to 1762 Parliament had voted £7000 per annum for the support of the royal forces in New York. In 1763 this grant was cut down to £2367, and thereafter was not paid at all. Macpherson's *Rights of Great Britain Asserted,* Appendix.

[3] 7 George III, Cap. 59 (Pickering's *Statutes at Large,* xxvii, 609). In February, 1767, Governor Carleton wrote

a most dangerous constitutional crisis which continued for several years until the New Yorkers were obliged by their necessities to yield.[1]

On closing the session of Parliament in April, 1764, the king expressed his hearty approbation of the wise regu· lations, as he called them, that had been made "to aug· ment the public revenues, to unite the interests of the most distant possessions of my crown, and to encourage and secure their commerce with Great Britain."[2] Pre· cisely how these regulations were likely to encourage colonial commerce with anybody was not stated. As to uniting the interests of two portions of the Empire, the words of the Virginia Committee of Correspondence were impressive, for they declared that no man or body of men had a right to do that which is contrary to reason and jus· tice or that tended to the destruction of the constitution.[3]

The presence of the revenue cruisers had aroused public attention, but nothing like the indignation which was excited by the news that the House of Commons was intending to levy a tax on the American planter "without the consent of his representative"[4] being asked. In those

from Quebec to Gage advising him to establish "a proper place of arms, near the Town of New York" because it is essential to establish that security and strength that can curb and overcome those who are "not thoroughly bound to their duty." Moreover, the establishment of such a post on the line of communication between New York and Quebec "will give security to the King's Magazines" and "will separate the Northern from the Southern Colonies." Massachusetts Historical Society's *Collections*, Fourth Series, x, 594, 595.

[1] From entries in the "Journals of the Board of Trade" (lxxvii, 122 and fol.) it appears that one of the clerks in the Plantation Office was in correspondence

with a relative in New York, and advised him, among other things, that if that province stood firm for one more year, the home government would be obliged to give way.

[2] *Parliamentary History*, xv, 1434.

[3] They wrote to their agent in London that no British subject could justly be made "subservient" to laws without his personal consent or that of his representatives, and that "no Man or Body of Men, however invested wth power, have a Right to do anything that is contrary to Reason & Justice, or that can tend to the Destruction of the Constitution." *Virginia Magazine of History*, xii, 13.

[4] Ballagh's *Letters of Richard Henry Lee*, i, 5.

days there was some subtle distinction between duties levied
at the customhouse and money collected directly from the
people. The colonists had clearly recognized and acknowledged the rights of the imperial government to regulate
trade and navigation, partly, no doubt, because up to this
time they had not thought much about the matter. Now
that there was a prospect of their trade being regulated
in earnest, more attention was paid to it. Of course, it
was difficult to separate the regulation of trade from
the collection of duties for purposes of revenue. Whatever was collected at the customhouse seemed to belong
to the regulation of trade; but when it was proposed
to extend the stamp duties to America by act of Parliament, there was no possibility of disguise. These were
taxes, direct taxes, to be collected in the interior parts
of the colonies as well as at the seaports. It was one
of the cardinal principles of political action that no
Englishman could be " taxed " without his consent being
given at least constructively; besides, the colonists were
paying enough taxes as it was. To ask them to submit
to new levies imposed upon them in what they regarded
as an illegal manner at the precise moment when
their trade was being restrained, was asking altogether too
much. Instead of suggesting alternative modes of taxation, as Grenville had requested,[1] they presented petitions
against being taxed at all, in any manner whatsoever,
except by vote of their own assemblies. The first of
these was laid before the Lords of Trade on December 11,
1764, and was promptly denounced as exhibiting " the most
indecent disrespect " to the legislature of Great Britain.[2]

---

[1] William Knox's *Claim of the Colonies Examined*, 31. This matter is
repeated in Appendix i of his *Extra
Official State Papers*, vol. ii.

[2] *Commons Journal*, xxx, 148, *Parliamentary History*, xvi, 121.

The Commons showed its sense of the matter by refusing to allow them to be presented, under the terms of an ancient rule of that body that no petitions against money bills were to be received from any one. After waiting the appointed time for suggestions, Grenville introduced into the Commons a bill extending the stamp duties to the colonies and it passed both Houses without arousing any opposition worth noting.[1]

Stamp duties were not new either in England or in America. They had been levied in the mother country since the reign of William III and had proved to be an easy and effective means of raising revenue. In 1763, they produced nearly three hundred thousand pounds sterling.[2] In America, also, stamp duties had been collected, although temporarily.[3] There had been many suggestions for extending the English duties to the plantations. As far back as 1722, Archibald Cumins, at the time naval officer at Boston, had made certain suggestions to the Lords of Trade, which anticipated Grenville's plan in almost every particular, even to the removal of the drawback and extending the stamp duties.[4] Other suggestions by other men[5]

[1] The debate as reported in *Parliamentary History* (xvi, 37) was very brief, hardly more than an extract from a speech against it which Isaac Barré is said to have delivered. This was reported only by Jared Ingersoll and possibly varied from the original as much as other speeches of the time. See Frothingham's *Rise of the Republic*, 175.

[2] Stephen Dowell's *Taxation and Taxes in England*, iii, 327.

[3] *Massachusetts Province Laws*, iii, 794, 867.

[4] "Board of Trade Papers" ("Philadelphia Transcripts, Plantations General," under date of November, 1723). Cumins had suggested a permanent military establishment for America of 6000 soldiers to be supported by taxes voted by Parliament and levied in the colonies. The removal of the drawback on European goods exported from England, would bring in £40,000; £33,000 more could be gained by duties on foreign rum, molasses, sugar, cotton, cocoa, and indigo imported into the colonies. Duties on foreign wines would produce another £20,000, and the stamp duties £30,000 more. On the other hand he suggested that some of the fees collected at the colonial customhouses should be reduced, so that the total net gain would be about £100,000 yearly.

[5] The best known of these is Sir William Keith's *Short Discourse on the Present State of the Colonies in America with respect to the interests of Great Britain* (London, 1728) and his *Two*

followed and toward the close of the French War Henry M'Culloh presented to Grenville an elaborate plan for an American stamp tax, coupled with a scheme for paper money to be issued in England for use in all the colonies.[1] In August, 1764, Halifax sent a circular letter to the colonial governors [2] directing them to report as to the legal documents that were used in their provinces. There can be no doubt as to the care with which the measure was framed. Much lighter duties were to be charged on ordinary documents than were levied in England, and in other respects the colonial rates were considerably less. It was even sought to make the new taxes useful as a restraint on land speculation by graduating the amount roughly in proportion to the number of acres involved in any one transaction. One clause in the act that arouses attention is that taxing newspapers and advertisements; but these were the same as those that were actually being levied in England.[3]

Papers, on the Subject of Taxing the British Colonies in America (London, 1767), p. 14.

[1] See Wm. A. Shaw, editor *Miscellaneous Representations relative to Our Concerns in America*, London, 1905. M'Culloh, besides suggesting the levying of stamp duties and certain duties on rum and molasses, advised establishing the same currency in all the colonies. The editor states that M'Culloh in 1763 presented a long, tabular statement of the proposed stamp duties to Grenville, who approved it. He says that this is among the " Hardwicke Papers " in the British Museum; but the Treasury Board was diligently searching for the best method of levying these duties two years later. It is noteworthy that Chalmers in a letter to Lord Mansfield (" Sparks Manuscripts," No. 7, p. 43) in describing the origin of the Stamp Act, makes no mention of M'Culloh.

[2] "Bernard Papers" (Ms.), x, 183, 185, under date August 11, 1764.

[3] Whately to Temple, February, 1765 (Massachusetts Historical Society's *Collections*, Sixth Series, ix, 49). He wrote that much lighter duties were to be charged on the ordinary documents than were paid in England. Bonds for the payment of small sums of money also were to be charged less than those for larger sums. Licenses to sell spirituous liquors in the colonies were to be taxed at the same rate as licenses to sell ale in England, while newspapers and advertisements were to pay the same rates in both countries. A few things, among which were certificates of marriage, pardons, and debentures, were not to be taxed at all in America, although they were in Great Britain. Upon the whole, one gets the idea that the stamp duties, which it was proposed to charge, were lighter than those which were actually being paid in England.

E

As a revenue measure, the Stamp Act was eminently fair and well constructed, the sole objection to it was in the mode of its passage.

The act[1] fills sixty-six octavo pages of the black letter type of the period, containing a preamble and one hundred and seventeen paragraphs. The duties were to be assessed on legal documents of every description, including letters of administration and ships' papers, on university degrees and similar certificates; on appointments to office, licenses to retail spirituous liquors, deeds, bonds, and leases, articles of apprenticeship, playing cards and dice, newspapers and pamphlets. On the other hand, school books, religious works, proceedings of assemblies, and all the ordinary papers of commerce, that were not sealed, were subject to no tax whatsoever. The administration of these duties was confided to the Commissioners of the Stamp Duties in Great Britain. Heavy fines and forfeitures were provided for infractions of the law, and these might be collected through the admiralty courts at the election of the informer or prosecuter. This last provision brought up a new principle, for it seemed a little strange to use the admiralty courts for the enforcement of inland duties. Doubtless, the reason for this was that there was no court of exchequer in the colonies and it was thought best to use the existing courts rather than to establish new ones. At the moment of its passage, no one in London had the slightest idea that the act would be opposed in America. Franklin and the other colonial agents had no thought

---

[1] 5 George III, Cap. 12 (Pickering's *Statutes at Large*, xxvi, 179); *American History Leaflets*, No. 21. Exaggerated ideas as to the amount of money to be raised under the act prevailed in America. For instance, Edmund Pendleton wrote to Madison that it was "supposed" that the contribution of Virginia would amount to £50,000 sterling a year. Massachusetts Historical Society's *Proceedings*, Second Series, xix, 109.

of the disturbances that a few months were to witness throughout the colonies. In America, too, politicians thought that the act would go quietly into effect; one of them, Richard Henry Lee of Virginia, even applied for one of the collectorships, — and found it rather difficult to explain away his conduct. Oftentimes the colonists had petitioned against proposed acts of Parliament, but when these had been passed, they had obeyed or had silently disregarded them. What would be the fate of this new enactment which was not only part and parcel of a new policy, but was itself a departure from all precedent?

NOTES

I. The Currency Act, 1764. — (4 George III, Cap. 34. Ruffhead's *Statutes at Large*, ix, 199.) The title is " An Act to prevent paper Bills of Credit, hereafter to be issued in any of His Majesty's colonies or plantations in America, from being declared to be a legal tender in payments of money; and to prevent the legal tender of such bills as are now subsisting from being prolonged beyond the periods limited for calling in and sinking the same." The justifications for this act are stated to be the great discouragement and prejudice of the trade and commerce of His Majesty's subjects, by occasioning confusion in dealings, and lessening credit in the said colonies. This was accomplished by enacting that every act, order, or resolution of any colonial assembly in contravention of this law shall be null and void and any governor assenting to such bill shall pay the sum of one thousand pounds, be immediately dismissed from his government, and be forever after incapable of any public office or place of trust. The act of 24 George II restraining paper bills in New England is also expressly confirmed.

II. The Quartering Acts. — The preamble of the Act of 6 George III, Cap. 18 recites that although the regular mutiny act provides for the government of the army, it may not be sufficient for the forces employed in America, especially as the conditions for quartering troops in the colonies are unlike those prevailing in Great Britain. The act provides, therefore, that the civil officers in the several towns, districts, and other places in the colonies must " quarter and billet the Officers and Soldiers, in His Majesty's Service, in the Barracks provided by the Colonies " and if there shall not be sufficient room in such barracks they shall billet them in " Inns, Livery Stables, Ale-houses, Victualling-houses," and the houses of sellers of wine, rum, brandy, cider, or metheglin; and in case there shall not be sufficient room in barracks and public houses then the troops may be quartered in uninhabited houses, out houses, barns or other buildings. Officers and soldiers, quartered in inns and public houses shall be fed by the keepers of such establishments at certain rates. Furthermore, the officers and soldiers in barracks and hired quarters shall be provided " with Fire, Candles, Vinegar, and Salt, Bedding, Utensils for dressing their Victuals, and Small Beer or Cyder, not exceeding Five Pints, or Half a Pint of Rum mixed with a Quart of Water, to each Man, without paying anything for the same." " If any Military Officer shall take upon himself to quarter Soldiers, in any of His Majesty's Dominions in America, otherwise than is limited and allowed by this Act; or shall use or offer any Menace or Compulsion" to any of the civil officers charged with the billeting upon conviction by a colonial court he shall "be *ipso facto* cashiered, and shall be utterly disabled to have or hold any military Employment."

Furthermore, the authorities were to provide carriages for the arms, clothes, or accoutrements of the soldiers, with able men to drive the same, the transportation to be paid for by the military officials at the rate of seven pence for twelve hundred pounds per mile, the province or colony to make provision for any charge in excess of that rate. The other sections of the law provided for the punishment of mutiny and desertion in the usual manner.

III. Bibliography. — The names of books, pamphlets, and articles concerning the legislation of 1764–1765 are given at great length in Winsor's *America*, vi, 68 and fol.; and in even greater detail in the *Bulletin of the New York Public Library*, i, 101–108. The latter is especially valuable on account of the list of pamphlets called forth at the time. The most important of these are mentioned in the footnotes of this volume. Among those to which no specific reference is given, the following may be mentioned: Richard Bland's *Enquiry into the Rights of the British Colonies* (Williamsburg, 1766); *Essay on the Trade of the Northern Colonies of Great Britain in North America Printed at Philadelphia* (reprinted London, 1764); *Copy of a Letter from John Huske, Esq; to the Committee of Merchants in Boston*, dated Westminster, 14 August, 1764; and *Reasons why the British Colonies in America should not be charged with internal Taxes by authority of Parliament* (New Haven, 1764). There is a copy of the last in the John Carter Brown Library. Oxenbridge Thacher's *Sentiments of a British American* (Boston, 1764) is an interesting little tract. The " Letters of Dennys de Berdt, 1757–1770 " (Colonial Society of Massachusetts, *Publications*, xiii) contain valuable matter on this period especially as to the impolicy of the new system from the point of view of a London merchant trading to America.

CHAPTER III

THE ROYAL assent was given to the Stamp Act on March 22, 1765. The ship bearing the news made a rapid passage across the Atlantic, but before her arrival the spiking of guns in a fort at Philadelphia on Sunday, April 14,[1] gave a premonition of what was to follow. Next, the colonial legislatures betook themselves to passing resolutions condemning the "fatal black act," as they not infrequently called the Stamp Act.

At the moment, Virginia politics were complicated by the probability that the financial irregularities of leading men in the assembly would be laid bare to public view. In the Old Dominion, the Speaker of the House of Burgesses also acted as public treasurer. He often had large balances of public money in his hands. As was the case with the paymaster of the forces and the treasurer of the navy in England, he looked upon these funds as his own property for the time being. In England, the officials often invested their balances in public funds, for they were able, owing to early information, to calculate with some degree of confidence as to the future of these securities. They retained the interest on the bonds and sometimes made large fortunes from their rise in value.[2] In default

[1] *Pennsylvania Gazette*, April 18 and May 23, 1765.

[2] Lord Holland had been paymaster of the forces in the last years of the French and Indian War. His executors retained £455,735 in their hands in 1778. Among those who benefited from the interest on this "balance" was Charles James Fox. *Parliamentary Register,* xxii, 365. The heirs of Charles Townshend and George Grenville, who had been treasurers of the navy, were also enjoying the interest of public money that had come into these statesmen's hands a quarter of a century earlier. The "balances" in all amounted to nearly a million pounds sterling.

of any such easy mode of stock jobbing, the Virginia
Speaker was accustomed to loan the balances in his hands
to his political friends.   These years were not prosperous
ones in Virginia, owing to one cause or another, and it
seemed likely that some of the debtors would be unable to
repay what they had borrowed.   To protect them, it was
proposed to establish a provincial loan office to which these
bad debts might be transferred and thus all traces of the
deficit be covered up.   Patrick Henry's eloquence in the
Parson's Cause, and the regard with which he was held in
the community, led to his rapid political advancement and
to his election as a burgess.   He defeated this measure, so
it is said ;[1] and as none of the recognized leaders were
interesting themselves in opposition to the Stamp Act, he
came forward with certain resolutions which were passed
rather reluctantly (May 29, 1765).   The records are confused
and it is impossible to tell definitely whether four, five, or
six resolutions were actually passed.[2]   It really matters
little, for the whole six were printed in the newspapers —
in the North and in the South — as the " Virginia Resolves."
They were, indeed, the "alarm Bell to the disaffected,"[3]

---

[1] This is given on the authority of
Jefferson who, many years later, recalled
the scene; but the recollections of that
venerable ex-President, in common with
those of other old men, must be received
with considerable caution.

[2] Edmund Randolph in his manuscript " History of Virginia " says that
all the Resolutions passed the committee of the whole House, but on report
the last two " as being too inflammatory
were laid aside."   The Resolves, so
Randolph asserts, were written by John
Fleming.   See Virginia Magazine of
History, x, 11.   The more usual account
comes from the London Gazetteer, an
extremely rare publication, through the
pages of George Bancroft ; see his History
of the United States, v, 277, and Henry's

Patrick Henry, i, 86.   See also Wirt's
Patrick Henry, 65; and Frothingham's
Rise of the Republic, 179.   Ample discussions of this episode and all the references will be found in the biographies
of Henry and the Virginia Magazine
of History, as above.

[3] This phrase occurs in a letter from
Governor Bernard of Massachusetts to
the Earl of Halifax, dated August 15,
1765, asserting that the vehement and
industrious opposition to the new policy
dates from the passage of the Virginia
Resolves.   The author of the Conduct of
the Late Administration Examined,
Relative to the American Stamp-Act
(London, 1767, p. 51) declared that
" publishing the Virginia resolutions
proved an alarum bell to the disaffected."

the spark that was needed to light the fire of discontent throughout the land.

Henry's resolutions recite the facts of the colonization of the Old Dominion and its early constitutional history. They assert that the settlers brought with them the rights of Englishmen which they transmitted to their posterity ; that taxation by themselves or by persons chosen by themselves is the distinguishing characteristic of British freedom ; that the right of the Virginians to be governed by their own assembly in the article of taxes has never been forfeited or given up, but has been constantly recognized by the British government, and that every attempt to invest such power in any other person or persons has a manifest tendency to destroy British and American liberty. So far, the first four resolves ; the fifth and sixth, which probably had no legal existence, denied that Virginians owed obedience to any laws designed to tax them, other than those passed by their own assembly, and that any person who maintained the contrary was an enemy to his Majesty's colony.

Throughout this period, sometimes consciously, sometimes without premeditation, Virginia and Massachusetts echoed and reëchoed each other's pronouncements and matched each other's actions. Now, the General Court of Massachusetts decided that a meeting of delegates from the several assemblies on the continent would be the best body to formulate a united protest. On June 8, therefore, a circular letter was adopted calling a congress to meet at New York on the first Tuesday in the following October.[1] At first, the response to this invitation was half-hearted and delegates from only nine colonies met at the appointed

---

[1] *Journal of the House of Representatives of Massachusetts Bay* for 1765, pp. 108–110.

time. Among the four that were unrepresented was
Virginia, for no session of the House of Burgesses had been
held between the reception of the invitation and the time
of meeting. The resolutions adopted by the Stamp Act
Congress were mild in tone; but they reflected general
colonial opinion more accurately than did the more outspoken resolutions of the radical assemblies.

After the customary expressions of affection for the
royal person and the Protestant succession, the Resolutions
of the Stamp Act Congress proceed by declaring that the
colonists owe the same allegiance and have the same
inherent rights as Englishmen born within the realm. It
is true that the colonists owe "all due subordination to
that august body the parliament of Great-Britain"; but
they, in common with other Englishmen, enjoy the
undoubted right to have no taxes imposed upon them
but with their own consent, given personally or by their
representative. They are not represented in the House of
Commons, but only in their own assemblies, which
therefore have the sole right of taxing them. The
Resolutions furthermore assert that trial by jury is also
an inherent right of every British subject, and declare
that the extension of the admiralty jurisdiction, by giving
it cognizance of cases which heretofore have been tried
before juries in the Common Law courts, is a subversion
of colonial liberties. The Stamp Act Congress was the
first general assembly to be held by concerted colonial
action without any prompting from royal officials.[1] It
pointed the mode for combined extra-legal resistance;
it proved to be the forerunner of other continental con-

---

[1] The convention, called by Leisler in the spring of 1690, met at New York and was attended by delegates from a few colonies only. The Albany Congress of 1754, and other conferences of the same kind, were called by royal officials.

gresses, and thus fully justified the declaration of the
Lords of Trade that it was a precedent of "dangerous
tendency."[1] Unfortunately, though unavoidably, voting
in this Congress was by colonies, and this example led to
the same procedure being adopted by the First Continental
Congress that met in 1774.[2]

Grenville decided to appoint the stamp distributors
from among the colonists themselves, possibly because
he thought that this might make the measure less un-
palatable. He asked the agents to nominate candidates.
They complied, one of them, Jared Ingersoll of Connecticut, securing an appointment for himself, — much to
his later sorrow.

The names of the stamp distributors were published
early in August, and public wrath speedily directed itself
against them, notwithstanding their colonial birth and
social respectability. Riotings, window breakings, house-
burnings, and personal indignities were visited upon them
from New Hampshire to South Carolina. The most
serious affrays occurred at Boston, because there the
rougher elements were thoroughly organized, and the
hostility against the royal officials was most intense.
This was due, in part, to the unwonted zeal which Governor Bernard and Chief Justice Hutchinson and those
beneath them had shown in the enforcement of the trade
laws and the new revenue act.

On August 14, a stuffed figure, which was supposed to
represent Andrew Oliver, the stamp distributor, was found
hanging from a tree. Later in the day, the effigy was
carried through the streets and beheaded in front of his

---

[1] *Parliamentary History*, xvi, 122.
[2] *Authentic Account of the Proceedings of the Congress held at New York,*

In *MDCCLXV, On the Subject of the
American Stamp Act* (1767).

house. A small building, which he was erecting in the
business part of the town, was pulled to pieces and the
lumber used for a bonfire. "It is said," so Bernard
wrote to Halifax, "that there were 50 Gentlemen Actors
in this Scene disguised with trousers and jackets on."[1]
The next morning, Oliver resigned his office. Twelve days
later, on the 26th of August, a much more serious riot
occurred also at Boston. In the interval, old stories as to
Hutchinson's and Bernard's connection with reports concerning the smuggling of goods by leading merchants of the town
were sedulously propagated and aroused great resentment.[2]
In the evening of that day a mob gathered, in which there
were no gentlemen, trousered or otherwise. The rioters
visited the houses of Hallowell and Story, two customs
officials, and that of Hutchinson. They burst open the
doors, carried furniture, books, and papers into the street
and kindled a bonfire. Among the manuscripts that
were consumed on this occasion were volumes of records
of the admiralty court, for Story was the "Registrar
deputed" of that tribunal, and documents which Hutchinson had collected to aid him in writing his "History of
Massachusetts," — this destruction has given the work
itself the immortality of an "original source." The
rioters then began the demolition of Hutchinson's house;
but it was so strongly built that sunrise found them with
the roof only partly uncovered. A revulsion of feeling at
once set in. That very day, the voters met in town

[1] Bernard to Halifax, August 16, 1765
(Ms.). Portions of this letter and of
other letters describing the events of
this time are in the *Parliamentary
History*, xvi, 126 and fol.

[2] Bernard to the Lords of Trade,
August 31, 1765 (Ms). From this time
on the governor's letters grow bitter
toward the radical party in the colony.
"So seditious a Nature, & so Flagitious
a tendency" becomes a standard form
descriptive of popular instructions and
resolves. His usefulness was over; but
in England politics blinded the leaders'
eyes to the necessity of taking prompt
action for his removal.

meeting[1] and expressed their "utter detestation of the
extraordinary violent proceedings" of "the last horrid
scene," although their hatred of the stamp tax burned as
fiercely as ever. Even Bernard was affected by the prompt
action of the townsmen and wrote that he wished some
means, consistent with the dignity of Parliament, might
be found to put an end to the Stamp Act[2] — the reformation of the colonial governments might be resumed when
resentment had died down.

Communication with North Carolina was slow in 1765
as it was throughout this period; but the tardiness of the
coming of information did not in any way lessen the indignation of the people when the news arrived. On
October 19, of a Saturday evening, nearly five hundred
assembled at Wilmington on the Cape Fear River. They
hanged and burned the "Effigy of a certain Honourable
Gentleman." They then visited every house in the town
and brought all the gentlemen to the bonfire, where they
insisted upon their drinking the toast of "Liberty, Property, and no Stamp Duty, and confusion to Lord B——te."
On November 16 "William Houston, Esq; Distributor
of Stamps for this Province" made his appearance. At
once three or four hundred persons with drums beating and
colors flying repaired to his lodging, took him to the court
house, and there extracted from him "a resignation satisfactory to the Whole." They then bore him in an arm-

---

[1] *Boston Town Records*, 1758–1769,
p. 152. So rapid was the reaction that
Bernard, who had summoned a meeting
of the council with a view to taking
energetic action, desisted from any such
display of vigor. With his family he
was residing at Castle William, the fort
in the harbor, for the summer months.
His letters describe vividly how rapid
was the change of opinion.

[2] Bernard's *Select Letters* (London,
1774), 28. Much of the material given
in the *Select Letters* is also to be found
in documents in the Appendix to the
second edition of *The Conduct of the
Late Administration examined, relative
to the American Stamp-Act* (London,
1777).

chair back to his lodgings, where " the best liquors " were
provided. After the customary bonfire in the evening and
more toasts the business was completed " and not the least
Insult offered to any Person." On the margin of the
printed sheet[1] from which this description has been taken
there appears a skull and crossbones with a legend " This
is the Place to affix the Stamp." Stuart, the publisher of
this paper, had been quite unwilling to keep on printing it
stampless, but had been obliged to do so " at the Hazard
of his Life, being maimed, or have his Printing-Office destroy'd."

As the stamp distributors were resigning, the stamps
themselves began to arrive; but everywhere on the continent, south of Halifax and north of St. Augustine, none
came before the stamp dispensers had laid down their
offices. In the excited condition of the public mind, the
governors were not anxious to take upon themselves any
duties in connection with distributing the stamps that
were not plainly theirs. At New York, Lieutenant Governor Cadwallader Colden turned the packages over to
the city fathers.[2] At Boston, Bernard sought the advice of
the House of Representatives and was told in reply that it
was none of that body's business[3] to advise him as to his
duty. Everywhere, indeed, there was " total Languor, and
Want of Energy "[4] on the part of the representatives of

---

[1] *Continuation of the North-Carolina
Gazette, Numb. 58.* November 20 [1765],
in the library of the Massachusetts Historical Society.

[2] Colden had attempted to carry out
his instructions; but, finding it impossible to do so, he made a declaration
that he would leave the whole matter to
his successor. See Massachusetts Historical Society's *Collections*, Fourth Series,
x, 559, 581; *The Conduct of Cadwallader
Colden, Esquire, late Lieutenant-Gov-*

*ernor of New York: relating to the
Judges Commissions, Appeals to the
King, and the Stamp-Duty.* Printed
in the year *MDCCLXVII*, p. 46; " The
Colden Papers," vol. ii, in the *Collections*
of the New York Historical Society for
1877.

[3] *Speeches of the Governors of
Massachusetts*, etc., 49.

[4] " Sparks Manuscripts," No. 4, vol.
x, Secretary Conway to Bernard, October
24, 1765. There are other official papers

the crown. Here and there a stamp or a piece of stamped paper was used,[1] but the number of instances in which the act was obeyed was so small that to all intents and pur poses it was a dead letter from the beginning.

On the 28th of November, a vessel from Virginia sailed into the Cape Fear River bearing the stamps that were designed for North Carolina; as there was no one to receive them, they remained on shipboard.[2] About a month later, in the early days of the new year, 1766, two vessels anchored at Wilmington without stamped clearances, but with written statements from customs officials at Philadelphia and St. Christopher's that no stamps could be procured at those ports, and a third vessel likewise circumstanced appeared soon after. A British cruiser, the *Viper*, was then lying at anchor in the river. Captain Lobb, her commander, seized these vessels, and, upon the advice of the attorney general of the province, prepared to take them to Halifax for adjudication. Upon this the principal gentlemen, freeholders, and other inhabitants of the neighborhood met and took an oath to resist the enforcement of the act to the death. They stopped the provisioning of the cruiser, thereby preventing her departure, and then sought out her commander. As they could not find him on shore, they sent a delegation to wait upon him on his own quarterdeck, and there so intimidated him that he gave up the

---

of this period in the same volume. The Lords of Trade were also disturbed by the doings of the colonists and made several representations to the crown. See "Journals," lxxiii, pp. 27, 263, etc.

[1] The *Halifax Gazette* for February 6-13, 1766, is on stamped paper; this number of the *Gazette* is also interesting because it contains an account of the seizure of ten boxes of stamped paper by the Haligonians and their destruction in a bonfire.

[2] *North Carolina Records*, vii, 122, 123, 143, 161. The ship *Portland* with

stamps and stamped paper for South Carolina, Georgia, Bermuda, and the Bahamas arrived at Charleston on November 21, 1765. The stamp distributor had already resigned. *Georgia Gazette*, November 21, 1765. Governor Fauquier of Virginia on March 12, 1766, wrote to Conway that "some merchants" had recently applied to him for Mediterranean passes and had given bonds on stamped paper; but his evidence is not conclusive on this point, or any other. It is to be remembered that the act was to have gone into effect on November 1.

vessels he had seized. They next secured the persons of the customs officials and extracted from them promises not to do anything to enforce the law until it should be accepted by the people.[1]

Custom house officials, generally, after ineffectual attempts at resistance, provided shipmasters with statements that stamped clearances could not be procured, or the provincial governors gave them "let-passes" that preserved them from seizure. Technically, all papers that were issued contrary to the provisions of the Stamp Act were null and void. Any decree of condemnation that Captain Lobb might have obtained in North Carolina would itself have been illegal; and it was for this reason that he wished to take his prizes to Halifax. Courts of law were generally closed for a time and this seriously affected creditors who could not secure judgments against those who owed them money. Administrators and executors also hesitated to pay out funds to heirs, and this doubtless inconvenienced widows and orphans. Edmund Pendleton of Virginia, who was naturally conservative, advised the opening of the courts, but suggested that no business should be done that required the use of stamps or stamped paper.[2] More radical counsels prevailed, however, and in a few weeks the courts were everywhere open and doing business.

The holding of the Stamp Act Congress was not the only evidence of a tendency toward colonial union that appeared in these months of excitement. Radical associations called "Sons of Liberty" were formed in New York, in the New England colonies, and elsewhere. The Sons of Liberty of

[1] Papers from "Tryon's Letter Book" in *Colonial Records of North Carolina*, vii, 169–186. These events are well summarized in R. D. W. Connor's *Cornelius Hartnett*, 33.

[2] Massachusetts Historical Society's *Proceedings*, Second Series, xix, 109. In the Library of Congress there is a broadside containing a petition from Peter Manigault and others asking for the opening of the courts at Charleston

New York and Connecticut formed a tentative union or
association which the radicals of Massachusetts and New
Hampshire were on the point of joining, or, perhaps, had
joined, when the news of the repeal of the Stamp Act put
an end for the time being to colonial excitement and prevented a revolutionary intercolonial organization being
formed in 1766. An interesting example of the disinclination of the colonists to obey "pernicious acts of Parliament" occurred at New Haven early in this year. A man,
who had come from the West Indies on a vessel with
Benedict Arnold, informed the collector that there were
smuggled goods on the ship. Thereupon, Arnold, with
others, seized him, tied him to the public whipping-post,
and gave him "near forty lashes with a small cord," for
which they were condemned to pay fifty shillings. Arnold
then wrote an indignant letter in a local paper, asking if it
was good policy for the people of a commercial town to
caress an informer; to his mind, every sensible man
should encourage trade.[1]

Meanwhile, the king had wearied of Grenville, who
lectured him as to his duties, and who gained his further
displeasure by omitting his mother's name from the list
of those from whom the regents or guardians should be
chosen in case he should again become insane. Grenville
had done this because he was afraid her enemies in Parliament would strike out her name, if it was in the bill; but
when the measure appeared without it, his opponents insisted
upon putting it in. The Marquess of Rockingham succeeded
him as the head of a ministry of those whigs who might
well be termed the "regulars." Rockingham came of the
great house of Thomas Wentworth, Earl of Strafford, who
lost his head on the block in 1641, and it was commonly
thought that the fate of ministers was ordinarily settled at

---

[1] Barber's *Historical Collections of Connecticut*, 166.

his dining table. The new ministers naturally opposed their predecessors' policy and, needing votes in the Commons, awaited anxiously the part that William Pitt and the few devoted souls who remained true to him would play. Moreover, advices from America became more and more menacing with the arrival of each packet. The disturbances growing out of the new system had created so much commercial distress in the colonies that merchants could not collect the moneys due them, and, therefore, could neither pay for goods which they already had on their hands nor venture to order new consignments. Exports to America fell from three million pounds in twelve months to one-half that sum ; at least, such was the current rumor in London.[1] Thousands of people were thrown out of employment in English manufacturing towns [2] and shipping centers, and merchants, manufacturers, and tradesmen from all parts of the kingdom petitioned Parliament to repeal or modify the acts of 1764 and 1765.

The question of what should be done with America was taken up in the House of Commons in January, 1766. Mr. Pitt at once took the leading part, for he was still burning with indignation at the defection of his wife's brother, George Grenville ; [3] but he had slight faith in the

[1] This statement is taken from an anonymous paper, Almon's *Political Register*, i, 251.

[2] Samuel Garbett to William Burke, Birmingham, December 14, 1765, *Calen-*dars *of State Papers, Home Office, 1760–1765*, p. 638.

[3] The relationship of Pitt and the Grenvilles is shown in the following table : —

HESTER, COUNTESS TEMPLE м. RICHARD GRENVILLE

| W. Pitt,
Earl of
Chatham | m. | Hester
Grenville
(Countess
of Chatham) | Richard,
Earl
Temple ;
d. 1779 | George
Grenville,
born 1712
Prime
Minister,
1763–1765 ;
d. 1770 | m. | Elizabeth
Wyndham |

F

Rockinghamites. Declaring that " Confidence is a Plant of slow Growth in an aged Bosom " — he was then fifty-eight years old — he exhibited great hesitation as to what course to pursue. Grenville defending himself with warmth, Pitt returned to the attack. In a fiery speech, he announced that Parliament had entire authority to bind the trade of the colonists, confine their manufactures, and legislate for them in all cases whatsoever, — " except that of taking the Money out of their Pockets without their Consents." [1] Franklin, who was then in London as agent for Pennsylvania and Massachusetts, was examined at the bar of the House of Commons. His testimony was conclusive as to the hopelessness of trying to enforce the Stamp Act, even in a modified form ; an army could not do it, although it might cause a rebellion.[2] The press was appealed to by both sides, and pamphlets appeared in great profusion. It will be well to examine the arguments set forth on either side with a view to discovering the ideas that urged on both parties to the disputation in America and in England in the next few years.

The resolutions of the Virginia House of Burgesses and those of the Stamp Act Congress have already been given in sufficient detail for the present purpose. The Pennsylvania Assembly went somewhat farther and declared that the government of Pennsylvania being founded on the

---

Richard Grenville, Lord Temple, represented the elder branch of the Temples of Stowe. John Temple, the surveyor general of customs at Boston, was descended from a younger branch of this family and on the decease of Sir Richard Temple, seventh baronet of Stowe, without children, succeeded to the title. After the Revolution, he was British consul general at New York.

[1] The Speech of Mr. P——. In a certain august Assembly On a late impor-

tant Debate, Printed in the Year —66, p. 33. In reference to Pitt's phrase, a member of the Irish Parliament is supposed to have said, " What a pother . . . whether money is to be taken out of their coat or their waistcoat pocket "; Three Letters to Dr. Price, 137 n.

[2] This examination has many times been reprinted since 1766. It may be most conveniently found in any edition of Franklin's writings or in the Parliamentary History.

natural rights of mankind and the noble principles of English liberty " is or ought to be perfectly free."

Among the many controversial tracts which were printed at this time, none states in clearer language the colonial position than Stephen Hopkins's "Rights of Colonies Examined." [1] He argued the matter as follows. If the British House of Commons is rightfully possessed of a power to tax the colonies in America, this power must be vested in it by the British constitution. Beyond doubt, the members of that body are the representatives of all the people of Britain, but their power cannot exceed that of their constituents. " And can it possibly be shewn," he asks, " that the people in *Britain* have a sovereign authority over their fellow-subjects in *America?* . . . It will be still more absurd, to suppose they can give a power to their representatives, which they have not themselves."

Among the pamphlets [2] printed in England dealing with the general subject of parliamentary taxation of the colonists, was one by Edward Bancroft who was then engaged in literary work, and whose later career as an English spy, or American spy, or both at one time, has occasioned much controversy. He declared [3] that every British subject possessing a forty shilling freehold within the limits of the empire was entitled to a vote for the member of the House

---

[1] This was printed at Providence, R. I., 1765. It was reprinted at London in the next year under the title of *The Grievances of the American Colonies Candidly Examined*. In the reprint, the sentences containing the argument noted above were not reproduced. On the other side, one of the ablest tracts written either in England or America is [Martin Howard's] *A Letter from a Gentleman at Halifax, to his Friend in Rhode-Island, containing Remarks upon a Pamphlet, entitled, The Rights of Colonies Examined* (Newport, 1765). This is replied to by James Otis in *A Vindication of the British Colonies, against the Aspersions of the Halifax Gentleman, in His Letter to a Rhode-Island Friend* (Boston, 1765).

[2] For the titles of the more important of these, see Note at the end of chapter.

[3] [Edward Bancroft] *Remarks on the Review of the Controversy between Great Britain and her Colonies* (London, 1769), p. 92.

of Commons for the county in which the freehold was situated, in addition to the right to vote for borough or city delegates which he might also enjoy. If the colonies are within the realm and the jurisdiction of its Parliament, every colonist having a freehold of forty shillings is entitled to vote for a member of the British House of Commons. Until that right is given them, Parliament will not be qualified to exercise jurisdiction over them. Somewhat similar ground was taken by Thomas Pownall in successive editions of his "Administration of the Colonies."[1] This statement of the arguments against colonial taxation by parliamentary grant might be extended almost indefinitely; but little new matter would be brought out by such elaboration.

The English point of view is stated in the speeches that are associated with the names of Pitt, Burke, and Grenville. In all of them the right of Parliament to legislate for America is distinctly set forth. Pitt limited it to external taxation; Burke thought that the exercise of legislative power was sometimes inexpedient; but Grenville asserted that the general legislative power and right of taxation were inseparable, if Parliament had not the latter, it had not the former. The most relentless analysis of the American position and refutation of the arguments set forth in the resolutions of the time is to be found in William Knox's "Controversy between Great Britain and her Colonies Reviewed." He especially seizes upon the phrases "natural born subjects" and "liege subjects" that are constantly to be found in those documents. In reply, he asserts that the rights and obligations of British subjects

<hr>

[1] The first edition was published in 1764; subsequent editions contain valuable appendices. On the circumstances of its publication, see Charles A. W. Pownall's *Thomas Pownall* (London, 1908), p. 174.

are inseparable. If the colonists are British subjects, they
have the rights of Englishmen and are bound by the laws
of the British Empire (namely, acts of Parliament); if
the colonists are not British subjects, they are not entitled
to the rights of Englishmen and may be taxed by Parliament regardless of whether they are represented or not.[1]
Adverting to the statement in the Pennsylvania Resolves
that the inhabitants of that province were perfectly free
and at the same time were entitled to the rights and
privileges of British subjects in Great Britain, he declares
that the enjoyment of privileges implies the performance
of obligations which cannot be associated with the phrase
"perfect freedom." As to Pitt's idea that there was a
distinction between external and internal taxation, Knox
declared that any act of Parliament occasioning expenditure
on the part of the colonists was in the nature of a tax ; it
was absurd to regard such a law as constitutional and to
hold that another law causing only a mere fraction of such
an expenditure was unconstitutional, on the ground that
it was internal taxation. Knox then shows his knowledge
of Locke's "Treatises of Government." That publicist had
asserted that society, being based on consent, " every man,
that hath any possessions, or enjoyment, of any part of the
dominions of any government, doth thereby give his *tacit
consent*, and is as far forth obliged to obedience to the laws
of that government, during such enjoyment, as any one
under it." [2] Knox applies this to the existing system by

---

[1] Hutchinson expressed the matter
thus : " You say you are British subjects ; you suppose you are constitutionally exempt from one of the obligations
which British subjects are under ; but
if you are exempt from the one, you
are exempt from all — and so, are not
British subjects." *Diary and Letters*,
i, 214.

[2] This is undoubtedly one of the weak
points in the theoretical arguments on
the basis of political organization. No
one is really ever free, nor does he " consent " in the meaning of the word as
used by Locke. It is also easily demon-
strated that no legislative body represents the unfranchised or even the
minority. Nevertheless, the broad un-

asserting that "every subject of Great Britain, when he is taxed by parliament, is taxed by his own consent, for he is then taxed by consent of those whom the society [on the Lockeian model] has impowered to act for the whole."[1]   If the colonists do not like this constitutional arrangement, they must reform the imperial constitution or separate from the empire.   Lord Lyttleton in a speech in the House of Peers developed this argument at greater length. This is "no question of expediency; it is a question of sovereignty till the Americans submit to this legislature."[2] The colonists, so he asserted, went out to America as subjects of Great Britain.[3]   Unless they can show a new compact between them and the supreme legislative of the empire, the Parliament of Great Britain, they are subjects still and liable to the laws of the country.   It is true that no subject is bound by any law to which he is not actually or virtually consenting.   If the colonists are subjects of Great Britain, they are virtually represented in Parliament and thereby consent to all the statutes made by it.   This idea was based on the theory that representation in the Commons was of classes in the community and was not in any sense a personal representation.[4]   In a private letter,

---

derlying generalities of Locke's scheme are perfectly clear and true now as they were in 1689 and 1776. The above quotation is from Locke's *Two Treatises of Government*, Book ii, § 119 (ed. London, 1728), p. 302.

[1] Knox's *Controversy*, 69.

[2] I am indebted to Mr. H. W. V. Temperley, Fellow of Peterhouse, Cambridge, for permission to use a copy of the debate in the House of Lords from the "Hardwick Manuscripts."

[3] *Parliamentary History*, xvi, 167. This phrase contains the crux of the difficulty. Englishmen in England looked upon the colonists as subjects of Great Britain and therefore owing obedience to it and to its legislature. The

colonists regarded themselves, as well as resident Englishmen, subjects of the British crown, and not at all as subjects of Great Britain. The matter was well stated by an English sympathizer, J. Shipley (*Speech Intended to have been Spoken on the Bill for Altering the Charters of the Colony of Massachusett's Bay* (second edition, London, 1774), p. 25). He said that the Massachusetts Government Act was "the highest and most arbitrary act of sovereignty, that one nation can exercise over another."

[4] Lord Mansfield, opposing the repeal of the Stamp Act (*Parliamentary History*, xvi, 172–175), brushed aside all the theoretical writings on the laws of nature and questions of expediency. "The law

written at this time, Sir Joseph Yates declared that by the constitution no money could be levied by the crown without the consent of Parliament: "To talk of personal representation of every individual is absurd ; for strictly speaking, no man is the personal representative of another, but who is actually chosen, and deputed by the person represented."[1] Technically, Sir Joseph Yates was no doubt right, for under the British form of government, Parliament was supreme in the empire. The mode of electing the members of the lower House had nothing to do with this particular point : all subjects of the crown were under its jurisdiction. Nevertheless, the unrepresentative character of the Commons,[2] using that word in its ordinary sense and not in its technical constitutional meaning, was patent to the colonists and to many good people in England as well.

A quarter of a century afterward, in 1793, Mr. Grey, who years later was the head of the government that secured the passage of the First Reform Act, presented a petition[3] to the House of Commons for a reform in the system

is made," he said, "and the question is, whether you had a right to make it." He could not agree that Otis's pamphlet was mad or silly, but even if it were, it was not to be disregarded, for many persons who had given forth foolish ideas had led people to rebellion and had overturned empires. He laid down two propositions : (1) that the British legislature represents the whole British empire and has authority to bind every part thereof and every subject of the crown, whether such subject has the right to vote or not; (2) that the colonists by the conditions of their settlement are more emphatically subjects of Great Britain than those dwelling within the realm. The British legislature has exercised the right of legislation over them without any dispute until the present matter came up. There is no distinction between the authority of Parliament within and without the realm. The colonists migrated with permission to form colonies and, therefore, from the very meaning of the word were, are, and must be subjects and owe allegiance and subjection to the mother country.

[1] Almon's *Biographical Anecdotes,* ii, 128.

[2] Edward Porritt's *The Unreformed House of Commons,* i, 37, 355, 408. Timothy Cunningham's *Historical Account of the Rights of Election of the several counties, cities, and boroughs of Great Britain* (London, 1783) is a useful and rare work.

[3] *Parliamentary History,* xxx, 787-925.

of representation. The statements that he made in debate and the facts that were given in the petition were as true in 1765 as in 1793. From these it appeared that a majority of all the members of the House was elected by less than fifteen thousand voters, most unevenly distributed over Great Britain.[1] Owing to the prevalence of rotten boroughs, in which there were few or no electors, one hundred and fifty-four individuals, among them the king and members of the House of Peers, named three hundred and seven members of the House of Commons.[2] Mr. Grey thought that had the reform, which he was then advocating, taken place immediately after 1763, the American Revolution would not have occurred. It is certain that the king by the use of national funds and the gift of places and pensions was able to keep a sufficient band of followers in the House of Commons from 1767 to 1781 to enforce his personal rule. At the very end of this period Lord George Germain, taunting the opposition with an unwillingness to impeach him, was instantly answered by George Byng that he was kept in power by "a band of hired men ready to support him, or any minister who will pay them. . . . Give us an honest Parliament and then see if the noble lord will repeat his suggestion."[3] In 1793, answering Mr. Grey and

---

[1] *Commons Journals*, xlviii, 739; *Parliamentary History*, xxx, 789. In *The Rights of Great Britain Asserted against the Claims of America* (tenth edition, London, 1776, p. 4) James Macpherson declared that scarce one resident of Great Britain in twenty-five is represented.

[2] The unrepresentative character of the Scottish delegation was even more glaring — if that were possible. The fifty-eight Scottish members were returned by less than seven thousand electors. One county contained fourteen thousand souls, but its vote was cast by twenty-one electors, of whom only one resided within its limits.

[3] *Parliamentary Register*, xxii, 147. Not only "King's Friends" but followers of all parties sat for nomination boroughs, as for example Isaac Barrè, who occupied a seat in the Commons by reason of Shelburne's favor from 1761 to 1790. The relation of the member for a "pocket borough" to his patron is well set forth in a note of Lord Sandwich to John Robinson, who was negotiating the sale of a seat in the gift of the First Lord of the Admiralty. The price was set at £2000 to be lent to Sandwich for five

those who spoke with him, Charles Jenkinson[1] pointed to
the repeal of the Stamp Act as justifying the existing system, and asserted that as soon as the American War became
unpopular in England, the North ministry was obliged to
resign, notwithstanding all the aid that the king and his
friends could give. The arrangement of the franchise, he
said, was a matter of wisdom and expediency. The object
was to constitute a House of Commons which should
be a just representative of the landed interests, the commercial classes, and the professions, including the army
and the navy. He admitted that if he were beginning
anew he would not arrange matters precisely as they were,
giving the franchise to Liverpool and Bristol, and not be-
stowing it upon Manchester and Birmingham ; but this
really made little difference, because commercial members
could be selected as well by the voters of two of these
cities as by the voters of all four. The case of Manchester
and Birmingham, to which Jenkinson alluded, had already
been referred to in the debate in 1766 to justify the thesis
that the colonists were represented in Parliament; for were
they not as much represented as the people of Manchester
and Birmingham? In point of fact under the broad colonial declaration that no one could be taxed who was not
personally represented, no legislative assembly that ever
existed could rightfully levy a tax. There are always persons and places " unrepresented," if representation is regarded as a right ; if, however, it is looked upon as a duty
by which the voter exercises one of the functions of the
State, then one comes back to Jenkinson's query how to

years and the cost of the election —
about £ 300. The conditions were " the
thinking and acting as I do in all
American points, and supporting the
present administration in their whole
system." *Abergavenny Manuscripts*,
p. 11, — the letter was written in 1775.
[1] *Parliamentary History*, xxx, 808–
820; see especially 815–817.

arrange the electorate to get the best assembly.   Probably
every country and every decade would answer this question
in its own way.   The colonists, certainly, had answered it
in their own way and in one which was unlike that which
prevailed in England.

   One of the curious phenomena that attracts the attention
of the student of colonial institutions is the way in which the
settlers repeated certain arrangements of the mother country and did not reproduce others.   They modelled their
criminal code on that of England, they based their local
government on that of the home land, but they built up
their representative systems entirely anew.   With few exceptions, their legislatures were chosen in accordance with
general laws.   In the middle and southern colonies, every
county or parish sent its members.   In New England,
every town was represented either by members elected
separately by the town voters, or, in the case of newly
settled towns in combination with other places.   There
were inequalities of apportionment in every colony, especially in Pennsylvania, New York, and South Carolina,[1] but
there was nothing that can be regarded as the counterpart
of the rotten borough system of England.   A few incorporated towns, a few manors, and one college enjoyed special
representation.   As the friction with the colonies increased,
the English government endeavored to limit the further
popularizing of colonial legislatures.   The governors of
the royal provinces were instructed to refuse their assent
to the establishment of new counties and towns, except on
condition that the question of summoning representatives from the new administrative unit should be left to

---

[1] See the acts of 1745, 1747, and 1759   iii, 656, 692; iv, 98.
in Cooper's *Statutes of South Carolina,*

the royal authority.[1] Apportionment of representation in the colonies, therefore, constantly grew less and less equitable; but the colonial ideal was far otherwise and, when unrestricted, was fairly well realized.

As with the apportionment, so with the franchise : in England, it rested upon the accident of historical descent ; in America, it depended upon general rules.[2] Sometimes it was regulated in the charter of the colony, as in Massachusetts, but usually every man who possessed a moderate amount of property could vote, although in some colonies it was provided that the property must be landed estate. The electors were not numerous in any colony,[3] but, as a rule, they were equitably distributed, both geographically and socially. The growth of the rotten borough system had led to the breaking down of residential qualifications for both the electors and the elected and, in England, a man possessed as many votes as he had technical qualifications. There are instances of plurality of voting qualifications in the colonies, but the tendency was to give no elector more than one vote.   In some colonies a representative might live outside of the district ; but ordinarily only residents were selected.[4]   Everywhere the idea that the representative

---

[1] See *Massachusetts Province Laws*, iii, 70–72; iv, 451 and H. A. Cushing's " From Provincial to Commonwealth Government in Massachusetts," 19–27, in Columbia University *Studies in History, Economics, and Law*, vol. vii. Between 1691 and 1761, fifty-nine towns were incorporated, of which one only was not to have representation in the General Court.   For this and other statements in these paragraphs, I am indebted to Mr. Waldo G. Leland.

An example of the aversion of the government at London to an enlargement of the colonial representation by colonial law is contained in a letter from Hillsborough to Governor Moore of New York, October 12, 1768. He writes that Albany County may be divided and that writs may be issued for the choice of two members for the new county ; " but his Majesty does not approve of its being made a part of the law."

[2] The Virginia law of 1736 regulating the franchise is typical; see Hening's *Statutes of Virginia*, iv, 475.

[3] On this point, see Albert Bushnell Hart's excellent study of the " Exercise of the Suffrage " in the *Political Science Quarterly*, vii, 316.

[4] The preamble of the New York law of 1769 (*Colonial Laws*, iv, 1094) states that doubts had arisen as to

was the personal deputy of the voters of his district either was established or was gaining ground. This brief survey of the representative systems of Great Britain and the colonies shows that very different ideas on this subject prevailed in the two parts of the empire. The phrase "no taxation without representation" in England simply meant that the executive authority could levy no money without the previous consent of Parliament, more especially of the House of Commons; in the colonies, it meant that taxes could be voted only by those bodies in which the voters were present in person or were represented by those in whose election they had actually taken part. In this respect, as in some others, colonial institutions had drifted so far away from those of the home land and had become so uniform in their principal characteristics that the colonies may well be considered as already forming an embryonic nation; but this was not realized by the settlers themselves or by any one in England. The political leaders of the old country firmly held to the idea of the imperial supremacy of Parliament; the colonists tried to harmonize their aspirations for freedom and the enjoyment of human rights with fealty to the British constitution, and this led them to the use of phrases like "due subordination to Parliament" and "free people" which were indefensible, for a free people cannot exist under the obligation of allegiance to a king.

Acting on the advice of Pitt and Franklin and other leaders, the Rockingham ministry attempted a resettlement of the colonial problem. Franklin had said that the

whether nonresidents could vote in districts where they possessed a freehold, the act gives them this right, but the delegate must have been a resident for six months in the district from which he was chosen to the assembly; freemen of corporations must have been actually residing within the corporate limits for three months next preceding the election.

Stamp Act must be wholly repealed; Pitt had suggested that the supremacy of Parliament should be declared by law. Both were now done. The Stamp Act was repealed absolutely; but the act declaring the supreme power of the British legislature, the Declaratory Act,[1] went far beyond what Pitt had advocated, in that it proclaimed the subordination of the colonies without any qualification as to internal taxation. It also annulled all votes and proceedings of colonial assemblies and other bodies in the plantations that had in any way denied parliamentary supremacy. In communicating these enactments to the colonial governors, General Conway, Secretary of State, adverted to the "Moderation, the Forbearance, the unexampled Lenity, and Tenderness of Parliament towards the Colonies, which are so signally displayed in those Acts." He expressed the hope that the colonists would return to that "chearful obedience to the Laws and legislative Authority of Great Britain and to those Sentiments of respectful Gratitude to the Mother Country"[2] for so much grace and condescension so remarkably manifested by king and Parliament.

Having thus entered upon colonial matters, the government next proceeded to renew the Quartering Act with some changes that were expected to make it more effective. Then they turned to the Revenue Act of 1764. The colonists evidently did not like the collection of duties at their custom houses, so it was now (1766) provided that the

---

[1] For the Declaratory Act see Note I. Pitt's followers in the Lords attacked it severely on account of the failure to exclude internal taxation of the colonists from the scope of parliamentary supremacy. *Parliamentary History*, xvi, 117.

[2] Conway's letter is printed in the *North Carolina Records*, vii, 192; *Prior Documents*, 89; Belsham's *Memoirs of the Reign of George III*, ii, 433; and in part in Mrs. Napier Higgins's *The Bernards of Abington and Nether Winchendon*, ii, 35. The definite news of the repeal of the Stamp Act reached New York April 25, 1766; Montresor's *Journals* in New York Historical Society's *Collections* for 1881, p. 362.

imposts on textiles that had been collected on importation
into America should in the future be collected at the time
of exportation from England.[1] The proceeds were to be
paid directly into the exchequer, where they could be used
for the general expenses of the kingdom instead of being
spent in America for the support of the soldiers.   The
cost to the colonial consumer would be the same, and the
benefits to British manufacturers, shipowners, and merchants would be as great as ever.   Edmund Burke and
other Rockinghamites believed fully in the legislative
power of Parliament in every case.   It was not always
expedient to exercise this power.   Possibly they thought
that this transference of the time of collection of the duty
would make its existence less noticeable and therefore more
expedient.   The duty on Madeira wine was retained, but
that on molasses was changed from threepence a gallon
on foreign molasses to one penny a gallon on all molasses
imported into the continental colonies, whether of British
or foreign production.   No one could for a moment pretend
that this was for the protection of sugar planters or of any
one else, except British taxpayers, or that it was in any
way a regulation of trade.   It was a tariff for revenue
only, nothing more nor less, — and was the work of the
Rockinghamites and of the followers of William Pitt.   It
marked the beginning of a new chapter in colonial policy.

These arrangements for extracting funds from colonial
consumers, together with the Declaratory Act, more than did
away with whatever of concession there may have been in
the repeal of the Stamp Act.   With an ignorance of English conditions that is comparable only to Englishmen's
lack of knowledge of American affairs, the colonists rejoiced
greatly over the repeal of the Stamp Act.   In their eyes,

---

[1] 6 George III, Cap. 52 (*Statutes at Large*, 1753–1766, vii, 619).

George III and William Pitt were deliverers from bondage. The New Yorkers voted statues to both. Pitt, in a toga, was carved in stone ; George, on horseback, was cast in lead and brass and richly gilded.[1] Really, the repeal of the Stamp Act settled nothing. Unconsciously, the American people had come to the determination to pay no more money levied by parliamentary grant. Many a stupider man than George Grenville and many a lighter headed man than Charles Townshend might well have been put on their guard by Franklin's answer to the inquiry whether the colonists, by the same line of reasoning which they had advanced against the Stamp Act, might not likewise object to external taxes levied by parliamentary law. " They never have hitherto," the philosophic statesman replied, and continued, " Many arguments have been lately used here to shew them that there is no difference, . . . At present they do not reason so, but in time they may possibly be convinced by these arguments."

[1] At the outset of the Revolution, the leaden part of the statue was melted into bullets, which were made into cartridges by the ladies of Lichfield, Connecticut. Roger Wolcott, in Massachusetts Historical Society's *Proceedings*, Second Series, iv, 291-298.

NOTES

I. The Declaratory Act. — The title is " An Act for the better secur‧ing the Dependency of his Majesty's Dominions in America upon the Crown and Parliament of Great Britain." [1]   The pream.b'e recites that several of the Houses of Representatives in the American colo‧nies have against law claimed to themselves or to the general assem‧blies the sole and exclusive right of taxing the colonists, and have passed votes derogatory to the legislative authority of Parliament and inconsistent with the dependency of the colonies upon the crown.   It is therefore declared that the said colonies have been, are, and of right ought to be, subordinate unto and dependent upon the imperial crown and Parliament of Great Britain and that Par‧liament " had, hath, and of right ought to have, full power and au‧thority to make laws and statutes of sufficient force and validity to bind the colonies and people of America, subjects of the crown of Great Britain in all cases whatsoever."   The second section declares that all resolutions, votes, orders, and proceedings, denying this right of Parliament are utterly null and void.

II. Tracts. — Among the arguments against the colonial conten‧tion are the following : —

[William Knox's] *The Claim of the Colonies to an Exemption from Internal Taxes imposed by Authority of Parliament, Examined : in a Letter from a Gentleman in London to his Friend in America* (London, 1765) ; Soame Jenyns's *The Objections to the Taxation of our American Colonies, by the Legislature of Great Britain, Briefly Consider'd* (London, 1765) ; and *An Examination of the Rights of the Colonies, upon the Principles of Law, By a Gentleman at the Bar* (London, 1766).   On the other side, John Dickinson published anonymously the following pamphlet, *The Late Regulations, re‧specting the British Colonies on the Continent of America considered; In a Letter from a Gentleman in Philadelphia to his Friend in London* (Philadelphia, 1765).   The American position is most clearly stated in a letter from William Pitkin, Governor of Connecticut, to W. S. Johnson, dated Hartford, 6th June, 1768, and printed in the Massa‧chusetts Historical Society's *Collections*, Fifth Series, ix, 276.

---

[1] 6 George III, Cap. 12. Pickering's *Statute at Large*, xxvii, 19; Running-   ton's *Statutes at Large*, vii, 571.

CHAPTER IV

THE TOWNSHEND ACTS

THE confusion in English politics that marks the first ten years of the reign of the third George occupies the journals and letters of the time, almost to the exclusion of references to American affairs. Whigs, tories, and "King's Friends" scrambled for office most desperately. They held with that transplanted placeman, Sir Francis Bernard, Governor of Massachusetts, that "it would be a strange piece of self denial"[1] for a minister to suppress an office which afforded lucrative patronage, no matter how much the people might profit by its abolition. To them the government was like a great plum pudding,[2] made to be enjoyed. They looked upon America as an asylum for those members of their families who could not live off the public at home. They essayed to extend the British administrative system to the old settled colonies, to treat them as integral parts of the empire, and to govern their inhabitants as " subjects of Britain."

Having dominated the parliamentary session of 1766, Mr. Pitt joined hands with the king to make an end of party government by establishing a new ministry in which all factions should be represented. He became a peer, with the titles of Viscount Pitt and Earl of Chatham, and took the office of Lord Privy Seal, to which great dignities

---

[1] " Bernard Papers " (Ms.), v, 282.

[2] This simile was used by Lord Barrington, a most successful office seeker, who, in 1780, had £13,000 of the public money in his hands as the result of having held the treasurership of the navy from 1762 to 1765. Almon's *Parliamentary Register*, xix, 69.

and few duties were attached. One of his followers, the
Duke of Grafton, became ostensible head of the government; another, Charles Pratt, now Lord Camden, presided
over the Peers as Lord Chancellor. Shelburne assumed
charge of colonial affairs, and his henchman, Isaac Barré,
held a minor office. These were all Pittites. Some of
Rockingham's adherents, as General Conway, remained in
place. Charles Townshend and Lord Barrington, who
belonged to no group except that of persistent office
seekers, were Chancellor of the Exchequer and Secretary
at War respectively. Finally, Lord North, a tory, held
the minor but lucrative office of joint paymaster of the
forces. It was a queer accumulation of politicians, the
"Mosaic Ministry," Burke, Rockingham's brilliant secretary, dubbed it.

Chatham almost at once betook himself to Bath, suffering from one of those strange disorders that sometimes
afflict humanity. Ordinarily, he was sane and reasonable,
but when one spoke of politics he shook like a person in
mild hysterics. His dominating personality removed, the
strongest men in the ministry seized control, regardless of
their political relationships to their departed chief. Of
these Charles Townshend astonished all observers by "the
extent and irregularity of his talents." [1] As Chancellor of
the Exchequer, his task was extremely difficult and was
not made easier by the factious opposition of Grenville

---

[1] *Letters to and from Henrietta,
Countess of Suffolk*, ii, 267. The account
of Townshend's "Champagne Speech,"
in Fitzgerald's *Charles Townshend*, ch.
xviii, gives a good idea of the levity of
the man who was much more responsible
than George Grenville for the loss of the
American colonies to England. The
cabinet meeting at which Townshend set
forth his policy is described by Shelburne
in a letter to Pitt in *Chatham Correspondence*, iii, 232. The debate on the
budget in 1767 is well described by Grenville in a letter to the Earl of Bucking-
hamshire in Royal Historical Manuscripts Commission's *Report on the
Lothian Manuscripts*, 275. See for
details Charles Townshend's "State of
the Nation" in Almon's *Collection of
Scarce and Interesting Tracts*, ii, 205-225.

and Dowdeswell, his predecessors in office. In opening
the budget for 1767, he estimated the expense of the colonial military establishment for the coming financial year
at four hundred thousand pounds.   Grenville and Dowdeswell at once intervened. They proposed to reduce this
by one-half and to make the Americans pay it all. Add
ing to the four hundred thousand pounds that would be
thus cut out from the appropriation bill the amount that
would be gained by the new export duties on goods sent
to America, it might be possible to strike off a shilling
from the land tax.[1] This proposition met with immediate
acclaim, for the great majority of the members of the
Commons were landholders or represented land holding
interests. Moreover, Townshend found it very difficult to
resist it, because he had always maintained the right of
Parliament to tax the colonists externally and internally,
and his chief had loudly proclaimed the supremacy of the
British legislature in all matters relating to external taxation. Townshend now pledged himself to gain a large
sum from America by reorganizing the customs service
and by laying new duties on goods imported into the colonies. These imposts were to be collected in America, and
it is worth while remembering that it was only a few
months since the collection of somewhat similar duties
had been changed from the colonies to Great Britain.
The result of all this was to add appreciably to the cost

[1] The land tax amounted to £2,037,854
and was four shillings in the pound on
the valuation of 1692.   One shilling
therefore brought in a little over half a
million.

[2] Townshend had voted for the repeal
of the Stamp Act on the ground of its
inexpediency, and not because he had any
doubt as to the constitutional power of
Parliament to tax the colonists in any way
it saw fit. In 1767 he said in debate that
he did not know "any distinction between internal and external taxes; it is a
distinction without a difference, it is perfect nonsense." W. S. Johnson to Wm.
Pitkin, London, Feb. 12, 1767, "Trumbull
Papers" in Massachusetts Historical
Society's *Collections*, Fifth Series, ix, 215.
Johnson was in London as agent for Connecticut. His letters, extending to March,
1771, give many details of Anglo-Ameri-
can politics.

of many manufactures of England and Europe, upon their sale in America. From the funds to be gained in this manner, Townshend proposed to maintain a colonial civil list which would be independent of assemblies. If there were any surplus, it could be used for the support of the troops. The scheme delighted the place holders, for it opened a long vista of good jobs.[1] It commended itself to those interested in administration, for it would free governors and judges from colonial control. If the plan worked well, assemblies would become unnecessary and provincial institutions might be entirely reconstructed.

Having decided to levy new imposts, the government took a good deal of pains to find out what articles would better be selected. One suggestion was that the Mediterranean trade might be opened to the colonists upon the condition that everything imported thence should be subject to duties upon arrival in America. This plan had something to be said in its favor, because it would grant a certain freedom of trade to the colonists. It was set aside, however, because it would not only deprive London merchants of the profits which they gained from handling goods on the way from Mediterranean ports to the colonies, but it would also divert from the exchequer the duties on those goods. As there were no longer any drawbacks paid on reëxportation, this would mean a distinct loss to the revenue. Another suggestion was that a tonnage tax should be levied upon all vessels entering colonial ports. Finally it was decided to lay duties on a few English manufactures, — paper, painters' colors, and glass, and also

---

[1] At the moment, several colonial salaries and many pensions to former colonial officers were paid out of the four and a half per cent Barbadian fund. The establishment of a continental colonial civil list would free this fund from the payment of some of these and the surplus could be used for purely English pensions. See the present work, vol. ii, p. 511.

upon tea.[1] As the colonial system acted as a protective tariff for English-made goods, the carrying out of this plan would turn into the treasury some portion of the extra price that British manufacturers and merchants were able to exact on all sales to the plantations. Another law provided for the reorganization of the American customs service,[2] and a third made more flexible the admiralty jurisdiction in the colonies.[3] Townshend died in September, 1767, and this last act was not passed until after his death. As it was designed to remove some of the hardships that necessarily attended the new system, it deserves remembrance to lessen the obloquy which his other doings have fastened upon his name.

The king now appointed an American Board of Commissioners of the Customs.[4] These were five in number

---

[1] 7 George III, Cap. 46 (Pickering's *Statutes at Large*, xxvii, 505). The following duties were collected at the American custom houses in 1768: —

		£	sh	d
25 Charles II	Enumerated goods from one colony to another (tobacco), per lb.			1
4 Geo. III, Cap. 15	Madeira & wine of the Western Isles from the Islands, per ton	7	0	0
4 Geo. III, Cap. 15	Wines through Great Britain from Spain, Portugal, or *elsewhere*, except French, per ton		10	0
6 Geo. III, Cap. 52	Foreign sugar, indigo, coffee (might be ware-housed or exported to Great Britain or Southern Europe). For coffee, per cwt.	2	19	9
	British grown coffee & pimento, per cwt.		7	0
6 Geo. III, Cap. 52	All molasses, per gal.			1
7 Geo. III, Cap. 46	Glass, lead, painters' colors, paper at varying rates; repealed 1770			
	Tea, per lb.			3

Instructions by the Commissioners of His Majesty's Customs in America (to John Mascarene).

[2] 7 George III, Cap. 41 (Pickering's *Statutes at Large*, xxvii, 447).

[3] 8 George III. Cap. 22 (*ibid.*, xxviii, 70). Papers elucidating the organization of the enlarged service are in *Colonial Records of North Carolina*, vii, 459; xi, 216.

[4] Their commission, with much material illustrating the history of the customs service from 1767 to 1775, will be printed by the Massachusetts Historical Society in a forthcoming volume. The commission bears date of September 8, 1767. It was printed at London in the

and were directed to make their headquarters at Boston. Their authority extended from Davis Streights to the Capes of Florida and included Bermuda and the Bahamas. They had entire charge of the customs service within these limits and were responsible to the Lords of the Treasury at London and not in any way to the British Commissioners of the Customs. The chairman of the board was Henry Hulton, who had been "plantation clerk" in the office of the British commissioners. Of the other members John Temple and Charles Paxton deserve remembrance. The former had been Surveyor General for the northern colonies since 1760. He belonged to the great Temple connection, although he himself was of American birth. He and Bernard had grown very hostile to one another, and had complained most vigorously to the home authorities of each other's behavior. The charges had been referred to Hulton, who had reported in favor of Temple. It is in this connection that Hulton first comes into American history. Paxton had been in the Boston custom house. He had become very unpopular with the merchants of the town and had also incurred the dislike of Temple. He had gone to England either to lay his grievances before the authorities there, or had been summoned home to advise them. He now returned to Boston on the same ship with Hulton and Burch, another commissioner. Bernard thought that they would not be allowed to land. As it happened, they disembarked at Boston on November 5, 1767. Guy Fawkes Day was still celebrated at that town. A procession of celebrants having figures of the Pope, the Pretender, and the Devil — the last being named "Charles" in dishonor of the return-

same year and is given, wrongly entitled "Instructions," in the *American Gazette,* 112. Six numbers of this interesting magazine were printed at London in the years 1768–1770. At the end of No. 6 is an index to the whole publication.

ing Paxton — met them at the wharf.   The paraders preceded the Commissioners on their way ; and whenever
Paxton paused to greet a friend, the Devil paused likewise
and faced conspicuously about.[1]   Beyond this pleasantry,
no indignity was offered them, but the attitude of the
townspeople was unmistakable.

On Tuesday, November 18, 1767, the Commissioners held
their first " Board of Customs at M[r.] Deblois's great Room in
Hanover Street." [2]   It soon appeared that Paxton had made
full use of his time on the voyage to poison Hulton's mind
against Temple, who found himself almost constantly in
a minority ; [3] but the majority insisted upon affixing his
name to whatever measures they adopted.   They also
refused to confirm his appointments and suspended the
official whom Temple had put in the place of the collector at Salem.   The Lords of the Treasury took the
former Surveyor General's part.   They directed the Commissioners to reinstate his appointee at Salem ; and
reminded them that their Board had been created not
only for the prosecution of unlawful traders but also for
the security of honest merchants.[4]   At this moment, the
English authorities had " the strongest desire," to use
Barrington's words, for quiet in America.   They especially
wished that there should be no more disputes between

[1] Letter to Lord George Sackville in
Stopford-Sackville Manuscripts, i, 126.

[2] *Boston Gazette*, November 23, 1767.

[3] Not anticipating his downfall, in
January, 1766, Temple had written to
Paxton that he desired " no further
intimacy" with him.   Nevertheless, he
seems to have been surprised at the
" unconquerable gloom " which appeared
on Paxton's countenance when they met
in November of the next year.

[4] The minute of the Board of Customs
Commissioners at Boston reciting this
order is interesting as showing their

relations to the Lords of the Treasury:
" Their Lordships [of the Treasury] having been pleased to signifie that they are
unwilling for many reasons to order the
suspension of M[r.] Fisher to be taken off
by an Imaediate Interposition of their
Authority.   But desire and direct that
this Act may be done by an order from
the Board."   " Temple Papers " (Ms.),
August 1, 1769.   There is a letter-book
in the Custom House at Boston which
throws light on the relations of the
commissioners to their subordinates in
the years 1772–1775.

the mother country and her colonies, or between governors and their assemblies.

Notwithstanding their internal wranglings, the Customs Commissioners performed their task very well. They reorganized the service and made it efficient. To do this they were obliged greatly to increase the number of employees, — there were three times as many of them at Philadelphia in 1770 as there were in 1767. The new men were almost all of them natives of the British Islands, a fact which did not tend to increase their popularity. Formerly, there had been great opportunities for peculation by the customs officials and for collusion between them and the importers. Even where there had been no criminality, there had been great laxness. At Charleston, in South Carolina, it appeared that the regulations had been constantly violated, the collector not requiring bonds to be given until a vessel cleared, instead of before a single bit of her outward cargo was placed on board. Business methods, some of them almost modern in character, were now introduced, and a system of intelligence was established which went far toward making the customs service work as one great machine.

The Revenue Act of 1767 added one more document to the sheaf which the master of every vessel had to have with him at sea. This was a "cocket," or list, enumerating every package in the cargo with its peculiar identifying marks. As soon as the Commissioners had made a good beginning with the reformation of the customs service, they set about enlarging the system of coast patrol. At Philadelphia and a few other ports, revenue cutters were stationed. These were manned by employees of the customs service and were directly under the control of the collectors. There were also many small vessels that were

commanded by officers of the navy. These received "deputations" from the Commissioners authorizing them to seize
suspected vessels, but their movements were directed by
the admiral on the station. They swept up and down the
coast, penetrating the smallest harbors in search of prizes,
as they termed their captures. They were not very successful, because lowering the duties on molasses had removed the principal inducement to illicit trade by making
it unprofitable. The high price that the English East
India Company was obliged to charge for its tea, owing to
the heavy exactions of the British government and its
own lavish expenses in India, invited smuggling in that
commodity.[1] And so did the heavy duty on Madeira; but
the amount of smuggling had dwindled to trifling proportions.[2] Bernard and the other governors were able to re-

[1] Under date of April 28, 1766, Bernard
writes that a vessel from St. Eustatia
had put into Barnstaple Bay to the southward of Boston. There her cargo of tea,
bales of duck, and other foreign European goods from Holland had been landed
and the ship herself had sailed away,
presumably for another cargo; "Bernard Papers" (Ms.), iv, 222. Again in
July, 1768, he informs Hillsborough that
a cargo of molasses which had been
seized had been taken from the schooner
that had brought it to Boston and carted
away. This vessel had been left at the
wharf, instead of being placed under the
guns of a man-of-war. Upon representations being made to the town authorities,
the selectmen summoned the captain
and directed him to restore the goods to
the vessel. This was done and elicited
from Bernard the comment that he, the
governor, could not have brought it
about. *Ibid.*, vi, 325; vii, 1. These are
the only cases noted by him after 1766.

[2] The following table is compiled from
the accounts of Charles Steuart, cashier
of the American Customs. The first
entry includes receipts from September
8, 1767 to January 5, 1769. The others
commence on January 5 and include the
following twelve months.

	To 1769	1769	1770	1771	1772	1773	1774	Total
	£	£	£	£	£	£	£	£
Seizures and penalties by customs officers	38	363	922	607	378	506	1403	4217
Seizures by ships-of-war	624	110	537	719	2017	815	992	5814
Totals	662	473	1459	1326	2395	1321	2395	10,031

port few instances, and the amounts received by the government from seizures was very small, only ten thousand pounds from November, 1767 to January, 1775. The expense and inconvenience to every one engaged in commerce was very great ; fees were exacted in all directions, for bonds and certificates as well as for clearances and other papers. The former were required of skippers of "little open boats" as well as from the masters of sea-going ships, and custom houses were few and far between, which occasioned much delay. The hardships of the regulations put an end to existing modes of trade in many cases and the profits on foreign commerce dwindled to so low a figure that importers were far readier to sign non-importation agreements in 1769 than they had been in 1766.

In the first years covered by this volume, the American customs had brought in less than two thousand pounds annually and the cost of collecting had been nearly nine thousand in each year.[1] Now, with the new organization and the new duties added to the old, they brought in over thirty thousand pounds yearly from 1768 to 1774 at an annual cost to the revenue of thirteen thousand.[2] More-

[1] See above p. 35 note.
[2] Amounts collected under the Commissioners, 1767–1775.

ACTS OF PARLIAMENT	To 1769	1769	1770	1771	1772	1773	1774	Total
	£	£	£	£	£	£	£	£
25 Charles II (tobacco)	945	539	660	806	320	643	1,533	5,446
6 George II and 4 George III } Wines	7,560	12,570	12,933	12,537	12,621	13,027	12,447	83,695
6 George III (molasses)	10,036	12,616	12,879	13,371	16,389	14,795	17,470	97,556
7 George III (tea, etc.)	9,723	8,189	3,413	4,596	1,677	4,170	987	32,755
Totals	28,264	33,914	29,885	31,310	31,007	32,635	32,437	219,452

over, the establishment of an effective American customs service was equivalent to reënacting the whole set of navigation laws from Charles II on. Hitherto, these had never been enforced. Now, they were carried out to the letter. Charles Townshend, by giving life to these obsolete enactments, established or reëstablished the colonial system. Regarding the amounts paid to the American customs officials in these years, and the salaries of civil officers in America that were paid out of these revenues, one hundred and fifteen thousand pounds in all, as so much profit to the placemen, and adding to it the one hundred thousand pounds actually paid over the counter of the exchequer, one would not be far from the truth in saying that in seven years the colonists had two hundred thousand pounds sterling taken from them by parliamentary grant and paid out by royal warrant. The new system was successful in that it enabled a swarm of officeholders to live on the fruits of colonial labor and industry.[1] It was disastrous because it led to riot, rebellion, and revolution.

In the absence of excitation through the medium of

In 1775 the total amount collected was £ 17,331, in 1776 only £ 520.

This table is compiled from the " Cash Account of Charles Steuart, Esq." Declared Accounts, Audit Office,Customs. Bundle 844. Roll 1137. Steuart was "Cashire and Paymaster" of the American Customs. This account will be printed in a forthcoming volume on the Commissioners of the Customs to be edited by Worthington C. Ford and the present writer. From the success of the Board in establishing an efficient organization in so short a time it seems beside the mark to call Hulton and his associates " little tricking pert office-clerks " as was done by a writer in the Boston Gazette of April 9, 1770.

[1] Actually there was no return whatever because the cost of the soldiers and sailors and vessels required to enforce these revenue acts far exceeded the gross returns. These were provided for in the army and navy estimates. Admiral Montagu was anxious to have the commissioners pay the cost of maintaining the Gaspee and other vessels employed in revenue duty ; but this was never done. On this general subject see the Observations on Several Acts of Parliament . . . and also on the Conduct of the officers of the Customs. Published by the Merchants of Boston, 1769. This was printed, without place of publication, in 1770, with the following title : Observations of the Merchants at Boston in New England upon Several Acts of Parliament.

the opera and the drama, the automobile and the aero
plane, our ancestors sought to refresh their spirits and
re-create their flagging energies by drinking enormous
quantities of cider, beer, wine, and rum. Ordinarily, the
humbler classes drank rum, the richer sorts substituting
Madeira and Fayal wines, which in America occupied
much the same position that the wine of Oporto then
held in England. The desire for alcoholic stimulants
was recognized in the colonies as a fruitful source of
revenue. In some, there were elaborate licensing systems,
in others, as in South Carolina, heavy import duties were
laid on wines and rum, — the duty on Madeira being
no less than eight pounds per ton, so that in that colony,
what with the parliamentary duty of seven pounds
sterling, and the colonial impost of eight pounds current
money, the premium on smuggling was very great. In
other colonies, the evasion of the parliamentary duty
was very profitable; in point of fact, the history of the
next few years turned upon the repeated attempts of
importers to bring in Madeira wine without paying the
impost. The earliest serious conflicts arose in Massachusetts, because the Boston customs officials were especially
vigilant.

Among the more strenuous and active Bostonians was
Captain Daniel Malcom. Being informed that he had in
his possession a few casks of wine, upon which no duty
had been paid, the customs officials visited his house on the
morning of September 24, 1766, and desired to inspect his
cellar. There, they suddenly espied a door which he refused to open, saying that it led to a room belonging to a
tenant. Malcom now armed himself with two pistols and
a sword, and declared that he would shoot the man who
attempted to force an entrance. The custom house men

argued with him in vain for a couple of hours, and then left.   In the afternoon they returned with a writ of assistance and the sheriff, but found the gates shut, the outer doors fastened, and the captain deaf to their repeated hailings.   He was more amenable to the callings of a bystander, who managed to open communications with him and informed the officials that the captain and friends, who had come to his aid, were determined to resist to the utmost.   By this time several hundred spectators had gathered.   They stood at a respectful distance, but the sheriff was informed that if the house was attacked the bell of the North Church would be rung, — which would call out hundreds more.   After some hours passed in this manner, the sheriff stated that it was too late to attempt anything that day, because after sundown [1] the writ of assistance would be of no avail, and so they all went home.   When the Commissioners, after arranging the preliminaries of the reorganization of the customs service, looked into this affair, they became conscious of their utter helplessness.   They wrote (February 12, 1768) to Commodore Hood at Halifax for a public vessel to protect them in the discharge of their duties.   On March 4 they repeated their request, this time for "two or more ships of war," in consequence of the "conduct and temper of the people of that town, & the aspect of things in general."   In answer to these repeated requests the *Romney*, man-of-war, Captain Connor, anchored off the Boston wharves.   The presence of this vessel did not satisfy the Commissioners, and on June 15 they requested a larger force.[2]   They had also written to Hillsborough and, probably, to Gage, requesting troops, because on

---

[1] Copies of the affidavits describing this occurrence are in the "Papers of Arthur Lee" (Ms.), i, 15–19, 22–25.

[2] "Sparks Ms.," No. 43, vol. iii 192

June 8 in that year we find Hillsborough writing to Gage
to send a regiment to Boston to support the civil magistrates and the officers of the crown in the discharge of
their duty, but for some reason he did not obey this order.

On May 9, 1768, the sloop *Liberty*, owned by John Hancock, a rich and popular merchant of Boston, sailed into
that harbor laden wholly or partly with Madeira wine.
Her cargo was placed on shore, two hundred barrels of
whale oil and twenty barrels of tar were put in her hold,
and she was about to sail on another voyage, when, on
June 9, Thomas Kirk, tidesman, sought the collector and
informed him that when the *Liberty* had arrived, he had
refused to permit the landing of several casks of wine before entry was made. Upon this he had been "hoved
down" into the cabin and confined there for three hours,
during which time he had heard "a noise as of many
people upon deck at work, a hoisting out of goods." When
the noise ceased he was given his freedom with the intima-
tion that his life would be in danger if he made any discovery of what had passed. On June 10, 1768, the day
following Kirk's information, Hulton ordered the seizure
of the *Liberty*.[1] Going to the wharf, the officials signalled
to the *Romney*, and a party of seamen, commanded by the
master of the ship, came on shore. A crowd at once assembled, but no opposition was made, except by way of
protest, as the seamen towed the vessel away from the

---

[1] Papers relating to the seizure and
subsequent riot are printed in *Letters to
the Ministry from Governor Bernard,
General Gage, and Admiral Hood* (Boston, 1769, pp. 114–146) and in *Papers Relating to Public Events in Massachusetts
Preceding the American Revolution*
(Printed for the Seventy-Six Society,
Philadelphia, 1856), p. 72. The examination of Hallowell, comptroller of customs
at Boston, before the Lords of the Treasury (July 21, 1768) is in *A Third Extraordinary Budget of Epistles and
Memorials between Sir Francis Bernard
. . . and the Present Ministry* (Boston).
Affidavits of the by-standers are in *The
American Gazette*, 101–112; the "Letter
from the Inhabitants of the Town of
Boston" giving the local version of the
affair is in *ibid.*, 97. See also Bernard's
letter-books.

wharf to anchor her under the guns of the warship. The
customs officials had gone hardly two hundred feet from
the wharf on their way to the custom house, when they
were set upon and so severely handled that two of them
were obliged to keep their beds for several days. When
darkness fell, the mob visited some of the Commissioners'
houses and broke the windows. The rioters also seized a
pleasure boat belonging to the collector, hauled her ashore,
and burned her on the Common.[1] Governor Bernard informed the Commissioners that he could not protect them,[2]
and with the exception of Temple, they repaired to the
Romney with their families, and, shortly after, to Castle
William, where Bernard was accustomed to pass the summers.[3] The *Liberty* was condemned in the admiralty court,
and Hancock, Malcom, and some others were sued by the
King's Advocate in the sum of nine thousand pounds each [4]
for obstructing the officers of the crown. Evidence had
been taken when, on March 25, 1769, the Advocate General prayed "leave to Retract this Information and says
our Sovereign Lord the King will prosecute no further
hereon." [5]

---

[1] Ten months later, at Philadelphia, an attempted seizure of uncustomed wine brought on a riot. In this case a writ of assistance, constables, and military men took part. A customs officer was brutally assaulted, but the whole matter was smoothed over. Massachusetts Histori- cal Society's *Collections*, Fourth Series, x, 611.

[2] Letters of Bernard and Gage in "Bernard Papers" (Ms.), xi, 205.

[3] The evidence bearing on the seizure of the *Liberty* is very unsatisfactory. Hallowell, the comptroller, stated that it was "common report" that more wine had been brought in on the vessel than had been entered, and that he had heard Hancock say he would run her cargo on shore. Another tidesman had accom-

panied Kirk to the *Liberty*. He had heard nothing and had fallen asleep, but Kirk stated that he had gone home drunk. There must have been other evidence than has come down to us or the admiralty judge would not have con- demned the vessel.

[4] *Observations of Merchants at Bos- ton*, 35 note.

[5] "Minutes of the Court of Vice Ad- miralty, Province of Massachusetts Bay, 1765-1772" (Ms.). Entries as to the con- demnation of the *Liberty* are in the same volume under date of June 22, July 7, 18, 25, 29, Aug. 1, 1768.

In the "Sparks Manuscripts" is the copy of an opinion of Attorney General William de Grey. He calls attention to the fact that Kirk did not see the un-

The Commissioners again renewed their demand for troops and Bernard asked the Council to join with him in requesting Gage to send soldiers to Boston. The Council, under the lead of Bowdoin, declining, he himself asked Gage to send troops on his own responsibility; but this Gage refused to do. In England, the government fell in with the wishes of the Commissioners and ordered two regiments for Boston, but there were so many delays that the first soldiers did not arrive until October 1, nearly four months after the riot.[1] The Quartering Act, which had been renewed in 1767, obliged each colony to provide barracks for the soldiers of the regular army who might be stationed in it. There were barracks for two thousand men on an island in Boston harbor, a mile or two from the wharves of the town. To station the men there would defeat the whole object of their coming, and Colonel Dalrymple, their commander, disembarked them on the mainland and applied for quarters within the town itself. Bernard laid the matter before the Council, which replied by calling his attention to the Act of Parliament. The provisions of this law were peculiar, because it was only when the colonial barracks were filled that soldiers could be billeted in taverns and stables, and only when this accommodation was insufficient that vacant houses could be hired for their shelter. Any officer quartering his men otherwise than as the law directed, or threatening a magistrate, was to be *ipso facto* cashiered upon conviction before

lading, but under the circumstances of the case advised going on with the suit and bringing actions against the persons concerned in obstructing the seizure (No. 43, vol. iii, 191). It is worth while contrasting with this guarded statement Hutchinson's declaration (*Copy of Letters sent to Great Britain*, Boston, 1773, p. 3) that the *Liberty* was seized " for a very notorious breach of the act of trade."

[1] On July 28, 1768, Hillsborough had informed the Lords of the Admiralty that two regiments were to go to Boston and asked for a frigate as a convoy. The destination of these troops was changed and instead soldiers were sent from Halifax.

two justices. Dalrymple refusing to remove his soldiers to the barracks, the General Court declined to provide them with the subsistence which was required by the act, and technically they seem to have been justified by the wording of the law. In the end, the governor, by the advice of the Council, appointed a commissary who should provide them with the necessary articles, taking the chance of reimbursement. For a time some of the soldiers camped on the Common, while others were lodged in Faneuil Hall and in the town house, where the Council and House of Representatives ordinarily held their sessions.[1]

While these events were enacting, the colonists had been busily employed in formulating protests and memorials against the policy which was set forth in the Townshend Acts. February 11, 1768, the Massachusetts House of Representatives adopted a Circular Letter to the other assemblies on the continent suggesting concerted opposition in the way of constitutional discussions and petitions.[2] The Representatives also voted an address to the British government in which, among other things, they took occasion to disclaim any thoughts of independence. In January of that year a third secretary of state was

---

[1] The *American Gazette*, 144, 159, 177, 225, 267; Bernard's account of this episode is given at length in *Letters to . . . Hillsborough from Governor Bernard, General Gage . . . with an Appendix containing Divers Proceedings referred to in the said Letters* (Boston, 1769).

[2] Frothingham's *Rise of the Republic*, 210; *Massachusetts State Papers*, 134. The story of these years in Massachusetts is told at length by Alden Bradford in his detailed and dry *History of Massachusetts from 1764 to July 1775* (3 vols., Boston, 1822). Hutchinson covered this period to 1774 in the third volume of his *History of Massachusetts Bay*, and G. R. Minot likewise treated it in his *Contin-*

uation of the History of the Province of Massachusetts Bay (2 vols., Boston, 1798, 1805). The title of the latter refers to the fact that only the first two volumes of Hutchinson's book were published when Minot wrote, the third volume not appearing until 1828. Most of the important documents are included in a volume edited by Alden Bradford and generally cited as "Massachusetts State Papers" from the running headline. In more detail it is *Speeches of the Governors of Massachusetts from 1765 to 1775; and the Answers of the House of Representatives . . . and other Public Papers* (Boston, 1818).

H

appointed to have especial charge of colonial affairs, but the Lords of Trade were continued in office, possibly because that body was considered to be a valuable school of business administration for young men of family [1] whose rank excluded them from nearer contact with the principles of trade. The new office was given to Wills Hill, Earl of Hillsborough, for Shelburne had retired on the adoption of the policy advocated by Townshend. Hillsborough seems to have taken his opinions mainly from Bernard. Eight years later, the king informed the indefatigable John Robinson that he had never known "a man of less judgment" [2] than he to whom he now intrusted the management of the most serious crisis in imperial affairs. One of Hillsborough's first acts as secretary was to direct Bernard in his Majesty's name to demand of the Massachusetts House of Representatives that it should rescind the resolutions which gave birth to the Circular Letter, and dissolve that body in case of a refusal; [3] also informing him that "proper care will be taken for the Support of the Dignity of Government," whatever that might mean. Not content with contesting this point of power and policy with one colony, Hillsborough widened the area of dispute by directing the governors of the other colonies to dissolve their respective assemblies, in case they showed any disposition to answer the appeal of Massachusetts in a favorable manner. The Commons, too, were for vigorous measures and addressed the king lamenting that the "arts of wicked and designing men" [4] should rekindle the flame of sedition in America; but the law officers of the crown were more cautious. They declared that there was no sufficient ground to fix the

[1] Almon's *Anecdotes of Chatham*, iii, Appendix (last unnumbered page).
[2] Royal Historical Manuscripts Commission's *Reports*, x, Appendix vi, p. 15.

[3] "Bernard Papers" (Ms.), xi, 173.
[4] *Parliamentary Debates*, xvi, 473.

charge of high treason upon any person in Massachusetts or to bring suit for the legal forfeiture of the charter.[1]

It is impossible, of course, to state what Hillsborough's expectations were in this matter; but it is inconceivable that either he or Lord North or the king could have supposed that the assemblies would prove amenable to these exhortations and demands. At any rate the Massachusetts House of Representatives refused by a vote of ninety-two to seventeen to rescind their obnoxious resolutions, and the other assemblies, whenever they had the opportunity, hastened to place themselves on the side of the Bay Colony. Nor did the dissolution convert the voters of Massachusetts to the royal way of thinking, for when the next General Court came together at Boston, instead of seventeen friends of government there were only ten.[2] This episode was another example of the ignorance of the English government as to colonial conditions which goes far to justify the contention of the colonists that they could not be properly governed from London and therefore must rule themselves.

These contentions induced many political essays which instructed the people and organized public opinion. Of these none was more widely read than " The Letters of a Pennsylvania Farmer" by John Dickinson, a prominent political leader of that province. He had already written effectively on the side of the colonists at the time of the

---

[1] "Sparks's Minutes" in "Manuscripts" No. 43, vol. iii, 195.

[2] Bernard to Hillsborough, June 1, 1769. "Bernard Papers," vii, 166. In England, a dissolution of the House of Commons brought upon its members great expenditure of time and money with no compensating advantages. In the colonies, elections were not usually attended with much expenditure; the representative was ordinarily a resident of his own electoral district; and in times of excitement was almost certain to be reëlected by his friends and neighbors with an increased majority and with a feeling that they were behind him. These dissolutions, therefore, strengthened rather than weakened the radical party in the colonies.

Stamp Act; but his opposition to the policy of Franklin in the struggle with the Pennsylvania proprietors had lost him his seat in the assembly. In "The Farmer's Letters" he begins by considering the act of Parliament which had denied a legislative assembly to New York because that body had refused to comply with the Quartering Act. In this connection he declares that "An Act of Parliament commanding us to do a certain thing, if it has any validity, is a tax upon us for the expence that accrues in complying with it." This idea found great favor with the colonists and went far toward preparing them to deny the general legislative power of Parliament over them.

In his letters, Dickinson involved himself in the contradictions and inconsistencies that were so common in colonial expressions of opinion at this time. In his second letter he stated that "the parliament unquestionably possesses a legal authority to regulate the trade of Great Britain, and all its colonies. . . . We are but parts of a whole and therefore there must exist a power somewhere, to preside and preserve the connection in due order. This power is lodged in the Parliament; and we are as much dependant on Great Britain as a perfectly free people can be on another." He goes on to declare that the doctrine that Parliament has authority to impose duties on the colonies, not for the regulation of trade, but for levying money is "an innovation," and denies that Parliament had any power to tax the colonies in any way whatsoever, external or internal. Finally, he says, "Let us consider ourselves as — MEN — FREEMEN — CHRISTIAN FREEMEN — *separated from the rest of the world,* and *firmly bound together* by the *same rights, interests,* and *dangers.* . . . What have these colonies to *ask,* while

they continue free ; Or what have they to *dread*, but
insidious attempts to subvert their freedom? . . . *They*
form *one* political body, of which *each colony* is a *member*." [1]
In these several extracts, Dickinson undoubtedly expressed the conscious opinion of the colonists. They
were joined together by community of sentiment and
possessed certain freedoms from social and constitutional
restrictions which were the inevitable result of their
frontier condition and distance from the seat of the
imperial administration. They, in theory, acknowledged
that Parliament had some undefined power in the regulation of imperial concerns, but whenever the English
government undertook to enforce this power, they at once
perceived that such exercise was in the nature of levying
a tax. Knox was right in saying that what they objected
to was not the levying of customs duties, but the collecting of them. Inconsistent and contradictory as " The
Letters of a Pennsylvania Farmer" were and hazy as
were many of the statements in them, Dickinson showed
the prescience of a true statesman. There was a latent
feeling of unity among the colonists from Maine to Georgia ;
the action of the British government brought this forci-
bly to the attention of the Americans and impelled them
to an expression of union sentiment.

Upon the dissolution of the Massachusetts House of
Representatives by Governor Bernard, the selectmen
of Boston requested the people of the several towns of
the province to elect delegates to a convention to be held in
Faneuil Hall. The convention met at the appointed time
and adopted resolutions that had nothing particularly new
in them ; but its meeting pointed the way to extra-legal
organization and action and therefore is noteworthy,

---

[1] *Farmer's Letters* (Boston, 1768), pp. 5, 7, 74.

When Parliament met in the autumn, papers relating to the disorders in America were laid on the tables of both Houses and several debates ensued. Lord Mansfield, the Chief Justice of England, was especially outspoken and suggested bringing the members of the Massachusetts House of Representatives to London for trial on the charge of treason. Acting, possibly, on this suggestion, the Peers addressed the king, praying him to have incitors of colonial rebellion brought to London and tried for their lives in accordance with an act that had been passed in the reign of Henry VIII for the " trial of treasons committed out of the Kings Majesties Realm of England and other his Graces Dominions." In the Commons, Grenville called attention to the words that have just been quoted, declaring that this was hard language to apply to colonies.[1] It is questionable whether the colonies were within the " Realm "; but surely they were of the " Dominions "; how then could a law that related solely to what happened outside of the Dominions be of any force within them? Nothing that Grenville and others could say was of any avail. The Commons joined in the address and this threatened action of the government proved to be the occasion of a new outflow of colonial constitutional resolutions.

New men had now come into prominence in Virginia. Francis Fauquier, the governor, was a gambler and otherwise a disreputable person.[2] He died in 1768. For a time,

---

[1] *Sir Henry Cavendish's Debates of the House of Commons during the Thirteenth Parliament of Great Britain . . . drawn up from the original manuscripts by J. Wright*, i, 191–225. The act of Henry VII had been used to deport persons from Ireland.

[2] On February 7, 1763, the Lords of Trade expressed to Fauquier their opinion of him. They charged him, among other things, with hanging out " by specious Words . . . an Appearance of Obedience to Orders, which in reality you render ineffectual." " Colonial Office Papers " (Ms.), v, 1369, Virginia, p. 213. Similar language might have been used as to many another colonial governor.

it seemed likely that Bernard would follow him as deputy
to Lord Amherst, in which capacity Fauquier had served ;
but suddenly, it became necessary to provide for Norborne
Berkeley, Lord Botetourt, a member of the House of Peers.
He was of the old Berkeley family that had so long been
associated with American colonization and, especially, with
Virginia. He had invested a portion of his inherited
property in an unincorporated copper company which was
on the point of failure. He hit upon the scheme of incorporating the associates before bankruptcy was declared,
thereby saving his property, although not his honor.
Chatham refused to affix the privy seal to this scandalous
patent, but was induced to place it for this purpose in the
hands of commissioners. The matter was now so notorious
that they refused to sanction the fraud.[1] To provide
Botetourt with an income, he was sent to rule Virginia,
where the opposition was led by George Washington,
Thomas Jefferson, Patrick Henry, and George Mason.

Heretofore, Washington had taken slight part in politics. He had served in military capacities, and, on
occasion, had defended the dignity of colonists. He was
one of the half dozen richest men in America and was a
successful planter and man of business. His wealth
and high character gave to anything that he did a standing, even at that period. He now introduced into the
House of Burgesses a series of resolutions which are known
in history as the " Virginia Resolves of 1769." These had
been drawn up by his friend and neighbor, George Mason,
who played a leading part in the history of the Old Dominion, although he seldom came into actual public notice.

[1] Ruville's *Pitt*, iii, 237, 241. William Wirt Henry (*Life of Patrick Henry*, i, 136) states that Botetourt was an ami- able and attractive man who was sent to Virginia to win the colony from the American cause.

Apart from that of Washington, the most interesting name affixed to these resolutions was that of Thomas Jefferson.[1] He possessed a peculiarly organized mind, in that he combined a love of literature and of science with a capacity to handle difficult political problems successfully and in conformity with the teachings of abstract political theorists. Jefferson's early life had been passed in the wilder parts of Virginia, and close communion with nature had powerfully affected his way of looking at political and institutional problems. Where more conservative men were guided by experience, he listened to the teachings of philosophy.

The Virginia Resolves of 1769 are remarkable for the absence of crudeness in political ideas which has been referred to more than once in the preceding pages. They declared that the sole right of imposing taxes is now and ever has been legally and constitutionally in the general assembly with the consent of the king or his governor; that the colonists have the right to petition the king to redress their grievances; that taking any person from the colony for trial beyond the sea is highly derogatory to the rights of British subjects; and they besought the king to avert those evils from his loyal people. These Resolves were at once sent to the other legislative bodies on the continent, and were reiterated by them as occasion served.

[1] One of the best brief accounts of Jefferson's career is in D. M. R. Culbreth's *University of Virginia*, chs. i–vii. The following, written by Jefferson in May, 1788, shows the radical nature of his opinions in the middle period of his life: —

"I am sorry that your first impressions have been disturbed by matters of etiquette, where surely they should least have been expected to occur. These disputes are the most insusceptible of determination, because they have no foundation in reason. Arbitrary & senseless in their nature, they are arbitrarily decided by every nation for itself. These decisions are meant to prevent disputes, but they produce ten where they prevent one. It would have been better therefore in a new country to have excluded etiquette altogether; or, if it must be admitted in some form or other, to have made it depend on some circumstance founded in nature, such as the age or stature of the parties." *Writings* (Ford ed.), v, 10.

At the time of the Stamp Act, colonial merchants, by
refusing to import any goods from England, had contributed greatly toward bringing about its repeal and the modification of the Revenue Law. A similar mode of action
was now taken, "associations" being formed in the several
colonies. The most famous of these was the Virginia
Association, which was drawn up by George Mason
and subscribed by Washington and Jefferson and many
others. The associators agreed to import no goods,
"which are, or shall hereafter be taxed by act of parliament for the purpose of raising a revenue in America."[1]
In other colonies where the importation of goods was in
the hands of merchants, many of these combined in similar
agreements, and the radical element in the population
looked about for legal and spirited measures to prevent
them being rendered abortive by seeing to it that other
merchants did not import any of the prohibited articles.
The case of the brigantine, *Good Intent*, is interesting as
showing the thoroughness with which this movement was
carried out.[2] She brought goods to Annapolis, Maryland,
consigned to James Dick and Anthony Stewart, and to
other merchants also. A committee of twelve leading
men of the vicinity promptly made its appearance, summoned the consignees before it, and questioned them narrowly. In this instance prohibited goods were packed
with others on which there was no ban of non-importation,
so that it was impossible to separate one part of the cargo
from the other. The consignees generally fell in with the
wishes of the committee and agreed to send back the goods.

[1] See K. M. Rowland's *Life of George Mason*, vol. i, 390.

[2] See *Proceedings of the Committee Appointed to examine into the Importation of Goods by the Brigantine Good Intent* (Annapolis, 1770). From letters of Governor Eden of Maryland to Lord Hillsborough, it would seem that he was blamed for this transaction; Massachu-setts Historical Society's *Collections*, Fourth Series, vol. x, 621–624.

Dick and Stewart objected, saying that if the vessel returned with the goods on board, both she and her cargo would be seized by the customs officials, — they wanted to know who was to secure them against loss. The silence of the committee on this point was ominous, and the *Good Intent*, with cargo intact, speedily departed.

At Boston, the publishing firm of Mein and Fleeming printed a pamphlet containing the names of merchants who had imported, or were alleged to have imported, goods contrary to the agreement, among the names being that of John Hancock. This publication greatly excited the ire of the radicals. They wrecked the shop, smeared Mein's house with filth, which they called " Hillsborough paint," and so severely handled him that his life was endangered. Another obnoxious Boston merchant, Nathaniel Rogers, was boycotted so thoroughly that, fearing the result, he fled to New York. There he saw his effigy suspended on the gallows and burned, and again took to flight. The customs officials were also treated with severity, being tarred and feathered, or otherwise abused. Usually this ceremonial was carried on at night, but Gage describes an instance of a New York informer who was tarred, rolled in feathers, and carted through the streets of that city at noonday. He states that these disturbances proceeded from the impossibility of carrying out the non-importation agreements by peaceable means, because many men had been forced into them against their inclination, and others, it may be added, had refused to sign them.[1]

In the general shuffling of placemen which followed the resignation of Chatham and the death of Townshend, Lord

---

[1] The non-importation agreements were differently observed in the several colonies, as appears from the following table which is given in a letter from W. S. Johnson to Jonathan Trumbull, dated " Westminster, March 6, 1770" (Massa-

North came out first, and for more than a decade he was the able chief clerk of his royal master in carrying on the affairs of the empire.   He had acquiesced in the levying of the Townshend duties, but he was anxious to avoid commotions in America which had cost English merchants and manufacturers much loss, and had most seriously reduced the purchasing power of wage-earners.   The duties on paints, glass, and paper had acted as a protective tariff in America, and had stimulated manufacturing there.   So much so, indeed, that William S. Johnson thought the colonists would do well to protest against taking them off. Lord North realized this.   Stigmatizing the Townshend duties on English manufactures as "uncommercial" and "preposterous," he moved for the repeal of all that part of the law ; but retained the tax on tea, which was not an English product.[1]   The duties levied under the older laws on tobacco, wine, sugar, and molasses were also retained, as was the whole administrative machinery of the new system.   This will be a favorable opportunity to pass

chusetts Historical Society's *Collections*, Fifth Series, ix, 424) : —

"Value [in pounds sterling] of all Goods exported from England to the Colonies in North America, from Christmas, 1767, to do. 1769, distinguishing each Colony" [from the Custom House books at London].

	1767 to 1768	1768 to 1769
Carolina	209,000	306,000
Georgia	56,000	58,000
New England . . .	419,000	207,000
New York	482,000	74,000
Pennsylvania . . .	432,000	199,000
Virginia and Maryland	475,000	488,000

For the operation of the agreements in Pennsylvania, see *Pennsylvania Magazine of History*, xiv, 41.

[1] 10 George III, Cap. 17. The act states that the duties are removed because " the said Duties, in so far as they effect the Produce and Manufacture of Great Britain, do in their Nature tend to the Prejudice and Discouragement thereof, and are therefore contrary to the true Principles of Commerce."

It was at this time (1769) that Mr. Burke declared Parliament had an undoubted right to tax the colonists, but " that the expediency of putting that right in execution should be very evident before anything of that sort passed," *Parliamentary History*, xvi, 605. At a later date (Sept. 11, 1774) the king wrote to Lord North : —

" I have no objection afterwards [after colonial submission] to their seeing that there is no inclination for the present to lay fresh taxes on them, but I am clear there must always be one tax to keep up the right, and as such I approve the Tea Duty." Donne's *Correspondence of George III with Lord North*, i, 202.

colonial commerce in view to see how limited it was, how meager was the list of colonial exports, how closely confined was American manufacturing, and how dependent the colonists were on the mother country for everything except the bare necessities of existence.

Among the officials of the American Customs Board was the Inspector of Imports and Exports. In his office were compiled detailed statements of colonial commerce. Some of these have been preserved, and repay consideration and study. Corn, wheat, bread and flour, tobacco, lumber and naval stores, fish dried and pickled, and the products of the whale, with rum, distilled from West Indian molasses, formed the staple exportations. There were also cattle, sheep, and hogs, alive and dead, butter, cheese, and lard, furs and skins, rice and indigo. The Middle Colonies produced a large surplus of breadstuffs which were exported mainly to the West Indies, — a million bushels of wheat and corn, and thirty-six thousand tons of bread and flour were sent out in the year 1771. It was one of the curious incidents of tropical industry that it was cheaper to feed the people of the islands on food brought from the north than to take them from their special labors and set them to work producing their own food. Even cattle, hogs, sheep, and poultry were imported from the north, — three thousand head of cattle, twelve thousand hogs and sheep, three thousand dozen poultry. Of salted meats there were twenty-two thousand barrels, and no less than three hundred thousand quintals of dried fish. The sugar planters had no time to devote to getting out lumber from their forests, and the oak of the north was better suited to making hogsheads for their molasses and sugar. The exports of lumber, therefore, were very large; sixty-two million shingles, forty-two million feet of pine and oak, and thirteen million staves, with accompanying shooks and hoops. Sometimes whole houses were sent out in sections, and there was no end of lesser articles, as boats, cartwheels, and ox-bows. To Great Britain went nearly all the tobacco that was exported from Maryland, Virginia, and North Carolina, — one hundred thousand hogsheads of it in this single year. The trade in the skins of the beaver and other small fur-bearing animals had been diverted to Canada, but deerskins, both dried and salted, were sent out in large quantities from Virginia and the Carolinas.

Of the importations, the most important was molasses: 4,159,008 gallons of it came in 1771; of which only 145,762 gallons were from the British plantations.[1] At first sight, this would seem to entirely justify the oft-repeated colonial contention that there was not enough molasses made in all the British sugar islands to satisfy the needs of the distillers of even one colony. To judge of the truth of this, however, one must remember that 2,160,790 gallons of West India rum were also brought in within these twelve months. The provision of the revenue act prohibiting the importation of foreign rum acted as a stimulus to the distillers of the British Islands. It may well have been this fact and not the scarcity of British molasses that aroused the resentment of northern importers and rectifiers. How much of the four million gallons of molasses was distilled into rum in the northern colonies is nowhere stated. Molasses was used for sweetening, instead of sugar, in many parts of the colonies, but there are many mentions of distilleries in New England and in the Middle Colonies. Possibly, we might be well within the mark to say that fifty

[1] Among other importations from the West Indies were 970,419 lbs. cocoa; 27,096 hides; 1,445,925 ft. mahogany; 448,830 lbs. coffee. The number of negroes brought into the continental colonies in 1771 was 1983 from the West Indies, 2754 from Africa direct.

per cent of the molasses was turned into rum, gallon for gallon. This would give about four million gallons of rum, New England and West Indian, as the yearly consumption. The exportations were large, — 298,622 gallons, — but this is nothing in comparison with the total. Some of it was also used in the Indian trade. When all has been said, there was too much left for the good of the people, especially when one recalls the amount of wine that was consumed, 213,201 gallons. All of this was heavy wine, six-sevenths of it being madeira and the rest port. Returning for a moment to the exportation of rum, 234,317 gallons of it, seven-eighths of the whole, was sent to Africa, and there exchanged for negro slaves, ivory, and palm oil. Of the other eighth, some was consumed by the Newfoundland fishermen, the rest went to southern Europe and to the Atlantic islands, where it may have been used to fortify the wines of Fayal and Madeira for transportation to North America.

Nearly a million and a half bushels of salt were brought into the continental colonies, one-half from the West Indies, and the rest in fairly equal quantities from southern Europe direct, and from Great Britain. This was the one absolute necessity that was not produced in the northern colonies. The other commodities that came from Great Britain were many of them eminently desirable,[1] but life

---

[1] The average annual value of British manufactures imported in the six years ending with 1774 was £2,216,970; of goods produced out of Great Britain and imported through that country £515,066. *Collection of Interesting and Important Reports*, 64.

Among the imports of British and foreign goods from Great Britain were the following: beer, 356 tons; "callicoes" (Br.), 121,942 yds., (for.) 200,-000 yds.; cottons (Br.), 87,462 yds., (for.) 30,000 yds.; cambric (for.) 10,000 yds.; playing cards, 21,819 packs; gun flints, 54,000; gunpowder, 72,401 lbs.; iron (wrought), 18,824 tons; nails, 201 casks and 11,479 pounds; tobacco pipes, 20,480 gross; paper, 20,299 yds.; stationery, etc., 54,109 pounds; painters' colors, 253,500 pounds, 1785 chests, and 93 boxes; pewter ware, 406,843 lbs.; tin ware, 241,195. lbs.; snuff, 74,545 lbs; silk stuffs, 74,145 lbs. The complete tables will be printed in the Massachu-.

could be carried on without them. There were, for instance, between forty and fifty different kinds of textiles
imported from Great Britain, thirty of them being manufactures of the European continent. Figures mean very
little in a case of this kind, but it may be said that the
four million yards of L.ish bounty linens which were taken
to the colonies formed one-half of the total exportation of
those commodities.[1] One of the colonial manufactures
that had aroused the interest of British lawgivers was
the making of hats and felts.[2] This industry had been
greatly restricted by legislation, as is evident from the fact
that no less than a quarter of a million of British-made
hats were imported in one year, in addition to nearly
twenty-five thousand leghorn and chip hats for women's
wear. These, with shoes and boots, ostrich feathers and
silk garters, mitts and fans, complete the tale of articles of
human covering and adornment. For the health of the
people there were nearly one hundred kinds of drugs, some
of which are still used, as opium, quinine, then known as
Peruvian or Jesuits bark, and benjamin or benzoin. The
amounts were not large, except in the case of jallap, of
which 685 pounds were imported. There were many
spices: mace, nutmeg, cloves, cinnamon, pepper, ginger,
and pimento or allspice. The quantity of pepper and
pimento, over 150,000 pounds, seems a great deal, but the
large consumption of these spices was one of the charac-

---

setts Historical Society's forthcoming
volume on the *Commissioners of the
Customs.*

[1] Anderson gives the total exportation of British bounty linens, at 4,411,040
yards, and Irish at 3,450,224. *Historical
Deduction of the Origin of Commerce,*
v, 197.

[2] Scarcity of capital and labor and
ineptitude had much to do with the
failure of the colonists to engage in
manufacturing. In 1771, 48,000 pounds
of tobacco and 75,000 pounds of snuff
were imported from Great Britain,
most of it being made from Virginia
tobacco. Four thousand pounds of it
were of foreign production, possibly
some of it was in the form of Havana
cigars, although the earliest mention of
tobacco in that shape in American
newspapers comes a little later.

teristics of the time. No study of colonial commerce would be at all complete without noticing the small quantity of iron and ironmongery that was sent out or brought in. The iron age was only just beginning, and steel was used hardly at all.

Of the commercial peculiarities disclosed by this study of statistics, a few things are worth mention. The glass business was still mainly confined to the Netherlands. Not merely the common glass was brought thence through England, but the making of lenses for spectacles was confined almost wholly to a few Dutch towns. Another thing that comes out is the fact that the colonies were, to a considerable extent, a halfway house. The heavy woods of the tropics, mahogany, brazil wood, and lignumvitæ, were sent to England, and so were dyestuffs, annatto and fustic ; there was even a little ivory and some coffee. Among other things, the exportation of 18,422 pounds of cotton attracts attention, for this was in the year 1771. Over 400,000 pounds of it were imported, and these figures, with the small quantities that were even then grown in South Carolina, show that the manufacture of cotton cloth was already carried on.[1] This commerce was from the West Indies to Great Britain ; in the other direction, also, there was a good deal going on in the exportation of furniture, carriages, sweetmeats, and manufactured tobacco to the islands. Such was the course of colonial trade carried on mainly from a few ports, Boston, New York, Philadelphia, Charleston, Savannah, and the harbors of the Chesapeake. The export trade of Philadelphia was in

[1] Smithers in his *History of Liver-pool*, p. 155, notes the following arrivals of cotton in 1770 : from New York three bales, from Virginia four bags or bales, from North Carolina three barrels. These figures are repeated in Thomas Ellison's *Hand-Book of the Cotton Trade* (London, 1858, p. 15) and W. B. Seabrook's *Origin, Cultivation, and Uses of Cotton* (Charleston, 1844, p. 12). For the early cultivation of cotton, see *ibid.*, p. 9.

greatest bulk, but Boston was still the leading center
of importation.   On March 5, 1770, the very day on which
Lord North moved the repeal of the duties on English
manufactures, an affray occurred in the streets of that
town which clearly showed that nothing less than a radical
change in policy could avert the impending conflict between Great Britain and her thirteen colonies on the
continent of North America, — no halfway measures of
" conciliation " would suffice.

NOTES

I. The Townshend Duties. — (7 George III, Cap. 46, 1767.) This is entitled " An Act for granting certain Duties in the British Colonies and Plantations in America . . . and for more effectually preventing the clandestine Running of Goods in the said Colonies and Plantations." The preamble recites that it is expedient to raise a revenue in the American dominions for making a more certain and adequate provision for defraying the charge of the administration of justice, and the support of civil government in such provinces where it shall be found necessary, and also towards further defending the said dominions. Among the duties were four shillings eightpence on every hundredweight of glass, except green glass, which was taxed one shilling twopence for each hundredweight; two shillings per hundredweight on red lead, white lead, and painters' colors; and threepence per pound on tea. Furthermore the act laid duties on sixty-five kinds of paper, ranging from twelve shillings per ream on " Atlas Fine " and " Imperial Fine " to sixpence three farthings for every ream of both fine and second " Genoa Pot " and threepence for " Small Ordinary Brown." On all other paper the duties were those that are charged in this act nearest in size and goodness to " the unrated paper." The money produced by this act might be disposed of by Parliament for defending the colonies; or applied to the charges of the administration of justice and support of the civil government by royal warrant as the king might direct.

New and stringent regulations were provided in the law to secure full information as to the progress of the voyage of any vessel coming into a colonial port. Moreover, this act expressly conferred the right on the Superior or Supreme Court of Justice in the several plantations to grant writs of assistance authorizing customs officers " to enter and go into any House, Warehouse, Shop, Cellar, or other Place in the British Colonies or Plantations in America, to search for and seize prohibited or uncustomed Goods," in the manner directed by the acts of 14 Charles II and 7 and 8 William III, which authorized the searcher, in case of resistance, to break open doors, chests, and trunks.

II. Controversial Tracts.[1] — The renewed propositions of taxation

---

[1] In using the controversial writings of the Revolutionary epoch I have been greatly assisted by a manuscript bibliography that was prepared some years ago by Mr. G. N. Fuller.

induced another stream of pamphlets and controversial tracts. From these the following have been taken as best showing, in connection with the *Farmer's Letters,* the position of the parties. *The Present State of the Nation : particularly with respect to its Trade, Finances, &c. &c., addressed to The King and both Houses of Parliament* (London, 1768). This has been attributed to George Grenville and to William Knox. It is a most useful pamphlet on account of the statistics given in the body of the work and also in an *Appendix* published the next year. Of almost equal value is the reply of Edmund Burke entitled *Observations on a late State of the Nation* (London, 1769), and certain *Remarks on the Appendix to the Present State of the Nation,* which was published anonymously at London in 1769. Another group of pamphlets is William Knox's *The Controversy between Great Britain and her Colonies reviewed ; Observations on the Review of the Controversy;* and *Remarks on the Review of the Controversy.* All of them were published at London in 1769. Another anonymous pamphlet of considerable interest published in 1768 is *The Constitutional Right of the Legislature of Great Britain to Tax the British Colonies in America, impartially stated.* With this may be read *The Right of the British Legislature to Tax the American Colonies Vindicated,* although it was published somewhat later, in 1774.

Two small volumes containing letters of Governor Bernard aroused the colonists to a vigorous reply. They are entitled *Letters to the Right Honourable the Earl of Hillsborough, from Governor Bernard, General Gage, etc.* (Boston, 1769), and *Select Letters on the Trade and Government of America* (London, 1774). The former evoked *An Appeal to the World; or a Vindication of the Town of Boston, from many false and malicious Aspersions* (Boston, 1769). This has been attributed to James Otis and to Samuel Adams. It was this tract that John Adams referred to, when he said that everything in the Declaration of July 4, 1776, had been long before set forth in a little pamphlet written by James Otis in one of his lucid moments and dressed up by Samuel Adams. It is an interesting publication, but would hardly seem to warrant the encomiums of John Adams or the violence of the claims for its authorship advanced by the descendants of Samuel Adams.

A very useful publication is *The True Sentiments of America : contained in a Collection of Letters,* which was compiled by Thomas Hollis and printed by Almon at London in 1768. A clear statement of the moderate American contention is contained in *An Humble*

Enquiry into the Nature of the Dependency of the American Colonies upon the Parliament of Great-Britain (Savannah or Charleston, 1769). This was written by John Joachim Zubly, a clergyman, who took for his motto, —

"A House divided against itself cannot stand" —

which events proved to be abundantly true.

III. Statistics. — The following statistics have been compiled from the tables of the Inspector of Imports and Exports: —

EXPORTS FROM NORTH AMERICA IN 1771

Commodity	Great Britain	Ireland	Southern Europe and Wine Islands	Africa	West Indies, British and Foreign	Total
Ashes, pearl and pot (tons)	2,530					2,530
Axes (no.)					2,385	2,385
Beaver skins (lbs.)	60,322					60,322
Beef and Pork (bbls.)			243½	988½	19,821¾	21,153¾
Bread and Flour (tons)	210	2,286	12,298	31	21,659	36,484
Bricks (no.)					1,546,480	1,546,480
Butter (lbs.)			300	3,340	118,920	122,560
Candles (lbs.)	4,214	225	13,750	3,980	467,154	489,323
Cattle (no.)					3,385	3,385
Cheese (lbs.)				1,600	112,488	114,088
Clapboards (no.)					30,709	30,709
Deerskins (lbs.)	628,937					628,937
Fish, Dry (quintals)	2,000		131,882½		195,983	329.865½
Fish, Pickled (bbls.)	4		269	3	32,695¼	33,004¼
Flaxseed (bu.)	15,379	164,351	7			179,737
Fustic (tons)	422					422
Hams (bbls.)	115½	14	10	3	1,371¾	1,514¼
Hides (no.)	1,562½					1,562½
Hogs and Sheep (no.)				70	12,693	12,763
Horns (no.)	55,065	200				55,265
Horses (no.)			25		6,365	6,390
Indigo (lbs.)	454,207½					454,207½
Iron, Bar (tons)	2,113	26	3	16	197	2,355
Iron, Pig (tons)	5,058	64			1	5,123
Lard (lbs.)	1,600				150,108	151,708
Laths (no.)					34,625	34,625
Lockstocks (no.)	20,660					20,660
Oak, boards and plank (ft.)	937,306	219,828	43,830		218,544	1,419,508
Oars (ft.)	345,149	3,000			87,143	335,292
Oats (bu.)					19,352	19,352
Oil, Whale (tons)	2,962		7			2,969
Peas and Beans (bu.)			1,326	124	31,196	32,646
Pine board and plank (ft.)	2,144,109	30,400	470,998	51,900	38,084,199	40,781,606
Pitch (bbls.)	7,382			51	690	8,123
Poultry (doz.)				9	3,424½	3,433½
Rice (bbls.)	97,200½		17,143½	116	30,947	145,406
Rum, N. E. (gals.)	3,612	4,560	38,972	234,317	5,151	286,612
Rum, W. I. (gals.)	4,015	4,875	2,140	120	860	12,010
Shingles (no.)					36,312,626	36,312,626
Shoes (no. pairs)					5,938	5,938

EXPORTS FROM NORTH AMERICA IN 1771 — *Continued*

Commodity	Great Britain	Ireland	Southern Europe and Wine Islands	Africa	West Indies, British and Foreign	Total
Shooks (no.)			236		61,492	61,728
Soap (lbs.)			850	2,000	121,000	123,950
Starch (lbs.)	50		360		20,090	20,500
Staves (no.)	6,054,583	2,734,007		7,500	12,912,945	21,709.035
Tar (bbls.)	104,398		171	175	3,303	108,047
Tobacco (hhds.)	108,922		11	22	181	109,136
Treenails (no.)	18,700	5,500				24,200
Turpentine (bbls.) . . .	14,196		27	51	1,143	15,417
Wax (lbs.)	76,298	7,300	27,487		568	101,653
Whalebones and fins (lbs.)	41,793				1,035	42,828
Wheat (bu.)	47,029	79,655	268,041¼		28	394,753¼

EXPORTS FROM PHILADELPHIA, 1771

Commodity	Great Britain	West Indies	Southern Europe and Wine Islands	Ireland	Africa	Totals
Candles (lbs.)		28,150	3,000			
Corn (bu.)		37,227	63,640			100,867
Wheat (bu.)			34,581	11,607		46,188
Bread and Flour (tons) .		12,253	8,832			
Rum, N. E. (gals.) . . .			2,237		9,825	
Rum, W. I. (gals.) . . .				3,500		
Oak lumber (ft.)	214,215	88,600	42,000	52,279		397,094
Staves (no.)	591,215	2,806,068		1,170,384		4,567,667

There were also sent out 22 tons pearl ash, 25 tons potash, 1499 tons pig iron, 1840 barrels tar, 2040 barrels rice, 5500 lbs. whale fins, 16,380 lbs. deerskins, 61,805 ft. pine lumber, 125,730 bricks, 109 tons bar iron, 10,750 lbs. lard, 18,650 ropes onions, 3360 barrels beef and pork, 18,670 lbs. butter, 4639 bbls. pickled fish, 3150 lbs. loaf sugar, 102,100 lbs. soap, 1500 pair shoes, 13,050 lbs. starch, 1 hhd. tobacco, 896,623 ft. pine plank, 2567 shooks, 190,190 hoops, 1,672,700 shingles, and 41,953 bu. flaxseed, — the last to Ireland.

CHAPTER V

RESISTANCE AND REPRESSION, 1770–1774

THE soldiers at Boston had generally conducted themselves in an exemplary manner, although there had been
some lapses from good behavior. There was a certain Captain Dundas who accosted John Rowe with : " Ha, John,
you are there — Dammy I expected to have heard of
your being hanged before now, for Dammy You deserve
it." [1]   Ordinarily Mr. Rowe, who turned a penny or two by
supplying British needs, was on friendly terms with the
officers of both army and navy and entertained them with
a lavishness that gives one an impression of anything but
gloom as prevailing in the Puritan capital.   A little later,
Otis, falling into a warm discussion with Robinson, one of
the Commissioners of the Customs and some of the army
men, was struck on the head and badly injured, so much
so that he was never the same man afterwards that he had
been in his earlier years.[2]   Otherwise the coming of the

[1] Anne R. Cunningham's *Letters and
Diary of John Rowe, Boston Merchant,
1759–1762, 1764–1779* (Boston, 1903), p.176.
Dundas also called Rowe a "Damn In-
cendiary," and said he hoped to see him
hanged in his shoes. Rowe noted the
names of those who were present; but
thought it prudent not to take any other
notice of these expressions. He was a
rather remarkable man in many ways,
being Grand Master of the Freemasons of
North America; his adopted daughter,
"Sucky Inman," married Captain John
Linzee, who commanded the *Falcon*,
British man-of-war. Rowe's *Diary* is
one of the most interesting of the time.

Selections from this manuscript are
printed in the Massachusetts Historical
Society's *Proceedings*, Second Series, x,
11.   See also, for other similar instances
of bad manners on the part of the British
soldiers, *ibid.*, First Series, xx, 9.

[2] Otis gradually became unmanage-
able, drinking excessively, and acting
queerly, as breaking the windows of the
town house, until he had to be taken
into the country.   This part of his career
is admirably stated by Tudor in his well-
known *Life of James Otis*. This early
revolutionary leader was killed by a
stroke of lightning in May, 1783.

soldiers, beside arousing sharp political controversies, lent an attractive bit of coloring to a rather gray existence.

The presence of British warships on the coast led to conflicts over the impressment of seamen.[1] In one of these a British officer was killed; but the prudence of the authorities prevented the radicals from making much of the affair. Again, an informer, being attacked by a mob, fired at his assailants from a window and killed a harmless eleven-year-old boy ; but beyond a demonstration at the boy's funeral, nothing happened. As the winter of 1769–70 wore on, the distrust of the military deepened. Especially the working people became irritated with the private soldiers, and threats of bloodshedding by the troops ran through the community.[2] The evening of March 5, 1770, opened with tumults between the troops and the citizens, and culminated in the incident that has come down in history as the "Boston Massacre." Snow was on the ground, but the night was mild. Boys and young fellows threw snowballs at the sentry in front of the custom house door. He called for aid, the guard turned out, and a crowd gathered. At length one of the soldiers, who was particularly objectionable to some of the townsfolk, was knocked down, and another was hit by a club. Either with orders or without them, six or seven shots were fired by soldiers in the street or by persons from the windows of the custom house just above them.[3] Four citizens were killed and

---

[1] See the case of Michael Corbet, Massachusetts Historical Society's *Proceedings*, February, 1911, 429, and *Works of John Adams*, ii, 224; Hutchinson's *History of Massachusetts Bay*, iii, 231, 419. From a view of the legislation, it would appear that sailors in the American trade were peculiarly favored.

[2] The soldiers "had Previously Cautiond some of their accquaintance not to be out at such a Time others Tell-

ing of more Blood would be spilt in Boston before the Next week was out," etc. Massachusetts Historical Society's *Proceedings*, Second Series, ii, 122.

[3] This statement is made on the authority of a paper in the Record Office at London, claiming compensation for losses sustained by an official falsely accused of firing out of the window of the custom house on the inhabitants of Boston on March 5, 1770; "Treasury

others were wounded. The people now collected, but with great prudence the soldiers were withdrawn in time to prevent further trouble. The officer commanding the guard surrendered himself to the colonial authorities, the privates were arrested, and the town watch, augmented, preserved order in the streets. Bernard had now returned to England. In his absence, Hutchinson, who was lieutenant-governor as well as chief justice, was acting governor. After much hesitation and some threatenings, he ordered the troops to be removed to Castle William. Some of the ablest lawyers in the country defended the soldiers who were accused of firing on the people. It was impossible to prove that any order to fire had been given, and the officer who had commanded the guard was discharged. Two of the privates were convicted of manslaughter, and, claiming benefit of clergy, were " burned in the hand " and dismissed.[1] After the removal of the troops, the atmosphere cleared. It seemed for a time that the colonists would at last obey the behests of Parliament, pay the

---

Board Papers," Bundle 482, No. 212. Clear copies of the Pelham-Revere engraving of the Massacre show the barrel of a musket protruding from one of these windows. The point is important because the occupants of this room could not have feared for their lives, as was advanced in defence of the soldiers.

John Mein, or whoever wrote *Sagittarius's Letters* (Boston, 1775, p. 106), referring to this story, called it an " atrocious villany," stating that " for this damnable purpose they suborned several of their adherents to perjure themselves ; and likewise by threats of imprisonment and promises of reward, so intimidated a servant of one of the Revenue-Officers, as to oblige him to swear that his Master, and several others, fired from the windows of the Board of Customs." The application for compensation for losses due to this very fact by an employee of the Commissioners would seem to give more credence to the affidavits than has sometimes been accorded them.

[1] An official " Short Narrative " prepared by a committee was printed, with ninety-six depositions, at Boston, and reprinted at London by Almon in the fourth volume of his *Collection of Tracts on . . . Taxing the British Colonies*. These, with the testimony given at the trial, are in Frederick Kidder's *History of the Boston Massacre*. The account in Tudor's *Diary* (p. 31) has been followed in the text because of its " unconscious " character. S. A. Green's paper in the *Proceedings* of the American Antiquarian Society (xiv, 40–51) is valuable for the moderation of its tone as well as because of the knowledge of the writer. The most complete modern account is that by Richard Frothingham in his *Life and Times of Joseph Warren.*

duties levied at the custom houses, and go about their
businesses.

The more conservative members of the radical party in
Massachusetts had grown tired of the revolutionary tactics
of the extremists, and were disposed to come to a halt.
At the opposite end of the line was Samuel Adams.[1] He
was distinctly a man of the people, gifted with incompar-
able tact in banding together the discontented, and endowed with consummate ability in setting forth in written
page the aspirations for liberty that impelled the masses,
or that Adams thought the masses should feel and show.
He knew how to arouse public attention by debates and
through the press. Resolutions written or moved by him
or by one of his lieutenants, time and again, gave the
signal for renewed agitation on the rights of colonists as
British subjects and as men. Samuel Adams possessed
an almost unparalleled cogency of style, and his closest fellow worker, Joseph Warren, had whatever qualities of a
successful revolutionist he himself lacked. With the
modern impatience of mental exertion and desire for the
sensational in literature, pre-revolutionary tracts and essays
seem dull, contradictory, and inconclusive. At the time
they were read with avidity and produced conviction.[2]

---

[1] In his *History of Massachusetts*
(iii, 295), Hutchinson states that
Samuel Adams "made defalcation" as
collector of taxes. At one time it was
supposed that Hutchinson used this
phrase to imply that Adams was neglect-
ful. Judge Mellen Chamberlain, after
an examination of the records, stated
that "Hutchinson undoubtedly meant
that Samuel Adams used the town's
money for his own purposes." Massachusetts Historical Society's *Proceedings*,
Second Series, iv, 141. See also *ibid.*,
First Series, xx, 213; and *Boston Town
Records*, 1758-1769, pp. 92, 143, 201, 218,
241, 243, 271; *ibid.*, 1770-1777, p. 69.
The way of looking at public financial
trusts in those days in both England and
America was very different from that
which prevails at the present time (see
above, p. 54). Justice seems to demand
the acceptance of the verdict of Adams's
fellow townsmen, who were certainly
convinced of his innocence of any criminal intent, although they themselves
were the victims of his carelessness.

[2] See letter of General William Cham-
berlin in Massachusetts Historical Society's *Proceedings*, Second Series, x, 494.

Adams and Warren[1] now devised a system of town committees of correspondence. The members of these conclaves would be the leading radicals in the several parts
of the province. They would foment discussion and revive interest in the colonial cause that seemed to be dying
down; they would also form a convenient organization
should occasion arise. Viewing the chain of incidents
leading up to the separation from England,[2] it is evident
that Samuel Adams was unalterably opposed to any
tightening of the imperial bond, and wished for increased
colonial self-government and probably for separation from
the mother country. It is also perfectly clear that he could
not have forced the issue, no matter how much he might
have wished to. That was the work of selfish placemen

[1] J. K. Hosmer's "Samuel Adams, the Man of Town Meeting" (*Johns Hopkins Studies*, vol. 2, No. iv) is strongly prejudiced in his favor, but it is the best analysis of his career. Richard Frothingham's *Life of Joseph Warren* tells the story of these years in Boston in great detail and with remarkable fidelity. Adams's and Warren's mode of working is best seen by turning over the leaves of the report of a committee appointed by the inhabitants of Boston (November 20, 1772), *Boston Town Records, 1770–1777*, p. 94, which includes a list of infringements of the rights of the colonists, a letter of correspondence to the other towns, and sundry documents which passed between Hutchinson and the town authorities. Six hundred copies were authorized to be printed and disposed of to the selectmen of the towns in the province and "such other Gentlemen as the Committee shall think fit."

[2] The War of the Regulation occurring in North Carolina at about this time has often been regarded as a part of the general revolutionary movement. In reality it was rather a "peasants' revolt" against the hard conditions then prevailing; and most of the "regulators" were tories a few years later.

Professor Bassett, whose detailed article in the American Historical Association's *Reports* (1894, pp. 141–212) is by far the best study that has yet been made, says (p. 211): "This investigation leads to the view that the Regulation could have no direct connection with the Revolution. I can see no continuity of influence. The Regulation did not make the later struggle inevitable." Although, as Professor Bassett states, there is no direct connection between the War of the Regulation and the American Revolution, and although most of the regulators were tories, these disturbances were doubtless influential in adding to the general spirit of unrest which was rising throughout the continent.

The documents are printed in the *Colonial Records of North Carolina*, vols. vii, viii, ix, x, xv. Especially valuable are Mr. Saunders's introductions to the first two of these volumes. See also Ashe's *North Carolina*; J. H. Clewell's *History of Wachovia*; M. de Lancey Haywood's *Governor William Tryon and his Administration*; Francis Nash's *Hillsboro, Colonial and Revolutionary*; and Herman Husbands's "Impartial Relation" in Wheeler's *North Carolina*, ii, 301.

in England, whose horizon was bounded by the narrow
seas of their own island, and of over-zealous and stubborn
officials in America, whose thoughts were ever intent upon
places and pensions, — Townshend, Hillsborough, and Lord
North in England; Hutchinson, Dudingston, and Tryon
in America. Without their aid, not even the superhuman
powers that have been attributed to Samuel Adams by
his enemies and his biographers could have brought about
the crisis of April 19, 1775.

In those towns where the radical spirit was strong,
brave answers were returned to the Boston letter. The
freeholders of Pembroke met on December 28, 1772. They
boldly resolved [1] that, although the British Parliament was
the "grand legislative of the nation yet according to the
original Compact" entered into between the first colonists
and the king, no legislative authority can be exercised in
the province "but that of the grate and general Court."
The enforcement of the present policy " will in a little time
issue in the total Dissolution of the union Between mother
Country and the Colonies to the infinight loss of the former
and regret of the latter." The Pembroke townsmen appointed a "Committee for greavinces" to correspond with
the other committees, but in general the response to the
suggestion of the appointment of local committees of correspondence at first was feeble.[2] Nor did the discovery

---

[1] These resolutions were copied for
me from the records by Henry W. Litch-
field. He has printed the one foretelling
independence in his *Ancient Landmarks
of Pembroke*, p. 181.

[2] J. W. Fortescue, in his *History of
the British Army* (iii, 43), makes the interesting suggestion that a great opportunity was lost in 1772 at the time of the
dispute with Spain over the Falkland
Islands " for removing the tea duty as a
graceful concession to the loyal spirit
shown in America, and inviting the colonial agents to a general conference on
the subject of Imperial defence." This
suggestion ignores the fact that the
opposition in America was due to other
causes than the tea tax; but possibly an
Imperial Conference might have convinced the authorities in England of the
inexpediency of asserting the supreme
legislative authority of Parliament in
any way whatsoever.

that Hutchinson and other governors and judges were being paid out of the customs revenue arouse burning indignation. No doubt the practice was fraught with danger to the colonists as subjects and as men; but it is difficult to incite rebellion for the privilege of paying other men's salaries directly out of one's own pocket.[1] Adams eagerly seized an opportunity, most unwisely given by Hutchinson, to bring on a discussion as to the nature of the British constitution; but it is not easy to arouse men to the fighting pitch by even the most acrimonious academic argumentation. At this point, Captain Dudingston of the *Gaspee* schooner came to Adams's assistance. He aroused the Rhode Islanders, and their doings impelled the ministry in England to issue orders that inflamed the continent from one end to the other.

Rhode Island had ever been the home of free traders, — pirates and smugglers, royal officials termed them. The great stretches of navigable waters within the limits of this smallest of colonies made illicit trafficking easy, and made correspondingly difficult the detection and punishment thereof. The Rhode Island government was practically independent: its governors were not confirmed by the home authorities, even though they appointed "naval officers" whose business it was to see to the carrying out of acts of Parliament.[2] There was a collector of customs at Newport, who held his office from the Commissioners, and revenue vessels were constantly cruising in Rhode Island waters. Two of these, the *St. John* and the

---

[1] See Note IV at end of chapter.

[2] 15 Charles II, Cap. 7, § 8, and 7 and 8 William III Cap. 22, § 5. These laws required colonial governors to be approved by the crown and to give bonds for the faithful performance of their duties in certain respects. Thurlow and Wedderburn, Attorney and Solicitor-Generals, in an opinion given on July 27, 1771, acknowledged the legality of the Rhode Island practice in view of the many precedents in its favor.

Liberty,[1] already had been destroyed by the Newporters, without any redress having been exacted. It was impossible for Captain Dudingston, or any officer of the revenue service, to stay on shore for any length of time without being arrested to answer suits that had been brought by Rhode Islanders whose vessels or cargoes had been seized; and it was practically impossible to secure condemnation in the Newport admiralty court on account of the opposition of the people. Admiral Montagu therefore directed Dudingston of the *Gaspee* and Linzee of the *Beaver*, who was also cruising in Narragansett Bay, to go on shore as little as possible,[2] and to send their prizes to Boston for adjudication. The serving of a writ on a naval officer was an "insult" to Montagu's mind; the presence of the *Gaspee* seemed to Governor Wanton of Rhode Island to require explanation. He wrote to Dudingston that complaints had been made of the presence of a "piratical vessel," and inquired if he had a commission authorizing him to make seizures; but only an insolent answer was returned.

On the afternoon of June 9, 1772, the *Gaspee* ran aground on a sand spit, about seven miles below Providence. Soon after midnight, the anchor watch discovered boats approaching. Hurrying on deck, Dudingston ordered them to stop; but on they came, and men — fifty to one hundred and fifty of them — swarmed over the bows and in an instant had the vessel at their mercy. Their surgeon bound up Dudingston's wounds, for he was the only man injured on either side. He and his sailors were then set on shore, while the flames were beginning to blaze on the schooner. The incendiaries then disappeared into the

---

[1] For the *St. John*, see *Rhode Island Colony Records*, vi, 427–430; for the *Liberty*, see *ibid.*, vii, 180.

[2] Montagu's "Journal," Monday, May 11, 1772.

darkness, from whence they have never emerged.[1] Soon, however, a sheriff appeared at Dudingston's bedside and served a writ upon him in the suit of many Greenes of Coventry for damages on account of the alleged unlawful conversion of sundry casks of rum and sugar. After three trials and three adverse decisions, Dudingston acknowledged himself beaten, and the Commissioners at Boston made good his losses to the amount of over three hundred pounds sterling.[2]

The burning of the *Gaspee* filled Admiral Montagu with indignation, and the authorities in England with furious wrath. Lord Dartmouth, who had succeeded Hillsborough in the management or mismanagement of colonial affairs, was usually a mild-tempered man. Now, he indited a long letter to officials in America, ordering them to ferret out the perpetrators of this outrage and bring them to condign punishment under an act that had recently been passed for the protection of his Majesty's dockyards. The law officers, being consulted before the letter was sent, pointed out that Narragansett Bay could hardly be regarded as a dockyard, but that the *Gaspee* burners might be indicted for treason either in Great Britain or in America. The secretary cancelled his letter. Instead, the king commissioned Governor Wanton of Rhode Island, the admiralty judge at Boston, and the chief justices of Massachusetts, New York, and New Jersey, to make an inquiry into the affair, and to communicate to the civil magistrates of Rhode Island all the information they could collect to the

---

[1] See Note I at end of chapter.

[2] Charles Steuart, Cashier and Paymaster, paid out by warrant from the Commissioners £ 363 to Dudingston and £70 to James Dundas, Master of the *Gaspee*, for losses. The only one of the Commissioners of Inquiry to secure compensation was Peter Oliver, who got £ 140 from the customs revenue, — another example of the facility with which the Hutchinson-Oliver family "fed off the public." The Commissioners of the Customs also paid £ 136 to the crew of the *Liberty*, revenue vessel, for compensation on account of loss sustained by the destruction of their vessel.

end that the participants in the attack might be arrested and delivered to Admiral Montagu, — and General Gage was ordered to give any aid that might be necessary. The commission held two distinct sessions at Newport in January and May, 1773, but not one bit of tangible evidence could be secured. The only person who could be found to say that he had been present on the schooner was Aaron Biggs, or Briggs, a runaway negro servant. He gave the names of several well-known men as having been concerned in the affair ; but his story was so badly constructed that Chief Justice Smyth of New Jersey, one of the commissioners, wrote that his testimony rather disgraced than aided the inquiry. Smyth also declared that no Rhode Island magistrate would ever lend a hand to commit any person to the custody of Admiral Montagu to be sent to England; there is " an universal abhorrence of such a proceeding not only in Rhode Island but in all the neighbouring Colonies in truth I am persuaded that nothing but an armed force w^d effect it." [1] He limited his opinion to the neighboring colonies, but the fiercest outburst of colonial wrath came not from them, but from far-off Virginia. [2]

In March, 1773, the Virginia Assembly was in session at Williamsburg. Under the guidance of Patrick Henry, Thomas Jefferson, and Richard Henry Lee, a standing committee of correspondence was appointed. [3] The first busi-

[1] At almost the same moment, January, 1773, William Eddis (*Letters from America*, 157, 168) wrote from Annapolis in Maryland : " Vast as this continent is, the inhabitants appear animated, to a degree of frenzy, with the same spirit of opposition " ; " The spirit of opposition to ministerial measures appears to blaze steadily and equally in every part of British America."

[2] March 17, 1773, Richard Henry Lee wrote to Thomas Cushing, inclosing the

Virginia Resolves and asking for the proclamation issued by the Commissioners and also for a copy of their commission.

[3] In Virginia, and also in some other colonies, the elected branch of the colonial legislative body had long been in the habit of appointing a committee of correspondence to transact business with the agent in England. See above, p. 7 n., and *Virginia Magazine of History*, x, 337.

ness of this body was to inform itself upon what principles and by what authority the *Gaspee* court of inquiry had been established. The other colonies were requested to appoint similar committees. If they should do so, and also should adopt Samuel Adams's plan of local committees, a revolutionary organization would be established against which royal officials and conservatives would find it very difficult to contend. There was no hearty response to this invitation because the entire failure of the *Gaspee* commission provided no object lesson of the dangers of despotism. At this moment, the London government stimulated the Americans to renewed action by giving the English East India Company a monopoly of the colonial tea business.[1]

[1] These figures are taken from an abstract prepared in the office of the Inspector of Imports and Exports and authenticated by the signature of his deputy.

Pounds of Tea IMPORTED AT	Jan. 5, 1768– Jan. 5, 1769	Jan. 5, 1769– Jan. 5, 1770	Jan. 5, 1770– Dec. 1, 1770	Dec. 1, 1770– Jan. 5, 1772	Jan. 5, 1772– Jan. 5, 1773	Jan. 5, 1773 to end of Customs Service
	lbs.	lbs.	lbs.	lbs.	lbs.	lbs.
Boston	298,251	95,567	48,070	265,884	107,193	119,809
Rhode Island	3,446	15,393	17,988	17,754	3,079	3,420
New York	352,488½	16,986	147	344	530	—
Philadelphia	146,763	112,159	65	—	128	—
Patuxent (Md.)	15,834	21,021	—	4,971	28,333	—
Virginia Ports	24,909	22,091	15,633	22,581	56,946	11,228
Charleston, S. C. . . .	28,695	20,918¾	862	26,402	22,138	4,319
Savannah	4,455	4,994	2,647	5,428	7,503	5,574
Tea imported: totals, including omitted ports .	877,193½	309,870¾	97,719	344,771	237,062	145,222
Duties collected	£9,723	£8,189	£3,413	£4,596	£1,677	£4,170

The amounts of duties collected are taken from the "Accounts of Charles Steuart, Esq." The discrepancies that will be noted are due no doubt to differences in time of entry in the offices of the cashier and the inspector.

By the act of 12 George III, Cap. 60 (1772), "Three-fifth Parts of the several Duties of Customs which were paid upon the Importation of such Teas" shall for five years be allowed on teas that are sold at the public sale of the English East India Company and which shall be exported to Ireland or to the plantations

Twice already, the English East India Company had
crossed the current of American colonization. The first
time was when Sir Thomas Smyth sent the *Susan Constant*
across the Atlantic, and, somewhat unwillingly, brought
about the settlement at Jamestown. The second was
when the Company, fearful of Scottish enterprise, stirred
the administration to the colonial reorganization of the
last years of the seventeenth century. Faulty government, inevitable native wars in India, and Dutch competition, with the greed of shareholders at home, kept the
Company's finances in a perilous state. Its political power
in India was so great and the possibility of profits from
the proper exploitation of that country so promising that
ministers intervened more than once to set the Company's
affairs in order. At length, in 1773, the Regulating Act
gave the government a share in the administration of
India. In return the Company was forgiven certain payments which it had agreed to make. At the moment it
had seventeen million pounds of tea stored in its English
warehouses. As a further measure of relief, it was
authorized to export a part of this directly to America,
free from all duties and customs levied in the mother
country, but subject to the threepenny tax payable in
America.[1] As all other exporters bought their tea at the
Company's regular auctions, they were obliged to charge

in America, upon rather stringent regulations being complied with. The figures
given above show that this relaxation
had not increased the sales of the East
India Company to America.

[1] The following resolutions were
adopted by the House of Commons on
April 27, 1773: —

"1. That, upon all teas, which shall
be sold at any of the East India Company's public sales, or be imported
under licence, after the 10th day of May,

1773, and shall be exported to any of the
British plantations in America, a drawback be allowed, of all the duties of
customs paid upon the importation of
such teas.

"2. That provision be made, for
empowering the commissioners of the
Treasury to grant licences to the East
India Company, to export teas to the
British plantations in America, or to
foreign parts; provided that, at the time
of taking out such teas for exportation,

a higher price than the Company, notwithstanding the relief in the way of drawbacks which was afforded them. This was a grievance to the London forwarders, but there might have been no trouble in America, had the Company chosen for its agents those merchants in the colonies who had been in the habit of handling the London tea trade. The importation and sale of tea in the colonies was extensive and no doubt profitable as nearly two million pounds of it were entered at the custom houses in the five years before 1773. Common tact, prudence, and justice would have led to the appointment of the colonial tea merchants to represent the Company in America. Instead of doing this, the business was given to men who had taken sides against the non-importation agreements and were unpopular; their employment was a grievance to all Americans of radical tendencies. The cry of monopoly was at once raised; the public mind was excited to a greater degree than at any time since the Stamp Act irritation.

The Company sent small consignments of tea to Boston, New York, Philadelphia, and Charleston. These were placed on ships that were loading at the London docks. The total amount was too small to yield any large financial relief to the Company. No notice of the shipments was sent to the governors in America.[1] The radical leaders there

there be left remaining in the Company's warehouses a quantity of tea not less than ten millions of pounds weight; and that, upon all teas which shall be so exported, a drawback be allowed, of all the duties of customs paid upon the importation of such teas, and an exemption from the inland duties charged thereupon;" *Parliamentary History,* xvii, 841. The act which was based on these resolutions is 13 George III, Cap. 44. This meant, to use Hutchinson's phrase (*History of Massachusetts Bay,* iii, 422), that their teas might be exported "on account of the company, to the colonies, there to be

sold by factors at a much lower price than it could be afforded by particular merchants who purchased it in England."

It is well to contrast this with Chalmers's disingenuous assertion that "the East-India Company were enabled to perform what every other subject could do; to export their teas to the Colonies, paying on the import three pence in lieu of a shilling on the export"; George Chalmers's "Letter to Lord Mansfield," p. 7 (Sparks Mss. No. 7).

[1] Royal Historical Manuscripts Commission's *Reports, Various Collections,* vi, 269. Hutchinson (*History of Massa-*

knew the tea was coming, but it is not certain that they
acted in concert, although, on the other hand, it is by no
means probable that the resistance offered to the landing
of the Company's property was anywhere spontaneous.
At Charleston, South Carolina, the tea was landed. It was
placed in a warehouse, whence it was removed three years
later and auctioned off for the benefit of the Revolutionary
government.[1] At Philadelphia[2] and New York[3] the consignees and the customs authorities proved amenable to public
opinion — after some demur — and permitted the tea to be
carried back to England without its being placed on shore.

At Boston, the Commissioners of the Customs, the
consignees, among whom were members of the governor's
family, and Governor Hutchinson himself were more
faithful to the trusts imposed upon them by their English
employers. Four ships sailed for Boston with East India
Company's tea as part of their cargoes. Three of them
arrived safely within ten days of one another ; the fourth
was wrecked on Cape Cod. The second of the vessels to
anchor in Boston Harbor belonged to John Rowe, the dia-
rist, who carefully noted her coming with " the Small Pox
& part of the Tea," [4] — both somewhat to his grief. The
colonists dreaded the smallpox beyond all other diseases;
but even more they dreaded monopoly[5] and corporations.

chusetts Bay, iii, 423) says the only
apparent discontent was among the
importers of tea; and the " complaint
was against the East India company for
the monopolizing a branch of commerce
which had been beneficial to a great
number of particular merchants."

[1] See Professor D. D. Wallace's interesting paper entitled " A Chapter of
South Carolina Constitutional History "
in the *Publications* of the Vanderbilt
Southern History Society, No. 4.

[2] See *Pennsylvania Magazine of
History*, xv, 385.

[3] A private consignment of tea was
thrown into the harbor by a New York
mob in the spring of 1774; see C. L.
Becker's *New York Parties, 1760–1776*,
ch. v. This essay would have been far
more valuable had it been compressed
into one-third of its size.

[4] Cunningham's *Diary of John Rowe*,
257.

[5] Previously on November 3, Governor
Tryon of New York had declared that if
the act of 1773 should be interpreted to
discharge tea of all duties whatsoever,
including the threepenny tax, the fact

Placards were posted declaring that that " worst of Plagues
The Detestable Tea, ship'd for this Port by the East India
Company " is now arrived. The " Hour of Destruction . . .
Stares you in the Face."   Measures of resistance to these
machinations of tyranny must be concerted.   Meeting followed meeting, attended by two thousand people and more;
but no impression could be made upon Hutchinson.   He
absolutely refused to sign a pass permitting either of the
ships to leave the harbor until she was regularly cleared,
which could not be done until all the cargo was discharged.
On December 17 the customs officers would take possession
of the tea on the vessel that first arrived, and sell it at
auction, unless before that time the tea was landed and
the duties were paid.   The consignees refused to resign, the
customs collector refused to abate the rules, the governor
refused to intervene, and the townspeople kept daily and
nightly watch to see to it that not a pound of Bohea or
Souchong found its way from hold to wharf.   On December 16, Hutchinson's final declination was communicated
to a crowded assembly at the Old South Meetinghouse.[1]
Instantly, the word was given, a band of Indians[2] boarded

that that act gives a monopoly to the
East India Company will be urged; and
Haldimand, on December 28, also writing
from New York, spoke of the " fear of the
introduction of a monopoly " as explaining the attitude of the " mercantile part "
in that city in opposition to the proposed
method of marketing tea; " Sparks
Manuscripts," No. 43, vol. i, 293; iii, 175.
Certain resolutions adopted by the " Inhabitants of the town of Hinsdale " in
New Hampshire in March, 1774, lend
color to this view. The third begins as
follows: " It is the Opinion of this
Town that the Tumult which now prevails in this Country Respecting the East
India Companys sending their Tea here
for sale does not arise by Reason by the
Act of Parliament which imposes a duty

on Tea for the Purpose of raising a Rev-
ennue but because the Intended method
of Sale in this Country by ye East India
Company woud probably hurt the private Interest of many Persons who deal
largely in Tea." On the whole subject
of the tea duty, see an admirable article
by Professor Max Farrand in the *American Historical Review*, iii, 266.

[1] The " Minutes of the Tea Meetings,
1773," are printed from the original
manuscript in the Massachusetts Historical Society's *Proceedings*, First Series,
xx, 10–17.   Other matter relating to this
subject is in *ibid.*, xii, 174, xiii, 151–215.

[2] " No one of its [the tea party's]
members are known by satisfactory
proof." See Edward L. Pierce's admirable paper on " Recollections as a Source

the vessels, opened the hatches, hoisted out the tea, and threw it over the side, while two thousand spectators stood approvingly by.

This picturesque activity of the Boston Puritans excited differing emotions in their contemporaries. John Adams, the next day, wrote in his diary that this was "the most magnificent Movement of all. There is a Dignity, a Majesty, a Sublimity in this last Effort of the Patriots that I greatly admire. . . . This Destruction of the Tea is so bold, so daring, so firm, intrepid, & inflexible, and it must have so important Consequences, and so lasting, that I cannot but consider it as an Epocha in History."[1] Harrison Gray, the Tory treasurer of the province had a very different prognosis, for he declared that God would punish " in the lake which burns with fire and brimstone "[2] those of the tea party who did not repent in time. Public opinion on both sides in London was against the destroyers. Franklin said it was an act of violent injustice that required a speedy and voluntary reparation.[3] Chatham wrote to Shelburne that it was " certainly criminal ; nor would it be real kindness to the Americans to adopt their passions and wild pretensions, where they manifestly violate the most indispensible ties of civil society."[4] Naturally, the king and the prime minister felt even more strongly. On March 7, 1774, Lord North asked Parliament to provide the means for putting down the disorders in America and for

of History " in the *Proceedings* of the Massachusetts Historical Society for March, 1896.

[1] Massachusetts Historical Society's *Proceedings*, 1873-75, p. 191.

[2] *A Few Remarks upon some of the Votes and Resolutions of the Continental Congress* (Printed for the Purchasers, 1775), p. 4.

[3] *Bulletin* of the New York Public Library, i, 244; this letter is also in the *Publications* of the Colonial Society of Massachusetts, v, 57.

[4] *Chatham Correspondence*, iv, 336. Later, May 26, in the debate on the Quartering Act, Chatham again severely condemned " the late illegal and violent proceedings at Boston." Ruville's *William Pitt*, iii, 278.

securing the "dependence of the colonies upon the crown
and Parliament of Great Britain." [1] This demand was quite
likely to be acceded to, for the existing House of Commons
was nearing the end of its seven years' existence. Those
who sat for royal boroughs or for constituencies that were
dominated by the King's Friends were more than usually
anxious to please their royal and noble masters.[2] There
was almost a scramble to see who should be foremost to
carry out the wishes of the king as embodied in the measures of the prime minister.

On the 14th of March, 1774, Lord North moved that
leave be given to bring in a bill for the immediate removal
of the custom house from Boston and to discontinue the
landing and shipping of goods at the town and harbor
thereof.[3] Three times the officers of the customs had been
obstructed in their duty; "our commerce" is no longer
safe at that town. The authorities had been asleep, as it
were, and, as had been the case with London, Edinburgh,
and Glasgow, it was only right that the whole town should
be fined for their neglect. Lord North furthermore declared
that "the laws of this country" had been defied at Boston
without the least interposition of the inhabitants.[4] On the
contrary they had held nightly watches to prevent the

---

[1] Hansard's *Parliamentary History*,
xvii, 1159. The debates on the Port Act,
Administration of Justice Act, Regulating Act, and other bills relating to the
colonies follow immediately after and
occupy the rest of the volume (1163–
1408).

[2] George III's greatest activity, as a
parliamentary boss, was in 1780, when
his bill for bribery and corruption
amounted to the equivalent of about
$ 1,000,000. Neither the king nor Lord
North was so active in the election of
1768 or in that of 1774, but the royal
wishes were fully known to those who

were in political life or who wished to
enter it.

This whole subject is admirably
treated in Edward Porritt's *Unreformed
House of Commons*, i, 309–364, 406–420.
Especially valuable are the long quotations that he gives from Donne's *Letters
of George III to Lord North;* but the
student will find it necessary to read this
correspondence through in order to understand the portion of George III in
bringing on the American Revolution.

[3] For an analysis of the Boston Port
Act itself, see Note II at end of chapter.

[4] *Parliamentary Register*, xxiii, 359.

landing of the tea, which was highly criminal in itself.
Boston had been the ringleader throughout ; the other
colonies, which were peaceably and well inclined, only
followed her example.   Whenever the town made full sat
isfaction to the East India Company for the loss of its tea,
an amount estimated at about fifteen thousand pounds
sterling, the port would be reopened.   One recommenda-
tion for this mode of procedure was that it could be executed by the navy without it being necessary to employ
the land forces at all.   The plan met with general com-
mendation in both houses of Parliament.   Isaac Barré,
Shelburne's mouthpiece in the Commons, gave the adher-
ence of the Chathamites, although, confused at finding himself for once in agreement with Lord North, he forgot his
grammar,[1] exclaiming amid much merriment :   " Boston
ought to be punished, she is your eldest son ! "   Gibbon,
the historian, who was then a member of the House of
Commons, wrote[2] to a friend that the Boston Port Act
bore " so mild an appearance " that it was agreed to without a division.   Thomas Pownall, once governor of Massachusetts, and up to this time a steadfast friend of the
colonies, wanted to go even further and to bring Adams
and " other principal Incendiaries "[3] to London for trial
and punishment as traitors.   A few voices were raised
against the punishment of the town, Major George Byng[4]
foretelling that it would " create that association in the
Americans which you had so much wished to annihilate."

The closing of Boston Harbor to inward and outward
commerce, which seemed so innocuous to the author of the

[1] *Parliamentary History*, xvii, 1169.
[2] *Miscellaneous Works*, ii, 118. Two
local American views of the act are
Josiah Quincy Jr.'s *Observations on the
Act of Parliament, commonly called the
Boston Port-Bill,* and *A Letter to a*

Friend. By T. W. A Bostonian, both
printed at the unfortunate town in 1774.
[3] Hutchinson's *Diary and Letters*, i,
183.
[4] *Parliamentary History*, xvii, 1175.

" Decline and Fall of the Roman Empire," bore an entirely different appearance to the people of the doomed town. They at once appealed to the other colonies for aid, promising to bear their trials with fortitude. The response was immediate and widespread.[1] In Virginia, the assembly, upon Jefferson's initiative, appointed a day of fasting. Being dissolved for this action, eighty-seven burgesses, as private gentlemen, expressed their sympathy with the distressed town and suggested that immediate steps should be taken for summoning a general congress. Subscription papers were handed about throughout the Old Dominion, and money and food were sent to Boston, — among other supplies nearly nine thousand bushels of wheat and corn. The Charlestonians contributed cargoes of rice; the Philadelphians gave more than one thousand barrels of flour, while from Connecticut came Israel Putnam with a flock of sheep.[2] The people of Providence hit upon the idea of building a new meetinghouse, and thus gave employment to the distressed carpenters of Boston. Never before in American history, and possibly never before in any history had the waves of sympathetic enthusiasm mounted so high as those which now rolled from South to North and from North to South. Hutchinson asserted that the act wholly failed to accomplish the object it was intended to effect, — the punishment of the radicals. On the contrary, it was the friends of government who were the greatest sufferers,[3] for they lost their jobs and received no aid.

The Boston Port Act went into operation on June 1, 1774.

---

[1] Eddis, in his *Letters from America* (p. 159, note), gives an animated account of the doings of the people of Annapolis on May 28, 1774 — before the Act was in operation.

[2] *New England Historical and Genealogical Register*, xxx, 374; Massachu-

setts Historical Society's *Proceedings*, First Series, iii, 259.

[3] Massachusetts Historical Society's *Proceedings*, First Series, xv, 326–334; and P. O. Hutchinson's *Diary and Letters of Thomas Hutchinson*, i, 158.

On that very day Hutchinson sailed for England, having turned over to General Gage the government of the province some weeks before. He had a rapid voyage. Almost on landing, without being given time to change his " New England dress," and much reduced by seasickness, he was led into the royal closet. The king received him kindly, questioned him closely about local matters, and showed an extensive knowledge of Bowdoin and Chauncey, of Samuel Adams and John Hancock, and other worthies of Boston. According to his recollection, Hutchinson informed the monarch that closing the port had alarmed the Bostonians.[1] The king related the interview somewhat differently. In a letter dated "Kew, July 1st, 1774, 2 min. pt. 9 p.m." he stated that Hutchinson told him the "Port Bill was the only wise and effectual method that could have been suggested for bringing them [the Bostonians] to a speedy submission" and that they "seemed much dispirited."[2] It is greatly to be hoped that the exiled governor was right in his recollection, and that he never gave such fatal misinformation to his royal master; but that personage was most accurate and painstaking as well as stubborn and self-willed.

For years Bernard and Hutchinson had been urging the reorganization of the government of Massachusetts on the Virginia and New York model. The prime minister now made some tentative propositions to that end, when Lord George Germain[3] suddenly intervened and won the notice of the king by advocating a much more thorough-going reformation. Massachusetts towns, he thought, should be

[1] Hutchinson's *Diary and Letters*, i, 357.

[2] W. B. Donne's *Correspondence of George III and Lord North*, i, 194.

[3] Lord George Sackville became Lord George Germain in 1777 on inheriting property from Lady Betty Germain; in 1782 he was made a peer, with the title of Viscount Sackville. See *Stopford-Sackville Papers*, i, 71, note, and Index under Lady Betty Germain, also p. 77.

turned into corporations, like the English boroughs; the jury system ought to be reformed, and the assembly, too, for it was a downright clog upon the administration.[1] Lord North declared that every one of these propositions coincided with his mind. Two weeks later he introduced bills providing that in the future Massachusetts councillors should be appointed by the king; that jurors, who had hitherto been chosen in town meeting, should henceforth be selected by the sheriffs; and that there should be no more town meetings except by permission of the governor. Thomas Pownall, who had once governed the province, asked how the people living in towns three hundred miles from Boston could manage their affairs, if they had to get the governor's permission before they could hold a meeting; but he was not much attended to. It was said that the bills did not take away the charter, but simply regulated the government, which was very necessary to be done to put an end to the tarrings and featherings, the plunderings and burnings. To this Pownall replied that the governor had ample power under the charter, if he would exercise it; the colonists were on the verge of rebellion, they should not be driven over the line. After more debate the bills all passed the Commons by large majorities.[2] In the Lords, a new Quartering Act attracted much attention. It provided, among other things, that when the bar-

---

[1] *Parliamentary History*, xvii, 1196. William Knox (Royal Historical Manuscripts Commission's *Reports, Various Collections*, vi, 257) relates that Governor Pownall suggested shutting up the port of Boston; that he (Knox) was for altering the Council. "Sir Francis Bernard unluckily came to town, and, with his old papers, infused the opinion into Lord North that the juries should be also regulated. The preventing town meetings came also from him." Knox represents himself as having opposed these suggestions when Bernard made them in 1770. Like most of the memoranda in the "Knox Papers," this one has no date. It is certain that Germain made the suggestions mentioned in the text. As he often acted on Knox's advice, it may well be that the latter had forgotten his own part in the business and given undue prominence to that of Bernard.

[2] The act regulating the government of Massachusetts passed the Commons, 236 to 64.

racks in any colony were not in the precise places where the
soldiers were required, the authorities must lodge them on
the desired spot.   It was at this time that Chatham ani-
madverted so severely upon the destroyers of the tea.   Going
on, however, he advised gentler methods, " for the day is not
far distant when America may vie with these kingdoms "
in arms and in arts.   " Clasp them [the Americans]
once more in your fond and affectionate arms ; and I will
venture to affirm you will find them children worthy of
their sire," but if they continue turbulent, he would be
among the foremost to make them feel what it is to provoke a " fond and forgiving parent."[1]

Meantime, General Gage had assumed the civil government at Boston in addition to his military duties as
commander-in-chief (May 17).   He was an amiable, well-
intentioned gentleman who had married an American wife
and was not at all desirous of leading any colonist to the
halter.   Supporting him were all the English soldiers who
could be spared from garrison duty in Canada and on the
frontier.   So complete had been the exodus from Halifax
that the Haligonians threatened to tar and feather a man
or two to bring them back, — for they were good customers.
After the Port Act had been in operation for a couple
of weeks, John Rowe walked around the wharves and
wrote that it was impossible to describe " the Distressed
Situation of this Poor Town — not one Topsail Merchant-
man to be seen " ; but sixteen days later, he with forty-
three ladies and gentlemen dined at the " Peacock," and
were very merry.[2]

General Gage had personally informed the king that
with four regiments he could overawe the Bostonians; they

---

[1] *Parliamentary History*, xvii, 1355,
1356.

[2] Anne R. Cunningham's *Letters and
Diary of John Rowe*, 275, 277.

will be very meek " if we take the resolute part." Now,
with his regiments and an attendant fleet of warships, he
found the colonists utterly impracticable. They would
not build barracks for the troops nor allow others to build
them ; they would not sell him food for his men ; they
burned the straw that he obtained for bedding, and split
the planks that he procured for the naval carpenters to use
in constructing some kind of housing for the soldiers. In
August the names of the royally appointed Councillors were
published. The Boston Committee of Correspondence at
once held a meeting with delegates from the neighboring
counties. They voted that the new Councillors were " unconstitutional officers," they denied the supremacy of Parliament, and suggested that a provincial congress should
take charge of the government of Massachusetts until constitutional officers should be appointed. With this incitement, which in truth was not needed, the country people
hunted the Mandamus Councillors out of their houses and
towns and drove them into Boston,—all who did not
promptly resign.[1] Gage fortified the narrow neck of land
leading from the country into the town, and promptly
found that his regiments, instead of terrorizing the people,
were themselves confined within strict limits. In October,
1774, he wrote to England, advising the suspension of the
punitive laws until an adequate force could be sent over.[2]

[1] On September 1, 1774, Richard
Lechmere, writing from Boston, said
that "1500 men, mostly under arms,
attackd Mr Payne of Worcester, one of
the new Council, and extorted a promise
from him to resign his seat at the Board ;
. . . Brigdr Ruggles has been hunted,
and oblig'd to take asylum here allso.
. . . Collo Leonard of Taunton had six
balls and some shot fir'd into his house."
Massachusetts Historical Society's *Proceedings*, Second Series, xvi, 287.

[2] "What turned us all so much
against Gage," says Knox, "was his
telling Governor Hutchinson that, in his
opinion, the only thing to be done was
to suspend the Acts, and, in the mean
time, make preparation for enforcing
them by hiring Hessians and Hanoverians, for it was absolutely necessary to
make an entire conquest of the New
England Governments, and not less than
twenty thousand men could venture to
take the field." Royal Historical Manu-

The laws which have been described in the preceding paragraphs applied directly to Massachusetts. They interested the other colonies only as precedents for later action. The law prohibiting the exportation of tools used in the cotton, linen, woollen, and silk manufacture,[1] and the Quebec Act,[2] both of which were passed in 1774, affected the concerns of several of the colonies and offended the sentiments of many people throughout the continent. In itself, the Quebec Act was the natural outcome of the conquest of Canada and the Proclamation of 1763. That document had been drawn up in haste and without perfect information. For ten years,[3] successive governments sought to place Indian affairs and the fur trade on a firmer footing, and to make better arrangements for the government of Canada. Coming in 1774, the Quebec Act seemed to be a part of the measures for reconstructing colonial governments in general. The Canadians had not taken kindly to the judicial procedure of Englishmen, and the exercise of their religion, which had been half promised in the Treaty of 1763, had not been fully permitted. The new

---

scripts Commission's *Reports, Various Collections*, vi, 257.

[1] 14 George III, Cap. 71, and 15 George III, Cap. 5.

[2] Victor Coffin has dealt with this subject at great length in his *Province of Quebec and the Early American Revolution*, and in briefer form in the *Yale Review* for August, 1895; the statements in the text are based primarily on this excellent research. William Knox's *The Justice and Policy of the Late Act of Parliament for making more Effectual Provision for the Government of the Province of Quebec, asserted and Proved* (London, 1774), is the best contemporary discussion. Justin Winsor's "Virginia and the Quebec Bill" (*American Historical Review*, i, 436–443) summarizes the colonial side. For the Roman Catholic

side of the case see *American Catholic Historical Researches*, vi, 150; viii, 129; xiv, 65. The debates are printed in Henry Cavendish's *Debates of the House of Commons . . . on the Bill for Making More Effectual Provision for the Government of the Province of Quebec*.

[3] As far back as May, 1765, the Board of Trade ("Journals," lxxiii, 151) had under consideration a report to the Lords of Committee of the Council upon the heads of a plan for allowing the free exercise of the Roman Catholic religion in the province of Quebec. In 1766 also there appeared *Considerations on the Expediency of Procuring an Act of Parliament for the Settlement of the Province of Quebec*. In 1771 the matter was again brought forward, but no act was passed until 1774.

act gave the French colonists in the province of Quebec the free exercise of their religion and summary judicial procedure, but made no provision for a representative legislative body.[1] Had these arrangements been confined to the province of Quebec, as it had been outlined in 1763, they might have attracted little attention in the old English colonies. By the act of 1774, however, Quebec was extended southward to the Ohio and westward to the Mississippi. The British government, in making this arrangement, had ease of administration in mind ; but the colonists thought that its wish was to prohibit settlements in the western country under the free institutions that existed on the seaboard. Besides, Virginia, Massachusetts, and Connecticut had claims to lands north of the Ohio. Already irritated by the *Gaspee* inquiry and by the laws for punishing the New Englanders, the colonists were annoyed and excited by this attempt to curb their further growth.

Resolutions and tracts now came out by the score. A few of them stand out from the rest, partly because of their intrinsic importance, but also partly because of the eminence of their authors. Of them all, Thomas Jefferson's " Summary View " is most worthy of analysis. Its author had been elected a delegate to the Virginia Convention of

---

[1] Professor Coffin points out that it was impossible to include the French Roman Catholics in any scheme of representation, and equally impossible to establish a representative system without them. The author of the " Considerations " (p. 15) states that giving the legislative power to the Protestants in Canada would be equivalent to giving 600 recent English settlers the rule of 90,000 French habitants; while to admit the Catholics would be " dangerous in these early days of their submission." Against this may be noted the language of Josiah Quincy, the elder. Writing to Franklin (March 25, 1775), he inquired, " Is not the King's power in Canada, by a late Law of the British Parliament, rendered as absolute, as that of an Asiatic Despot ? . . .

" If Despotism is established in Canada, why may it not, by another Law be established in all the Colonies upon this Continent? The Idea is horrible! " Massachusetts Historical Society's *Proceedings*, 1863–64, p. 119.

The act is defended in *An Appeal to the Public stating and considering the Objections to the Quebec Bill*, London, 1774.

1774, which, among its other duties, was to choose delegates to the forthcoming Continental Congress. Before
leaving home, he prepared a set of instructions for these
delegates. Illness preventing his attendance, he sent copies
of this paper to Patrick Henry and Peyton Randolph; but
the Convention preferred a milder series of instructions
that were formulated by Henry himself. Thereupon,
Jefferson's friends procured the printing of his paper as a
small pamphlet.[1] At the outset the delegates are directed
to propose what the author terms "an humble and dutiful
address" to the king, who is described as the "Chief
Magistrate of the British Empire," — thus removing George
III from his throne in the very first sentence. In this
address, moreover, the king's attention should be called to
the unwarrantable encroachments and usurpations which
the legislature of one part of the empire has made "upon
those rights which God and the laws have given equally
and independently to all," — thus denying parliamentary
supremacy absolutely. His Majesty is also asked to reflect

[1] *A Summary View of the Rights of British America, Set forth in some Resolutions intended for The Inspection of the present Delegates of the People of Virginia, now in Convention. By a Native, and Member of the House of Burgesses* (Williamsburg, printed by Clementina Rind). This was reprinted in the same year (1774) at London, Philadelphia, and again at Williamsburg. Modern reprints are in *American History Leaflets* No. 11, and in P. L. Ford's *Writings of Jefferson*, i, 427, with a bibliography on p. 423. Other resolutions and papers of the time will be found in Force's *American Archives*, Fourth Series, i. One of the very best discussions of the opposing views of theory, politics, and conduct is to be found in the letters signed "Novanglus" and "Massachusettensis" which were printed in the Boston papers in 1774 and 1775. The author of the former series was John Adams; of the latter Daniel Leonard — otherwise not well known. They were gathered into book form in many editions and are easily accessible. At one time "Massachusettensis" was believed to be the pen name of Jonathan Sewall, the Attorney-General of the province, and the letters are often cited under his name.

Notable English tracts of this time are Edmund Burke's *Speech on American Taxation, April 19, 1774*, and his *Speech for Conciliation with the Colonies, March 22, 1775*; Samuel Johnson's *Taxation no Tyranny; an Answer to the Resolutions and Address of the American Congress* (London, 1775); and *An Answer to a Pamphlet entitled Taxation no Tyranny. Addressed to the Author, and to Persons in Power* (London, 1775).

" that he is no more than the chief officer of the people, appointed by the laws . . . . to assist in working the great machine of government, erected for their use."

Jefferson declares the right of expatriation to be a natural law, and describes how the Saxon ancestors of the Virginians had left their native wilds in the north of Europe and possessed themselves of the island of Britain, whence some of their descendants had come to America, — thus preceding the enunciation of the same idea by an English historian by about one hundred years. There was no proof that the dwellers in the old Saxony regarded themselves as the supreme governors of those who went to England; and there is no more reason why the people remaining in Britain should now presume to govern their kinsfolk in America. These acquired lands for their settlement by the expenditure of their own blood and fortunes, and then they adopted the system of laws of the mother country. He reprobates the whole colonial policy, asserting that free trade to all parts of the world is a natural right. He takes up one act after another, in the period preceding 1760, before the accession of George III, and then calls attention to that " rapid and bold succession of injuries" which mark the reign of that monarch. "Single acts of tyranny may be ascribed to the accidental opinion of a day; but a series of oppressions begun at a distinguished period, and pursued unalterably through every change of ministers, too plainly prove a deliberate and systematical plan of reducing us to slavery." Jefferson then enumerates the wrongful acts with which we are so familiar in the later Declaration of Independence. He especially notes the law for suspending the legislature of New York, and asks if any reason can be assigned why 160,000 electors in the island of Great Britain should give laws to four millions in the states of America, particularly as each one of the British electors is removed from the reach of fear, "the only restraining motive which may hold the hand of a tyrant." In concluding this part of the subject, he asserts that these are "acts of power, assumed by a body of men, foreign to our constitutions, and unacknowledged by our laws, against which we do, on behalf of the inhabitants of British America, enter this our solemn and determined protest." The misdeeds of Parliament having been thus reviewed, he runs over those of the government, condemning especially the policy of restricting the growth of colonial legislative bodies. Finally, he exhorts George III to open his breast to liberal and expanding thought and let not his name be a blot on the page of history! He has no minister for American affairs because he has none taken from among us. "No longer persevere in sacrificing the rights of one part of the empire to the inordinate desires of another; but deal out to all equal and impartial right."

The First Continental Congress met at Philadelphia on the fifth day of September, 1774. From Virginia there came Washington, Patrick Henry, and Richard Henry Lee; from Massachusetts, the two Adamses; from New York, John Jay and Philip Livingston; from Connecticut, Roger Sherman; from Rhode Island, Stephen Hopkins; from Pennsylvania, Joseph Galloway, Thomas Mifflin, and John Dickinson; from Delaware, Cæsar Rodney, Thomas McKean, George Read; from North Carolina, Richard Caswell; from South Carolina, the two Rutledges and Christopher Gadsden. Georgia, alone, was unrepresented. The general sentiment of the members was more conservative than the expressions which had come from the several colonies, and much more conservative than the resolutions

L

of counties and towns, since only the more radical of these minor divisions had felt it necessary to take action. For a time it seemed that the Congress would endorse a plan of union which was brought forward by Galloway,[1] with the approval of some of the leading royal officials. In these weeks, rumors had come from Boston that Gage had already attacked the colonists. On September 17, resolutions, which had been drawn by Joseph Warren and adopted by a convention in Suffolk County in Massachusetts, were laid before Congress and by it entered upon its journal. These " Suffolk Resolves "[2] asserted that no obedience was due to the acts of Parliament of 1774, and that no public money ought to be paid into the province treasury until the government should be replaced on a constitutional foundation, or Congress should direct otherwise. Sentiment suddenly turned toward radical measures, and the " Declaration of Rights,"[3] which was adopted on October 14, 1774, undoubtedly expressed the thoughts of very many colonists. After reciting the misdeeds of king and Parliament, the Declaration contains ten resolutions which for their moderation and calmness of tone are worth a detailed study. They base the rights of the inhabitants of the English colonies of North America upon the immutable laws of nature, the

[1] For a brief synopsis of this plan, see below, ch. vii.

[2] Printed in Richard Frothingham's *Life and Times of Joseph Warren*, 529, from the *Essex Gazette* of September 20, 1774. Other texts are in *Journals of Congress* (Ford ed.), i, 32; Force's *American Archives*, Fourth Series, i, 901.

[3] *Journals of Congress* (Ford ed.), i, 63. There are many editions, more or less incomplete, of the *Journals of Congress*. In 1904, the Library of Congress began printing a definitive edition under the editorship of Worthington Chauncey Ford. With the volumes for 1780, Gaillard Hunt, his successor, as Chief of the Division of Manuscripts, became editor. Lists of the official publications of Congress are in successive volumes. A minute bibliography of books and articles relating to Congress, 1774–1789, is in the *Bulletin* of the New York Public Library, i, 125, 159, 191, 227, 257, 289, 323. See also Dr. Herbert Friedenwald's articles in American Historical Association's *Report*, for 1896, vol. i, p. 85; *Pennsylvania Magazine of History*, xxi, 161, 361, 445.

principles of the English constitution, and the charters or compacts. The colonists are entitled to life, liberty, and property regardless of their migration from their mother country. They are not represented, and from their local and other circumstances cannot properly be represented in the British Parliament, and, therefore, are entitled to a free and exclusive power of legislation in their several provincial assemblies. Nevertheless, from a regard to the mutual interest of both countries, " we cheerfully consent to the operation of such acts of the British parliament, as are bona fide, restrained to the regulation of our external commerce." They enumerate the successive acts of Parliament from the Revenue Law of 1764 to the Quebec Act of ten years later. To these grievous laws Americans cannot submit, " but in hopes that their fellow subjects in Great-Britain " will restore them to their former prosperity, they have resolved for the present only to prepare addresses to the king and the people of Great Britain and British America.

The most important work of Congress was the adoption (October 20, 1774) of an agreement or " Association " [1] by which the delegates from the several colonies bound themselves and the inhabitants whom they represented to attack England on her industrial side. They proposed to do this by enforcing a stringent non-importation, non-exportation, and non-consumption agreement throughout

[1] The " Association " and other documents of the First Continental Congress were printed widely at the time, and have been constantly reproduced since. The best reprint is in the *Journals of the Continental Congress* (Ford ed.), i, 75, and in facsimile at the end of the volume. The proceedings, including the papers, were printed at Philadelphia by William and Thomas Bradford in October, 1774, with the following title, *Extracts from the Votes and Proceedings Of the American Continental Congress, Held at Philadelphia on the 5th of September 1774. Containing The Bill of Rights, a List of Grievances, Occasional Resolves, the Association, an Address to the People of Great-Britain, and a Memorial to the Inhabitants of the British American Colonies.*

the continent, and also by discouraging every species of extravagance and dissipation. Committees were to be chosen in every county, town, and city who were to publish the names of all delinquents. Any colony that generally violated the agreement should itself be placed under the ban, but this was not at all necessary. Everywhere agreements, covenants,[1] and associations were entered into and committees were appointed for enforcing the general association. They summoned before them whomsoever they suspected, looked into their books, and dealt with them according to their deserts. The extent of this organization and the unanimity of sentiment in the colonies are graphically portrayed in the certificate which the Charlestown Committee of Correspondence gave to Joseph Lee, a resigned Mandamus Councillor of Massachusetts. He wished to travel for his health, but felt that it was not safe for him to do so without a statement from the local committee that his resignation had been voluntary. Certificateless, he assuredly would have done well to avoid Wilmington, North Carolina, where there was now as much zeal displayed as there had been at the time of the Stamp Act. The associators of that town boycotted Andrew Miller, resolving that they would not purchase any goods from him and would have no commerce or dealing with him.[2] They visited all the housekeepers in the town with the local agreement in hand, to the end that all who refused to sign might be "set forth to public view"; and the names of Dr. Thomas Cobham and ten others who refused to sign were published that they might be treated

---

[1] In Massachusetts, the agreement in remembrance of its seventeenth-century predecessor was called the "Solemn League and Covenant." See Massachusetts Historical Society's *Proceedings*, First Series, xii, 45, which also contains (p. 47) Gage's proclamation for discouraging certain illegal combinations.

[2] *North Carolina Records*, ix, 1098, 1102, 1150, etc.

with the contempt they merited. The Wilmington Committee, having thus performed with thoroughness one part of their duty, next proceeded to put down extravagance and dissipation. They wrote to Mrs. Austin, who was intending to give a ball at her house, that she would better " decline it," and determined that private dances even were contrary to the spirit of the Association, as was the public use of billiard tables. In January, 1775, Demsey Bond and others, having been concerned in a horse race, expressed sorrow for their misconduct, and promised " to make proper atonement for such our enormity."

In Maryland, Anthony Stewart of Annapolis, who had already made himself obnoxious to the radicals, again found himself in trouble upon the arrival of his brig, *Peggy Stewart*, with seventeen chests of tea (October 15, 1774). Meetings were held and measures were in train to deal effectually with him and the consignees of the tea, when he set fire to the brig, which was burned to the water's edge.[1]

The story of tarrings and featherings, riotings and burnings becomes monotonous, almost as much so as the reading of the papers that poured forth from counties, towns, conventions, meetings, congresses, and private individuals. In reality this universality of protest is the most interesting thing of the year. Samuel Adams and Joseph Warren were among the most astute politicians this country has

---

[1] Eddis's *Letters from America* (171-184) contains a full account of this incident. See also *Pennsylvania Magazine of History*, xxv, 248; Kate Mason Rowland's *Life of Charles Carroll of Carrollton*, i, 128. It is worth noting that in his defense Stewart declared that " the duty on tea has been paid hitherto, both in Virginia and Maryland."
Invoices in the Library of Congress confirm his assertion. From these it appears that the ship *Fanny*, coming in 1772 from London to Piscattoway, Maryland, had 417 pounds of tea in her cargo; and the *Adventure*, from London to Portobacco, also in Maryland, in 1774, had 400 and odd pounds of fine green and Bohea tea, valued in all at fifty-nine pounds sterling.

ever seen ; but there is no reason to suppose that they furnished models for the writers of these articles.   Nor would
men like Jefferson and Mason have taken kindly to suggestions from New England.   These papers held the same
language and shadowed forth the same ideas, because their
authors drew inspiration from the same sources.   America
was united ; not that all Americans thought alike or were
opposed to England, but everywhere the radical party had
come to the same conclusion.   This one fact should have
warned George III and his subordinates that they no
longer had to deal with Boston, or Massachusetts, or New
England, but were face to face with a rebellion as widespread as the continental settlements.   No hint of the
danger appears in the voluminous correspondence of the
king and his premier.   On the contrary, on November 18,
the king tells Lord North that " the New England Governments are in a state of rebellion, blows must decide
whether they are to be subject to this country or independent."

NOTES

I. The Gaspee Affair. — The standard work on this episode is
W. R. Staples's *Documentary History of the Destruction of the Gaspee*
(Providence, 1845). J. R. Bartlett's *History of the Destruction of the
Schooner Gaspee* (Providence, 1861) is hardly more than a reprint
of the same material. Other matter will be found in Arnold's
History of Rhode Island and the *Rhode Island Colonial Records* and
in the publications of the Rhode Island Historical Society. The
names of the participants are unknown. The idea that Commodore
Whipple, as he afterwards became, led the boarders rests upon a
letter written by Ephraim Bowen in 1839, when he was eighty-six
years of age. Previously, in 1826, John Mawney, also an old man,
had written an account of his own participation in the affair for the
American Gazette (Staples's *Gaspee*, p. 8). These accounts name
Mr. John Brown as one of the leaders; but the recollections of contemporaries as to events of their early careers are so treacherous
that too much weight should not be given to them. Judge Staples
expresses surprise at the small amount of evidence that was collected
by the commissioners. Their supineness was remarkable in view of
the fact that a few years saw all of them in the guise of fugitive
loyalists. The new matter upon which the account in the text is
largely based was placed in my hands by Mr. Walter A. Edwards of
Providence, who collected it from several places in Rhode Island and
from the Record Office in London.

The papers that are preserved in the suit brought by the Greenes
are especially interesting. From them and from a letter of Governor Wanton, it would seem that Dudingston technically was without authority to make seizures in Rhode Island. He had a deputa-
tion from the Customs Board at Boston, but it was not under seal
and had never been recorded in Rhode Island. When Wanton
asked him to show his authority, he sent an order from the Lords of
the Admiralty assigning him to the command of the *Gaspee*, and also
a letter from them to the Commissioners at Boston. The act of
Parliament authorizing the use of naval vessels is 3 George II, Cap. 4.
The Order in Council directing the disposition of the proceeds of
seizures in conformity with this law bears date of June 1, 1763.
The pay of a lieutenant in Dudingston's circumstances was four
shillings per diem, — which accounts in part for the eagerness with
which naval men entered the revenue service.

II. Boston Port Act, 1774. — It is entitled " An Act to discontinue, in such Manner, and for such Time as are therein mentioned, the landing and discharging, lading or shipping, of Goods, Wares, and Merchandise, at the Town and within the Harbour of Boston, in the Province of Massachuset's Bay, in North America."[1] The preamble recites that dangerous commotions and insurrections have been fomented and raised in the town of Boston, that certain valuable cargoes of teas have been destroyed, all of which has made the carrying on of commerce there unsafe and the collection of his Majesty's customs impossible. It is, therefore, necessary to remove the customs offices from the said town forthwith. After the first day of June of that year (1774), it shall not be lawful for any one to lade or put off from any wharf or other place whatsoever, at any part of Boston Harbor onto any vessel or boat of any sort, any goods whatsoever to be " carried into any other Country, Province, or Place whatsoever, or into any other Part of the said Province of the Massachuset's Bay " ; or to discharge or lay on land out of any boat or vessel, any goods brought from any other place or other part of the province upon pain of forfeiture of the goods and vessel. The same penalty applied to the transportation of goods in small boats, from ship to shore, or shore to ship, within the proscribed limits.

This act did not extend to military stores, " nor to any Fuel or Victual brought Coastwise from any Part of the Continent of America, for the necessary Use and Sustenance of the Inhabitants of the said Town of Boston," provided the vessel had received the necessary permission from the customs officers in the port of Salem ; nor to any vessels which were within the port on the day when the act went into effect.

III. The Massachusetts Government Acts, 1774. — The first of these[2] provided for the impartial administration of justice in the case of persons who were questioned for any acts done by them in the execution of the law, or for the suppression of riots or tumults in Massachusetts. Whenever it should appear to the governor or

---

[1] 14 George III, Cap. 19 (Pickering's *Statutes at Large*, xxx, 336).

[2] 14 George III, Cap. 39. Pickering's *Statutes at Large*, xxx, 367. This act and the next one are not printed at length in the ordinary compilations, but may be read in the original black letter copies ;

abstracts are in the *Annual Register* for 1774, " Chronicle," 238. In the original draft of the bill the consent of the council was not required. See *A Bill for the Administration of Justice . . . in the Province of the Massachusets Bay in New England.*

lieutenant-governor that an indifferent trial could not be had in the province, he might direct, with the advice and consent of the council, that the trial should take place in some other colony or in Great Britain and bind over all such witnesses as the accused person shall desire for their personal appearance at the time and place of such trial, and appoint a reasonable sum for the expenses of all witnesses who were to be free from arrest during their necessary absence from home in any suit to be commenced against them in their absence.

The second [1] is entitled " An Act for the better regulating the Government of the Province of the Massachuset's Bay in New England." It provides that from and after the first day of August, 1774, the charter is revoked so far as the mode of electing councillors is concerned, and is modified to give the governor power to appoint and remove judges, sheriffs, and other officers without the consent of the Council. Elaborate provisions were also made for the selection of jurors, who in future should be summoned by the sheriffs instead of being elected by the freeholders. Town meetings were no longer to be held without the leave of the governor in writing, save only that an annual meeting might be held for the election of officers.

IV. The Quebec Act, 1774.[2] — This act extended the boundaries of the Province of Quebec as they were outlined in the Proclamation of 1763 to include that part of the Ohio Valley which lies north of that river, west of Pennsylvania, extending to the Mississippi River and to the Great Lakes, provided that nothing in this act shall in any wise affect the boundaries of any other colony, nor make void any rights formerly granted. Within the Province of Quebec as thus outlined the inhabitants may enjoy the " Religion of the Church of Rome, subject to the King's Supremacy," but no inhabitant professing that religion shall be obliged to take the Oath of Supremacy or any other that had been substituted for it, but shall swear allegiance to the king and make known all treasons and traitorous conspiracies. The criminal law of England shall be continued in the province to the exclusion of any other rule of criminal law. The king shall appoint not exceeding twenty-three persons nor less than seventeen to act as a Council, and with the governor to make ordinances which shall be laid before his Majesty for his approbation. This power did not extend to the laying of taxes, and ordinances affecting religion must be approved by the king before they became effective.

---

[1] 14 George III, Cap. 45 (Pickering's *Statutes at Large*, xxx, 381).

[2] 14 George III, Cap. 83 (Pickering's *Statutes at Large*, xxx, 549).

V. Salaries of Governors, etc. — The following amounts were paid out of the American customs revenue by order of the government, for compensation for services rendered between June, 1768, and July 5, 1776.[1]

Name	Office	Annual Salary	Total Amount
		£	£
Thos. Hutchinson . .	{ Governor of Massachusetts { Chief Justice of Massachusetts	1500 200 +135 extras	6677
Andrew Oliver . . .	Lieutenant-Governor of Massachusetts	300	1169
J. T. Kemp	Attorney-General of New York	additional salary 200	1400
Robt. Auchmuty . . .	Judge Vice Admiralty, Boston	600	3968
Foster Hutchinson . .	Assistant Judge, Massachusetts	200	100
Jonathan Sewell . . .	Judge Vice Admiralty, Halifax	600	1657 } 2032
Jonathan Sewell . . .	Attorney-General, Massachusetts Bay	150	375 }
Jared Ingersoll . . .	Judge Vice Admiralty, Philadelphia	600	3164
Lord Dunmore . . .	Governor of New York	2000	3032
Frederick Smith . . .	Chief Justice of New Jersey	400	1400
Thos. Oliver	Lieutenant-Governor of Massachusetts	700	320
Peter Oliver	Chief Justice of Massachusetts	400	800
Samuel Quincy . . .	Solicitor-General of Massachusetts	50	125
William Tryon . . .	Governor of New York	2000	7000
D. Horsemander . . .	Chief Justice of New York	500	1012
Aug. Johnston . . .	Judge Vice Admiralty, Charleston	600	88
		Totals	32,287

[1] These figures are compiled from the " Accounts of Charles Steuart, Esq." The salaries of the governors and other officials of Virginia, North Carolina, and Georgia were provided out of permanent revenues or from parliamentary grant. The facts shown in this table justify the assertion that the beginning of a colonial civil establishment — out of the control of the colonists — had been made before April, 1775.

CHAPTER VI

THE CRISIS, 1775

MEANTIME, Thomas Gage, Lieutenant-General commanding His Majesty's forces in America and Governor of
Massachusetts Bay, with five thousand troops and abundant
ships-of-war, had been idling away his time in and near
Boston. He had been ordered to secure the persons of John
Hancock and Samuel Adams and send them to England for
trial for their lives, and also to disarm the inhabitants.
Gage was no military genius, nor was he a man of force
or conspicuous ability; but he judged well the hopelessness
and danger of any attempt of this kind. The slightest
suggestion on his part or on the part of anybody else of
bodily violence to the radical leaders or of seizure of
colonial powder or other articles of war gave the signal
for disturbances, riotings, and military exercisings.

On the first day of September, 1774, a party of British
soldiers seized three hundred barrels of powder stored in a
public magazine a few miles from Boston. At once,—the
wildest rumors ran through the colony,— six colonists, so
it was said, had been killed by the ministerial troops. By
midnight messengers had gone forty miles from Boston to
Worcester; within half an hour, fifty men had assembled;
they started for Boston the instant they were equipped.
All the way from that town to Cambridge, a traveler, who
recounted his impressions, found the greatest excitement as
he rode forward on the second day of September. Everywhere men were leaving their farms; in one town the

landlord of the tavern was the only able-bodied man left. Between two thousand and three thousand men reached Cambridge before it was discovered that no American had been killed. After a demonstration, they returned to their homes. No less than forty thousand men, and possibly double that number, started for the front on this occasion. General Gage was quite fortunate in maintaining peaceful possession of Boston through that winter.[1] Instead of seizing Hancock and sending him to London for trial and execution as a traitor, he found it necessary to ask him to use his best offices to induce men to build barracks for the soldiers before the cold weather set in.

As the winter approached its end and spring drew nigh, Gage sent out parties of officers in disguise to survey the roads and discover the colonial stores of military supplies and ammunition.[2] The experiences of one of these parties has come down to us and is instructive as showing how thoroughly united the people of eastern Massachusetts were in opposition to the policy of the English government. In every town through which these officers passed they found

[1] F. B. Dexter's *Literary Diary of Ezra Stiles*, i, 457; "Letters of John Andrews" in Massachusetts Historical Society's *Proceedings*, First Series, viii, 352, 368.

Armed opposition was not confined to Massachusetts. On December 14, 1774, New Hampshire men led by John Langdon and John Sullivan broke into the fort at Portsmouth, N. H., notwithstanding the defense by a small garrison, and took away powder, muskets, and cannon. *New Hampshire Provincial Papers*, vii, 420–422; T. C. Amory's *Military Services and Public Life of Major-General John Sullivan*, 10, 295. On Sunday, February 26, 1775, Gage sent one hundred and fifty men to destroy military stores at Salem. They went by vessel to Marblehead, and thence set out for their destination. Thirty or forty Salem men led by Colonel Timothy Pickering met them by an open drawbridge. The British tried to cross over in boats that lay near by. For a moment or two it seemed that a serious conflict was at hand, but it was arranged that, if the draw was closed, the British would turn around and go back to Boston after completing thirty rods beyond the bridge. *Essex Institute Historical Collections*, xxxviii, 321; an ample bibliography on p. 327. See also Octavius Pickering's *Life of Timothy Pickering*, i, 60–68.

[2] *General Gage's Instructions, of 22d February 1775, To Captain Brown and Ensign D'Berniere, . . . whom he ordered to take a sketch of the roads, passes, heights &c., from Boston to Worcester* (Boston, 1779), reprinted in Massachusetts Historical Society's *Collections*, Second Series, iv, 204.

some tory who was willing to shelter them, but they and
their hosts were appalled by the hostility of the inhabitants.   In the preceding autumn the Provincial Congress
of Massachusetts had appointed a Committee of Safety consisting of nine members, three of them from Boston, — John
Hancock, Dr. Joseph Warren, and Dr. Benjamin Church.
In the evening of Tuesday, April 18, 1775, bodies of troops
were noticed marching to the water side.   Warren, who was
then in Boston, at once despatched William Dawes to Lexington to inform the country of the impending excursion and
to apprize Hancock and Samuel Adams, who were at that
town, of their danger.   Fearing that this messenger might
be intercepted, at ten o'clock Warren sent for Paul Revere
and desired him also to set off for Lexington.   Before this
it had been arranged that in case of a movement by the British troops, signal lanterns should be displayed from the
tower of the North Church.   Asking a friend to make the
appointed signal, Revere accoutred himself, crossed the river
to Charlestown, borrowed a horse of Deacon Larkin, mounted
and rode away.[1]   Pursuing a shorter route, he reached
Lexington half an hour before Dawes, but was captured by
a party of British officers while on his way to Concord.

The British expeditionary force of about one thousand
men was ferried across from Boston to the mainland.   As it
proceeded up into the country, the booming of cannon, the
firing of guns, and the ringing of church bells informed
the officers that their coming was no secret.   In the early
morning light, as they approached the green at Lexington,
they saw some fifty armed men standing in military array.

[1] Revere's own account is in E. H.
Goss's *Paul Revere* (2 vols.) ; C. F.
Gettemy's *True Story of Paul Revere ;*
and Massachusetts Historical Society's
Proceedings for 1878, p. 371.   See also
articles in *ibid.*, for 1876–1877, p. 163;
for 1879–1880, p. 120; J. L. Watson's
Paul Revere's Signal; and R. Frothingham's *The Alarm of the Night of April
18, 1775.*

Suddenly a shot rang out; it was followed by a volley, and before the militiamen could escape, eight of them were killed and ten others were wounded. The British then passed on to Concord, occupied the village, and stationed a party beyond the bridge across the Concord River. It was at this point that the minutemen from that and the neighboring towns came into conflict with the picket. After destroying a few stores that had not been removed, the British left the town on their homeward march. By this time the embattled farmers from far and near had gathered at sound of bell and gun. From behind rock, fence, and building, they picked off the brightly clad soldiers as they hurried along the dusty road.[1] Half a mile after leaving Lexington, the exhausted men were received by Lord Percy[2] and fifteen hundred soldiers whom Gage had sent with two field pieces to their aid. After resting, they again set out. As soon as they cleared the village, the attack began again, and continued with unabated fury until they gained a position of safety at Charlestown, whence they were ferried across to Boston in the course of the night.[3] The pursuers withdrew to

[1] The American loss was approximately 49 killed, 39 wounded, 5 missing, or 93 in all; the British 73 killed, 174 wounded, 26 missing, or 273 in all.

The men of Colonel Smith's regiment, the Tenth Infantry, wore three-cornered cocked hats bound with white lace, scarlet coats faced and turned up with bright yellow and ornamented with white lace, scarlet waistcoats and breeches, white linen gaiters reaching above the knee, and white cravats (R. Cannon's *Historical Record of the Tenth or North Lincolnshire Regiment of Foot*, 35). These gorgeous figures in the road, and the farmers in their workaday clothes behind the hill-tops and stone-walls offered a contrast which reminds one of the events in South Africa, one hundred and twenty years later.

[2] Earl Percy was the eldest son of Hugh Smithson, whose wife was the inheritor of the Percy property. In 1750, Smithson succeeded to his father-in-law's title and also to his name, and was created Duke of Northumberland by George the Third on account of his political influence. It is said that when the king refused him the Order of the Garter, he reminded the monarch that he was the first Northumberland to be so denied, and that George III replied that he was the first Smithson who had asked for the honor.

[3] The bibliography in Winsor's *Memorial History of Boston*, iii, 101, is very detailed. Hudson's *History of Lexington* goes into the matter with

Cambridge, secured what refreshment they could, and settled down to blockade the ministerial army.

The first accounts of this pregnant day were carried to England by Captain Derby, who had with him depositions from eyewitnesses asserting that the British at Lexington had fired the first shot. The news came as a thunderclap, because much had been expected from Lord North's conciliatory propositions. At first Lord Dartmouth was "too much affected to say much." When he recovered himself, he sought to minimize the affair. Eleven days later, Gage's own account reached London. There was no longer any doubt. The king determined to stand firm, — "America must be a colony of England or treated as an enemy," he wrote to Dartmouth.[1] "Distant pos-

---

great detail, but with nothing like the space given to it by Ellen Chase in the second and third volumes of her *Beginnings of the American Revolution*, — unfortunately her quoted matter is sometimes not accurately printed and is not always correctly cited. Frothingham has given long quotations from the original papers in his *Siege of Boston* and his *Life of Joseph Warren*. Colonel Smith's report to Gage is printed in Massachusetts Historical Society's *Proceedings*, for May, 1876, and in the Appendix to Lord Mahon's *History of England*, vi, p. xxv. An excellent English account is Lieutenant Mackenzie's diary (Massachusetts Historical Society's *Proceedings* for March, 1890). Other material is in *ibid.* for 1869–1870, p. 306; 1879–1880, p. 315; and 1896–1897, p. 304. See also "Proceedings against John Horne" for libel on the British government in Howell's *State Trials*, xx, and in briefer form in John Winslow's paper in the *Publications* of the New York Society of Founders and Patriots of America, No. 2. Dr. G. L. Goodale's " Address on British and Colonial Army Surgeons on the 19th of April, 1775 " is an excellent paper. With this may be read Dr. Rush's " Directions for Preserv-

ing the Health of Soldiers " adopted by the Board of War in September, 1777, and reprinted in the Appendix of Cutbush's *Observations on the means of Preserving the Health of Soldiers and Sailors* (1808). Full accounts of the events of this memorable day were printed in the *Salem Gazette* for April 21 and reprinted in facsimile with much other matter in the *New York Herald* for April 19, 1875. Whole No. 14, 119.

[1] Royal Historical Manuscripts Commission's *Reports*, xiii, Part iv, p. 502. This may be said to justify Adams's assertion that the king had declared: " Let the consequences be what they may, it is his *unalterable* determination to *compel* the colonists to *absolute* obedience "; Samuel Adams to James Bowdoin, Philadelphia, November 16, 1775; Massachusetts Historical Society's *Proceedings* for 1872, p. 227.

R. S. Rantoul's " Cruise of the ' Quero ' " in the *Century*, xxxvi, p. 714, is a lifelike account of this dramatic voyage. The interest aroused in Europe by the tidings of " la grande scaramucia a Concordia " may be seen in the space given to American affairs in *Lettere Istoriche . . . sopra gli Affari Correnti*, printed at Venice in 1775.

sessions standing upon an equality with the superior State is more dangerous than being deprived of such connections." On his part Lord George Germain asserted that "a pistol accidentally fired occasioned all the mischief." He suggested turning the Canadians loose on the New England frontier as being one means of bringing the rebels to reason. With a politician's eye, he noted "the joyful faces upon this event," thinking that it might lead to a change of ministers.[1] It led, indeed, in no long time to Dartmouth's retirement to the less arduous place of Lord Privy Seal and to Germain's appointment to the colonial secretaryship, for which he was so signally and providentially unfitted.

On the morning of April 19, about ten o'clock, while the Concord men were deciding as to their course of action, the Committee of Safety hastily drew up a statement as to the attack at Lexington. This they sent by a messenger to Connecticut; and followed it with another describing the later conflict. From one Committee of Correspondence to another these went,[2] reaching Philadelphia at 5 P. M. on April 24. Six days later, the news crossed the Potomac into Virginia ; and another week saw it at Newbern, North Carolina. On May 8 it reached Charleston by water. From the seaboard, the tidings were carried westwardly to the remotest borders. The response was instant and emphatic. From every part of New England minutemen streamed to Cambridge. Knowlton and Putnam led the men of Connecticut; John Stark those of New Hampshire, and Nathanael Greene those of Rhode Island. At Mount Vernon in Virginia Washington de-

---

[1] *Stopford-Sackville Manuscripts*, i, 134, 135.

[2] "It is admirable to see the alteration of the Tory class in this place since the account of the engagement in New England." Christopher Marshall's *Diary*.

clared that now it was either war or slavery, and in
far-off South Carolina two regiments of infantry were
recruited. "The people of Charleston are as mad as they
are here in Boston," wrote Gage. In the upper regions of
North Carolina the frontiersmen were even more overflowing with wrath and more outspoken in their indignation
at the doings of the government. On the last day of May
some of them, at Charlotte in Mecklenburg County, resolved that all civil and military commissions "heretofore
granted by the Crown, to be exercised in these colonies,
are null and void, and the constitution of each particular
colony wholly suspended."[1] They also provided for carrying on their own affairs "until laws shall be provided
for us by the Congress."

While the news of Lexington and Concord was speeding
southward and westward to the uttermost confines of the
colonies, the delegates to the second Continental Congress
were making their way to Philadelphia, where that body
began its sessions on May 10, 1775. In January, Lord
Dartmouth had addressed a circular letter[2] to the colonial
governors, directing them to prevent the choice of delegates
to this body. The members of the second congress, there-

---

[1] Hoyt's *Mecklenburg Declaration*,
23, quoting the *South-Carolina Gazette*
of Tuesday, June 13, 1775; Ashe's *North
Carolina*, i, 437; H. Addington Bruce in
North American Review, clviii, 47.
These authorities are united in discredit-
ing the so-called Mecklenburg Declaration of May 20, 1775, which has never
been found in any contemporary publication. These facts have been most
succinctly stated in a leaflet issued by
Van Noppen, at Greensboro, N. C.
Among the names appended to this
little brochure are those of the president
and former president of the University
of North Carolina; Professors Phillips,
Hamilton, and Raper of that institution;
Bassett, now of Smith College, and W.

E. Dodd, now of Chicago; and Stephen
B. Weeks and R. W. D. Connor, two of
the closest students of the history of that
state. The last named most kindly
furnished me with a copy. Historical
students are now of the opinion that
the "Mecklenburg Declaration of Independence" of May 20, 1775, was
simply an old man's attempt to reproduce from memory what had been written
a quarter of a century earlier. Possibly,
as W. G. Wickens of Cleveland suggests,
the difference in dates may be explained
by the fact that the people of Mecklenburg
had not as yet adopted New Style in the
calendar. Both sets are printed in the
North Carolina Records, ix, 1263, 1282.

[2] *North Carolina Records*, ix, 1108.

M

fore, were chosen by irregular revolutionary conventions or congresses in the several colonies, instead of by the regular assemblies, and were more representative of the radical elements in the colonies than might otherwise have been the case.   The new congress was a revolutionary body, and in no sense a representative of constitutional authority. Among the new members was Benjamin Franklin, who had now returned from his last embassy to England. Before long Thomas Jefferson succeeded Washington, when the latter left Philadelphia to assume command of the army at Cambridge.   From every quarter the delegates brought with them resolutions in favor of sustaining Massachusetts; many of them also brought suggestions for the formation of local revolutionary governments.   In every colony, however, there were men of influence and character who thought that nothing should be done looking toward a definite separation from the British empire.   Only sixty days before, John Adams had pronounced against independence and the Massachusetts Provincial Congress had declared that even the blood of the 19th of April had not detached them from their lawful sovereign.   Independence in any form was out of the question for the time being. Resistance to the ministerial army was quite another thing. Congress took the soldiers that were blockading Boston into the continental service, appointed Washington commander-in-chief, and published a " Declaration setting forth the Causes and Necessity for taking up Arms." [1]   It represented the opinions of the majority, but was not phrased in the vigorous language that Jefferson had suggested. After recounting the course of the estrangement from Great

---

[1] As to the authorship of this declaration, see Stillé *Life and Times of John Dickinson*, 161, 353 and Massachusetts Historical Society's *Proceedings* for October, 1890, and the books cited therein.

Britain, this memorable document goes on to declare that "In our own native Land, in Defense of the Freedom that is our Birthright, and which we ever enjoyed till the late Violation of it; for the Protection of our Property, acquired solely by the honest Industry of our Forefathers and ourselves against Violence actually offered, we have taken up Arms: We shall lay them down when Hostilities shall cease on the Part of the Aggressors, and all Danger of their being renewed shall be removed, and not before." Congress also formulated a petition to the king which was popularly denominated the "Olive Branch."

The actual governing body in Massachusetts ever since October, 1774, had been the Provincial Congress and its committees. Money had been found by advising the tax gatherers to turn in the funds that they collected to the receiver-general appointed by the Provincial Congress instead of to the public treasurer.[1] Three days after the affair at Lexington, this congress resolved that an army of thirty thousand men be immediately raised, of whom thirteen thousand six hundred should be recruited in Massachusetts, and the other New England colonies were asked to furnish the rest. The raising of new regiments was at once begun, and by June a more permanent force was in front of Boston than that of the minutemen who had rushed to the field on the first alarm; but the terms of service of the new men were generally confined to the current year. The more important positions were given to veterans of the French and Indian wars, some of whom were too old for active service in the field. Others were assigned to popular leaders whose influence would bring men into the field. The inexperience of some of these political

---

[1] *Journals of each Provincial Congress of Massachusetts*, 148.

colonels and majors led to lamentable mistakes and failures when the next important conflict took place. Gage had also received reënforcements, including three major-generals, Howe, Clinton, and Burgoyne. The situation was peculiar in the extreme: a veteran army of six or seven thousand men, supplied with every requisite for the conduct of war, was confined on an island, for Boston was practically an island in those days, by a blockading force three or four times as numerous, constantly changing, unsupplied with the requisites of warfare, and woefully undisciplined. Gage had effectually closed the narrow isthmus which connected Boston with the mainland, so that direct assault was out of the question; the blockaders had stationed themselves on ground commanding the approaches to this isthmus, so that all egress in that direction was practically impossible. On the mainland to the east and south of Boston were Dorchester Heights, across a narrow strip of water; and to the west and north, on the other side of the Charles River, on a hilly peninsula, stood the village of Charlestown. Bunker Hill formed the western part of this peninsula, terminating in a low eminence to the eastward that was occupied by pastures, Breed's pastures and others. The occupation of the Dorchester and Charlestown hills was essential for the safety of Boston, but otherwise was valueless, because they in their turn were commanded by neighboring heights. Eastern Massachusetts, indeed, was one succession of easily fortified hilltops. Apart from political purposes, there was no reason for the retention of the British army at Boston, for New York was the strategic center of the Atlantic seaboard. The prestige of the British forbade an early retirement. From the colonial point of view, it would have been well to have tempted the enemy into the country for another

bushwhacking like that of April 19. Politically, such
an idea was impossible; the thought of the ministerial
army immured in Boston, living on salt rations, was too in-
spiring. Nor was it possible for a volunteer army to stand
inactive until the enemy either attacked or moved away.
At almost the same moment both combatants resolved on
taking a decisive step; the British to occupy Dorchester
Heights, from which the harbor as well as the town could
be threatened; the Americans to seize the Charlestown
hills, because most of their soldiers were nearer that point.
Originally the plan had been to fortify the hills on the
mainland commanding the crest of Bunker Hill, but men,
guns, and ammunition for so large a plan were lacking.
On the evening of June 16, 1775, Colonel William Prescott
led his own regiment and some other soldiers to Bunker Hill.
Possibly because the soil was very refractory at that point,
the detachment proceeded to the eastward extremity, just
above Charlestown. When morning dawned (June 17),
the lookout on the nearest British man-of-war, which was
swinging at her moorings just below, was astonished to
see a redoubt some six feet in height crowning the top of
Breed's Hill. The warships and a land battery on one of
the Boston hills opened fire at once. Prescott's men were
thirsty and hungry and anxious to be relieved, but he refused to let them go back because they had become accustomed to the roar of artillery and had witnessed the
small amount of damage which the cannonading had
caused. He asked for more men and food; but so poor was
the organization that reënforcing him or supplying him
was a matter of difficulty and great confusion. Knowlton
from Connecticut and Stark[1] from New Hampshire led their
men to the front, and occupied a line extending from the

---

[1] G. F. Willey's *Semi-Centennial Book of Manchester* [N.H.], 293.

BOSTON AND VICINITY, 1775

(Sketch of part of a map made by a British officer. From the *Proceedings* of the
Massachusetts Historical Society for 1879–1880, Frontispiece.)

redoubt to the River Mystic. Adventurous soldiers from many regiments, in groups or individually, made their way to the firing line, notwithstanding the cannonading from British ships and floating batteries.[1] The most notable figures among these later comers were Joseph Warren and Israel Putnam. The former, although a major-general, served as a private in the redoubt, while Putnam by example and exhortation made the defense more vigorous and more prolonged. Stark and Knowlton built a defensive breastwork from the material furnished by stone walls and rail fences, — and thus gave their troops a feeling of security which was most helpful.

Upon the sudden appearance of the redoubt, Gage summoned a council of war which, unlike most councils, was unanimous in advising immediate attack. The danger of being caught between the main American force at Cambridge and the detachment on the Charlestown hills[2] determined Gage and Howe to assault the position in front, although Clinton and Burgoyne advised the contrary. The command in the field was assigned to Howe, who was the senior major-general. Sir William Howe came of a distinguished family. His eldest brother, Lord Howe, had been killed at Ticonderoga in 1758; Richard, the second brother, was the Admiral Lord Howe of the Revolutionary

---

[1] Soldiers from sixteen American regiments, or more, were present at Bunker Hill. Reckoning them or half of them at their ordinary strength would give four thousand men and more; but most of these regiments had only a handful of men in the fight. It is therefore impossible to give the numbers.

[2] In commenting upon the battle of Bunker Hill, Colonel Carrington (*Battles of the American Revolution*, 113, New York, 1888) says: "A prompt occupation of the isthmus, under the guns of the fleet, [would] have enabled the British commander to have seized Bunker Hill summit in the rear of the American works, and would have placed those works at his mercy." See also C. F. Adams's "Battle of Bunker Hill" in *American Historical Review*, April, 1896, p. 401. Mr. Adams served in the Army of the Potomac through the War for Secession, and was brevetted as a brigadier-general at its close. His military experience, in combination with his marked historical insight, give a peculiar value to this and other papers criticising military operations.

War. General Howe himself, had led the forlorn hope
of twenty-four that seized the entrenched path which ascended from the St. Lawrence to the Heights of Abraham
and cleared the road for Wolfe's advancing column. He
was now forty-six years of age, and at the moment few
British officers had a more brilliant position in the public
mind.

Gathering the British troops in Boston and ferrying
them across the harbor to the seaward end of the Charlestown peninsula was a work of time. As soon as Howe
closely observed the American lines and the broken nature
of the ground over which the assault must be made
he sent to Gage for more men. It was afternoon before
the British attacked.[1] The soldiers, burdened with blankets, knapsacks, and provisions, for it was intended to
pursue the retreating rebels upon their flight, stumbled
heavily over the plowed land, slowly climbed the fences and
stone walls, and gradually advanced up the slope toward
the redoubt. Along the American line the order ran:
"Wait until you see the whites of their eyes!" "Aim at
the hips!" "Aim at the handsome coats!" The firing,
when it began, was so heavy and continuous that the Brit-

---

[1] The battle of Bunker Hill and the
"Siege of Boston" occupy a large
portion of the general histories of the
war, and of most of the special works
noted under Lexington. In addition
may be mentioned the publications of
the Bunker Hill Monument Association,
especially the article by General Horace
N. Fisher in the number for 1907. The
controversy over the command at
Bunker Hill produced many books and
articles. Increase N. Tarbox and
W. F. Livingston have both written
biographies of Putnam. All accounts
of his share in the battle are largely
based on the depositions of the veterans that were taken in 1825. The
account by Judge William Prescott,
Colonel Prescott's son, is in Massachusetts Historical Society's *Proceedings*,
1875–1876, p. 68; although singularly
void of filio-pietism, the letter should
be read with this relationship in mind.
Caleb Stark's *Memoir and Official
Correspondence of Gen. John Stark* (Concord, N. H., 1860) may be supplemented
by articles noted in "Bibliography
on John Stark" in Manchester Historic
Association's *Collections*, i, 205–211.
There is a good article on Colonel
Knowlton in *New England Historical
and Genealogical Register*, xv, p. 1.
An interesting anonymous English account is in Royal Historical Manuscript
Commission's *Reports*, xiv, Appendix 1,
p. 2.

ish went down in ranks.   In some companies only eight or
nine men were uninjured.   Back the survivors rushed out of
musket range.   Again they formed and marched to the attack, and once more were driven back.   Clinton with four
hundred marines now came to the aid of Howe.   The
third assault was made with greater attention to the tacti-
cal problems, and artillery was used with effect.   Again
the slaughter was great; but, suddenly, the redoubt was
silent.   The last cartridge had been burned.   In this time
of direful need it is related that one man having some
spare powder in his pocket " tare off some part of his
shirt to make wadding of, & when he had fir'd away all
his powder he retreated without hat or wigg, & almost
naked." [1]   Some of the Americans had bayonets, but most
of them were without defensive weapons, and they could
not withstand the greater number of the British.   They retreated without confusion, first to Bunker Hill, then to the
mainland; the pursuers bivouacked for the night on the
hill.   One thousand or fifteen hundred British soldiers
were killed or wounded on this ever to be remembered
day,— a greater proportionate loss than had befallen any
detachment of the British army in the Seven Years' War
made memorable by the battles of Minden and Quebec.[2]

[1] This sentence is quoted in a letter
dated " Newbury Port, 21st June,
1775," in Massachusetts Historical Society's *Proceedings*, 1869–1870, p. 226.
The amount of care required to scruti-
nize history, when told by contemporaries
in their old age, is illustrated by the depositions of the forty survivors of the
Battle of Bunker Hill who were present
on the occasion of the laying of the
corner stone of the monument commemo-
rating that event.   These testimonies,
for the most part, were " mixtures of old
men's broken memories and fond im-
aginings with the love of the marvellous.
Some of those who gave in affidavits

about the battle could not have been in
it, nor even in its neighborhood.   They
had got so used to telling the story for
the wonderment of village listeners, as
grandfathers' tales, and as petted representatives of ' the spirit of '76,' that they
did not distinguish between what they
had seen and done and what they had
read, heard, or dreamed." *Ibid.*, First
Series, ii, 231 note, 232 note.

[2] The losses of the British at Bunker
Hill were extraordinary, as appears from
Lieutenant Inman's lists (*Pennsylvania
Magazine of History*, xxvii, 176).   The
total number of officers killed in the
twenty battles of the war was 198;

On the American side, one hundred and forty were killed, two hundred and seventy-one wounded, and thirty were reported as missing. It is a "most decisive blow against the Bostonians," wrote Lord George Germain (July 26) on first hearing the news.[1] "I wish we could sell them another hill at the same price," was the ardently expressed desire of Nathanael Greene.[2]

Lexington and Concord and Bunker Hill decided the matter; there could be no going back. Since the beginning of the year, and even before, the king had anxiously watched every move. Over and over again he wrote to Lord North and to Lord Dartmouth and in repeated messages to Parliament that the colonists must submit, — after that conciliation might be possible. There was not the slightest doubt in his mind, nor was there in the mind of any Englishman in authority or within the ranks from which those in authority were drawn, that Great Britain was supreme in the empire and that the British Parliament was the supreme legislative power in Great Britain, and in the empire, too. The broadest minded and friendliest of Englishmen, the Earl of Chatham, himself, had no question on this point. In February, 1775, he offered a provisional act for settling the troubles in America. The further title of this proposed law was "for asserting the Supreme Legislative Authority and Superintending Power of Great Britain over the Colonies."[3] It was in the form

wounded, 387. Of these 27, or about one-eighth, were killed at Bunker Hill, and 68, or about one-sixth of the total number, were wounded on that day.

[1] *Stopford–Sackville Papers*, i, 136.

[2] G. W. Greene's *Life of Nathanael Greene*, i, 95; Frothingham's *Siege of Boston*, 210.

[3] The Marquess of Rockingham seems to have stood alone. In the debate on the disturbances in America, in February, 1775, he declared "he would neither risk nor hazard life or fortune in such a cause [crushing America]. . . . He should not tread in the steps of his noble, but ill-fated ancestor (Lord Strafford), who first courted popular favour, and then deserted the cause he had embarked in; for as he had set out by supporting the cause of the people against the tyranny and arbitrary measures of ministers, so he should never, for

of a declaratory act containing among other things
the statement that the colonies were subordinate to the
British Parliament.   Edmund Burke likewise asserted that
the Parliament of Great Britain sat at the head of the empire in two capacities, one as a local legislature, the other
in " her imperial character."   As such, " she superintends
all the several inferior legislatures."   A minister who had
announced as a part of his policy, in 1775, the giving up of
the idea of parliamentary supremacy could not have held
his office for a day; a king who had proposed such a
thing would have lost his crown.   Between parties in
England, the question was as to the assertion of this
power in point of time and object.   The shedding of
blood in America, both British and colonial, only deepened
the determination to compel submission to the " parent
state " and its Parliament.   Gage was recalled and the chief
command given to Howe, with authority to transport the
army from Boston.   Negotiations were at once begun
with foreign powers for a supply of veteran soldiers to
compel the undutiful children to obedience, and arrangements were made to recruit British regiments to their
war strength and to furnish the army in America with
food and equipment.

The determination to coerce the colonists was the more
readily reached because no stiff resistance was expected.
The Americans were looked upon as cowards by those
high in office.   General James Murray, who had so gal-
lantly defended Quebec in the winter of 1759–60, wrote
to Germain that the native-born American was " an effemi-
nate thing, very unfit for and very impatient of war."   He
took it for granted that Washington would have to rely

any temptation whatsoever, desert or betray them."   *Parliamentary History,*
xvii, 267.

on the emigrants from Europe who had not yet been "mollify'd by an American possession."[1] Lord Sandwich averred that Sir Peter Warren had represented the conduct of the New Englanders at the siege of Louisbourg "as in the highest degree dastardly." He himself, the First Lord of the Admiralty, answered for it that they "will bluster and swell when danger is at a distance, but when it comes near, will like all other mobs throw down their arms and run away."[2] These opinions reflected the contempt of military men for citizen soldiery in the day when tactics demanded that opposing armies march slowly toward one another and fire into each other's faces. The colonists had learned a different mode of warfare, more suited to a broken and forested country. Whenever possible they got behind trees or logs or sheltered themselves in a hole in the ground and shot down the first enemy who came within range. In Europe, war was a profession; in America it was only waged for life and family. Before the conflict ended there was something plaintive in the complaints of Englishmen and Germans that the Americans fought like savages, — the frontier had taught them a more modern method of warfare.

The stand made by the colonists at Bunker Hill aroused a spirit of exultation throughout the continent, which was not at all lessened by the fact that, in the end, their troops had been obliged to retreat. A few days before this battle, the Continental Congress had begun the reorganization of the army by taking the force that was blockading Boston

[1] *Stopford-Sackville Papers*, i, 371. Wolfe's opinion of American cowardice has already been noted in the present work (ii, 579 note 2).

[2] Richard Price to Josiah Quincy, Jr. (Massachusetts Historical Society's *Proceedings*, May, 1903, p. 287). Dr. Price stated that he heard Lord Sandwich make these assertions. The notorious Dr. Shebbeare thought that, had not England interfered in 1754, "the colonists, like the herd of swine possessed by the Devil, would, otherwise, have run headlong into the Atlantic ocean and been drowned, through fear of the Canadians."

into the service of the continent and appointing general
officers to command it. The jealousy of New England,
which was high even at this time, and the great proportion
of New England officers in the army led to the selection of
Washington as commander-in-chief [1] and to the appointment, as major-generals, of Horatio Gates and Charles Lee,
who had been officers in the British army, but were now
living in Virginia. Washington hastened to Cambridge,
and entered earnestly upon the task of making more efficient the troops that he found there and in the neighboring
towns.[2] Supplies of powder and munitions of war were
so scanty, and the discipline of the troops so lax that he
was obliged to remain inactive for nearly eight months.
In the interval the force that he at first commanded melted
away, owing to the terms of enlistment coming to an end
with the close of the year, and a new army had to be recruited and schooled in the discipline and art of war.
The seizure of Ticonderoga, on May 10, 1775, and the capture of a British ordnance brig six months later, supplied
him with warlike material when the snows of the winter
made it possible to drag the guns captured at the former
place from Lake Champlain to the seaboard.

The forts at Ticonderoga and Crown Point, which had
performed such great services to the French and the English in preceding campaigns, had been used as storehouses
and magazines after the conclusion of the Peace of Paris
in 1763. In order to keep a proper force at Quebec and
to provide even the weak detachment that was sent to

---

[1] On the circumstances of this appointment see the *Works of John Adams*,
ii, 415–418; Massachusetts Historical
Society's *Proceedings* for 1858–1860,
68–75. Worthington C. Ford has examined this subject with his usual care
in a long note to p. 476 of the second
volume of the *Writings of Washington*.
He set forth the same facts in a more
popular form in *The Nation* (June 13,
1889) reprinted in his *Spurious Letters
attributed to Washington*, pp. 138–147.

[2] See Note at end of chapter.

Boston, the interior garrisons and posts had been denuded. Possibly Gage, from his knowledge of the weakness of the radicals in New York, had not felt apprehensive for these magazines. They were guarded by very small forces; a few officers and about forty men at Ticonderoga, and even smaller numbers at Crown Point, Fort George, and St. Johns. It occurred to Benedict Arnold, an enterprising Connecticut militia officer, who was hastening to Boston on the first alarm, and also to Ethan Allen, one of the most outstanding of the settlers in the New Hampshire Grants, that the seizure of these posts was entirely feasible, if undertaken immediately without apprising the garrisons of their danger. Arnold asked the Committee of Safety for a commission and authority to recruit a force for this purpose. Both were given him, and he started for western New England; but found that Ethan Allen had already embodied his expedition. Without recruiting his men, therefore, Arnold joined as a volunteer. Ethan Allen and his followers lived in what is now southern Vermont, on lands which had been granted to them by New Hampshire authorities. New York claimed jurisdiction over this tract, and from time to time officials from Albany attempted to enforce this jurisdiction; those who escaped without a severe beating were fortunate. Allen and the Green Mountain boys were frontiersmen inured to hardship and capable of exceedingly rapid and vigorous movements. They now marched to Lake Champlain, where as many as possible embarked on whatever boats could be seized, crossed the lake to Ticonderoga, entered the fort at night without opposition, and captured it with its startled garrison. Two days later, Crown Point likewise succumbed to their vigorous rapidity of movement. Soon Arnold was joined by fifty recruits. These he placed on

a schooner, and, sailing to the outlet of the lake, captured
Fort St. John and an armed sloop that lay anchored near
by. More recruits joining him, he assumed command of the
forces on the lake.[1] This arrogation of authority aroused
so much resentment that Arnold returned to Cambridge;
but his ardent spirit was not daunted, and he soon joined
with others in suggesting the feasibility of surprising
Quebec by a rapid march through the wilderness of Maine.

During the summer of 1775 the blockade of Boston
became so effective that no supplies from the country
reached the British soldiers and the other inhabitants of that
town. From this time, they were obliged to procure food
and clothing, as well as all military supplies, from Halifax,
or from the other colonies, or from England itself. It
occurred to Colonel John Glover of Marblehead, who was
as much at home on ship as on shore, that it would be perfectly practicable to capture some of these transports on their
way to Boston and thus add greatly to the distress of the
garrison. He laid the matter before Washington, who commissioned him to fit out one or more vessels at the continental
expense to perform this service. Soon several small fishing schooners, the *Hancock*, *Lee*, *Franklin*, and *Warren*,
sailed from Marblehead. The *Lee* was commanded by
John Manley, born in England, in Devonshire. He came
to Marblehead, was married there, and was known to his
townsmen as John Russell. His crew consisted of fifty
men of Glover's regiment. The *Lee* carried ten swivels
and four four-pounders, and was provided with twenty
rounds of ammunition. On October 29, she sailed from
Marblehead, and for a month met with slight success.
Late in November it was reported from Boston that the

---

[1] The circumstances of the Ticonderoga campaign are fully set forth with
ample citations by Justin H. Smith in *Our
Struggle for the Fourteenth Colony*, vol. i.

British officials at that place were anxious over the non-appearance of an ordnance brig, the *Nancy*, laden with a very valuable cargo of military stores.   Manley at once sailed in the hope of intercepting her, and three days later sighted her off Cape Ann and brought her into Gloucester Harbor.   Two thousand muskets and   bayonets, eight thousand fuses, thirty-one tons of musket balls, barrels of gunpowder, and military tools of many descriptions formed the cargo of this "instance of divine favor," as Washington termed it.   To some of those immured at Boston the sending a vessel laden with such a valuable cargo, so poorly manned, and taking no steps whatever to meet her at some distance from port, as Peter Oliver wrote, "looks very odd."   There were eight or ten "pirate vessels" cruising between Cape Cod and Cape Ann, he informed Hutchinson, and the British men-of-war were chiefly in the harbor.   " Now for Bombardment, &c." [1]

When the spring of 1776 opened, Washington deter-mined to drive the enemy from Boston.   With the lesson of Bunker Hill before them, one might have expected that the British would have seized and fortified every hill which commanded the town and the anchorage in the har-bor.   Yet through all this time General Sir William Howe had neglected to possess himself of Dorchester Heights, the very hill which Gage had intended seizing in the preceding June, now nine months agone.   Washington decided to oc-cupy the hill.   He intrusted the details of this operation to Generals Heath and Thomas, who commanded the troops stationed at Roxbury.   The movement was carried out with a celerity and success that seldom rewards the sol-dier.[2]   Providing himself with means to deaden the noise

---

[1] Hutchinson's *Diary*, i, 581.
[2] There is no adequate life of General Thomas, but an excellent article by Charles C. Smith is in the Massachusetts

and with barrels to be filled with stones to roll down on an attacking force, Thomas seized the highest of the Dorchester hills, and there with incredible swiftness built a redoubt. Howe at once put his men into boats to drive off the Americans before they could make their works impregnable; but a severe storm prevented the carrying out of this plan for several days, by which time the works were so advanced that an assault was out of the question. It was likewise out of the question to remain longer in Boston. Unofficially and informally, a sort of agreement was entered into between the opposing forces that if the British were not attacked on embarkation, they would leave the town substantially as it was. There was no formal communication between Washington and Howe, but this was the understanding. The British commander offered transportation to those Americans who wished to leave the town. About one thousand took advantage of this offer.[1] The members of Governor Hutchinson's family who had not accompanied him in 1774, with a few others, were

Historical Society's *Proceedings* for November, 1904. There is some matter in Heath's *Memoirs* under date of February 15 to March 18, 1776. Miss Rowena Buell's *Memoirs of Rufus Putnam* (p. 54) has some very interesting material on the seizure of Dorchester Heights. Five interesting letters bearing on this movement are printed in the *Proceedings* of the Bunker Hill Monument Association for 1909.

[1] The case against the American radicals was vigorously stated by " E. B—— ": [possibly Edward Bentham] in *The Honor of the University of Oxford defended against the Illiberal Aspersions of E——d B——e, Esq;* (London, 1776). After noting English contributions to learning, to the propagation of the gospel, and money given by Parliament " to cultivate, adorn, and protect the American Colonies," to defend them from Frenchmen, Spaniards and Indians, to alleviate their military expenditures, and to pay premiums on their products, he glows with the benefits of unrestricted migration from the home land. American gratitude for these favors far exceeds Punic perfidiousness and ingratitude. " Long have these insidious practices prevailed; . . . Long have this iniquitous people wreaked their insatiate malice on the friends of the British name in North America," etc. The sins of the revolutionists are recounted at even greater length in two recent books: Arthur Johnston's *Myths and Facts of the American Revolution* (Toronto, 1908) and James H. Stark's *The Loyalists of Massachusetts and the Other Side of the American Revolution* (Boston, 1909), and in the early chapters of Belcher's *First American Civil War* (London, 1911).

taken directly to England. The rest of the exiles accompanied the departing troops to Halifax,[1] whence a few crossed the Atlantic to weary the ministers directly with their personal applications for relief.

One of the peculiar features of the Revolutionary War was the idea, which was always prevalent in British minds, that the loyalists were formidable in numbers in some other place than the particular spot where the British army then was. At Halifax, New York loyalists were expected to rally in great numbers to the aid of His Majesty's army, whenever it should appear; at New York, the same hopes were held as to the Pennsylvanians; always the Carolinas were looked upon as loyalist strongholds. In the upper regions of North Carolina there were many Scottish Highlanders. These held their lands directly from the crown and had been active in the "Regulation," which was largely a movement in opposition to those who were native born, or had been longer in the country, and were now at the head of the radical party. The Scottish leaders entered into communication with Governor Martin, Tryon's successor. Finally, a plan was formulated, according to which a British force was to act in conjunction with these Scottish loyalists. Accordingly, in February, 1776, Donald McDonald, acting under instructions from Governor Martin, summoned the up-country tories to Cross Creek to enlist in the service of their royal master. Thousands of Scots assembled; but only sixteen hundred remained when it was found that no royal troops had arrived. Under McDonald, the faithful started on their march to

---

[1] One of this band of "Loyalist refugees" was a London merchant who bore the pleasant name of Jolley Allen. The vessel bearing him, his family, and their effects was wrecked on Cape Cod. Allen's journal is chiefly interesting as bearing testimony to the inveteracy of the people against the loyalists. Massachusetts Historical Society's *Proceedings*, First Series, xvi, 69.

Wilmington. They were met at Moore's Creek Bridge,[1] eighteen miles above Wilmington, by the radicals on February 27, 1776, and were killed, captured, or dispersed to a man. This complete crushing of the southern loyalists brought to the fore the question of the secession of the thirteen colonies. The decision lay in the hands of the Pennsylvanians and of the king. If the former held back, New England and the South could not secede; if the London Government gave way, or even stood still, the radical party in America could not carry out its policy of independence.

[1] J. G. Wright's *Address*, delivered February 27, 1857, contains a clear statement of this episode. The best modern account is in Samuel A. Ashe's *History of North Carolina* (Greensboro, N.C., 1908), 496–512. Caswell's and Moore's reports are printed in *ibid.*, 510. R. D. W. Connor gives a very brief, but accurate account in his *Cornelius Harnett*, 116–118. The papers relating to Cross Creek and Moore's Creek Bridge are in the *Records of North Carolina*, x, 429, 441–445, 465, 482–493; those on Clinton's expedition to Cape Fear are in *ibid.*, x, 313, 412.

The husband and son-in-law of the famous Flora McDonald were at Moore's Creek Bridge. There is an article on the American part of her career in *American Historical Register* for April, 1897, pp. 97–112. Some accounts for expresses, guns, etc., are calendared in *Headquarters Papers*, i, 117; ii, 7.

NOTES

I. Washington at Cambridge. — Washington arrived at New York City on his way to Cambridge on June 25, 1775. He was escorted through that town by a body of local militiamen, which then performed a similar function for the newly appointed Governor Tryon, who disembarked from England on the same day. On June 25, also at New York, Washington first exercised his office of commander-in-chief, by directing Philip Schuyler[1] to take command of the soldiery and especially to keep "a watchful eye upon Governor Tryon." He then journeyed through Connecticut to Cambridge, reaching that place on July 2. The next day he reviewed the soldiers[2] stationed there and in the neighborhood, and set about bringing what order he could out of the existing military chaos.

Two days after his arrival, on July 4, in general orders, Washington reminded the soldiers that they were now "the Troops of the United Provinces of North America" and that all local distinctions should be laid aside. Again and again, in general orders, he adverted to the necessity of preventing invasions of private property, and of limiting the supply of rum to the private soldiers. The practice of applying for furloughs and of deserting from one regiment to enlist in another filled him with astonishment, for "Brave Men, who are engaged in the noble Cause of Liberty; should never think of removing from their Camp, while the Enemy is in sight." The laxness of sentries and communications with the enemy alarmed him greatly. He alone was the judge of the propriety of holding such intercourse; and no man who is not "a Native of this

---

[1] *Writings of Washington* (Ford ed.), ii, 497.

[2] Paul Lunt, who was stationed at Cambridge or near by, noted in his diary on Sunday, July 2, "General Washington came into the camp." On Monday, July 3, is this entry: "Turned out early in the morning, got in readiness to be reviewed by the general. New orders given out by General Washington." Massachusetts Historical Society's *Proceedings*, 1871–1873, p. 194. Other information as to these days is summarized in the *Cambridge Tribune* for April 28 and July 28, 1900. The *New England Chronicle* for July 6, 1775, contains the following account of Washington's arrival and his doings at Cambridge for July 2–5: "Last Sabbath came to Town from Philadelphia, his Excellency George Washington, Esq; appointed, by the Continental Congress, General and Commander in Chief of the American Forces, and was received with every Testimony of Respect due to a Gentleman of his real Worth and elevated Dignity. His Excellency was accompanied by the Hon. Charles Lee," etc. The remainder of the entry is a description of Lee and other notables. July 3 is not even mentioned.

Country or had a Wife or Family in it" should be stationed at the outposts. Washington's distrust of foreign recruits was somewhat justified by the fact that of 1134 deserters who found their way into Philadelphia from Valley Forge, in March, 1778, only one-quarter were native Americans.[1]

One of his most trying tasks was to review the findings of court-martials that were held on soldiers accused of cowardice at Bunker Hill. Some of the sentences were probably unjust. One of them, that of Captain Callender, an artillery officer, is of singular interest, because the cashiered officer enlisted as a private and so distinguished himself at Long Island that Washington ordered his commission to be restored to him.

A perusal of the "Diary of Jabez Fitch, Jr.," in Massachusetts Historical Society's *Proceedings* for May, 1894, will give an inside view of the conditions prevailing in the American army from August to December, 1775.

II. Precursors of the American Navy. — The story of Glover, Manley, and Mugford is told by Robert E. Peabody in an article on the "Naval Career of Captain John Manley of Marblehead," in the Essex Institute's *Historical Collections*, xlv; Henry E. Waite's *Extracts relating to the Origin of the American Navy ;* C. O. Paullin's *Navy of the American Revolution*, chs. i and ii ; and Massachusetts Historical Society's *Proceedings*, First Series, i, 203.

The first British naval vessel to be captured after the destruction of the *Gaspee* was the *Margaretta*. She was seized by Jeremiah O'Brien and citizens of Machias, Maine, after a stiff fight. See Foxhall A. Parker in *Magazine of American History*, i, 209; A. M. Sherman's *Life of Captain Jeremiah O'Brien;* and the local histories.

---

[1] C. K. Bolton's *The Private Soldier under Washington*, 58, citing Stevens's *Facsimiles*, No. 2094.

CHAPTER VII

THE DECLARATION OF INDEPENDENCE

BEFORE 1775, independence was outside of practical American politics, and, in that year, few of the leading men among the radicals wished for separation from England, or believed it to be possible. Earlier, the bogy of American independency had been used in England in the hope of compelling the ministry to retain an extra sugar island or two at the cost of restoring Canada to its former owners. French statesmen, also, had tried to save New France from Britain's conquering grasp by dilating on its usefulness as a check to colonial aspirations.[1] In America these thoughts had never occurred to any number of men. The colonists were not at all opposed to monarchical institutions, nor were they hostile to the British kingship. They had outgrown the colonial condition and desired to be permitted to govern themselves or to be given a share in the imperial councils on an equal footing with the dwellers in the parent state. Jefferson's "Summary View" may be taken as expressing the thoughts of an advanced radical in the year 1774. In it he pictures the king holding the scales even between the several parts of the British Empire. To Jefferson Parliament was merely the local legislature of Great Britain. The political theories to which he and his fellow

[1] The argument that Canada in the weak hands of France was to be feared by the colonists after independence more than Canada under the rule of the strongest colonizing power the world has yet seen is difficult of comprehension. There is no evidence that any such reasoning had any weight with the American radicals. See the present work, ii, 596, and note on p. 602.

radicals so closely clung provided for kings and emperors, as well as for presidents and governors; each and every political society had the right to settle for itself which of these forms was best suited to its welfare. There was nothing fixed in the framework of government; the rights of man were unalienable and eternal. Imperial federation, not independency or democracy, was in Jefferson's mind; but in 1774 he was in advance of public opinion, even in Virginia.

Political leaders in Great Britain, from the king and Chatham to Burke and Barré, were united in proclaiming the colonists to be subjects of Great Britain and absolutely dependent on the legislation of its Parliament. It is true that Chatham, at the time of the Stamp Act, had attempted to qualify this position by excepting internal taxation of the colonists by the British legislature, but the Declaratory Act in its final form made no such exception. Edmund Burke, whose speeches on American affairs entitle him to everlasting gratitude, had no uncertainty as to the supremacy of the British Parliament in all cases whatsoever; it was the injustice and inexpediency of American taxation that he reprobated, not its unconstitutionality. Thomas Hutchinson, the foremost of Massachusetts tories, disapproved of the Stamp Act, the Port Act, and the Regulating Act; but he vigorously reprehended the resistance of the colonists to the supreme authority of the empire. The governing classes in England were determined to abate not one jot or tittle of the sovereignty of Great Britain and its legislature — their own supremacy, in fact. Both sides had reached the point where neither could give way without abandoning its whole case; but this did not hinder men from proposing conciliatory measures.

Several plans of compromise were proposed in America. One of these is associated with the name of Joseph Galloway, a Pennsylvanian of education and wealth who sacrificed property and position for loyalty to his king. In 1774 he introduced a plan of union [1] into the Continental Congress. This scheme closely resembled the Albany Plan of twenty years earlier, except that by it acts of Parliament relating to the colonies might be vetoed by a federative colonial council. He also proposed that Congress should declare its abhorrence of the idea of independence. In the same year William Henry Drayton of South Carolina, a radical, made a similar suggestion for the establishment of a High Court of Assembly of North America to be summoned by the king; but its members were to be chosen by the colonial assemblies. As a part of the plan, Drayton suggested that the present councils should be abolished and new ones established by the king appointing members from leading American families. As the two houses in each colony were to be equally represented in the High Court, this body would be quite different from the federative assembly suggested by Galloway which would represent the existing assemblies.[2]

In England both the Earl of Chatham and Lord North brought forward suggestions [3] which they, or people around them, regarded as conciliatory. Really there was nothing hopeful in either of them. Chatham, on his part, sug-

[1] *A Plan of a Proposed Union, between Great-Britain and the Colonies.* This is also in *Journals of Congress* (Ford ed.), i, 49.

[2] *A Letter from Freeman of South-Carolina to the Deputies of North America assembled in the High Court of Congress at Philadelphia.* South-Carolina, Charles-Town, Printed by Peter Timothy, M, DCC, LXXIV. A copy of this interesting pamphlet is among the books from Washington's library in the Boston Athenæum.

[3] *Parliamentary History,* xviii, 198, 221–358. Chatham's plan is printed in F. Thackeray's *William Pitt,* ii, 293.

gested that Parliament should again declare its supremacy, and that this should be acknowledged by a general colonial congress. The colonists, having yielded on the vital point, were to be given concessions. For the future, no tax should be levied in America without the consent of the assemblies, and colonial judges were to hold office during good behavior. Lord North's resolutions were based on an "Address" in which the two Houses had pledged themselves never to "relinquish any part of the sovereign authority over all his Majesty's dominions, which by law is vested in his Majesty and the two Houses of Parliament." This being premised, the minister proposed that whenever a colonial legislature should make financial arrangements that were satisfactory to Parliament, the supreme legislature should levy no tax upon such colony, except for the regulation of commerce, and the net proceeds of such dues should be credited to colonial account. Lord North called this a symbol of peace and prophesied that it would put an end to combinations and commotions in America. The king also approved it; to use his own words, it "certainly in a most manly manner shews what is expected, and gives up no right."[1] The bill embodying this specious plan passed both Houses by substantial majorities, but it meant nothing. The trade laws and the acts of 1774 were to remain unrepealed; standing armies were still to be kept in the colonies; "and the other numerous grievances of which ourselves and Sister-Colonies separately and by our representatives in General Congress have so often complained, are still to continue without redress."[2]

[1] Donne's *Correspondence of George the Third and Lord North*, i, 232.

[2] *Journals of the House of Burgesses of Virginia, 1773–1776*, p. 219. In 1776 a pamphlet entitled *Observations on the* *Reconciliation of Great-Britain and the Colonies* was first published at New York. It purported to be by a "Friend of American Liberty," and was in the form of a "compact" which was really

The colonists were to be free from Parliamentary taxation if they taxed themselves to the satisfaction of Parliament; but their trade was still to be confined to Great Britain. Governor Tryon at New York judged the temper of the Americans more accurately. Again and again he warned the ministry of the dangers of the situation. On July 4, 1775, he wrote that no one province could possibly accede to Lord North's proposals, — "Oceans of blood may be spilled, but . . . America will never receive Parliamentary taxation." He declared that he had never met one colonist who showed the smallest inclination to draw the sword in support of that principle. Two months later he wrote that no arguments could persuade the Americans that Great Britain would not tax them; he wished for "some explicit declaration" that it would refrain from exercising this right.[1]

When the Second Continental Congress met at Philadelphia in May, 1775, its members at once realized the difficulties of their task. Some of them were moderate men like Joseph Galloway, John Dickinson, John Jay, and James Wilson. Others were radicals, as the Adamses, Patrick Henry, and Christopher Gadsden. Between these groups stood Washington and Franklin. Lexington and Concord had aroused the fighting spirit in America, but not even Bunker Hill impelled toward independence. The first ten months of 1775 was a period of waiting and of disheartenment for those who advocated extreme

---

in the nature of a federal constitution. Its essence consisted in the condition that Parliament should not tax the colonies or interfere in their internal policy. The king was to continue to appoint all officers of government, but these were to be paid by the colonists. A general Convention or Congress of deputies of the several assemblies was to have a general colonial legislative power, but its enactments must receive the royal assent. Twelve thousand British troops might be stationed in the colonies, but no more could be sent from England without the consent of the Convention. In return for the protection afforded by Britain, the colonists were to pay into the imperial exchequer eight per cent of the value of all goods that they imported from foreign countries.

[1] "Sparks Manuscripts," No. 43, vol. iii, 223, 224.

measures. In May, Congress declared war; in June, it
adopted as its own the army blockading Boston, and appointed Washington commander-in-chief; but these meas
ures had no constitutional significance; they were simply
an attempt to organize the resistance to what were looked
upon as the unconstitutional acts of Lord North and his
abettors in London. In June, also, Congress advised
Massachusetts to revive her charter government as if the
Regulating Act had never been passed, for that too was
unconstitutional. In July, the conservatives, led by Dickinson and Jay, compelled Congress again "to whine in the
Style of humble Petitioners" to the king.[1] Congress adjourned on the first of August, and did not again transact
business until September 13. The current was now running strongly against separation. In September the North
Carolina Provincial Congress disclaimed any thought of
independence. In November and December, 1775, and
even as late as January, 1776, Pennsylvania, New York,
New Jersey, and Maryland instructed their delegates in
Congress to vote against independence, and the town of
Portsmouth, New Hampshire, which had been the scene of
one of the earliest disturbances, also declared against separation. The tide now turned; the king, coming to the aid
of the radical party in Congress, made measures palatable
which hitherto had seemed quite out of the question.

The "Olive Branch Petition" had been entrusted to Mr.
Richard Penn, who was returning to England. In August
he presented a copy to Lord Dartmouth, and was soon given
to understand that no answer would be returned to it.[2]

---

[1] *Journals of Congress* (Ford ed.), ii,
158. The phrase is that of Daniel Dulaney in his "Preface" to *Considerations
on the Propriety of imposing Taxes in
the British Colonies.*

[2] *The Declaration by the Representatives of the United Colonies of North
America. . . . Their Humble Petition
to his Majesty* (London, 1775), p. 19 and
note.

For some time the king had had in mind issuing a proclamation declaring the Americans rebels and warning all persons against giving them aid and comfort.   Lord North had forborne drawing up the document, but on August 18 the king wrote to him that Lord Suffolk would show him one that had been drafted by royal order which ought to be issued at once if it met with the Prime Minister's approval. Accordingly on August 23 one was promulgated.[1]   While it cannot be regarded as an answer to the petition, it certainly showed the line of conduct which the king thought the situation demanded.   Two months later, in opening the new session of Parliament,[2] he declared that " the rebellious war now levied is become more general, and is manifestly carried on for the purpose of establishing an independent empire."   He promised that a speedy end should be put to it " in such a manner as may be the least burthensome to my kingdoms."   After long debates, Parliament finally passed an act to prohibit all trade and intercourse with the thirteen colonies on the continent, during the continuance of the present rebellion therein.   It was this royal and parliamentary casting out that brought many an American conscience to consent to secession.[3]

For some time Congress had been debating as to what advice should be given to the four colonies that had been omitted by Parliament from the acts [4] restraining the commerce of the other nine to ports within the empire.   It had also under discussion the question of what answer should be given to

[1] Force's *Archives*, Fourth Series, iii, 240.   American Antiquarian Society's *Transactions and Collections*, xii, 228.

[2] *Parliamentary History*, xviii, 696.

[3] 16 George III, Cap. 5 (Pickering's *Statutes at Large*, xxxi, 135).   The debates are given in the 18th volume of the *Parliamentary History*, 1028–1106, and in *Parliamentary Register*, iii, 236–287.

[4] 15 George III, Cap. 10 and Cap. 18. Force's *American Archives*, Fourth Series, i, 1691, 1716; the parliamentary debates preceding the enactment of these laws are also printed in the same volume.   The colonies omitted were New York, Delaware, North Carolina, and Georgia.

New Hampshire and South Carolina as to forming more permanent revolutionary governments than the provincial congresses and committees of safety. The royal proclamation
of August 23 was known at Philadelphia on one of the last
days of October. Hesitation at once vanished. The four
colonies were strongly urged not to take advantage of their
favored commercial condition, and New Hampshire and
South Carolina were advised to establish new governments
forthwith. Before the end of the year, a committee was
appointed to enter into correspondence with foreign powers,
and other revolutionary measures were adopted.

The month of January, 1776, brought to Congress renewed reports of the royal determination and the news of
the burning of Norfolk, Virginia, by order of Lord Dunmore. At this opportune moment a thin pamphlet entitled " Common Sense " was published at Philadelphia.
The author was Thomas Paine,[1] an Englishman, one of
those literary spirits whose birthright is the faculty of in-
fluencing their fellow men in writing and in print. The
diction of " Common Sense "[2] would not appeal to a modern professor of rhetoric ; but it was admirably fitted to
convince ordinary Americans, which a more polished performance might not have done. Paine offered " nothing

[1] Moncure D. Conway's *Life of
Thomas Paine*, vol. i, has a detailed and
rather uncritical account of this part of
Paine's life.

[2] The complete title of the second
edition is *Common Sense ; addressed to
the Inhabitants of America, On the
following interesting Subjects. I. Of
the Origin and Design of Government
in general, with concise Remarks on
the English Constitution. II. Of Monarchy and Hereditary Succession. III.
Thoughts on the present State of American Affairs. IV. Of the present Ability
of America, with some miscellaneous
Reflections* (Philadelphia, 1776). This

was reprinted again and again. In 1776,
*Large Additions to Common Sense . . .
To which is added and given an Appendix
to Common Sense,* was published at
Philadelphia and widely reprinted.
Among Paine's other contributions to
American freedom, the numbers of *The
American Crisis* stand foremost. The
first of these was issued on December 19,
1776, and begins with the imperishable
words: " These are the times that try
men's souls: The summer soldier and
the sunshine patriot will, in this crisis,
shrink from the service of his country ;
but he that stands it *now,* deserves the
love and thanks of man and woman.''

more than simple facts, plain arguments, and common sense,"
so he wrote. "The period of debate is closed. Arms, as
the last recourse, decide the contest. The appeal was the
choice of the king and the continent hath accepted the
challenge. . . . The sun never shined on a cause of greater
worth." The present moment is the seed time of continental union, faith, and honor. Everything pleads for
separation. "The blood of the slain, the weeping voice
of Nature cries, ''Tis time to part.'" As British subjects the American revolutionists would never be received
abroad; independence from every point of view was
necessary. Edition after edition of Paine's tract was
printed and sold in all parts of the colonies. We have
Washington's own testimony of the powerful change that
it worked in the minds of many men in Virginia; it
unquestionably converted thousands to the necessity of
separation.

The change of sentiment coincident with the turn of the
year is marked in the attitude of Washington and the army
then blockading Boston. In June, 1775, while on his way
through New York, he had promised the provincial congress assembled at that city to make every exertion to
restore peace and harmony, and declared that he would
sincerely rejoice when he could return to a private station
in the bosom of a free, peaceful, and happy country.[1] On
the first day of January, 1776, he raised the Continental

---

[1] October 9, 1774, Washington had
written to Captain Robert Mackenzie: —
"But I have done. I was involun-
tarily led into a short discussion of this
subject by your remarks on the conduct
of the Boston people, and your opinion of
their wishes to set up for independency.
I am well satisfied, that no such thing is
desired by any thinking man in all North
America; on the contrary, that it is the
ardent wish of the warmest advocates
for liberty, that peace and tranquillity,
upon constitutional grounds, may be
restored, and the horrors of civil discord
prevented." Ford's *Writings of Washington*, ii, 444.

As late as February 7, 1776, John
Hancock wrote to Thomas Cushing that
Lord North's motion of "20 Nov[r] bodes no
Good . . . the mak[g] all our Vessels law-
ful Prize don't look like a reconciliation."

flag in front of his headquarters at Cambridge[1] and in a few weeks was openly advocating independence. Even at that time Nathanael Greene had gained the confidence of his chief. On January 4, we find Greene writing to one of the Rhode Island delegates in Congress that a declaration of independence ought to be at once made, for God and the world were witnesses to the necessity, propriety, and rectitude thereof.

In the first quarter of the year 1776 there was a marked change of sentiment in the attitudes of the States themselves. In January, the New Hampshire Provincial Congress framed a temporary government, which was to continue only during the present unhappy and unnatural contest, and protested that they had never sought independence.[2] In March the Provincial Congress of South Carolina likewise framed a constitution for " regulating the internal polity of this colony " until the unhappy differences then existing might be accommodated.[3] Even as late as July 2, the New Jersey men in drafting their constitution provided that it should be null and void whenever a reconciliation with Great Britain should take place.[4] In the same months, however, South Carolina and other States, replying to letters from their delegates in Congress, authorized them to join in whatever action might be deemed best for the good of all. The North Carolinians went further, and on the 12th of April instructed their delegates to vote for a general declaration of independence.[5] The reliance that was placed on the general

[1] As to the origin and history of the American flag, see G. H. Preble's *History of the Flag of the United States*; P. D. Harrison's *Stars and Stripes*; J. H. Fow's *True Story of the American Flag*. A reference list of books is given on p. 106 of H. H. Horner's *American Flag*.

[2] *Charters and Constitutions of the United States*, ii, 1279.

[3] *Journal of the Provincial Congress of South Carolina, 1776*, p. 112.

[4] *Charters and Constitutions of the United States*, ii, 1314.

[5] " Resolved, That the delegates for this Colony in the Continental Congress be impowered to concur with the delegates of the other Colonies in declaring Independency, and forming foreign

Congress is noteworthy; but it was sometimes qualified by later action. In August, the Marylanders in their Bill of Rights declared that the people of that State "ought to have the sole and exclusive right of regulating the internal government and police thereof."[1] The Connecticut General Assembly in October, its first meeting after the passage of the general declaration, gave its approval to that document, but resolved that "this Colony is and of right ought to be a free and independent State."[2] Opinion in the Continental Congress changed with greater rapidity. In January, James Wilson of Pennsylvania moved the adoption of a resolution denying that the colonies aimed at independence. The preliminary motion was agreed to, but when a few weeks later an address to the king embodying the same ideas was brought in, it was not even honored with a vote. On the contrary, Congress opened the ports of the continent to the commerce of the world, excepting Great Britain, sent Continental soldiers to disarm the Long Island tories, directed the arrest of Governor Eden of Maryland, and extended its sympathy to the Pennsylvania radicals in their struggle for political freedom.

In none of the colonies, not even in Massachusetts, were the leading men so desirous of freedom from England as they were in Virginia. It was natural that the people of Massachusetts should advocate separation, for their trade had been greatly injured in the last few years, and their

---

alliances, reserving to this Colony the sole and exclusive right of forming a Constitution and laws for this Colony," etc. *Records of North Carolina*, x, 512. The history of the resolve is traced in detail by R. D. W. Connor in the *South Atlantic Quarterly* for July, 1909.

[1] *Charters and Constitutions of the United States*, i, 817

[2] *Records of the State of Connecticut*, i, 3. This resolution is also interesting because it declared that the king had "abdicated the government of this State," thereby absolving the people from their "allegiance and subjection to the Crown of Great Britain" by unjustly levying war "against this and the other united States of America."

leading town had experienced the weight of royal displeasure. In Virginia the conditions of living were in many ways not unlike those that prevailed in England. The landed aristocracy there was very strong, socially and politically, although the smaller proprietors were beginning to find their way into power. Many of the more prosperous families were still in the habit of sending their sons to England for their education. Reading between the lines of letters and other writings of the Virginians, one gets the idea that the prosperity of the Old Dominion was already on the wane, and that the business of producing tobacco could no longer bear the heavy burdens with which it was weighted by English laws. Sentiment, too, had a place in turning the scale, because the Virginians, acquainted as they were with Englishmen, felt themselves to be fully their equals, and not to be governed by them. Richard Henry Lee was the head of one of the greatest families. At this moment his sons were attending school in England, his brother was an alderman of London, and he himself was dependent for his living upon the production and sale of tobacco. Yet in April, 1775, he wrote to Patrick Henry [1] advising an immediate declaration of independence, for the acts of the British government had placed the colonists " in the high road to anarchy." It was impossible for the Virginians to be rebels, as the act of Parliament defined them, and at the same time serve as magistrates under a royal commission. Moreover, it was indispensably necessary to form a new government at once for the preservation of society and to strengthen the hands of the radicals in neighboring States.

For ten months or so Lord Dunmore and the Virginians had been at odds. He had won some popularity by his

---

[1] Ballagh's *Letters of Richard Henry Lee*, i, 176.

o

strenuous Indian policy ;[1] but this did not save him from annoyance.   He removed with his family from the "palace" at Williamsburg in June, 1775, and took up his residence on the *Fowey*, a man-of-war that lay at anchor in York River. The estrangement constantly grew more bitter, until a condition of war existed.   Revolutionary bodies denominated conventions exercised authority on shore, although the assembly met time and again.   At length, in May, 1776, the Convention then sitting appointed a committee to draw up a bill of rights and a frame of government, and instructed the Virginia delegates in Congress to move a resolution declaring the United Colonies " free and independent States."   Moreover, they were authorized to give the assent of the colony to such a declaration and to whatever measures might be thought necessary for forming foreign alliances and for bringing about a confederation of the colonies.   In this resolution there was one important condition that the power of forming the government and regulating the internal concerns of each colony should be left to the respective colonial legislatures.   These resolutions were forwarded to Richard Henry Lee, the chairman of the Virginia delegation at Philadelphia, but it was not until June 7, nearly a month later, that he acted under them.

Meantime, in Virginia, the Convention proceeded with the formation of a constitution, which was adopted on June 29. Besides a bill of rights and a frame of government, it contained a declaration of independence which had been drawn up by Jefferson, then one of Virginia's delegates at Philadelphia.   The Virginia declaration [2] recited that " George

---

[1] Until recent years, the importance and meaning of Dunmore's War were uncertain. This is no longer the case, since the publication of Thwaites and Kellogg's *Documentary History of Dunmore's War* (Madison, 1905).   See also

Virginia Magazine of History, xiv, 54; and Clarence M. Burton's " John Connolly," in American Antiquarian Society's *Proceedings*, New Series, xx, 70.

[2] The similarity in the language of the category of royal offenses in this Virginia

the third, King of Great Britain and Ireland, and elector
of Hanover, heretofore entrusted with the exercise of the
kingly office in this government, hath endeavoured to pervert
the same into a detestable and insupportable tyranny. . . .
By which several acts of misrule [enumerated in the
omitted sentences] the government of this country, as formerly exercised under the crown of Great Britain, is totally
dissolved."[1]

The lukewarmness of North Carolina, Maryland, and the
three Middle Colonies was due to a dread of mob rule
that was felt by many of those who had hitherto led in the
resistance to England. John Adams, returning to Massachusetts, was horrified to hear one of his constituents declare that there was no reason for having judges or courts,
and he asked indignantly: " Is this to be the result of all
our efforts and bloodshed ? " Samuel Johnston, one of
the foremost of the North Carolina radicals, wrote to
James Iredell, in December, 1776, that every member of the
North Carolina constitutional convention who had " the
least pretentions to be a gentleman " was suspected by
the others, whom he describes as " a set of men without
reading, experience, or principle to govern them." His
colleagues in the first legislature were many of them " fools
and knaves, who by their low Arts have worked them-

Declaration and in the Declaration of
Independence adopted by the Continental
Congress on July 4, 1776, has been advanced to justify the surmise that Jefferson, in writing the latter, had borrowed
from George Mason, who had the principal
hand in drawing the other parts of the
Virginia constitution of 1776. Paul
Leicester Ford has shown that Jefferson
wrote the Virginia declaration at Philadelphia some weeks before he formulated
the more famous document. See Ford's
Writings of Jefferson, ii, 7, and note,
and fol. It is well to remember that

while Jefferson's statement of his part
in these proceedings was not written
until 1825, George Wythe's letter to
Jefferson telling him of the action of the
convention bears date of July 27, 1776;
ibid., ii, 8 note.

[1] *A Collection of all such Public Acts
of the General Assembly, and Ordinances
of the Conventions of Virginia, Passed
since the year 1768, as are now in force*
(Richmond, 1785), p. 34. For Jefferson's
drafts, see *Writings of Jefferson* (Ford
ed.), ii, 7.

selves into the good graces of the populace."[1] Governor Caswell gives similar testimony as to the inexperience and ignorance of his supporters. In Maryland a coterie of wealthy men in each county had for a long time dominated the politics of the colony and had usually acted in conjunction with the representative of the proprietor. These men were opposed to Britain's coercive measures, but they dreaded democratic rule, which they feared would be the result of separation. They were so averse to precipitate action that even as late as May, 1776, the Maryland Convention instructed its delegates in Congress to oppose any such declaration. Only at the last moment were Samuel Chase and Charles Carroll able to turn the scale and swing Maryland into line for independency.[2] In New York, too, there was so much hesitation that her delegates were still uninstructed on the ever memorable Fourth of July, 1776. The contest between the two parties in Pennsylvania exerted the greatest influence on the proceedings of Congress, because its sittings were held in the very center of the fight.

The people of Pennsylvania were roughly divided into three groups; the English, the Germans, and the Scotch-Irish. The old English colonists, living in the eastern counties, were mostly Quakers, were engaged in commerce, and many of them were men of considerable wealth. In the middle belt of counties dwelt the Germans. These were agriculturists, were mostly non-Quakers, and, while well-to-do, they had not acquired such substantial fortunes as one associates with the names of Galloway and

[1] *North Carolina Records*, x, 1041; xi, 504, 627; see also G. J. McRee's *Life and Correspondence of James Iredell*, i, 338.

[2] J. V. L. McMahon's *Historical View of the Government of Maryland*, i, 426, 430; Eddis's *Letters*, 258; Agnes Hunt's *Provincial Committees of Safety*, 107; K. M. Rowland's *Charles Carroll of Carrollton*, i, 177.

other Philadelphians. In the western counties the Scotch-Irish Presbyterians were predominant. They were frontiersmen, living by agriculture, and having nothing in common with the people of the eastern part of the province. The representative system, which dated back to the charter of 1701, gave power in the assembly to the easterners,[1] although they were now in the minority in the population. The richer men and those engaged in commerce found their interests at variance with the adoption of extreme measures. The Quakers were opposed to war by reason of their religion and also on account of their close relations with the English Friends. The Germans and the Scotch-Irish were generally in favor of armed resistance and independence. They felt that their interests had not been fostered by the Assembly, and were believers in democracy rather than in the Pennsylvania aristocratic institutions. The Quakers and their allies from

[1] Apportionment of representation in 1775, 1776, and in the Constitution of 1776.

County	1775	1776	Constitution of 1776
Philadelphia City	2 ⎫	6 ⎫	6 ⎫
Philadelphia County	8 ⎬ 26	8 ⎬ 30	6 ⎬ 24
Chester County	8 ⎪	8 ⎪	6 ⎪
Bucks County	8 ⎭	8 ⎭	6 ⎭
Lancaster County	4 ⎫	6 ⎫	6 ⎫
York County	2 ⎪	4 ⎪	6 ⎪
Northampton County	1 ⎪	4 ⎪	6 ⎪
Berks County	1 ⎬ 13	4 ⎬ 28	6 ⎬ 48
Cumberland County	2 ⎪	4 ⎪	6 ⎪
Bedford County	1 ⎪	2 ⎪	6 ⎪
Northumberland County	1 ⎪	2 ⎪	6 ⎪
Westmoreland County	1 ⎭	2 ⎭	6 ⎭
	Votes of Pennsylvania, vi, 546.	*Votes of Pennsylvania*, vi, 693 (March 14, 1776).	*The Proceedings relative to calling the Conventions of 1776 and 1790*, p. 59.

From the above table it will be seen that in 1775 the voters in the original settlements returned two-thirds of the members; by the end of the next year the situation had been precisely reversed.

Philadelphia and the older counties had opposed the commercial and financial aggressions of England, and had driven out the proprietor's representative. There they wished to stop, and were quite unwilling to give power to a revolutionary organization, a convention, or a provincial congress, which would uproot the representative system under which they controlled affairs. They realized that something must be done, and gave added representation to the Germans and the Scotch-Irish. The concessions were entirely inadequate, more especially because the right to vote was still withheld from the smaller tradesmen and the mechanics of Philadelphia. Meantime, county committees had been formed, a committee of safety had been appointed by the Assembly, and an Association had been set on foot. This was composed of those who volunteered for military service,— Quakers and others, who had religious scruples against fighting, could not belong to this organization.

As the spring of 1776 advanced, the spirits of the radicals in Congress and in the country rose, week by week. In May, reports reached Philadelphia that German soldiers had been hired by the royal government to coerce the Americans into obedience,[1] and that a large army would at once be sent over. On May 15, the Continental Congress passed a resolution recommending the establishment in each colony of such a form of government as should, in the opinion of the representatives of the people, best conduce to the happiness and safety of their constituents in particular and of America in general. The passage of this resolve so heartened the extremists in Congress that

---

[1] In view of the irritation which the employment of the German mercenaries aroused in America, it is significant that nowhere in the published writings of Hutchinson or other tories is there to my knowledge any expression of regret for this action on the part of the London government.

they at once brought forward a preamble to explain the resolution that had already been adopted. The preamble was drawn by John Adams. It asserted that the exclusion of the colonists from the royal protection, the refusal of the king to answer petitions, and the employment of foreign mercenaries required the suppression of royal authority throughout the continent and the assumption of government by the people for the preservation of internal peace and defense against their enemies. The preamble and the resolution, taken together, formed a statement of congressional conviction that the colonies were no longer parts of the British empire.

The action of Congress emboldened the Pennsylvania revolutionists. A "conference" of county committees met at Philadelphia on June 18, 1776, and called a convention. In this body, the several parts of the colony were to be represented according to numbers, as nearly as the members of the conference could guess at them. Only associators were to vote for members, — thus disfranchising the conservatives. It was this body that formed the first constitution of Pennsylvania and advised Franklin and his colleagues in Congress that they would do well to vote for independence.[1]

By June 7, 1776, the time seemed ripe to Richard Henry Lee to agitate the question of separation and confederation. He therefore brought the matter before Congress in three resolutions for (1) declaring the United Colonies free and independent states, (2) forming foreign alliances, (3) forming a plan of confederation which should be

---

[1] On this bit of Pennsylvania history, see Charles H. Lincoln's essay on "The Revolutionary Movement in Pennsylvania" in *Publications* of the University of Pennsylvania, History Series, No. 1. A good bibliography is on p. 288. A much briefer article is "The Adoption of the Pennsylvania Constitution of 1776" by P. L. Ford, in *Political Science Quarterly*, x, 426.

submitted to the respective colonies for their consideration
and approbation.   The assertion was at once made by
John Dickinson and others that the organization of stable
governments should precede or at least accompany a declaration of independence, and that a premature declaration would lead to anarchy in some colonies.   This party
was still so strong that it secured the postponement of the
further consideration of the first resolution until July 1.
The radicals were, however, able to secure the appointment of committees to consider the three matters that had
been brought forward.   The idea at the time undoubtedly
was that independence and confederation should go hand
in hand.   The formulation of the declaration turned out
to be a much simpler matter than the devising any scheme
of confederation that had the slightest chance of adoption.
The task of drafting the declaration was confided to Jefferson by the committee of which he was a member;[1] but
Franklin and John Adams, who were also on the committee,
went over the paper carefully and made some important
suggestions.   As the author of the "Summary View" and
the Virginia declaration of independence, Jefferson had
already prepared what might be termed rough drafts of
the document under consideration.   Without "book or
paper," he set to work to put into undying phrase the

---

[1] As to the authorship of the Declaration see an illuminating paper by Albert
Matthews in the *Proceedings* of the
Massachusetts Historical Society, xliii,
241 — treating especially of the claim
advanced on behalf of Thomas Paine,
which seems to have no foundation. Dr.
I. M. Hays notes six drafts of the
declaration still in existence. Three of
these have been reproduced in facsimile:
(1) with his article in the American
Philosophical Society's *Proceedings*,
xxxvii; (2) in Randall's *Jefferson*, i;
and (3) in Gilpin's edition of the *Madison*
Papers, iii, at end. Dr. Hays has also
given a list of printed copies in the *Pro-*
ceedings of the Philosophical Society
(vol. xxxix). The *Bulletin of the New*
York Public Library, vols. i, ii, iii, contains an exhaustive bibliography. The
whole subject has been treated at length
in J. H. Hazelton's *The Declaration of*
Independence, its History (New York,
1906), and in lesser bulk in Herbert
Friedenwald's *The Declaration of In-*
dependence, an Interpretation and an
Analysis (New York, 1904).

ideas which were generally held by the radical revolutionists. He did not regard it as a part of his business to
evolve new ideas, but merely to put into shape those that
were generally recognized.

On July 1, Lee's first resolution came up for debate.
No record of the discussion remains except in the letters of
contemporaries that were written long after the event.
From these it appears that John Adams took the leading
part for the resolution, and John Dickinson against it. By
this time the latter had brought himself to consent to
eventual independence, but he thought that the time was
inopportune. Many other members must have joined in the
discussion, for the debate seems to have been prolonged.
At its close the opposition secured the postponement of
the vote until the following day. At the moment the
Delaware delegation was divided ; that of Pennsylvania
was opposed, Dickinson, Robert Morris, and James Wilson
outvoting Franklin and Morton ; and the South Carolina
and New York delegates had no definite instructions. The
vote, therefore, had it been taken, would have had only
nine states in its favor. That night must have been a busy
one at Philadelphia. Cæsar Rodney, the third member of
the Delaware delegation, who was absent at the moment,
was hastily summoned. He mounted and rode as rapidly
as horse could carry him to Philadelphia, reaching Independence Hall in time to give the vote of his State for
independence. Dickinson and Morris were induced to stay
away and James Wilson consented to vote for the resolution,
and thus Pennsylvania was brought into line. The South
Carolinians had been directed to join the other colonies in
such measures as would promote the best interests of their
State and of the Continent. They were persuaded to regard this as sufficient authority to vote for the adoption of

independence.   The resolution was therefore carried by the vote of twelve states, the New Yorkers remaining silent.

The declaration itself was then brought up for debate. In general the document met with the approval of the members of Congress ; but some important changes were made. One of these was the omission of the clause condemning the slave trade in no measured terms. This displeased not only the Southerners, but some of the New Englanders, for many of their constituents had been engaged in that commerce. The last paragraph was also reconstructed. The insertion in it of the words "hold them [the British people] as we hold the rest of mankind, enemies in war, in peace, friends" certainly added strength to the document ; but the omission of the phrase "we must endeavor to forget our former love for them . . . we might have been a free and a great people together" was unfortunate, because it so exactly expressed the feelings of the great majority of the people, even of ultra radicals like Jefferson.

Never in the whole range of the writings of political theorists has the basis of government been stated so succinctly. The ideas are drawn directly from Locke, the words are generally his, sometimes whole phrases are taken from the "Second Essay of Government," but the reader will go to Locke in vain for so lucid a statement of his ideas. Jefferson possessed the faculty of combining words in phrases that remain in one's memory throughout life. He stated ideas that were well known, that were common, that were hackneyed ; but they are ideas which the American people have not yet grown tired of reading and hearing. In the last analysis, government depends upon the consent of the governed and is for the public good ; whenever this is not the case, government should be opposed and destroyed.

The governing power, a king, or whatever it may be, exercises authority by virtue of a compact. Whenever the ruler breaks this compact, the government is itself destroyed. Certain essential facts lie at the basis of society. These are the natural equality of men and their inherent right to life, liberty, and that which they gain by their labor.

The remainder of the Declaration is a statement of the facts of colonial misgovernment which justify the Revolution. In this long array will be found fact after fact which have been described on preceding pages of the present work. The king is especially charged with having entered into a combination with the two Houses of Parliament which are described under the phrase "jurisdiction foreign to our constitution and unacknowledged by our laws; giving his Assent to their Acts of Pretended legislation." In this connection are enumerated the Quartering Act, the Restraining Act, the Quebec Act, to which Franklin added the phrase "abolishing our most valuable Laws," thus referring to the constant exercise of the veto power as to colonial legislation, long after it had become entirely obsolete as to bills which had passed both Houses of Parliament; — "a Prince, whose character is thus marked by every act which may define a Tyrant, is unfit to be the ruler of a free people."

In using the phrase "free people," which Congress substituted for Jefferson's original words "people that mean to be free," it involved itself in the same seeming contradictions that pervade the earlier documents of the Revolutionary epoch. It is true, using language in absolutely accurate terms, that men in society are not free, and that a people which has a king to rule over it is not free; but to the student of the papers of that time and of the writings of political theorists the meaning is sufficiently clear. The phrase a " free people " meant a people possessing and exercising the inalienable rights which are described in the opening paragraphs of the great Declaration and which appear constantly in the pages of Locke and Hooker. In a society where a man's life is safe, his liberty secure, and his property not to be taken from him, except with his consent, a man is free, even though the customs, rules, regulations, or laws of the society to which he belongs agree to give the executive power to an hereditary ruler. Even though, for the good of society, a man submits to the execution of fundamental laws that in some circumstances may deprive him of his property, his liberty, or even his life, he is still regarded as " free." The makers of the Declaration were stating the principles underlying the condition of men gathered into society ; they had no thought of resolving society into a state of nature, or of anarchy. So, too, the phrase " all men are created equal " in the earlier paragraph is easy to understand as Jefferson and his contemporaries [1] used it. They had in mind the idea of equality as it was expressed by their great masters, that all men are born to the use of the same advantages of nature and to the use of the same faculties, and that ideas come by experience and not by inheritance. Moreover, by men, they meant members of society, — they had no thought of slaves.

The Declaration of Independence, with the amendments that had been made to it in Congress, was then referred

---

[1] Edmund Randolph says that " the declaration in the first article of the Bill of Rights [of the Virginia Constitution], that all men are by nature equally free and independent, was opposed by Robert Carter Nicholas, as being the forerunner, or pretext, of civil convulsion. It was answered, perhaps, with too great an indifference to futurity, and not without inconsistency, that with arms in our hands, asserting the general rights of man, we ought not to be too nice and too much restricted in the delineation of them, but that slaves, not being constituent members of our society, could never pretend to any benefit from such a maxim." M. D. Conway's *Edmund Randolph*, 30.

back to the committee that had drafted it, that the language
of the amendments and that of the body of the document
might be made harmonious.   This was done by the committee during the evening of July 4.   A few copies of the Declaration were printed and sent on July 5 to the governors
of the several States and to the commanding officers of the
Revolutionary armies, authenticated by the signatures of
John Hancock and Charles Thompson, the president and
secretary of Congress.   On the 8th, the Declaration was
read to the people of Philadelphia gathered in State House
Square.[1]   Everywhere the document was well received,
and gave new life to the cause of revolution.

The New York Provincial Congress met early in July,
and authorized its members to give the consent of that
state to the Declaration.   It could now fairly be said to be
the unanimous declaration of the thirteen United States in
Congress Assembled.   On July 19, therefore, it was determined to have the instrument engrossed on parchment and
signed by the members.   On August 2 the document was
ready, and the members, who were then present, affixed their
signatures to it.   A number of those who had voted for
the resolution on July 2 and for the Declaration on July 4
were no longer in Congress, and other members signed
who had not been in Philadelphia in the first part of July.
Later some of the former were permitted to affix their
signatures, and one man who was not in Congress at all in

---

[1] The commemoration of independence on July 4 began early, as we find
under that date, 1778, Ebenezer Wild, at
Brunswick, N.J., noting in his diary : —
" This afternoon at 5 o'clk the army
turned out & fired a fudey joy [feu de
joie] to celebrate the Glorious Independence of Americay."   Massachusetts
Historical Society's *Proceedings*, Second
Series, vi, 111. Thomas Burke, writing
to Governor Caswell from Philadelphia,

July 5, 1777, notes the celebration at
that city on the preceding day, at which
" a Hessian band of music which were
taken at Princeton performed very
delightfully, the pleasure being not a
little heightened by the reflection that
they were hired by the British Court for
purposes very different from those to
which they were applied." *North Carolina Records*, xi, 512.

the summer of 1776 was given leave to place his name on the honored roll.[1]

So many difficulties were found in drawing up the articles of confederation and in securing their adoption by the several States that they did not go into effect until the summer of 1781, — too late for their inadequacy to interfere with the military operations, which practically came to an ending at Yorktown in October of that year. It will be well, therefore, to postpone all consideration of them until the years following the peace are reached, when the baleful effects of a weak central government became apparent and extorted the federal constitution from the necessities of the country.

[1] There is an admirable article on "The Authentication of the Declaration of Independence" by the late Mellen Chamberlain in the *Proceedings* of the Massachusetts Historical Society for November, 1884. Herbert Friedenwald would add Elbridge Gerry to the list of "late signers," *American Historical Review*, viii, 199.

NOTES

I. The Doctrine of Equality. — Sir Henry Sumner Maine, in his *Ancient Law*, says that the Americans, in the Declaration of Independence, combined the French idea that all men are equal with the assumption, more familiar to Englishmen, that men are born free.[1] No phrase in the great Declaration is more frequently misquoted. The words are " all men are created equal." The phrases " all men are born free and equal" and " all men are by nature equally free and independent" occur in the Bills of Rights prefixed to the Massachusetts constitution of 1780 and to the Virginia constitution of 1776. An English writer might easily misplace these phrases, but the further dictum that Jefferson's Gallic predilections led him to join the specially French assumption of equality with the English idea of natural freedom is not so easily accounted for. The idea of equality is found in English theoretical writers from Locke backward to Hooker, while Rousseau's *Social Contract* begins with the words " Man is born free." Moreover, there is no evidence whatever that Jefferson in 1776 was influenced to the slightest degree by the ideas of Rousseau.

II. Revolutionary Tracts. — The publication of the official documents issued by Congress and the rebellious actions of the colonists aroused great interest in England, and led to an outpouring of tracts that is comparable only to the flood of such literature in America. Among these may be noted as of especial interest two commentaries on the Declaration of Independence. The first of these was entitled *Strictures upon the Declaration of the Congress at Philadelphia; in a Letter to a Noble Lord, etc.*, London, 1776. The author's name is not given on the title-page, but Thomas Hutchinson, under date of November 13, 1776, made the following entry in his diary : —

" Called upon Mr Ellis. By his advice I wrote the following, to accompany the letter to a noble Lord, &c.

" ' Governor Hutchinson, being prompted by zeal for your Majesty's service, and a desire to expose, and as far as may be to frustrate,

[1] "We cannot doubt," says Sir Henry Maine, " that it was sympathy with the peculiar ideas of the French jurists which led him [Jefferson] and the other colonial lawyers who guided the course of events in America to join the specially French assumption that ' all men are born equal ' with the assumption, more familiar to Englishmen, that ' all men are born free,' in the very first lines of their Declaration of Independence." *Ancient Law* (London, 1861), p. 95.

the very criminal designs of the leaders of your Majesty's deluded unhappy American subjects, has wrote, and caused to be printed a small Pamphlet, which he begs leave to lay at your Majesty's feet, humbly entreating your Majesty's forgiveness of this presumption'" (*Diary and Letters of Thomas Hutchinson*, ii, 112).

The other, entitled *An Answer to the Declaration of the American Congress* (London, 1776), was the work of John Lind, a hack-writer employed by the government. Previously, the Declaration of Congress of 1775 "setting forth the Causes and Necessity of their taking up Arms" had evoked a notable rejoinder in the shape of a pamphlet entitled *The Rights of Great Britain Asserted against the Claims of America* (London, 1776). This pamphlet went through ten or a dozen editions before the end of that year. It has been attributed to no less than three notable personages, Sir John Dalrymple, James Macpherson, and Lord George Germain, and it is said to have been published by order of the British government.

The speeches of Edmund Burke on American taxation,[1] on conciliation with America,[2] and his letter to the sheriffs of Bristol[3] called forth many replies. Among these, as of especial interest, is the *Letter to Edmund Burke, Esq; in answer to his Printed Speech by Josiah Tucker, D.D., Dean of Glocester* (London, 1775). This was only one of several tracts by this reverend gentleman[4] in which he argued that separation would be better for both parties. Other pamphlets called forth by this controversy are *Thoughts on the Letter of Edmund Burke Esq.*, by Willoughby Bertie, Earl of Abingdon (London, 1777); and another, an anonymous one, purporting to be *An Answer from the Electors of Bristol to the Letter of Edmund Burke, Esq.* (London, 1777).

Other writings to attract great attention were those of Richard Price and John Wesley. The former are interesting combinations of theory and statistics. They seem rather turgid nowadays, but

---

[1] See above, p. 183.

[2] *Speech of Edmund Burke, Esq. on moving his resolutions for Conciliation with the Colonies, March 22, 1775* (London, 1775).

[3] *Letter from Edmund Burke, Esq; . . . to John Farr and John Harris, Esqrs. Sheriffs of that City [Bristol] on the Affairs of America* (3d ed., London, 1777).

[4] Some of the others are *Four Tracts, on Political and Commercial Subjects* (3rd ed. Glocester, 1776); *Tract V. The Respective Pleas and Arguments of the Mother Country, and of the Colonies* (Glocester, 1776); *A Series of Answers to Certain Popular Objections, against separating from the Rebellious Colonies* (Glocester, 1776); and *The True Interest of Britain, set forth in regard to the Colonies* (Philadelphia, 1776).

his *Observations*[1] ran through five editions in one month in London, in 1776. To the successive editions, Price added appendixes, additions, supplementary observations, etc.; finally gathering the whole into *Two Tracts on Civil Liberty*[2] which was published at London in 1778. Wesley's *Calm Address* was calm only by comparison, and had a good deal of the vigor which signalized its author's pulpit utterances. Among the rejoinders was Augustus Montague Toplady's *Old Fox Tarr'd and Feather'd. Occasioned by what is called Mr. John Wesley's Calm Address to our American Colonys, By an Hanoverian* (2d ed., London, 1775). The author of

> Rock of ages, cleft for me,
> Let me hide myself in Thee

had no mercy on Dr. Wesley, whom he denominated "a low and puny tadpole in Divinity," and accused of cribbing and carving from Dr. Johnson. Other reverend gentlemen joined in, and theology, politics, and personalities became inextricably mixed.

---

[1] *Observations on the Nature of Civil Liberty, the Principles of Government, and the Justice and Policy of the War with America. To which is added An Appendix, Containing a State of the National Debt, an Estimate of the Money drawn from the Public by the Taxes, and an Account of the National Income* and *Expenditure since the last War* (London, 1776).

[2] *Two Tracts on Civil Liberty, the War with America, and The Debts and Finances of the Kingdom: with a General Introduction and Supplement* (London, 1778).

CHAPTER VIII

THE REVOLUTIONARY WAR IN THE YEAR 1776

In the first days of 1776 the British held Boston town and harbor. Twelve months later New York and Newport were in their grasp, but Boston had been long abandoned. Another year saw Philadelphia added to their possessions; but by January, 1779, that city had been given up, and Savannah in Georgia had been wrenched from colonial control. And so the conflict proceeded. The Americans could not prevent the capture of any seaboard town; they could prevent the enemy making any prolonged excursions inland north of Virginia, or occupying effectively any large extent of territory, anywhere, at any time. Even in the South, in Carolina, Virginia, and Georgia, the soldiers of Britain had no real hold on the country outside of their military lines. On the other hand, the Americans were never able unaided to eject the British from any position which was regarded as important. The two armies were stalemated until time gave the weight of numbers and wealth to the opposers of Britain and her world-wide imperial aspirations.

At the outset, those who were responsible for the management of British military matters foretold failure in the prosecution of the design to conquer America by a land war. General Harvey, the Adjutant-General, wrote that it was " as wild an idea as ever controverted common sense." [1]

[1] To General Irwin, June 30, 1775, quoted in Fortescue's *British Army*, iii, 167. See also W. B. Donne's *Correspond-* *ence of George III with Lord North*, ii, 7.

Lord Barrington, Secretary at War, who had served in the same capacity in the glorious years of Pitt's great administration, declared in August, 1775, that the Americans never could be reduced to obedience by the army. His plan was to bring them back to their duty by interrupting their commerce and fishery, by seizing their ships in their ports, all of which could be accomplished with little expense and less bloodshed. To conquer America by land meant not only armies beyond Britain's strength, but, if successful, soldiers and fortresses, "the expense of which would be ruinous and endless."[1] Undoubtedly, if reconciliation was the object of coercion, a blockade was preferable. It would arouse far less animosity than the shedding of blood with accompanying outrages to person and property. It was not so to be. A British army was in America. Until that army could be extricated with honor the land war must go on, or the demands of the rebellious colonists be fully granted.

A land war being thus forced upon the British government, whether or no, it became necessary to secure men to carry it on. Ordinarily, there were some fifteen thousand troops in Great Britain, and as many more in Ireland.[2] In

[1] Barrington to Dartmouth, November 12, 1774; December 24, 1774; to Lord North, August 8, 1775. *Political Life of William Wildman Viscount Barrington* by his brother Shute, Bishop of Durham, pp. 140–152. These thoughts were set forth by an anonymous Scottish pamphleteer: "When an effectual stop is put to their export-trade, the boasted power and strength of the rebellious Colonies must soon be annihilated." *Considerations on the late Act for Prohibiting all Commercial Intercourse with the Rebellious Colonies: or The weakness of America Exposed* (Edinburgh, 1776), p. 6. A copy of this rare tract is in the John Carter Brown Library.

[2] J. W. Fortescue's *British Army*, vol. iii, using index. There is an interesting account of the "Forces of the Crown" in Henry Belcher's *First American Civil War* (i, chs. vii, viii) — but much the same matter is given by Fortescue in ch. xxvi of his third volume. In the library of the Wisconsin Historical Society at Madison there are several manuscript volumes of "Returns of his Majesty's Forces." From these, it appears that in July, 1767, there were, on paper, 11,001 soldiers in North America and the West Indies, but the actual figures were 8737, of which 6595 were in North America. From this, it will be seen that all the figures of the establishment should be considerably reduced.

October, 1775, Barrington informed Lord North[1] that the whole effective rank and file in England and Scotland numbered only 4,480, beside the 42nd Regiment that was recruiting in Scotland.[2] There were some thousands of troops in Ireland and other thousands in the garrisons at Gibraltar and Minorca. The bulk of the British army was in America, either on the continent or doing garrison duty in the West Indies. The nine thousand men[3] who were cooped up at Boston formed the only available field force, and this Washington and the lack of transports held immovable in the capital city of New England. About a year before, Gage had declared that "if these misunderstandings proceed to the last extremities" an army of twenty thousand strong at the beginning will save Great Britain both blood and treasure, and foreign troops must be hired to make up the necessary numbers.[4] This was true because the conditions of the service, the harsh discipline and the poor pay had no attractions for the classes from whom the ranks might have been filled. It was cheaper, indeed, for Great Britain to hire foreign troops than it was to make the service attractive to the people of the home land. At once efforts were made to recruit the regular regiments to their war strength, and negotiations were opened with the princes of Europe for the employment of twenty thousand veterans. Four thousand Hanoverians were dispatched to the Mediterranean, setting free that number of British

---

[1] Royal Historical Manuscripts Commission's *Reports*, x, Appendix, Pt. vi, p. 12. This volume contains a calendar of the manuscripts of the Marquess of Abergavenny. Many of them are printed in full. The volume will be cited hereafter as *Abergavenny Manuscripts*. In 1777 Great Britain was so denuded of troops that Germain declared there was not a single artilleryman on the island. *Stopford-Sackville Papers*, ii, 66.

[2] According to Belcher (*First American Civil War*, i, 259) there were 921 Scots and 3 Englishmen in this regiment. He gives the total strength of the British forces in the summer of 1775 at 49,575; of these 14,122 were in America, including Canada and the West Indies.

[3] Fortescue's *British Army*, iii, 177, citing Howe to Germain, May 7, 1776.

[4] "Sparks' Manuscripts." No. 43, vol. iii, pp. 182, 188.

troops. The English garrison in Ireland was also reduced,
much to the relief of the Irishmen, and added a few
thousand more for service in America. Recruiting sergeants
also visited that island and did everything possible to fill
the ranks of the regular regiments with Irishmen, both
Protestant and Catholic. Scotland furnished other recruits,
and many were bought in Germany. For years, indeed,
the depleted ranks of the " British " army had been filled
by the Hamburg contractors at the rate of seven guineas
for each recruit furnished.[1] The jails, too, were scoured
for material, and the magistrates were directed to enforce
vigorously the vagrancy acts, enlistment being an alternative
for imprisonment.[2] As a fighting machine, whatever its
composition, the British army was superbly disciplined, as
its losses in many a hard contest testify. At Bunker Hill
the killed, wounded, and missing were about two fifths of
the numbers engaged ; at Guilford Court House fully one
quarter.

At first, efforts were made to induce Catherine, Czar-
ina of Russia, to loan twenty thousand Cossacks and
other Russian soldiers.[3] For a moment she looked
favorably upon the proposal, but then suddenly changed
her mind, either because the compensation offered was
not sufficiently attractive, or because she did not

[1] Barrington to Howe, October 31, 1776, *Head Quarters Papers*, i, 67 ; Barrington to Howe, May 28, 1776. The battalions of the Royal American Regiment had been kept to their strength in this way for some time.

[2] J. W. Fortescue's *British Army*, iii, 173 ; Henry Belcher's *First American Civil War*, i, 251.

[3] On this somewhat curious episode, see Edward Gibbon's *Life and Writings*, ii, 146 ; Cunningham's *Letters of Horace Walpole*, vi, 252, 266, 275, 277 ; *Parliamentary History*, xviii, 798, 811, 848, 850 ; Adolphus's *History of England*, ii,

268 ; *Recueil des Instructions données aux Ambassadeurs et Ministres de France*, ix, 329. (Vergennes to Marquis de Juigné, Versailles, September 21, 1775.) September 5, 1775, Dartmouth, who was then at the colonial office, wrote to Howe that " the hope of having a large army in America in the spring rests on the ground of an assurance from the Empress of Russia that she would give any number of infantry that might be wanted, and that a requisition has thereupon been made for twenty thousand men." *Head Quarters Papers*, i, 7.

like the word "mercenaries," which the British ambassador had used somewhat incautiously.   Attention was
then centered upon the Germans, and they proved more
complaisant.

For many years, the Prince of Hesse-Cassel, the Mar-
grave of Anspach and Bayreuth, the Duke of Brunswick-
Luneburg, the Prince of Anhalt-Zerbst, and others of
their kind had sold the bodies of their subjects for military purposes to the highest bidder.   They were now
glad to further the desires of the English monarch at their
own price.   George, with his economical instincts, was
inclined to haggle a bit, for the Germans recognized his
necessities.   He consoled himself with the thought that
there would be no half pay to provide for officers until
the grave closed upon them ; nor would there be one-
armed and one-legged veterans to draw pensions for the
rest of their natural lives.   The contract with the Duke
of Brunswick provided that the British king should pay
seven pounds, four shillings, four pence ha-penny "levy
money" for each one of the forty-three hundred Brunswickers.   The duke also was to receive an annual subsidy
of eleven thousand five hundred and seventeen pounds,
seventeen shillings, and three ha-pence until the soldiers
returned, and double that sum for two years after their
coming back.   For each man killed he was to be paid
an amount equal to the levy money, and one third
as much for each one wounded.   The soldiers were
to have the same pay and food as the British troops ;
but the money was to be paid to them directly and
not through the duke's officials.   The other contracts
were similar ; but the Landgrave of Hesse-Cassel seized
this favorable opportunity to compel his cousin of
England to pay a disputed debt of over forty-one thou-

sand pounds that had been owing since the close of
the Seven Years' War.[1]

Thirty thousand German soldiers came out to America
under these agreements with the German princes; how
many more came in the guise of recruits for British
regiments is not known, but there are many references
to them. The Hessians, the Brunswickers, and the rest
were well drilled troops. They obeyed their officers;
but both Howe and Burgoyne declared that they did
not fight any harder than they had to, and why should
they? Undoubtedly they were the cheapest soldiers
that could be procured; but their employment was a
sad mistake, if conciliation with the erring colonists was
to be accomplished. In the early campaigns the Hessians
looked upon themselves as being in an enemy's country,
and treated the inhabitants most cruelly. It had been
the practice for generations to use them in European
wars, but their intervention in a civil contest between
two sections of the British empire was felt to be a very
different matter. This employment of the Hessians led to
similar suggestions in America. Charles Carroll thought,
all else failing, that six thousand Germans, or Swiss, or
the Irish Brigade might be engaged for service on the
American side; but the members of Congress to whom he
mentioned the idea did not seem to relish the introduction
of foreign " mercenaries." [2]

Besides the English, Scottish, Irish, and German com-
ponents of the British forces in America, there were also
regiments of American loyalists, and from time to time
bands of Indians were employed. The largest number of

[1] Edward J. Lowell's *Hessians in the
Revolutionary War*, is an excellent
work with a complete bibliography. See
also *Pennsylvania Magazine of History*,
xxiii, 157.

[2] K. M. Rowland's *Charles Carroll of
Carrollton*, i, 209; the letter is dated
"Doohoragen, Anne Arundel Co., August
12th, 1777."

loyalists at any one time seems to have been in December, 1780, when the provincial forces were stated at just under nine thousand men.[1] The total number of provincials in the British army has been rated at from thirty thousand to fifty thousand.[2] As these regiments formed a fairly permanent force, it is possible that even the smaller of these estimates is too large. The characters of the individual loyalists, their devotedness to the cause, and the length of service of many of them made the provincial regiments a most notable addition to the armies of Howe, Clinton, and Cornwallis. Among them were three of the most famous and efficient regiments in the British service : Ferguson's American Riflemen, Simcoe's Queen's Rangers, and Tarleton's Legion.

The British also essayed to enlist the Indians as partisans, either attached to the regular armies or for harrying the frontier settlements. As auxiliaries they proved to be of slight utility. As long as everything went well, they were faithful, but when their masters fared ill, they disappeared into the forests. On separate expeditions against lonely frontier farms, either by themselves or accompanying a few hardy pioneers, they were more successful, and caused much suffering in many an outlying hamlet. The Americans had been first to employ the red men in this conflict, for some Stockbridge Indians were in the army blockading Boston, and shot down a few British sentries. These particular Indians were civilized and Christianized, and formed a part of the Massachusetts militia. Elsewhere the

[1] The exact figures are 8954, *Writings of Washington* (Sparks ed.), v, 544. Germain stated in the same year that 8091 was the whole number of "provincial effectives in the British service"; *Parliamentary Register*, xviii, 155.

[2] Professor Van Tyne, in his admirable *Loyalists in the American Revolution* (p. 183), thinks "we may safely state that 50,000 soldiers, either regular or militia, were drawn into the service of Great Britain from her American sympathizers."

Americans would have been glad to secure the services of the savages; but in this they were not very successful, so that many more Indians were employed by the British than by the revolutionists. The comparative size of these contingents and the priority of their employment is of slight importance in arguing the question of humanity; it was bad enough to use the Indians against trained troops of the enemy; but employing them to despoil and massacre non-combatant pioneer families was atrocious.[1]

The advantages of distance, dislocation of the fields of war, and climate were all on the side of the Americans; their greatest disadvantage was the small proportion of the people of the continent who desired separation from England and were willing to fight for it. Probably less than half of the people favored independence. Not that the larger half were militant loyalists, or even loyalists. Merely that very many Americans thought with Robert Beverley of Virginia that "altho' our political rulers may have gotten together by the ears" there is no reason for "private peoples" joining in the fray.[2] His particular business was to grow tobacco, and not at all to fight on either side. The number of loyalists who were willing to enlist in the British service at the risk of their lives was considerable, but nothing like one half of the male population of military age.

In the first flush of resentment at the attempt to disarm

---

[1] Andrew McF. Davis has treated this subject with his usual thoroughness and skill in Winsor's *America*, vi, ch. viii. The bibliography is especially good. Among the episodes treated by him is the Wyoming Massacre. The books and articles relating to this massacre are cited on pp. 662–665. Other matter is noted by him in Massachusetts Historical Society's *Proceedings*, Second Series, iii, 340; and he has also treated the general theme in an article in the *English Historical Review*, ii, 709.

[2] Robert Beverley's "Letter Book" in the Library of Congress. The fortunes of a Pennsylvania conservative may be followed in the pages of James Allen's "Diary" in *Pennsylvania Magazine of History*, ix, 176, 278, 424. He opposed the despotic acts of the British government, but could not bring himself to declare for separation.

the New Englanders and the first burst of enthusiasm after
Bunker Hill, it might have been possible to raise a volunteer army of thirty thousand men, or even fifty thousand,
for the war. After 1776 this was impossible. As the
years went on, the difficulty of getting men became greater
and greater, except that everywhere the militia were always ready to turn out for a few weeks, unless their services were required far from their homes. The coming of
the French armies, instead of stimulating the Americans
to the pursuit of military glory, had quite the opposite
effect. In the spring of 1781, when it was necessary to
make every possible effort, there was a greater disinclination than ever to enlist. By this time bounties had
risen to enormous sums. In Massachusetts they began
at ten dollars, and had run up to one thousand, — in
continental currency. Even then drafting became necessary, and many schemes were devised to avoid it. Some
Massachusetts towns appointed committees to hire men for
the town's quota, getting them wherever they could, — at
the lowest rate.[1] In Connecticut, any two men who would
keep one man on the rolls were themselves excused, this
led to the employment of many negroes. In Pennsylvania,
the inhabitants were divided into as many classes as there
were recruits to be provided, each class to furnish one or
pay fifteen pounds in specie. In Pennsylvania deserters
from the United States army might be accepted,[2] but not
those from the navy or from the British army. In Virginia [3] the highest bounties were offered, eight thousand or

[1] See, for example, the *Records of the
Town of Weston*, index under " committee."

[2] *Pennsylvania Statutes at Large*
(ed. 1896), x, 260.

[3] Hening's *Statutes of Virginia*, x,
331. A similar arrangement was made
in North Carolina, *State Records*, xxiv,
338. See also *ibid.*, vol. xi, 490, 491, 494,
520, 522. For South Carolina see Salley's
*Documents relating to the History of
South Carolina during the Revolutionary
War*, p. 67. By an act of 1780 each soldier of that State in the Continental Line
was to receive one sound negro for each
year of service.

twelve thousand paper dollars down, and, at the close of the war, three hundred acres of land and "a healthy sound negro, between the ages of ten and thirty years, or sixty pounds in gold or silver at the option of the soldier." If these inducements did not fill the quota, the necessary numbers were to be drafted for eighteen months. The difficulty in raising men was not due altogether to lukewarmness in the cause or disinclination for a military life. It was owing partly to the great demand for labor which the growing industries of the country stimulated. There was doubtless some diminution in the number of seamen required in commercial enterprises, especially in the fishery. The possible gain from privateering and the constant demand for men on the public armed ships more than made good this lack of employment. In fact, labor was so scarce in some places that it was difficult to cultivate the soil and harvest the crops.

The composition of the American army after 1776, at least, was very nearly, if not quite, as varied as that of the British. It reflected the heterogeneity of the American population. As there were Englishmen, Scots, Irishmen, Germans, Dutchmen, Frenchmen, and Jews among the colonists, so there were representatives of all these nationalities in the American regiments. Soldiers of the Pennsylvania line, at the time of the mutiny in 1781, were mainly descendants of the Scotch-Irish and German immigrants to that province in the first half of the century.[1] A study of muster rolls shows a large proportion of foreign names in the regiments of almost every state. This, however, does

---

[1] This is the statement of the editors of the *Pennsylvania Archives*, printed by Stillé in his *Major-General Anthony Wayne* (p. 248 note). He also makes the further statement from Egle that there were not over "300 persons of Irish birth (Roman Catholic and Celtic)" in the Pennsylvania regiments during the war.

not imply that the bearers of these names were new-
comers.   They might well have been the children or grand-
children of earlier immigrants.   The word " Irish " was
doubtless used at that time to include both Scotch-Irish
Presbyterians and the Celtic Roman Catholic natives of
Ireland and their descendants.   There certainly were many,
very many, foreign immigrants in the American regiments.
Five of Morgan's Virginia Riflemen deserted into Boston in
one month ; of these four are described as Irish.[1]   In 1779
Paul Revere's State Artillery lacked seventy-five deserters ;
among them were twenty-seven foreigners.   Turning over
the files of the " Maryland Journal " for 1777, one comes
across repeated advertisements for deserters.   From Captain Lynch's company there were six of them, three Irish,
one English, and two natives ; from Thomas Yates's company two Irishmen.   At another time four deserters from
Whetstone Fort are advertised for, three of them were
described as Frenchmen, the other was an Englishman.
Even on the march to Yorktown, men fell out by the way.
From Colonel John Lamb's regiment of artillery eleven
men were missing ; one of these was a Scot, three were
Irishmen, and seven were native born.   These are only examples taken at random, which might be continued almost
indefinitely.   It would not do to argue from these proportions that the army was composed in any such ratio of
natives and immigrants, but they certainly show that there
were many foreigners in the army.   Fortescue, the English
historian of the British army, states that so many Irish
deserted from the Americans to the British that a regiment was recruited from them.[2]   The number of Irish

[1] " Kemble's Journals " pp. 55–60, in
New York Historical Society's Collections for 1883.
[2] Fortescue's History of the British
Army, iii, 270, citing Clinton to Germain
under date of October 23, 1778. Probably this was the Provincial Corps of
Roman Catholic Volunteers mentioned
in " Kemble's Journals."

serving in the British army was also very large. They, too, were constantly deserting to the American side, in such numbers, indeed, that the proposition was made to embody them as a separate colonial regiment. There is frequent mention in orderly books of deserters from the British. They came from all parts of the army, even from the loyalist regiments, as N. Kearney from the Queen's Rangers, and J. Connely and J. McCue from the New Jersey volunteers. Judging from the number caught by the British and sentenced by court martial to receive five hundred or a thousand lashes or to suffer death, there must have been a great many of them.

As to the actual size of the armies, one can say nothing accurately. The number of enlistments on the rolls of the American army was very large in proportion to the radical population. Taking the highest estimate of three million as the total population of the continental colonies in 1775, and regarding forty per cent as militant revolutionists, this would be twelve hundred thousand, of whom one fifth would be men of military age, or two hundred and fifty thousand at the outside. Yet we read in the returns of 89,651 in 1776.[1] This figure included the opponents of Clinton in South Carolina, those who turned back the Highlanders at Moore's Creek Bridge, the regiments in the "flying camp" in New Jersey, the soldiers with Washington at Boston, and those with him in New York, New Jersey, and Pennsylvania, the members of the Canada expedition and those who went to their relief, together with

[1] These figures are from Henry Knox's " Letter to the House of Representatives, May 11, 1790 " in *American State Papers, Folio, Military Affairs*, i, 14. In his letter of transmittal, General Knox, then Secretary of War, refers to the inaccuracies of the records, except as to the " regular troops." In many books a table is given which purports to show the numbers furnished by the several states. This table was constructed from Knox's report, but is so misleading and inaccurate as to be entirely worthless. See an article by Justin Winsor in the *Proceedings* of the Massachusetts Historical Society for January, 1886.

isolated commands at various points along the seaboard.
As against this large total should be placed the fact that
Washington, including the sick and ineffectives, never had
more than sixteen thousand in the summer of 1776, and
that at the end of the year, just before Trenton, five thousand was all that he could place in the field. On the other
hand, Great Britain was paying for from 60,000 to 200,000
soldiers.[1] In 1781 Clinton had nominally under him
34,000 men. These were enlisted for long terms, so that
there was no seasonal variation in numbers in the British
army as there was in the American; but there was an
equal dissipation of force. Howe's command included the
garrisons of Pensacola in West Florida, St. Augustine in
East Florida, and Clinton had under his orders troops in
the West Indies. Every town or bit of land that was occupied had at once to be fortified, and this meant a garrison.
Howe was able to take thirty-six battalions, or about
seventeen thousand men, with him to Pennsylvania in his
campaign against Philadelphia; but Clinton never had so
many available for service in the field. On his return to
New York from the South in 1780 he was obliged to leave
troops for the garrisons at Charleston and Savannah and
for Cornwallis to complete the conquest of the Carolinas
and Georgia. How inadequate this force was may be

[1] *Commons Journals*, xxxviii, 34.
The total number on the establishment
in 1781 was a little over 100,000, but this
did not include the militia, the "foreign
troops," the provincials, or those on the
"Irish establishment." No less than
35,000 were needed for garrisons in
Europe, Ireland, and possessions outside
of America. These figures represent
"effective troops," the "present and fit
for duty" appear to have averaged about
three-fourths of the "effective" force.
In 1781 the Treasury was supplying
52,000 rations for America. Robinson
thought that this was out of all proportion to the troops stationed there, and
complained to Clinton that "the expence
to the public in sending out all these
supplies from Great Britain is very
heavy." (*Head Quarters Papers*, ii, 256).
The loyalist refugees at New York and
Charleston were responsible for the increased consumption,—but they could
not be allowed to starve. In fact, every
loyalist driven into a British garrison
brought the end of the war just a little
nearer, as Washington realized.

gathered from the fact that Cornwallis had only 2239 men at Camden, including 500 militia, hardly 1500 British troops at Guilford,[1] that he marched with only 1723 men from Wilmington to Virginia, and after uniting all the various expeditions that were within reach, he surrendered 7000 fighting men at Yorktown. On the American side the actual forces engaged in the decisive conflicts of the war were very small, and might even be described as diminutive in comparison with the results achieved. The American army that marched from the Hudson to Yorktown numbered only some 2000 men, and never exceeded 6000 regulars at any time during the siege.[2] Morgan won the battle of the Cowpens with only 800 men, while Greene fought at Guilford Court House with 4300 men, more than half of whom were militia, who were with the army for only a few weeks.

It is one of the easiest things in the world to judge a nation's actions, or the doings of individuals, by the standards of other times and the successes of other men. One of the commonest animadversions of students of American history is to set forth in darkest colors the inertness of the revolutionists, the inefficiency of congresses and the members thereof, and to conjecture as to what a Napoleon or a Frederick would have done in the place of Washington, Howe, or Clinton.[3] These are matters beyond the historian's ken. He must take nations, congresses, and generals as he finds them. It is possible, of course, that Congress in 1776

---

[1] Immediately before this battle the strength of Cornwallis's army is given as follows in a contemporary return: in the field with his lordship, 2700; at Camden, 1400; at Charleston, 1200; at Ninety-six, 350; at Georgetown, 200; on the Peedee, 150, making a total of 6000.

[2] H. P. Johnston's *Yorktown Campaign*, 55, 112, 195.

[3] As to the British generals, Lord North is said to have remarked that he did not know " whether they will frighten the enemy; but I am sure they frighten me whenever I think of them." *Life of Barrington*, 185.

might have enlisted an adequate army of regular soldiers
for the war and by taxing the people have suppiied them
bountifully with arms, ammunition, clothing, food, and all
the paraphernalia of war, including horses; but the Continental Congress did not raise such an army, nor did
it levy such taxes. The world has seldom seen abler
political leaders than those who gathered at Philadelphia
in 1775 and 1776. They were not great administrators,
but they were politicians of the first order. They did
not believe themselves possessed of the authority to raise
armies on such a scale or to tax the people, nor did they
think it wise in the critical conditions of that time to
do either of these things. It is idle to speculate as to
whether they were right or were wrong, but one hardly
likes to think of what might have happened had unwise
and premature measures added ten per cent to the loyalist
side.

The military annals of the Revolution are devoid of the
spectacular; they are lacking in useful lessons on the progress of the art of war. No remarkable soldier emerges
from the conflict, for Washington was a moral force rather
than a general; and of second-rate characters Nathanael
Greene, alone, shines conspicuous. On the British side,
Howe, Clinton, Burgoyne, and the rest were mediocre men.
No great siege stimulates one's emotions almost to the
breaking point. The brilliant feat of arms at Trenton,
the hurrying flight of Greene across North Carolina, and
the sudden stroke at Stony Point stand almost alone in
exciting the imagination. The task of the British was to
conquer territory; that of the Americans to prevent their
accomplishing this object. In war the enemy's army is
the main objective. So it was in this conflict; but the
American army was not the force that actually stood in

arms from year to year; it was the potential power of the
farmers and planters of the continent. They formed an
army, not actually in being, but capable of rapid mobiliza-
tion for brief periods. It was the certainty of opposition
by masses of poorly trained but determined men that kept
the British confined to small districts on the seaboard and
prevented their possessing territory which was essential
to the reconquest of the continent.

While Howe with his soldiers lay uneasily at Boston,
awaiting the first chance to get away, two expeditions
were set on foot, both of which led to most important
consequences. One, by the Americans to the northward,
had for its object the conquest of Canada, and the addition
of a fourteenth state to the potentially budding American
Union. The other, by the British to the southward, was
designed to wrench the country beyond Virginia from
radical control, and thus to limit the number of rebellious
colonies to ten. Both expeditions were based on the supposed friendliness of the dwellers in the regions to be in-
vaded. Both were unsuccessful owing to the lukewarmness or the hostility of those upon whom reliance had
been placed. Had the South been conquered in the first
half of 1776, it is entirely conceivable that rebellion would
never have turned into revolution. The northern expedition ended in failure and even in disaster. Nevertheless,
it served well the American cause by drawing away from
Howe the troops which otherwise would have formed
his first reënforcements. The dispatch of this expedition
from England to the St. Lawrence delayed his departure
from Halifax for the Hudson until June. The diversion
of field equipment from New York to Quebec postponed
the opening of the Long Island campaign until August,
when other material arrived from England. The turning

Q

aside of British effort from the most important objective
to a secondary operation at this particular period was of
the utmost importance to the American cause. It was
indeed the hand of Providence that pointed the road to
Quebec to Richard Montgomery and Benedict Arnold.[1]

The troops for the southern attempt came with Cornwallis from Ireland directly to the Cape Fear River.[2] Sir
Henry Clinton, the commander of the expedition, with
a few men only, was detached from the army that was
blockaded in Boston. This project worried Barrington. He protested vigorously against it to Dartmouth,
who was still colonial secretary. He dilated on the
dangers attending upon a march "up the country," and
besought him to consult fully with able military men.[3]
His protestations were not listened to. Clinton touched
at New York and Virginia on his way to Wilmington,
North Carolina, where Cornwallis joined him. Loyal
Scots from the interior were to meet them there; but
these had been dispersed weeks before at Moore's Creek
Bridge. It being useless and dangerous to operate in
the Cape Fear River district without them, Clinton
again turned southward for Charleston. This city stands
open to the sea; but it is defended by sandy shoals
through which are channels that come together near the
western end of Sullivan's Island. At that point the
Southerners built a redoubt open at the rear. Its walls
were sixteen feet thick, of sand held in place by palmetto
logs, and it was amply armed with cannon, — many of
large caliber. It was named Fort Moultrie for the South
Carolina leader. Clinton landed his troops on the next

---

[1] This expedition is described briefly
in the next chapter.

[2] *Correspondence of Charles, First
Marquis Cornwallis*, i, 21.

[3] *Political Life of Viscount Barrington*, 151.

island to the northward. On June 28, 1776, while the
British ships bombarded the fort in front, he tried to

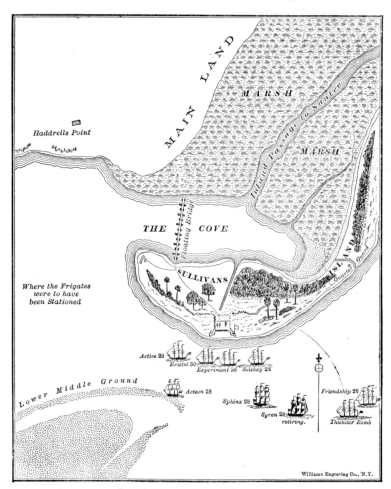

THE ATTACK ON FORT MOULTRIE
(From John Drayton's *Memoirs*, ii, 290)

cross the narrow bit of water between the two islands
to attack the Americans in flank and rear, and thus to
effect the capture of the fort and its defenders. The

event was otherwise, for the ships were more injured than was the fort, and the soldiers were unable to gain Sullivan's Island at all.[1] The vessels, save one, sailed out of the harbor as well as they could. Clinton re-embarked his men and the fleet proceeded northward for New York, which was to be the principal point of attack in 1776. At Moore's Creek and Sullivan's Island the Carolinians turned aside the one combination of circumstances that might have made British conquest possible.

As early as August, 1775, Howe had written to his brother that "the theatre of the now inevitable war [must be changed] to the province of New York."[2] The lack of shipping had put off the abandonment of Boston

---

[1] McCrady's *South Carolina in the Revolution, 1775–1780* (pp. 135, 170), gives by far the best account of this gallant defense. The clearest map is that given by Joseph Johnson in his *Traditions and Reminiscences of the Revolution*, 96; this is reproduced in McCrady (p. 140). A British plan by Faden is given in *Charleston Year Book*, 1883, p. 414. Further references will be found in McCrady's footnotes, and in Winsor's *America*, vi, 168, and notes. Three letters from Charles Lee describing the defense are in the *Records of North Carolina*, x, 618–618*d*. Charles Lee had been detached by Washington from the army before Boston to direct the fortification of New York; Congress had ordered him southward to organize opposition to Clinton. To his military eye the crude structure on Sullivan's Island seemed destined to be a slaughter pen; it required the united efforts of Governor Rutledge of South Carolina and of General Moultrie to prevent the withdrawal of the soldiers from that place. There are two interesting letters from Jacob Morris at Charleston to his father, General Lewis Morris, dated June 10 and 29, 1776, in New York Historical Society's *Collections*, 1875, pp. 435, 438.

[2] *Stopford-Sackville Manuscripts*, ii, 9. Gage had earlier expressed the same opinion, and so had Barrington. As early as November, 1774, the latter had suggested the removal of the seven regiments then at Boston and the establishment of a naval blockade. In December he reiterated his suggestion, and advised their removal to Canada, Nova Scotia, and East Florida. On August 2, 1775, Dartmouth had written to Gage, suggesting the occupation of New York in addition to Boston, or even moving his whole force to Halifax and Quebec, leaving to the future the settlement of the plan of operations for 1776. Belcher's *First American Civil War*, i, 199. Belcher states that this letter reached Boston about September 13, 1775, at the same time as the commission to Howe appointing him commander-in-chief in Gage's absence. In August and again in October, 1775, Sir Henry Clinton wrote from Boston to Lord Dartmouth, suggesting an immediate removal from Boston to New York and "Rhodes Island" (*Ibid.*, 204). See also Dartmouth to Howe, September 5, 1775, in *Head Quarters Papers*, i, 7.

until March, 1776, when Washington compelled a rapid
evacuation. Howe embarked his soldiers and the Massachusetts loyalists on the vessels in the harbor. The mot-
ley fleet being unsuited to the voyage to New York, he
steered for Halifax. There he was detained awaiting re-
enforcements and equipment until June. It was July
before his troops disembarked on Staten Island. There
they waited for more reënforcements and more equipment
and August had come in before they landed on Long Island
and marched toward Brooklyn Heights. Had Howe gone
to New York in September or October, 1775, or even in
April, 1776, it is conceivable that he might then have
occupied enough territory to have furnished food and forage for man and beast and thus have completely changed
the character of the conflict.

Realizing that the weight of the British attack would
fall on New York, Washington had detached Charles Lee
to undertake its defense, and, upon the British evacuation of Boston, had himself repaired thither with the
bulk of his army. The city of New York then stood
on the southern end of Manhattan Island. It was exceedingly difficult to defend, owing to its being commanded by the heights of Brooklyn on the western end
of Long Island and being accessible on either side to
the guns of ships of war. Military considerations, alone,
would have dictated its abandonment, but other reasons
demanded that the Americans should attempt to retain
it.[1] Washington, therefore, fortified Brooklyn Heights,
and stationed a large portion of his small force on the

[1] John Jay and Nathanael Greene,
after the retreat from Long Island, suggested the abandonment and destruction
of New York City. Jay even suggested
desolating the country as far north as
the Highlands. (William Jay's *Life of*
John Jay, ii, 7, and G. W. Greene's
Greene, i, 212.) The reasons that
prompted Washington to hold Manhattan
Island and with it Long Island are unknown.

hills in front of that position.[1] The American army
was decimated by sickness; among those in the hospital
at the moment was Nathanael Greene, to whom the
command of this important post had been given. It fell,
therefore, to Israel Putnam and John Sullivan, neither of
whom seems to have been fully aware of the precise part
he was expected to play. Most skillfully Howe attacked
(August 27, 1776) the outlying body of Americans, marched
a formidable portion of his soldiers by night far to the
right of the American position, captured a mounted patrol
that had been sent to watch the road, thrust his detachment between the two American forces, and captured nearly
the whole of Sullivan's command with its leader. He
stopped his soldiers in front of the heights. By a miracle
of good fortune, Washington rescued the garrison and transported it across the East River to Manhattan Island.

Then came delay after delay on the part of the British
commander; but time did not strengthen Washington's
hands. The British and Hessian army under Howe was the
finest force that had yet appeared on one side in America,
and in the open field could not be opposed by any troops that
Washington could summon. It followed, therefore, that
notwithstanding some brilliant strokes, as at Harlem
Plains[2] and Chatterton Hill[3] the Americans were finally

---

[1] On the battle of Long Island, see
Henry P. Johnston's "Campaign of 1776
around New York and Brooklyn" (Long
Island Historical Society's *Memoirs*,
iii). This is a most valuable study, and
is abundantly supplied with maps and
documents. C. F. Adams's "Battle of
Long Island" in *American Historical
Review* (i, 650) is an excellent critical
study.

[2] Henry P. Johnston's *Battle of Harlem Heights* (New York, 1897). In 1782
the British engineers drew a map of
Manhattan Island, based on surveys that

had been made during their occupation
of the island. It is ten feet long, has
been reproduced in facsimile, and is exceedingly useful for the study of these
operations. Excellent maps illustrating
the operations around New York are in
H. P. Johnston's "Campaign of 1776."

[3] This hill formed the right of the
American position at White Plains. On
this campaign, see Henry B. Dawson's
Westchester in the Revolution, 240 and
fol.; Charles W. Baird's *History of Rye*,
234.

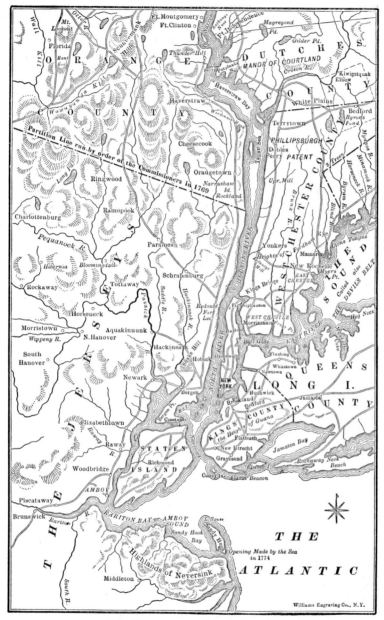

NEW YORK AND THE LOWER HUDSON
(From *The Documentary History of New York*, i, 774)

driven from Manhattan Island and the mainland immediately north of it.[1] With the main body Washington
retreated slowly across the Jerseys, and, finally, in December, passed the Delaware into Pennsylvania. The one
serious disaster in this movement was the loss of Fort
Washington at the northern end of Manhattan Island, with
its entire garrison and all its munitions of war.[2]

The dilatoriness of Sir William Howe has sometimes
been ascribed to licentiousness, at others to lack of soldierlike qualities. It has frequently been suggested that he
did not wish to beat the Americans, but to bring them
back to their allegiance by force mixed with conciliation.
The Howes belonged to a family that had been friendly
to the colonists for years; they were also commissioners
to grant amnesty to repentant rebels. The union of the
sword and the olive branch in their hands, coupled with an
entire lack of sympathy with the policy of the government,
doubtless diminished their zeal; but the difficulty of securing supplies and the inefficiency of many of their subordinates had something to do with failure to push matters
to the extremest limits. It is also to be remembered that
the British army was a professional force. Officers and
privates alike had no desire to endure the hardships of
winter campaigning, or to see hostilities come to a sudden
termination which meant half-pay, or garrison duty, or
return to private life without trade or profession.

[1] See R. P. Bolton's *History of the
Defence and Reduction of Mount Wash-
ington*, and W. R. Benjamin's article in
Empire State Chapter of the Sons of the
American Revolution's pamphlet on *Fort
Washington*. There is much interesting
and valuable matter in J. C. Schwab's
*Revolutionary History of Fort Number
Eight*, and in H. B. Dawson's *West-
chester-County, New York, during the
American Revolution*, which has an

excellent map. See also C. W. Baird's
History of Rye; Abbatt's *Battle of Pell's
Point.*

[2] The treason of Adjutant William
Demont of Magaw's Pennsylvania regiment simplified the task of the British;
but the fort would probably have fallen
in any event. See an article by E. F.
De Lancey in *Magazine of American
History*, i, 65.

The American cause seemed well nigh hopeless; Congress retired from Philadelphia to Baltimore because as soon as the Delaware froze the crossing of the river by the British could not be prevented. Washington's army dwindled to five thousand men or less, and the terms of service of most of the soldiers would cease with the year. The British lines now extended across New Jersey, the extreme outposts being at Trenton and Bordentown, both being held by Hessian regiments. The foreigners had pillaged the inhabitants mercilessly,[1] converting resentment for England's unconstitutional acts into hatred of her rulers. More than once Colonel Rall, the commander of the Hessian outpost at Trenton, had been ordered to construct one or more redoubts; but this he had neglected to do. He kept one of his three regiments under arms each night, and established patrols on the roads leading out from the town into the country, a full mile from the village. Washington projected an attack upon the detachments at Bordentown and Trenton. His plan provided for a simultaneous passage of the Delaware by three bodies of troops. One of these was to attract the attention of the Hessians at Bordentown and prevent their going to the succor of those at Trenton where the main attack would be delivered. Another detachment was to cross the river just below Trenton and seize the line of communication between the two Hessian outposts. The third column was to pass the river at McKonkey's Ferry, eight or nine miles above Trenton, and capture Rall and

---

[1] On the pillaging by the Hessians in New Jersey see the "Journals" of Adjutant-General Kemble of the British Army (New York Historical Society's *Collections*, 1883, p. 91) and the "Journal" of J. P. C. von Krafft of the Regiment von Bose (*ibid.*, 1882). Outrages were not confined to the British side; the loyalists were often most cruelly treated, as is noted by De Lancey in Jones's *New York during the Revolutionary War*, **i,** 185, 669. From the viewpoint of political results the former is important; the latter has only a personal interest.

his regiments. The first detachment managed to cross the river, but the ice on the Jersey shore prevented the landing of the artillery and the whole body regained the Pennsylvania side in safety. The central column likewise failed to carry out its part of the general plan.[1] The main attack was brilliantly successful.

Washington went with the northern column, having Sullivan, who had returned from captivity, and Greene in command of the two divisions of his little force of about twenty-three or twenty-four hundred men. The young ice[2] which had formed in the river greatly retarded the crossing, and must have sorely tried the commander-in-chief's constancy as he watched the slow and hazardous passage of the troops who literally formed the forlorn hope of the Revolution. Most fortunately a false alarm on the preceding evening had made the Hessians relax something of their vigilance and satisfied Rall that he had defeated an American attack on his force.[3] Once over the river, Washington's two divisions proceeded by roads that ran almost parallel, one by the river, the other farther inland. On the latter, was Greene's command accompanied with artillery, and with it went Washington himself. Proceeding painfully through a storm of sleet and

---

[1] These were the times that tried men's souls, and few stood the test. At one period Washington had only 3000 effectives, possibly only 2500, and the terms of enlistment of most of these expired with the year. Pennsylvania militia proved to be a timely aid at this crisis; then came the remnant of the force that had been left on the eastern side of the Hudson, and finally some hundreds of the northern army joined him.

The operations in New Jersey have been admirably elucidated by Colonel Stryker in his *Battles of Trenton and Princeton.*

[2] *Writings of Washington* (Ford ed.), v, 132, 135, and note.

[3] Just before midnight on Christmas Eve, General Grant, the British commander in New Jersey, wrote to Von Donop at Bordentown that Washington was aware of the weakness of the Hessian garrisons and that he would better be on his guard "against an unexpected attack at Trenton." This warning does not seem to have reached Von Donop in time for him to apprise Rall of the impending blow. See Stryker's *Trenton and Princeton,* p. 115.

rain, and being troubled to keep their muskets and powder
dry, the soldiers pressed on, and both columns struck the
pickets of the enemy at almost the same moment at about
a mile from the village. Pursuing the fleeing enemy, the
Americans entered the town with them. Sullivan was
unable to seize the bridge leading over the Assunpink
toward Bordentown in time to prevent a few Hessians and
some English cavalrymen getting away. Surprised by this
sudden and overwhelming attack, Rall tried to escape with
his regiment, which was under arms that night, by the
road leading toward. Princeton; but Greene had artillery
already in position commanding the road. The Hessian
chief was mortally wounded, and his men, about one
thousand in number, surrendered (December 26, 1776).
Washington hastily returned to Pennsylvania. His success and the sight of the German prisoners gave new life
and hope to the cause.

Cornwallis was on the point of embarking for England
when the news of Rall's death and the capture of his
men reached New York. Howe sent him to the front to
drive away the Americans, or, at any rate, to rescue the
other Hessian detachments. When Washington again
passed the Delaware, he found himself facing a greatly
superior British force. By a clever stratagem he kept the
enemy immovable during a night while he passed around
their flank and rear to Princeton. Several British regiments were at that place on the way to Cornwallis's main
army. Thinking that the van of the American army was
an isolated force, the British attacked, and a fierce encounter
took place before they were driven off. From Princeton
Washington sought the high lands of central New Jersey;
his position there was so threatening that Howe felt obliged
to recall his detachments to within easy supporting dis-

tance of New York.   The end of the year 1776, therefore, found the continent in American possession, except New York City and its environs and Newport in Rhode Island, which had been seized by the British in the preceding autumn.

NOTES

I. General Military Bibliography. — Henry B. Dawson's *Battles of the United States*, because of the documents that he prints at the ends of his chapters, is the most useful book of its kind. The chapter in Winsor's *America* (vol. vi) on the "Struggle for the Hudson" was written by General G. W. Cullum, but the bibliographical portion was the work of Mr. Winsor. The other chapters on military operations were the work of civilians, but the bibliography of these other campaigns is equally detailed. Force's *American Archives* stopped with the third volume of the fifth series, thus containing papers only to the end of 1776. As far as it goes, it is an exceedingly useful publication, but one does not always feel entirely confident of the accuracy of the text. There is no official collected printed series of volumes giving the military papers on both sides, or even on one side. The reports and letters must be looked for in countless places, — the writings of Washington, Greene, and other leaders, the publications of states, as the *New Hampshire State Papers;* the proceedings of learned societies, and publications of the time, as Almon's *Remembrancer,* the *Gentleman's Magazine,* and the *Annual Register.* A documentary publication of official papers arranged chronologically and confined strictly to the military part of the American Revolution would enable historical writers to secure more accurate and broader views of the period.

The Royal Historical Manuscripts Commission in its various publications has thrown a great deal of light on American annals, and never to greater purpose than on the military side of the Revolution. Foremost of these is the *Report on American Manuscripts in the Royal Institution of Great Britain* (4 vols.). This is a calendar of the papers of successive British commanders-in-chief, which came to the Royal Institution in a roundabout way from Sir Guy Carleton. Of almost equal importance is the *Report on the Manuscripts of Mrs. Stopford-Sackville* (2 vols.). The second volume of this work contains the letters of Lord George Germain, while Colonial Secretary, and also letters to him. The sixth volume of the *Report on Manuscripts in Various Collections* contains a similar collection of the correspondence of William Knox, Germain's under-secretary, to.

gether with much matter of anecdotal nature.   Appendix vi to the *Tenth Report* of the Commissioners is a calendar of the Abergavenny Manuscripts, which include the correspondence of John Robinson. These four publications taken together have cast a new light on much that has hitherto been obscure.   They can be obtained separately, and might well be on the shelves of every considerable collection relating to the Revolutionary war.

J. W. Fortescue in the third volume of his *History of the British Army* has used this material in manuscript or in print to very good purpose.   This volume, indeed, is the best account within reasonable compass of the military annals of the American Revolution. Mr. Fortescue is well known to American students from his slanderous statements upon the American people and their government[1] and the introductions which he wrote to a few volumes of *Calendars of State Papers.* In the chapters of his *British Army* devoted to our Revolution, he has showered blame in no uncertain language on Americans and British alike.   Another recent English work of somewhat similar type and owing much to Fortescue is Henry Belcher's *First American Civil War*, in two volumes, stopping for the present at 1778.   This work is written from the point of view of a loyalist descendant.   The author sees little that is good in Americans ; and, like Fortescue, he has had no military training.   Nevertheless, his chapters on the forces of the crown and the American armies, by bringing together a mass of out-of-the-way matter, have their place.   Carrington's *Battles of the American Revolution* was the work of a man of some military training, but is marred by enthusiastic prejudices.   The same may be said of F. V. Greene's *Revolutionary War*, which was published in 1911, but does not show the use of the material that has just been referred to.   Captain Mahan, in his *Influence of Sea Power on History*, correlates the several parts of the world-wide contest.   Usually the campaigns in North America are treated as quite apart from general world history.

Benson J. Lossing, sketchbook in hand, traveled over the scenes of the Revolutionary campaigns and incidents at a time when many participants in those events were still alive.   His *Pictorial Field-Book of the Revolution* (2 vols., 1851–52) contains the result of his sketchings and conversings.   As it is arranged according to his

---

[1] *British Statesmen of the Great War.* The sentences referred to are quoted at length in the *American Historical Review*, xvii, 402.

journeyings and not according to the chronology, it is sometimes dis-
connected; its author had not then acquired the critical ability he
showed in later works. Notwithstanding, it is a valuable and stimulating book. The military portions of works on the American
Revolution by Lecky, Trevelyan, Fiske, and Washington Irving are
all interesting, but were all written without that intimate knowledge of the documents in the Record Office in London which is
essential to any judgment of the virtues and failings of the British
commanders. Charles Francis Adams, who combines historical
genius with military experience, has written a series of articles[1]
dealing with certain phases of the contest, — the family dislike of
Washington seems sometimes to surcharge his historical conscience.

Two contemporaneous American accounts stand somewhat apart,
because of the position of the writers and the intrinsic merits of
the narratives. These are the *Memoirs of Major-General* [*William*]
Heath . . . written by himself (Boston, 1798),[2] and *A Military
Journal . . . from 1775 to 1783, by James Thacher, M.D. late
surgeon in the American Army* (Boston, 1823).[3] The *Journals* of
Stephen Kemble, Adjutant-General in the British army, are in the
New York Historical Society's *Collections,* for 1883 and 1884.
They cover the period from June, 1773, to February, 1781. After
June, 1778, they have to do with affairs in the West Indies. Howe's
*Orderly Book at Charlestown, Boston, and Halifax, June 17, 1775 to
1776, 26 May,* to which is added a précis of his correspondence with
the home authorities during the siege of Boston (London, 1890) contains matter that is not in Kemble's *Journals.* Among the older
English works, the *History of the Origin, Progress, and Termination
of the American War,* which is always attributed to Charles Stedman, a "commissary" in the British army during the war, is based
partly upon personal observation and partly upon what was gathered
from other participants. In the John Carter Brown Library there
is a copy of this work with marginal comments by Sir Henry

---

[1] These have been brought together
and rewritten in his *Studies, Military
and Diplomatic, 1775–1865* (New York,
1911). They are well worth reading by
all students of the Revolutionary epoch.

[2] A limited edition was issued in 1901
under the editorship of William Abbatt.

[3] The rough diary or orderly book of
Jacob Turner of the North Carolina Line
throws a great deal of light on the

character of the conflict, and the
heart-rending conditions with which
Washington had to reckon (*North Carolina Records,* xii, 455–548). Another
diary giving homely details from day
to day is the "Journal of Ebenezer
Wild," 1776–81, in Massachusetts Historical Society's *Proceedings,* Second
Series, vi, 78–160.

Clinton, who seems to have been given to annotation. Stedman's work is probably the best of its kind, although necessarily inaccurate in places and oftentimes lacking in perspective. It is abundantly supplied with excellent maps and plans. The most successful attempt to combine the position of troops as given in the official accounts with actual surveys is in Avery's *History of the United States;* the same maps are given in F. V. Greene's *Revolutionary War.*

CHAPTER IX

THE DECISIVE YEAR OF 1777

THE campaigns of 1777 were decisive of American independence. The capture of Burgoyne and his army at
Saratoga stimulated Frenchmen and Spaniards openly to
take up the cause of the rebellious colonists, — the one
in formal alliance, the other less sympathetically, although
hardly less effectively. To understand the British plan of
campaign which led to this glorious catastrophe, it will be
necessary to study the Quebec expedition of 1775 and to
trace briefly the ejection of Arnold and his soldiers from
Canada in 1776.

The plan of wrenching the province of Quebec from
British grasp and adding it to the number of free American states came from the thought that the "habitants" of
ancient New France were languishing under a foreign yoke
and would gladly join their deliverers, especially if success
came to these in the beginning. Possibly, had the matter
been better managed, these expectations might have come
true. It was difficult to efface the impression made on the
Canadians by the outburst of indignation which swept
over New York and New England in 1774 and 1775, at the
passage of the Quebec Act. John Carroll, a Maryland
Roman Catholic, and Dr. Franklin, combined, were not
able to stimulate the Canadians to rebellion. Their lukewarmness was doubtless enhanced by receiving in payment
for supplies continental paper money that in Canada was
not worth the material it was printed on. On the other

hand, they did as little as possible to help their British masters. When Governor-General Sir Guy Carleton, as the feudal head of the seigneurs, summoned them with their retainers to the royal standard, the habitants saw their opportunity, and refused to perform their services.[1]

The American plan of invasion provided for two expeditions. One was to follow the old route by the way of Lake Champlain, seize Montreal, and then proceed to Quebec. The other was to march through the wilderness of Maine and take Quebec by surprise. The former was commanded by Richard Montgomery, once an officer in the British army, who had settled in New York; the latter was led by Benedict Arnold. Unforeseen difficulties on the route delayed Arnold. Quebec was warned, and, notwithstanding the valor of the assailants, proved impregnable. Montgomery was killed, and Arnold was wounded. In the winter the soldiers suffered from scanty rations, cold, and sickness, culminating in the most dreaded of all diseases, before the days of vaccination, the smallpox.[2]   By

---

[1] Professor W. B. Munro writes me that "If the American Revolution did nothing for Canada but to strike a blow at feudal institutions, it rendered therein a good service."

[2] Winsor, in his *America*, vi, 215–229, has an extensive bibliography down to the date of publication, 1888. Justin H. Smith has re-studied this part of the Revolutionary conflict with great zeal, and has embodied his researches with ample bibliographical detail in *Our Struggle for the Fourteenth Colony* (2 vols., New York, 1907). C. H. Jones's *History of the Campaign for the Conquest of Canada* (Philadelphia, 1881) carries the story down to the end of the year 1776. J. J. Henry's *Accurate and Interesting Account of the Hardships and Sufferings of that Band of Heroes who traversed the Wilderness in the Campaign against Quebec in 1775* (Lancaster, 1812, reprint Albany, 1877) is an excellent example of the type of books with which our grandfathers were familiar, and which fixed the traditional ideas of the Revolutionary struggle in the minds of succeeding generations.

Verreau's *Invasion du Canada* (Montreal, 1873) is valuable as giving a Canadian view of this episode; see also a "Journal of the most remarkable occurrences in Quebec" by an "Officer of the Garrison." (New York Historical Society's *Collections*, for 1880, p. 175.) George Morison, a Pennsylvanian, served as a rifleman from the beginning of the expedition until he was captured at the time of the assault. In his *Interesting Journal of Occurrences during the Expedition to Quebec* (Hagerstown, Maryland, 1803) he states that a few days before the assault two men deserted to the enemy, and adds "to this infernal act of treachery the failure of the enterprize may in a great degree be attributed."

May Day, 1776, the original force had dwindled to nineteen hundred; of these nine hundred were on the sick list, and three hundred more refused to do duty because their time had expired. Everything that Congress could do to succor the Americans before Quebec and strengthen them to complete their work was done. Generals Wooster, Thomas, Sullivan, and Gates, and soldiers by the hundreds and thousands went northward. Sickness, distance, and poverty worked against them, to the accompaniment of a powerful army from England.

Meantime in London the news of the American raid on Quebec had awakened great interest, far more than Lexington and Concord, or the cooping up of Sir William Howe and his army at Boston. The action of the Americans in leaving their own country and invading a separate section of the British empire excited great indignation. Soldiers and supplies for Sir William Howe and his army were being brought together in England. It seemed of the utmost importance to send the first detachment of troops to the St. Lawrence for the purpose of assuring the continued occupation of Quebec or recapturing it, if it had been taken. The Canadian expedition of 1775–1776, which seemed so foolhardy in thought and fruitless in result, was really of the highest importance to the American cause. It divided Howe's army into two parts, thus depriving him of the preponderance of force that was necessary for the conquest and occupation of the Middle States in 1776; and the attempt to reunite the two portions of his army in the next year brought about the first serious disaster to British arms.

An extract from this very rare book is in the *Pennsylvania Magazine of History*, xiv, 434. A manuscript of the journal is in the Harvard Library. An excellent brief modern account is G. W. Cullum's *Major-General Richard Montgomery*.

Sir Guy Carleton was now Governor-General of Canada. Like so many men who have won renown in that country, he was born in Ireland, his family having migrated from England. He and Wolfe were intimate friends, and the latter took him to Quebec, technically as quarter-master-general, but in reality as confidential engineer. Carleton stayed in Canada and advanced from one post to another until he reached the position of Governor-General. He was a man of marked administrative ability, and after the independence of the United States, returned to Quebec, and under the title of Lord Dorchester achieved an unpleasant prominence in our history. Carleton's second in command was John Burgoyne. He was a typical military man of fashion of that day, passing his winters at Bath on account "of his health." In the springtime he would hasten to the front, take command of an army that had been carefully nursed all the winter by the lower officers, and undertake some dashing adventure. In the course of the Seven Years' War, Burgoyne won considerable éclat at the storming of Valencia d'Alcantara and the enemy's camp at Villa Velha. He married a daughter of the Earl of Derby, and naturally found himself in Parliament talking vehemently on subjects of which he knew little. He also wrote plays, one of which was brought out by David Garrick in 1775. In all, from his various public employments he had managed to gain an income of three thousand five hundred pounds sterling a year and the favor of the king. He went with reënforcements to Boston in 1775, and there found fault with Gage so energetically that he was sent out to Canada in the spring of 1776, that he might have active service in the field and win glory and renown for self and country.

The prospect of Carleton's intervention in the campaign in New York was displeasing to Sir William Howe, for although he had been appointed commander-in-chief, Carleton ranked him on the army list. In the summer of 1776 Howe was in high favor with the government. Upon learning of his fears as to the delicacy of his situation in case his troops and Carleton's should come together, Lord George Germain wrote to Carleton directing him to remain in Canada or to return thither in case his troops had passed the boundary between that province and New York, because he was needed at Quebec. He was also ordered to turn the command of the army in the field over to Burgoyne. This letter never reached Quebec as the vessel bearing it had been thrice blown out of the Gulf of St. Lawrence by westerly gales. Meantime, Carleton had driven the Americans southward to Lake Champlain. There he had been obliged to stop while a flotilla was built to gain control of the water from a naval force that Arnold had organized on the lake.

On October 11, 1776, the two fleets came together off the Island of Valcour, and again a little later at Split Rock. In these combats the Americans were overcome by superior force, but not before they had fully justified the cost and time that had been spent in building and equipping their vessels.[1] To these delays to the British advance was now added a three weeks' stop at Crown Point, which has never been explained. When, at length, Carleton found himself able to advance to Ticonderoga, he declared that

---

[1] On this part of the campaign, see Peter S. Palmer's *History of Lake Champlain*, ch. vii. Arnold's description of the battle of Valcour Island and following events is in Force's *American Archives* (Fifth Series), ii, 1038; *Journals of the Provincial Congress of New York*, ii, 344; I. N. Arnold's *Life of Benedict Arnold*, 118 note; and H. B. Dawson's *Battles of the United States*, i, 171. See also Hadden's *Journal*, 22. Captain A. T. Mahan has set this action in its rightful place in history. *Scribner's Magazine*, xxiii, 147–160 from W. L. Clowes's *The Royal Navy: a History*, iii, ch. xxxi.

it was too late in the season to attack the fortress, and with his whole force returned to Canada.

Having seen his troops in comfortable quarters in New York and New Jersey, Howe busied himself with planning for the future. On November 30, 1776, he wrote to Germain that he needed fifteen thousand new troops with an additional battalion of artillery and three hundred horses to mount his light dragoons. This would give him a total force of more than thirty-five thousand men, which would enable him to hold New York and Rhode Island and place in the field three expeditions, to operate from Rhode Island toward Boston, from New York northward, and also from New York southward. This last force might capture Philadelphia and possibly invade Virginia. On December 20, Howe wrote again. By this time he had become convinced that the Pennsylvanians were disposed to peace. He therefore proposed to defer offensive operations against Boston, "that there may be a corps to act defensively on the lower part of Hudson's River to cover Jersey on that side, as well as to facilitate, in some degree, the approach of the army from Canada," which he thought could not reach Albany before the middle of September. Germain, in replying to the first letter, cut his reënforcements nearly in halves, as he could promise only eight thousand at the most, with no artillerymen and only one hundred horses. On March 3, 1777, Germain wrote again, expressing himself as confident that Cornwallis had made good progress in East Jersey, although he could not help expressing the very great concern he felt for the loss of the Hessians at Trenton. He had received another letter from Howe dated December 31, 1776, in which the latter declared that Rall's defeat "has put us much out of our way." The loss, Germain thought, was especially

grievous because he would be able to send Howe only
about fifteen hundred new troops, instead of the eight
thousand that he had promised in January, having
been disappointed in negotiations for more Germans.
The king, he wrote, approved of Howe's plans for the following campaign, but was also of the opinion that many
good results would flow from a " warm diversion upon
the coasts of the Massachusetts Bay and New Hampshire."
He and Lord Howe were to take the matter into serious
consideration. This was the last letter that Howe received
from the secretary before his departure for the conquest of
Pennsylvania and contained no hint that the commander-
in-chief was to subordinate his plans to the reception of
the Canadian contingent.

Meantime, Burgoyne had returned to England and laid
before the king a scheme for utilizing the bulk of the British and German soldiers in Canada. In the dearth of recruits, it was imperative to place this force in touch with
Howe's army. This could be accomplished by proceeding
to Albany by way of Lake Champlain, or by putting the
seven or eight thousand men who were not needed in Canada on shipboard and taking them to New York by sea.
The king disapproved the latter plan because, if the Americans were to discover how greatly the army in Canada had
been weakened, they would surely undertake another invasion. The first proposition was adopted, Burgoyne being
retained in command of the field force. On March 26
Germain wrote to Carleton, who was still in Canada,
stating that in the preceding August he had directed
him to return to Canada, giving the command of the
field expedition to Burgoyne, who was to join General
Howe as soon as possible ; but this letter had never
reached Quebec and had been carried back to England.

Since then he had been mortified, so he said, to learn that Carleton's repassing Lake Champlain in the preceding year had set free a considerable number of the Americans, who had promptly marched southward and had made possible the midwinter successes of Washington's army.[1] "Upon these accounts, and with a view of quelling the rebellion as soon as possible" it was necessary that the junction of the armies in New York and Canada should be speedily effected. Carleton was to retain between three and four thousand men, and send the rest, numbering about eight thousand, southward under Burgoyne and St. Leger, giving them orders to proceed to Albany and put themselves under Howe's command. A copy of this letter was sent to Howe, and reached him at the end of May. That general had already written to Germain and to Carleton; to the former he announced his determination to invade Pennsylvania by sea, although this would probably necessitate the temporary abandonment of the Jerseys. He also would be able to leave only enough troops at New York and Rhode Island to hold those posts; but a corps of provincials, under Governor Tryon, could demonstrate on the Hudson or on the coast of Connecticut. He informed Carleton, that "from the want of sufficient strength in this army" he would be unable to detach a body up Hudson's River in the beginning of the campaign; but he would endeavor to open the communication for shipping through the Highlands. Upon receiving Howe's letter of April 2, inclosing this one to Carleton, Germain at once replied

[1] Writing to Knox, Germain observed that Carleton must see that the "particular directions" of the instructions of 1777 proceed from the inactivity of his last campaign. Royal Historical Manuscripts Commission's *Reports*, "Various Collections," vi, 132. It is certain that Pennsylvania and New Jersey troops were at once ordered southward the moment the pressure from the north lessened. See Capt. Ichabod Norton's *Orderly Book* (Fort Edward, N. Y., 1898, p. 58).

(May 18, 1777) that his Majesty approved the alterations
which he had made in his plans, " trusting, however, that
whatever you may meditate, it will be executed in time for
you to coöperate with the army ordered to proceed from
Canada." This letter was received by Howe on August 16,
while on his voyage up Chesapeake Bay, when it was
impossible for him to go to the assistance of the
northern army.[1] Burgoyne understood that the purpose
of his going southward was either to join the main
army, or, by remaining upon the Hudson, to enable Howe
to act with his whole force to the southward by holding
in northern and central New York troops that might otherwise join Washington.[2] The steps by which the plan of
campaign of 1777 was slowly wrought out in England and

[1] The letters on which the preceding
paragraphs are based are printed at
length in the *Stopford-Sackville Manuscripts*, ii, 49, 52, 53, 56, 58, 60, 63, 65, 66.
   William Knox, one of Germain's
under-secretaries, at some later date,
wrote in his reminiscences that after the
orders for Carleton had been prepared,
he observed to Lord George that no letter
had been written to Howe telling him of
Burgoyne's expedition. Germain thereupon directed the military under-secretary to write to Howe himself, inclosing
a copy of Burgoyne's instructions.
(*Various Collections*, vi, 277.) This letter
was received by Howe on May 24, 1777
(*Stopford-Sackville Manuscripts*, ii, 63);
but the letter itself has never been
printed. Shelburne, in his biographical
note on Germain (Fitzmaurice's *Shelburne*, i, 358; Fonblanque's *Burgoyne*,
233), states that the orders for Howe's
coöperation with Burgoyne were prepared and ready for Germain's signature,
but were pigeonholed and forgotten,
owing to the secretary's desire to go to
his country seat. Fonblanque adds that
the unsigned dispatch was found in the
colonial office after Burgoyne's surrender. No authority is given for either
of these statements, and no such paper
has ever been produced. The whole an-

ecdote is repeated in E. F. De Lancey's
Note lxi to Jones's *New York in the
Revolutionary War*, i, 696. Possibly
the later stories grew out of Knox's
anecdote.
   From the moment of Burgoyne's
surrender to the present day, efforts
have been made to saddle the failure of
the 1777 campaign on Howe; especially
Galloway, a Philadelphia loyalist whose
performances had not measured up to
Howe's expectations, was bitter in de-
nunciation. Stedman, in his *History of
the American War*; Carrington, in his
Battles of the American Revolution; and
Charles Francis Adams, in sundry
papers, have all reflected on Howe's
conduct with severity. See Massachusetts
Historical Society's *Proceedings*, xliii
and xliv. For Howe's defense, see the
*Narrative of Lieut. Gen. Sir William
Howe* (London, 1780). A convenient
" schedule " of Howe's correspondence is
sometimes found between p. 487 and the
index of the *Parliamentary Register*,
vol. xi.
   [2] See Burgoyne's " Thoughts for conducting the War," dated February 28,
1777, in his *State of the Expedition, Appendix*, p. iv, and his letter to Howe of
October 20, 1777, in *Head Quarters
Papers*, i, 140.

in America have been stated at length without any attempt at valuation, but simply to show the ideas of the government at London and of their generals in America. It does not appear from these letters that the authorities in England or America had in mind any permanent conquest of the Hudson Valley by Burgoyne. The design was to place within Howe's reach reënforcements which he needed to take the place of those that had not been obtained in Germany.

As the months after Trenton and Princeton one after the other passed away, the American army slowly grew in numbers. When the ground dried in the later spring, Washington was puzzled at the inactivity of the British. In May they left their camps and advanced into the country, but the attack was not pushed home, and, indeed, did not seem to be made in earnest. After desultory marchings and counter-marchings, Howe withdrew his troops once more to their quarters in New York and the vicinity. On July 5 the British embarked on transports, but lack of wind held the fleet immovable for eighteen days. When the ships at length crossed the bar and disappeared from the view of the watchers on the Jersey shore (July 23, 1777) Washington was even more uncertain as to what the enemy was purposing to do. One surmise was that Howe had gone to the eastward to take up matters again with the recalcitrant New Englanders. Such, indeed, was the royal desire; but Howe had at heart the capture of Philadelphia, the seat of the Continental Congress and the capital city of the rebellious provinces. His earlier movements in New Jersey had been merely a reconnoissance to test the feasibility of an attempt upon Philadelphia from the north, and had convinced him of the danger attendant upon any such operation. He had decided, therefore, to approach that

city from the south, either by the way of the Delaware
or the Chesapeake. A week before he left New York,
a letter from Burgoyne had announced the occupation
of Ticonderoga and the dispersal of the whole northern
American army. It was with a light heart, therefore,
that Howe saw the land fade from view.

The news of the reappearance of the British army from
Canada also came to Washington, but the abandonment
of Ticonderoga did not fill him with dismay. He realized
to the full the strength of the New Englanders ; Burgoyne
might have some temporary successes, but would not
win his way to Albany and to New York. His own
place was with the main American army in opposition
to the main British force, wherever that might turn up.
Nevertheless, Washington sent Morgan with some picked
troops to the aid of the northern army, while he waited
attentively for tidings of the reappearance of Howe.
The first reports placed the British fleet off the Delaware,
for Howe had designed disembarking at Newcastle or
somewhere thereabouts. Captain Sir Andrew Snape Ham-
mond, who had cruised for months in that bay, reported
so adversely on the feasibility of disembarkation at this
point that the British put to sea and again turned their
ships southward.[1] Washington was now more uncertain
than ever as to the destination of the enemy ; it might
be Virginia, Charleston, or the West Indies. The progress
of the British armada was painfully slow, and it was
not until three weeks later that the news of the presence
of the fleet in the upper Chesapeake showed that the
intention was to land at the Head of Elk, only seventeen
miles distant from Newcastle on Delaware.

[1] This officer for a year and a half
had been in command of a squadron
cruising in the Delaware and off the
Virginia coasts, and knew this region
better than any other man in the fleet.

Being now assured of the British plan, Washington led his army southward from Philadelphia, taking up a strong position at Chad's Ford, where the road from the Head of Elk crossed Brandywine Creek. The battle which followed was, in many ways, a repetition of that of a year earlier on Long Island. At Brandywine the Americans were not so numerically inferior as they had been in 1776, but the results achieved by the British were out of all proportion to their excess of numbers, especially when one regards their long confinement on shipboard under the most trying conditions. At Brandywine Howe again pretended a frontal attack as a feint for the real blow which was delivered on the flank. In 1777, as a year earlier, Sullivan commanded the exposed American division, and, as in that year, was the victim of a surprise.[1] Washington was compelled to abandon the position (September 11, 1777); but it speaks volumes of praise for him and his men that after such a disaster the military organization remained intact and in effective working order. With a fixedness of purpose all his own, and admirably supported by his troops, Washington strove to retard Howe's advance upon Philadelphia. On September 20, a detachment under Wayne was surprised and badly cut up at Paoli, and six days later the van of the British army entered Philadelphia. Even then Washington was not satisfied that he had done everything in his power to break the hold of the British on the Delaware. On October 4, in the early

[1] Bancroft and other older writers were inclined to use severe language as to Sullivan's military career, and it was also charged that he received money from the French minister while a member of Congress. These imputations have been warmly resented, especially by his descendant, Thomas C. Amory, in his *Military Services of Major-General John Sullivan* (Boston, 1868); *General Sullivan not a Pensioner of Luzerne* (Cambridge, 1875); *Daniel Sullivan's Visits*, and other papers printed in the *Proceedings* of the Massachusetts Historical Society, especially vol. xiii of the First Series, p. 383. See also Alonzo H. Quint's address in *Dedication of the Sullivan Monument at Durham, New Hampshire*.

morning he suddenly delivered a fierce attack upon the enemy at Germantown. Accidents and an untimely fog prevented proper coördination of his columns, and he was obliged to retire, without accomplishing anything decisive.[1]

Below Philadelphia the Americans had constructed a carefully devised system of defenses consisting of forts on islands in the river and on its banks and obstructions in the waters themselves. These were so vigorously defended that it was the end of November before British shipping was able to pass up and down the river. While all this had been transacting in Pennsylvania, Burgoyne and the army from Canada, instead of reaching Albany and New York, or drawing any considerable body of troops from Washington, had itself been forced to surrender at Saratoga.

Sir Guy Carleton was stung to the quick by the tone of Germain's letter of March 26, as well as by its contents. Standing by itself, the restriction of his command to Canada would have been unpleasant, even if the original letter of August, 1776, had reached him before the lame conclusion of the campaign of that year. Now, when it was coupled with the assertion that the disaster at Trenton was due to his supineness,[2] his anger knew no bounds; in one letter to Germain, he referred to the "private resentment"

---

[1] The authorities on this campaign are cited in Winsor's *America*, vi, 414–436. To these should be added the papers printed by the Royal Historical Manuscripts Commission (see above, p. 237); S. G. Fisher's *Struggle for Independence* (ii, 17–53); and Fortescue's *British Army*, iii. C. F. Adams's *Studies, Military and Diplomatic* has some interesting criticisms. The *Valley Forge Orderly Book of General George Weedon* (New York, 1902) describes this campaign, and is, for an orderly book, interesting. Washington's plan for the attack of Germantown is in the *Pennsylvania Magazine of History*, xxvi, 387. Other

articles in the same periodical are "Diary of Lieutenant James McMichael, of the Pennsylvania line, 1776–1778" (xvi, 129), and the journal of the German Captain Münchhausen (*ibid.*, xvi, 197). Samuel W. Pennypacker's address on "The High Water Mark of the British Invasion" (*ibid.*, xxxi, 393) has to do with the campaign after Brandywine.

[2] This paragraph is not in the letter as printed in the *Parliamentary Register* (xi, 401) or in Burgoyne's *State of the Expedition*, Appendix, p. vii; it will be found in the *Stopford-Sackville Manuscripts*, ii, 60.

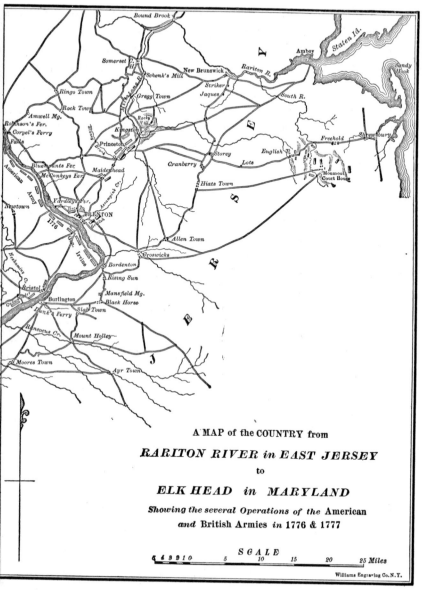

A MAP of the COUNTRY from

RARITON RIVER in EAST JERSEY

to

ELK HEAD in MARYLAND

Showing the several Operations of the American *and* British Armies *in 1776 & 1777*

SCALE

5   5 3 2 1 0   5   10   15   20   25 Miles

Williams Engraving Co. N.Y.

of a secretary ; in another, he expressed the " ardent wish "
that " the dignity of the Crown may not appear beneath
your Lordship's concern." [1]   To judge Carleton fairly, it
must be remembered that he had been wounded in the
battle which sealed the fate of Quebec, while Germain had
been dismissed from the British army for disobedience of
orders at Minden.   Nevertheless, Carleton promised that
Burgoyne should have every assistance in his power, and
the latter stated in the House of Commons that Carleton
could not have been more assiduous, had he been personally
in command.[2]   The whole episode, however, is a good illus-
tration of the difficulty of carrying on military operations
at so great a distance from the office of the minister responsible for the conduct of affairs.

The composition of the forces to operate southward
from Canada was carefully determined in England, and
most detailed directions were sent to Carleton.   He was
to give Burgoyne seven thousand troops, British and German, including all of the latter except six hundred and

[1] *Canadian Archives, 1890,* "State
Papers," 84; A. G. Bradley's *Lord Dorchester,* 169. It has often been stated
that Germain disliked Carleton because
the latter had testified against him at the
court martial. This can hardly be, as
Carleton had no personal knowledge of
the battle of Minden, and the printed
minutes contain no mention of his name.
See Donne's *Correspondence of George
III with Lord North,* i, 44 and note; ii,
76 note; Fortescue's *History of the
British Army,* iii, 208; Lucas's *History
of Canada, 1763–1812,* p. 139. See also
*Proceedings of a General Court-Martial
. . . upon the trial of Lord George
Sackville* (London, 1760) and *A Complete
History of the Late War* (London, 1760,
ii, 396–417 ; 491 and fol.). Furthermore,
Germain in replying to Carleton's "very
extraordinary" letter of May 20, 1777,
assured him that he had no "personal
dislike" to him, adding, "I have at no

time received any disobligation from
you." These two letters are printed at
length in *Canadian Archives,* 1885, pp.
cxxxii, cxxxvi. Carleton's letter of May
20 is also printed at length in Kingsford's
Canada, vi, 129. It has also been said
that Germain resented Carleton's refusal
to appoint Major Christie to an office in
Canada and that he was jealous of Carleton's appointment to the sinecure office
of commander of Charlemonte in Ireland ;
but there seems to be no evidence of this.
Germain was certainly right in his assertion that the idea of restricting Carleton
to his governorship was not due to any
dissatisfaction, for only four days after
Germain's original letter, Lord North
wrote to Carleton that the king intended
to confer upon him a pension of one
thousand pounds per annum for three
lives (*Abergavenny Manuscripts,* 14).

[2] *Parliamentary History,* xxvi, 194.

fifty whom he was to retain. All the artillery, except "such parts as shall be necessary for the defence of Canada," was also to be given to Burgoyne. Six hundred and seventy-five soldiers were to be placed under Lieutenant Colonel St. Leger, who was to proceed down the Mohawk to Albany. Both detachments were to be provided with as many Canadians and Indians as might be thought necessary, and to be given "every assistance which it is in your power to afford and procure." In his orders to Burgoyne and St. Leger, Carleton was to inform them that until they received orders from Howe, they must "act as exigencies may require . . . but that in so doing they must never lose view of their intended junctions with Sir William Howe as their principal objects."[1]

Burgoyne's total force, at the outset, numbered only 6840 foot soldiers, and 357 artillerymen. Of these 3116 were Brunswickers. The soldiers were ready on time, with the exception of some recruits, whose late arrival delayed the actual embarkation. Carleton had contracted for the transportation of the artillery and ordnance; but, notwithstanding that he levied a corvée of five hundred habitants,[2] he was unable to make any adequate provision for the transportation of food and general military equipment. Draft animals were not plentiful in Canada, nor were wheeled vehicles. Also, it took time to get land transportation to the place where it was needed. Ticonderoga was easily captured, for St. Clair, who commanded the American garrison, had not deemed his force sufficient to include within his

[1] *Stopford-Sackville Manuscripts*, ii, 63. It will be noticed that nowhere in any of the letters that have been referred to is there the slightest hint of effecting a permanent conquest of central New York, or, indeed, of doing anything, except to further Howe's plans either by joining him or by keeping troops from Washington's army.

[2] *Canadian Archives, 1890*, "State Papers," p. 89.

s

lines an almost inaccessible hill that dominated the position only fourteen hundred yards away.[1] With enthusiasm and skill, the British crowned the top of this height with a battery, and there was no hope of successful resistance. St. Clair wisely decided to evacuate the position in the following night by means of a floating bridge that connected Ticonderoga itself with the eastern shore of Lake Champlain. Unfortunately at that moment, when secrecy was essential to give the Americans a good lead through Vermont, a building burst into flames, and the blaze apprised the invaders of their opportunity. They at once occupied the deserted fort, and started in pursuit of the fleeing garrison. At Hubbardton, they came up with the rear guard, and a smart action followed. The Americans were defeated, but they gave a good account of themselves and regained their spirits, which had been somewhat damped by the early evacuation of Ticonderoga. The pursuit of the Americans drew Burgoyne and his army away from the line of advance by Lake George to its southern end, and thence overland to Fort Edward, where the Hudson, after flowing eastwardly for a few miles, turns sharply and runs southward by Saratoga and Albany to New York. The army reached Fort Edward on July 29. It had now outrun its supplies, and was obliged to wait until these could be brought up. The distances are nowhere great, but the obstacles to easy transportation provided by nature were many and formidable. The Lake George route from Ticonderoga required first of all overland

---

[1] Hadden's *Journal*, p. 84. St. Clair's numbers were too small to defend so extended a position. Schuyler advised concentration on Mount Independence (June 5, 1777). If, as St. Clair contended, that position also was indefensible, why was not Sugar Loaf Hill occupied? Why was not a new fleet constructed? No answer to these questions is given in the records of the court-martials of either Schuyler or St. Clair. New York Historical Society's *Collections* for 1879 and 1880.

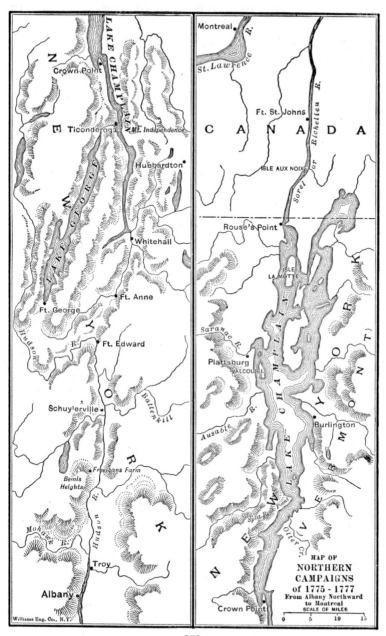

LAKE CHAMPLAIN

N

Crown Point

E

Ticonderoga • Mt. Independence

LAKE GEORGE

Hubbardton

W

Whitehall

Ft. Anne

Ft. George

O

Hudson R.

Ft. Edward

Batten kill

Schuylerville

R

Mohawk R.

Freemans Farm

Bemis Heights

Hudson R.

K

Troy

Albany

Williams Eng. Co., N.Y.

Montreal

St. Lawrence R.

Ft. St. Johns

C A N A D A

Soret or Richelieu R.

ISLE AUX NOIX

Rouse's Point

ISLE LA MOTTE

LAKE CHAMPLAIN

N E W

Saranac R.

Plattsburg
VALCOUR

Ausable R.

Burlington

M O N T

Y O R K

V E R

Split Rock Point

Otter Cr.

MAP OF
NORTHERN
CAMPAIGNS
of 1775 - 1777
From Albany Northward
to Montreal
SCALE OF MILES

0   5   10   15

Crown Point

carriage from Lake Champlain to Lake George, which is two hundred and one feet higher. Next goods and soldiers had to be laden on boats and taken by water from the northern end to Fort George at the southern end of the lake. Then came another bit of overland transport to Fort Edward and the Battenkill, from which point the Hudson was navigable for boats and rafts,—with occasional interruptions. An alternative route led southward from Ticonderoga by Lake Champlain and thence overland to Fort Edward. There was not much choice between the two; what advantage existed was in favor of the way by Lake George, owing to its being less exposed to attack from the East.

During the year that the soldiers had passed in Canada they had accumulated many personal belongings which they were anxious to transfer to their new quarters in New York. Some of them, also, as Baron Riedesel, the commander of the Brunswickers, had their wives and children with them, together with their attendants. These families could hardly be transported without a considerable amount of baggage in addition to that with which a soldier was ordinarily supplied. Taking the boats to pieces at Ticonderoga, carrying them up the rough road to Lake George, and putting them together again took time. From Fort George to Fort Edward was a distance of only fourteen miles, but the Americans had done everything they could to break up the road and add to the difficulties of the enemy. All this labor discouraged the Canadians, who escaped to the woods as opportunity served. Days turned into weeks, and the weeks into a full month and more before Burgoyne had gathered thirty days' stock of food on the Hudson. While at Fort Edward, the thought occurred to him that a raiding expedition to the east-

ward might aid him greatly in securing grain and beef
cattle that were said to have been gathered at Bennington. He was informed that the inhabitants of this
region were very loyal to the king. In addition to food and
beef, horses and even recruits might be procured. Burgoyne's ideas of American geography were possibly not
as hazy as those of his chief at London; but they were
misty enough,[1] as he seems to have thought that it would
be rather easier to get to Newport on the island of Rhode
Island than it would be to go to Albany. At all events,
he determined to try the experiment to the eastward.
For this he selected five hundred Brunswickers, under
the command of Lieutenant-Colonel Baum. These were,
for the most part, dismounted dragoons who might procure horses in the course of the expedition. Thurlow,
the attorney-general, when he expected to be compelled to
defend the government in a parliamentary inquiry as to
the failure of Burgoyne, asked Knox how it happened that,
both at Trenton and at Bennington, the Germans had
been selected for the most dangerous duty. He was informed that in both cases the Germans happened to be
on the left of the line, and, therefore, etiquette required
their employment. "So," ejaculated the lawyer, " because

[1] While at Fort Edward, Burgoyne
requested Carleton to provide a garrison
for Ticonderoga, thus releasing for
active service in the field the troops that
had been left at that place. Carleton
replied that his instructions forbade
this; but he took advantage of a clause
in a letter from Barrington to deviate
from Germain's orders by sending the
"additional companies" then in Canada
to join their regiments under Burgoyne's
command (*Canadian Archives, 1890,*
"State Papers," p. 95). About a month
later, Germain, who had specified
minutely what regiments were to stay in
Canada, wrote to Burgoyne that he

presumed Ticonderoga would be garrisoned from Canada (*ibid.,* 97). His
geographical knowledge was derived
perchance from *The North American
and the West Indian Gazetteer.* Under
"Bristol, a county and town in New
England," it states that the town
is laid out with great regularity, "the
capital is remarkable for the King
of Spain's having a palace in it, and
being killed there; and also for Crown
the poet's begging it of Charles II." It
may be that Burgoyne thought Bristol
would be a convenient stopping place for
an army proceeding from Lake Champlain to Newport.

one damn'd blockhead did a foolish thing, the other block-head must follow his example."

As the fiery cross summoned the Scottish clansmen to the slaughter of the hated Southron, so did the bruit of the advent of the German trooper call the New England frontiersman from his lonely dwelling to the fray. In New Hampshire, especially, was there enthusiasm mixed with fear. John Stark at the moment was out of the service on account of some slight from Congress. The New Hampshire legislature authorized him to enlist a force to serve under his command and to inflict as much damage as possible upon the enemy. With surprising speed Stark raised his men and marched over the mountains to Man-chester in Vermont. There some difference of opinion developed between Schuyler, Lincoln, and himself as to the best use that could be made of this force. While they were still debating, Baum and his Brunswickers began their march for Bennington. At once all doubt vanished from Stark's mind. With skill comparable to that he had shown at Bunker Hill in defending the rail fence, he now manœuvred his men for the capture of the enemy. Most of the British soldiers and the Indians who were with Baum escaped ; the Germans were killed or cap-tured, almost to a man. Not liking the looks of affairs, Lieutenant-Colonel Baum, some days earlier, had asked Burgoyne for reënforcements. This led to the dispatch of another body of Brunswickers, commanded by Lieu-tenant-Colonel Breyman. Colonel Seth Warner, with some of the remnants of the Ticonderoga garrison, was not far away. To him Stark had sent most urgent calls for assistance. The weather in the intervening time had been very rainy, and had made the roads almost impassable for artillery. Breyman's men, therefore, had marched very

slowly. It fell out, in this way, that Warner and Breyman
came in contact not far from the precise spot where Stark's
men were still plundering the Brunswickers. The fighting
was sharp for a time, and then Breyman went back much
faster than he had come, leaving a goodly portion of his command behind him. In all Bennington (August 16, 1777) cost
Burgoyne about eight hundred men, — a serious diminution
of his small force. Six days later (August 22, 1777), Lieutenant-Colonel Barry St. Leger abandoned the siege of
Fort Schuyler, and endeavored to reach Burgoyne by way
of Canada and Lake Champlain.

The idea was that this expedition "as a diversion would
facilitate every proposed operation,"[1] presumably by attracting to itself Canadian frontiersmen and New York
Indians, and also by relieving the pressure upon the main
army. St. Leger had about six hundred European soldiers, a
large body of Indians, and an unknown number of provincials. Fort Stanwix, or Schuyler, to give it its Revolutionary name, stood at the carrying place between the Great
Lakes and the Mohawk Valley. The fort was supposed to
be in a ruinous condition; but it had been practically rebuilt
by Colonel Gansevoort and his New York men and a detachment under Marinus Willett. St. Leger had no artillery of
any size with him, and was therefore obliged to enter upon
a siege that was likely to be prolonged, although every
week's delay was of almost vital concern. As the people
of western New England rushed toward the Hudson
to strike at Burgoyne, so the German settlers of the
Mohawk Valley set out to succor Fort Schuyler and its

---

[1] Burgoyne's *State of the Expedition*,
App. p. vi. This sentence occurs in a
paper entitled "Thoughts for conducting
the War from the Side of Canada. By
Lieutenant-General Burgoyne." This
document begins by calling attention to a
report that the Americans were building
a new flotilla on Lake Champlain. It
refers to a "former memorandum,"
which is not printed.

beleaguered garrison. They were led by General Herkimer, and marched straight into an ambush that the enemy had craftily prepared for them, where the road crossed a very difficult bit of ground at Oriskany. The position has been well described as having the general conformation of a bowl. The attack was unexpected, but the frontiersmen were too much at home in forest fighting to give way. They took to the nearest cover, and fought Indian fashion. Herkimer was wounded early in the fight, but directed the battle astride his saddle, which was placed on the ground at the foot of a tree. A terrific thunder storm stopped the fighting for the moment, and when it cleared, the British returned to their camp in front of Fort Schuyler. While this had been going on at Oriskany, the garrison of the fort had plundered the quarters of the absentee besiegers, and had returned safely to the walls with stores that were of great service to them. Two thousand men were now detached from the American army, which was then at the mouth of the Mohawk, and sent under Arnold up that river. The enemy did not await their coming. Hearing of his approach from messengers, whom Arnold sent in advance, the Indians deserted in a body and St. Leger returned to Oswego and Canada, abandoning his tents and heavy equipment.[1]

Of Burgoyne's seven thousand soldiers, nearly one thousand had been left behind at Ticonderoga to garrison the fort and guard the lines of transportation, and eight hundred had been lost at Bennington. His force on paper, therefore, was only about fifty-five hundred men, exclusive of a varying number of provincials and Indians. By the

[1] In 1779 Sullivan, with three thousand men, dealt a severe blow to the Iroquois. See Andrew McF. Davis in Winsor's *America*, vi, 638, and in Massachusetts Historical Society's *Proceedings*, Second Series, ii, 436; G. S. Conover, *Journals of the Expedition of John Sullivan in 1779* (Auburn, N. Y., 1887). See also "Journal of Lt. Robert Parker" in *Pennsylvania Magazine*, xxvii, 404, and xxviii, 12.

first of September, most of the Indians had vanished into the forest, and the larger part of the provincials had also abandoned the expedition. Even with the diminished numbers, the question of transport remained exceedingly difficult. The number of horses that had been asked for had never been provided, and the carts that had been supplied were constantly breaking down. It was found necessary to bring hay from Canada to feed the animals that were with the army, for there was little grazing to be found in the forested country between the Hudson and the lakes. On the marches to Hubbardton and Bennington, and wherever any part of the army went, the soldiers were obliged to carry their own food and equipment, and, indeed, to turn the horses out of the traces and themselves pull the artillery and ammunition wagons through the mire, which was exceedingly deep that year, and up the steep hills that abounded in that region. Up to Fort Edward and to the check at Bennington, the expedition had borne the aspect of a pleasant summer promenade. Thirty wagons were required for Burgoyne's baggage. Even at Saratoga, after the retreat from in front of Bemis Heights, champagne was served at the general's table. The delays made necessary by the opening of the Lake George route were annoying, but until Bennington the Americans had avoided serious fighting. Burgoyne, himself, was said to have suggested the coming of General Riedesel's wife and children to Fort Edward. When the army was about to leave Fort Edward on the next stage of its journey to Albany, there was a question whether the Baroness and her family should continue with the troops or return to Canada ; and it was again at Burgoyne's suggestion that they remained with the army. In those days women played an active part in war. They sailed on the frigates and ships of the line, and accompanied the armies in their marches over the cultivated lands of France or through the wildernesses of America. At Cambridge, at Christmas time, in 1777, there were still three hundred women and children included in the fifty-five hundred who drew rations under the guise of "Convention troops."[1]   How many had fallen out on the way from Saratoga to Boston cannot be said, but gossip at the time placed the number of women with the Canadian army at very much more than three hundred.   The roster of the troops, therefore, gives little indication of the number of mouths to be fed.   At all events, Burgoyne's men and women consumed provisions nearly as fast as these could be brought to the front, and compelled the long wait at Fort Edward and the Battenkill from the middle of July to the middle of September.

The providential halt of the Canadian expedition enabled American reinforcements to reach the front. Washington sent two brigades from the troops on the lower Hudson, and forcefully implored the New England governors to set the militia in the field. The response was hearty.   By September the American forces, regulars

---

[1] "Heath Papers" (Ms.), vol. vii. As to the navy, Samuel Leech notes the birth of two children on the *Macedonian*, while she was blockading the French naval ports.   Similar conditions prevailed in the American Revolutionary forces, for the "Heath Papers" also note the presence of seventy women and children among the "American Soldiers Familys & others in the barracks." Enos Hitchcock, a Rhode Island chaplain, recorded in his "Diary" (Rhode Island Historical Society's *Publications*, vii) that in the months of May and June, 1779, he baptized two children and united four couples in the holy bonds of matrimony, all belonging to the army. Washington, writing to Robert Morris from Newburgh on January 29, 1783, stated that the number of rations for women had been limited to one fifteenth of the issues to non-commissioned officers and privates; "Sparks Manuscripts," No. 65, vol. iv, p. 36. See also, on this general subject, *Records of North Carolina*, xii, 480.

The presence of Jane McCrea in the vicinity of Burgoyne's army, and her death at the hands of the Indians while on the way to join her betrothed, who was among the provincials in the British service, affords another glimpse of that domesticity in arms which marked that time. Her death incited thousands of New Englanders to join in repelling the invader; but it is extremely doubtful whether it was an American or a British Indian who ended her life. See W. L. Stone's *Campaign of Burgoyne*, Appendix iv.

and militia operating against Burgoyne, had increased
to ten thousand; by the end of that month the numbers had grown to over twenty thousand, four times
Burgoyne's field force. Most of this array was of
an extremely temporary type of troops, — the New
England farmers who came with their own firelocks
and subsistence for a few weeks' service; but they came
in such numbers that Burgoyne was not merely blocked
in front and rear, his army was enveloped. During the
first weeks of the campaign Schuyler was in supreme
command. Then Lincoln, a New Englander, was sent
to receive the militiamen as they assembled and to organize them, so far as this could be done in the field.
Schuyler was intensely unpopular among the New Englanders; he was an aristocrat, while they were farmers,
and the mere fact of his being a New Yorker was chilling
to the settlers of New Hampshire and of Vermont, who
stoutly denied the claims of New York to the lands
between the Connecticut and Lake Champlain. Horatio
Gates had commanded at Ticonderoga in 1776, when
Carleton had turned back. In 1777 the command was
again offered to him. He refused to serve under Schuyler,
and St. Clair had been appointed to that post. Congress
now asked Washington to appoint a commander-in-chief
for the northern department in succession to Schuyler.
On his refusal to take this responsibility it gave the
place to Gates. Lincoln and Arnold with Morgan bore
the chief subordinate parts. Schuyler had withdrawn
to the islands at the confluence of the Mohawk and
the Hudson; but Gates's increasing numbers enabled
him to occupy a more northern position at Bemis
Heights, where the high ground closely approaches the
western bank of the Hudson. On the opposite side

of the river, steep hills and deep ravines at right angles to the stream prevented the passage of an army, except at some distance inland. As the British were dependent upon the river for transport, they could not go far away from its banks, and were thus compelled to take the road that led directly beneath Bemis Heights. On the top an entrenched camp was constructed, the whole being protected by a deep ravine in front. Probably the plan was to await attack within the lines; but the failure to occupy a hill that commanded the western end of the American line necessitated encountering the British at a distance, when they seemed intent upon passing the ravine to the westward to gain possession of this high ground. At the foot of the heights, between the road and the river, an entrenchment had been thrown up, and a bridge of boats connected the western and eastern shores at this point.[1] There is no information as to who selected this position or arranged for its fortification; in the absence of direct evidence, whatever credit there may be would seem to belong to Gates and to his engineer, Kosciusko, the Polander.

Crossing the Hudson, on September 13, just above the Battenkill at a place now known as Schuylerville, the British slowly made their way down the river, a few miles daily, until on the 18th signs of a hostile force in

---

[1] An interesting historical pilgrimage may be made by trolley car from Albany to Fort George. The entire distance can be covered in a few hours, and the speed with which the trip is now made compared with the slowness of Burgoyne's movements and also the changed aspect of the country can truthfully be described as startling. At Fort George a steamer can be taken up the lake to the head of the old portage to Lake Champlain, which lies over two hundred feet below. Any one who thinks that Burgoyne's fleet could have sailed from Lake Champlain into Lake George and so made the passage from Fort Ticonderoga to Fort George in two days or so, would do well to walk along the three-mile gorge which separates the two lakes.

the neighborhood became more and more evident. The next day, September 19, Burgoyne sent his army forward by three different roads or paths. In the afternoon, as the westernmost regiments came out of the woods into the cleared lands of Freeman's Farm, they were attacked. A stubborn fight followed, in which the British lost, in killed, wounded, and missing, nearly five hundred men. When darkness fell, the Americans retired, thus giving Burgoyne the chance to make out to himself and to his superiors in England that he had won a victory. This affair is known as the Battle of Stillwater, or the first Battle of Freeman's Farm. In reality it was a check for British arms, for the Canadian expedition had reached its farthest south. Burgoyne placed his troops in camp a little retired from the battle ground. His information as to the number and position of the Americans, and as to the whereabouts of the other British armies, was astonishingly vague. Sounds of felling trees and of roll-calls came to the British from the southern side of the ravine in front of Bemis Heights, and occasional attacks were made on the right of the British line, which was two miles from the river; but as to the size and disposition of the American force, Burgoyne was as ignorant as when he left Fort Edward. On September 21 a messenger came announcing the definite intention of Clinton to attack the American forts on the Hudson. Possibly it was this information that kept Burgoyne immovable, when all other considerations dictated immediate retirement to Fort Edward and Ticonderoga.

Earlier in the year, when making arrangements for the summer's campaign, Howe had written to Carleton that he could give no great assistance to the army operating from Canada. It would be possible for him at a later time to

send an expedition from New York to capture the forts
guarding the passage through the Highlands, thus opening a
way to Albany whenever Burgoyne should reach that
point. Clinton, whom Howe left at New York, did not
feel justified in leaving that post until reënforcements
from Europe arrived. Then, in the early days of October,
he organized a combined naval and military expedition
which proceeded rapidly up the Hudson. Israel Putnam,
the American commander in that quarter, promptly crossed
to the eastern bank of the Hudson with most of his soldiers, expecting the attack to be made on that side. The
British control of the river enabled Clinton to take his
men over to the west bank and to prevent Putnam re-
crossing. The forts, Montgomery and Clinton, surrendered
on the 5th of October, and Fort Constitution, on the eastern bank, was later abandoned.[1] Clinton then returned
to New York with most of his men; others, on shipboard,
went up the Hudson as far as Kingston, burning and pillaging. Above that point the river is shallow in places,
quite impracticable for sea-going vessels of any size. Indeed,
as Clinton wrote to Burgoyne, it was impossible for him
to go as far as Albany with the force at his disposal.

On October 3, the very day that Clinton started up
the river from New York, Burgoyne issued an order
reducing the daily ration by one third. Three days later
he determined to attack the American left, with a view
to ascertaining the possibility of breaking through to
the southward. He also hoped to obtain forage for his
horses and cattle, which had been only half fed for some
time. At noon of October 7, word was brought to Gates

---

[1] Isaac Q. Leake, in his *Memoir of
General John Lamb*, treats this part of
the campaign with considerable detail,
as Lamb was the commander of Fort
Montgomery.

that British soldiers with artillery "were disposed to fix themselves on an eminence that lay opposite to our [the American] left."[1]   Upon this Gates directed that a strong force should be sent to deliver a counter attack, and this brought on a general engagement.   The accounts of the combat that followed are unusually conflicting and vague. The idea of the American commander-in-chief was merely to prevent the enemy's effecting a lodgment, whence his entrenched camp could be attacked; he did not wish for a general battle.   Once begun, the ardor of the Americans carried them to the British line and into it.   Most of the fighting was in the woods, where the well-aimed American muskets proved to be much better weapons than the more modern arms of the British and Germans.   This conflict is most conveniently called the Second Battle of Freeman's Farm.   For the numbers engaged, the losses were heavy.   Remembering the slight force at Burgoyne's disposal, his loss was fatal.

Retreat rapidly conducted and pushed through every obstacle was the only chance that was left to Burgoyne to save his army.   Already parties of Americans had been operating on his line of communication with Canada. They had captured the hill overlooking Ticonderoga, but had not been able to seize that fort.   They had also sailed on Lake George, but had not broken up the transport service on the lake.   They were in force on the eastern bank of the Hudson; but as yet had not made their positions too formidable for successful attack.   When haste was so urgent, Burgoyne seemed strangely inert, and acted as if he preferred

---

[1] This statement is made on the authority of a paper written by J. M. Hughes, aid-de-camp to Gates, in Massachusetts Historical Society's *Proceedings*, First Series, iii, 279. Hughes was a major in a New York regiment, but nothing more seems to be known of him. Henry Dearborn was in both battles of Freeman's Farm.   See his "Journal" in Massachusetts Historical Society's *Proceedings* for 1886.

surrender to flight.   Riedesel offered to cut his way through, and a contingent of Canadian auxiliaries with the Indians did succeed in escaping to Canada.   The weather was stormy, the roads nearly impassable ; but the distance to Fort George was so small that it could easily have been made by soldiers carrying their own food within forty-eight hours — unless they had been obliged to stop and fight.   Baroness Riedesel has left us a most dramatic account of the last days : the burial of General Fraser ; the breaking down of military discipline; and the incessant cannonading of the British position.   She has also noted for us the gayety of the commander-in-chief.   She was accustomed to army life and to warfare as it was conducted on the European continent.   The novel conditions of the wilderness oppressed her, and doubtless caused some exaggeration ; but when all is said, it is impossible to account for Burgoyne's doings after the disaster of October 7 on any other ground than that he was, for the time being, mentally unbalanced.

The Convention of Saratoga was completed on October 17.   The British army, after surrendering its arms and public property, was to march to Boston.   There the soldiers were to embark on transports, to be provided by the British on condition of not serving in North America during the present war.   In being thus lenient to a foe whom he held securely in his grasp, Gates was influenced by the knowledge of Clinton's successful attack on the forts in the Highlands and by the news of the burning of Kingston, which seemed to argue for an ascent of the river in force. Several hundred New Yorkers, their time being up, had taken themselves off while the negotiations were proceeding.   There was much sickness in the army, and discipline was necessarily slack when the bulk of the troops were militia. A stronger soldier might have pushed the enemy to unconditional surrender. A man of statesmanlike mind might have peered into the future and discerned the impolicy of the terms granted. Gates's one idea was to wrench the arms from the enemy's grasp. Yet it was a great victory, and brought Britain face to face with the trading nations of western Europe. From being a local conflict between two sections of the British empire, the war took on the form of a world-wide contest for dominion.

NOTES

I. Burgoyne's Expedition. — Authorities on the campaign and capture of the Canada army under Burgoyne are set forth in detail in Winsor's *America*, vi, 346–366. W. L. Stone's *Campaign of Lieut. Gen. John Burgoyne* (Albany, 1877) is still the most important compendious account of the campaign. So many documents have been made accessible in recent years that it would be well to have this important episode in our military annals again described for popular perusal. From the British side the standard account is E. B. de Fonblanque's *Political and Military Episodes derived from the Life of The Right Hon. John Burgoyne* (London, 1876), which is usually cited as Fonblanque's *Burgoyne*. Accounts in C. P. Lucas's *History of Canada, 1763–1812*, and in J. W. Fortescue's *History of the British Army*, vol. iii, are written with the aid of the papers in the Record Office; they are necessarily brief and prepared without special knowledge of the ground or the American sources, — relying on Fiske as the standard American account. The more important dispatches of the commanders on both sides are printed at the ends of the successive chapters of Dawson's *Battles of the United States*. Many documents illustrating different phases of the campaign are calendared, sometimes at length, in the *Canadian Archives* (1890, "State Papers"), and in the *Reports* of the Royal Historical Manuscripts Commission, which have already been noted. Of the numerous journals, orderly books, etc., which have been printed, the *Journal Kept in Canada* by Lieut. James M. Hadden, Roy. Art., and edited by General Horatio Rogers (Albany, 1884); *Journal of Lieut. William Digby*, edited by J. P. Baxter (Albany, 1887); and Thomas Anburey's *Travels through the Interior Parts of America, in a Series of Letters* (London, 1789) are the best. Burgoyne's *Orderly Book*, edited by E. B. O'Callaghan, illustrates the difficulties of the expedition and contains a good map. Madame Riedesel's *Die Rerufs-Reise nach America* (Berlin, 1800) has been twice translated into English. She was the wife of the commander of the Brunswickers; but the interest of the book lies in its hints as to army customs and life in rural New England rather than in military information. Less known is Eelking's *Memoirs of Major General Riedesel*, also translated by W. L. Stone (Albany, 1868).

Estimates of numbers on the two sides are conflicting. The Americans are given at from 11,098 to 22,348, or 22,000 in round numbers; and the British from 13,677 to as low as 3719. In the former case the smaller estimate, which is from the " Gates Papers," probably did not include thousands of militiamen, possibly not even Stark's Independent Command that won the battle of Bennington. In the latter case the larger figure included garrisons all the way to the Canadian boundary, the smaller figure excluded every one who was not able to stand up in the firing line with a musket. See Thomas Jones's *New York in the Revolutionary War*, i, 674; Hadden's *Journal*, lix; Digby's *Journal*, 354. Gates's return of October 16 (Burgoyne's *State of the Expedition*, Appendix lix) gives the numbers as 18,624. Of these 13,216 are " present fit for duty." A note states that the total is exclusive of " the upper staff of the army, the bateau-men, the artificers, and followers of the camp." These discrepancies have been a source of delight to depreciators and defenders of both Gates and Burgoyne.

II. **Bennington.** — The bibliography appended to Foster and Streeter's article on Stark in New York State Historical Association's Bennington volume is complete and discriminating. Other lists are those of S. C. Gould in Manchester (N.H.) Historic Association's *Collections*, i, 205, and in Winsor's *America*, vi, 354. The documents are printed in *New Hampshire State Papers*, viii; Vermont Historical Society's *Collections*, i, 163–249; Burgoyne's *State of the Expedition;* Caleb Stark's *Memoir of Gen. John Stark;* and Stevens's " Facsimiles." The facts have been brought together in chronological order and with abundant citations by Professor Herbert D. Foster and Thomas W. Streeter in the article above noted. C. E. Potter's *History of Manchester* (N.H.) and the *Collections* of the Manchester Historic Association have a good deal of matter relating to Stark and the other members of the family who lived in that town. An earlier account is that by Hiland Hall, which was first printed in the *Bennington Banner*.[1] Owing to state jealousies and state pride, the part taken by the sons of

[1] It has been twice reprinted in *The Bennington Battle Monument and Centennial Celebration* (Milford, Mass., 1877); and in *Centennial Anniversary of the Independence of the State of Vermont and the Battle of Bennington* (Rutland, 1879), p. 166.

New Hampshire, Massachusetts, Vermont, and New York has been the subject of controversy, as has the site of the battle-ground, some New Yorkers averring that the three hundred foot monument, which is in Vermont, is a mile and a half from the location of the redoubt, which they say was in New York. The excellent map which is reproduced on the opposite page is found in "Sparks Manuscripts," No. 28.

III. Gates and Arnold. — The attempt to appoint Gates to chief command in Washington's place and the wilting of his laurels at Camden have inclined American writers to take from him the glory of Saratoga. On the other hand, the desire to deepen the dye of Arnold's treason has led them to exalt his soldierlike qualities and performances, and especially to give him the credit of burgoyning the Canadian expedition. Gates's position was a very trying one, for the friends of Schuyler were bitter against him. They played upon Arnold's vanity[1] and urged him on to quarrel with his chief, who had been a very good friend to him. The trouble began at least a week before the First Battle of Freeman's Farm. With the great accession of numbers, the army had to be reorganized. Lincoln, being the senior Major-General was necessarily second in command. Arnold made claims which Gates could not and would not admit.[2]   In reporting to Hancock the First Battle of Freeman's Farm, Gates stated that he had ordered out Colonel Morgan's corps and had reënforced the original body with four more regiments. The good behavior of all the troops on this occasion "cannot be surpassed by the most Veteran Army, to discriminate in praise of the officers would be Injustice."[3]   Somehow it came to the notice of Arnold, that neither his name nor that of his division was mentioned. On the same day, Arnold wrote to

[1] Letters of Varick and Livingston in the "Schuyler Papers" in the Lenox Library at New York. These are printed in Wilkinson's *Memoirs of my Own Times* and in I. N. Arnold's *Life of Benedict Arnold*. It is in one of these that Gates is represented as staying in his tent while the battle was raging without, and it is in them that Arnold is lauded to the skies. They are valueless as historical material, except as showing Gates's trying position.

[2] John Austin Stevens's "Summary of the Case against Arnold" (*Magazine of American History*, iv, 181–191) is still the best brief statement. Bancroft had before him a very complete collection of transcripts and originals, which are now in the Lenox Library. His account is excellent. The student must read the documents themselves as printed in Wilkinson's *Memoirs*, i, ch. vi.

[3] Gates to Hancock, President of Congress, dated "Camp Heights above Behmus's Septem 22d 1777." Library of Congress, "Washington Papers," Letters to Washington, xci, fo. 48.

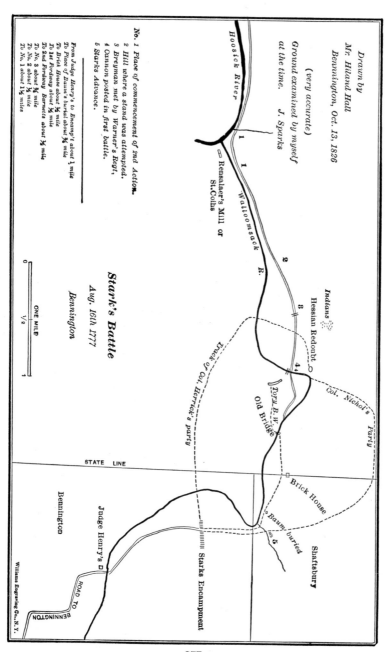

Drawn by
Mr. Hiland Hall
Bennington, Oct. 13, 1826

(very accurate)

Ground examined by myself
at the time.   J. Sparks

No. 1 *Place of commencement of 2nd Action.*
2 *Hill where a stand was attempted.*
3 *Breyman met by Warner's Regt.*
4 *Cannon posted in first battle.*
5 *Starks Advance.*

From Judge Henry's to Encamp't about 1 mile
To Place of Baum's burial about ¾ mile
To Brick House about ½ mile
To 1st Fordway about ¼ mile
To 2nd Fordway Barnetts about ½ mile
To No. 3 about ¾ mile
To No. 2 about ½ mile
To No. 1 about 1½ mile

Stark's Battle

Aug. 16th 1777

Bennington

Hoosick River

Rensalaer's Mill or
St.Coits

Watloomsack
R.

Indians
Hessian Redoubt.

Col. Nichol's
Party

Tory B. W.
Old Bridge

Track of Col. Herrick's party

STATE LINE

Brick House

Baum
buried

Shaftsbury

Bennington

Judge Henry's

Starks Encampment

ROAD TO
BENNINGTON

0   ½   1
ONE MILE

Williams Engraving Co., N.Y.

277

Gates,[1] complaining that certain dispositions as to his division had not been made according to Gates's alleged promise.[2] As to the events of the 19th, he said that he himself had suggested attacking the enemy and that Gates had desired him to send Morgan and to support him, and that accordingly he, Arnold, had sent out his whole division, except one brigade and one regiment. Finally, he averred that Gates had told him when Lincoln arrived he would be without a division. On the next day (September 23), not having received a reply, Arnold wrote again, and on September 27 and October 1 he wrote other letters. Getting no satisfaction, Arnold said that he wished to go to Congress, and applied for a pass. Gates thereupon gave him a letter of introduction to Hancock. This Arnold returned, saying that what he wanted was a pass. Gates thereupon gave him one, but Arnold was still with the army on October 7. Lincoln was in command in the field on that day. In writing to Hancock of this battle, Gates stated that among the wounded was the "Gallant Major General Arnold; whose Leg was fractured by a Musket Ball, as he was Forcing the Enemies Breast Work."[3] All the evidence seems to point to the following facts: (1) that Arnold was not present on the field at the First Battle of Freeman's Farm; (2) that he declared his intention of leaving the army while in the presence of the enemy; and (3) that he was practically a volunteer without command on October 7. The credit of Saratoga belongs to Horatio Gates, and with him to Daniel Morgan, Benjamin Lincoln, and Thaddeus Kosciusko. *Prima facie* the verdict is for Gates; the burden of proof is on the other side.

---

[1] This and the other letters in this series are in the "Gates Papers" in the New York Historical Society's Library. They are printed correctly in Wilkinson's *Memoirs*.

[2] Lincoln was appointed major-general on February 19, 1777, and Arnold on May 2 following (*Journals of Congress*, Ford ed., vii, 133, 323).

[3] Gates to Hancock, Library of Congress, "Papers of the Continental Congress," No. 154, vol. i, fo. 272.

CHAPTER X

CHARLES TOWNSEND, William Knox, and their kind would make of rebellious America another Ireland. Had Virginia and New England been no farther from Bristol and the Thames than Dublin and Cork, this daydream might have become a reality. The people of Great Britain outnumbered those of the continental colonies four or five to one, and exceeded them in wealth even more largely. Nevertheless, the task to which King George and his ministers addressed themselves in the summer of 1775 was wellnigh hopeless from the beginning, and was absolutely futile after France, Spain, and the other trading nations of Europe joined the insurgents.

Instead of being near at hand, the Atlantic seaboard of North America was three thousand miles distant from the British base. In those days of sailing ships New York, Philadelphia, and Charleston were more remote from London and Southampton than Cape Town and Australia are to-day. Practically everything, from men and horses to flour and gunpowder, had to be carried from England to America. It is hard to realize how long it took to cross the Atlantic and how uncertain was the crossing. On the first day of October, 1775, John Robinson, the abnormally efficient secretary of the Lords of the Treasury, wrote a long letter to Howe, then commanding at Boston, telling him of the money and supplies that were going forward. The store ships " will be coming out to you every two or three

days "[1]   It was a vain expectation, for in June of the next
year we find Robinson expressing great concern on learning
that only one of the ships sailing between August 28 and
November 11, 1775, had reached Boston.   Again, in March,
1776, Howe wrote from Boston to Lord Dartmouth, whom
he supposed to be still in the colonial office, that he had
received no letters from him since the preceding October.[2]

In one of his burning speeches Chatham declared it to be
impossible to conquer a map ; yet America was little more.
The settlements extended in a long thin line from the
Penobscot to the Savannah.   Now and then around excellent harbors thriving commercial towns had arisen.   Away
from these, the villages and plantations were dispersed,
especially to the southward of Pennsylvania.   The field of
operations was attenuated in shape and no large part
of it was easily accessible.   Great rivers and bays divided
the   colonies   into   distinct   zones   of   military   operations.   The   Hudson isolated New England from the
rest of the country ; the Delaware intervened between
New York and Philadelphia ; and the occupation of
Georgia and the Carolinas produced little effect, if any, on
the attitude of Virginia and Maryland.   Government was
equally dislocated, in place of one there were thirteen.
The Congress had its headquarters at Philadelphia ; but
the seizure of that town had no important bearing on the
course of the war, — except that its occupation kept a British
army from the field.   New York was the strategic center
of the continent, but the shallowness of its approaches and
the danger from floating ice that came down the Hudson

---

[1] *Head Quarters Papers*, i, 15, 46.   secretary to Lord George Germain in
[2] *Parliamentary Register*, xi, 302.   November, 1775.
Dartmouth had given place as colonial

in the winter made naval men wary of it.   Rodney, indeed, declared that from his point of view Newport was better; but it had no military significance.   The fortification of a naval base on the Chesapeake was at length determined on, and the capitulation at Yorktown followed.

American climatic conditions and difficulties of transportation had also to be reckoned with.   The severe cold of northern winters, the excessive heat of southern summers, and the malarial disorders incident to the autumn months, especially in Virginia, made against the full and constant employment of armies.   Transportation by land for any distance was impossible; there were few wagons to be had, and fewer animals to draw them.   An anonymous and exceedingly indignant pamphleteer declared that Bunker Hill was a " bicoque " to marching into the country "without oxen, without horses [to] drag your cannon, your bread waggons, and your baggage through the woods." [1] The winds and currents of the coastal waters contributed greatly to the uncertainty of conducting operations by water at any distance from New York.   A vessel might make the run from Sandy Hook to Hatteras in three or four days, or might take as many weeks.   Calculations as to the length of time it would take to reënforce an army in the Carolinas or in Virginia, or to send supplies to those regions from New York, were very nearly as likely to turn out to be wrong as were those for voyages across the Atlantic.

After July, 1776, the British forces were always superior in fighting power to any that the Americans could maintain in the field, even with the aid of the treasuries and arsenals of western Europe; but every victory won by England's armies only added to her difficulties.   " Why ! " ex-

---

[1] *A Letter to Lord George Germain* (London, 1776), p. 25.

claimed Chatham in the House of Lords, on May 30, 1777,
" what would you conquer ? . . . What will you do out
of the protection of your fleet ?   In the winter, if together,
they are starved ; and if dispersed, they are taken off in
detail."   He was experienced in spring hopes and vernal
promises; " but at last will come your equinoctial disappointment."   The ministers assert that the " army will be
as strong as last year, when it was not strong enough.
You have got nothing in America but stations."   The
soldiers you have there are too many for peace and too few
for war.[1]   Burgoyne's surrender and Howe's useless conquest of Philadelphia gave point to Chatham's prediction.
His further assertion that France " must be as self-destroy-
ing as England, to make a treaty while you are giving her
America at the expense of twelve millions a year " was
not equally well founded, for the Convention of Saratoga
induced His Most Christian Majesty openly to throw in
his lot with the rebellious subjects of his brother of England.

From the very beginning of the war England was really
embarked on a contest with her enemies the world over.
The greatness of her empire was a positive injury, because
at any moment any one of her colonizing rivals might
throw off the mask and seize some desirable possession.
She had to be armed at all points and places and be prepared for all possible contingencies.   Thus, even before
1778, England was exposed to many of the dangers of war
without enjoying any of the advantages in the way of
captures on sea and land which its actual existence might
confer.   As soon as resistance to Britain became a continental matter and no longer a New England affair merely,
Congress opened the provincial ports to the commerce of

---

[1] *Parliamentary History*, xix, 317.

the world, excepting that of Great Britain. Committees
and agents began negotiations with foreign powers, and
sought their aid more or less openly. In France, Spain,
and Holland, great encouragement was given. American
vessels were sheltered in Bilbao, Nantes, and Rotterdam;
their cargoes were bought, and manufactured goods were
placed in their holds. In France Beaumarchais, in Spain
Diego Gardoqui, acted as go-betweens to preserve the
formal peace, while supplying the rebels largely at the
expense of those neutral governments. A fund was provided by Paris and Madrid to enable Beaumarchais and
Gardoqui to place contraband of war drawn from royal
arsenals on board vessels sailing for America. These men
and their friends supplied additional funds which were
thus invested. Payment was received, so far as it ever
was received, in American goods. The Farmers General of
France took American tobacco directly, instead of importing it through England. The Spanish government did not
go so far, but Spanish officials had a convenient habit of
not knowing exactly what was going on, or of taking into
their own keeping a cargo and crew that was violating the
laws of Spain and the nations.

The mode of procedure was much the same in the case
of both France and Spain. Around the doings of Beaumarchais and Silas Deane[1] an almost impenetrable darkness has gathered; but the transactions of the Spaniards,
while veiled in more obscurity at the time, are more
transparent to-day. At Bilbao was the mercantile firm

---

[1] See bibliography in Winsor's
America, vii, 78. To the books there
enumerated may be added those listed in
Blanche E. Hazard's *Beaumarchais and
the American Revolution*, p. 4. Of
especial interest is C. J. Stillé's *Beaumarchais and the Lost Million*. Silas
Deane's part in the whole transaction
may be studied in the five volumes of
The Deane Papers, in the New York
Historical Society's *Collections*. Miss
Hazard's article is an extremely useful
summary of the whole subject.

of Josef Gardoqui and Sons. Diego Gardoqui at Madrid collected funds which he sent to Paris to the order of Arthur Lee who had sole charge of this business on the part of the revolutionists, and did his work very well. Gardoqui also exerted his influence with government officials to favor the Americans. Lee sent his orders to the Bilbao firm, who bought the goods, shipped them off, and drew on his bankers for payment. In this business everything was done on a cash basis so that no perplexing questions ever arose as to payments due from Congress. In France Lord Stormont, the British ambassador, did everything in his power to hinder the outgo of military stores and supplies. In Spain Lord Grantham and his agents were ever on the alert;[1] but they accomplished even less than did Stormont. In the year 1778 alone, the Gardoquis shipped on public account 18,000 blankets, 11,000 pairs of shoes, 41,000 pairs of stockings, and shirtings, tent cloth, and medicines in great quantities. Their bills amounted in that year to 600,000 riales of vellon, on which they charged five per cent commission. Besides this, an extensive private commerce was carried on between Bilbao and other Spanish ports with merchants in America. In this business the Gardoquis charged only two and a half per cent commission, which gives point to Lee's protests that in their transactions with the public they were taking advantage of their position.

In 1776, Benjamin Franklin joined Arthur Lee and Silas Deane at Paris, and other American agents sought other European ports to secure as much recognition and aid and comfort as they possibly could. The three men at Paris did not get on well together. Franklin's Vandalia scheme had displeased Lee, who had referred to

---

[1] For material on Spain, see chapter xiii.

him and his partners as "ministerial tools" and had declared that there was not "a greater set of knaves under the sun." As to Deane, the Virginian regarded him as a shopkeeper, and was jealous of his confidential dealings with Beaumarchais. Franklin had his hands full to keep even a semblance of peace in the commission. The French government was unwilling to come out openly for America, and for months all the wiles of the diplomatic philosopher, coupled with the pressure of French sentimentalists, was unavailing. Nevertheless, wise observers in England felt that this situation could not last. "The sight of Banquo's ghost could not more offend the eyes of Macbeth than the knowledge of this old man [Franklin] being at Versailles should affront the minds" of Wedderburne[1] and other ministerialists who had grossly insulted him. The news of the Saratoga victory aroused to action all parties in Europe. At this moment Franklin seems to have been in even closer communication than usual with his English friends. They certainly had quite accurate information as to what was going on in Paris, although there is no evidence that any tangible offers

[1] In 1773 Franklin somehow secured letters that Hutchinson had written to the British government. He sent these to Boston with a request that they should not be published. They were printed. They added to the resentment against Hutchinson, and led to a petition for his removal. At the hearing of this petition Alexander Wedderburne referred to Franklin as a thief. Hutchinson was not removed at the time, but Franklin was dismissed from his office of deputy postmaster general in America. A duel also occurred before Franklin acknowledged his part in obtaining the letters. In thinking of this incident, it is well to remember that Franklin and the Bostonians felt that the circumstances justified them in what they had done. On June 3, 1774, Dartmouth asked Gage to secure certain letters of Franklin and Arthur Lee that "a proper proceeding" might be grounded thereupon. Massachusetts Historical Society's *Collections*, Fourth Series, x, 712, and *Proceedings* for 1878, pp. 41–49. See also *Copy of Letters Sent to Great-Britain, by his Excellency Thomas Hutchinson, the Hon. Andrew Oliver, and several other Persons, born and educated among us* (Boston, 1773); *A Collection of Scarce and Interesting Tracts*, iv, 222 (Wedderburne's speech). The circumstances of the duel are described in Almon's *Anecdotes*, iii, 236. Franklin later had his revenge on Wedderburne by dedicating to him a tract entitled *Rules for reducing a Great Empire to a Small One*.

were made to any responsible British political leaders. Foreseeing the dangers of the enlargement of the sphere of conflict, Lord North brought forward conciliatory bills; but these were too full of "artifice and deceit" to close the chasm of successful revolt;[1] besides, they were too late. Chatham, at the risk of his life, came forward as the exponent of British imperialism and of her aspiration for world-wide supremacy on the sea. He would throw the whole weight of England on the French colonies in the Indies, West and East. The thought of temporizing with the Americans at such a crisis was to him unbearable. The excitement and effort of this great outburst were too much for his enfeebled frame. He sank down, and was taken home to die. With him perished the one hope of making head against the trading nations of Europe and their American allies.

Vergennes and Louis XVI were now as eager for alliance with America as before they had been wary. On the 6th day of February, 1778, two treaties were signed at Paris,[2] one of alliance, the other of amity and commerce between

[1] 18 George III, Cap. 12. The act contains a declaration that in the future Parliament will not impose "any Duty, Tax, or Assessment whatever" payable in the colonies, except for the regulation of commerce, and the net produce shall always be expended in the colonies in which it is levied. The Townshend Revenue Law and all the laws relating to tea were repealed.

[2] On the general subject of the diplomatic history of the Revolution, see the papers printed in Jared Sparks's *Diplomatic Correspondence of the American Revolution*, or Francis Wharton's *Revolutionary Diplomatic Correspondence of the United States*. The "Introduction" printed in the first volume of the latter work is one of the most valuable essays on the Revolutionary period yet written — although few students will agree with all of the

author's conclusions. In 1882 the government acquired a mass of transcripts and original manuscripts from Mr. Henry Stevens of London, which is known collectively as "The Peace Papers," and is in the Library of Congress at Washington. Many of these papers have been printed in Sparks and Wharton, copies of others are in "Sparks Manuscripts" and in the "Bancroft Manuscripts." Hale's *Franklin in France*, 2 vols. (Boston, 1887–88), is founded upon a study of this material, but touches only the fringe of it. A review of this book by Professor J. B. McMaster is in the *Atlantic Monthly*, lx, p. 318. In using these papers, it cannot be too often pointed out that transcripts are likely to be inaccurate and that letters printed from letter books and from letters actually sent will often not agree.

the thirteen United States of America and His Most Christian Majesty. By the first of these, the two parties agreed
in case war should break out between France and Great
Britain, during the continuance of the existing contest, to
make common cause and not to conclude a truce or peace
with the enemy without the formal consent of the other,
and not to lay down their arms until the independence of
the United States shall have been assured. The French
king, on his part, renounced forever the possession of any
portion of the North American continent which in 1763
belonged to Great Britain; but this did not in any way
apply to the West Indies. On the contrary, the United
States guaranteed to France her present possessions in
America as well as those which might be acquired by success in the war. On his part the French king guaranteed
to the United States their liberty, sovereignty, and independence, and also their possessions, together with such
additions as they might obtain during the war from British
dominions in North America. Spain did not immediately
join in the warfare against England, for with the accession
of Florida Blanca to power in 1778 a change had come
over the policy of the government at Madrid.[1] The new
chief minister was anxious to distress Spain's colonizing
rival; but assisting rebellious colonists in America seemed to
him to be highly impolitic, — the planting of a republic in
the New World would be a deplorable example to her
own colonists. Besides, the revolutionists, if they were
successful, would not remain long grateful. Nevertheless,

---

[1] "Montmorin, dans un billet confi-
dentiel (n° 71) qui accompagne ce rap-
port, explique d'après M. de Florida-
blanca que S. M. C. ne reconnaîtra l'
indépendance des États-Unis que lorsque
les Anglais y seront forcés eux-mêmes
par la paix; qu'elle leur fournira tous
les secours nécessaires, mais non la
garantie demandée par eux: 'Il donne
pour raison de cette répugnance du roi
son maître la crainte de l'exemple qu'il
donnerait à ses propres possessions.'"
Henri Doniol's *Histoire de la Participation de la France à l'Établissement des
États-Unis d'Amérique*, iii, 753, note 3.

he permitted aid to be given surreptitiously, and in 1779 Spain joined in the attack on perfidious Albion as the ally of France, but not of the United States.[1]

From the moment that France joined in the war, the British felt to the full the impolicy of the restoration of Cuba, Martinique, Guadaloupe, and St. Lucia that had been made in 1763 at the impotent close of the Seven Years' War.   The Lesser Antilles extend in a long bow-shaped line from San Domingo to Trinidad off the mouth of the Orinoco.   In this great stretch of islands the winds blow persistently from the southeast.   They were, therefore, the maritime outposts of the more valuable and larger islands and mainland colonies to the west.   Of them the most advantageous, as a naval base, was Martinique, which had been returned to France in 1763, as had Guadaloupe, also of strategic value.   The English held the southern end, St. Vincent, Tobago, and Trinidad, while out at sea to windward was Barbadoes.   This island, from its position, furnished an excellent naval base, but the lack of another toward the northern end of the line diminished England's naval strength fully one quarter.   The Treaty of Amity and Commerce was communicated to the British government in insolent language that made war inevitable.   At once the dockyards of England were pushed to their utmost, and those of France were set at work to provide a fleet capable of coping with England in the Channel and the Indies.   On April 5 Comte D'Estaing sailed from Toulon with twelve sail of the line and several regiments of soldiers.   He passed Gibraltar safely, but loitered on his way across the Atlantic to drill his men and perfect his officers

---

[1] The comparative strength of British, French, and Spanish fleets in 1778 was about as follows : British, 70 vessels of 50 guns and over ; French, 58 ; Spanish, 63, or 121 for the Bourbon powers.

in manœuvers.   It was not until July 8 that he made the
mouth of Delaware Bay.

It was time for succor to arrive.   The credit of the Continental Congress was lower than it ever had been.   Loy-

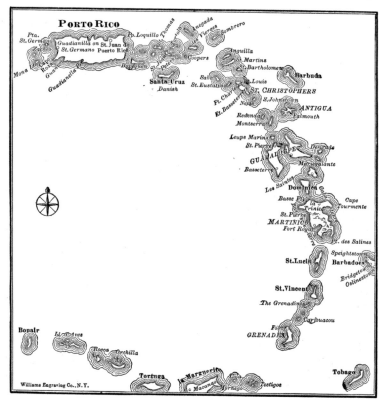

THE LESSER ANTILLES

alists flocked into the British lines; soldiers deserted from
the thin ranks of Washington's army; the loss of the
"capital city" seemed almost to overbalance the capture
of an army at Saratoga.   One indication of the desperate
condition of affairs is to be found in the lavishness with
which the farmers of eastern Pennsylvania supplied the

British at Philadelphia with food, while the American soldiers lay starving at Valley Forge, less than thirty miles away. Of course they got good British gold and silver for whatever they carried into Philadelphia, and Continental paper money for whatever they sold to the commissary of Washington's forces; but the lengthening contest had disheartened many who hitherto had been constant, and the successes of the British had a seeming value in ordinary eyes. Confidence in Washington, too, was on the decline. His failure was unfavorably contrasted with the success of Gates. Washington, as an aristocrat, was disliked by the New England democrats, by Samuel Adams and the rest, — and it was the force of New England that had stopped Burgoyne's onward march. Fortunately no one could be found to take his place. The egregious Charles Lee was still in the hands of the British, and Horatio Gates was the only hope of the anti-Washingtonians. The attempt to displace Washington is enshrouded in the mists of what is known as the Conway Cabal which in turn is intimately connected with the story of James Wilkinson, whose life as he himself relates it was a mystery from beginning to end. New Englanders, at the moment, were puffed up with pride at the thought of their prowess at Bennington and Saratoga; but even to this hour it is impossible to say how much the attack on Washington was part of a popular revolt, and how far it was merely an attempt of a coterie of self-satisfied officers to push themselves to the foremost positions in the army. In this attempt they were aided by those who were dissatisfied with Washington's treatment of themselves.[1]

---

[1] Winsor notes the older books in his *America* (vi, 446). Of later treatments that by L. C. Hatch in his *Administration of the American Revolutionary Army* (23–34) is by far the best. See also Wharton's *Revolutionary Diplomatic Correspondence*, i, 272–283. Richard Henry Lee and other Virginians were also

Thomas Conway, around whose name this plot centered, was an Irishman from France, who had come to America and had found himself on Gates's staff. The tiresome years of peace that had followed the war of the Seven Years had filled veteran officers of continental armies with discontent and redoubled their desires for pay and glory. Some of them, even of the French, applied for service in the armies of Britain ;[1] others besieged the doors of the American commissioners at Paris and Passy. Silas Deane's shopkeeping sensibilities were impressed by the importunity of these sons of war. He engaged them by the hundreds. Most of the foreigners proved to be unavailable for one reason or another, and went back to France by the shipload. Some of them gave help of inestimable value to the cause of America.[2] Of these Lafayette was the exemplar. He belonged to one of the greatest families in France, was hardly more than a boy, and was much affected by the gallant fight for freedom that the American colonists were waging against the traditional enemy of his country. Washington was disconcerted by the crowding in of so many foreign officers, but he at once recognized Lafayette as unlike the rest. He took him into his military family, and soon became exceedingly fond of him. Others whose memories should always be gratefully revered are Baron Steuben, John Kalb, and the Chevalier Du Portail.

---

dissatisfied with Washington's conduct, and Dr. Rush expressed the opinion of more than one man when he wrote to Dr. Ramsay, on Nov. 6, 1778, that "Conway, Mifflin, and Lee [Charles] were sacrificed to the excessive influence and popularity of *One Man*" whom he plainly would like to have seen ostracized. *Pennsylvania Magazine of History,* xxix, 20. See also Paul Leicester Ford's "Dr. Rush and General Washington" in the *Atlantic Monthly,* lxxv, 633.

[1] Letter of Col. Horace St. Paul, British Chargé d'Affaires at Paris, May 1, 1776. "Stevens Facsimiles," No. 1333.

[2] The "Letters of Col. Armand" (New York Historical Society's *Collections* for 1878, p. 289) give the anxieties of a meritorious French officer, and show the difficulties and perplexities of Washington's position.

The last was an accomplished military engineer whose knowledge and experience were of great value to Washington. Kalb came over originally to ascertain the prospects of a French prince being called to the chief command. He found no encouragement in this design, but American aspirations so appealed to him that he offered his own services, and, wounded in thirteen places, fell at Camden doing his duty as major-general commanding the detachment of the Continental Line on that ill-omened field. Of them all Steuben stands first in services performed. He was no mere tyro when he came to America, for he had already seen much service under one of the best of military masters that the world has known, Frederick the Great, King of Prussia. He presented no exorbitant claims, but asked merely for employment. He became inspector-general or chief drill master. He trained the soldiers admirably, adapting Prussian military ideas to the needs of his pupils. As a part of this duty, he devised and published a book of tactics, which was adopted by Congress and became the basis of the American system.

British military and naval authorities realized that the American war was now distinctly secondary. Orders were sent to Sir Henry Clinton, who had succeeded Sir William Howe, to remove his army from Philadelphia to New York, but for the present to keep the post at Newport. There was no hope of reënforcements for him, but a squadron under Commodore Byron, " foul weather Jack," as he was called, was sent to the assistance of Lord Howe, who had not asked to be relieved with his brother. The British forces in the West Indies were strengthened ; the Channel fleet was released from its moorings, and the reorganization of the militia was undertaken. Notwithstanding the inefficiency and the administrative chaos, everywhere patent to the historical seeker, great progress was made; but the utmost that Britain could do was far below her needs. The soldiers who had surrendered with Burgoyne were eagerly expected, for by the terms of the Saratoga Convention they could be employed anywhere in Europe as reënforcement for the force at Gibraltar or to hold Brest or any other French port of which the navy might gain possession, or they might be sent to the West Indies.

By the terms of the Convention, Burgoyne and his troops were to march from Saratoga to Boston, there to embark upon transports to be furnished by the British, on condition of not again serving in North America during the war, unless exchanged. At once, so the Baroness Riedesel tells us, the soldiers began stripping the ensigns from the staffs and concealing them about their persons, or in their baggage; and when they piled their arms, they retained many articles of military equipment. Most of them arrived safely at Cambridge in the vicinity of Boston, although some fell out by the way, especially the Germans, who were attracted by New England country life. The impolicy of the Convention was at once apparent to Washington and to Congress. Unless the British government refused to confirm it or evaded its conditions, it must be carried out; but if the departure of the soldiers could be delayed long enough, it would be impossible to transport from Europe those whom they would replace in time to take part in the ensuing campaign. The nautical fears of Lord Howe ably seconded these desires. He had no transports fit for this service that could be sent over Nantucket Shoals to Boston in November and December;[1] so he suggested that the Convention troops might be embarked at Rhode Island. Washington

---

[1] Belcher's *First American Civil War*, i, 294.

and Congress at once seized on this proposed alteration of the terms of the Convention, and the discussion was easily prolonged into the winter months. The troops were thus forced to remain in the vicinity of Boston, and difficulties and discontents daily increased. It was only right that the British should support their own soldiers, while awaiting the arrival of the transports, but Congress had no other hold upon that government than the possession of Burgoyne and his army. It therefore demanded that all the accounts should be settled and all balances discharged in coin before a single man or officer left America. Descriptive lists of all the Convention troops were also required as means of identification. This Burgoyne looked upon as an outrage. In an insolent letter he declared " The public faith is broke." [1] By this time, the knowledge of the Treaty of Alliance had found its way across the Atlantic and had added to the desire to find some excuse for not carrying out the terms of the Convention. Congress pitched upon this strong though ungrammatical phrase as evidence that the British government itself would not regard the Convention as binding. In 1778 the authorities at London refused longer to support the troops, — Congress evidently regarded them as prisoners of war, and therefore must feed and lodge them at its own expense. Upon this they were marched to the interior parts of Maryland and Vir-

---

[1] *Journals of Congress* (Ford ed.), x, 13 and fol. Charles Deane took a gloomy view of the actions of Congress with regard to the Convention troops in a paper which he read before the American Antiquarian Society in October, 1877, and which was printed in the *Proceedings* of the society and also separately.

Washington's ideas may be gathered from his letters to Heath of November 5 and 13, 1777. In the first he says that if the Convention troops sail in December they may be in time to take the place of others who may be sent to America. As the principal difficulty in their transportation will arise from the want of provision, he advises Heath not to " furnish an ounce for sea store, or suffer it to be purchased in the country." In the second letter he strongly advises against permitting any change in the port of embarkation from Boston to Rhode Island or anywhere else.

ginia, where they were out of the reach of rescuing
British parties and could be maintained after a fashion at
slight expense.

Sir William Howe and his soldiers had passed the winter
months at Philadelphia most agreeably.   The feeble American army, two days' march away, invited attack, but none
was made.   In the late spring, in May, there was an affair
at Barren Hill, in which neither side covered itself with
glory.   It was at this time that Howe sailed for England
and obscurity, after being the victim of a fulsome fête
gotten up by Major André and others.   The change from
Howe to Clinton was not much of a gain in celerity of
movement.   Moreover, the orders from Germain were
singularly confusing and inapplicable to the situation.   One
thing comes out clearly in them : the government actually
thought that there was a chance that the Commissioners appointed in virtue of Lord North's conciliatory resolutions
might induce the rebels to return to their allegiance.[1]   Clinton was ordered to detach eight thousand men to the West
Indies, five thousand of them for the conquest of St. Lucia.
In any case he was to abandon Philadelphia, and if the
proposals of the Commissioners ended in failure, New York
also if necessary.   The royal anger against the New Englanders was still keen, as may be gathered from a letter
of March 8 before the signing of the French Alliance was
known, for in it Clinton is urged to forbear offensive oper-

[1] As showing the nature of the conciliation to be dealt out to the conquered
colonists, Lord George Germain's instructions to Governor Robertson of New
York of July 9, 1779, deserve passing
notice. He says that the king wishes to
have an assembly called to dispel the
idea that there is any intention of governing by military law. Moreover, the
Assembly can annul all the pretended
proceedings of the rebel government,
arm the executive with power to prevent
another insurrection, recompense the
loyalists for their sufferings, provide a
permanent support for the provincial
government, and arrange for the payment of New York's contribution to the
general charge of the empire. From this
it will be seen that the crushing of rebellion would be the opening sign of an
imperial millennium !

ations against Washington and to devastate the ports along the coast from New York to Nova Scotia.[1]

Clinton clearly understood the necessity of leaving Philadelphia ; but it was by no means easy to remove his army and the crowd of loyalists that had sought protection within the lines of British occupation. They had cherished belongings in the shape of household goods, some of which had come down from father to son for generations, and the British officers and soldiers had also accumulated effects. Loading as much as possible on the shipping, Clinton set out with the soldiers to march overland to New York. He left Philadelphia on June 18, 1778. Washington had early notice of the movement, and a detachment of his army under Arnold entered Philadelphia as the British rear guard was crossing the river. Clinton had issued stringent orders for camp followers to be left behind and for the impedimenta to be sent by water. But his directions had not been much regarded. The baggage train extended over twelve miles of road, and the army hardly made more than thirty miles in ten days. On June 28 it was in the vicinity of Monmouth Court House. By this time Washington, with his soldiers well in hand, caught up with the British, and a sharp action took place. He had designed the command of the attacking force for Lafayette, but Charles Lee had returned from captivity just in time to demand the post of honor as the senior major-general. At first all went well. It seemed that now, at last, Washington was to be victorious in a pitched

---

[1] The instructions to Clinton of March 8, 1778 ("Stevens Facsimiles," No. 1062, *Stopford-Sackville Papers*, ii, 94), were written before the existence of the Franco-American treaties was surely known in England. It is interesting to read it in connection with the dispatches of March 21, after the French attitude had been disclosed. These are printed in "Stevens's Facsimiles," Nos. 1068, 1069.

Sparks had seen these papers, and gives the gist of them very accurately (*Life and Writings of Washington*, v, 548-551).

battle with a British army. Then Lee made some incomprehensible and wholly disastrous movements which lost to the American soldiers the advantages they had gained and gave the enemy a chance to threaten their left flank. Washington, coming to the front, sent Lee off the field and reëstablished the fight.[1] The happy moment had passed, and the following night Clinton made off by the "light of the moon." He pursued the rest of his march more expeditiously than he had the first part of it, and reached the shores of New York Bay in safety.

In those days French naval policy and that of Spain demanded fine large ships, splendidly armed, but there their ideas stopped. There was no adequate permanent personnel, and training and discipline were of the slightest. At this moment, too, naval officers as a class were abnormally inefficient; it was necessary to seek admirals from the army. It was thus that Count D'Estaing, a soldier, found himself in command of the Toulon fleet, one of his captains being Suffren, whom youth and naval tradition kept from the highest command. French tactics looked to the gaining of some definite object as the result of a naval campaign and not the winning of fleet battles or single ship combats. Thus De Guichen's constant refusal to give battle to the British in 1779 won for France the West Indian campaign of that year; while, on the other hand, Rodney's destruction of a part of De Grasse's fleet in 1782

[1] Journal of Henry Dearborn in Massachusetts Historical Society's *Proceedings* for 1886, p. 115. John Fiske has an interesting and scholarly paper on "Charles Lee, the Soldier of Fortune" in his *Essays, Historical and Literary*, i, 55. It is well to remember that Charles Lee, although living in Virginia in 1775, was no relation to the Virginia Lees. The *Proceedings of a General Court Martial*, which was held in July and August, 1778, were printed by Dunlap in 1798, but may most conveniently be consulted in the volumes of the New York Historical Society's *Collections*, "Lee Papers," ii. These four volumes contain nearly everything appertaining to Lee, including a reprint of George H. Moore's *Treason of Charles Lee*, which was originally published in 1860.

turned the scale in favor of the British. Had De Grasse succeeded in holding off Rodney in 1782, as De Guichen did in 1779, the terms of the treaties of 1783 might have been quite different. One's sympathies are always with the dashing fighter, and American naval ideas have gone with those of England rather than with those of France, which has somewhat obscured the part actually played by the French in the later portion of the Revolutionary War.

D'Estaing reached the Delaware on July 8, to find that Howe had sailed thence with his warships and a miscellaneous fleet of transports and cargo ships for New York. He followed him, and anchored off Sandy Hook three days later. For eleven days the French held their station there, being busily engaged in sounding the channels leading over the bar. Lord Howe's American command was not the glorious period of his career,[1] but now he showed a degree of energy worthy of the victor of June 1, 1794. Distinctly inferior to the French, he gathered every possible bit of assistance that could be found within the British lines, the crews of the transports and privateers volunteering to make good his deficiencies in numbers. Suddenly, on July 22, when the depth of water on the outer bar rose to thirty feet — ample for the passage of the biggest French liner [2] — D'Estaing stood out to sea, and was next heard from off Newport. Treachery or unwillingness of pilots has always been alleged as the reason for this sudden turn-about; but the

[1] Admiral Howe was severely criticised for his naval mismanagement in America, as in Joseph Galloway's *Letter to the Right Honourable Lord Viscount H— E, on his Naval conduct in the American War*, London, 1779. On the other side may be noted a *Candid and Impartial Narrative of the Transactions of the Fleet under the command of Lord Howe . . . by an Officer then serving in the Fleet*, London, 1779. This is reprinted in C. Ekins's *Naval Battles from 1744 to the Peace in 1814 critically Reviewed and Illustrated* (London, 1824, pp. 57-73). This volume has also a plan showing the disposition of Howe's fleet.

[2] *Ibid.*, p. 62.

necessity of keeping his fleet intact, or possibly some
knowledge of the approach of Commodore Byron, may
have impelled him to this action.

The holding of Newport by the British was due partly
to the king's sentimental desire to retain a bit of New
England soil within his grasp; but crude geographical
conception may have had something to do with it, for
it certainly had no place in any well-considered military
scheme. An attack on New York being out of the
question, one upon Newport was substituted for it,
General Sullivan being in command of the land force,
with Greene and Lafayette under him. Delays were
inevitable in combined military and naval operations,
especially where the coöperating forces belonged to different nations. In this case, also, the army consisted
partly of New England militiamen who had to be assembled for the occasion. For one reason or another the
attack was postponed until well into August. Meantime
reënforcements had at length come to Howe. His strength
was still inferior to that of the French, but nevertheless
he sailed from New York to give them battle. A terrific
storm came upon the fleets while they were still manœuvering for position. D'Estaing's flagship was dismasted
and other vessels were so injured that he sailed for Boston
to refit. His going left the Americans in rather bad case,
for they had crossed over to Rhode Island from the
mainland; but fortune and skill enabled them to retire
with small loss. The whole affair aroused so much
bitterness of feeling between the New Englanders and
the French that Washington and Lafayette had to
intervene.[1]

---

[1] The story of this abortive operation is told by Winsor, with abundant citations, in his *America* (vi, 592–603). See also Edward Field's *Diary of Colonel Israel Angell, 1778–1781.*

In November, D'Estaing sailed for the West Indies and was preceded and followed by two English squadrons In September, the Marquis de Bouillé had taken Dominica from the British, but this success was neutralized by the loss of St. Lucia in December, owing largely to the delays of D'Estaing. On the other hand, the arrival of the British squadrons threatened the very life of the French fleet; but in January, 1779, D'Estaing made good his retreat to Fort Royal, Martinique. In the summer, the French renewed their victorious career, capturing St. Vincent and Grenada. In September D'Estaing sailed from Hayti. At first it was supposed he was bound for Jamaica; but he was next sighted off the coast of Georgia, for he had gone northward to aid the Americans in an attempt to drive the British from Savannah, which they had seized in the preceding December. This particular enterprise failed ignominiously. The presence of the French fleet on the coast, however, induced Clinton to withdraw the British garrison from Newport. On the whole, D'Estaing's cruise greatly assisted the American cause by bringing about a detachment from Clinton's army to the West Indies, by securing the evacuation of Philadelphia and Newport, and by causing very considerable expenditures in British men and money in the islands.

In Europe, too, although the battle off Ushant in July, 1778, had been one of those indecisive actions in which both sides claimed to have been victorious, French intervention had produced important results. The necessity of defending the British islands from invasion and of being prepared for rebellion in Ireland, with or without French assistance, meant greatly increased expenditures and the diversion of labor and capital from productive employment

1778] 301

to the pursuits of war. With the beginning of hostilities between France and Great Britain, a safe basis for action was opened to American privateers for the whole length of the Channel and along the greater part of the shores of the Bay of Biscay. Hitherto, they had operated under every disadvantage of distance from home, and with only clandestine connivance in French and Spanish ports. Now they were able to devote their whole energies to the despoiling of the British, even within sight of their own shores. It was hard to distinguish between French and American privateers in those days, for many of the most enterprising American seamen were employed at high wages by French shipowners. Combined, they certainly inflicted great damage on British property, and caused vast expenditure on the part of the government and the local authorities in preparing to repel invaders who never appeared. In June, 1779, Spain joined France, and the area of war again widened. At once the Spaniards began the blockade of Gibraltar, which was so seriously pushed that it amounted almost to a besiegement. In July a combined French and Spanish fleet appeared in the Channel, and might have effected a lodgment on the British coast at Plymouth or elsewhere, had they attacked at once. Such was not the habit of Frenchmen and Spaniards in combination. At this time, too, a virulent plague turned the Spanish vessels into pest ships. They returned to their several ports, having aroused panic in many parts of England, but without much other result. In America, owing to the unsanitary conditions of Spanish ships and armies, little was accomplished in proportion to the great efforts that were made. Soldiers were sent over by the thousand, and a great fleet appeared in 1780 at San Domingo. Plans were laid for the capture of Jamaica and for turning the British out of the West Indies,

entirely. The only results, beyond holding their own possessions, were the capture of Mobile and Pensacola, in March
and May, 1780, the possession of St. Joseph in the Great
Lake region for one day, and the encouragement given to
the trans-Alleghany pioneers in their warfare against the
British.

One of the most significant facts of the Revolutionary
period is the constant migration that was going on from
the old colonies to the country west of the Alleghanies.
It did not cease with Lexington and Bunker Hill, but
continued well into the war. North of the Ohio were the
old French settlements in the Illinois country, at Kaskaskia
and Vincennes, and the stations on or near the Great Lakes,
at St. Joseph and Detroit. Lieutenant-Governor Henry
Hamilton was active in urging the Indians of the Northwest to attack the settlers across the Ohio, in Kentucky
and Tennessee. This pressure, in turn, brought George
Rogers Clark and a small band of Kentuckians across the
river into the Northwestern country. Clark had a commission from Patrick Henry, who was then governor of
Virginia, but his supplies and men were pitifully inadequate to turn the British out of the Illinois country. With
commingled craft and military spirit, he captured the
French villages. In the winter following, Hamilton came
southward from Detroit and occupied Vincennes. Now
Clark showed wonderful audacity. He gathered recruits
from the French villagers. With them and a few of his
original band, he marched through storms and floods and
appeared before Hamilton as one dropped from the sky.
No adequate preparations had been made to repel so
formidable and unexpected an attack. Hamilton surrendered, and the Northwest definitely passed into American
hands. The Illinois country was made into a Virginia

county, and was governed or misgoverned as such.[1]   A
Frenchman, La Balme, once of Armand's legion, led a
mixed band of French and Indians toward Detroit.   He
was killed and his followers disappeared, but the attempt
itself has the marks of underhandedness on the part of the
French.   The same might be said as to the Spanish expedition from St. Louis in 1781; but the evidence on these
points is still so vague and contradictory that it will be
best to leave them here and turn to the war on the Atlantic
seaboard.

The years 1778–80 saw no improvement in the condition of Washington's army.   Every winter his force
dwindled to three or four thousand, to be increased by new
levies in the summer.   All the time his soldiers were half
starved and half clothed.   Continental currency was at its
point of lowest discredit.   The prospect of French assistance in men and money paralyzed whatever efforts the
radicals might otherwise have made.   In these years, too,
the British plan of campaign on the continent underwent
a radical alteration.   There was no longer any thought of
an immediate military conquest of the northern colonies.
The attention of the British was toward the South; they
confined themselves in the North to holding what they
possessed and to making predatory attacks on New England seacoast villages.   Washington had not force enough

---

[1] See F. J. Turner's "Western State
Making in the Revolutionary Era" in
American Historical Review, i, 70.
    Clarence W. Alvord's "Introduc-
tion" to the Virginia volumes of the
Collections of the Illinois State Historical Library, while not containing a
formal bibliography of printed books,
refers to practically all of the more
important ones in the footnotes.   This
volume, with C. E. Carter's *Great Britain
and the Illinois Country, 1763–1774,* and

J. A. James's forthcoming life of Clark,
will furnish, practically, a complete
treatment of this part of our history.
W. H. English's *Conquest of the Northwest* (2 vols. Indianapolis, 1896) is important on account of the documents
printed at the end of the first volume.
An interesting address by Judge John
P. Hand of the Illinois supreme court is
in the *Henry County Advocate* for
August 20, 1908.

to justify an assault on New York, so that the American
northern army was for the most part quiescent.   The
storming of Stony Point and the treason of Benedict
Arnold stand forth almost alone as requiring record.

In May, 1779, Clinton ascended the Hudson and took possession of Verplanck Point and of Stony Point opposite, and
thus held the lower end of the Highlands.   This compelled
Washington with the main army to draw in his posts. On the
night of the 16th and 17th of July, General Wayne, with a
picked body of troops made a well executed attack on
Stony Point.[1]   He captured the post ; but Washington had
not force enough to justify its permanent occupation, and,
being abandoned, it was again occupied by the British,
and by them finally evacuated in the closing months of
the year.   The success to British arms that could not be
gained on the field of war might possibly be purchased
by money.

In Britain the king was buying support in Parliament.
Why should he not purchase radicals in America as well
as whigs in England ?   American generals or British parliamentarians, — what was the difference ?   Germain had
already informed Clinton that their royal master would
be glad to encourage treachery and would not mind the
expense.   There is an interesting memorandum in Clinton's handwriting as to the probability of purchasing
American military men with money and rank in the
British army.   He recognized the hopelessness of corrupt-
ing Washington, but suggested the possibility of pur-

[1] Stony Point has attracted attention
on account of the brilliancy of the action
and also by reason of the later career of
General Wayne. See H. B. Dawson's
study in his *Gleanings from American
History*, Pt. xi; H. P. Johnston's *Storming of Stony Point ;* and the descriptions
of the battle in the memoirs by Isaac
Wayne (*The Casket* for 1829, No. 7), by
Charles J. Stillé, and by J. R. Spears.
There is a copy of Wayne's letter to
Washington of July 17, 1779, in *Historic
Letters* compiled by G. M. Philips. In
substance this is the same as the letter
printed by Dawson.

chasing that somewhat incapable soldier, Major General
Israel Putnam.   There has been a good deal of debate as to how far Clinton proceeded with various
personages, but there is no doubt whatever as to Benedict Arnold.   The only question that can arise as to him
is as to his motives.   Was he seeking to play the part of
General Monk, the restorer of the Stuarts, or was he
guided by a genuine belief in the hopelessness of the American cause, and a desire to end the ills of his countrymen
for their good?   Ten thousand guineas [1] and a major-general's commission were the price for which West Point,
with its garrison, stores, and outlying forts, was to be
placed in the hands of the British.

The correspondence which had been going on between
Arnold and the British headquarters for some time had
been conducted with John André, Clinton's adjutant, who
concealed his identity under the name of John Anderson.
André was the logical person to conclude the negotiations,
with the potential traitor, and he went at his own request.
In sending him on so dangerous a mission, the British commander-in-chief charged him not to go within the enemy's
lines, not to disguise his person, and to have nothing to do
with incriminating papers.   André sailed up the Hudson
in the sloop-of-war *Vulture*, which anchored off Teller's
Point, almost opposite Haverstraw and from sixteen to
eighteen miles below West Point.   There a boat containing Joshua Hett Smith and two rowers came off to the
man of war.   Smith gained the deck unannounced, and
stated that his errand was to convey John Anderson to the
shore to meet General Arnold.   Throwing a long military
cloak over his scarlet uniform, André went ashore, found

[1] In January, 1781, James Meyrick of
London invested for Arnold five thousand pounds sterling in " the new consolidated annuities " at 72¼ per cent: see
Magazine of American History, xv, 89.

x

Arnold, and passed the night conferring with him. About daylight Arnold suggested that they would better go to Smith's house to conclude their debate. He had horses near by, and, mounting, the two rode between four and five miles to the mansion. On the way André was startled by the challenge of a sentry, but the password and the counter-sign were given by the commandant, and the conspirators entered the American lines without attracting notice. While they were breakfasting, or perhaps a little later, they suddenly heard the sound of guns, and looking out discovered that the *Vulture* was being fired upon from the opposite shore. It seems that Colonel James Livingston, seeing a hostile vessel so near to the bank, had borrowed a four-pounder and had opened fire on his own responsibility. The *Vulture* fell down stream, and when evening came, Smith refused to convey André by water to the vessel. Arnold had long since departed for West Point, after entrusting André with plans of the fortification, which the latter placed inside of his stocking. Smith said that he would set him across the river, provide him with a horse, and accompany him to the outposts, Arnold having given André a pass for this purpose. To avoid accident in case the cloak should blow up and one should see the scarlet uniform, Smith advised André to substitute for it a long blue coat. It was thus in disguise and with concealed papers, that André was captured two days later by a band of irregulars on the Neutral Ground between the outposts of the two armies on the eastern bank of the Hudson River. His captors refused to permit him to proceed, although he offered a large sum if they would release him. Instead, they took him to the nearest American outpost. The commander there at once sent a note to Arnold, apprizing him of the capture of John Anderson.

Without an instant's delay, Arnold embarked on a boat, and descending the river reached the *Vulture*, and in her proceeded to New York.[1] Shortly after his departure, Washington arrived at West Point. He at once realized that all was not right, and made dispositions to guard against any possible danger. When, at length, after a long roundabout journey, André was brought to Fort Putnam near West Point, Washington requested the general officers of the American force in the Highlands to inquire into the status of the captive and report to him. The chairman of this court of inquiry was General Nathanael Greene. Among those who aided him were Lafayette and Steuben. No soldier in America was better versed in the military art in all its details than Greene ; Steuben in the course of long experience had gained familiarity with the practice of European armies, while Lafayette spoke both English and French, and could, therefore, interpret everything that passed. The report of the fourteen officers was that " Major André ought to be considered as a spy from the enemy, and that agreeably to the law and usage of nations, it is their opinion he ought to suffer death." It is well to add, that on his examination by the board, André explicitly stated " that the boat in which he came ashore carried no flag "; that he did not consider himself under the protection of a flag, " and that if he had, he certainly might have returned under it." Steuben's words are also interesting : " It is not possible to save him. He put us to no proof, but in an open, manly manner confessed everything, but a premeditated design to deceive." On the second day of October, 1780, he was executed as a spy.

---

[1] What one English officer at New York thought of Arnold comes out in a letter written to Lord Herbert, October 26, 1780, stating that Arnold is to " raise a regiment of as great scoundrels as himself, if he can find them." Royal Historical Manuscripts Commission's *Reports*, ix, Pt. ii, p. 383.

The winter of 1780–81 saw the turning of the tide of war. In October preceding, at King's Mountain, the settlers of the southwest had set a term to Cornwallis's conquering career. In April of the following spring the van of De Grasse's mighty armament was descried by the lookouts on the British fleet coming around the southern end of Martinique. His advent was to give sea power to the allies for one supreme month in the coming autumn and place an English army at their mercy. Throughout the war American ships had sailed the ocean and had powerfully affected the fortunes of Britain, but they had never acted together in formidable array. Of them all, the *Bon Homme Richard* stands first in recollection, although she was scarcely American, except for the flag that flew at her peak. She was a decayed fourteen-year-old French Indiaman, provided by His Most Christian Majesty for that prince of sea-fighters, John Paul Jones. Her decks were too weak for her guns, her guns were too old for service, and her crew was ill-assorted, and of many nationalities. Jones himself was a Scotsman who had settled in America shortly before the war. Of her 227 officers and men, only seventy-nine were " Americans," the rest being Jones's own countrymen, Irishmen, Scandinavians, and Portuguese, while 137 French soldiers served as marines. She had four consorts, the American frigate, *Alliance*, commanded by Landais, whose mind was even then clouded with insanity, and three French vessels, one of them being the *Pallas*, whose captain was named Cottineau. On September 23, 1779, Jones sighted a fleet of British merchantmen bound for the Baltic under the convoy of two vessels, one a fine new large frigate, the *Serapis*, the other a smaller ship. The merchantmen at once put back and gained the shelter of Scarborough Head; the warships remained to guard their charge. In due course, Jones with the *Bon Homme Richard* came up with the *Serapis*, the *Pallas* looking after the smaller vessel and the *Alliance* remaining aloof. The *Richard* was dull and heavy in the water, and the light wind gave the newly launched Englishman great advantage. With consummate seamanship, Jones placed his reformed Indiaman alongside the British frigate and lashed her there with a two-inch hawser. At the first discharge one of his heaviest guns burst, killing its crew— the rest of the battery was abandoned. With the lighter guns Jones made play as long as he could, but the balls from the *Serapis* soon ranged almost at will through the *Richard's* gun deck. Again and again she caught fire, and one officer after another came to Jones, entreating him to surrender. The English prisoners in the hold were treacherously set free, but they were compelled to man the pumps before they were able to do mischief. Meantime, the fire of the Frenchmen in the tops had cleared the spar deck of the *Serapis* of officers and men. Then some men running along the yard from the *Richard* to the *Serapis* gained the British maintop and threw hand grenades down her open hatchway to the deck beneath. One of these caught some loose powder, and flashing along set fire to the cartridges that stood near the guns. At almost the same moment, the *Alliance* coming up, fired into friend and foe alike, shrouded as they were in the smoke of the conflict and conflagration. The *Serapis* surrendered, as did her consort. After the battle the *Richard* was abandoned. The effect of this exploit was tremendous. It is reflected in the letter of Sandwich, First Lord of the Admiralty, imploring Captain Reynolds to get to sea instantly, declaring that if he took Paul Jones, he would be as high in public estimation as if he had beaten the combined fleets of France and Spain.

Jones in the *Serapis* sought refuge in the Texel where she
was taken from him to satisfy the laws of neutrality.   He
was never able, for one reason or another, again to have
a fleet under his orders during the last years of the war.

There were many other valiant deeds on the seas; but
they had little effect on the war as a whole.   Among the
national ships was the *Trumbull*, Captain James Nicholson.
On the first day of June, 1780, she fell in with the British
letter-of-marque, the *Watt*, carrying more guns and a larger
crew.   For three hours they bombarded one another at
a distance of from fifty to eighty yards.   Then Nicholson
bore away to try to save his masts that were tottering;
but two of them went over the side.   The Englishman,
too, had had enough of it, his loss in killed and wounded
exceeding that on the American ship.   In the next year,
while carrying a cargo of flour to Havanna, the *Trumbull*
was set upon and captured by two British ships.   Nicholson fought this action under every disadvantage.   Only a
few hours before the *Trumbull's* foretopmast had been
carried away in a squall.   Of her crew of one hundred
and eighty men only forty took part in the combat.
Among the rest were forty-five British prisoners who
had enlisted as the price of release from confinement
on shore.   Some of the States had warships of their
own.   The most famous of these was the Massachusetts
ship *Protector*, of twenty-six guns, Captain John Foster
Williams.[1]   In June, 1780, while cruising off the Grand
Banks, she met a British West Indiaman of equal force,
the *Admiral Duff*.   She was the larger, floated higher in
the water, and her guns were well served.   From the tops
of the *Protector* sixty marines, all Americans, killed the
British topmen and then shot down the men at the wheel.

[1] "Memoirs of Captain Luther Little" (Ms.).

The two ships came together; the *Duff's* rigging caught fire and the flames, running downward, exploded a hogshead of cartridges under her quarterdeck and blew it off. She sank, only fifty-five of her crew being rescued.[1]

More than two thousand American privateers ranged the seas at one time or another. They swarmed in the West Indies; they cruised along the Atlantic coasts; they sought their prey in the British Channel and the North Sea.[2] They actually cruised off the ports of Spain, in plain sight from the shore, capturing British vessels laden with fish from Newfoundland, — selling ships and cargo to the Spaniards at much below their value. In 1781, the Cabots of Beverley received six hundred thousand riales of vellon for their half share in five prizes, the Gardoquis getting the rest. The Derbys of Salem[3] got over sixty thousand dollars on account of prizes that were sold at Bilbao. In one way privateering was an evil, because the privateers and letters of marque attracted men from the decks of regular warships, from the ranks of the army, and from the fields and shops. But they added greatly to the expenditure of the British, interfered with the transport service, and made government and people more willing to acquiesce in American independence.

[1] The bibliography of the naval history of the Revolution is given by Mr. Winsor himself, in his *America*, vi, 589. Books which have appeared since this list was made will be noted, with the best of the older ones, in Gardner W. Allen's forthcoming *History of the Navy in the Revolution*.

[2] Some of these privateers were really French or Spanish vessels with foreign crews, the captain and possibly one or two other officers being American. After 1777 many American seamen were to be found in French privateers. See Almon's *Remembrancer*, v, 141, 142, etc. On the general subject of Revolutionary privateers see Maclay's *American Privateers;* Goodrich's "Naval Side of the Revolutionary War" in the *Papers* (vol. xi) of the Military Historical Society of Massachusetts; "Revolutionary Letters" from George Williams to Timothy Pickering in the *Essex Institute Historical Collections*, vol. xlii, 313 and fol. Among the local histories are Currier's *Newburyport* and Stone's *Beverly*. See also *New England Historical Genealogical Register* for 1869, p. 50; the *Deane Papers* and the *Lee Papers* in the *Collections* of the New York Historical Society; and the *Journals of Congress*. The estimate as to their number is taken from the advance sheets of Dr. Gardner W. Allen's *History of the Navy in the Revolution*.

[3] See Robert E. Peabody's paper on "The Derbys of Salem" in Essex Institute's *Historical Collections*, vol. xliv.

NOTES

I. Foreign Views. — Carlo Botta's *Storia della Guerra dell' Independenza degli Stati Uniti D'America* (4 vols., Paris, 1809) is the best extended foreign view. It was translated into English by G. A. Otis as *History of the War of the Independence of the United States* (3 vols., Boston, 1820–21). Of less bulk and more philosophical is Adolphe de Circourt's "Conclusions Historiques" appended to the second volume of his translation [1] of Bancroft's tenth volume (pp. 251–344). Henri Doniol's *Histoire de la Participation de la France à l'Établissement des États-Unis d'Amérique* (Paris, 1886, 5 vols.) approaches as nearly as any historical work can to finality, and tends to the destruction of feelings of American gratitude to France and Vergennes. François Soulés's *Histoire des Troubles de L'Amérique Anglaise* (4 vols., Paris, 1787) is contemporaneous, and sometimes reflects the opinions of participants.

II. Arnold and André. — Isaac N. Arnold's *Life of Benedict Arnold* (Chicago, 1880) says all that can be said for Arnold.[2] Around André's tragic fate has arisen a mass of literature which is listed in William Abbatt's *Crisis of the Revolution, Being the Story of Arnold and André* (New York, 1899). This volume, which was issued under the auspices of the Empire State Society, Sons of the Revolution, has about all there is to say on this subject, and is superbly illustrated. An older book which is still a standard work is Winthrop Sargent's *Life of André*, which was first published with a slightly different title. The *Proceedings of a Board of General Officers respecting Major André* was published at Philadelphia in 1780, and has been reprinted more or less fully in various places. The subject of the execution is most carefully examined by Herbert

[1] The title of this work is *Histoire de l'action commune de la France et de l'Amérique pour l'Independance des États-Unis par George Bancroft . . . traduit et Annoté par le Comte Adolphe de Circourt, Accompagné de documents inédits.* The documents form vol. iii. Circourt's "Conclusions Historiques"

is translated in the *Proceedings* of the Massachusetts Historical Society, First Series, xv, 16–64.

[2] "The Treason of Benedict Arnold, as presented in Letters of Sir Henry Clinton to Lord George Germain" is in *Pennsylvania Magazine of History*, xxii, 410.

Haines, with specific references to authorities, in the *English Historical Review*, v, 31. An excellent brief article is that by Henry P. Johnston in the *Magazine of American History*, viii, 717.

André's case has often been compared with that of Nathan Hale; but the two are strikingly dissimilar. Hale was securing information for his general; André was seducing the enemy. Henry P. Johnston's *Nathan Hale* possesses all the high qualities of workmanship of this author.

Charges of treasonable conduct have been made against General John Sullivan and General S. H. Parsons, and repelled most vigorously by descendant and biographer. See C. S. Hall's *Life and Letters of Samuel Holden Parsons* (Binghamton, 1905), ch. xxiv; and G. B. Loring in *Magazine of American History*, xx, 286. These charges originated in "Clinton's Secret Intelligence" in *Magazine of American History*, x, 503. The statements upon which Sullivan's memory was attacked are in *ibid.*, xi, 156. Ever anxious for his ancestor's fame, T. C. Amory defended him in *ibid.*, xi, 353, and also in the *Proceedings* of the Massachusetts Historical Society, Second Series, i, 47. See also, on a somewhat similar subject, his *General Sullivan not a Pensioner of Luzerne*.

III. John Paul Jones. — Because of the *Bon Homme Richard* episode and of his own meteoric character, Jones's career has attracted great interest. The biographies of him that have been printed up to the present time[1] are all poor reading except that by Buell. This last is a work of fiction — as its author invented manuscripts and books, whenever so doing served his purposes. See C. O. Paullin in the *Proceedings* of the United States Naval Institute, for March, 1910.[2] C. H. Hart and E. C. Biddle in their *Life and Works of Jean Antoine Houdon* (Philadephia, 1911, p. 152) point out that Buell cites as authority for the height and physical proportions of Jones a volume which has no existence, and never had. Curiously enough, it is upon this mythical book that the identification and the recovery of the body of the father of the American navy depends.[3]

The *Bon Homme Richard-Serapis* combat is admirably described

---

[1] See "Editorial Note" in Winsor's *America*, vi, 589. In 1903 the Library of Congress published a *Calendar of John Paul Jones Manuscripts* in that Library.

[2] Buell's account of Jones's Virginia estate is exposed in "Some Facts about John Paul Jones" by Junius Davis in *South Atlantic Quarterly*.

[3] The government, in 1907, printed a volume on the *John Paul Jones Commemoration at Annapolis, April 24, 1906*, giving details of the finding of the body and its removal to America.

by Captain Mahan in *Scribner's Magazine*, xxiv, p. 22. Jones's account and that of Captain Pearson of the *Serapis* are widely printed, and they may advantageously be compared and read in connection with the account in the *Memoirs* of Captain Nathaniel Fanning, p. 41, and with those of onlookers from the shore, as that by Samuel Beilby in Royal Historical Manuscripts Commission's *Reports*, xiv, Appendix, Pt. i, p. 21. See also *The Logs of the Serapis — Alliance — Ariel under the command of John Paul Jones, 1779–1780*, and Fanning's *Narrative*, both edited by John S. Barnes and included in the publications of the Naval History Society, as vols. i and ii.

CHAPTER XI

THE WINNING OF INDEPENDENCE

In the winter of 1779–80, Lafayette returned to France and convinced the king and his ministers that it was absolutely necessary to send an army to continental America, if the guarantee of independence in the Treaty of Alliance was to be something more than a mere writing. Probably the separation of the British empire into two parts was fore-ordained. The tremendous conflict that Britain now had on her hands was already straining her resources to the very utmost. France, too, was rapidly descending into bankruptcy. The outcome of the war, indeed, was dependent upon whether Great Britain or the Bourbon powers could hold out the longer, and the probabilities all pointed to the former's prior exhaustion. In the determination of this issue, it mattered little whether Rochambeau's army was in North America, the West Indies, or Ireland. Nevertheless the king yielded to Lafayette's entreaties, and a force of 7500 men, comprising some of the best regiments in the French service and officered by men whose names were famous, or were to become so, was gathered together and marched to the seaboard for embarkation.[1] It was found to be impossible to send them all at once, but enough vessels to carry 5500 of them with supplies and equipment were procured. Lafayette himself desired the command of this expedition, but it was given to the

[1] For the books relating to the French coöperation, see Note II at end of chapter. Among the officers in Rochambeau's force were two of Napoleon's marshals, Berthier and Dumas. One of his aides was Count Fersen, who drove Louis XVI on the first stage of his ill-omened flight. See Wharton's *Diplomatic Correspondence*, i, 401, 404, 407.

Comte de Rochambeau, a much older and more experienced soldier. On July 10, 1780, this fleet anchored in

THE WAR IN THE SOUTH

(From Gordon's *History of the Independence of the United States*)

Newport Harbor. At the moment Sir Henry Clinton was
at New York, whither he had hastily returned after

receiving the surrender of Charleston from General Benjamin Lincoln.

The plan of the southern campaigns came from England, and was due to the persistent counselings of the exiled royal governors of South Carolina and Georgia. These represented that the loyalists were numerous in those States and would coöperate most efficiently with a British army. A whole State might be conquered, or even two or three, and from this southern base the army might work northward to the conquest of Virginia. A beginning was made by the seizure of Savannah in one of the last days of December, 1778. No serious opposition was offered, and the British spread into the interior with the assistance of a force that came from St. Augustine in Florida, under the command of General Prevost. When it became clear that the attack on the South was no mere raid, but was the beginning of a serious attempt at occupation, a few thousand men were detached from the main continental army and sent southward under the command of Benjamin Lincoln, who had gained renown in the Saratoga campaign. The details of the operations in the year 1779 in South Carolina are somewhat vague.[1] Prevost was unable to capture Charleston, although he seriously threatened that town. On the other hand, Lincoln, while he was able to compel Prevost to let go his hold on Charleston, could not turn him out of Savannah. Affairs were in this order, when D'Estaing sailed into the Savannah River with a portion of his fleet and essayed the capture of the town in conjunction with Lincoln. Here, again, coöperation was not successful, although exactly why the attempt failed is still a matter of dispute. D'Estaing's men were sickly;

---

[1] The "Journal of Major F. Skelly" (*Magazine of American History*, xxvi, 152, 393) covers this operation to June, 1779.

he was acting more or less against the general tenor of his instructions, and possibly hastened operations unduly. At all events, after a futile assault he gave over the attempt and sailed for France, passing up the coast on his way. The end of the year, therefore, found the southern combatants in much the same situation that they had been in the spring. The departure of D'Estaing for Europe left the sea open to Clinton. He promptly took advantage of this by sailing from New York with about seven thousand men for South Carolina on December 26, 1779.[1] Instead of again attempting to take his troops into Charleston Harbor he disembarked them at some distance to the southward and advanced overland to the conquest of the city. Lincoln might have left Charleston to its fate and preserved his soldiers for a field campaign. He chose to shut himself in the town, and was captured with his army by the British in May, 1780.[2] Clinton had with him the two most enterprising military men who appeared on the British side during the war, Lord Cornwallis and Lieutenant-Colonel Banastre Tarleton. In the weeks after the capture of Charleston they won several battles in the interior, and these early successes misled Clinton as to the scope and permanency of his conquest. He issued two proclamations direfully threatening those who remained contumacious. He then sailed northward to look after Rochambeau and the Frenchmen. The fleet, which was commanded by Admiral Arbuthnot, reached Newport too late to do more than blockade the port, and Clinton while trying to act in coöperation with the navy was promptly called back by

---

[1] "Journal of Captain Peter Russell, Dec. 25, 1779–May 3, 1780" in *American Historical Review*, iv, 479–501. This journal is very useful for identifying dates and other particulars.

[2] Besides the authorities noted in Winsor's *America*, vi, 524, see the papers printed in the Appendix to the *Charleston Year Book* for 1897, and in the *North Carolina Records*, xiv, xv.

the appearance of ten thousand men or more with Washington at their head in the neighborhood of the Harlem
River.

When Lincoln's misfortune was known in the North,
several regiments were detached from the main army
to act in conjunction with the militia of Virginia and
of the Carolinas. The task of rescuing the South from
the invader was entrusted to Horatio Gates, General Kalb
having command of the Continental contingent. All went
well with the little force until North Carolina was reached,
when progress became every day more painful. The
country was sparsely settled, the farmers were very
poor, and the roads were few and far between. Militiamen from Virginia and North Carolina joined the expedition, and added to the difficulty of procuring supplies in
sufficiently large quantities for the soldiers' needs. Gates
and Kalb used every endeavor to push forward, but their
progress was necessarily slow. By this time the British
had collected stores at Camden, which stands on the
principal road from Charleston to the interior. Gates
concentrated his force at Rugely's Mills, about seventeen
or eighteen miles to the northward. Cornwallis had been
absent from the front for some time, but returned
at this moment. The two commanders determined
each to surprise the other, and set out from their
respective quarters in the same night. The heads of
the two forces came together near Sanders Creek about
midway between the two starting points. The position
in which the Americans found themselves was trying
to undisciplined soldiers, as most of Gates's men were.
They took up their stations in good order, but, when the
dawning light of August 16 showed the enemy in motion
to attack them, the militiamen made off without firing

many shots.   The regulars, on the other hand, stood so
firmly in their ranks that the British killed or captured
nearly every one of them.   Caught in the mass of fleeing militiamen, Gates was hurried to the rear.   Night
found him miles and miles away from the scene of the
battle.[1]   His career was at an end.   No inquiry was ever
held as to his conduct, for Greene advised against it; but
he was not again employed in the field.

This victory, which is always called the battle of Camden, greatly heartened the British, but nothing could
dismay Sumter, Marion, Pickens, and other partisan
leaders in the Carolinas.   They were many times defeated
and driven into hiding, but they always appeared again
in unexpected places.   They beset the roads, shot down
the messengers from one British force to another, and
captured convoys of supplies and bands of loyalists.
Moreover, local loyalist levies could not be relied on for
faithful service, — they constantly surrendered to inferior
bodies of radicals and sometimes went over to the Americans without any visible reason.[2]   It fell out in this way,
therefore, that although the British had captured one
American army and destroyed another, Cornwallis was ex-
periencing to the full the perils of operating in the interior
of the Southern States, which had been so graphically set before Lord Dartmouth by Lord Barrington in October, 1775.

---

[1] Selections from the " Gates Papers "
in the fourteenth volume of the *North
Carolina Records* (pp. 496–768) form an
important   addition   to   the   printed
sources.   Governor   Martin   was   at
Camden during the battle; his account
is in *ibid.*, xv, 49.   Gates's force is given
in a return (*North Carolina Records*,
xv, 162) as 2604 in all; of these the
Continentals numbered 1053.   Of the
total number 431 were sick and 109 were
on furlough. An account by a participant,

but when written is not known, is " A
Sketch of the Military Services performed
by Guilford Dudley " (*Southern Literary
Messenger*, xi, 146).

[2] " Col. Robt. Gray's Observations on
the War in Carolina " (*South Carolina
Historical Magazine*, xi, 140–159) is one
of the best statements from the loyalist
side that we have.   He notes especially
the mistaken policy of the British and
the relentless cruelty of the radicals.

" There must be great danger," he wrote, " of its [a British expedition] wanting many essential necessaries, where there is so little to be had, so much desire to prevent the having that little, so much difficulty in conveying artillery, stores, provisions, &c. and so much hazard of losing communication with the ships." [1] Eight weeks after Camden, these uncertainties were brought home to Cornwallis by the disaster which befell Ferguson and his riflemen at King's Mountain.

Major Patrick Ferguson was an active officer, well skilled in frontier fighting, and his command was one of the best loyalist regiments in the British service. At the moment he had wandered far away from headquarters to secure recruits among the tories of the Upper Regions. The appearance of this expedition aroused the ire of the radical settlers in the mountains. Led by Sevier, Shelby, and Campbell, they gathered secretly and rode rapidly on the track of Ferguson and his men. Scenting danger, he had started backward to gain touch with the main army. The pioneers suddenly came upon him on a small elevated plateau, known as King's Mountain.[2] The battle that followed (October 7, 1780) was the severest action of the war since Bunker Hill. Again and again the Americans charged up the hill, and were driven back at the point of the bayonet. At last Ferguson himself was killed, hundreds of his men were dead or disabled, and the rest surrendered. Ordinarily the loss of a thousand men more or less would not mean much in war, but with an expedition like that of Cornwallis's, consisting of a few thousand only, isolated

[1] *Political Life of William Wildman, Viscount Barrington, compiled from Original Papers*, by his brother, Shute, Bishop of Durham, p. 152.
[2] Lyman C. Draper's *King's Mountain and its Heroes* is still the standard work. Not many documents eluded Draper's scent or grasp; but a few have been printed in the *North Carolina Records* (vol. xv), that were unknown to him. Oliver P. Temple's chapter on the battle in his *East Tennessee and the Civil War* is good — although somewhat uncritical in places.

in the interior parts of Carolina, the disaster was a most telling one. Its immediate effect was to induce him to order Leslie, who had been sent to Virginia by Clinton, to take his men to Charleston as fast as he could, and then to march with all speed for Camden.

The year 1781, that was to end so gloriously for America, began in deepest gloom. Every winter the army dwindled to almost nothing. Hitherto those who remained in arms had generally borne starvation and exposure with a fortitude that still arouses admiration. In the first months of this year a mutiny by the Pennsylvania line[1] for a moment seemed to foreshadow the end. At least so Sir Henry Clinton thought. He sent emissaries to extend a welcoming hand to the mutineers, but they contemptuously repelled the British beguilers. They were weary of the tergiversations of their rulers and worn down by starvation. They left the service at the first opportunity which the vacillation of the Pennsylvania governors afforded them. When some of the Jersey line, following their example, mutinied a few weeks later, Washington himself took the matter in hand. He sent a superior force from other regiments to overawe the mutineers. They returned to their duty, a few of them being at once executed. The finances were in a more deplorable condition than the army; and the people, except in the neighborhood of British forces, seemed indifferent. Washington and a handful of resolute men alone stood forth as the embodiment of a national spirit.

[1] Previously, in May, 1780, two Connecticut regiments had mutinied. The soldiers declared that they must have food or would seek it at the point of the bayonet; but their officers induced them to return to their quarters. General Knyphausen, the Hessian commander, was in charge at New York during Clinton's absence. He conceived that this moment of confusion would be opportune for a timely stroke, but he marched only a little way into New Jersey when the rising of the countryside convinced him that the sooner he regained the shore of New York Harbor, the better.

For England the case was even more desperate than it was for America. She was still on a specie-paying basis, it is true, but her credit was nearly gone. No new sources of taxation appeared, and the last loan was raised at a ruinous discount. At this moment another enemy appeared openly on the water.

Since 1776 the Dutch had permitted the Americans to make the freest use of the roadsteads and warehouses at St. Eustatia and St. Martin in the West Indies, and had received them most hospitably at Amsterdam and Rotterdam. The supply of saltpeter, which formed the basis of gunpowder, was then in the hands of the Dutch East India Company and its rival of England. The latter sold its stock to its own government; the Dutch sold much of theirs to the Americans. They took Virginia tobacco in exchange, and when this was lacking sold them gunpowder and steel and whatever else they wanted on credit. Toward the close of 1780, the English became aware that a treaty was actually in agitation between America and Holland, and declared war. England's commercial success and her arrogant attitude toward her competitors had angered others besides the Spaniards, the French, and the Dutch. The sea traders of northern Europe saw their opportunity in the prevailing contest. They set up their own rules as to the rights and duties of neutrals in time of war, and announced their determination to enforce them by warships if necessary. This league is hence known as the Armed Neutrality.

In the autumn of 1779 a new man was appointed to chief command of the British fleets in American waters, Sir George Brydges Rodney. He was a tory, was sixty-six years of age, and so far had distinguished himself rather as a gamester than as a sea fighter. In December,

1779, he sailed from Portsmouth, convoying a fleet of transports and supply vessels for the relief of Gibraltar. On the way he captured a small squadron of Spanish line of battle ships, saw his charge safely under the guns of the famous batteries, and then steered westward. The French commander in the West Indies was the Comte de Guichen. His fleet was superior in numbers and guns, and he was a good officer. Nevertheless Rodney was able to defeat his attempts to recapture St. Lucia, although he could not bring him to a decisive action. The fall of 1780, during the hurricane season, Rodney spent at New York, much to the dismay of Arbuthnot, who lost several thousand pounds of prize money owing to the presence of his superior on the station.[1] Besides thus getting on the worst possible terms with the admiral, Rodney also fell out with Clinton, whom he accused of overfondness for the fleshpots and theatrical entertainments of the town. Each of them wrote home refusing to serve with the other, and Arbuthnot requested to be relieved as speedily as possible.[2] Those were the days of port and gout. On the famous 12th of April, 1782, the day of his great battle with De Grasse, off Dominica, Rodney passed most of the time sitting in an armchair on the quarterdeck of the *Formidable*, a three-decker of ninety-eight guns, directing the greatest naval combat of the generation. Age, disease, and disappointment had made him a physical wreck, and account for much of the dislike which his equals and inferiors felt for him. The ill feeling between him and those

---

[1] Admiral Marriot Arbuthnot in 1780 had been fifty-five years in the navy, having entered it when he was fourteen. His encounter with Destouches was his most important service as commander-in-chief; see brief notice of him in the *Naval Chronicle*, xxiii, 265.

[2] He wrote to Stephens, secretary of the Admiralty (February 16, 1781) that all order was "violated and the Board and myself equally insulted by Sir George Rodney."

with whom he worked was among the potent providences
that made for American independence.

In December, 1780, Sir Samuel Hood sailed from England with a reënforcement of battleships for Rodney's
fleet and a large convoy of merchantmen. At about the
same time, Comte de Grasse, with a great armament, sailed
from Brest. The news of the war with Holland reached
the West Indies shortly before De Grasse. For a long
time St. Eustatia had been hated and coveted by Rodney.
It was to all intents and purposes a military and naval
arsenal for the American revolutionists and their allies.
Moreover, the British West India planters were none too
loyal, and British merchants were making fortunes at St.
Eustatia, dealing in American produce and selling to the
Americans and to British planters those things that were forbidden by acts of Parliament and dictates of patriotism
and many things, too, that Rodney needed for his ships.
It was a nest of rebels and thieves, so he said. Leaving
Hood to look out for De Grasse, Rodney himself pounced
upon St. Eustatia before the Dutch governor had begun
to prepare for defense. The spoils were tremendous, and
variously estimated from two million pounds to three
millions. The British also pursued a fleet that had left
the island a short time previously for Holland, and captured
it. For a month they kept the Dutch flag flying, and
thereby lured a vessel a day under their guns. At length
Rodney felt that his financial future was secure. He personally oversaw the selling of much of the loot, and sent the
rest to England ; the vessels carrying the latter falling into
the hands of La Motte Piquet and a French fleet. In his
rage against the cupidity of British colonial merchants, and
quite forgetful of his own, Rodney had not realized that
legally he had no right whatever to the goods that had

actually belonged to loyal Englishmen before the declaration of war. They pursued him in Parliament and
courts of law, made miserable the last ten years of
his existence, and preserved for us the facts as to St.
Eustatia and its commerce. Meantime De Grasse had
slipped by Hood and joined the French squadron at Fort
Royal, Martinique.[1]

Since July, 1780, the French army and fleet had remained
at Newport. Their presence there had brightened the
monotonous life of many a New England lady, and the
good French gold and silver had cheered the farmers and
tradesmen of Connecticut and Rhode Island. Otherwise
Rochambeau and his Frenchmen had not as yet affected the
war, except by keeping a large force immovable at New York.
In May, 1781, Barras with a few ships newly arrived from
France anchored in Newport Harbor. He brought no
troops, but reported that in the summer De Grasse would
bring his fleet northward, and with it three thousand
soldiers. Washington suggested that this accession of
force would enable the allies to capture New York. Rochambeau disapproved of the project. His published instructions
were to place himself under Washington's orders, but he
must have had secret directions, because he had no hesitation in advising De Grasse to seek the Chesapeake instead
of Sandy Hook. He further told him of the weak condition
of the American army and of the depleted state of the
Continental finances. With admirable skill De Grasse
subtracted himself and his fleet from British observation,
and sought the French colony of Hayti. There he secured
three thousand soldiers and some artillery, and borrowed
bullion from a neighboring Spanish governor. De Grasse

---

[1] Hood maintained that his failure to stop De Grasse was due to Rodney's hampering orders. See *Letters of Sir Samuel Hood*, 17–24.

sent word to Washington and Rochambeau that he was sailing for the Chesapeake with ships, soldiers, and money, that his stay on the coast would be brief, but that he hoped something solid might be accomplished. In the midst of these transactions Cornwallis sat himself down at York-town and awaited his fate. Rodney, remembering his unpleasantnesses at New York, never dreaming that De Grasse would take his whole fleet northward, and wishing also to keep in touch with the St. Eustatia treasure, sent Hood with fourteen sail of the line to follow the enemy, and himself left for England to recuperate his health in the pump room at Bath.

In the three months after King's Mountain, affairs in the Carolinas had taken on a new aspect, for Cornwallis had been given a free hand by his superiors in England and Nathanael Greene had been placed in charge of the American forces in the South. It made little difference who was in chief command in America ; Germain always encouraged insubordination in his second. When Howe was first, he encouraged Clinton ; when Clinton was first, he encouraged Cornwallis. In the latter case he even went so far as to make him practically independent of the titular commander-in-chief. The result was that between them Germain and Cornwallis again took up the design of invading North Carolina. It was in the first stages of this renewal of invasion that Nathanael Greene appeared in the South.

Of all the soldiers of the Revolution, Greene most nearly approached genius. Of Quaker family, he had perfected himself in all that pertains to war by reading every book within reach or that could be procured and by serving in the militia of his colony. He came to Boston at the head of the Rhode Island troops, attracted the attention of

Washington, and rose rapidly in rank and responsibility. He reached Charlotte in North Carolina on one of the first days of December, 1780. On his way south he gathered together what he could of men, food, clothing, and military necessaries, and left Steuben in Virginia to gather more and forward them to him. Greene had only a few hundred regulars and a variable body of militia, but his officers were of the best and could be implicitly relied upon. Foremost of them was Daniel Morgan,[1] whose presence on many a hardly contested field has been frequently noted. As yet he had exercised no important independent command. Greene, instead of keeping his little force in one body, divided it into two parts; one on either flank of the route by which Cornwallis must seek the interior of North Carolina, — if he were to carry out his intended invasion. The western body Greene entrusted to Morgan.

As soon as Morgan's presence to the west was reported to Cornwallis, he detached Tarleton and his "Legion" and some other troops to capture him, or to drive him away. It turned out far otherwise, for Morgan disposed his men so skillfully at the Cowpens (January 17, 1781) that he killed or captured nearly all of Tarleton's men, that leader and forty or fifty more escaping only by the speed of their horses. At once Morgan set about withdrawing from the field. He sent his prisoners to Virginia, without even taking time to count them. When the news of this victory came to Greene, he, too, put his part of the army in motion for Virginia, by way of Guilford Court House, and rode rapidly across the country to be at the post of danger. Now followed one of the most dramatic retreats in military annals. Cornwallis burned his heavy baggage

[1] James Graham's *Life of General Daniel Morgan* (New York, 1856) is an admirable book in point of view as well as in content; but Morgan deserves to be more widely known.

and destroyed quantities of military supplies that his men might march all the faster; but in vain. The American retreat was admirably conducted, and the forces of nature fought for the revolutionists. One river after another rose in flood, when the Americans had crossed, detaining the British a day or so. By Greene's orders all the boats on the River Dan, which flows by the boundary of Virginia and North Carolina, had been collected at one place. Passing Guilford, Greene united his two detachments, marched to the Dan, and crossed over to the Virginia side, his last boat leaving just as the head of the British columns appeared.

Cornwallis now called the loyal people of North Carolina to the royal standard. Some of them answered the summons, but the Carolina loyalists had been so harshly treated by their radical neighbors that they generally preferred to wait until the British forces had gained some decided advantage. A party of them fell into the hands of the Americans, which did not add to their enthusiasm. In a short time Greene was able to collect a numerous body of recruits. He then recrossed the Dan, entirely unannounced, and advanced with his whole force to Guilford Court House. Unhappily illness obliged Morgan to leave the field, but Greene adopted the tactics that had been so successful at the Cowpens. He placed his militia in two lines in the front; his regulars he posted on a strong position in the rear. The battle that followed was one of the severest in modern times. The British and Hessians lost in killed and wounded between one fourth and one third of their whole number.[1] The American militia fought as they seldom did, and the regulars beat off all attacks; but Greene, unwilling to risk his army further, ordered a retreat. Cornwallis called it a victory, but an-

[1] Fortescue's *History of the British Army,* iii, 373.

other such would have ruined his army beyond repair. As it was, he left his wounded to the care of his opponent, and marched as fast as he could to Wilmington, where supplies had been gathered for him.

At first Greene thought of pursuing the British, but he, too, was in need of powder and lead, and many of his troops had only a few days left to serve. Realizing that he could not catch up with Cornwallis in time to deal an effective blow, he turned southward, and marched with his regulars to the vicinity of Camden, where were some British troops whom Cornwallis had left behind when he started in pursuit of Morgan. These were commanded by Lord Rawdon. Greene stationed himself on Hobkirk's Hill, not far from the British post, and was most unexpectedly attacked (April 25, 1781). This time an accident suddenly placed his whole army in danger, and again he was obliged to retreat. Rawdon on his part retired from Camden to Charleston, where there was a considerable garrison. Greene now laid siege to a frontier post, Ninety-six. In this operation he did not show himself so skillful as in the field. Rawdon now received reënforcements from Ireland, and again marched up into the country. Greene could not meet him in battle, and retreated. Taking the garrison with him, Rawdon returned to Charleston, and from this time the interior of South Carolina was free from the enemy. In the autumn (September 8, 1781) one more battle was fought, this time at Eutaw Springs. Here, again, Greene was obliged to retire from the field; but here, again, all the fruits of victory were his, for the British returned to the seaboard.[1] In these campaigns in North

---

[1] Greene described this battle in a letter to Washington, September 11, 1781 (*Pennsylvania Magazine of History*, xxx, 359). The North Carolina brigade, all new levies, "fought with a degree of obstinacy that would do honor to the best veterans." He sent substantially the same letter to the president of Congress. See Loubat's *Medallic History of the United States*, i, 52.

Carolina and South Carolina with insufficient forces and
with scanty supplies, by skillful manœuvering Greene had
compelled the British to abandon all the posts they held in
the interior.   In this accomplishment he had been powerfully assisted by Sumter, Marion, Pickens, and their partisan
troops.   The ultimate reason for British failure in the
southernmost states was their inability to place a sufficiently
large force in the field to overcome the odds that nature
and man raised against them.

Sir Henry Clinton, on the one side, and Germain and
Cornwallis, on the other, were now hopelessly at odds.
Clinton, having the responsibility weighing on his shoulders,
and realizing the insufficiency of his means to accomplish
anything in the way of conquest, wished to worry the
Americans by sending formidable expeditions, first in one
direction and then in another, to destroy their commerce
and break down their economic life.   Cornwallis, over-
valuing his successes, gave Germain a wrong impression of
their importance.   The result was that the Secretary, acting on information that was already three months old,
gave Cornwallis permission to carry out plans that were
unsuited to the actual condition when the consent reached
America ; and Cornwallis, feeling that the minister was
behind him, was inclined to take his own line.

Pursuing his idea of desultory expeditions, and also to
relieve the pressure on Cornwallis, Clinton had carried the
war into Virginia.   In October, 1780, he sent Leslie with
twenty-five hundred men to the Chesapeake ; but this force
Cornwallis had drawn to himself.   In December, therefore, Clinton dispatched Benedict Arnold, now a British
major-general, to the Old Dominion with fourteen hundred
men, most of them loyalists.   Arnold acted with his usual
vigor, and inflicted much damage.   Washington and Ro-

chambeau thereupon formed a plan for a combined naval
and military expedition to capture the traitor and bring
him to a place where his deserts could be meted out to
him.   To this end, Lafayette with a picked body of men
marched southward in February, 1781.   The idea was that
ships and men from Newport should act with him to
capture the traitor.   Intelligence of this scheme induced
Clinton to send General Phillips with three thousand men
and a strong naval escort to the Chesapeake.   There were
the delays inevitable to coöperative ventures, and the French
retired without having accomplished anything except to
draw more British troops to Virginia.[1]   Instead of returning to New York, Phillips disembarked his soldiers and
joined Arnold.   This was the situation when Cornwallis
at Wilmington took into consideration plans for the
future.   To invade North Carolina again was plainly
out of the question.   The logical thing would have been
to go to Charleston by sea and from that point again
take up the conquest of the interior.   Any movement
of this kind savored too much of failure and retreat.
Besides, Cornwallis argued that as long as Virginia was
able to pour men and supplies into North Carolina, the
conquest of the latter was hopeless.   He decided to
go northward and join Phillips in the hope, perchance,
that fortune might smile more sweetly upon him.   On
April 25, 1781, the day of Hobkirk's Hill, with seventeen hundred men[2] he left Wilmington for the north —
and Yorktown.

---

[1] See Charlemagne Tower's *Lafay-ette*, ii, 221–242; *Virginia Magazine of History*, v, 374 and vi, 55; and G. M. Philips's *Historic Letters*, 26.   The naval action between Destouches and Arbuthnot is treated at length by Mahan in Clowes's *Royal Navy* (iii, 488) and in his own *Influence of Sea Power* (385); and in

Ekins's *Naval Battles*, 102.   See also Lord Robert Manners to the Duke of Rutland in Royal Historical Manuscripts Commission's *Reports*, xiv, Appendix i, p. 31.

[2] In May a reënforcement from New York of another seventeen hundred reached him.   This brought the paper strength of the British in Virginia up to

The military situation was now complicated in the extreme. The British forces were scattered along the coast. At Halifax there was a small garrison; on the Penobscot, at Castine, a few hundred men held a fort. At New York was the main army strictly confined within its lines; at Charleston, Savannah, and St. Augustine were other garrisons, likewise immovable, while each British island in the West Indies had also its military protectors. The seven thousand men with Cornwallis formed the only force that was free to move. The safety of every one of these detachments and of the main army at New York depended upon the control of the sea, for the Americans and the French were free to move on the land. At any moment when sea power passed from the British to the allies, not one of their garrisons or detachments was safe.

Lafayette's total force in Virginia was less than one quarter of that which Cornwallis now had under his orders; but in Virginia, as elsewhere, the militia were active and compelled the British to keep together in large bodies. Cornwallis chased Lafayette from one side of the State to the other, and then returned to the seaboard, closely attended by the Marquis.[1] Wayne with the remnant of the Pennsylvania Continentals had joined Lafayette. The British caught them while crossing the James at Green Spring; but fortune favoring the Americans, Wayne and his men extricated themselves. It was at this time that Clinton became obsessed with the idea that a formidable attack on New York was about to be made. He directed Cornwallis to fortify a naval station

---

7800, including those with Arnold and Phillips. The latter died within a few days, and Cornwallis sent the former to New York.

[1] Jefferson's agility in keeping out of harm's way pleased his political opponents and led to explanations. See Ford's *Writings of Jefferson*, viii, 363–374.

at Old Point Comfort or Yorktown, and send some
thousands of his men to New York. They were actually
on shipboard, when another letter arrived countermanding
the order for their return. In the midst of these dis-
couragements and contradictions, Cornwallis fortified
Yorktown, for there the water was deep and conditions
favored a naval base, which was much desired by the
seamen. At almost the same moment word came to
Washington from De Grasse that his fleet with three
thousand soldiers on board would be at the mouth of
the Chesapeake on the first day of September or thereabouts; his leading ship sighted Cape Henry on August 29,
five days later the van of the allied forces reached the
Head of Elk. For years Washington had ardently desired
to regain possession of New York City. He had suggested this, and certainly the time was most opportune,
for De Grasse's fleet combined with the French naval
armament at Newport greatly outnumbered the squadrons
of Graves and Hood. It was not so to be, and Washington, thinking only of doing well that which his hand found
to do, made the best arrangements possible for the defense of the Hudson against Clinton's army;[1] then with
two thousand Americans and five thousand French, he
passed through the Jerseys and was across the Susque-
hanna before Clinton realized that Cornwallis and not
himself was the objective of the allies.

Before leaving for England, Rodney sent a dispatch to
Arbuthnot, whom he supposed to be still in command on
the North American station, that De Grasse was going

[1] Washington left Heath in command
of the posts of the Highlands with five
thousand men. These included ten
Massachusetts continental regiments,
with the exception of the "light companies." There were also New York
state troops and some militia regiments.
Other militia regiments, principally from
New England, were stationed to the
northward of Albany under General
Stark to guard against another invasion
from Canada.

northward with some of his ships and that he would be
followed by Hood with a portion of the British West
India fleet. At first Rodney ordered only eight line-of-battle-
ships to the northward, but this number was later increased to fourteen, and another dispatch vessel was also
sent to New York.[1] At this time Graves was away to
the eastward with his fleet, and these dispatch vessels,
seeking him, were captured. It fell out, therefore, that
Hood himself brought the news of De Grasse's coming
northward. When at length Graves and Hood joined
at New York, it was necessary for the former to spend
some days in replenishing supplies, and it was the 5th of
September when his leading frigates made the mouth of
Chesapeake Bay. There a number of great ships at anchor
were seen extending across the entrance of the bay, from
Cape Henry northward to the Middle Ground. De Grasse at
once slipped his moorings and stood out to sea. For once
the Frenchmen sought the battle.[2] The wind was light.
The water was shoal in places. The two fleets approached
each other cornerwise. Graves signaled his captains to
lay their ships alongside the enemy. They refused to
break away from tradition — for which they got a pen
lashing the next day. The foremost ships suffered severely.
After some hours the fleets separated, and, although in
sight of one another for several days, did not renew the
fight. The losses in men were about equal and were not
heavy, but the British suffered severely in the foundering
of the *Terrible*, a line-of-battle-ship, three days after the
encounter, and in serious damage to the masts of the
Intrepid. Graves was in no position to renew the combat,
and returned to New York. De Grasse went back to his

[1] *Letters of Sir George Brydges Rodney*, p. 146.   [2] See Note III at end of chapter.

anchorage, and there found that Barras, making a wide
sweep from Newport, had safely passed the enemy with
five liners, some frigates, and vessels bearing a train of
siege artillery.

While De Grasse was away on this important business,
the American and French troops from the northward had
been ferried down the bay.   Soon all were united in front
of Yorktown.   They numbered sixteen thousand in all,
two thirds of them Frenchmen.   Outside of the actual
lines of investment were Virginia militiamen in undefin-
able numbers.   They watched the roads and occupied important points for miles around, insuring that the British
would not get very far into the country, provided they
were able to escape from the town.   The York River, like
its companions, the Potomac, the Rappahannock, and the
James, is really an arm of the bay.   It is formed by the
coming together of the Pamunkey and Mattapony.   For
the greater part of its length, it is wide and deep.   Not
far from the mouth the two banks suddenly approach one
another.   At this point on the southern side is Yorktown,
and directly opposite is Gloucester Point.   In front of
Yorktown to the west and south, except along the river
bank, the ground was low and marshy with a few bits of
upland, but to the eastward, it was firm.   The position
was strong for operations on a small scale, but was cir-
cumscribed for so large a body of men as Cornwallis had
with him.   On the other hand, he did not have enough
to defend an outer line of works which had been thrown
up and to hold Gloucester Point.   At all events, he did
not try to maintain the outer line, but at once withdrew
to the inner forts, retaining possession only of two advanced redoubts on the eastern face.

The French engineers were well trained and experienced

officers, and made no mistakes in their arrangements.
Parallels were opened at proper distance (October 5) and
in an orthodox manner, and the siege went on steadily
and successfully for ten days or so. By this time the

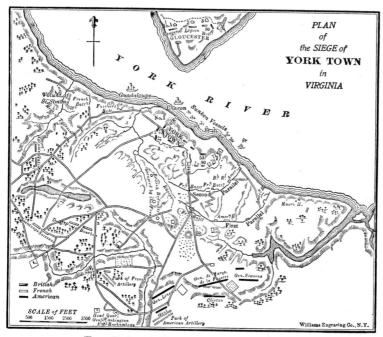

(From Stedman's *History of the American War*)

trenches had so far advanced that the capture of the two
redoubts had become necessary. The performance of this
task was given to two bodies of troops, one French, the
other American. To the former was entrusted the assault
on the larger work. Both were carried without much
difficulty and without serious loss, Alexander Hamilton,
then a colonel, leading the way into the smaller. The
trenches were at once extended to include the captured
redoubts within the allied lines. The condition of the

z

besieged had now become critical, for their inner defenses were commanded by the captured works. They made a determined effort to regain the redoubts, but although they seized some of the entrenchments, they were not able to hold them and were compelled to retire. Cornwallis now bethought him of flight. The only possible mode of escape was to ferry his troops across the York River to Gloucester Point and then march hurriedly through Maryland and Pennsylvania, crossing the Delaware into New Jersey, where Clinton could hold out a helping hand. There is little reason to suppose that the attempt would have succeeded under the most favorable circumstances. It never came to trial, because a severe storm put an end to the movement, and when ferriage again became feasible, Cornwallis seemed disheartened. Instead of fighting or fleeing, he sounded the parley and asked for terms. His men were worn down by sickness and fatigue, and only a few thousand were left to man the works. Nevertheless it does not seem that the case was desperate; but, for reasons best known to himself, Cornwallis surrendered, October 19, 1781.

The next day, while the Americans were counting their prisoners and the spoils of war, Graves, with a relieving force from New York, was approaching the Chesapeake. On the return of the fleet after the battle with De Grasse, Clinton had at length realized the pressing necessities of Cornwallis's condition. He had done his best to induce the admiral to take him with reënforcements to within reach of Yorktown. Graves, better judging the danger of the undertaking and its probable uselessness, in view of the superiority of De Grasse, now that Barras had joined him, refused to weigh anchor until his vessels had been put in fighting trim. The shipwrights and riggers made all

possible haste, but it was not until October 17 that the
last ship passed Sandy Hook.   Then the progress was slow,
as was always the case with a large fleet of sailing vessels
of different types.   Throughout the greater part of the
siege Clinton and Cornwallis had been in communication,
their messengers crossing the bay to the Eastern Shore,
thus eluding the French fleet at anchor in the lower Chesapeake, and it would seem that Cornwallis must have known
that help was coming.   Clinton and Graves appeared off
Cape Henry on the 21st.   It was then too late.   There
was nothing for them to do but to return to New York.

The articles of capitulation were in the precise terms of
those which had been imposed upon Lincoln at the surrender of Charleston, and that general was appointed to
oversee the giving up of arms and the reception of prisoners.   The capitulation included the British vessels that
were lying in the York River; but Cornwallis was permitted to send one of these to New York with dispatches.
It is said that this opportunity was used to secure the
safety of the more objectionable loyalists who were with
the British army, but the ship was not large enough to
hold them all.   Anxious to make the fullest use of the
force that was assembled in front of Yorktown, Washington tried to induce De Grasse and Rochambeau to join him in
further conquest, the capture of New York, or the seizure
of Charleston.   They were deaf to all appeals; De Grasse
was especially anxious to restore to Hayti the troops that
he had borrowed from the governor there.   He sailed away;
Rochambeau remained in Virginia for the winter with his
men; and Washington, with the American contingent,
marched northward to the Hudson.

It is interesting to note the unanimity of opinion with
which the surrender of the British army at Yorktown was

received on both sides of the Atlantic. In America, in England, and in France, the uselessness of any further attempt at colonial reconquest was apparent. Almost alone the king thought of going on. When he first learned of Cornwallis's dangerous position, he wrote to Lord North of the confidence he had " in the assistance of Divine Providence." As to the unnatural alliance between the Americans and the Bourbon powers, he declared " Duplicity can never withstand any disasters, but those who act on other motives ought ever to support any misfortune from the consciousness of the rectitude of intentions."[1] When the news of the surrender arrived, he wrote to Lord George Germain that " when men are a little recovered of the shock felt by the bad news . . . they will find the necessity for carrying on the war, though the mode of it may require alteration." Parliament was no longer of this way of thinking, nor was the country.

In the first years of the war an increased demand for English manufactured goods on the European continent replaced the loss of American trade and made it impossible for those opposed to the king's policy to raise a clamor on the score of the decay of commerce. Now the case was very different. With the widening of the area of conflict, the markets for English products became more and more restricted. With the increasing number of her enemies, it became more difficult to carry English productions to the markets that remained open. Besides, privateers, American, French, and Dutch, preyed upon British shipping to so great an extent that insurance rose to such high figures that the delays and expenses consequent upon convoys had to be borne. The national income had decreased and the expenditures of the government had in-

---

[1] Donne's *Correspondence of George III with Lord North*, ii, 387.

creased over those of peaceful days to an amount of fully
one hundred million pounds sterling. The British debt
had grown even faster, by no less a sum than one hundred and twenty-one millions. This condition of affairs
was due to the world-wide nature of the conflict, to the
low credit of the country, and to the corruption that per-
meated every branch of government.

Everything that was needed by the soldiers in America
had to be brought from the home land. The coals to warm
the troops and loyalists in New York came from Newcastle;
the bread they ate was made from English wheat; their
beef and pork, fresh and salted, were likewise brought from
Great Britain and Ireland; even the hay and oats for the
army horses were carried across the Atlantic. And the
cost of transportation was not light. The forage laid down
at New York in the single year 1781 cost eighty-one thousand pounds sterling, of which more than one half was for
transportation.[1] At times Robinson, who had charge of
this business as well as of the buying and selling of boroughs,
was nearly beside himself at the inefficiency and minor
pilferings of his underlings. His agents in America would
not send him proper accounts. His contractor at Cork
was accused of providing moldy flour for the army,[2] but
nothing could be proved against him, because no one
at New York had noted down the marks on the packages as they came to hand. In England in the dockyards, the case was just as bad. Rodney's flagship, the

[1] *Account of Extraordinary Services
incurred, and paid by . . . Richard
Rigby, . . . and not provided for by
Parliament* (London, 1782), p. 19. On
this general subject, see *Head Quarters
Papers*, i, 34, 37, 42, 52, 54, 55.

As partly accounting for delay in
shipments the contractors informed Howe
that "there is scarce an article of all

those things to be found ready made."
Robinson also complained of the scarcity
of shipping.

[2] Owing to the scarcity of staves,
after the American supply was cut off,
the flour was packed in bags, and soon
deteriorated in the moist air of the
ship's hold.

Gibraltar, was sent home because her rudder was hung on iron pintles, although the rudder itself and the ship's bottom were coppered.   Another great ship went to sea with two-stranded rigging instead of the three-stranded that she was supposed to have; her masts went over the sides, and she was towed back to port by her consorts.   After this it is not surprising to read that naval storekeepers kept their own pigs, instead of the nation's cordage, in the warehouses in the dockyards, and fed them on the ships' biscuit.

The dissipation of military strength was peculiarly striking.   In June, 1782, 149,514 men were on the returns, [1] not including those on the Irish Establishment; seventy thousand represented the garrison of Great Britain, of whom one half were militiamen, whose whole time probably was not paid for by the nation.   Of the other eighty thousand there were 34,177 British and German troops with Sir Guy Carleton at New York; 6081 were strictly besieged at Gibraltar; and the rest were scattered over the world, in the East Indies, the West Indies, in Africa, and in Canada.   There were Germans to be had for the money to replace the army lost at Yorktown, but there was no money with which to buy them from their masters.   Lord North floated a new loan at a ruinous rate.   He told the king that it was the last one that he could raise and handed over the government to the whigs.

[1] *Returns of His Majesty's Forces, June, 1782*, in the Wisconsin Historical Society.   I am indebted to Mr. R. G. Thwaites for an opportunity to consult these interesting little volumes.

NOTES

I. Bibliography. — Books, articles, and reports relating to the war in the southern department were listed by the present writer, so far as they had appeared before 1886, in Winsor's *America*, vi, 507–555. The most notable books that have since appeared are the third and fourth volumes of McCrady's *South Carolina*[1] and the only volume yet published of Ashe's *North Carolina*. These works are interesting on account of the local knowledge of their authors, and are examples of the dangers of writing history from the local standpoint. This appears more especially in McCrady's treatment of Greene, which is a bit of pleading well worthy the author's standing as a lawyer, but not at all fitting his reputation as an historian. At the same time McCrady's assertion that sufficient credit has not been given the southern partisan leaders is doubtless true. Possibly the excessive hero worship of Francis Marion has made students wary of them all. Ashe's book would have been a boon had it appeared before the volumes of the *North Carolina Records* on the Revolutionary epoch. The publication of the volumes of the *North Carolina Records* covering the years 1776–82 has changed the whole problem of writing the history of the Revolution in the South. They are now made usable by Stephen B. Weeks's excellent index.

II. Yorktown. — The Yorktown campaign was so intimately connected with the coming of the French troops, that it will be convenient to treat these two subjects as one. A. P. C. Griffin has contributed a convenient list of works to De B. R. Keim's *Rochambeau*, 607–645 (U. S. Senate Doc. No. 537, 59th Congress, 1st Session). To the same volume Mr. Keim has contributed an article entitled "Army of De Rochambeau on Land and Naval Exploits of De Ternay, Destouches, De Barras and De Grasse in American

[1] *The History of South Carolina in the Revolution*, 1775–1780 and *ibid.*, 1780–1783. These are frequently referred to as vols. iii and iv of McCrady's *South Carolina*. The letters from Greene to Sumter in the *Charleston Year Book* for 1899, "Appendix," 71–135, throw a new light upon the relations of these commanders.

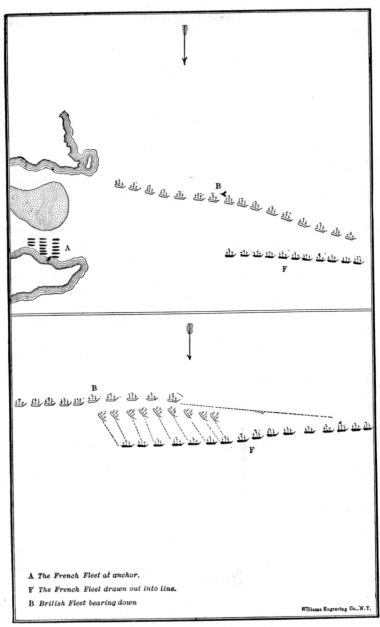

A *The French Fleet at anchor.*
F *The French Fleet drawn out into line.*
B *British Fleet bearing down*

THE BATTLE OFF THE CHESAPEAKE

(From Ekins' *Naval Battles*; the lower sketch shows the mode of attack proposed, but not carried out.)

Waters: 1780–1781 " (pp. 261–510). Other lists of books are in Winsor's *America*, vi, 547, and H. P. Johnston's *Yorktown Campaign*. The latter is the best account of this operation; a briefer statement is in J. B. Perkins's *France in the American Revolution*, chs. xviii, xxi.[1] A more specialized work is Balch's *The French in America* (2 vols. Philadelphia, 1891; the second volume has a particularly valuable list of French officers with some biographical details). Among other works may be mentioned the *Mémoires Militaires, Historiques, et Politiques de Rochambeau* (vol. i, pp. 225–307 [2]), and S. A. Green's edition of Count Deux-Ponts's *Campaigns in America*. Charlemagne Tower's *Marquis de La Fayette* (vol. ii) contains an elaborate account of this part of his career.

The documents relating to the responsibility of Clinton and Cornwallis for Yorktown are printed in B. F. Stevens's *The Campaign in Virginia, 1781*. This is a reprint of six controversial pamphlets with copious notes and extracts giving material from manuscripts and rare books.

III. De Grasse and Graves, 1781. — The leading authority on the battle off Cape Henry from the French side is *The Operations of the French Fleet under the Count De Grasse in 1781–2, as described in two contemporaneous Journals* (Bradford Club Series, No. 3). A footnote to page 72 of this publication contains extracts from Graves's report to Stephens, Secretary of the Admiralty, dated September 14, 1781. In the conflict off the Chesapeake, Thomas Graves, afterwards Lord Graves, endeavored to introduce the tactics that were so successfully employed by Lord Howe and himself in 1794.[3] See Julian S. Corbett's *Signals and Instructions, 1776–1794* (Navy Records Society's *Publications*, vol. xxxv, pp. 53 and 259). Graves severely reflected upon Hood's failure to act, Hood upon Graves, and Rodney upon both; see *Letters of Samuel Hood*, pp. 24–48, and *The Barham Papers*, i, 120–136. See also the accounts in Ekins's *Naval Battles*, 122; Hannay's *Short History of the Royal Navy*, ii, 267; and especially that by Mahan in Clowes' *Royal Navy*, iii, 494.

---

[1] Asa Bird Gardner has an interesting attempt to state "the disposition and order of battle of the allied armies" on the march from Williamsburg, September 27, 1781, in the *Magazine of American History*, vii, 267.

[2] This portion is translated in M. W.

E. Wright's *Memoirs of the Marshal, Count de Rochambeau*.

[3] Corbett's words are interesting (p. 56), "Had Hood but acted with one-half of the spirit that Nelson showed at St. Vincent, would De Grasse have been able to get back to the Chesapeake? And if he had not, what then?"

CHAPTER XII

INDEPENDENCE AND PEACE

In their desperation after Yorktown, the king and his ministers turned for salvation to the garrisons at Savannah, Charleston, and New York. If the thirty-four thousand men stationed there could be withdrawn from the continent and sent to the West Indies, such a blow might be dealt to France and Spain that the whole fate of the empire might be changed. These very soldiers might even be needed in Britain to preserve the country from foreign conquest. This was no time to consult men's prejudices. Sir Guy Carleton was appointed commander-in-chief in succession to Clinton. Germain at once withdrew from the cabinet[1] but the retirement of this master marplot did not save the ministry. On March 27, 1782, the Marquess of Rockingham again became First Lord of the Treasury, with Lord Shelburne and Charles James Fox as secretaries of state. There was no longer any need of a third secretary for colonial affairs. Shelburne and Fox, therefore, divided the management of business between them, — the colonies falling to Shelburne's share, foreign relations to Fox. The change of ministers brought no change to the military problem, — the necessity of extri-

---

[1] "The Ghost of Minden is forever brought in neck and shoulders to frighten him with," so wrote George Selwyn in 1775 (*Carlisle Papers*, 311). On his elevation to the peerage at his retirement from office after Yorktown a debate sprang up in the House of Lords as to whether he should be permitted to sit in that august assembly. *Parliamentary Register*, xxv, 105–112, 217–229. Germain's defense is on p. 220. Walpole relates (*Last Journals*, London, 1910, ii, 396) that when North told Germain he must go, the latter exclaimed, "Very well — but pray, why is your Lordship to stay?"

cating the army at New York was as great as ever. On
April 4, instructions to Carleton were signed ordering him
to transfer the garrison at New York to Halifax, even at
the price of "an early capitulation." He was furthermore
strictly charged to "keep in recollection, that the removal
and reservation of his Majesty's troops for his future service is the *immediate* object to which all other considerations must give way."[1] Had the administrative capacity
of the new government matched the feeling of peril that
comes out in these instructions, the garrisons at Charleston
and New York would have been removed in the summer
of 1782. The disorganization in the admiralty office[2] was
so great that transports were not provided and the soldiers
were still at New York twelve months later.

Already, in the winter and spring of 1781–82, English
emissaries had appeared at Paris and at The Hague, seeking
the conditions upon which the war in America might be
ended. No more than this could be done then because the

---

[1] To Sir Guy Carleton on his leaving
England to take command in America
(April 4, 1782) : —
"The first object of your attention
must be the withdrawing the garrison,
artillery, provisions, stores of all kinds,
& every species of public property
from New York & its dependencies to
Halifax. The same steps are to be taken
with reference to the garrisons of
Charleston & Savannah. The garrison
of St. Augustine you will determine
upon according to circumstances on your
arrival. The execution of the whole,
both in point of mode & time is left to
your discretion. In case you should
meet with obstructions by any attack
supported by a formidable force, or from
disappointments, so that it will not be in
your power to effect the evacuation without great hazard of considerable loss an
early capitulation, which may secure
the main object, is thought preferable
to an obstinate defence of the place

without hope of answering any rational
hope by it."
"In the execution of his Majesty's
commands, you must always keep in
recollection, that the removal & reservation of his Majesty's troops for his
future service is the *immediate* object to
which all other considerations must give
way. But you must likewise lose no
time to avail yourself of the change of
measures, which has lately taken place
for the purpose of reconciling the minds
& affections of his Majesty's American
subjects, by such open and generous
conduct as may serve to captivate their
hearts & remove every suspicion of
insincerity." Sparks Mss., No. 58,
fo. 145, and Library of Congress,
"British Transcripts," Colonial Office, 5,
vol. 106.

[2] *Letters and Papers of Charles, Lord
Barham*, ii, 72, 77–80 (Navy Records
Society's *Publications*, xxxviii).

ministers could not advise the king to acknowledge the independence of the United States until an enabling act for that purpose had been passed by Parliament. A bill giving this authorization was introduced into the House of Commons, but politics and not patriotism being uppermost, its passage took time. Franklin at Paris and Adams at The Hague had little faith in Lord North's professions of peace; but the former thought it worth while to write a friendly letter to Shelburne, with whom he had been intimate before the war. Shelburne, as soon as he was in office, sent an agent to Paris to sound Dr. Franklin. This newcomer was Richard Oswald, a Scotsman, who had considerable property in America. Franklin received him kindly, took him to see Vergennes, and informed him that the United States, France, and the other belligerents would better negotiate separately with Great Britain. When everything was arranged, he added, there would "only remain to consolidate those several settlements into one general and conclusive Treaty of Pacification." In the course of the next few months, Oswald made several journeys to London to confer with his chief. On Rockingham's death in July, his followers retired from the government and Shelburne became prime minister. Toward the end of that month, the passage of the Enabling Act authorized him to issue a commission to Oswald and to give him definite instructions as to the negotiation with the Americans. Unfortunately, the Lord Chancellor and the Attorney-General and other officials had betaken themselves to the country, the moment Parliament was prorogued. The commission, therefore, that Oswald exhibited to the Americans was not under the great seal, and, indeed, was only a copy or exemplification of the original. Franklin and Jay, who had by this time joined the doctor, thought that this was unsatisfactory, especially as the phraseology of the instrument was dubious as to independence. Oswald's instructions [1] directed him to secure peace even " at the Price of acceeding to the complete Independence of the thirteen States"; but this was not communicated to Franklin and Jay at the time. Shelburne intended to deal fairly and uprightly with the Americans, but both he and the king were very unwilling to acknowledge their independence. The prime minister, as a follower of Lord Chatham, believed that with the division of the empire, the star of Britain would forever set. He wished to bring about a federal union between the parent state and her former colonies, and had, indeed, more than once used the equivocal phrase " dependent states " [2] when referring to them. The royal pride dreaded independence ; the king was perturbed at the thought of going down in history as the first English monarch of modern times whose death had seen his dominions smaller than they were at his coronation.

[1] He is instructed to open negotiations with the American commissioners at Paris and to express to them the king's earnest wish "to restore Peace and Amity between Our Kingdom and the said American Colonies"; the fourth section authorized him to even purchase peace " at the Price of acceeding to the complete Independence of the thirteen States," and (fifth) to agree to cede the town and district of New York, and any other town or district, "within the limits of the said Colonies which may be in our possession at the time of signing our Treaty."

He was furthermore instructed to secure repayment of all debts "incurred to the subjects of Great Britain before 1775." " Oswald Correspondence " (Sparks Mss., No. 40, fo. 47).

[2] This phrase came to Franklin from Shelburne through David Hartley or Benjamin Vaughan, and annoyed him. He wrote to Vaughan that if Shelburne really had such a project in mind " our Negotiation for Peace will not go very far; the Thing is impracticable & impossible, being inconsistent with the Faith we have pledg'd, to say nothing of the general Disposition of our People." Vaughan showed Franklin's letter to Shelburne. Meantime Oswald had written to Shelburne, who was then Prime Minister, suggesting that Townshend, Secretary of State, should take better care of his papers. Replying to Oswald, Shelburne (September 3, 1782) took upon himself all blame in the matter, and sent Vaughan to Paris " for the single Purpose of satisfying Dr. Franklin's mind." Shelburne's letter was marked "Private." It was not copied for Sparks; a transcript is in the Library of Congress.

Later in the month, Vaughan sounded Franklin on the subject of a " Federal union," but reported to Shelburne that there was little hope. " Letters of Benjamin Vaughan " in Massachusetts Historical Society's *Proceedings*, Second Series, xvii, 409.

At the moment both would have granted independence and almost anything else for the sake of having in hand the thirty thousand troops who were uselessly living in America at terrific cost to the exchequer. Fox, while still in power, had also sent a representative to Paris. When his chief resigned, he too retired, declaring as he did so that Shelburne had no thought of granting independence.[1] All in all, bearing in mind Shelburne's unhappy reputation for deceit, Franklin and Jay might well have felt uneasy, and they did.

The American commissioners at Paris found themselves in a very difficult position. The Treaty of Alliance between the United States and France precluded a separate peace with Great Britain, and Congress had instructed them to conform absolutely to the terms of the treaty, and to negotiate only in harmony with the French government. Doctor Franklin had now lived some years in France at Passy, near Paris. He had attracted great attention by reason of his achievements in science, and with his long unpowdered hair and plain dress he fulfilled admirably the Parisian ideal of a forest philosopher. With a facility peculiar to himself, he charmed the ladies, young and old, received the embraces of Voltaire, and did not mind, in the least, the adulation that was poured upon him. Realizing the obligations of the United States to France, and the necessity of continuing French aid, in his correspondence with Vergennes and his secretary, Franklin sometimes pushed conciliation almost to the point of servility;[2] but

[1] William Knox, writing to Germain, now Lord Sackville, July 6, 1782, says that Fox found yielding to the Americans' claim of independency was unpopular. The whole letter is full of interesting political gossip, among other things referring to the death of Rockingham as the "providential removal of the Marquis," *Stopford-Sackville Papers*, i, 78.

[2] When Franklin learned that Vergennes was disturbed at not being apprised of the earliest propositions from the British, he wrote to Rayneval,

his shrewdness and acumen were as great as ever, and his love of country was beyond reproach. John Jay, the second commissioner to have conferences with Oswald, came of an old French family, long resident in America. With the inherited prejudices of a Huguenot, he had no faith in the rectitude of the Bourbon monarchy. He believed that the Frenchmen were in league with the Spaniards to confine the newly born nation within the strictest geographical limits, and in this he was entirely right. The third commissioner to reach Paris was John Adams. Born and bred in the town of Braintree, Massachusetts, he found the manners and customs of the French capital quite unlike those of his New England village. He thought that the excessive respect shown to the venerable doctor was entirely misplaced, and feared lest his aged colleague had fallen too much under the influence of the French court.

It was unfortunate that Franklin and Shelburne could not have brought matters to a head in the spring of 1782, when British prospects were darkest. On the twelfth of April, a few days after the instructions to Carleton were signed, Rodney defeated De Grasse in a naval battle off Dominica, in the West Indies, and thereby relieved the pressure in that quarter. Rodney's report reached London, on May 18;[1] but the condition of affairs remained sufficiently grave to urge the British to come to some arrangement with the Americans by which danger to the garrison at New York might be removed. Whenever the negotiators at

March 22, 1782, apologizing for not sending the letters from and to Hartley and Digges: —

"With this I have the honour of sending you *all the Letters* I have received from or written to England on the Subject of Peace. M. de Vergennes should have seen them sooner if I had imagined them of any Importance: for I have never had the least Desire of keeping such Correspondence secret. I was, as you will see, accidentally drawn into this; & conceiving it of no Use, I have been backward in continuing it." "Peace Papers," Box 1, Library of Congress.

[1] *A Short Account of the Naval Actions of the Last War* (London, 1788), 70 note.

Paris came together and discussed the matters confided to them, difficulties inevitably recurred. Supposing that the British embarked on transports and prepared to sail away, how could it be expected that Washington would stand idly by without at least attempting to pick off a detachment? In point of fact, how could he do so, without transgressing the treaty with France? Moreover, while the war had died down on land, it was being vigorously prosecuted on the water. British vessels were constantly capturing American merchantmen; there seemed to be no way to put a stop to it. At one time it was suggested that Carleton might enter into a capitulation with Washington by which the British soldiers should become prisoners on parole and thus secure a safe retreat from New York. The Americans insisted, however, that a treaty properly signed and communicated to Washington and Carleton was the only practicable means of securing the object that Oswald and his employers seemed to have so much at heart.

In one of the early conferences Franklin had stated in a general way the conditions upon which the United States would be willing to make peace. First and foremost was the recognition of the independence of the old colonies or new states; this must be granted in the widest sense of the word. The settlement, whenever it should be made, would be a division of the empire, and therefore the people of the United States would be entitled to their share in the imperial assets, among which Franklin enumerated the Newfoundland fisheries. These conditions were essential. Franklin thought that to promote an enduring peace other things would be desirable, as the cession of Canada. As a gilding to this rather bitter pill, in a moment of complacency and charmed with the guileless simplicity of his British conferee, he made the further suggestion that if this was done, the United States might be willing to recompense the loyalists for their losses in the older colonies by grants of wild lands in Canada. Oswald was certainly very anxious for peace, thereby reflecting the desires of his chief. Fascinated by the genial doctor's ingenuousness, he asked for and obtained a paper [1] containing in black and white these intimations of Franklin's pacific disposition. He took the paper to England. The ministers regarded these propositions much more seriously than Franklin could have expected they would, and used them in fact as a kind of protocol.

On May 17 David Hartley left a paper at Shelburne's house. It was entitled "Preliminaries, May, 1782." [2] Its origin is unknown. Whether it represents Hartley's lonely lucubrations, or was Shelburne's own scheme which Hartley had borrowed and now returned cannot be divined. It contains five sections, beginning with the proposition that the British troops should be withdrawn from " the thirteen provinces of N. America " and a truce made between them and Great Britain for ten or twenty years. Negotiations should at once be opened with the allies of America. Should this not be successful, " America sh⁴ act, & be treated as a neutral Nation." If peace should be made with France and Spain, these articles should be converted into a perpetual treaty. Moreover, the " independence of America shall be admitted and

---

[1] Richard Oswald to Earl Shelburne, July 10, 1782.

" 1ˢᵗ Of the first Class, *necessary* to be granted, Independence full & complete in every sense to the 13 States, & all Troops to be withdrawn from thence.

2ᵈ A settlement of the boundaries of *their* Colonies, & the loyal Colonies.

3ᵈ A Confinement of the Boundaries of Canada, at least to what they were, before the last Act of Parliament, I think

in 1774, if not to a still more Contracted State, on an ancient footing.

4. A freedom of fishing on the Banks of Newfoundland & elsewhere, as well as for Fish as whales."

" Entire Correspondence of Richard Oswald," Sparks Ms., No. 40, fol. 20; " Peace Papers," Box v, Library of Congress; Sparks's *Franklin*, ix, 354 note.

[2] " Peace Papers," Box 2. This is printed in Sparks's *Franklin*, ix, 296.

2 A

guaranteed by G. Britain ; and a commercial treaty set
tled between them." Dependence and independence seem
to have been convertible terms with the followers of Lord
Chatham, but the meaning is clear enough that the
British troops were to be taken from New York and used
elsewhere, the Americans standing calmly by while the
armies of France were being overwhelmed. It is true
that negotiations were also to be opened between Great
Britain and France, and whenever these were successful the
independence of the United States was to be acknowledged
and a commercial treaty arranged. Whatever the origin
and standing of these propositions, they are interesting
as foreshadowing the course the negotiations were to take.

The third party to the negotiation was the French
monarchy, which was largely guided by the desires of
the Spanish government. In 1780, Spain had joined
in the conflict. She had entered into no formal alliance
with the United States, her object being to drive the
English from the Floridas, and once more become supreme on all the shores of the Gulf of Mexico. Spanish
forces had been successful in the South, and St. Augustine was all that now remained to England of her former
possessions in Florida and eastern Louisiana. Moreover,
an expedition from St. Louis had seized the British post
of St. Joseph near Lake Michigan and had held possession
of it for twenty-four hours.[1] Dreading the spread of

---

[1] F. J. Teggert's "Capture of St.
Joseph, Michigan, by the Spaniards in
1781 " in *Missouri Historical Review*, v,
214. Professor Clarence W. Alvord
(*ibid.*, ii, 210) has maintained that the
expedition was French rather than
Spanish; but Professor Teggert appears
to have the better of the argument.

Two facts are interesting in this
connection: in March, 1778, Grantham
wrote to Weymouth that Florida Blanca
had expressed a willingness to mediate
on the basis of confining the United
States to the Atlantic seacoast, giving
the St. Lawrence Valley to Great Britain,
and keeping the Mississippi Valley for
himself. See also Jay to Livingston,
November 17, 1782. It appears from this
that the Spaniards were willing to
give the Northwest to the United States
provided they could be kept out of the
Southwest. Wharton's *Diplomatic Correspondence*, vi, 23.

republican ideas which would be the inevitable outcome
of the colonization of the country between the Mississippi
and the Alleghanies, Spain wished to see the lands
northwest of the Ohio remain in British possession rather
than have them transferred to the United States. There
were already so many Americans in the country south
of that stream that it would be impossible to make a
similar disposition of that region; but it might be feasible to limit the western extent of American settlement
by a meridian line, and thus keep the radicals away from
the Spanish villages on the Mississippi. These matters
had been discussed between the Spaniards and the
Frenchmen, and Vergennes had easily understood the
reality of Florida Blanca's anxieties, and was willing to
second his wishes. His own ideas went somewhat
farther than those of the Spaniards, and, as a matter of
fact, were contrary to them. He had in mind, at some
future time, to secure the retrocession of Louisiana from
Spain and again to make France a power on the continent
of North America. It is true that by the Treaty of
Alliance with the United States the French were pledged
not to recover any of the lands in North America that
belonged to England and that once had been hers; but
French statesmen, like those of England at a later time,
affected to regard the country south of the Great Lakes
and between the Alleghanies and the Mississippi as Indian
property and not as included within the limits of the
old English colonies or of the United States.[1] Moreover,
there were a few old French towns in that country.
These had been ceded to England in 1763, and had since
been occupied by Virginians led by George Rogers Clark,

[1] See F. J. Turner's illuminating article on " The Policy of France toward
the Mississippi Valley " in the *American
Historical Review*, x, 249-255.

and had, indeed, been organized into the Virginia county of Illinois, under an act of the legislature of that state. Nevertheless there seems to have been some kind of an intrigue set on foot by French and Spanish emissaries for the purpose of again adding these settlements and others in the Great Lake region to Spanish or French possessions.

When Oswald brought his commission to negotiate with the Americans, it was shown to Vergennes. The wording of this document was peculiar in that it did not authorize Oswald to negotiate with the representatives of the United States, but only to deal with commissioners to be named by the colonies, or bodies corporate, or assemblies, or descriptions of men, — this being the phraseology of the Enabling Act.[1] Vergennes at once declared that the dignity of the United States required that they should be recognized as a separate power, and negotiated with as such. The significance of this attitude appears from a letter which he wrote to Luzerne that if the United States are recognized as independent, they will have to take their chances in the general negotiations. In other words, once their independence is acknowledged, the object of the Treaty of Alliance will have been attained; henceforth they will have to look out for themselves, and it will be easy to play off their demands against those of Spain and Holland, and thus secure those which French policy requires.

As American minister to Spain, Jay had had a most uncomfortable time. He knew something of the wishes of Spain as to the western lands and as to the willingness of France to abet Spanish pretensions. He surmised, and correctly, a good deal that was beyond his actual knowl-

1 22 Geo. III, Cap. 46.

edge.[1] In the midst of the intrigues and plottings at
Paris, his fears were aroused. One day, he suggested to
Oswald that the British should remove their army from
New York, take it southward, and drive the Spaniards
from Florida.[2] This proposal was so attractive that
Oswald communicated it to the government at London.
Thomas Townshend, who as Secretary of State spoke the
mind of the government, replied that the matter was one
with which the ministry "in some points of view . . .
might be tempted to close," yet as the Americans did not
offer to guarantee a quiet evacuation of New York, nothing further could be done, especially as it would be dangerous to carry so large a force "to the Southward of all
our West India possessions." The anti-Bourbon feeling
of Jay found expression, however, in a clause of the projected treaty that Strachey took to London with him, by
which, in case the British should repossess themselves of
West Florida before the actual conclusion of peace, the
southern boundary of the United States, instead of following the Proclamation Line of thirty-one degrees from the
Mississippi to the Chattahoochee, should be run due east
from the confluence of the Yazoo and the Mississippi, thus
giving the British a strip of territory about ninety miles
wide. This clause was not inserted in the preliminaries,
as they were actually signed on November 30, for these
were to become public. It was appended as a separate

---

[1] The perusal of a mass of notes which
Professor F. J. Turner most kindly
placed in my hands has confirmed the
impression that the policy of France and
of Frenchmen toward the United States
was not straightforward. Jay's intuitive
suspicions were well founded, although
the specific bits of evidence that have
been adduced to justify his attitude do
not carry conviction. The letter from
Barbé Marbois, which the British caused
to be placed in Jay's hands, has been
often printed, as in Pitkin's *United
States*, and Jay's *Life of Jay*. The
whole subject is examined by Jay and
Wharton. A. C. McLaughlin, in his
volume in Hart's *American Nation*
Series, argues for the good faith of the
French and gives a bibliography.

[2] See Notes at end of chapter for the
correspondence.

and secret article.   As the Spaniards were still in possession of the former province of West Florida at the time of
the signing of the definitive treaty, nothing further was
done in the matter, but the separate and secret article
remained to give trouble to American negotiators when
they came to settle the question of the southern boundary
of the United States.

Franklin's suggestion of the recognition of the independence of the colonies was adopted as the basis of discussion,
in London and in Paris.   When it came to explaining and
defining, the Americans laid down the general proposition
that by the colonies was meant the colonies as legal corporate portions of the British Empire.   To recognize their
independence was to recognize them as independent sovereign states with the boundaries that they had legally
possessed as colonies and with all the jurisdictions and
territorial rights that had formerly belonged to the British
crown.   The Americans had never recognized the legality of the Quebec Act so far as it diminished the extent
of colonial territory and extended the boundary of that
province.   They insisted on going back to the Proclamation
of 1763 and the Peace of Paris of that year.   The English
ministry acceded to this general proposition, although later
they brought forward reservations and started doubts.   According to the settlement of 1763, the western boundaries
of British dominions, as far north as the southern boundary
of the Hudson Bay Company, was the Mississippi River,
which was then thought by some geographers to have its
source as far north as the fifty-sixth parallel; the Mississippi would, therefore, be the natural western boundary
of the United States.   The southern limit would be the
southern boundary of Carolina and Georgia, as determined
by charter and proclamation; this would be the thirty-first

parallel from the Mississippi to the Chattahoochee, for this
was the 1763 boundary of West Florida. From the confluence of the Chattahoochee and the Flint, the boundary
would be the old northern limit of East Florida, which
was a straight line from the confluence of the Chattahoochee and the Flint to the source of the St. Mary's and
down that river to the Atlantic Ocean. On the northeast,
from the point where the forty-fifth parallel crosses the
St. Lawrence, the southern boundary of the province of
Quebec according to the proclamation was followed first
along that parallel to the Connecticut, to the head of that
river and thence along the highlands which separate the
rivers flowing into the St. Lawrence from those which fall
into the sea to the northwestern angle of Nova Scotia.
From this point, the line ran due south to the St. John's
River and thence by that stream to its mouth in the Bay
of Fundy.[1] On thinking the matter over and looking at the
maps, it appeared that this last line was beyond the existing limits of Massachusetts, which then included Maine.
This oversight was remedied by continuing the north and
south line to the head of the St. Croix, and thence following that stream to its mouth. Unfortunately, owing to
the carelessness of the American commissioners, or, possibly, to sharp practice on the part of some one in London,
" Atlantic Ocean " was substituted in the treaty for " the
sea " which was in the proclamation. This change gave
rise to considerable trouble later on, when the United

---

[1] Richard Oswald to the Right Hon.
Thomas Townshend, Paris, October 7,
1782: —

" After considering the terms as they
stand in the Treaty, I thought there was
no reason to object to the boundary lines
of the Thirteen States, excepting that
there is a part of Nova Scotia cut off on
the Bay Fundy.

" I called on M.ʳ Jay this morning
and found him willing to sett that matter
to rights, so as the Massachusets Government shall have no more of that
coast than they had before the War.
He took his directions from maps, and
they are not distinct, nor do they agree
in this matter." Sparks Mss. No. 40,
fo. 150.

States and Great Britain endeavored to delimit this part
of the boundary on the spot.[1]

The part of the boundary that caused most trouble was
that portion which extended from the St. Lawrence to
the Mississippi. In the first project of the treaty that
was agreed to on October 8, this part of the frontier was
described as running from the point where the forty-fifth
parallel strikes the St. Lawrence to the southern end of
Lake Nipissing and thence straight to the source of the
Mississippi. There was no available knowledge as to this
latter point. Mitchell's map of 1755 was used by the
negotiators.[2] It was very unsatisfactory, because that car-
tographer had placed a sketch of Hudson's Bay over the
unknown tract in the northwestern corner of the map.
The Mississippi is thus shown as issuing from underneath
this sketch, but a legend printed on the map states that
the river is believed to rise to the northward. There was
so much doubt on this point that the Americans asked Oswald to procure a collection of the best maps in London.
He did so, but the maps when they arrived were accompanied by Henry Strachey, an under official in one of the
departments, in whose knowledge of American geography
Shelburne had great confidence, and who had not been exposed to the seductive fascinations of Franklin and his
colleagues. The Americans had gained so much more in
the way of territory than they had dreamed possible, that
Strachey soon returned to London with two other suggestions as to this part of the line, and the British government
was invited to choose one of the three propositions, the
Americans thus leaving the ultimate decision to them.
The two new suggestions were (1) to follow the forty-fifth

[1] This subject will be considered in a later volume, when the question of the Northeastern Boundary will be taken up.

[2] Franklin to Jefferson, April 8, 1790, in Sparks's *Works of Franklin*, x, 447, and W. T. Franklin's *Franklin*, vi, 564.

MITCHELL'S MAP OF 1755
(The Northwestern Corner)

parallel from the St. Lawrence westward to the Mississippi, or (2) to run the line by river and lake to the northwest corner of the Lake of the Woods and thence due west to the Mississippi. The British ministers thought this last line preferable. They selected it, and it was so written in the treaty. In all the discussions as to boundaries, there does not appear to have been any strenuous give and take. The principle of utilizing the old colonial limits once having been adopted, the Americans were clearly not disposed to haggle over the ownership of a few thousand square miles more or less of wild lands.[1] As to the other questions which came up the conferences were more heated and became acrimonious before the end was reached.

Every month that passed saw the British in a better position from a military standpoint. Gibraltar, which had been straitly besieged by the forces of France and Spain, had now been supplied with provisions and troops (October 10, 1782); the defeat of De Grasse had relieved all apprehension of danger for Jamaica; and the armies on the American continent seemed to be preserving the *status quo*. In the Far East alone was there danger, and this was so remote that little could be done one way or another to remedy it. It was under these circumstances that the question of loyalists, debts, and fisheries came to the fore. The royalist refugees, to give the fugitive loyalists a designation, had drawn heavily upon British funds and were likely to do so for years to come. Some of them were Englishmen, as the Commissioners of the Customs, who had fled from America, but had continued to receive their

[1] It will be noticed that Clark's conquest of the Northwest has been given no place in the text as a decisive factor in inducing Great Britain to relinquish her hold upon that region. No doubt the knowledge of recent events in the Illinois country influenced both the American and the British negotiators; but there is no reference to Clark or his conquest in any of the diplomatic papers that have been consulted in this research.

salaries as colonial officials. Others, like Judge William
Smith of New York, were native-born Americans whose
families had so long enjoyed the emoluments of office that
they formed a class by themselves. Then there were the
officers and men of the loyalist regiments to be cared
for, — De Lancey, Skinner, Benjamin Thompson, who later
as Count Rumford won renown in the scientific world.
These had been given pensions and occasional gifts of
money, — the pensions, alone, in 1782, amounting to sev-
enty-three thousand pounds sterling.[1] The great mass of
refugees had no other claim on the government than their
allegiance to the king; but they could not be allowed to
starve, and their number was increasing rapidly as one
town after another was evacuated. A thousand or more
had gone from Boston in 1776, between four and five thousand men were on the point of embarking from Savannah
and Charleston,[2] and thousands would be taken from New
York whenever that place could be abandoned. Many
English families of position and power, as the Carterets
and the Penns, had great financial interests in America.
Few indeed had more at stake than Shelburne and his connections. The wife of his youth and mother of his children was the daughter of John Carteret, Earl Granville,[3]
and granddaughter of the only Carolina proprietor who
had refused to sell his rights to the king. His aunt was
the relict of Thomas Penn, and entitled to an annuity from

[1] *Parliamentary Register*, xxiv, 245.

[2] Massachusetts Historical Society's *Proceedings*, Second Series, iii, p. 95.

[3] *Ibid.*, Second Series, June, 1903, p. 428; Collins's *Peerage of England*, iv, 382; viii, 33. Of native-born loyalists Benjamin Thompson of Woburn, Massachusetts, achieved greatest fame. In 1781 he was appointed under-secretary by Lord George Germain, to whom he had given much information. In 1781 he recruited a regiment of horse among the tories of New York and Long Island. After the war he devoted himself to scientific pursuits, especially on the subject of heat. For his discoveries the King of Bavaria made him Count Rumford. The only formal biography of him is the *Life of Count Rumford* by G. E. Ellis; it is very inadequate as to his early life. See *Stopford–Sackville Papers*, ii, 13, 249–256.

his estate. Anxiety for the royal exchequer, sympathy for those who had been faithful, and personal interest, all combined to arouse the ministers to activity in behalf of the loyalists. The American commissioners were equally determined that nothing should be done for them.

The triumphant Revolutionists regarded the loyalists with hatred and loathing. To them it seemed that the misinformation of royal officials and loyalists in general had induced the British government to embark upon the policy of taxation and coercion which had led to war, and that the conflict itself had been continued, long after its hopelessness should have become apparent, by the mis-statements constantly reiterated of the adherents of the king both as to the numbers and the devotion of their fellows in different parts of the continent. The loyalists, too, had aided, and efficiently, in carrying on the war by enlisting in the British service by the thousands. Washington was outspoken in his detestation of them. To him they were "abominable pests of society," against whom vigorous measures ought to be taken.[1] In 1782, the Virginia House of Delegates stigmatized them as "vicious citizens who side with tyranny and oppression," and Washington publicly declared that they ought to be treated as traitors. The state legislatures confiscated their property, outlawed them, and in some cases, attainted them of high treason, both women and men.[2] The commissioners at Paris felt precisely as did their fellow-citizens in America. Franklin, who was generally so kindly, in this case was actuated by

---

[1] Professor C. H. Van Tyne has collected many instances of Washington's distaste of tories, in his *Loyalists of the American Revolution*, 57, 125, 149, 223, etc.

[2] See act of New York of 1779, which attainted Mrs. Beverly Robinson, Mrs. Roger Morris, and Mrs. Inglis with their husbands. The editor of the *Barclay Correspondence* (p. 137 note) says: "This is believed to be the only case, here or in England, in which women were attainted of high treason, and banished and threatened with death."

feelings of personal resentment on account of the part which his son William Franklin had played. The latter had not only remained faithful to the king, but, as President of the Board of Associated Loyalists, had authorized and urged on measures that were harassing and unjustifiable. Jay reflected the general opinion of the Revolutionary leaders when he informed Oswald that " there were certain of those refugees they never would forgive . . . they would not suffer them to live in their neighborhood . . . nor would those persons be sure of their lives there." [1]

At first Oswald, acting on instructions from London, proposed that the loyalists should be compensated by the Americans for their losses and sufferings. The commissioners declared this to be impossible because they had no instructions and because Congress had no power to provide compensation or to compel the States to do so. At the outset of the negotiations, Franklin had let fall a suggestion that if Canada was ceded to the United States, the loyalists might be given lands in that province. As the boundaries were finally arranged, a large portion of the province of Quebec, according to the Act of 1774, was included within the limits of the new nation. Why should not the king retain these ungranted western lands as a fund to be disposed of for the benefit of the refugees? Shelburne, with his idea of the United States as forming a dependent nation, saw nothing incongruous in the idea. The commissioners did; they replied that the colonies must be recognized as independent states with all governmental and territorial rights that had belonged to the crown. The loyalists might be cared for by the British govern-

---

[1] "Oswald Correspondence," Sparks Mss. No. 40, p. 179. A writer in the *Pennsylvania Journal* (January, 1783) expressed the general opinion when he described the loyalists as embarking at New York for Nova Scotia, "there to drag out the residue of a life more intolerable than death."

ment or their property might be restored by the States which had confiscated it, but no clause requiring this to be done could be inserted in the treaty.

Side by side with this discussion, there proceeded another providing for the recovery of debts contracted by American colonists to British merchants before the beginning of hostilities in 1775. Franklin disliked this proposition fully as much as he did that for compensating the loyalists. He likened the demand to that of a burglar who sold a piece of goods to a merchant, then broke into his store and stole it, and finally demanded payment. The British had plundered private property, burned towns, and seized goods entirely beyond the necessities of military operations. They had destroyed the means of productive employment, and could not reasonably make demands with which they had made it impossible to comply. When Adams joined Franklin and Jay toward the close of the conferences, he assumed an entirely different attitude: if his countrymen owed money, as honest men they ought to pay it. Nay, more, he saw no reason for limiting the time to 1775; American citizens should pay their creditors, no matter when the debts had been contracted.

On the subject of the fisheries, the commissioners were not unanimous, and the British government was disposed to limit the privileges asked for in every way. In his preliminary memorandum, Franklin had stated rather loosely that the Americans would expect to share in the Newfoundland fisheries. Although a New Englander by birth, he had not lived there since his boyhood, and was not fully informed of the later development of the fishing industry. Moreover, in drawing up the memorandum, he had no idea it would have great importance attached to it, or that it would be used as an informal basis of negotiations. The British government fully understood the details of the fisheries, and was cognizant of the desire of the French ministry to exclude the Americans from that industry, although there is no reason for supposing that Vergennes sent Rayneval to London to urge their opposition. When the matter came up for discussion, therefore, Townshend noted that Franklin had confined his demand to the Newfoundland fisheries; he had said nothing about those of the Gulf of St. Lawrence, nor had he suggested that the Americans should continue to enjoy the right of drying their fish on the unoccupied shores of the British provinces, as they had in colonial days. When Adams reached Paris, he took very firm ground on this question. As a New Englander, he realized the great importance of the fishing industry, and was able to point to a clause in his earlier instructions, as sole commissioner for making peace with Great Britain, directing him to secure complete rights in this direction. He now declared that he would never put his name to a treaty that did not give his countrymen their full share in the northern fisheries, including the drying of fish on the unoccupied shores of British America.

Continual haggling over these questions discouraged Oswald. He was still desirous for peace at almost any price, and possibly did not realize the improved position of Britain from a military point of view. Shelburne could not well displace him, but he sent Strachey to stiffen his resistance to Franklin and Jay. When Strachey, too, seemed to be growing compliant, he instructed Oswald not to sign any treaty without the consent of Alleyne Fitzherbert, who afterwards won high distinction as Baron St. Helens. He was now conducting negotiations for peace with the French government. With the coming of Adams, with this stiffening of the attitude of the British govern-

ment, and with the interjection of loyalists and debts into
the debate, the discussions at Paris became disheartening.
It was then that Franklin brought the affair to a crisis by
pulling from his pocket a paper upon which he had made
a tentative list of unwarrantable British depredations for
which compensation might well be exacted. Moreover,
he informed the British commissioners that a committee
of the Pennsylvania Assembly, at that very moment, was
drawing up a list of spoliations for which the British
were liable. He showed Oswald a Philadelphia newspaper containing some information on that subject, and
added that the other States were certain to follow this
example. At length Oswald acted quickly and with determination. The Americans had said Congress had no
power to order the States to return loyalist property, that
the utmost it could do was to recommend such legislation.
He now suggested that a clause to this effect should be inserted in the treaty. The Americans, gratified by this
concession, also took a step forward and provided that no
legal impediments should be placed in the way of the collection of debts which American citizens owed to British
subjects, no matter when they had been contracted. This
was evidently as far as Franklin and his colleagues would
go. Fitzherbert authorized Oswald to affix his name to
the instrument, and the preliminary articles were signed at
Paris on November 30, 1782.

The Americans felt very doubtful as to the reception of
the treaty in the United States. They had broken their
instructions as to treating in harmony with the French government, and had proceeded without making any definite
communication to Vergennes. They had secured ample
boundaries, but had given way on the subject of debts,
and had seemed to give way as to the loyalists. The pro-

vision as to debts proved to be the salvation of the treaty in England. It did away with all opposition on the part of merchants trading to America, and it contributed to the government's ease of mind, because it enabled the ministers to refuse to pay whole classes of loyalist claims on the ground that they were debts that could be collected in the ordinary way.

The task of communicating the preliminary articles to Vergennes was left to Franklin, and he, with his abounding knowledge of human nature, felt that it would be a good plan to couple the announcement of the favorable terms which "the love of peace" had torn from the British ministers with a request for a fresh loan of twenty million francs. The delicacy and kindliness of manner with which he accomplished his double purpose can be imagined by those familiar with the characteristics of this many-sided man, — they cannot be described. Vergennes thought that the signing of the articles was premature,[1] but he made no inconvenient remonstrances, and procured six millions of the twenty. The commissioners had broken their instructions; but was their action equivalent to pledging the United States to a breach of the treaty of 1778 with France, which obliged the contracting parties to fight on until a general peace should be made? Technically, the United States had observed this requirement. Negotiations for a general peace were being carried on. All the treaties could not be concluded at one given moment, and the American commissioners had been careful to insert in the instrument that what had been agreed to were merely preliminary articles which should constitute a treaty

---

[1] Vergennes knew of the beginning of the negotiation between Franklin and Oswald. With all the resources at his command, it is inconceivable that he should have been unaware of its continuance. He was surprised, as were probably both the Americans and the British at its sudden and favorable ending.

eventually, "but which treaty is not to be concluded un-
till terms of a peace shall be agreed upon between Great
Britain and France, and His Britannic Majesty shall be
ready to conclude such treaty accordingly." Nor can it
be called a desertion of America's allies, for the preliminary articles between France and Great Britain were
agreed to two weeks later,[1] although they were not signed
until another month had passed away.

It is the custom of historical writers to regard this
treaty as being greatly to the advantage of the United
States [2] and as having been extracted by three remarkable
Americans from the complaisant Oswald and the second-
rate Strachey. Such, at any rate, was not the view of
the negotiators themselves. In sending the articles to
Robert R. Livingston, Franklin, Adams, and Jay adopted
an apologetic tone.[3] They clearly felt that they had not
obtained as much as their countrymen expected and had
agreed to some things that required explanation. They
also thought that a few phrases in the articles themselves
needed alteration, and Franklin suggested the desirability
of at once beginning deliberations "upon the additional
clauses to be inserted in the definitive Treaty." Probably
he had reference to commercial matters, but Fitzherbert
was annoyed. He wrote that the Americans should be
obliged "to declare explicitly whether they do or do not
mean to adhere to the letter of the provincial Articles."
Evidently, to his mind, Oswald and Strachey had made a

---

[1] "*December 14th.* I have this day
learned, that the principal preliminaries
between France and England are agreed
on"; Franklin to Livingston, in *Works
of Franklin*, ix, 442.

[2] For instance, W. E. H. Lecky
(*England in the Eighteenth Century*, iv,
284) says: "It is impossible not to be
struck with the skill, hardihood, and

good fortune that mark the American
negotiation. Everything the United
States could with any shadow of plausi-
bility demand from England they
obtained."

[3] See Franklin to Livingston, December 5, 1782, and Adams, Franklin, Jay,
and Laurens to Livingston, December 14,
1782.

good bargain. The latter apparently had misgivings. He wrote to Oswald that some things needed explanation. His idea as to the "Article of Refugees" was that the "Resolution of Congress to the different States concerning the Restitution of Property will be equivalent to a Message from the King to Parliament and that it is not probable any refusal will be given except to a very few who are particularly obnoxious." Why should not Oswald talk familiarly with Jay about it and secure "as Compleat a Dissertation upon it [Article 5] as possible." Oswald was so well satisfied with the Articles as they were that he thought it best not to agitate the matter, but these letters [1] are interesting as showing the expectations of the British negotiators.

The conclusion of this treaty which Shelburne had expected would confirm him in power had precisely the contrary effect. The opposition, especially in the House of Commons, made it the subject of fierce and unprincipled attacks. Memoirs, and diaries, and letters of the day give no satisfying reason for the distrust of Shelburne that was felt by all parties. He certainly made a sad mistake by declaring in the House of Lords that the grant of independence was temporary, while at the same moment William Pitt, the younger, his Chancellor of the Exchequer, was stating in the House of Commons that it was irrevocable. Doubtless, Great Britain could have revoked her recognition of the United States whenever she had the power and will to do so; but this statement of Shelburne's, coming when it did, went far to justify the distrust of him that was felt on both sides of the Atlantic. The king's keen political insight convinced him that a time of

---

[1] The quotations in this paragraph are taken from the transcripts in the "Peace Papers" in the Library of Congress.

political chaos was nigh. He withdrew his protection
from Shelburne. Soon the King's Friends became less
constant in their attendance. Before long, North and Fox
were seen amicably sitting side by side on the same bench.
On February 24, 1753, Shelburne resigned, but Pitt strug-
gled on for a few weeks longer. Charles James Fox was
personally displeasing to the king, and Lord North's coalition with him seemed to George the basest of ingratitude.
After holding out as long as he could, the king was obliged
to yield to the inevitable, and the ill-starred coalition came
into office with the Duke of Portland as Prime Minister
and Fox and North as Secretaries of State.

Unlike Shelburne, Fox had no scruples about granting
independence to the United States, although he had forced
his predecessor out by securing an adverse vote on the preliminary articles. Personally, he favored having a commercial treaty with America and entering into an alliance
with the new republic. He selected David Hartley to go to
Paris and take up the thread of the negotiations.[1] Fox
instructed Hartley to behave "ingenuously" to the United
States minister. There is no occasion for reserve, he
said, because it is "his Majesty's earnest desire to renew
the Intercourse and Commerce so beneficial to both Countries, and his wish that some treaty or provisional convention may be speedily concluded wch may establish that
commerce upon a just and equitable footing."[2] Trade

---

[1] David Hartley had known Franklin
before the war. The two continued in
correspondence throughout the period of
hostilities. Hartley's letters give the
impression contained in the text. His
appointment, like that of Oswald, was
far removed from the ordinary British
practice. The former was an early
example of "dollar diplomacy"; but
the combination of Fox's carelessness
and levity with Hartley's muddling

mediocrity put an end to a most favorable
chance for making a fair and honorable
commercial arrangement between the
United States and Great Britain.

[2] These paragraphs are based on the
"Hartley Papers," which are in the
possession of Mrs. Levi Z. Leiter of
Washington, who kindly permitted me to
see them. Many of the same letters
are in the "Peace Papers" in the Library
of Congress. There are many minor

between the two countries might well revert to the footing of colonial days, so far as the produce and manufactures of the two countries were concerned. As to the West Indies, " there is no objection to the most free intercourse between them and the United States," but American ships might not carry any other merchandise to those colonies than the produce of their own countries. Fox also directed Hartley to secure better terms for the loyalists, and was informed that it was intended to remove the troops from New York at the earliest possible moment to save expense. He also sent Hartley certain regulations that had been proposed by merchants interested in the fur trade of the St. Lawrence and the Great Lakes. Among other suggestions was one for the continued occupation of the Northwestern posts for three years, this being necessary to avoid Indian troubles.

David Hartley was a well-meaning person, albeit somewhat opinionated and perhaps a little dense. Without reading his instructions carefully and studying the meaning of every word and phrase, he proceeded to substitute his own opinions for the wishes of the government, and suggested to the Americans an arrangement by which trade should be reopened between all parts of the British empire and the United States. Fox was distinctly annoyed. He wrote to Hartley that he had forgotten all about the limitation of American trade to the West Indies. He prayed him to do nothing to bind the government to permit the produce of the West India plantations to go even to America in American bottoms. Hartley was much disconcerted by this, and his sensibilities were not at all relieved when the American commissioners handed him an

differences in the wording of the two sets. These are partly due to the fact that one set consists of original letter books and letters; the other of transcripts of the corresponding set of original letters and letter books.

Order in Council absolutely closing the British West Indies to American commerce. Hartley's usefulness was gone, for, as Adams wrote to Livingston, he was plainly not in the secrets of his government. Nevertheless, he lingered on, although Fox wrote to him that the representations from persons interested in this matter "do undoubtedly make me rather wary in this business." The Jamaica merchants had intervened and had been powerfully seconded by the ship owners. In fact nothing could be done except to convert the preliminary articles into a definitive treaty, which was signed at Paris on September 3, on the very day that Great Britain came to terms with France and Spain, at Versailles.[1]

Independence was won, but it remained to disband the army without another civil war and to see to it that the British evacuated the posts held by them and did whatever else the treaty required. The first of these was accomplished with difficulty, but a dozen years elapsed before the last British soldier retired from the limits that had been assigned to the United States in the treaty of peace. In the beginning, the American armies had lacked that corporate spirit which is so essential to success, but later, with the establishment of the Continental Line, the military organization had become more closely knit. In the end it was a "regular" army, and as the close of the contest came nearer, those dangers which the colonists had dreaded in regular military organizations seemed

[1] On January 20, 1783, preliminary articles had been signed by representatives of Great Britain, France, and Spain. The time contemplated by the provisional treaty between Great Britain and the United States for a cessation of hostilities had now arrived. On February 14, Franklin, Adams, and Fitzherbert signed an agreement to this effect. The Americans issued a proclamation accordingly, February 20, 1783, which was followed by a British one at London on February 27. The ending of hostilities between France and Great Britain was proclaimed at the same time. The definitive treaty was signed on September 3, 1783. It was ratified by Congress, January 14, 1784, by the king on April 9, and ratifications were exchanged at Paris on May 12, 1784.

about to be realized. Many of the officers were ambitious and not at all anxious to return to humdrum civilian existence. Unfortunately, the incapacity and bad faith of Congress had placed it within the power of these men to arouse the discontent of the rank and file of the army.[1] The splendor of Washington's character and the stupendous influence which he possessed over his men alone turned away the storm.

Successive congresses, since that of 1774, had comprised in their numbers able and influential men, but they had been drawn, for the most part, from those portions of the community that were inexperienced in administration. Congress had sought to perform executive functions through committees. These acted slowly, constantly changed in personnel, and, undoubtedly, caused much useless expenditure and bad administration. From the beginning, avoidably and unavoidably, supplies had run low, and hardships had been great. In one of the last years of the war, Robert Morris became financier or sole executive of the financial department. He brought some order out of the existing chaos, and in the years following Yorktown, the soldiers were better fed, housed, and clothed than they had ever been before. They now had time to think of their lot in the not far-off to-morrow, when the army would be disbanded and they would return to the towns and hamlets which many of them had left half a dozen years before.

The officers' pay had never been satisfactory, and, at first, had been small in proportion to that given to the privates. Gradually, the pay of the officers had been raised in proportion to that of the men ; but, owing to the tre-

[1] This whole subject, including the disbanding of the forces, is thoroughly elucidated with a bibliography by L. C. Hatch in "The Administration of the American Revolutionary Army" in *Harvard Historical Studies*, No. x.

mendous depreciation of paper money, even the increased compensation had been entirely inadequate. Those officers who had families dependent upon them were especially badly off, but even those who had no family ties could not look forward with any hope to the future. Aided by Washington, they appealed to Congress, but it was impossible to pay them properly, for there was not enough gold and silver in the country to have answered their just demands. Promises for the future were the utmost that Congress could give. These finally took the form of an assurance of half pay for seven years after the war, and then, when that assurance did not suffice, of half pay for life. The soldiers had other equally just claims upon Congress, because the stipulations as to food and clothing had never been fulfilled. Then, too, those in service could not desert those who had been dismissed on account of the disbandment of companies and regiments, — "the deranged officers," as they were graphically termed. The case of the privates too, aroused the sympathies of the officers. It was determined to make an appeal to the States for justice, and Massachusetts was selected as the first to be approached, for there was a good deal of sympathy for the soldiers in that State. Possibly, something might have come of this plan, but most inopportunely, when the legislature seemed about to act, a letter arrived from one of the Massachusetts delegates in Congress, stating that it would itself reconsider the whole matter.

The officers from six States now decided to send a joint petition to Congress by a committee of their own number. This document contained no threats. It merely asserted that it would be criminal to conceal any longer the dissatisfaction that prevailed in the army. General McDougall of New York presented the case to Congress, which

handled the matter with great skill, through the medium
of Robert Morris, Alexander Hamilton, and James Madison.
Washington took the opportunity to write a private letter
to one of the Virginia delegates, seriously suggesting the
adoption of " soothing measures." The mild language held
by McDougall must have powerfully seconded Washington's advice, for he was one of those men who was ordinarily most vociferous. After some months, Congress
voted to commute the half pay for life to full pay for five
years. To this determination they were brought by the
incident which is usually referred to as the Newburg
Addresses.

Republics, and, especially, federative republics, were
novel in the range of political governments. Monarchy
was still the standard form of rule in the world, and no
country had a man better fitted to occupy a throne than
America had in George Washington. Inevitably, men in
different walks of life thought that his coronation would
be the outcome of the Revolution. This idea was distinctly distasteful to Samuel Adams and others among the
radicals, but there were men who looked upon it as desirable. In the spring of 1782, Colonel Lewis Nicola wrote
to Washington that a limited monarchy was the best form
of government, and plainly hinted that Washington himself would be the best of monarchs. Congress would not
do justice to the army, but the soldiers would welcome
their chief as king. Washington's reply is, possibly, the
grandest single thing in his whole career. He declared
that no occurrence had given him more painful sensations
than the " information of there being such ideas existing
in the army "; he was at a loss to conceive what part of
his conduct could have given encouragement to a thought
that was " big with the greatest mischiefs that can befall

my country." No such scheme had any chance of success; Washington had not fought for personal aggrandizement, — and no one else could have gained an American crown in the face of his displeasure.

About a year later, on March 10, 1783, there appeared in the camp of the main army at Newburg on Hudson an anonymous address, written with great skill, and with it an invitation to the officers to assemble and consult as to their future plans. In powerful phrase the writer related how he had left private life with regret, had served throughout the war, and had hoped, as the sunshine of peace broke in upon them, the coldness and severity of government would relax, — but there were points beyond which faith and temper could not be stretched. Would his fellow officers consent to be the only sufferers and to grow old in poverty, wretchedness, and contempt, — and "owe the miserable remnant of that life to charity, which has hitherto been spent in honor?" Let them especially suspect the man who should advise more moderation and longer forbearance.

Learning of the designs of the addressers, Washington condemned the anonymous summons and himself called a meeting of the officers. At the appointed time, he unexpectedly appeared, and began reading from a paper which he held in his hand. After the first paragraph, he suddenly stopped, and, drawing his spectacles out of their case, remarked that he had grown gray in their service and now found himself growing blind. Resuming, he reprobated the address as appealing to passion and not to reason, and the advice given by the anonymous writer proved that he was a foe to the army, and, possibly, he was a spy from the enemy. On their sacred honor, he conjured them to express their horror of him who would overturn their country's liberties and deluge their rising empire in blood. Give one more proof of unexampled patriotism, that posterity may say, "Had this day been wanting, the world had never seen the last stage of perfection, to which human nature is capable of attaining." Washington then read a letter from a member of Congress, describing the perplexities of that body and pointing out that when soldiers once assumed undue power, they go farther than they at first intended; attempts were being made to lessen the popularity of the commander-in-chief, with what results no one knew. Washington then retired, and the officers passed resolutions expressing confidence in the justice of Congress, and asking their chief to plead their cause. This he did in an official letter in which he stated that if the picture drawn in the anonymous address was true, he should learn what ingratitude is and realize a tale which would embitter every moment of his future life. Privately, he wrote to a member of Congress that the need of taking measures which would prevent renewed disturbance was imperative, for, although force could not help the officers, passion might easily carry them away. In this extremity of danger, Congress voted full pay for five years in money or in six per cent securities. Soon afterward, news of the cessation of hostilities was received, and on April 19, 1783, eight years to a day since the excursion of the ministerial troops from Boston to Lexington and Concord, the end of the war was proclaimed to the army. At first, it was not at all certain whether the officers and privates would consent to be peaceably dismissed. With great difficulty, enough money was procured for three months' pay.[1] With this partial payment

---

[1] The difficulties of the time come out graphically in Robert Morris's diary (Ms. Library of Congress). On May 23 is this entry: "Genl St Clair called to

in hand, most of the soldiers accepted furloughs and repaired to their homes. A few, with Washington, remained before New York until November 25, when the last of the British left that town.[1] On December 4, he bade an affectionate adieu to the principal officers who still remained at headquarters. Repairing to Annapolis, he surrendered his commission to Congress, and received with calm countenance the parting benediction of its president that his future days might be happy as his past had been illustrious and that "He will finally give you that reward which this world cannot give."

The story of the infractions of the treaty by the United States and Great Britain, and the growing estrangement of the two powers until the signing of Jay's treaty averted hostilities, belongs properly to a later volume, but it will not be amiss to call attention to a few points, while the facts and dates are fresh in the reader's mind. For strictly military reasons, the British ministry wished to withdraw the troops from Charleston, Savannah, and New York. But there was no military necessity whatever for withdrawing those from the posts under control of Henry Haldimand, Carleton's successor as Governor General of Canada. It happened, therefore, that orders for evacuation were issued to Carleton, in April, 1782, but none to Haldimand, and the latter steadily refused to surrender the posts on the Great Lakes to the Americans until he was ordered to do so. The communication of the prelim-

---

enquire respecting the pay intended for the Army. I told him that unless Congress will agree to disband them I am fearfull they will eat up the only means which I have left for making any pay." And again, under date of September 16, 1783: "Gen¹ St Clair again applied for money his necessities are so urgent that I cannot resist them and desire Mʳ Swanwick to supply 320 Dollars from my own monies to be hereafter taken from the Generals Pay."

[1] Professor H. P. Johnston has an interesting article on the "Evacuation of New York by the British, 1783," *Harper's Magazine*, lxvii, 909.

inary articles did not induce him to change his mind in the least, nor did the notification of the cessation of hostilities incline him to alter his conduct. He refused again and again to surrender any of the posts in his government until he received instructions so to do from his superiors in England. Meantime, the London merchants trading to Quebec had represented to the ministers the impolicy and danger of abandoning these posts which were in the heart of the fur country. Haldimand seconded these representations by relating the fears of the fur traders and residents on the spot. Looking about for some excuse for postponing their surrender, the ministry pitched upon the fact that loyalist estates were not being restored and that new laws, making the collection of British debts more difficult, were constantly being enacted by the state legislatures. Accordingly, on April 8, 1784, Lord Sydney, more than a month before the ratifications were exchanged, wrote to Haldimand[1] that "the posts in the United States will not be evacuated till the Articles of the Treaty of Peace are fully complied with."

The only way to have secured the evacuation of the Northwest was to bring military pressure to bear in that part of the country as on the seaboard. Washington contemplated detaching a few men of the Continental Line to take charge of the nearest posts; but New York at once objected because the troops were Massachusetts regiments. These particular places were within the territory then in dispute between New York and Massachusetts. The other posts were within the limits claimed by Virginia under her old charter and by the operations of George Rogers Clark. The supineness or lack of interest of Washington

[1] *Canadian Archives*, 1885, p. 286. The "Haldimand Papers," which are calendared in these archives, contain much valuable material on this subject.

may be referred to one or the other of these causes. There was also jealousy displayed in Congress at the idea of Continental troops taking possession of lands that were clearly within the limits of the several States and which ought to be occupied by state troops.[1] Indeed, under the Articles of Confederation, the Continental authorities had no constitutional right to maintain any troops whatever.

Somewhat similar considerations as to the binding force and meaning of the Preliminary Articles as to the removal of negroes and other property prevailed. At Savannah, Charleston, and New York, besides the British garrisons, there were thousands of loyalists and negroes. The Articles provided that all prisoners on both sides should be set at liberty and that the British army should speedily withdraw "without causing any destruction, or carrying away any negroes or other property of the American inhabitants." In what category were the loyalists and their property? Were they American inhabitants? Was their property to be left behind when they themselves fled? Not much question was raised about them, for the Americans were glad to have them go, and most of their real estate had been confiscated long before; but there was abundant friction in regard to the negroes. British commanders had invited slaves to leave their masters and come within the lines, promising freedom to all who did so, and thousands of other slaves had been captured. Carleton thought it would be dishonorable to

---

[1] E. L. Hommedieu to George Clinton, Princeton, September 3, 1783: "I was observing that I found many of the States disposed to have the frontier Posts garrisoned by the States in whose Territory they were, and not by the Continentals." As to Virginia, see *Report of Committee of Congress to whom were referred the Act of the legislature of Virginia of January 2, 1781*, as to reimbursement of G. R. Clark's expenses. It is dated June 6, 1783. For this and other material on the general subject of the Northwest posts, I am indebted to Worthington C. Ford, who most kindly permitted me to make use of papers which he and his brother, Paul Leicester Ford, collected some years ago.

restore to their masters those slaves who had come in under the proclamations.   As to the rest, he felt differently. But it was very difficult to prove the facts in any one case, and practically impossible where thousands were concerned, although American commissioners attended the embarkation at New York.   To Washington and the other leaders, the invitations to the negroes to desert the plantations seemed to be highly reprehensible.   The rebellious colonists, according to them, had been entitled to belligerent rights at the outset, or at any rate, from an early period.   To them their slaves were as much their property as their horses and cows, and equally protected by the clause in the treaty.

With the peace, therefore, there came a fresh batch of grievances that bade fair to bring on another conflict with Great Britain at no distant date.   It was not until the formation of a powerful national government under the Constitution that the United States was able to compel obedience to the treaty by either American citizens or foreign powers.

NOTES

I. Bibliography. — Winsor's "Notes" on the peace negotiations in the seventh volume of his *America* are full and complete down to the year 1887. Sparks's *Diplomatic Correspondence of the American Revolution* was compiled under many difficulties, as the authorities on Washington exercised something of a censorship. Sparks also was guided by the editorial canons of his day, and was not always fortunate in his transcribers. None the less, the book, like his *Washington* and his *Franklin*, is a monument to his industry and his historical insight. Francis Wharton's *Revolutionary Diplomatic Correspondence of the United States* is founded upon Sparks's work, and, as has been the case with other followers of Sparks, he constantly notes errors in the older work. Sparks's *Writings of Benjamin Franklin* also contains much matter on the negotiations, as does *Franklin in France* by Edward Everett Hale, father and son.

In the "Sparks Manuscripts" is a volume entitled "The Entire Correspondence of Mr. Oswald in the Negotiation of the Peace of 1782 with the American Commissioners in Paris." This was copied from the Lansdowne papers, and also contains selections from the correspondence of Henry Strachey, Thomas Grenville, and Alleyne Fitzherbert, which were copied from the papers in the British Foreign Office. The same matter is in the "Stevens Transcripts" in the Library of Congress at Washington, but the Sparks volume, showing the American negotiation by itself almost day by day, is convenient to use. Transcripts of some of the papers are in the "Bancroft Collection" at the Lenox Library at New York. In preparing the foregoing account, it was thought desirable to compare the three sets. They were made by different transcribers, and in some cases from different originals, but the variations are trifling. Owing to the proximity of Paris and London and to the great difficulty of communication between France and America, Oswald's and Strachey's letters are much more numerous than those of the American commissioners, and also much more detailed. On the American side, the journals kept by Franklin to July, 1782, and by Adams after his arrival give the same kind of information, but they are not so complete or so minute.

Of the briefer articles[1] one by George Ticknor Curtis in *Harper's Magazine*, lxvi, 666 and 833 is readable. Usually the descriptive narratives of the negotiation are so controversial as to be of slight assistance.

II. Jay and West Florida. — On October 2, 1782, Oswald wrote to Townshend a letter, from which the following is an extract.

" I have given M͏ͬ Jay an account of it; and he greatly approved of the Proposal. He is indeed anxious that Great Britain should regain possession of that Colony on the same footing it stood before the War, since he said their States would not by any means like that the Key of that part of the Gulph should be in the hands of the spainards, as the whole or greatest part of the Trade and Produce of that great Back Country, would most naturally and beneficially issue there; and which he says would soon be very considerable and would ultimately fall into the hands of the English on the Mobile and Missippi; both in the supply of English merchandise, and Importation of American Commodities in return. Rather than leave it in the hands of the Spaniards, he said it would be worth while to embark some of the Troops from New York and Charles Town, and retake it. I mention this only to shew how desirous they are that the Colony should not remain with the Spaniards; and in confirmation of the opinion I took the liberty to give on that subject in my former letters; " " Oswald Correspondence," fo. 131 ; see also fo. 133.

October 26, 1782, writing to Oswald, Townshend refers to this proposition : —

" There was one part of your letter which referred to a Proposal of M͏ͬ Jay's which seems to have been frequently and eagerly urged by him. I mean that of an Expedition against West Florida. I do not think he went so far as to guarantee a quiet evacuation of New York,

---

[1] The chapter on the " Peace Negotiations " in Winsor's *America* (vii, ch. ii) was written by Jay's grandson and takes the family view, strongly; Wharton in the "Introduction" to his *Revolutionary Diplomatic Correspondence* and the Appendix to the third volume of his *International Law Digest* argues against the Jay tradition. Owing to their form these articles are by no means easy to use.

See also the biographies and writings of Franklin, Adams, and Jay.

On the British side Fitzmaurice's *Life of Shelburne*, iii; and G. C. Lewis's *Administrations of Great Britain;* and Earl Russell's *Memoir of Fox* present the two main views. The " Supplementary Note " on pp. 81–84 of Lewis's *Administrations* is especially important.

" This is a matter of great delicacy, and though in some points of view the Proposal appears to be one, with which we might be tempted to close, yet we might put ourselves too much in the Power of Friends very newly reconciled to Us, as well as of those who might remain our enemies, by carrying a large Force to the Southward of all our West India possessions." *Ibid.*, fo. 171.

In the project of a treaty that Strachey took to London, in the early days of November, 1782, the northern boundary of West Florida was to extend from the 31st degree of latitude to a line to be drawn due east from the place where the Yazoo River falls into the Mississippi to the River Appalachicola, and a separate article appended to the draft repeated this arrangement. *Ibid.*, fo. 194, 196. These letters are also in the " Peace Papers " or " Stevens Transcripts " in the Library of Congress.

III. The Three Boundary Propositions. — In the project of a treaty that was agreed on between the American commissioners and Oswald, October 8, 1782 (" Oswald Correspondence " in " Sparks Ms." No. 40, fo. 154; Wharton's *Diplomatic Correspondence*, v, 805), the northern boundary is described as running from the point where the 45th parallel strikes the St. Lawrence " straight to the south end of the Lake Nipissing and then straight to the source of the river Mississippi." This was the southwestern boundary of the Province of Quebec as far as Lake Nipissing according to the Proclamation of 1763, and appears in the instructions that were issued to Adams in 1779 (Wharton's *Correspondence*, iii, 301). The extension of the line to the source of the Mississippi, which was also in those instructions may have been chosen to make the boundary reach the southern limit of the Hudson Bay Company's territory as laid down on the maps.

On November 8, 1782, Strachey, then on his way to England, wrote from Calais to Townshend as follows : —

" The moment I arrive at Dover, I shall dispatch a Messenger, with the enclosed new Terms of Treaty, as a paper which you will be most anxious to see. It is accompanied with a Map, upon which are drawn the Boundary line originally sent to you by Mr Oswald, and two other lines proposed by the American Commissioners after my arrival at Paris. Either of these you are to choose " (" Oswald Correspondence," fo. 189).

The three propositions were (1) the old Nipissing line of the Oswald project which now seems to have been obsolete. (2) The

2 c

45th parallel from the Connecticut to the Mississippi. This was written in the Strachey project merely because it was contained in lesser compass than the alternate proposition. (3) The lake and river boundary. As to the two new boundary propositions, they were proposed by the American Commissioners "if more agreable than those in the Treaty," by which was meant the first or Oswald project. See *ibid.*, 193, 197.

It will be observed that Strachey says that the line by the 45th parallel and that by lake and river were both proposed by the American commissioners and that the final choice was left unreservedly to the British government. It would appear from this that Franklin and his colleagues placed no very great importance upon the possession of any particular portion of the Northwest. See, however, Annah M. Soule's "International Boundary of Michigan" in *Michigan Pioneer and Historical Collections*, vol. xxvi.[1]

IV. The Loyalists. — C. H. Van Tyne's *Loyalists in the American Revolution* is the standard work. Unfortunately it has no bibliography, but this is supplied in the same author's volume on the *American Revolution* in Albert Bushnell Hart's *American Nation Series* (ix, 338).[2] Of the more detailed books, those by Sabine

---

[1] In 1820, Samuel Preston of Stockton, Pennsylvania, wrote that Franklin, in conversation, remarked that he had drawn the line through Lake Superior to include the largest supply of copper in the American possessions and that the time would come when this would be considered "the greatest service I ever rendered my country." See Wisconsin Historical Society's *Proceedings*, Forty-ninth meeting, p. 214. According to Preston, Franklin stated that he had access to the journals and charts of a corps of French engineers who had explored the Lake Superior region. No trace of them can be found, and the Forty-fifth parallel, which was suggested as an alternative to the Lake Superior line, passes far to the south of the metalliferous belt. Probably Preston had forgotten the facts of a conversation nearly a quarter of a century old, or Franklin, himself, then a very old man, may have misplaced events. He certainly joined in offering the British government one of two lines, and as certainly they chose the natural instead of the artificial line.

In confirmation of Strachey's letter see Adams to Livingston, November 6, 1782, stating that " we have offered them the choice of a line through the middle of all the great lakes, or the line of 45 degrees of latitude." Wharton's *Diplomatic Correspondence*, v, 856.

[2] There is an interesting analysis of the Revolutionary test acts and other laws against the loyalists in Van Tyne's *Loyalists*, Appendix B and C. As to the payment of claims by Great Britain, something is printed in the *Pennsylvania Magazine of History*, xv, 350. In New York, especially, loyalists were plenty and claims persistent; see A. C. Flick's *Loyalism in New York* in the Columbia series and Rives's *Correspondence of Thomas Barclay*, 121 and 138. As to their fate in Massachusetts see *The Confiscation of John Chandler's Estate* by A. McF. Davis; the " Narrative of Jolley

and Ryerson stand first. The *Second Report of the Bureau of Archives for the Province of Ontario* contains a most appalling list of loyalist claims. It is well to read in this connection John Eardley-Wilmot's, *Historical View of the Commission for enquiring into the Losses, Services, and Claims, of the American Loyalists.* Of the older expositions of loyalist sufferings and deservings, Joseph Galloway's *Claim of the American Loyalists* (London, 1788) and his *Letters from Cicero to Catiline the Second* (London, 1781) are worth reading. Of modern articles those by Professor M. C. Tyler[1] in the *American Historical Review*, i, 24, and G. E. Ellis in Winsor's *America*, vii, are the best. The loyalist side is well stated in W. Kingsford's *Canada*, vii, ch. v.

Allen " in *Proceedings* of the Massachusetts Historical Society for February, 1878 (also printed separately) ; and *Report of the Claim of William Simpson.*

[1] This same matter is in ch. xiii of Tyler's *Literary History of the American Revolution,* i.

CHAPTER XIII

ECONOMIC ADJUSTMENT

THE years between the cessation of hostilities with Great Britain and the inauguration of President Washington were memorable over all others in American annals for readjustments in politics, society, commerce, and industry. In politics, the governmental systems of the States were worked over and developed, and the weak Articles of Confederation were replaced by the Constitution. In society, distinct advances were made toward the realization of religious freedom; educational facilities were improved and enlarged and were placed within the reach of many more people; and a beginning was made in the reorganization of the labor system. Side by side with these changes, commerce and industry were readjusted to suit the needs of a nation which was emerging from the colonial condition.

The thirteen States had achieved their independence by preserving their economic well-being while the contest with the sea-trading nations of continental Europe had sapped England's strength for the moment. The war brought hardships to the Americans; but these had mostly disappeared by 1779 and the last years had been marked by speculation in business and extravagance in living. In 1783, the New Englanders and the dwellers in the Middle States were enjoying a degree of comfort unknown before 1775. This was not true of the country south of Mason and Dixon line because the ravages of the British and loyalists left Virginia and the Carolinas in a straitened condition and stripped of laborers without whom their natural resources could not be worked.

Lexington and Concord found colonial warehouses bare of British and European manufactured goods owing to the policy of commercial coercion by which the American radicals had striven to bring the mother country to their way of thinking. Hostilities once begun, both Parliament and Congress further hindered American commerce. The former forbade loyal Britons trading with rebellious colonists; the latter closed American ports to British ships and British goods. In April, 1775, Congress opened the harbors of the thirteen colonies to European ships and commodities and, later on, the prohibition against British goods was taken off. Merchants, manufacturers, and shipowners of France, Holland, and Spain welcomed with eagerness the new markets that insurrection opened to them, and the Americans were equally desirous of utilizing to the utmost the facilities that foreign enterprise placed in their hands. Time was needed to discover the best means of evading the vigilance of British cruisers and privateers, and to establish commercial relations with European forwarders and commission merchants. In the interval, before this was done, there was a scarcity of many articles that were essential to an easy existence and of military supplies that were necessary for the effective prosecution of the war. By 1777, the storerooms began to fill up and after that year to the end of the conflict, necessities, luxuries, and even superfluities were abundant. Prices were high when measured in hard money, and absurd when stated in terms of continental currency. Rates of freight and of insurance[1] were naturally far above those of peaceful days,

---

[1] The normal rate of insurance on a voyage between North America or the West Indies and Great Britain was 2 per cent or 2½ per cent and about 2 per cent

and the necessity of pursuing circuitous routes also added to the expense of laying down goods on American wharves. But the people desired European goods, and there was a constantly increasing flow of foreign commodities to America from 1778 onwards.

Capital, labor, and transportation facilities were all in urgent demand and were often lacking. The supply of labor had been far below the demand before 1775. After that year the situation grew worse and worse. Recruits were needed for the armies, seamen were required for the ships of war and the privateers, and sailors were hired at almost any price for the cargo carriers that sailed across the Atlantic or plied between continental shores and the West Indies. Thousands of loyalists fled to England, Halifax, or New York. Many of these were of the capitalistic class, but many of them were white or black workers in the field, shop, or house. Thousands of negroes also found refuge within the British lines and others were taken from the plantations, especially in South Carolina, to be sold into West Indian slavery. Putting all these facts together, it is evident that there was a great lessening in the supply of labor for farm and factory at the very moment that need was greater than it ever had been.

In the interim between the cessation of importation from Great Britain and the establishment of commerce with the rest of the world, the demand for manufactured goods became intense. After that time the high rates of freight

between North America and the Sugar islands. In 1777 and 1782 the Browns of Providence paid 33 per cent and 40 per cent. In 1777, the rate on British vessels on the run across the Atlantic rose to 23 per cent; in 1778, it dropped to 15 per cent or only 5 per cent with convoy. After that time all British vessels were convoyed (G. W. Bridges's *Annals of Jamaica*, ii, 167). Adams saw a fleet of more than " four hundred sail, for New York, Quebec, Newfoundland, and Ireland " convoyed by six ships of the line, besides frigates, and armed transports. (*Works*, iii, 207.) In 1780 Hood with seven sail of the line and five frigates convoyed one hundred odd vessels from England to the West Indies (D. Hannay's *Letters Written by Sir Samuel Hood*, p. xxii).

and insurance served as a stimulant to local production. Many articles were especially needed for the army : canvas for the soldiers' tents, and arms and ammunition for their use in battle. Also heavy guns and all kinds of camp equipment were urgently required. Blankets were always necessary, for the men could not use, in bivouac, the quilted coverlets that were so common an article of homely economy. Stockings and shoes and other clothing generally wore out with great rapidity on the march and in the camp. Salt, molasses, and rum were the most important articles of food and drink that had been obtained from abroad. The first was not only essential for the health of man and beast ; it was the only means of preserving meat and fish for domestic consumption and for exportation before the days of cold storage and the canning factory. Molasses was widely used for sweetening instead of sugar, but much of it was distilled into rum. The supply of this cheap alcoholic stimulant was cut off at the moment when the hardships and privations of campaigning, the freedom of military life, and the relaxation from ordinary standards that are inseparable from war affected all classes. The demand for all these articles was keen and attempts were made to supply it.

Everywhere new industries were started and people embarked in speculative enterprises without much thought of the welfare of the country or of their fellow-countrymen. The casting of guns and of camp kettles was taken up in earnest in Pennsylvania, on the banks of the Hudson, and elsewhere. Before long these and other heavy iron castings were turned out in sufficient quantities to supply American needs. At Philadelphia, the making of stockings was carried on with success, and in Boston the weaving of sailcloth from flax proved to be a profitable

occupation for women and children. Every effort was
made to procure nitre, which was the basis of gunpowder,
and the making of that explosive was undertaken. Roofs
were stripped of their lead for bullets, and the lead mines
at Chiswell, Virginia, were worked to their fullest capacity.
Cloth making as a household industry was taken up with
redoubled vigor and some beginnings were made toward
the manufacturing of textiles by machinery. Fortunate
captures from the enemy and timely importations from
France tided the people over the dangerous years of commercial stagnation ; but there undoubtedly was a good deal
of suffering and privation in the first half of the war.

The one necessary article that was in great demand and
high in price throughout the period of hostilities was salt.
A great deal of it had been used in preserving fish and
provisions for export, but none of this had been made in
the colonies. At once, Congress, the States, and private
individuals began making salt.[1] The sole method employed was to evaporate sea water in shallow pans, for the
riches of the country in mineral salts were then unknown.
The pans were expensive to import and difficult to make
without skilled and experienced iron workers. When one
had pans and sea water, the process was slow and demanded
labor. In 1774, salt sold in Philadelphia for eighteen
pence the bushel ; in 1780, it brought from £125 to £348
in continental currency ; and in 1781 was purchased by
the quartermaster general of the army for six hard dollars
the bushel.[2] The lack of a cheap and constant supply of

[1] There is a brief article on "Salt
Making in the Revolution" by Charles
C. Smith in the *Proceedings* of the
Massachusetts Historical Society for
1876, p. 221. Charles Carroll of Carrollton wrote to Franklin on August 12, 1777
that the cast-iron salt pans cost £100 per
ton and were liable to crack; he hoped
that means might be found to make
them of "plate-iron." "Sparks Manuscripts," No. 57, fo. 218.

[2] Pickering to Washington, Newburgh, May 10, 1781.

this preservative added greatly to the difficulty of providing food for the soldiers and for the people.

The most surprising feature of the time to the modern
observer is the enormous prices that were paid for commodities, as in the case of salt ; but these were largely fic-
titious. Instead of levying taxes, Congress emitted quantities of bills of credit and the States put out large amounts
of paper money. In the early flush of enthusiasm, farmers
and storekeepers willingly parted with their produce and
goods for these paper promises. Until the beginning of
1778, the value of the paper money held fairly well, one
hundred dollars in specie being then equivalent to about
one hundred and fifty in paper. The decline then went on
rapidly. In July of that year one hundred silver dollars
could be exchanged for three hundred paper bills, in December for six hundred, in August, 1779, for sixteen hundred
in paper currency, and in March, 1780, for four thousand.[1]

[1] SCALE OF DEPRECIATION OF CONTINENTAL MONEY SHOWING THE VALUE OF 100
CONTINENTAL DOLLARS IN SPECIE.

	1777			1778			1779			1780			1781		
	Dollars	90ths	8ths	Dollars	90ths	8ths	Dollars	90ths	8ths	Dollars	90ths	8ths	Dollars	90ths	8ths
January				67	85	1	12	85	1	3	40	0	2	45	0
February				61	83	6	10	85	6	2	89	1	2	45	0
March.				56	79	6	9	87	1	2	45	0	2	45	0
April				48	74	4	8	89	7	2	45	0	2	45	0
May				42	77	5	7	89	5	2	45	0	2	45	0
June				36	86	1	6	89	2	2	45	0	2	45	0
July				32	79	3	6	40	0	2	45	0			
August				27	87	3	5	89	6	2	45	0			
September	100	00	0	24	78	5	4	88	5	2	45	0			
October	90	77	3	20	84	5				2	45	0			
November	82	73	0	17	88	0	3	89	6	2	45	0			
December	74	70	0	14	89	2	3	30	0	2	45	0			

May 31, 1781, Continental money
ceased to pass as currency, but was
afterwards bought and sold as an article
of speculation, at very uncertain and
desultory prices, from 500 to 1000 to 1.

From Pelatiah Webster's *Political Essays*, 503. See also *American State
Papers, Finance*, v, 772, and contemporary almanacs as Nathanael Low's
Almanack for 1788.

Washington said that it took a wagon load of paper money to buy a wagon load of flour. This rapid and continuing depreciation is startling, but if one did not hold the paper for any length of time, the loss was not great in any one transaction. The hardship involved was nothing like what it would be nowadays. Few people then had settled incomes. They lived on farms or supported themselves by shop keeping, commerce, and the mechanic arts. The amount of money actually used in buying and selling was small, for many people kept a running account with the village storekeeper, giving him their produce and taking whatever goods they needed in exchange.

Whenever one thinks of these subjects, the spectre of Valley Forge at once appears. The sufferings of the soldiers are always painted in saddest hues; the men are shoeless; their progress over the frozen ground is traceable by the blood from their naked feet, and their clothing is so tattered that the spectators' sensibilities are shocked. Far away from Valley Forge and more than a year later, the colonel of a Virginia regiment wrote that half of his men were without a coat, a waistcoat, or a shirt, and more than half of them were without shoes and stockings.[1] In camp or garrison there was little to eat, and less to drink; there was never meat on hand beyond the requirements of the immediate future and often there was none. Flour, too, was difficult to procure and to keep. In 1781, General Patterson at West Point wrote that his troops had nothing whatever to eat, and apparently no prospect of getting anything. On one occasion, while at Valley Forge, Washington ordered the commander of a

---

[1] *Bland Papers . . . Selections from the Manuscripts of Colonel Theodorick*   *Bland, Jr.*, ed. by Charles Campbell (Petersburg, 1840), i, 136.

foraging party to seize wheat, flour, beef, hogs, and pork ; and to assure the owners that some time they would be compensated. Volumes might be filled with the instances of starvation and hardship. Wherever the army went, hunger and want at once appeared. Ten thousand soldiers encamped at any one spot for a couple of weeks created famine. But in 1779, in the very year when the soldiers were starving in New Jersey and on the Hudson, bread-stuffs were practically unsaleable at Philadelphia, less than one hundred and fifty miles away.[1] The inefficiency of Congress, the lack of administrative experience of the people generally, and the covetousness of contractors con-tributed to the sufferings of the soldiers; but the primal cause of these distresses was the lack of transportation. It was impossible to clothe and feed thousands of soldiers for any length of time far away from the ordinary routes of water carriage.

Before 1776, transportation had been almost entirely by water. South of the Potomac there was scarcely a road to be found. With the war, ordinary means of trans-portation were dislocated, and the demand for drivers, draft animals, and wheeled vehicles far outstripped the supply. There were no magazines of food. Everything had to be collected from the farmers. When food and clothing for a regiment or two had been gathered, it was often impossible to forward them to the camp. In June and July, 1780, Jefferson wrote that supplies for the Virginia troops were already on shipboard, but they could not be dispatched owing to the presence of

---

[1] This statement as well as others as to prices in Philadelphia is based on the figures given in the "Day-book of a Philadelphia Merchant," in the manu-script collections of the Pennsylvania Historical Society. This nameless store-keeper bought wheat for 6s. per bushel in 1774, 7s. 6d. in 1777, and 3s. 9d. in 1779. In the same years he paid for salt by the bushel 18d., £5, and £7.

the enemy's privateers in the Chesapeake.[1] Land transportation could not be procured. Indeed, so little had
it "been practiced in this country" that there were
few wagons at any time, and a great part of what
there were had been recently drawn to the southward.
Two years earlier, a vessel with a cargo of clothing had
dodged into a North Carolinian port; to get the uni-
forms to the soldiers, wagons had to be sent all the
way from Pennsylvania.[2]

Throughout the war, agricultural operations went on
very nearly as they did in peaceful days, except in the
neighborhood of the contending armies. The conflict began in New England, but after the spring of 1776, excepting for the occupation of Newport and a few raids on seacoast towns, that part of the country was free from the
invader. British privateers watched the mouth of the
Chesapeake and occasionally a plundering expedition
visited plantations up the Rappahannock, or the James,
or the Potomac; but, until the winter of 1780–81 plantation work went on much the same as if the Declaration
of Independence had never been signed and was taken up
again in 1782. Life, indeed, was so placid in the Old
Dominion that Robert Beverley, unmindful of war, sent
his son to England for his education, as he himself had
gone years before. South Carolina and North Carolina
knew the contest only by hearsay until 1780. Even in the
Middle States, which were the scene of marching armies
and garrisoned posts, war was no unmixed economic evil.
The British and the French were well supplied with gold
and silver and paid good prices for whatever they could
buy. The farmers of southern New England welcomed

---

[1] Ford's *Writings of Jefferson*, ii. 315,   [2] *North Carolina Records*, xiii, p. v.
317.

the latter as allies and charged them fifty per cent or so extra. The farmers of eastern Pennsylvania closed their ears to the groans of Valley Forge and brought meat and flour in great abundance to the British commissaries at Philadelphia. Even the American soldiers, sufferers that they were, contributed to the garnered hoard of fore-stallers, engrossers, and speculators who were even then "preying upon the vitals of this great Country." [1] As years went on, the scene changed, commerce grew and was exceedingly profitable, and the privateers poured their prize goods upon the markets. There was a constant supply of luxuries and superfluities that found a ready sale, and at the end of the war, people were living in un-wonted ease.

By the summer of 1779, the shelves of the importers and of the storekeepers were filled with foreign and do-mestic commodities of all kinds. On the first day of August in that year, a Newburyport merchant took an account of his stock. It occupies six pages of forty lines each. No less than sixty lines are given up to textiles of all kinds; flannels, yellow broadcloth, shalloon, forty dozen Bilbao handkerchiefs, four dozen of Barcelona and six dozen of English weave, besides oznabriggs, British and Irish linens, and sheetings. Then come soap, shot, bung borers, powderhorns, shoes, pumps, and boots, pint mugs, looking-glasses, and scented hair powder. Of iron-ware there were hammers, nails, knives, razors, muskets, and cutlasses. For food and drink, there were flour, rice, salt, beef, sugar, molasses, pickled herring, alewives, Geneva, starch, and coffee.

Privateering grew out of the speculative mania which

---

[1] Washington to Burwell Bassett, Middlebrook, April 22, 1779 (*Writings of Washington*, Ford ed., vii, 413). See also Massachusetts Historical Society's *Proceedings*, 1871–73, p. 56.

is an ordinary concomitant of war.[1] The profits were often large, not only to the owners, but to the captain and crew as well. Sometimes a year's operations did not turn out favorably, owing to vessels being captured by the British. Many firms made money, a great deal of it. There were the Cabots of Beverley and the Derbys of Salem who grew rich during the war.[2] The privateersmen often sold their prizes and cargoes in European ports, sending home those which were captured near the American coast or were unsaleable in Europe. The proceeds of prizes that could be disposed of abroad were invested in goods that the privateer herself carried home, or were sent across the ocean in a chartered vessel. The same Newburyport merchant carefully inventoried goods that came from his armed ships. Among the privateers in which he was interested was the *America*. The list of goods from her prizes is a formidable one. It includes tea, Florence oil, glass, tin, butter, loaf sugar, spelling books, glass, bar iron, gunpowder and rifles, and all kinds of textiles from Queen's cord to common duck. There were also " Hows acid " and " Stoughton's Elixir," and other things that would naturally be found in vessels plying across the Atlantic, or bound to or from the West Indies. Prize goods might well be regarded as the substratum of a general storekeeper's stock. Whatever additions were made to them by foreign importations would be the consequence of orders sent out from America or of ventures made by foreign commission houses. The duplication of these importations year after year from 1779 through 1783

---

[1] General Greene noted that the Carolinians even in 1780 "appear, not-withstanding their danger, very intent upon their private affairs." *North Carolina Records*, xv, 174.

[2] See Robert E. Peabody's "Derbys of Salem, Mass." in Essex Institute's *Historical Collections*, xliv, 193.

is convincing proof not only of the demand for them, but of the ability of the people to pay for them.[1]

These goods were brought over from the Netherlands, France, and Spain. The records of European custom houses have disappeared and so have those of American ports, for the most part. It is possible, however, to get some suggestion from invoices and account books that have been preserved [2] and from statements in contemporary diaries and newspapers. Among the captains was William Haydon of Boston who made three voyages to Amsterdam and back in 1779, 1780, and 1781. The name of the earliest ship commanded by him has not come down to us, but the *Hannah* which sailed from Amsterdam in 1780, and the *Juno* which came in 1781 were armed cargo carriers or letters of marque. The cargo of the former was invoiced at thirty-three thousand florins; that of the latter at sixty-seven thousand. Among other articles in the hold of the *Hannah* were necessaries like German steel, china ware, brushes, tea kettles, window glass, and cutlery. There were also desirable things, — tea, spices, coach glasses, and silk mitts, as well as children's toys, blue-flowered velvet, and superfine scarlet broadcloth. Of expensive articles, there came from Amsterdam to New England ports in these or other ships one box of tea that was valued at nearly three hundred florins, and a " fire

---

[1] "Tho' the *public treasury was so very poor and distressed*, yet the States were *really overrun with an abundance of cash :* the *French* and *English* armies, our *foreign loans, Havanna trade,* &c. had filled the country with *money*, and *bills on Europe* were currently sold at 20 to 40 per cent. *below par.*

"This induced the merchants to buy these bills, and remit them to *Europe*, and in return to import great quantities of *European* goods, which arrived under the great expense of a *war freight* and insurance; yet their *scarcity*, the great *plenty of cash*, and the *luxury and pride* of the people were such, that they sold rapidly and to *great profit*." Pelatiah Webster's "Sixth Essay on Free Trade and Finance" in *Political Essays* (Philadelphia, 1791), p. 267.

[2] These details as to the commerce of Amsterdam are gathered from a " Facteur Boëk " of De Neufville and Son in the Library of Congress; the fragment of a letter book of the same firm is in the same collection.

burnt chiney table sett" of one hundred and fifty-seven pieces that was invoiced at two hundred and twenty florins It will be noted that some of these goods came from Germany and it may be said that others came from England, as two trunks that were sent to Amsterdam by Mr. George Harlay of London and were taken by the *Dolphin* to Boston on account of Mr. Christopher Champlin of Newport, Rhode Island. Besides Captain Haydon's vessels others sailed from Holland for Philadelphia and the Chesapeake, either directly or by way of St. Eustatia. Among these was the *General Washington*, which left Amsterdam in July, 1780, consigned to George Mason of Alexandria, in Virginia. Her cargo was not valuable, but the number of the articles was extensive, ranging from one dozen packs of playing cards to scissors, buttons, sewing silk, rhubarb, and Venice treacle.

No invoices of cargoes from France have appeared, but there are many indications of vessels and goods from that country in American ports during the Revolution. In February, 1778, rather before the time that we are considering, a certain Monsieur Roulhac wrote to Henry Laurens that five vessels of his Bordeaux firm were then in American ports. About the same time the cargo of the *Marquis de Cassigny* from Bordeaux was advertised in the Boston papers and she may have been one of Roulhac's ships. Her cargo, besides window glass, tea, sugar, and soap, included almonds and anchovies, claret and brandy, figs and lemons, brandied fruits, and a long list of materials for women's dress. A few days later another ship came in from Martinique with forty cases of gin, two of lavender water, and hogsheads of sewing twine, pins, and needles. Everywhere throughout the States French goods were constantly being offered for sale, but recorded details of cargoes are scanty. On July 3, 1778, an Englishman, Joseph Hardy by name, wrote from Cadiz to Lord Weymouth, then Secretary of State, that a French frigate and a sloop of war had arrived at that port to convoy a fleet of American merchantmen across the Atlantic. Throughout the war there was a large commerce with southern Spain.[1]

Before 1775, the colonists had been allowed to trade to the Spanish peninsula south of Cape Finisterre ; they carried rice there and brought home large cargoes of salt. They also had availed themselves of the situation of Finisterre to run along the northern Spanish coast to Bilbao in the Basque Provinces, next to the French boundaries. They were hospitably received there by the Spaniards, especially by the firm of Joseph Gardoqui and Sons. In 1779, these enterprising merchants informed the Committee of Foreign Correspondence that Bilbao was the only free port in the Spanish kingdom [2] and offered their best services to public and private traders alike. The public commerce that went on through this port has already been described. In addition to this, Bilbao proved to be a useful rendezvous for American privateers, whether in search of supplies and shelter, or for the purpose of selling their prizes and their prize goods. Among the ships that sought

[1] The *Pennsylvania Journal* for March 26, 1783 reported six American vessels lying in Cadiz Bay.

[2] "Papers of the Continental Congress" in the State Department at Washington, 92, 459. There are many letters from Diego Gardoqui in the "Lee Manuscripts" and the "Sparks Manuscripts." The latter also contain many letters from Stormont, Grantham, and York, which are full of information on these themes, and the same is true of the "Stevens Facsimiles." Professor H. N. Sherwood, who is preparing an essay on this general subject, assisted me in this research — of which I have given the barest outline.

Oliver Pollock served as agent for the United States at New Orleans. There are many letters from him in the collections above mentioned. See also A. B. Woodward's *Representation of the Case of Oliver Pollock* (Washington, 1803) ; an interesting article about him is in the *Magazine of American History,* xxii, 414. From all this it appears that the Spanish authorities at Havana and New Orleans were very favorably disposed toward the United States and that there was a considerable exchange of goods between Havana and the northern ports.

2 D

this haven was the *Rambler* belonging to the Cabots of Essex
County, Massachusetts.   On two of her outward voyages,
she carried tobacco from the Chesapeake direct; on her homeward trips she brought brandy, two hundred casks of it in
1783; blankets, tarred yarn, cordage, the ever present window glass, gunpowder, and iron, and four hundred dozen
silk handkerchiefs, formed an important part of her cargo
on her last trip, which was valued in all at 383,512 riales
of vellon.[1]

Advertisements in the newspapers throughout the States
confirm the impression that foreign goods were everywhere in large supply after 1778.   Not only this, but
foreign goods that ministered to the æsthetic desires and
the craving for delicate stimulants are everywhere offered
for sale.   At Charleston, in the winter of 1779–80, in the
interval between Prevost's abortive siege and Clinton's
successful one, one could buy "Spanish segars with cases
for ditto," fine Turkey coffee, silver-tipped razors, and
superfine India chintzes.   At Philadelphia, besides the
usual array of tea, handkerchiefs, looking-glasses, playing
cards, and Madeira there were offered for sale English and
French gold watches and " very thick plated elegant Table
Chafing Dishes of the newest fashion."   Across the Delaware, at Trenton, at Morristown, hard by the headquarters
of the American army, and at Captain Carter's at Bottle
Hill, one could buy goods by the newspaper half column of

---

[1] An idea of the value of a thousand
riales of vellon may be gathered from
the statement that a vessel, the *Savage*,
was bought at Bilbao for 16,623 riales,
which was stated in the account as equal
to 180 pounds sterling. These details
are taken from the papers that were
placed in the hands of Nathan Dane by
the Cabots when he was employed by
them to prosecute a suit against the
Gardoquis. They are now in the cabinet
of the Massachusetts Historical Society.
My attention was drawn to them by
Mr. Samuel E. Morison. Don Carmelo
de Echegaray, Chronicler of the Basque
Provinces, very kindly made a search
for the Gardoqui papers at Bilbao; but
account books and the family too have
disappeared. The *Rambler* was a letter
of marque and was bonded for $ 20,000.
See C. H. Lincoln's *Naval Records of the
American Revolution* (Washington, 1906).

unleaded type : laces and rattinet, white gauze and moreen, chocolate and ginger, "Geneva" and brandy, "patent medicines," and pickled sturgeon.

Account books tell a similar tale of display and drink. At Hartford, Connecticut, Nathan Bolles kept a general store and the best daybooks that have come down to us. On October 9, 1781, a week before the drummer boy mounted the ramparts at Yorktown and beat a parley, Mrs. Rhoda Chapel had charged to her account at his shop, satin and ribbon to the amount of one pound, thirteen shillings, and three pence, to which she added one "Orstrech Feather" and a gauze handkerchief, together valued at ten shillings. Three months later, Mrs. Polly Goodwin visited Mr. Bolles's and bought tea, coffee, chocolate, and sugar, all of which were charged on one bill. The gayeties of Philadelphia are recounted in the letters of the members of Congress and of the French representatives. Elsewhere there was dancing and horse racing. Cosmo Medici, writing from Halifax, North Carolina, in March, 1778, mentions "an elegant Ball" which had been held at that place.[1] In 1779, a French dancing master advertised for pupils in the "Maryland Journal," and the same paper informed its readers that the Bladensburg races would be run as usual for purses of one thousand dollars and five hundred. Frenchmen who traveled over the country in the last years of the war declared that it was difficult to conceive of the prosperity which they saw ; in 1782, Robert R. Livingston wrote that necessities and even luxuries were in ample supply ;[2] and four years later Stephen Higginson stated that the people at large had been living in an expensive and luxurious manner.[3]

[1] *North Carolina Records*, xiii, 69.
[2] Wharton's *Diplomatic Correspondence*, vi, 146.
[3] American Historical Association's *Reports*, 1896, vol. i, p. 740. Charles Jenkinson, who had been one of the

Goods that came from abroad were paid for by export-
ing the products of the fields and forest. So constant and
large was the outgo that Congress and the States several
times interfered and sought by embargoes and restrictions
to keep foodstuffs at home, not realizing that the want of
supplies in camp and elsewhere was due to lack of means
of transportation and inefficient modes of management
and not to any scarcity of beef and flour. Notwithstanding
these hindrances, exportations were very large. Tobacco,
flour, and rice were constantly sent out on public account
as well as by private persons. In 1781, Congress gave the
control of public commerce to Robert Morris, who prosecuted it with his usual energy and success.[1] Private
traders appear to have thought that they would elude
British cruisers as they had in the French and Indian
wars. Now, there was more activity on the part of the
naval men, and the details of their prizes and cargoes furnish information as to the course of the export business.
Five hundred and seventy vessels were taken by ships of
the squadrons commanded by Admiral Lord Howe and
Admiral Gambier in the years from 1776 to 1779. Most
of these captures were made near the coast, either by
ships on the American station or by British privateers
fitted out at New York. Of the captured vessels more than
one hundred were bound to or from the West Indies.
About the same number were engaged in commerce with

secretaries to the Lords of the Treasury
throughout the war, stated that the
Americans had never lacked British
goods, although they had been high in
price. See " Report of the Lords of the
Committee of Privy Council, January
28, 1791 " in *Collection of interesting and
important Reports and Papers on the
Navigation Trade*, London, 1807,
" Printed by order of ' The Society of
Shipowners of Great Britain,' " p. 112.

[1] " Papers of the Continental Congress," No. 137, ii, 287. In 1783, the national ship *Duc de Lauzun* brought from
Havana sugar, wine, hides, cotton, and
peltry; the *General Washington* brought
from L'Orient a cargo valued at £9680
consigned to twenty-two persons, and
the frigate *Alliance* sailed from the
Chesapeake for Amsterdam with a cargo
of tobacco.

the European continent, and the rest were on coasting voyages. Their cargoes included large quantities of tobacco and other American products that were on their way to European or West Indian markets. As late as the spring of 1783, losses are reported in the newspapers. Among them were vessels bound out from the Chesapeake and the Delaware laden with tobacco, and flour, and also ships bound in from Europe. One of these had 29,000 pounds of tea as part of her cargo.

Some of the vessels taken by the British cruisers and privateers were engaged in collusive commerce — their captains sailing from Philadelphia with the expectation of unloading their cargoes on the wharves at New York. An active traffic was also prosecuted across Long Island Sound and over the marshes of eastern New Jersey. No estimate can be made as to the amount of this traffic. It was sufficiently extensive to provoke an act of the New Jersey legislature providing for the summary disposal of goods that had come through the lines. The proprietor of the Burlington stage also thought it desirable to publicly warn prospective passengers that no "run goods" would be taken by his conveyances. There was no dearth of finer foreign dress fabrics in New Jersey shops, but one can only surmise as to the proportion of them that came from London by way of New York.

Of all American products, tobacco was the most important because of its value in comparison with its bulk and the constant demand there was for it not only on the European continent, but also in Great Britain. Old English laws forbade the importation of Chesapeake tobacco into England except from the colony of production or by way of some other British plantation. Nevertheless, twenty-four million pounds of it were entered at the

British customhouses in the years 1777–80. How the consciences of customs officials were salved is uncertain; but doubtless they felt convinced it came from some British plantation, which very likely it did indirectly. In 1780, Parliament legalized the importation of tobacco by way of neutral ports. Tobacco was also brought in under the guise of prize goods. All in all, enough reached Great Britain to provide for about one-third of the ordinary annual consumption, and small quantities of tobacco were exported from England during every year of the war.[1] In the autumn of 1781, owing to the presence in Virginia of warring armies and navies, the price of tobacco in London rose to three shillings a pound, but in a few months it had fallen to two shillings.[2]

American, French, and Dutch vessels took on board tobacco at the plantation wharves on the banks of the Potomac, the Rappahannock, and the James. Waiting for a favorable gale from the north and west, they stood boldly down the bay and out to sea by Cape Henry. Almost always there were British vessels watching for them; but the wind that drove them prosperously outward compelled the blockaders to run for shelter under the nearest protecting bit of land. When the enemy became so numerous that it was too dangerous to attempt the passage by the Capes, the tobacco was taken overland

---

[1] These statements are based upon the figures given in a report of a committee of the House of Commons (*Parliamentary Register*, xxiv, 324–336 and Appendix No. X); Lord Sheffield's *Observations on the Commerce of the American States* (second edition, London, 1783), Appendixes i, ii, iii; George Chalmers' *Opinions on Interesting Subjects of Law and Commerce arising from American Independence* (London, 1785); and Anderson's *Historical and Chronological Deduction*, v, 250. The acts of Parliament are 20 George III, Cap. 39 and 22 George III, Cap. 38. In 1780 no less than 19,478 hhds. of tobacco were shipped to Great Britain by way of British Islands; *Case of R. D. Jennings*, p. 8.

[2] The best James River tobacco sold at Amsterdam for sixteen florins in 1781, in comparison with seven florins in 1783, De Neufville's "Prices Current," in the Massachusetts Historical Society's library.

to North Carolina or to the Delaware and shipped thence to market.

Once at sea, the tobacco ship was comparatively safe until she approached her port of destination. Many of them sailed directly across the Atlantic, but many sought the hospitable roadsteads of the Dutch St. Eustatia or the French Martinique. The former island was only a few miles long and of narrow width. Its soil was worthless for sugar cane; but it was one of the most profitable European possessions in that part of the world. Lying at the northeastern angle of the Greater and Lesser Antilles, it was a natural port of call for vessels bound to and from the Windward and Leeward Islands. The Dutch recognized its commercial possibilities. They declared it a free port and received with hospitality merchants of all nations who came to reside there. Gladly, too, they welcomed vessels from the rebellious colonies,[1] and the island became a clearing house for traffic between Europe and North America. Not only were American, French, Dutch, and Spanish vessels to be found in the anchorage there, but English vessels, too, some from British or Irish ports, others from the British West India Islands. Rodney found one hundred and twenty-five vessels lying at anchor there when he captured the place in 1781, twelve of them were English.[2] The warehouses were overflowing with Eu-

[1] Under date of March 21, 1776 the *Remembrancer* (iii, 32) notes the capture by the English of eight American vessels from Curacoa and St. Eustatia with powder and warlike stores; five others escaped. In 1780 they seized seven American vessels at anchor in the Dutch port of St. Martin's, *Parliamentary Register*, xviii, 77.

[2] Beatson's *Naval and Military Memoirs*, v, 160 note. Robert Beverley wrote that the capture of St. Eustatia seriously interfered with the commerce between Virginia and England, "Letter Book" under date of February 25, 1782.

Rodney's statement as to the number of vessels captured is in *Letters from Sir George Brydges now Lord Rodney relative to the Capture of St. Eustatius*, p. 8. In a letter in Mundy's *Life and Correspondence of Lord Rodney* (ii, 9) the number is given as one hundred and thirty. General Vaughan, Rodney's military colleague, says "upwards of two hundred ships" (Almon's *Remembrancer*, xi, 260). On the trade of St. Eustatia and

ropean goods and the beach was piled high with hogs-
heads of tobacco and tierces of rice. The neighboring
Dutch island of St. Martin and the Danish islands of St.
Croix and St. Thomas shared in this beneficent trade,[1] but
Statia led them all.

The cessation of hostilities was proclaimed by Washington at the head of the army on April 19, 1783, and the
news spread rapidly over the country. The most joyful
anticipations were entertained as to the future. With
free trade with all the world, with liberty to exploit their
great domain free from quitrents and parliamentary protection, with their political well-being absolutely in their
own hands, what doubt could the American people have of
their successful pursuit of happiness! The next three years
belied every one of these expectations. Commerce did
not prosper, the settlement of the country halted, and
government in State and nation seemed to be on the edge
of collapse.

Once independent and free, the thirteen States found
themselves face to face with the commercial barriers of
France, Spain, and Great Britain. It was one thing to
encourage rebellious colonists against an ancient rival; to
continue to give them commercial privileges, after their
usefulness was gone, was quite another. The French
government annulled its decrees giving Americans peculiar
rights;[2] Spain closed many ports to their shipping; and

its capture, see also Hannay's *Letters
Written by Sir Samuel Hood* (Navy
Records Society, London, 1895); *The
Case of Richard Downing Jennings who
Resided at Saint Eustatius as a Merchant*
(London, 1790); and an excellent article
by Professor J. F. Jameson in the *Ameri-
can Historical Review*, viii, 683–708.

[1] The Swedes having acquired French
St. Bartholomew made it a free port,
and the king of Denmark abolished all

custom fees in his West Indian possessions. *Maryland Journal and Baltimore Advertiser*, April 29, May 13, 1785.

[2] "Ordinance. Of the King's Council
of State concerning the Commerce of
foreigners with the French Islands of
America, 30th August 1784." Copied
from the Registers of the Council of
State. See also *Recueil des Anciennes
Lois Françaises*, xxvii, 459–464. The
Ordinance of 1778, admitting foreign

the navigation system of Great Britain automatically excluded them from the commerce of the empire. The
British government went so far in relaxation as to admit
unmanufactured American products to ports of Great
Britain, without paying any alien duty, even when brought
in American ships; but they closed the trade of the West
India sugar plantations to American vessels absolutely,
although they permitted the lumber and breadstuffs of
the continent to be imported in British bottoms. This permission did not extend to salted meats and fish, for this
would interfere with the commerce of Nova Scotia, Quebec,
Newfoundland, and Ireland. Instead of enjoying freedom
of trade with the rest of the world, therefore, American
shipowners and producers found themselves cut off by
law from some of the most profitable commercial activities
of colonial days.[1] Three years of hard times followed,
and it was not until 1786 that the outlook began to
brighten.

With the ending of hostilities, modes of living and
obtaining one's livelihood underwent many changes.

---

vessels into French colonial ports, was
annulled in 1783. The United States by
the commercial treaty of 1778 enjoyed
the right of the most favored nation.
The effect of these ordinances, therefore,
was to admit American vessels to the
French West Indies in 1778; exclude
them for the most part in 1783; and
give them certain privileges in 1784.
See *Loix et Constitutions des Colonies
Françoises*, vi, 314. France in 1778 had
opened the ports of Dunkirk, L'Orient,
Bayonne, and Marseilles to American
commerce, and this privilege was continued after the peace. A document in
the "Sheffield Papers" in the John
Carter Brown Library states that France
opened the ports of the sugar islands to
American commerce in articles that the
home land could not supply on July 23,
1783; but no such ordinance has been
found.

[1] On November 8, 1783, Edward Bancroft wrote from Philadelphia to William
Frazer, one of the British Under Secretaries of State, that the proclamation
as to West India trade had very much
surprised and alarmed the people of the
United States, who confidently expected
continued trade with the British West
Indies and considered the prohibition as
an injury. The writer seems to have
been in the United States at that time in
the guise of confidential agent. About
a year earlier, Fitzherbert had informed
Shelburne that Bancroft was an invalu-
able treasure and had advised that he be
given the arrears of his former salary.
See also Sir John Temple to Camarthen,
New York, January 5, 1786, confirming
Bancroft as to the Order in Council.

For one thing, the prices of American products fell far below those that had been obtained during the war, even when the high rates of freight and insurance were taken into account. Moreover, it was difficult to disband armies, recall privateers, and fill the gaps in the stock of labor made by the war and by the removal of thousands of negro slaves. Labor and capital had been diverted from agriculture to manufacturing enterprises that could not be profitably prosecuted in competition with British and European mills now that war no longer served as a protective tariff. Had there been any adequate political machinery for waging commercial war, something might have been done to remedy this. With a powerless central government and thirteen separate States, each one looking out for itself, concerted action was impossible. Industry and economy, alone, could bring prosperity to the farmer, manufacturer, and shipowner; and this required time and patience. Weeks and months were required to bring the disbanded soldiers home; and much longer time to recall the privateers and turn them and their crews into peaceful fishermen. The manufacturers could only slowly be convinced of the hopelessness of their endeavors and turn their energy and that of their workmen into more profitable occupations.

Nowhere was the immediate prospect more gloomy than in South Carolina. The ravages of war and the taking away of thousands of negroes by the British and the fleeing loyalists had seriously lowered her productive capacity. In 1784, negroes and goods to the amount of nearly two million pounds sterling were imported into the State, but the crops of 1783 and of 1784 combined did not amount to seven hundred thousand pounds. The yield was not much better in 1785, and the large importation had meantime gone

on. In Massachusetts, at the other end of the line, the case
was as bad, if not worse. The ending of the war found the
warehouses full of goods, and more had been ordered from
abroad and were on their way to the coast. British merchants
trading to America vied with one another in loading vessels with goods for the States, and sending them across the
Atlantic. But the market was already glutted. There
was no reckless "dumping" of British goods on American
wharves, but the increased amounts that came in were far
greater than the market could absorb. The New Englanders had less to give in return even than the South
Carolinians. Until the fishermen returned from the Banks
and trade could be reëstablished with the sugar islands, the
resources of New England were insufficient to pay even
what was then owing.[1] The case of New York was even
more desperate, and for the moment Philadelphia alone
seemed prosperous, for the wastage of the later years of
the war had been severely felt in Virginia.

All attempts of the State legislatures to remedy these
conditions proved of little avail, nor did the efforts of the
United States ministers at London and at Paris amount
to much more. Representations of British tobacco merchants and of French and Spanish sugar planters proved
to be more efficacious. The first were anxious to regain
the monopoly of handling the Chesapeake tobacco crop
that they had once enjoyed, and the government was
willing to help them. Certain ports of Great Britain
were appointed to which tobacco might be brought and
landed without the payment of any duty, bonds being
given for such payment in case the goods were not re-

---

[1] The *Independent Chronicle* of
March 9, 1784 quoted from a London
paper the statement that two vessels
had recently arrived in the Thames from
Boston in ballast "not having been able
to procure cargoes of any kind, though
they had (what is most desirable in that
country) specie to pay for all they should
have brought away."

exported.[1] All Jefferson's wiles could not induce the French government to open the tobacco trade to private merchants, for the Farmers General were still financially supreme. The French sugar planters were more successful. They convinced the government that cheap American food and lumber was necessary for them. Half a dozen of the most important ports in the French West India Islands were opened to the Americans. These could bring any American products in their own vessels, with the exception of salt pork, but could take away only molasses and rum in exchange.[2] Spain also relaxed her system somewhat and permitted American vessels to trade with Havana and with Trinidad, which was then in her hands[3]; and the ports of Louisiana and Florida seem to have been always open. In this way, by 1785, the West Indian trade was fairly unshackled and once more began to form an important element in American prosperity. All this time, the Dutch and Danish Islands had been open and had, indeed, been the salvation of American West Indiamen. Beginning with 1786, this traffic, in common with American commerce

---

[1] By orders in council of May 14, and June 6, 1783, the British government opened trade between America and Great Britain in oil and unmanufactured goods to include naval stores, tobacco, and indigo. In November of the same year, another ordinance established six ports at which tobacco might be imported and warehoused under bonds, and one of December expressly permitted the importation of any unmanufactured American goods not prohibited by law. These could be brought in by Americans or by British subjects in American or British vessels upon payment of the duties that were paid by British subjects importing the same goods from British Islands. In the case of rice the British, finding that the American exporters were sending quantities of it to the Netherlands, removed the import duty and re-

gained a large part of the business of distributing this commodity to northern Europe. The orders in council of May 14, June 6, and July 2, 1783 are printed in the Appendix to A. Stokes's *View of the Constitution of the British Colonies.*

[2] Goods imported under the ordinance of August 30, 1784 were to pay local duties, and there was a further duty of one per cent on all exports and imports. An additional duty of three livres per quintal was to be charged on salted beef and fish. The conditions under which this commerce was carried on proved to be burdensome; sixteen American vessels were seized by the French in 1785. See *Pennsylvania Packet,* February 17, 1787.

[3] *Pennsylvania Packet,* May 30, 1785; *Maryland Journal and Baltimore Advertiser,* February 27, 1789.

in general, grew with wonderful rapidity and, by 1788, had regained the position that it held before the war.

In those days there was so much irregularity in the observance of the laws of one's own country, or of any other, that it is necessary in studying commercial subjects to leave the statute book and the customhouse regulations and try by other means to pierce the gloom of historic doubt, and see the facts as they really were instead of as they should have been had every one, from skippers and supercargoes to collectors and governors, done his duty. Newspapers were beginning to improve in the matter of providing news; the war had broadened the outlook and given men more interest in what was going on in other parts of America. Especially ship news that formerly had served to fill the vacant spaces becomes of first importance. The " Pennsylvania Packet " published at Philadelphia made a specialty of maritime news. Its lists of arrivals and departures were never complete, but they grew better with each year from 1783 to 1789. Its correspondence was not well organized, but it was fair in 1783 and grew better with each year. The editors were clearly much more interested in arrivals than they were in departures, for the former were of much greater importance to their shopkeeping customers than the latter. Tabulating these arrivals from foreign ports throughout the years under review and comparing them with an official list of pre-Revolutionary days gives one the opportunity to make rough generalizations. Fortunately the customhouse books of St. Eustatia and St. Martin were taken to Holland many years ago and are there to-day.[1] Like the lists in the newspapers they

[1] The St. Eustatia and St. Martin shipping lists have been copied for me under the direction of Dr. H. T. Colenbrander, Director of the Bureau of His-

were not always accurate, but they are useful in checking the latter and have a fund of information of their
own.

From pre-Revolutionary customhouse returns it appears
that in the twelve months preceding October 10, 1766,
twenty-three hundred topsail vessels, sloops, and schooners
entered at the ports of the thirteen old English colonies
from foreign parts. From 1783 until 1785, the number of
arrivals reported was very small and probably reflects the
inadequacy of the records[1] as well as the paucity of
the commerce; but in the latter year 754 vessels are recorded as entering at the important ports from foreign parts.
In 1786, the number had grown to 1738; in 1787, there is a
slight falling off; but in 1788, almost two thousand arrivals
are noted. This number should be increased somewhat
for unrecorded vessels, so that it is safe to say that in the
year of the ratification of the Constitution of the United
States, the foreign commerce had been reëstablished.
Moreover, as the average size of vessels had increased within
twenty years, the commerce was actually greater than it
was in the earlier time. Many interesting things come
out from a study of these tabulations. It appears that the
old triangular trade was not regained, and that the traffic
with the Atlantic Islands was not resumed with anything
like its old vigor. The business of supplying slaves to the
foreign sugar planters had passed into other hands, and the

torical Publications at The Hague, who
has been most kind and helpful. The
transcripts fill some eight hundred pages,
giving arrivals and clearances with the
date, the name of the ship and of the
captain, and, in some cases, details as to
the cargo. These last are given only of
vessels arriving at St. Eustatia. The St.
Martin lists are more complete in this
respect, but the trade of that island is
not so interesting for the present purpose.

These transcripts are deposited in the
Harvard University Library, where they
may be used by students.

[1] A committee of the Pennsylvania
Assembly reported in 1785 that only
about one-half of the wine, brandy, and
rum imported into that State had paid
duty. After this time there seems to
have been greater efficiency; but the
customs service throughout the States
was very lax before 1789.

wines of France and Germany were fast taking the place
in aristocratic estimation that had once been held by the
vintages of Madeira and Fayal. In time, the trade with
the Far East and with Russia filled the place once held by
that from the Guinea coast. But now it was only in its
infancy. The *Empress of China* entered at New York from
Canton in May, 1785, and the *Grand Turk* sailed into Salem
harbor from the same port in 1787. The trade grew
rapidly. In 1789, of forty-six foreign vessels reported at
Canton, eighteen were American. Among them were the
old Derby privateer, *Astrea,* and the Boston ship, *Columbia,*
Captain Robert Gray,[1] which was then halfway on that
memorable voyage that for the first time carried the American flag around the world. The Baltic trade also grew
until twenty-five vessels were reported from Hamburg
and from Russia. These were the beginnings of what was
to develop into a profitable commerce, but for the time it
was no substitute for the lost African trade.

From the figures in the preceding paragraph, it is a
fair inference that commerce was reëstablished so far as
a study of arrivals from foreign ports may be taken as
evidence. Confirmation of this view is found in a comparative study of goods exported in the years 1771 and
1790.[2] From these, it appears that there was some falling
off in bricks, iron, candles, shooks, and tar. As to the
iron, in the earlier time, the law had contemplated all
later processes of manufacture being carried on in England; now the native ore was more and more being worked
up within the country. The other declines in exportations
were probably accidental, for although shooks declined,

---

[1] From the list in the "Hamilton
Papers," No. 8, Library of Congress.
Phineas Bond, British consul at Philadelphia, feared that the Americans would
"run" Oriental goods into Europe and
Ireland. American Historical Association's *Reports,* 1896, vol. i, p. 542.

[2] See Note II at end of chapter.

staves increased, and the same thing was true as to tar and turpentine. Nearly all other commodities as to which comparisons are possible show an increase. The largest increases were in breadstuffs. Of the great staples, tobacco, rice, indigo, and rum, the first two show no increase, but both indigo and rum gained decidedly. In live stock also there was an increase and the fishery had been reëstablished, as the gain of twenty per cent in exportation shows. Finally, the trebling of the exportation of whalebone is evidence that the whale fishery was becoming firmly established.

Charles James Fox and his Whig and Tory colleagues in the Coalition Ministry had no thought of building up American trade with Great Britain for the benefit of Americans, nor had their successor, the younger William Pitt. What they wished to do was to give employment to Englishmen in the handling and distribution of the Chesapeake tobacco and to regain the monopoly of the American markets for manufactured goods that they had enjoyed in the older days. They succeeded to a remarkable degree in both these attempts. American palates took kindly to the beverages of the Continent, but for clothing and cutlery, they preferred the products of the looms and shops of England. In the last three years of this period, continental trade, apart from that to the Baltic, scarcely grew at all, and that with France declined nearly one-half, while that with England grew apace. This is especially noticeable as to the ports of Virginia and Maryland. In 1766, there were 133 recorded British arrivals in the Chesapeake; in 1788, the newspapers noted 111. The serious economic condition of France and the Netherlands no doubt partly account for the stagnant or declining condition of trade with those countries, but the wiser policy of Great Britain and the desires of Americans were powerful factors.[1]

It is as to West Indian trade that these tabulations are especially valuable. Vessels by the hundreds sailed to the British West Indies from the United States and returned northward laden with products of British and foreign sugar fields. In 1766, 1442 vessels entered northern ports from the islands. Of these 851 came from the British West Indies, and 591 from all the rest. In 1788, 1170 arrivals at United States ports were noted in the "Pennsylvania Packet"; of these 467 came from the British Islands and 703 from the others. From this it appears that the British had given place to the other West India Islands. But this transference was more seeming than real, for commerce that apparently centered in the Dutch, French, and Spanish islands was actually British. The nationality of vessels is not given either in the papers or in the custom-house books, but this matters little, for those were the days when the nativity of a ship and her master depended upon the port that she was sailing for or upon the probable nationality of the first man-of-war whose sails appeared above the horizon.

The St. Eustatia shipping lists contain much interesting information on these matters. From them it appears that in 1785 no less than 321 vessels arrived at that island from the United States. Of these one-third came from New England. The vessels that unloaded their cargoes at

---

[1] There was a British and a French packet service to America after 1783. The latter was not successful, being hampered by high rates and petty regulations and also because letters carried were often opened, even those directed to the American minister at Paris. Goods brought by these vessels were frequently advertised for sale. Miss Julia Post Mitchell has studied this subject most carefully and has placed her manuscript at my disposal. See also Robert [St. John) de Crèvecœur's *Saint John de Crèvecœur, sa vie et ses ouvrages* (Paris, 1883). The enterprise is interesting rather as an example of French political desires than as throwing light on commercial conditions.

St. Eustatia put enough goods on shore to supply the inhabitants of that island for years. Of the vessels that came from the States, one-third returned directly home, and one-fifth cleared for other West Indian free ports. The remainder dropped out of sight. If we could trace them, they would doubtless be found in forbidden harbors. Mingled with these vessels that plied between St. Eustatia and North America, or that cleared for Danish, French, or Spanish islands there were others that made hundreds of voyages each year between Statia and the neighboring British islands. Presumably they were British vessels; but he must have been a superconscientious collector who inquired too closely into the origin of the register that the captain of one of these vessels or of the "lost ships" presented for their inspection. The temptation to connive at evasion of the regulations was very great, for the prosperity of British planters, governors, and collectors depended upon their producing molasses and sugar as cheaply as their neighbors.[1] If the Frenchmen got cheap American food and lumber, the British planters must do likewise or go into bankruptcy. The regulations permitted governors to suspend the orders on account of famine and hurricanes or other emergencies, and no one could refuse the hospitality of a British port to a vessel that was in danger of foundering or of other perils of the sea. Horatio Nelson was then second in command on the Caribbean station. Reading the "Admiralty Statutes," the customs regulations, and the Orders in Council, he became imbued with

---

[1] No official statistics have been found as to Jamaica, but that island must have been prosperous at this time. Between 1768 and 1786 the number of sugar plantations nearly doubled, slaves increased from 166,900 in 1768 to 255,700 in 1786; cattle from 135,750 to 224,500; and the production of sugar rose from 68,160 hhds. to 105,400. See W. Beckford's *Descriptive Account of the Island of Jamaica*, i, p. xxx. In 1786 lumber was plentiful at Jamaica and "much lower in price than we have known it" according to a letter from two Kingston merchants in the "Sheffield Papers," in the John Carter Brown Library.

the conviction that his duty to his country required him to enforce the law. His orders were to protect the commerce of Great Britain. How could he do that if he permitted "Rebel Americans" to frequent the ports of Nevis, St. Kitts, Antego, and other British islands? After unloading their cargoes there, they could sail to Martinique or some free French port and there load with molasses and rum and proceed homeward. No British vessels could compete with them, for the laws of many of the States taxed goods imported in British bottoms at a higher rate than those brought in in American ships. Whenever Nelson came across an American vessel in a British port he seized her, regardless of whether she had a British register or not. He soon found governors, customhouse officials, and planters upon him. Even the law officers, for the most part, refused to give him advice or draw a writ, unless their fee was paid down in cash in advance. The residents of the island, he declared, were Americans by interest and "as great rebels as ever were in America, had they the power to show it." On one occasion, he seized four vessels which were condemned; but not before their masters had procured writs charging him with assault and false imprisonment, laying the damages at four thousand pounds. He reported to the authorities in England that some of the vessels that he examined had certificates of British registry that had done duty for years, and that new ones were easily procured at many ports. After a time, American vessels with British registers became scarce, owing to his endeavors but, instead, American vessels appeared with Spanish papers. Under a regulation that dated back more than a century, Spanish vessels were permitted to enter the ports of the British islands for certain specified purposes, and the number of these purposes had been increased from time to time by the easy process of writing on the margin of the official document on file at the customhouse. Oftentimes, Americans who had neither British nor Spanish certificate were permitted by the official to unload their cargoes under the plea of having sprung a leak or lost a topmast. Some captains, according to Nelson, would "swear through a nine inch plank" to get permission to sell their produce.[1]

Sir John Temple, British consul general at New York, and Phineas Bond, vice consul at Philadelphia, detected another means by which American shipowners continued to enjoy the advantages of British trade which they had had in colonial times. At Philadelphia, forged Mediterranean passes were openly sold. Temple bought one for twelve guineas and sent it to the Lords of the Admiralty, asking them to note the clever way in which their signatures had been imitated. With one of these and a certificate of British registry, an American ship captain in an American ship might sail boldly into the Mediterranean, scorning British cruiser and Barbary corsair alike. The British consul complained to Jay,[2] but without much result. Bond undertook to list the vessels having these passes, but he soon found that this would require a corps of officials to make it effective.

One of the most interesting plans for the evasion of national regulations had nothing to do with the British, but is mentioned here as further evidence of the general laxness of the period. Diego Gardoqui was now in America as the representative of His Catholic Maj-

---

[1] Nicholas, *Dispatches and Letters of Lord Viscount Nelson* (London, 1845), i, 113–203. See also letters in the *Pennsylvania Packet* for June 10, 16, 1785.

[2] There is some correspondence on this matter between Jay and Temple in *The Diplomatic Correspondence of the United States of America, 1783 to 1789*, vi, 29. At this time Jay was in charge of foreign affairs.

esty. In combination with Massachusetts shipowners, who had traded with his firm at Bilbao during the Revolution and before, he proposed to utilize an American-built ship for trading between Spain and the Spanish colonies, — a bit of commerce that was confined by Spanish law to Spanish vessels alone. The ship was fitted out and sent to Spain, but the project came to an abrupt termination because he could not obtain a Spanish register ; but the intention of evading all regulations was the same whether it succeeded or not.

To return to the British. By 1786, it had become evident that the Order in Council closing West Indian trade to American shipping was practically a dead letter, except when Nelson with the *Boreas* was in sight. By two acts, one passed in 1786,[1] the other in 1787,[2] Parliament tried to make the system more efficient. The former of these laws was designed to put an end to fraudulent registration of American vessels. After the 1st of May, 1786, no foreign ships should be registered as British, and persons holding certificates were to give bonds not to sell or lend such certificate, nor dispose of it in any way, except to return it to some customhouse in case the vessel was wrecked or burned, perchance the certificate had survived the catastrophe. The law of 1787

---

[1] 26 George III, Cap. 60, " An Act for the further Increase and Encouragement of Shipping and Navigation."

[2] 27 George III, Cap. 7. The act of 28 George III, Cap. 6 brought into one law the regulations as to British colonial trade. In 1785, Parliament had provided that no goods should be imported from the United States into Nova Scotia, New Brunswick, Prince Edward Island, Cape Breton, and Newfoundland, except in British vessels. The only exceptions of this general closing of British colonial ports to American shipping was as to Turk's Island, to which American vessels

might go in ballast and from which they might take salt, but nothing else. In emergency the governors in any colony might permit any vessel to bring food and lumber. Even before the passage of the act of 1787, a committee of West India merchants informed Mr. Fox, November 26, 1783, that it was impossible for the British sugar islands to compete with the French islands, and suggested that lumber and provisions should be admitted from the United States on the cheapest terms. " Bancroft Manuscripts," 1783–86, i, 99, in the New York Public Library.

prohibited the importation of American goods by way
of the foreign islands. So many loopholes were necessarily left open in both of these acts that slight effect was
produced by them in the immediate future. For instance,
in the earlier law, it was provided that foreign vessels
built before the 1st of May, 1786, were not to be deprived
of the privileges they then enjoyed; this led to the elonga-
tion of the life of many a ship, or at least of her register.
As to the later law, the colonial governors were authorized
to suspend its operation in case of emergency, — and disasters and famines grew in frequency.

The three years 1787, 1788, 1789, saw an increase of the
American commerce on the whole, but this was due
mainly to the reabsorption by Britain of the business that
had formerly been hers. The West Indian trade maintained itself, but did not increase. Combining the arrivals
at St. Eustatia from the United States and the departures
for the ports of that country, it appears that the trade
was at a stand, there being fifteen fewer in 1789 than in
1787.[1] These figures afford a fair indication of the course
of trade, because St. Eustatia was not only an entrepôt for

[1] Mr. Albert L. Kohlmeier of Indiana
University has placed at my disposal
tables which he has compiled from these
lists in the prosecution of a research into
West Indian commerce. Below are some
of the results.

In the following table the vessels
touching at St. Eustatia from the French
and Spanish West India Islands are in-
cluded in the clearances from St. Eustatia
for the United States. Of the 827 vessels
clearing from St. Eustatia to the British
Islands in 1788 only 8 were to Jamaica.
Of the vessels coming from the United
States in 1788, one-third were from New
England; of those clearing for the United
States, one-half were bound for New
England.

YEAR	NUMBER OF VESSELS				
	Arriving at St. Eustatia from the United States	Clearing from St. Eustatia for the United States	Arriving at St. Eustatia from French W.I. and Clearing for U.S.	Arriving at St. Eustatia from Spanish W.I. and Clearing for U.S.	Clearing from St. Eustatia for the British W.I.
1785	321	366	119	0	1230
1786	328	436	158	10	1010
1787	256	421	168	14	883
1788	249	427	203	20	827
1789	254	408	169	3	712

goods on their way to and from British sugar plantations, but was a port of call for ships bound northward from Martinique and the other islands of the Lesser Antilles. The number of arrivals and clearances of vessels sailing between St. Eustatia and St. Martin and the British Islands diminishes steadily after 1786, which would seem to show that British policy was beginning to produce results in limiting American trade — at least to the British West Indian sugar islands. It is evident, however, that the collectors at Nevis and St. Kitts, now that Nelson was ashore in England, had reverted to their former modes of action. Otherwise it is difficult to explain the fact of vessels coming to the Dutch Islands from America with American goods on board, sailing thence with cargo intact to Nevis or St. Kitts, and reappearing with the same cargo on the way to Jamaica. Notwithstanding these subterfuges, the West Indian trade was not growing. The expansion of commerce was in that with the British Islands, the Mediterranean, and the Far East.

The American people were ambitious to make themselves really independent of the world by manufacturing their own goods wherever it was possible to do so; but the difficulties of carrying out any such plan were very great in view of the prevailing high price of labor, the scarcity of capital, and the lack of raw materials.[1] In some cases the States gave bounties; in others societies, by prizes and premiums, sought to encourage industry and had a good

[1] There is an interesting article on this subject by William Barton in Carey's *American Museum*, 1790, First Part, 285. The statements in the text are taken from the "Hamilton Manuscripts" in the Library of Congress.

September 10, 1785, Patrick Henry wrote to Jefferson that "the high price of labor, scarcity of money, and other difficulties" had prevented the establishment of an arms factory in that State Immigration set in with renewed vigor in 1784, from the European continent as well as from Great Britain and Ireland. *American Historical Review*, xvi, 572. The demand for labor, what with the establishment of new industries, the migration to the West, and the replenishing of the waste of the war continued unsatisfied.

measure of success. In Massachusetts, Rhode Island, Connecticut, and Pennsylvania, mills were erected for working up linen, wool, and cotton. As yet the policy of Great Britain in prohibiting the exportation of textile machinery or patterns thereof had prevented the extended use of machinery in the United States, for the inventive genius of Americans had not yet manifested itself. Efforts were made to reproduce the machinery that had been invented in England, but up to 1789, these efforts had not borne much fruit, and many mills that had been opened were obliged to suspend operations. At Providence in Rhode Island, successful beginnings had been made, judging from the statements that were drawn up by a committee of that town and also from letters that were written by Moses Brown. From these it appears that with the aid of Samuel Slater, who had worked with the new machinery in England, Almy and Brown had been enabled to take the first steps in what proved to be the beginning of a profitable cotton manufacture in America.[1] They were making twelve thousand yards of cottons in each twelve months besides thirty thousand yards of woolen cloth. Providence also produced quantities of hats, a good deal of leather, and worked up much of this into shoes, — fifteen thousand pairs of them, besides saddlery and harness. Small articles of iron and brass were also made there as joiners and molders' tools, scythes, axes, and drawing knives. Among the articles noted were three million nails. These were also made throughout New England to such an extent, indeed, that they were no longer imported into that section of the country, but some were even exported to the other States of the Union. The development of

[1] *The Slater Mills at Webster*, issued in 1912 by S. Slater and Sons, contains an interesting and concise account of Slater and the introduction of textile machinery into the United States.

spinning machinery led to the increased demand for cotton and wool cards. These were made extensively in Massachusetts, sixteen hundred women and children being employed in that State alone, using one hundred and fifty casks of imported wire. Two-thirds of these cards were exported to other States. At Boston there was a sailcloth factory employing two hundred women and children. There were thirty looms. These produced about two thousand yards of duck each week. Double the amount might have been made if flax could have been bought at a reasonable price. This enterprise was sustained by a state bounty, making less than one per cent net over what was received from the treasury. Nearly fifty thousand yards of lace and edging, valued at £1869, were made at Ipswich in one year.

Manufacturing was carried on at many places in Connecticut, at New Haven, Glastonbury, Middletown, New London, Killingly, Hartford, and elsewhere. At these towns woolens, linens, thread, and lace were manufactured, and wood, iron, and leather worked up into articles of everyday use. The woolen factory at Hartford had been established in 1788 with a capital of £1280 raised by subscription in shares of £10 each. It was still in operation in 1791, but was greatly embarrassed in its working by the difficulty of procuring wool of suitable quality and by the scarcity of labor. It would already have suspended operations had the State not given it the right to hold a lottery. Turning to Virginia, it does not appear that there were any factories in that State, but the household production of cloth, stockings, and shoes was so large that in some counties five-sixths of the amounts required were produced on the plantations. In King William's County, twenty families including 96

whites and 205 negroes made in one year 3814 yards of
cloth, and 260 pairs of stockings, all valued at £500.
In other counties, in Princess Anne, Norfolk, and Nanse-
mond, conditions were similar, and at Norfolk there was
a tannery which produced leather that was worked up in
the vicinity.   Everywhere, indeed, throughout the States,
more attention was being paid to manufacturing every
year.

   This period was signalized not only by activity in commerce and industry, but also by the desire to make better
communications between the different parts of the country.   Washington, especially, interested himself in plans
for improving the navigation of the Potomac and the
James and connecting them with western rivers.   He also
thought well of a project to unite Virginia and North
Carolina by a canal through the Dismal Swamp.   In relation to this general subject, he also watched with care
the attempts of James Rumsey to apply steam to the
propulsion of boats by sucking water in at the bow and
ejecting it at the stern.   At Philadelphia John Fitch,
William Thornton, and Henry Voight produced a steam-
boat that actually ran eighty miles in one day.[1]   They
were ahead of their time, and no immediate revolution in
water transportation attended their efforts.   For another
generation people were content with the river sloop and
periagua, with the coasting schooner and small square-rigged
vessel whenever necessity or pleasure compelled them to
embark upon a voyage — short or long.

   It is clear that the American people in 1789, at the moment when the new Constitution went into operation, had

---

[1] The early experiments with steam
navigation are well summarized by Mac-
master in his *United States*, i, 432–436.
He gives abundant citations. For the
reference to Thornton, I am indebted to
Mr. Gaillard Hunt, who has placed me
under deep obligations by his kindness
in many ways.

already regained their footing in the commercial world
and were experimenting in many directions to effect a
diversification of their means of livelihood.[1]   In politics
and society they were open to new ideas and were prepared to take advantage of the opportunities which the
success of the new government would shortly place within
their reach.

[1] Professor Callender in the introduction to the fifth chapter of his *Selections
from the Economic History of the United
States* says that the effect of the changes
which he has enumerated in the preceding sentences was " gradually to change
economic conditions from extreme depression to almost normal prosperity,
before the new government came into existence in the spring of 1789, and before
any of its measures had time to produce
an effect."

NOTES

I. **British Commercial Policy.** — The act of 23 George III, Cap. 26, repealed the previous laws prohibiting trade with America. Chapter 39 of the acts of the same year gave the king power to regulate the trade between the " Subjects of his Majesty's Dominions and the Inhabitants of the said United States." This authority was given originally for one year, but was extended by subsequent laws. Under this authority, the customs officers admitted American vessels to ports of Great Britain without manifests and other documents formerly required by law; and the king by Order in Council of July 2, 1783 closed the West Indies to American shipping. This ordinance is printed in full in Brian Edwards's *Thoughts respecting the Trade of the West India Islands*, 7 note. It was quite within the ordinary course of events that the British should close their West Indian ports to American commerce, now that the United States were independent. William Knox prided himself upon having drafted this Order in Council. See Royal Historical Manuscripts Commission's *Reports, Various Collections*, vi, 199: " When Lord North became Secretary of State I made all the arrangements for America without office and without allowance, and the Order of Council of July 2, 1783, was of my suggesting and preparing, and I carried it thro' against the opposition of Mr. Fox and Mr. Burke, and thereby saved the navigation and maritime importance of this country and strangled in the birth that of the United States."

Some of the most important essays and compiled works dealing with this subject have been mentioned in the footnotes to this chapter. Other writings that have been useful in tracing commercial relations before 1789 are given here: Lord Sheffield's (J. B. Holroyd) *Observations on the Commerce of the American States* (6th ed. enlarged, with an index, London, 1784) ; Tench Coxe's *Brief Examination of Lord Sheffield's Observations* (Philadelphia, 1791); *A Free and Candid Review of a Tract, entitled, " Observations on the Commerce of the American States "* (London, 1784) ; Richard Champion's *Considerations on the Present Situation of Great Britain and the United States* (London, 1784) ; George Chalmers's *Opinions on Interesting Subjects of Public Law and Commercial Policy; arising from American Independence* (London, 1784) ; Brian Edwards's *Thoughts on the late Proceedings of Government respecting the Trade of the West*

India Islands with the United States of North America (London, 1784) ;
John Stevenson's *Address to Brian Edwards, Esq.* (London, 1784) ;
William Bingham's *Letter from an American . . . containing Strictures
on . . . Commerce* (London, 1784); Christian Febiger's " Extracts
from a Merchant's Letters, 1784–1786 " in *Magazine of American
History,* vol. viii, Pt. i, p. 351 ; Tench Coxe's *View of the United States
of America* (Philadelphia, 1794); Timothy Pitkin's *Statistical View
of the Commerce of the United States of America* (New Haven, 1835) ;
Theodore Sedgwick, " Letter to Caleb Strong, August 6, 1786 " in
American Historical Review, iv, 328–330 ; and *The Commercial Conduct of the United States of America considered . . . by a Citizen of
New York* (New York, 1786).

Professor Guy S. Callender has printed much useful matter bearing on the subjects treated in this chapter in his *Selections from the
Economic History of the United States,* 1765–1860, pp. 122–238.

II. A Comparative Study of Exports. — These figures are compiled from the table of exports for 1771 given on a preceding page and from the earliest government statistics.[1]

	1771	1790[2]
Ashes, pearl and pot (tons) . .	2,530	8,598
Beef and pork (bbls.)	21,153¾	69,124
Bricks (no.)	1,546,480	870,550
Candles (lbs.)	489,323	225,582
Cattle (no.)	3,385	5,406
Cheese (lbs.)	114,088	144,734
Fish, dry (quintals)	329,865½	378,721
" pickled (bbls.)	33,004¼	36,804
Hogs and sheep (no.)	12,763	15,362
Horses (no.)	6,390	8,628
Indigo (lbs.)	454,207½	612,119
Iron, bar (tons)	2,355	200
" pig (tons)	5,123	3,555
Oats (bu.)	19,352	98,842
Peas and beans (bu.)	32,646	38,752
Pitch (bbls.)	8,123	8,875
Poultry (doz.)	3,433½	3,704
Rice	145,406 (bbls.)	100,845 (tierces: [3])
Rum, N. E. (gals.)	286,612	370,331
" W. I. (gals.)	12,010	12,623
Shingles (no.)	36,312,626	67,331,115
Shooks (no.)	61,728	52,558
Staves (no.)	21,709,035	36,402,301
Tar (bbls.)	108,047	85,067
Tobacco (hhds.)	109,136	118,460
Turpentine (bbls.)	15,417	28,326
Whalebone (lbs.)	42,828	121,281
Wheat (bu.)	394,753¼	1,124,458

[1] In 1786 Jefferson sent to Lafayette an "Estimate" of the Imports and Exports of the United States. This he had compiled from the best accessible information; but he warns his correspondent that it "cannot pretend to accuracy." The estimate of West India commerce "does not present its present face." The values are given in French money of the day. Notwithstanding these limitations, the table is interesting because in many cases quantities are given. *Writings of Jefferson*, iv, 258.

[2] *American State Papers, Commerce and Navigation*, i, 23–34. These figures cover more than a year, as "from inadvertence in some of those offices, the space of time prior to the 1st of October, 1789, was blended with the quarter following." The custom houses were opened on various days in August.

[3] A tierce is intermediate in size between a barrel and a hogshead.

CHAPTER XIV

THE STATES AND THE CONFEDERATION

FOR generations the dwellers in each of the thirteen original colonies or states had regarded themselves as forming a distinct administrative entity ; the planters of Virginia were Virginians, otherwise they were Englishmen. When Parliament and king thrust the colonists out of the protection of the British constitution,[1] the people in each colony looked upon themselves either as being in a "state of nature" or as forming a "society." They were absolutely free from all outside control, sovereign in fact and in law. Through their representatives, they adopted certain rules and regulations for the future government of their State,[2] — constitutions, as these came to be called.

Side by side with these particularistic ideas, there had developed a sense of unity. The political institutions of all the colonies were bottomed on those of England. The settlers had grown to power in conflict against imperial control. The colonists of the continent in their own eyes and in those of the dwellers in the other sections of the British

---

[1] This conception of being ejected from the empire comes out clearly in the New Jersey constitution of 1776, providing that it should become null and void if the colonies "be taken again under the protection and government of the crown of Great Britain."

[2] The Georgia constitution of 1777 stated the current ideas very clearly: "We, therefore, the representatives of the people, from whom all power originates, and for whose benefit all government is intended, by virtue of the power

delegated to us, do ordain . . . that the following rules and regulations be adopted for the future government of this state."

Professor J. B. Thayer stated the matter in these words: "The Revolution came and what happened then ? . . . There was no longer an external sovereign. . . . 'the people' took his place; that is to say, our own home population in the several States were now their own sovereign." *Origin of the American Doctrine of Constitutional Law*, p. 5.

empire formed a group by themselves.   In 1760, when Boston was devastated by fire, the settlers to the southward
as far as South Carolina contributed to her relief; in
Maryland [1] no less than seven religious organizations gave
nearly two thousand pounds to alleviate her sufferings.
The "Thirteen" opposed the new imperial policy in union.
They associated themselves together to enforce their rights
by a boycott as extensive as the continental settlements.
United, they declared their independence, and had it
acknowledged by Great Britain and the powers of the
civilized world.   Friendly union was prior in point of
time; in the eye of law and legal sanction the state organizations were first.   The earliest legal obligation that any
continentalist owed, after the severance of his allegiance
to the British crown, was to his State.   On the other
hand, the mere fact that all the state governments were
republican in form and that not one of them reproduced
the monarchical institutions of the motherland evinces
more strongly than anything else the unity of political
thought that prevailed among the people throughout continental America.

The prevalent confusion in ideas comes out clearly in
the debates and reports of the Continental Congress.   In
1780, Congress informed the States that "our very existence
as a free, sovereign and independent people" depends upon
the establishment of the federal union on a fixed and permanent basis. [2]   Two years later the report of a committee
stating "Facts and Observations in support of the several
Claims of the United States" to lands and to the fisheries
was presented to the Congress of the Confederation.   In
this document the representatives of the United States at

---

[1] Gambrall's *Church Life in Maryland*, 46.

[2] *Journals of Congress* (Hunt ed.),
xvii, 806.

Paris were instructed to push the claims of the successful
revolutionists to the ungranted western lands on the ground
that they belonged to individual States.   If this could not
be maintained, they are "to be deemed to have been the
property of his Britannic Majesty . . . and to be now
devolved upon the United States collectively taken."
Theodorick Bland and Richard Henry Lee were at once on
their feet and moved that this clause in the report be
expunged.   The latter asserted that the United States
individually were in existence before Congress was; "they
were sovereign free and independent & retained all the
rights of sovereign free and independent states, except
what they voluntarily gave to Congress by the Confederation."[1]   And so one might go on piling up instances on
one side or another to prove one's case, or on both sides, to
follow the historian's method.   Enough has been given to
show the indistinctness of conviction that prevailed and
how easily arguments could be constructed, and can be, for
nationalism or for States'-rights.

The state constitutions were framed by bodies termed
congresses and conventions.[2]   These words were used

[1] "The Papers of Charles Thomson" in the *Collections* of the New York Historical Society for 1878, pp. 141, 146. James C. Welling has brought together much useful information on this general theme in his "States'-Rights Conflict over the Public Lands" in the *Papers* (iii, 411) of the American Historical Association.

[2] "Convention" in earlier English history denoted an irregular meeting of Parliament, or the House of Commons before it was formally organized. Next it was applied to that pregnant assemblage that formulated the Bill of Rights and recognized William and Mary as king and queen. The word crossed to America and was used by the revolutionary bodies of that period. In 1768 the Boston selectmen invited the towns to send delegates to a "convention" to consider the grievances under which the people were laboring (see J. F. Jameson's "Early Political Uses of the word 'Convention'" in American Antiquarian Society's *Transactions*, xii).

The word "Congress," in its earlier political meaning, connoted a meeting of ambassadors or of delegates from sovereign states. In the colonies it was first used of conferences between representatives of the imperial government, the colonies, and Indian tribes; or to describe conferences between colonial agents simply. It seemed to be peculiarly applicable to extra-legal revolutionary representative gatherings.

2 F

almost interchangeably and denoted irregularity in origin
and standing as compared with assemblies.   These
revolutionary bodies performed all functions of government,
executive, legislative, judicial, and constituent.[1] The Virginia Convention of 1776 compensated Lucretia Pritchett
for a slave who had been killed, discharged Moses Riggs
from the public jail, levied taxes, passed laws of all kinds,
deposed George III, formulated a constitution, and put it
into force without seeking any fresh mandate from the
voters.   All this they did as representative of the sovereign
people of Virginia.   In 1808, the Supreme Court of the
United States confirmed the view of 1776 that the several
States from the time when they declared themselves independent were entitled to all the rights and powers of sovereign States and that their laws were obligatory upon the
people of such State from the time of their enactment.

At first there was much irregularity in the conception of
a constitution.   Underlying all human regulation were the
rights of man and the fundamental law.   Government was
an attempt to work the machinery of society in conformity
with these underlying obligations.   A constitution was an
effort to set down in writing the most important of these
rules.   By it the people conferred authority upon governors,
judges, and assemblies, and also limited it.   Constitutions
took the place of charters, commissions, and instructions of
the colonial time.[2] So long as the people were in the

[1] Thus the New Hampshire constitution of January, 1776 and that of South
Carolina of March, 1776 were made by
" congresses," those of Virginia and
Pennsylvania in the summer of the same
year were framed by " conventions."

[2] The first American colonial charters
were designed for the guidance of commercial corporations or land companies.
As precedents, their framers had before
them the charters of the East India
Company and other commercial corporations; these in turn were modeled on
the charters of the boroughs. Lilburne's
" Agreement of the People " that had
been proposed to the New Model Army
for its approbation was the earliest
attempt in the history of English
speakers to set forth in detail the more
important functions of the state. The
" Instrument of Government " of Cromwell's time was the earliest written

colonial condition, their laws and the decisions of their courts had been reviewed in England, and often annulled or reversed because they were contrary to acts of Parliament or were against the customs and usages of the realm. The people of the States were, therefore, accustomed to a written organic law, and to a fundamental law explanatory of it. When there was no longer the possibility of an appeal to England, and no superior government in America, their own judges found themselves obliged to review the acts of the state legislature in the light of the state constitution as interpreted in accordance with the underlying fundamental law. Thus there came into being four distinct laws : the political theory at the basis of human society, the fundamental law which was no other than the Common Law of England, the written state constitution, and the laws made by the legislature ; their authority was in precisely this order.

The Virginia constitution of 1776[1] was the first detailed organic state law that had any extended life. It stands on the statute book as Chapters I and II of the acts of the General Assembly and was capable of amendment or repeal like any other legislative enactment. It consists of

organic law to be put into actual everyday use. It contained many ideas that had already been worked out in New England and Virginia. See Alfred Borgeaud's *Rise of Modern Democracy in Old and New England* (London, 1894) ; S. R. Gardiner's *History of the Great Civil War* and *History of the Commonwealth and Protectorate*.

[1] See *A Collection of Acts of the General Assembly of Virginia* (Richmond, 1803) ; this is often cited as the *Revised Code of 1803*. The convention that met in the winter of 1775–1776 declared that constitutional government was "obstructed" and that "the people of this country" must adopt some other mode of providing for the general safety.

The new convention that was chosen in consequence of this resolution may be said to have had a mandate from the voters to frame a new organic law. See J. P. Kennedy's *Journals of the House of Burgesses of Virginia, 1773–1776; Proceedings of the Convention of Delegates* (Williamsburg, 1775, 1776; reprinted at Richmond in 1816.) It is interesting to compare the list of members of these two bodies.

David A. Pulliam's *The Constitutional Conventions of Virginia* (Richmond, 1901) and J. N. Brenaman's *History of Virginia Conventions* (Richmond, 1902) contain much valuable information conveniently arranged.

three parts : a Bill of Rights, a Declaration of Independence
of Virginia, and a Frame of Government. Jefferson, at
Philadelphia, had formulated a complete constitution for
his native State, distributing representation according to
population and providing for the reference of the constitution to the voters. In other respects also his organic law
was more in accord with modern ideas than the instrument
that was actually adopted. It was too radical for the
members of the Convention, and all they took of it was
the Declaration of Independence, which was printed in
the form of a preamble to the Frame of Government.
The idea seems to have been that the Bill of Rights stated
the fundamental law, while the Frame contained the rules
for the guidance of the state government, the Declaration
being a justification of the secession from the British empire and the institution of a new government.

The Bill of Rights begins with the statement that "All
men are by nature equally free and independent" and
have the inherent right to the enjoyment of life and
liberty with the means of acquiring and possessing
property and pursuing and obtaining happiness and
safety. Power is derived from the people. Government is instituted for them and can be reformed or altered
at any time or in any way by a majority of the voters.
Magistrates are trustees and servants, and the legislative,
executive, and judicial powers ought to be distinct. The
members of the first two branches ought to be reduced
to private stations at fixed periods that they may be restrained from oppression. As to the definition of the
people, all men having "sufficient evidence of permanent
common interest with, and attachment to, the community"
ought to have the right to vote. These could not be taxed
or bound by any law to which their own consent or that

of their representatives had not been given. Then followed declarations against suspending laws, wrongful trial, excessive bail, cruel and unusual punishments, general warrants, and laws restraining the freedom of the press. Finally, the assertion is made that all men are equally entitled to the free exercise of religion.

The Frame of Government in twenty-one sections was in general terms. It provided for a legislative department of two houses. One of these, the House of Delegates, consisted of two members from each county and from such cities and boroughs as might be given representation. These were elected yearly. The other branch was termed the Senate and consisted of twenty-four senators elected by districts, one-quarter being replaced in each year. Bills were to originate in the House. They might be rejected by the Senate, or amended by it with the consent of the delegates; but money bills must be approved or rejected as they came from the lower branch. The chief executive, following colonial practice, was termed the governor, which is noteworthy, as the Convention did not perpetuate the title of burgess in the new organic law. The governor was to be annually chosen by both Houses with the consent of the Privy Council. This last-named body consisted of eight members chosen by joint ballot of both Houses who also appointed delegates to the Continental Congress, the judges, secretary, treasurer, and attorney-general. Every three years the two Houses were to remove two of the eight members of the Privy Council; the delegates held office for one year. All other officers were appointed during good behavior and might be impeached by the House of Delegates. The trial in such cases was not by the Senate or the Privy Council, but by the General Court, the prosecution being conducted by the attorney-general.   Impeachment was a new idea in America, but it is interesting to see that the makers of this early constitution did not look upon the Senate as possessing the functions of the House of Peers in England. Besides the General Court, Court of Chancery, and lower courts, the Virginia constitution provided for the establishment of a Court of Appeal to decide on the constitutionality of laws and to hear appeals from other courts.   This constitution once adopted by the Convention, that body declared itself to be the House of Delegates, chose the officers which were to be selected by both Houses and made provision for the election of a Senate.   In this way was established the first organic law of Virginia.

Another constitution to be made in 1776 was that of Pennsylvania.[1]   It, too, was the work of a body termed a convention, but the Pennsylvania Convention was quite unlike that of Virginia, because it was in the hands of the radical elements of the community.   Franklin, who presided over its deliberations, is usually regarded as a moderate, but he does not seem to have exerted himself to curb the eagerness of the Scotch-Irish Presbyterian radicals who held the balance of power.   This organic law was most democratic in many respects and was otherwise peculiar. The legislature of the new State was to consist of only one chamber which in itself would have marked off this constitution from all the rest.   It is often said that Franklin secured the adoption of this arrangement by likening a bicameral legislature to a wagon with one horse hitched in front and another behind, pulling in opposite directions.

[1] Delaware seized this opportunity to separate entirely from Pennsylvania, and adopted a constitution of its own. See an excellent article by George B. Palmer in the Wilmington *Every Evening* for Saturday, April 21, 1900.   Professor Max Farrand discussed some aspects of the Bill of Rights adopted in connection with this instrument in *American Historical Review*, iii, 641.

Dr. Benjamin Rush relates, on the other hand, that Franklin regarded such a body as a monstrosity and "strongly reprobated" placing supreme power in its hands.[1] The right to vote for members of this powerful legislature was given to every freeman of twenty-one years of age who had resided in the State one year and had paid taxes. No one could serve in the House for more than four years in seven, and every representative must declare his belief in God and acknowledge the divine inspiration of the Old and New Testaments. The apportionment for the immediate future was arbitrarily settled in the constitution, but after three years it should be arranged according to the number of taxables in the several parts of the State.

Democratic dread of one-man power is shown in the establishment of a multiple executive. The presiding officer of this Executive Council was dignified by the name of president, but he was not in any way a chief magistrate. This council had no negative voice on the acts of the legislative body and had no power to act in emergencies. The only restraint upon the legislature was to be found in the Council of Censors which was to be chosen by the voters every seventh year. Its business was to inquire whether the constitution had been observed. It could not annul laws made by the legislature, nor dismiss officers of the State. It was devised to enlighten public opinion. By a two-thirds vote it could summon a convention to amend the constitution and thus give an aroused public conscience an opportunity to make itself felt. Curiously enough in Pennsylvania, where this measure originated, it never

[1] *Pennsylvania Magazine of History*, xxix, 29. Rush further stated that in 1763 Franklin had declared in print that three branches were better than two; but he does not give the name of the publication. The *Minutes of the Proceedings of the Convention of the State of Pennsylvania, 1776*, were printed at Philadelphia in 1782. On the history of the formation of this organic law, see above, pp. 196–198.

amounted to anything in practice; but in Vermont, which was the only State to copy it, the Council of Censors were several times elected and with good results.

The Virginia and Pennsylvania constitutions were made in 1776, but the vicissitudes of war delayed the adoption of an organic law in New York until 1778.[1]   Among the members of the convention that framed this instrument were Robert R. Livingston, John Jay, Gouverneur Morris, and Robert Yates.   Radicalism had spent its force in New York and the new government was of the regular American type with a few abnormal features.   The governor had no appointing power himself, nor could he veto bills that had passed the legislature.   These functions were intrusted to two councils.   One of these, a Council of Appointment, was to be chosen yearly by the Assembly from the members of the Senate.   The governor presided at its meetings, but had only one vote.   The other, the Council of Revision, consisted of the governor, the chancellor, and two or more of the judges of the Supreme Court.   This body had power to revise bills that had passed the two Houses, but its objections might be overruled by a two-thirds vote.   One of the difficulties that most troubled revolutionary constitution makers was to devise some means by which the two branches of the state legislature should represent different interests in the community.   In New York, they sought to accomplish this by dividing the State into four senatorial districts, the members of the Assembly being apportioned among the counties.   The senatorial districts were geographical divisions, the senators being apportioned three-fifths to the southern district and two-fifths to the other three put together.   In choos-

---

1 *Journals of the Provincial Congress of the State of New York* (2 vols.   Albany, 1842).

ing the Council of Appointment, the Assembly was to elect one senator from each district, thus making that body geographically representative rather than basing it on population or on wealth. These two councils seem to modern students rather crude in design, but they attracted considerable attention at the time and narrowly escaped being widely copied.

The Massachusetts constitution of 1780 is still in working order as the organic law of that State, although, of course, it has been amended in some important particulars. It is not only remarkable for its long term of life, but also because it was the first constitution to be made by a convention specially elected for that sole purpose, and to be submitted to the voters of the State for their ratification.[1] The people of Massachusetts were able to postpone making definite arrangements because their provincial charter had served very well as a framework for their revolutionary government. They had regarded the governor, lieutenant governor, treasurer, and other officers that were appointed by the king under its provisions as being absent. In such cases executive power devolved upon the Council. For some years, therefore, Massachusetts had been governed by a legislature consisting of two Houses, each having a negative upon the other, and the upper House acting as a multiple executive. In 1777, an effort had been made to draft a new constitutional law, the Council, and the House of Representatives in joint session forming a convention for this purpose. This constitution had been submitted to the voters, and had been negatived by a vote of

---

[1] A different procedure was followed in Maryland. There, when the constitution had been formulated by the Revolutionary Assembly, it was submitted to the voters for approval and suggestion, but not for decisive action. At its next session the assembly reconsidered the constitution in connection with these suggestions and enacted it as amended into law.

about five to one.[1]   In 1779, the advocates of a new constitution again bestirred themselves and brought about the
holding of a convention elected for that sole purpose.
This body met at Cambridge on September 1, 1779 ; its foremost members were the two Adamses and James Bowdoin.
These three men acted as a subcommittee of a larger committee,[2] and they seem to have intrusted the actual drafting
of the instrument to John Adams.   Upon its adoption by
the Convention, it was submitted to the adult freemen for
their consideration.   About sixteen thousand, out of a total
population of three hundred and sixty-three thousand,
voted on it.   The Convention thereupon declared the Constitution to be ratified and it went into force.

The form of the Massachusetts constitution of 1780 is
peculiar in that it begins with a preamble setting forth
the end of government and the means by which it is
constituted.   The body politic is defined as a voluntary
association of individuals " by which the whole people
covenants with each citizen, and each citizen with the

---

[1] *A Constitution and Form of Government for the State of Massachusetts-Bay.
Agreed upon by the Convention of said
State, February 28, 1778, to be laid before the several Towns and Plantations
in said State, for their Approbation or
Disapprobation* (Boston, 1778).

The arguments against its adoption
were set forth in elaborate detail in the
*Result of the Convention of Delegates
holden at Ipswich in the County of Essex,
who were deputed to take into Consideration the Constitution . . . proposed by
the Convention* (Newburyport, 1778).
This paper is always cited as the " Essex
Result." It was drawn up by Theophi-
lus Parsons and is printed in the Appendix of the *Memoir* of him prepared by
his son. Mr. L. Kenneth Clark placed
at my disposal material which he had
gathered from the local records. The
document deserves to be better known.

[2] Letter of Samuel Barrett, Secretary
of the Convention to Professor Wiggles-
worth, dated Boston, 5 Nov. 1779 (Ms.).
*The Report . . . Agreed upon by the
Committee* (Boston, 1779); *An Address
of the Convention for framing a New
Constitution* (Boston, 1780); *A Constitution . . . Agreed upon by the Delegates
. . . in Convention . . . To be submitted
to the Revision of their Constituents*
(Boston, 1780); and *The Constitution or
Frame of Government for the Commonwealth of Massachusetts. Boston:
Printed by Benjamin Edes and Sons.
Printers to His Excellency the Governor,
the Council and the Senate of the Commonwealth of Massachusetts, MMCC,
LXXXI.* The whole of this imprint has
been given because it is significant of the
time. These papers deserve a careful
examination by students of the science
of government.

whole people, that all shall be governed by certain laws for the common good." Following this preamble is a declaration of the rights of the inhabitants which is rather lengthy, but not unlike in principle the other bills of rights of the period. Having thus stated the origin of government and the rights of man, the constitution proceeds to set forth in form the actual compact. By this the people " hereby solemnly and mutually agree with each other, to form themselves into a free, sovereign, and independent body politic."

The legislative and executive branches were not unlike those provided in the other States, but the governor inherited from the old colonial system a great sweep of power. He is commander-in-chief and is directed to encounter, repel, resist, expel, and pursue by force of arms and by all fitting ways, enterprises, and means whatsoever, all persons that shall attempt the destruction or even the annoyance of the commonwealth. To render him independent of the legislature, he was to be provided with an honorable stated salary. The restriction upon the governor's power was the necessity he was under of acting with the advice of the Council of nine persons who were to be elected annually from the senators by joint vote of the two Houses of the legislature. The judges of the Supreme Court and of the other courts were to be appointed by the governor with the consent of the Council and might be removed by them upon address of the two Houses. One further clause of this constitution deserves mention, the one enabling the executive and legislative branches to demand of the judges of the Supreme Court their opinions " upon important questions of law, and upon solemn occasions."

From this analysis of four constitutions it is evident

that the American people in the Revolutionary epoch had certain well-defined ideals as to political organization, although they differed in some respects as to how these ideals could best be carried out. Especially noticeable is the insistence upon the separation of the different branches of the government, of rotation in office, and of the mutability of the written organic law. The Virginia constitution was merely an act of the legislative body which could be changed at any time. In Pennsylvania, every seventh year the Council of Censors would have to consider the desirability of going over the ground again, and in Massachusetts a provision was made for holding a new constitutional convention in 1795. Jefferson even advocated the automatic termination of all written laws at certain definite periods so that the people should be brought face to face with the problems of social organization. In all this it must be remembered that the inalienable rights of man and the principles of the fundamental law were eternal and immutable. It was only the means of realizing these that were to go through the sifting process.

American continental unity had long been the dream of imperial administrators and political theorists.[1] The interests of the several colonies had been so divergent, their ideals in Church and society so repugnant, and their economic interests so opposed that hitherto nothing had been accomplished in this regard. The New England Confederation had served its purpose in earlier years and remained a valuable precedent for action ; but the scheme

[1] For lists of plans of union and extracts from some of them, see Winsor's *Narrative and Critical History*, v, 611; Frothingham's *Rise of the Republic*, 107–121; H. L. Carson, editor, *History of the Celebration of the Anniversary of the* *Constitution of the United States*, ii, Appendix by F. D. Stone; W. E. Foster's *Life of Stephen Hopkins*, i, 155, and ii, Appendices G, H, and W; *North Carolina Records;* and *New York Colonial Documents.*

that was most often in the minds of the radical leaders when the pressure of war demanded union was the Albany Plan of 1754, which had so signally failed of popular appro- bation at that time.

The Albany Plan contemplated an intercolonial union with an executive appointed by the crown and a legislative chosen by the assemblies. To this body Massachusetts and Virginia were each to send seven members, and the other colonies smaller numbers, Georgia and Delaware not being provided for at all. After the beginning, the members of this council were to be apportioned according to the contributions of the several colonies to the general treasury. The powers of this general government extended to the management of Indian affairs, to the making of new settlements, and to the defense of the colonies by land and water. For these purposes, they might make laws and lay and levy whatever taxes were most equal and just "rather discouraging luxury than loading industry with unnecessary burthens." They could appoint whatever officers were necessary for the carrying out of these functions. This plan received the unanimous consent of all the delegates at Albany. The colonists would have none of it. At Boston, the townsmen voted to instruct their representa- tives in the General Court "to Use their utmost Endeav- ors" to defeat this scheme and to oppose any other like it whereby the liberties and privileges of the people were endangered.[1]

The colonists came to the struggles of the Revolutionary epoch without any formal general organization. Jeffer- son's idea of the imperial constitution appears in the "Summary View." It was that of a federative empire

---

[1] *Boston Town Records, 1742 to 1757*, p. 266.

composed of states, independent of one another and united
only through the executive. There was no general legislative body, each member making laws for itself, the executive by his veto preventing friction between them. The
first working federal organization in America was the
American Association by which the radical party carried
into effect the determination of the Congress as to the non-
importation of British goods.

In July, 1775, Dr. Franklin read to Congress a scheme
of a confederative constitution that he had prepared. His
idea was that the United Colonies of North America should
form a league of friendship for the common defense and
the general welfare. Each should retain its peculiar jurisdiction within its own limits. A general congress was to
be annually appointed for the management of the interests of the confederacy. Its powers should extend to all
affairs of war and peace, to disputes between different
colonies, to the planting of new settlements, to the making
of ordinances relating to the general commerce, and to the
establishment of a common monetary system, intercolonial postal arrangements, and the regulation of military
matters. The Congress should have the appointment of
all the general officers, civil as well as military. The
share of each colony toward the general expenses and the
number of its delegates in Congress should be in proportion to the number of the males between the ages of sixteen
and sixty years. Each delegate was to have one vote and
might be represented by proxy. One-half of all the delegates must be actually present, however, in order to enable
Congress to transact business. Among other officers, Congress should appoint twelve executive councilors from its
own body. One-third of these should retire in each year
and not again be eligible for three years. This executive

council in the recess of Congress was to execute what had been intrusted to it and in general manage Continental interests. Congress should propose such amendments to this scheme as might be found necessary, which were to go into effect whenever approved by a majority of the assemblies. Franklin was fond of planning constitutions and probably had no expectation of this particular scheme meeting with general favor. At all events he did not press it.

John Adams, like Franklin, was fond of cogitating upon constitutional matters, but at this time he was in favor of proceeding slowly. In 1776, the North Carolina Provincial Congress sought his advice as to taking up government. In reply he wrote that he saw no occasion for a Continental constitution. " Let every Colony please itself without Control in its own Constitution." Then if an equitable representation of every colony appeared in Congress, if the authority of that great council were sacredly confined to war, trade, and disputes between colony and colony, and a confederation were agreed to by Congress and the Assemblies, the Thirteen Colonies would be unconquerable by all Europe. At first sight there seems to be an inconsistency between Adams's scorn of a Continental constitution and his advocacy of a confederation. Probably his idea was that no formal written pact was necessary or desirable, but that whatever was necessary could be done by votes of Congress and the Assemblies. In this way a constitution might grow up piecemeal, being fitted year by year to the changing needs of the country. There was a good deal to be said in favor of letting constitutional matters remain as they were. At the moment, the revolutionists were accepting the authority of the Continental Congress without question. It was in fact a revolutionary body and was exercising many of the attributes of sovereignty which were quite certain to be taken away from it by any hard and fast written organic federative law that had any chance of adoption. The education of the American people had been otherwise; they were accustomed to written organic laws controlling and limiting the powers of governors and legislatures. Moreover, existing federative republics possessed written constitutions, and the American colonists had behind them a long line of abortive attempts to frame plans of union.

In the critical moments of the contest with the mother country national feeling expressed itself. In December, 1765, Christopher Gadsden of Charleston wrote to the South Carolina agent in London, " There ought to be no New England men, no New Yorker, &c., known on the Continent, but all of us Americans." [1] In 1774, at the first sitting of the Continental Congress, Patrick Henry uttered the oft-quoted words, " Where are your landmarks, your boundaries of Colonies? . . . I am not a Virginian, but an American." [2] No general government for the united colonies could be formed or even thought of until separation from Great Britain was decided upon. The final impulse for both came from the Virginia resolutions of May, 1776, that were introduced into Congress in the following June. By that time the psychological moment had passed. The committee for drafting the Declaration of Independence was made up of the first men in Congress ; second-rate characters were placed on the one to which the drafting of the federal constitution was confided.

---

[1] Quoted by Ulrich B. Phillips in *American Historical Review*, xiv, 531; from Gibbes's *Documentary History of* the *American Revolution: . . . chiefly in South Carolina, 1764–1776*, p. 8.
[2] John Adams's *Works*, ii, 366, 367.

Moreover, the task of reconciling opposing ideas was formidable. Dickinson, the chairman of the committee, did not present his report until July 12, and then the brothers Howe with their great military and naval armaments had arrived in New York Harbor and were giving the members of Congress and the people generally other things to think about than the drafting of a federal constitution that very likely could never go into operation. At all events little interest was taken in it. From time to time some parts of it were debated, but that was all.

Three things in the committee's plan especially aroused argument. These were the apportionment of taxation according to the population, the giving each State one vote, and conferring upon the governing body of the proposed confederation the right to meddle with the boundaries of the States. As to the first of these, the Southerners were indignant at the idea of rating the several States according to the number of inhabitants, counting the whites and blacks, both slave and free. Samuel Chase of Maryland promptly moved to insert the word " white " before the word " inhabitants." He asserted that the slaves were property and " should not be considered as members of the state, more than cattle, and that they have no more interest in it." Lynch of North Carolina carried the idea further, observing that slaves being property should be no more taxed than the lands, sheep, cattle, or horses. This brought from Franklin the remark that there certainly was a difference between slaves and sheep, because the latter will never make any insurrection. This debate [1] was held

---

[1] *Journals of the Continental Congress* (Ford ed.), vi, 1079, 1099. Both John Adams and Jefferson made notes of these debates. They will be found in any edition of the writings of those statesmen and are printed by Worthington C. Ford at the end of the third and sixth volumes of his admirable edition of the *Journals of the Continental Congress.*

within four weeks of the adoption of the Declaration of Independence with its assertion of the equality of man [1] by the very same persons who had then immortalized themselves.

The proposition to give the States one vote apiece in the Congress of the proposed Confederation aroused Franklin's indignation. At the moment, he was the presiding officer of the Pennsylvania Convention as well as one of the delegates from that State in Congress. The equal representation of the States, large and small, was against equity and justice, he asserted. He thought they should be represented " in proportion to their Importance, arising from their Numbers of People, and the Share and degree of Strength they afford to the United Body." He wished that the Convention should at once announce its dissent, but, " from some prudential Considerations " [2] was induced to desist. In Congress, sitting behind closed doors, he was not actuated by the same motive of delicacy, and moved that the committee's plan should be amended so that the votes in Congress should be according to numbers. Middleton of South Carolina moved that they should be in proportion to contributions. In the debate that followed Franklin adverted to the extraordinary assertion which had been made that the States would not come into the confederation, " unless we would let them dispose of our money." On the contrary, he exclaimed, " Let the smaller Colonies give equal money and men and then have an equal vote." If they had an equal vote without bearing equal burdens, no government that was based upon such iniquitous

---

[1] As to the meaning of this phrase in the Declaration of Independence, see above, pp. 203, 204 n.

[2] *Journals of the Continental Congress* (Ford ed.), v, 554 note, from the Franklin Manuscripts in the Library of Congress.

principles could long endure.[1]   In reply, great stress was laid on the difference between an " incorporating and a federal union."   The proposed government would be of the latter type.   It was a league of friendship for certain specified purposes, and therefore it was only right that each member of it should have one vote.

The third point, that as to the congressional settlement of boundary disputes between the States, found a different alignment in Congress, because the claims to western lands were not related to the existing size or populousness of the several States.   There was Georgia.   So far as population was concerned, she was one of the smallest of the thirteen; but she had most extensive claims as to western lands.   Pennsylvania, on the other hand, was one of the three States having the largest number of inhabitants, but she had no claims to lands west of her charter limits. These differences were so great and so vital and the number of votes so much on the side of the smaller States and of those which had no claims to western lands that a reasonable settlement was out of the question.   There was an entire lack of interest in the scheme on the part of

[1] The working of the equal vote is shown in the following table which is taken from the *Pennsylvania Packet,* for December 11, 1786.

STATE	No. OF INHABITANTS	PROP. OF TAXES AS FIXED REVENUE OF CONG. IN $	MEAN PROP. OF VOTES	PRESENT VOTES IN CONG.
N. H.	150,000	76,268	3	1
Mass.	400,000	324,746	11	1
R. I.	59,670	46,764	2	1
Conn.	192,000	191,135	6	1
N. Y.	250,000	185,567	7	1
N. J.	150,000	120,619	4	1
Penn.	300,000	296,908	9	1
Del.	50,000	32,475	1	1
Md.	320,000	204,775	7	1
Va.	650,000	371,186	14	1
N. C.	300,000	157,732	6	1
S. C.	225,000	139,017	5	1
Ga	56,000	23,288	1	1

Franklin, Adams, and Jefferson.   As long as they were in Congress, nothing more was done.   In the autumn of 1777, however, the plan was adopted and sent to the States for their ratification.

The Articles in their final form announce a perpetual union for common defense and general welfare between the thirteen States, under the style of the United States of America.   Each retained its sovereignty, freedom, and independence, and every right that was not expressly delegated.   The free inhabitants of each State were to be entitled to all the privileges of free citizens anywhere within the Union.   Each State shall accord full faith and credit to the records and the judicial proceedings of every other State, and fugitives from justice shall be delivered up.   Delegates to the Congress were to be annually appointed.   In number they were to be not less than two nor more than seven, but each State was to have one vote. The management of warlike matters and foreign relations was confided to the general government.   The charges of war and other general expenses were to be defrayed out of the common treasury.   To this each State should contribute in proportion to the value of surveyed lands and the buildings thereon.   The quota thus determined was to be levied and collected by the several States.   As to disputations between States, Congress was authorized to appoint in a complicated and roundabout way a commission or court whenever any one State should request it to do so.   This commission or court [1] was to hear and determine the matter submitted to it, but " no state shall be deprived of territory for the benefit of the united states."   Congress could not engage in war, enter into a treaty, coin money

---

[1] The history of this "court" is traced by J. C. B. Davis in the Appendix to vol. cxxxi of the *Reports of the Supreme Court.*

or emit bills of credit, unless nine States assented.   All
the pecuniary obligations of the Continental Congress were
to be deemed a charge against the new government.   These
Articles of Confederation were to be ratified by the several
States before going into effect, and no alteration could be
made in them except by the vote of Congress and subsequent confirmation by the legislatures of all the States.

Looking backward, and having in mind the success
which followed the government under the Constitution of
1787 and the failure which attended on the Articles of
Confederation, one is astonished, not at the delay in ratifying them, but that they were ever ratified at all.   To many
men of that time, they seemed to provide for an ideal federative state.   The people in their local organizations
would rule, the "United States in Congress assembled"
carrying out their wishes.   The Congress, indeed, was not
to be a legislative body at all.   It was to be a federal executive and was to execute only those things that were
desired by nine of the thirteen individual members of the
Confederation.   Many men even then saw more clearly,
and the defects of the proposed government became apparent even before it was adopted ; but where thirteen separate legislatures had to be consulted before the slightest
change could be made, the best thing that could be done
was to have this feeble federal government demonstrate
its inadequacy for the task of the hour.

The delay in the ratification of the Articles was not due
in any way to the undesirableness of the form of government to be established under them, but to the jealousy of
the States that had no claims to western lands towards
those who were more fortunate in this respect.   Five
States, New Hampshire, Rhode Island, New Jersey, Delaware, and Maryland, had definite western limits.   At the

moment, the unoccupied lands west of the Alleghanies were expected to be a valuable asset and to fill the treasury by the proceeds of direct sales to the settlers. As the case stood, the five States that have just been mentioned would have no participation in these riches which would flow into the coffers of the other eight. The Articles of Confederation were so favorable to the smaller States that Delaware, New Hampshire, and New Jersey ratified them without insisting on any awkward demands as to sharing in the prosperity of their land-claiming brethren. This was not the case with Maryland. Lying between Virginia, which had pretension to enormous territories west of the Alleghanies, and Pennsylvania, which had great masses of unoccupied lands within her borders, her case was a hard one. Looking into the future, it was easy to picture the revolutionary obligations of Virginia and Pennsylvania being liquidated by sales of wild lands. Their soldiers could be pensioned in this way, and by this means their debts could be extinguished. Taxation would be Maryland's only resource, and her people would be so burdened that they would cross the boundary, either to the northward or to the southward. Congress appealed to the land-claiming States to cede their rights to the United States in Congress assembled that the backlands might be used for the benefit of all.

Nowadays, the claims of Virginia, the Carolinas, Georgia, New York, Massachusetts, and Connecticut to these vast spaces between the Alleghanies and the Mississippi, when their own existences were in doubt, seem fantastic. They did not so appear to Franklin and his brother commissioners at Paris in the summer of 1782, nor to the British government. The treaty was based upon the acknowledgment of the independence of the thirteen colonies

with their boundaries as they were before 1774. To them
Virginia was the old Virginia with her charter limits [1] reduced by later grants from the crown constituting the
colonies of Carolina, Maryland, and Pennsylvania. In the
constitution of 1776, Virginia acknowledged the rightfulness of these royal grants, but asserted her title to all the
rest of the land within her charter limits east of the Mississippi. Since then, the conquest of the Northwest by
Clark had reënforced this claim, which had been still
further strengthened by Virginia's establishment of the
County of Illinois. The claims of the Carolinas and
Georgia to lands south of Virginia extending to the Mississippi were of the same general character, except that
Georgia had done very little toward occupying or, indeed,
toward claiming the lands west of the Chattahoochee.

Three northern States, Massachusetts, Connecticut, and
New York, also had claims to lands west of the settled
parts of the country. The two first put forward pretensions to large portions of what are now the States of New
York and Pennsylvania as well as to lands farther west.
These claims went back to the New England Charter of
1620. This had limited the patentees to lands not occupied by the subjects of any Christian prince. Their
claims therefore stepped over the lands settled by the
Dutch, and thenceforward ran to the Mississippi. Charles
II had given the territory between the Connecticut and
the Delaware to his brother James and had later given
Pennsylvania to his friend, William Penn. Connecticut's
claim [2] to the northern part of Pennsylvania was certainly

---

[1] On the Virginia claim, see especially
Kate M. Rowland's *Life of George
Mason*, i, 321; W. C. Rives's *Life and
Times of James Madison*, i, 207, 257,
447, 450; H. S. Randall's *Life of Thomas
Jefferson*, i, 248, 256.

[2] On Connecticut's claim, see Charles
Miner's *History of Wyoming*, 62–92;
Pennsylvania Archives (First Series),
ii, 147, 156, 174, 303; ix, 568; x, 116, 146,
204, 213, 216; J. A. Chapman's *Sketch of
the History of Wyoming*, 66 and fol.;

awkward, to say the least.   As to Massachusetts' claim to western and central New York, similar difficulties were certain to arise.   New York's assertions as to western lands were not limited to territory east of Lake Erie, but extended into the Ohio Country and thus came into competition with the claims of Virginia as well as with those of Connecticut and Massachusetts.   The line of argument was about as follows: The League of the Iroquois owned and occupied central and western New York, and tribes tributary to it lived in the Ohio Country; the Iroquois had submitted to the governor of New York, and therefore, to the province of New York.   It followed that all the territories of the Iroquois were within the limits of New York.   In these conflicting claims lay possibilities of interminable wranglings and wars.   Congress wisely determined to have nothing to do with the discussions as to the rights and wrongs of them.   Instead it asked the claimant States to cede all their rights and pretensions, good, bad, and indifferent, to the United States in Congress assembled for the benefit of all.

At first the reply to the suggestion of Congress was not reassuring.   Virginia, indeed, offered to cede a portion of her western lands if the Congress would guarantee her right to the rest; but this Congress was unable or unwilling to do.   In March, 1781, New York cut the knot by offering to cede to Congress all her claims to lands west of Pennsylvania.   This offer was at once accepted and proved to be an example to the other States.   Without waiting for them to act, Maryland ratified the Articles of Confederation, and in March, 1781, they became the measure of federal authority in the United States.

Massachusetts Historical Society's *Collections*, Fifth Series, ix ("Trumbull Papers"), 381, 413–416, 443; B. Trumbull's *Plea in Vindication of the Connecticut Title to Contested Lands* (New Haven, 1774).

NOTES

I. Bibliography. — The constitutions of the several States have been several times printed by the government, but never with the attention to accuracy in proof reading that modern scholarship requires. The first series of constitutions attracted much attention in America and in Europe, for revolution was then the order of the day. In 1781 Francis Bailey, a Philadelphia printer, published "by order of Congress" *The Constitutions of the Several Independent States of America; the Declaration of Independence ; the Articles of Confederation between the said States; the Treaties between His Most Christian Majesty and the United States of America* (Philadelphia, 1781). This became the basis of many reprints and translations [1] in Great Britain and Europe as well as in America.

II. Cessions of Western Lands. — Professor Herbert B. Adams, whose untimely death deprived American historical students of a valued guide and friend, treated the matter of the cessions in a stimulating paper entitled "Maryland's Influence upon the Land Cessions to the United States" in *Johns Hopkins University Studies*, Third Series, No 1. The following table was compiled by Payson J. Treat and is taken from his *National Land System*, 14.

1780, February 19.   Act of New York Legislature.
    March 7.   Laid before Congress.
    October 10.   Act of Connecticut Legislature.

1781, January 2.   Act of Virginia Legislature.
    March 1.   New York deed of cession executed in Congress.

1782, October 29.   New York cession accepted by Congress.

1783, September 13.   Virginia cession rejected.
    October 20.   Second Virginia Act.

1784, March 1.   Virginia cession completed.
    June 2.   Act of North Carolina Legislature.
    November 13.   Act of Massachusetts Legislature.
    November 20.   Act of North Carolina Legislature repealed.

1785, April 19.   Massachusetts cession completed.

[1] The following are among the most interesting: London, 1782, 1783; Glasgow, 1783; Switzerland, 1778; Paris, 1783, 1792; Gand, 1790.

1786, May 11.   Second Act of Connecticut Legislature.
      May 28.   Connecticut cession completed.

1787, March 8.   Act of South Carolina Legislature.
      August 9.   South Carolina session completed.

1788, February 1. First Act of Georgia Legislature.
      July 15.   Georgia offer rejected.

1789, December 22. Act of North Carolina Legislature.

1790, February 25. North Carolina cession completed.

1802, April 24.   Articles of Agreement and Cession entered into
                   between the Commissioners of the United
                   States and of Georgia.
      June 16.   Ratified by the Georgia Legislature.

III. Conspectus of the Constitutions. — The following tables were
suggested by those in William Smith's *Comparative View of the Constitutions of the Several States with each other, and with that of the
United States* (Philadelphia, 1796). See also Sydney G. Fisher's
Evolution of the Constitution of the United States (Philadelphia, 1897).

THE EXECUTIVE

State and Constitution	Mode of Appointment	Length of Appointment	Reëligibility	Appointing Power	Veto Power
New Hampshire, 1784	Voters	One year	Reëligible	With Council	None
Massachusetts, 1780	Voters	One year	Reëligible	With Council	Qualified
Connecticut, 1662	Voters	One year	Reëligible		None
Rhode Island, 1663	Voters	One year	Reëligible		None
New York, 1777	£100 Freeholders	Three years	Reëligible	With Council of Appointments	With Council of Revision
New Jersey, 1776	Legislature	One year	Reëligible		None
Pennsylvania, 1776	Council elected by voters	Three years	Reëligible after four years	Appoints judges, attorney-general, etc.	None
Delaware, 1776	General Assembly	Three years	After three years	With General Assembly	
Maryland, 1776	Legislature	One year	Three years in every seven	With Council	None
Virginia, 1776	Legislature	One year	Three years in every seven		None
North Carolina, 1776	Legislature	One year	Three years in every six	Only temporary	None
South Carolina, 1778	Legislature	Two years	After four years	With Council	
Georgia, 1777	Representatives	One year	One year out of three	Temporary	None
United States, 1787	Electors	Four years	Reëligible	Senate confirms	Qualified negative

THE LEGISLATIVE

State and Constitution	Number of Branches	Mode of Election	Duration	Qualification of Members	Qualification of Voters	Peculiar Powers
New Hampshire 1784	Two — Senate (12) and House of Representatives; called the General Court	Voters	Annual		Paying a poll tax	Representatives originate money bills and impeach. Senate tries impeachment
Massachusetts, 1780	Two — Senate and House of Representatives: called the GENERAL COURT. The former, 31 members; the latter, 356	Voters	Annual	Senator: freehold of £300 or personal estate of £600 and inhabitant five years. Representative; freehold of £100 or personal estate of £200	£3 income from freehold or any estate of £60 value	Representatives originate money bills and impeach. Senate tries impeachment
Connecticut Charter of 1662	Two — General Court: Council (12); Representatives (179)	Voters	Council annual: Representatives semiannual	Freeman of Corporation	Freehold £2 income or £40 estate	General Court possesses judicial powers
Rhode Island Charter of 1663	Two — General Assembly: Council (10); Representatives (70)	Voters	Council annual: Representatives semiannual	Freeman of Corporation	Freehold £2 income or £40 estate	General Court possesses judicial powers
New York 1777	Two — Senate (24): Assembly (70)	Voters	Senate four years, annual rotation of one-fourth: Assembly annual		For senator: freehold of £100. For representative; freehold of £20 or rent £2	Assembly by two-thirds vote impeaches. Senate by two-thirds vote convicts
New Jersey 1776	Two — Legislative Council (13): Assembly	Voters	Annual	Councilor: £1000 estate. Representative; £500 estate	Inhabitants of £50 estate. (Under this women voted)	Legislative Council cannot originate or alter money bills
Pennsylvania, 1776	One — House of Representatives	Voters	Annual	Freeman who pays taxes	Freeman who pays taxes	Has supreme legislative power

				Freeholders	Freeholders	
Delaware 1776	Two — General Assembly: Assembly (21), Council (9)	Voters	Assembly annually; Council three years, with annual rotation of one-third	Freeholders	Freeholders	Assembly originates money bills, may be amended by Council
Maryland 1776	Two — GENERAL ASSEMBLY: Senate (15); House of Delegates (80)	Senate by electors chosen by voters: Delegates by voters	Senate five years: Delegates annual	Senator: £1000 and three years' residence. Delegate: £500	Freehold 50 acres or £30	House of Delegates originates money bills and appoints treasurer during pleasure
Virginia 1776	Two — GENERAL ASSEMBLY: Senate (24); House of Delegates (150–160)	Voters	Senate four years, annual rotation of one-fourth: Delegates annual	Must be freeholder	Freeholders	House of Delegates initiates all laws. Senate cannot alter money bills. Impeachments voted by House and tried by law courts
North Carolina, 1776	Two — GENERAL ASSEMBLY: Senate (60); House of Commons (120)	Voters	Annual	Senator; freehold of 300 acres. Commons; freehold of 100 acres	Senator; freehold 50 acres. Commons; taxpayer and one year's residence in county	House of Commons impeaches. Trial by law court
South Carolina, 1778	Two — General Assembly: Senate and House of Representatives	Voters	Two years	Protestant, and five or three years in State	Free white man and freeholder	Money bills originate in Representatives. Senate cannot alter money bills
Georgia 1777	Representatives and Executive Council	Representatives by voters: Council by and out of Representatives	Annually	Protestant and £250 estate	Male white inhabitant paying taxes	Representatives pass all bills: Council may propose changes with their reasons
UNITED STATES, 1787	Two — CONGRESS: Senate; House of Representatives	Senate by state legislatures: Representatives by voters	Senate six years, biennial rotation of one-third: Representatives two years	Senator; 30 years old and 9 years citizen. Representative; 25 years old and 7 years citizen	For Representative: the same as for the most numerous branch of the state legislature	Representatives originate money bills and impeach. Senate tries impeachment; two-thirds to convict. Confirms President's nominations

THE JUDICIARY

State and Constitution	Mode of Appointment	Tenure of Office	Removability
New Hampshire, 1784	President and Council	Five years	Impeached by Representatives; tried by Senate
Massachusetts, 1780	Governor and Council	Good behavior	Impeachment; and by Governor and Council on address of both Houses
Connecticut, Charter of 1662	Legislature	Annually	
Rhode Island, Charter of 1663	Legislature	Annually	
New York, 1777	Council of Appointment	Good behavior	Retired at sixty years of age
New Jersey, 1776	Council and Assembly	Seven years	Impeachment by Assembly; trial by Council
Pennsylvania, 1776	By Council	Seven years	Impeachment by Assembly; trial by Council
Delaware, 1776	President and General Assembly	Good behavior	
Maryland, 1776	Governor and Council	Good behavior	Conviction in Court; or by Governor on address of two-thirds of both Houses
Virginia, 1776		Good behavior	Impeached by Delegates; trial by General Court
North Carolina, 1776	Legislature, nominated by Governor	Good behavior	Impeached by Assembly or Grand Jury; trial by Special Court
South Carolina, 1778	Legislature	Good behavior	By Governor on address of Senate and Representatives
Georgia, 1777			
United States, 1787	President and Senate	Good behavior	Impeached by Representatives; tried by Senate

CHAPTER XV

FOUR YEARS OF CONFUSION, 1783–1787

THE framing of the Articles of Confederation had taken much time and their ratification by the State legislatures had occupied more. They were obsolete when signed by members of Congress and antiquated when the Maryland delegates gave the consent of that State to their ratification. The ideal federative system led to the continued poverty of the general government,[1] to failure to adopt and enforce any effective commercial measures against hostile outsiders, to dangerous disagreements between several States, and to internal disorders in New England, Virginia, North Carolina, and elsewhere. All these led to reaction which found expression in the Constitution of 1787.

In war, money was the fulcrum upon which the existence of armies depended. With money in plenty, Washington could have had men, food, and munitions in abundance; without it an evanescent militia and requisitions that might or might not be paid in kind were the only resources. In Washington's military family was one of the most remark-

---

[1] Charles J. Bullock summarizes the financial history of the Government of the Confederation for the years 1784–1789, as follows: "The expenses of government, domestic and foreign, had been about $3,476,067, of which amount $189,906 remained unpaid on September 12, 1789. The principal of the domestic debt had been decreased $960,915 by the receipts from the public lands; while the arrears of interest had increased from $3,109,000 to $11,493,858 at the end of 1789, in spite of the fact that $2,371,000 of indents had been drawn in by taxes. The principal of the foreign debt had increased from $7,830,517 to $10,098,707, while the arrears of foreign interest had grown from $67,037 to $1,640,071 at the end of 1789." "The Finances of the United States from 1775 to 1789, with Especial Reference to the Budget" in *Bulletin of the University of Wisconsin* (Economics, Political Science, and History Series), vol. i, no. 2, pp. 117–273.

able men to whom the United States is indebted for its place among the nations, Alexander Hamilton, a native of the island of Nevis in the West Indies.   In 1780, he wrote to James Duane, then in Congress, of the distresses of the army and the necessity there was for greater vigor in government.   He proposed that the existing Congress should reassume the revolutionary character that formerly had given it its power.   Then there might be held "a convention of all the States, with full authority to conclude finally upon a general confederation."[1]   The suggestion that Congress had relaxed a part of its authority while awaiting the ratification of the Articles is full of meaning, as is Hamilton's unveiled distrust of the Articles.   Congress had no power to coerce the States.   They replied to its requisitions for men and money as seemed fitting to them, and often not at all.   Unable to secure funds at home, the government borrowed from the French king and the bankers of the Netherlands.   When the Articles of Confederation went into operation in March, 1781, the case was no better; if anything it was worse.   The Articles gave Congress no power to levy taxes by its own authority.   The nearest approach to this was the issuing of great quantities of paper money, which depreciated rapidly as it passed from hand to hand, each holder thereby paying the modicum of a national tax.

In February, 1781, before the actual ratification of the Articles, Congress had asked for authority to collect certain duties within the several States.   In 1783, the request was repeated in a somewhat different form.   To the first of these applications all the States had acceded except Rhode Island, which feared anything that looked like an

[1] Alexander Hamilton to James Duane, September 3, 1780, Hamilton's *Works* (Lodge ed.), i, 213.

infringement on her sovereignty.[1] To the second, twelve
States — Rhode Island among them — consented; but
this time New York refused. As the conferring of this
power on Congress necessitated an amendment to the
Articles of Confederation — requiring the consent of all
the States — these projects failed. Besides, Congress
could not apportion the requisitions for public contributions according to the mode prescribed in the Articles,
because there was no money with which to pay for the
necessary appraisal of houses and lands. New Jersey
seized upon this as a pretext for refusing to contribute at
all. In fact, throughout this time had it not been for the
emission of Continental bills of credit, it is difficult to see
how the government could have been carried on, even in
the feeble manner in which it was.

In 1785, John Adams appeared in London as the ac-
credited minister from the United States. The king received him civilly and gave him the chance to make his
famous avowal that he had no attachment but to his own
country. With the foreign secretary he was not so happy,
for when he approached him with suggestions as to taking
up negotiations for a commercial treaty, the British minister replied by demanding the presence of thirteen
ambassadors, one from each American State, since the
general government of the Confederation seemed to be
unable to secure the observance of the treaties. There
was a good deal that might have been said on both sides
of this question; but the British government was not at
all ready to listen to any arguments or explanations from
the American minister. The only way that Britain could
have been brought to reason was by boycotting her com-

[1] F. G. Bates, " Rhode Island and the Impost of 1781 " in American Historical Association's *Reports*, 1894, pp. 351–359. See also on the general subject Timothy Pitkin's *Statistical View of the United States*, p. 29.

2 H

merce as had been done more than once before the war.
Congress had no power to make commercial regulations,
and the States refused to confer it upon the general
government. They tried to deal with the matter themselves, but their interests were so divergent and their
administrative systems so lax, that no effective pressure was brought to bear upon British merchants and
manufacturers and through them upon the king and his
ministers.

The government at London was fully aware of the
difficulties which beset the ruling powers in America.
At New York was Sir John Temple, Consul General, and
at Philadelphia was Vice Consul Phineas Bond. Both
constantly reported to their chiefs describing the disorganization that prevailed in America, and especially adverted
to the low state of commerce and credit. Edward Bancroft was also at New York, but not in a public capacity.
He, too, reported indirectly to Lord Carmarthen, who was
foreign secretary in Pitt's administration. In his letters [1]
Bancroft represents the great difficulty of securing the
attendance of a sufficient number of members of Congress
to give that body the quorum of nine States, without which
it could not transact important business. He describes
the financial difficulties of the general government, the
States, and individuals, and writes that France and Spain
seem determined to reëstablish " their former systems of
monopolizing the Commerce and Productions of their
several Colonies." This extraordinary intriguer then sailed
for L'Orient with Luzerne, the French minister to the
United States. At Paris he conversed familiarly with
Jefferson and then passed over to London, where he doubt-

[1] Copies of these letters are in the
" Manuscripts of George Bancroft " in
the Lenox Library, 1783–86, i, 139–150,
213.

less gave accurate accounts of the prevailing weaknesses of the new republic.

The penurious condition of the members of the Confederation caused them to look with jealous eyes upon any one of their number that seemed to be prosperous and to endeavor to build up their own trade and fill their treasuries at the expense of their neighbors. Connecticut and New Jersey, to use a favorite expression of that day, were each of them " between the hawk and the buzzard." Both had little foreign commerce and paid tribute to New York. Connecticut also contributed to the prosperity of Newport and Boston, as did New Jersey to that of Philadelphia. They tried to secure foreign trade for themselves and in a measure succeeded, although the New Yorkers checkmated them as well as they could. In 1785, the New York Assembly passed an act by which foreign goods that were brought into her limits from the neighboring States were to be taxed as if they had been imported in a British vessel, unless the owner could satisfy the collector that they had not been brought into the United States in a British ship. The New York Assembly increased the duties on foreign goods on April 11, 1787,[1] and took the occasion to extend the entrance and clearance fees to all vessels coming from or bound to Connecticut and New Jersey. If these were freighted with United States goods, the fee was only two shillings for vessels under twenty tons, but if there were any goods on the boat that were subject to duty, the fee was four times greater; open boats only were to pay no fee. Connecticut took no official notice of this law, partly no doubt because the new constitution which was in

[1] Acts of New York of 1787, Chap. 81: An act imposing duties on goods imported; clause providing for collector's fees.

agitation would obviate all these differences, if it was adopted. The wrathful Jerseymen tried to retaliate by laying a tax of thirty pounds per month on a few acres that New York had bought at Sandy Hook[1]; and the high sheriff of Monmouth County was directed to collect the tax at once.

In these modern days of interstate commerce commissions, federal corporation taxation, and a nation-wide excise, it is difficult to realize the hostile feelings with which the people of some States looked upon their neighbors. There was Lewis Morris of New York, father of Gouverneur Morris, the writer of the Constitution. He drew up his will in 1760, but saw no occasion to change the following words, before he died in 1800. He charges his executor to give his son the best education that is to be had in England or America, outside of Connecticut. The lad must never be sent to that colony, lest he imbibe in his youth "that lowe craft and cunning so incident to the people of that country" which no art could disguise, although " many of them under the sanctified garb of religion have endeavored to impose themselves on the world as honest men." Not so thought Timothy Dwight, Joel Barlow, and the literary men of Yale College, as appears in the following lines : —

> " Shall lordly Hudson part contending powers,
> And broad Potomac lave two hostile shores ?
> Must Alleghany's sacred summits bear
> The impious bulwarks of perpetual war ?
>
> *　　*　　*　　*　　*　　*
>
> Ere death invades, and night's deep curtain falls,
> Through ruined realms the voice of UNION calls;

[1] Acts of New Jersey, Chap. 29, supplement to Act for raising revenue from stages, ferries and taverns, passed at Burlington, June 7, 1787. For particulars concerning these statements, see *American Museum*, December, 1787, " Chronicle," p. 1, and *Pennsylvania Gazette*, June 27, 1787. McMaster has treated this episode at length in his *United States*, i, 404.

*   *   *   *   *   *

On you she calls ! attend the warning cry :
'Ye Live United, or Divided Die !' " [1]

It was not only in New England and the Middle States
that there was friction and ill feeling. The people of North
Carolina had no sympathy with Virginia's attempts to
regulate British commerce, and the Marylanders were constantly legislating in a manner that defeated the designs
of the statesmen of the Old Dominion.   There were abundant causes of estrangement between these last two.
When Lord Baltimore asked the king to carve a province
for him out of Virginia territories, it was arranged that
the southern limit of the province of Maryland should be
the southern bank of the Potomac River.   A vessel lying
at anchor in the stream, or even tied up to a Virginia
wharf was in Maryland ; her cargo from England might
be designed for Mount Vernon or Gunston Hall and her
outward freight might be tobacco grown on these plantations.   All the time she was subject to Maryland laws
and regulations, but the moment her cargo swung over
the ship's side onto the land it was in Virginia and liable
to her customs laws.   On the other hand, whatever tobacco came into her hold from the Virginia shore must have
been subjected to all the requirements of the inspection
laws of that State, but the hogsheads that came from boats
alongside might well have been brought from some Maryland plantation and produced under more lenient regulations.

Both Virginia and Maryland had tried to restrict British
commerce.   They had passed tonnage duties and levied
imposts.   In 1783, the Marylanders had laid a tax of two
per cent on all goods imported in British vessels, besides a

---

[1] *The Anarchiad* (*New Haven Gazette*, 1786–87; reprinted at New Haven, 1861),
p. 62.

tonnage duty on the ships themselves. In 1784 and again in 1785, these were changed. In these years, Virginia laid imposts on all goods imported from Britain. These were increased year by year, until in 1785, they were above those of Maryland; but Virginia levied no discriminating duties on British shipping. The Virginians owned both sides of the mouth of the Chesapeake. The lighthouse at Cape Henry and beacons and buoys marking the channels through the shallows of the lower bay were all in Virginia. Many of the vessels using these channels were bound to or from Maryland; it seemed only right that they should contribute toward maintaining these aids to navigation. Somewhat similar conditions obtained as to the navigation of the Pokomoke, a river of the Eastern Shore, that had its source in Maryland and its mouth in Virginia. Dues were collected of all vessels bound in or out of Chesapeake Bay, no matter whether they carried Virginia or Maryland commerce. The successful collection of these fees could not fail to suggest to the Virginians the possibility of putting pressure upon the people of Maryland to secure more favorable treatment on the Potomac and the Pokomoke and to compel them to join in a vigorous attempt to restrict British commerce.

As early as 1777, the Virginians had tried to come to terms with the Marylanders as to the navigation of Chesapeake Bay, the Potomac, and the Pokomoke. A conference of delegates from the two States was held in 1778; but nothing came of it because those from north of the Potomac had such rigid instructions that nothing could be done. The next overture for joint action came from Maryland and related to the defence of Chesapeake Bay. A Maryland commissioner visited Richmond on this errand. In reply the Virginia Assembly suggested the propriety of harmonizing the navigation system of the two States. It is at this point that James Madison becomes a prominent figure in American history. He was a Virginian, but much younger than Washington or Jefferson. In 1784, he became chairman of the committee of the Virginia Assembly on commerce. Many petitions had been presented, complaining of the British monopoly and of the fact that so much of the inland trade of the State was in the hands of foreigners. Madison thought that if all commerce with the outside world were confined to Norfolk and Alexandria, it might be possible to regulate it. No sooner was this idea mooted abroad than the people of other districts hastened to present their claims to a share in the monopoly. So many other places had to be given these rights that the Port Act, when it was passed, was practically worthless. Madison was happier in bringing about renewed conferences with the Marylanders who were especially well disposed toward the Virginians on account of the recent liberality of the latter with regard to western lands. The Virginia legislature appointed him with Mason, Edmund Randolph, and Alexander Henderson to meet commissioners to be appointed by Maryland to devise "such liberal and equitable measures" concerning the Potomac River as might seem mutually advantageous. They were to report to the Assembly which retained the right to confirm or not as it pleased. Maryland promptly appointed four commissioners, Samuel Chase, Daniel of St. Thomas Jenifer, and two others, and authorized them to confer with the Virginians not only as to the Potomac, but also as to the navigation of Chesapeake Bay and the Pokomoke River. They came to Alexandria, but the Virginia commissioners had not been apprised of the time and place of meeting or of the restrictions of their functions to the Potomac navigation. Mason and Henderson conducted the conference on the part of Virginia. Before they had been long debating they adjourned to " the general's seat " at Mount Vernon, near by. Washington does not seem to have taken any part in the actual business, but no doubt his advice was sought by Mason. In their report, the commissioners suggested an agreement between the two States as to commerce and defence and that each State should make application to Congress to enable them to carry out these plans. They also thought that the prosperity of both States depended upon their having similar duties on exports and imports. Finally, they suggested that annual conferences should be held on commercial matters of general interest.[1]

The Alexandria agreement was ratified by the legislatures of Virginia and Maryland in the autumn of 1785. But there was evident need of more definite and more far-reaching action being taken. A great deal of the commerce of the upper Chesapeake and the western parts of Maryland as well as of Virginia was by the way of the ports of Pennsylvania and Delaware. Maryland suggested, therefore, that these two States should be asked to join in the proposed settlement of commercial regulations. In January, 1786, the Virginia Assembly in agreeing to this proposition extended the invitation to all the States and authorized the delegates who were appointed " to take into consideration the trade of the United States, to examine the relative situations and trade of the said States," and to report a plan which would enable the United States in Congress assembled to act with vigor toward foreign nations, especially England.

[1] Rowland's *George Mason*, ii, 81–86; Hunt's *Writings of Madison*, ii, 100. Dr. Elliot H. Goodwin very kindly placed at my disposal a mass of material that he gathered on the relations of the States in this period of readjustment.

May, 1786, was the time set for holding this convention, and Annapolis was the designated place. The meeting was thinly attended and the members were very slow in assembling. Maryland did not send any representatives at all. Her Assembly had just authorized the levy of a federal impost and gave this as a reason for not engaging in any other agitation. Pennsylvania was represented by one delegate only; Virginia, indeed, was the only State to send the full number. Massachusetts and New Hampshire appointed delegates; but they had not reached Annapolis before the convention adjourned.[1] The opportune moment had not yet arrived. That much is clear; although the precise history of the convention and its dissolution is still uncertain. Hamilton took the leading part and was probably acting in harmony with Madison and Washington and other advocates of a stronger government. Resolutions that he had drafted were adopted by those who were on the spot and were sent out with a letter justifying their early adjournment. The resolutions dilated upon the weakness of the Confederation, the necessity for strengthening it, and the desirability of having this done by a convention which should report directly to the State legislatures.

The idea of amending the Articles of Confederation or remaking them wholly was by no means new in 1786; neither was the plan of having this done by a convention instead of by the Congress. Hamilton's letter to Duane, which was written in 1780, has been already mentioned. In 1782, the New York legislature had proposed that a con-

---

[1] A letter from the Massachusetts delegates to Hamilton, dated New York, September 10, 1786, stating that they were on their way to Annapolis, is printed in J. C. Hamilton's *Works of Alexander Hamilton*, i, 432. Bancroft printed some matter on this convention in his *History of the Formation of the Constitution*, i, 502; ii, 378, 389. See also the writings of Washington, Madison, Jefferson, and Monroe.

vention of the States should be held to revise the Articles. In 1784, Madison mentions the possibility of holding a convention in such a way that it is plain there had been much discussion on the subject that has not come down to us.[1] In the next year, 1785, in May, James Bowdoin, who was then governor of Massachusetts, described with vigor the unfortunate commercial conditions of the time. He asserted that the American people could not regulate the trade of the country because of the helplessness of the United States in Congress assembled. He suggested that the several States should appoint delegates who should meet in convention to determine exactly what powers could safely be given to Congress for the regulation of commerce. Bowdoin's suggestion met with favor in the Massachusetts legislature; an appropriate resolution was passed and sent to the delegates of that State in Congress. These were Elbridge Gerry, Samuel Holten, and Rufus King; the first and third had distinguished careers before them; Holten is less known nowadays although he had quite a reputation at that time. They refused point blank to present the resolution to Congress, because any attempt to alter the existing organization of the federal government would be the signal for the advocates of aristocracy to strike for the accomplishment of their designs.

Ever since that time it has been a commonplace of historians to pooh-pooh the dangers of an aristocratic or monarchical reaction in the twenty years following the Revolution. Probably the fears of the radicals and moderates had no basis, but there are indications that men high in official rank had some such scheme in mind and even had done something toward its realization. Years afterwards, in 1825, it was stated in debate that

[1] Hunt's *Writings of Madison*, ii, 99.

Rufus King had known of a plan to establish a monarchical form of government in the United States under Prince Henry of Prussia, and that Nathaniel Gorham of Massachusetts, who was president of Congress, had actually caused Prince Henry to be approached on the subject.[1]

The evident necessity for restudying political organization with a view to providing a more effective government for the United States as a whole led to several plans being put forward. The earliest of these was the work of Pelatiah Webster, a native of Connecticut, who was then living at Philadelphia. The title of this essay is "A Dissertation on the Political Union and Constitution of the Thirteen United States, of North America."[2] Webster lays down as his first premise that the supreme authority of any state must have sufficient power to effect the ends of its appointment. This supreme authority ought to be limited and checked to prevent abuse, but not so far as to diminish its power of doing good. "A number of sovereign states uniting into one commonwealth, and appointing a supreme power to manage the affairs of the union do necessarily and unavoidably part with and transfer over to such supreme power so much of their own sovereignty, as is necessary to render the ends of the union effectual." Sufficient powers must be vested in every department of government to make effectual the ends for which it is

---

[1] A suggestion was made in 1786 by some one looking toward the offering of the regency of the new United States to Prince Henry of Prussia, brother of Frederick the Great, — at least Richard Krauel demonstrates the strong probability of this in *American Historical Review*, xvii, 44.

[2] The original edition of 1783 does not bear Webster's name; but the "Dissertation" was printed with his *Political Essays* at Philadelphia in 1791. It has again been reprinted in Hannis Taylor's

"Memorial in behalf of the Architect of our federal Constitution" (Senate Documents, 60th Cong., 1st Sess., No. 461). The quotations in the following paragraphs of the text are taken from pp. 3, 35, 39, 41, of the edition of 1783.

Among other important discussions which appeared in these years are Noah Webster's *Sketches of American Policy* (Hartford, 1785); [William Vans Murray's] *Political Sketches inscribed to His Excellency John Adams* (London, 1787).

designed.   Thus the supreme authority, besides having
power to make war and conclude peace, to appoint officers
and regulate trade, must necessarily be vested with a
power of taxation.   If ill used, this will be a "dreadful
engine of oppression"; but to give supreme authority without power is a "solecism in government" and naturally
absurd.   Webster advised a congress of two houses, but
he made no suggestion as to any line of differentiation
between them.   His scheme provided for no chief executive, but it did suggest the appointment of certain depart-
mental heads.   These were to possess no direct veto, but
they might secure a reëxamination of any act by Congress.

Abuses were inevitable in any government, strong or
weak; but Webster was not willing to give up all
attempts to form a stable administration for that reason.
It was irrational to place it in the power of a single State
to destroy the prosperity of the country as a whole.   He
suggested that any State might petition the proposed Congress to repeal or reverse any law or decision that had been
made.   If more than half the States joined in such a petition, it should be regarded as mandatory, and the law or
decision was to be recalled.   One exception had to be made
to this general rule, because it would be destructive of all
financial credit if acts of Congress levying taxes could be
repealed or recalled unless other measures equally effective
were adopted in their stead.   If any State were to obstruct
or oppose the execution of any act ordered by the supreme
authority, the Congress might send troops into such a State
to enforce it.   The danger of such an expedient was
patent.   Webster tried to avoid it by compelling every
person to obey the supreme authority under pain of "the
censure of the great supreme power."   Every one disobey-
ing might be compelled to appear before Congress and be

fined or imprisoned as it should deem best. The weakest point in Webster's whole scheme was the provision for a dictator in case of a deadlock between the two houses. It is not perfectly clear that the framers of the Constitution were acquainted with Webster or with his "Dissertation," but whether they were or no, and whether the Constitution owed anything to him or not,[1] this essay is one of the most interesting dissertations ever printed in America.

As the time approached for the elections to the proposed constitutional convention, James Madison applied himself to the study of federations, ancient and modern, including the existing one in America. He drew up papers giving the results of his historical studies of the Achaiæn League and other federations of the past; he enumerated the essentials of strong national government; and set down the vices of the Confederation of the United States in Congress assembled. The results of these lucubrations he communicated to Edmund Randolph, then governor of Virginia, and a little later to Washington.[2] Like so many men of that day, Madison combined scholarship with politics. He is not in the first rank of Americans with Washington, Jefferson, and Lincoln; but as a constructive statesman, he stands almost alone by reason of the acumen with which he judged of the possible and impossible, conjoined to a knowledge of the present and the past. He conceived the individual

---

[1] Professor Farrand of Yale University has well expressed the opinion of students who "have generally believed that the American Constitution would have taken its present form if the pamphlet in question had never been written, or, indeed, if Webster had never lived." This sentence is taken from his review of Hannis Taylor's *Origin and Growth of the American Constitution* in *American Historical Review*, xvii, 162. In a note to the present writer Professor Farrand adds that he has "not a scrap of evidence that Webster's dissertation directly influenced a single member of the convention. In fact I have found practically no reference to it at that time."

[2] Hunt's *Writings of Madison*, ii, 336, 344, 361.

independence of the States to be utterly irreconcilable
with their aggregate sovereignty; but the consolidation
of them all into one "simple republic" would be as inexpedient as it was unattainable. He sought a middle
ground which would permit a due supremacy of national
administration, while not excluding the local authorities
whenever they could be of use. He proposed to make a
change in the principle of representation by doing away
with the equality of the States in Congress. He thought
that the "national Government," besides the powers it
possessed under the Articles, should have positive and
complete authority in all cases that require uniformity of
action as the regulation of trade, including the right of
taxing both imports and exports. He thought that the
national supremacy ought to extend to a negative on the
legislative acts of the State; in other words, that the national judiciary ought to be supreme. Madison wrote that
a central executive ought to be provided; but up to the
time of his departure for Philadelphia, he had not ven-
tured upon an opinion as to how it should be constituted
or as to the functions with which it should be clothed.
He suggested the division of the national legislature into
two Houses. The members of one of these should serve
for a longer term than the members of the other and
should go out of office by some system of rotation. Madison thought well of the New York plan of the Council of
Revision to have a suspensive negative on the acts of the
national legislature; but he did not look upon this as
necessary. Neither Webster nor Madison suggested that
one branch of the proposed national congress should represent the States in their corporate capacities. Neither
of them recognized the difficulties which arose the moment
that the attempt was made to adjust representation and

taxation between the distinctively slave States and those in which slave labor played an unimportant part. Webster's idea that sovereignty could be distributed was new in 1783; his distinction between sovereignty and supremacy was highly significant. His proposition that the supreme authority should operate directly on the individual citizen aroused the ire of one who signed himself "a Connecticut Farmer." [1] The thought that a member of the General Assembly of Connecticut might be "dragged down to Congress" and subjected to fine, imprisonment, and possibly corporal punishment was to him distinctly distasteful, not to say abhorrent.

There seems to have been a public consciousness that the convention which was summoned to meet at Philadelphia, in 1787, was on a very different footing from that which had met in the preceding year at Annapolis. This is seen in the letters of the leading personages of the day and also in the fact that the foremost men were asked to take part in the work of the new constituent body. Some of them had been members of the First Continental Congress and had been prominent in public life ever since. Foremost among these were Washington, Franklin, and Dickinson. The presence of the first named had been secured with difficulty. Washington was disinclined to reenter public life. Moreover, it was undesirable for him to take part in an abortive attempt to reorganize the existing government. At first he refused point blank. He had made up his mind to retire from the presidency of the Society of the Cincinnati. This body was to meet at Philadelphia at the same time as the proposed convention.

---

[1] *Remarks on a Pamphlet entitled* "*A Dissertation on the political Union . . . by a Citizen of Philadelphia*" *with some brief Observations . . . by a Connecticut Farmer;* (Printed, M,DCC,LXXXIV).

He was tired of the intriguing that went on within that society. He wished to withdraw from it, but did not see how he could do this decently, if he were to be at Philadelphia when the society was in session there. Madison wrote to Washington repeatedly. He stated his reasons for wishing Washington's presence so cogently, that at length he induced the master of Mount Vernon to consent to accept the appointment as a delegate. It is interesting to note the reverential way in which Madison wrote to him and spoke of him to others. It is particularly noticeable, as is the affection which the older man exhibited towards his younger correspondent. Indeed, it is in a letter to Madison written at a little earlier date that Washington made one of the very few confessions of physical weakness to be found in his writings, when he apologized to his junior for not making a fair copy of his letter, because he had a headache. With a good deal of shrewdness Madison proposed to make the best use of the general's position and influence. He thought it would be well for Washington to put off announcing any decision until it was more certain what the outcome of the movement would be. If the convention were foredoomed to failure, he might stay away altogether, or having accepted he might be late in arriving. The news of the appointment of Franklin by Pennsylvania at first gladdened Madison, for it gave a certainty that the convention would have a presiding officer of dignity and prestige. On second thought, his mind was filled with foreboding lest Washington coming late should find the first place occupied by another and thus lose position in the eyes of his countrymen. He, therefore, wanted him to be at Philadelphia from the beginning. Among the younger men to attend were Madison, himself, Alexander Hamilton, and Gouverneur Morris. The Constitution owes to them primarily its form, its phrasing, and, indeed, its existence. Besides the men whose names have just been given, there were others hardly less noteworthy who, indeed, would have given any body historical distinction had they been by themselves. These were Robert Morris, James Wilson, George Mason, and Roger Sherman.

The consciousness of imminent public danger and the sudden willingness of the States and of the people to meet it was due to three principal causes: internal disorders in different parts of the country; a threatened secession of the southwestern settlements; and the inability of the existing government to provide for the colonization of the lands northwest of the Ohio River. Between 1783 and 1787, the country had passed through a period of economic readjustment. This was now coming to an end, and commerce and industry were beginning to thrive; but this fact was not recognized at the time. Contemporary evidence as to actual conditions is always very misleading. The onlooker sees only a small portion of any field, is influenced by local and personal considerations, and is governed largely by his own immediate experience. Statistics that are accessible to us, but were unattainable by the voters in 1786 and 1787, demonstrate the truth of the theory that commercially and industrially the country had regained its prosperity by 1788 and was on the high road to it in 1786. The organization of the government under the Constitution came at precisely the right time to give added movement to the favorable forces that were already in motion. To the men of 1786, this was unknowable and unknown. They were "hurt by the injustice, folly, and wickedness" of the state governments[1] and seemed

---

[1] M. D. Conway's *Omitted Chapters of History as disclosed in the Life and Papers of Edmund Randolph*, 86.

2 I

ready for almost any change. They were hampered by debts and could not see their way clearly from day to day. Washington and Mason were reputed to be among the richest of Virginia planters. The former was a forehanded man and a good manager. Yet we find him writing to John F. Mercer in September, 1786, that he is greatly in need of two hundred pounds that Mercer owes him to pay the workmen who had been employed in remodeling his house. Mercer could not pay the money. In January, 1788, Washington informed him that he was so straitened for funds he had been obliged to put off the tax collector three times, and unless he could collect something, he must let the sheriff seize some of his land and sell it to discharge his debt to the county.[1] George Mason, the owner of one of the greatest plantations on the Potomac, in April, 1787, was obliged to anticipate the payment from the treasury for his services as delegate or not attend the Convention at all. He had nearly six thousand pounds owing to him, but without the sixty pounds that were obtained from Governor Randolph, he could not have crossed the Potomac.[2] Virginia was honeycombed with debt. There were loud cries for paper money, and the legislature yielded to popular clamor to the extent of allowing taxes to be commuted by the payment of commodities — tobacco, flour, hemp, and deerskins — at specified rates.[3]

In South Carolina, the planters were even more heavily in debt than were those of Virginia, although they were rapidly regaining their old-time prosperity as is evident

[1] *Writings of Washington* (Ford ed.), xi, 63, 177 note.

[2] Rowland's *George Mason*, ii, 98. In a letter to Bart. Dandridge, dated Orange, February 26, 1785, Madison writes that he sends him sixty pounds and would have paid him sooner had he not been distressed by a prior debt and been " un-genteely treated " by those who owed him money. " Madison Papers " in Library of Congress, xiv, 10. See also [W. C. Ford's] " Letters of Joseph Jones " issued by the State Department in 1889, pp. 138, 153.

[3] Hening's *Statutes of Virginia*, xi, 302, etc.; see index under " commutables."

from a study of the importations at Charleston. These
favorable circumstances had not produced visible results in
1787, but they were there. The case of Thomas Bee [1] is to
the point. His creditors had secured executions against
him; the sheriff had seized his property and had sold it
at one-thirteenth of what it would have brought at private sale in ordinary times. He declared that he would
rather go to jail than see his property dissipated in this way.

New York was rapidly recovering from the occupation
of her principal town by the British and from the devasta-
tions of the armies in the near-by counties. This growth
toward prosperity was not realized by persons living there
who were conscious of the high imposts that were charged
on goods imported into the State. A nameless writer
in "Thoughts on Taxation in a Letter to a Friend" that
was printed at New York in 1784 advocated a system
of direct taxes levied on sixteen classes of persons according to the value of their houses and an "equivalent tax"
to do away with whatever inequalities the system might
disclose.

In New England the distress was even greater, and the
demand for paper money and for the passage of laws favoring the debtor was so strong that the leading men found it
difficult to make head against it. In Rhode Island the
bonds of society seemed to be broken. For many years
that State had been the home of paper money. Now, it
surpassed its former excessive reliance on paper money by
issuing it in enormous amounts and forcing it upon
creditors and upon those who had goods for sale, until at
length it deprived those who refused to receive it of their
political rights. The governing classes in Massachusetts
were able to defeat all attempts to issue paper money or

[1] Ulrich B. Phillips in *American Historical Review*, xiv, 540.

to scale down debts by means of "tender laws."[1] The pressure of poverty there was very great, and the General Court tried to moderate the demands of the poorer people by issuing an address[2] which was to be read by the ministers to their congregations on Thanksgiving Day. This paper contains a clear and detailed statement of the finances of the State since 1780. More than one and one-quarter million pounds had been collected by the State since that year. Of this £830,000 had been contributed to the Confederation or used to extinguish the state debt. In addition to this the towns had collected and paid out £700,000. The State had raised more money for the public service than was justifiable in time of war and in the period of economic disturbance that followed on the declaration of peace.[3] Besides this campaign of financial education by the authorities many among the well-to-do associated together to refrain from the excessive use of foreign articles of luxury, hoping in this way to encourage domestic industry, restore public credit, facilitate payment of debts, and promote the happiness and welfare of their country.[4] They were well-meaning persons, but if they

[1] In 1784, forgetting the lessons of the past, the Massachusetts legislature had passed an act imposing duties on licensed vellum and paper for discharging the war debts, etc. These were levied on bonds, deeds, notes, writs, newspapers, bills of lading, certificates for admission to the bar, and other documents by requiring them to be written or printed on parchment or paper previously stamped by commissioners (Acts of 1784, ch. 75). This law was changed in the next year by omitting newspapers, almanacs, and notes of hand and then repealed.

[2] James Swan's *National Arithmetic: or, Observations on the Finances of the Commonwealth of Massachusetts . . . by a late Member of the General Court* (Boston, 1786), pp. 2–5. Professor C. J. Bullock called my attention to this valuable tract. See also his " Historical Sketch of the Finances of Massachusetts " in the *Publications* of the American Economic Association for May, 1907, ch. ii.

[3] In 1774, before the outbreak of the Revolution, Virginia and Massachusetts had been nearly on a par in the matter of exportations, the Massachusetts trade being about ten per cent less than that of Virginia. In 1786, however, while Virginia's trade had more than regained its pre-Revolutionary standard, the exports of Massachusetts were only about one-fourth of what they had been twelve years earlier.

[4] The " Agreement " with signatures is printed in Massachusetts Historical Society's *Proceedings*, Second Series, viii, 496.

had opened their purses and spent money freely at this crisis, they would have done more to further the welfare of their less fortunate fellow-beings.

The first indications of trouble in Massachusetts were the attempts of mobs and riotous assemblies to prevent the opening of the courts of law. The movement was not confined to any one locality. The people threatened the judges at Groton in the northeast, at Taunton in the southeast, and at Worcester in the center; but it was especially in the western counties that there was grave disorder. Everywhere, debtors were numerous and creditors were pressing. Popular meetings were held at which a good deal of inflammatory talk was heard and fiery resolutions were passed. At one of these, in Hampshire County, resolutions were voted recommending the towns to instruct their representatives "to have emitted a bank of paper money, subject to a depreciation, making it a tender in all payments, equal to silver and gold." The idea underlying this panacea was more clearly expressed by a Connecticut man who advised making "a bank of paper money, big enough to pay all our debts, which will sink itself (that will be so much clear gain to the state)." [1]

The Massachusetts legislature refused to act on these suggestions looking toward a scaling down of debts; they had in mind the first article of the Declaration of Rights in the constitution of 1780, among which is enumerated that of acquiring, possessing, and protecting property. The malcontents, thereupon, proceeded to take the law into their own hands. They decided to resist with force all attempts on the parts of sheriffs and constables to carry out the orders of courts of law. Springfield on the Connecticut River had been the abode of gun makers

---

[1] Libby's *Distribution of Vote on the Federal Constitution*, 56, 58.

in colonial days. During the Revolution, the United States had established a manufactory of arms and an arsenal there. Within its walls were 7000 new muskets, 13,000 barrels of gunpowder, and lead proportionable. According to the Articles of Confederation, the United States in Congress assembled could not maintain an army in time of peace. War, actual or constructive, was always the fate of the frontier. This had justified the retention of about 750 soldiers who were distributed in posts west of the Alleghanies, and the appointment of General Henry Knox, Secretary of War. Recognizing the danger attendant upon the plundering of the arsenal at Springfield, Knox came to Boston and obtained from Governor Bowdoin authority to call upon the militia to protect property of the United States. He did so, and a body of militia from the western part of the State commanded by General Shepard reached Springfield in time to prevent a party of the disaffected under command of Captain Daniel Shays from looting the storehouses; but it was not until a fieldpiece was discharged, killing three of their number, that they understood General Shepard's earnestness and realized that he was in control of the situation. Knox also applied to Congress and asked for authority to recruit a " legion," consisting of infantry, cavalry, and artillery to the total number of two thousand men. This force was designed ostensibly for service in the Indian country; but being raised in Connecticut and Massachusetts, the soldiers would be on the spot in case of further trouble at Springfield. Neither Congress nor Knox had any money for this purpose, but the Secretary was supplied with funds by private subscriptions, and a few hundred men were enlisted.

Meantime, Governor Bowdoin and the Massachusetts

legislature had acted with vigor and success. General
Benjamin Lincoln was given command of a body of militia taken from the eastern part of the State where dis-
affection was least. With them he marched westward
through the storms and cold of a New England winter;
the snow was eighteen inches deep when he came to the
towns of Hampshire County, but news that Shays and
his men were in the neighborhood served only to increase
his indomitable resolution. Lincoln and his men surprised
the insurgents at Petersham, reaching that place after
a night march. Most of the insurgents escaped, but some
of them were taken. Lincoln asked their commander
what he and his men wished to do. The answer was
that they wanted to go home, to which Lincoln replied
that was the very best thing that they could do. The
vigor that he displayed on the one hand and the leniency
that he showed on the other brought the insurrection to
an abrupt ending. Shays and a few more escaped to
Vermont. Those who could not get away were treated
with harshness by the General Court; but ultimately
an act of indemnity set free nearly all of them. In the
coming election Bowdoin was defeated, Hancock being
chosen in his place, and a year later, those who had been
"out with Shays" and their sympathizers formed a large
portion of the party which opposed the ratification of the
new federal Constitution.

Public opinion was also powerfully affected by the condition of affairs in the settlements west of the Alleghanies,
especially in those in the region south of the Ohio. Ever
since 1775, even during the war, there had been a constantly increasing flood of colonists into what are now the
the States of Kentucky and Tennessee. After the peace,
this stream constantly grew in volume and in vigor. The

Kentuckians from the beginning recognized the authority
of Virginia over them, but the Tennessee settlers had been
inclined to dispute the right of the North Carolinians to
rule them.   By 1786, this had been changed and they had
come to recognize the legality of North Carolina's position.
In the Treaty of 1783, Great Britain had passed on to the
United States the right to the free navigation of the Mississippi that France had conferred upon her twenty years
earlier.   The Spaniards were desirous of putting an end
to this privilege, for the Mississippi flowed through their
territories for a couple of hundred miles.   In 1785 Don
Diego Gardoqui came to New York as Encargados de
Negocios or Minister to the United States.   He drew up a
" Representation " dilating upon the inconvenience of this
arrangement.   To his mind the Mississippi was in a way
analogous to the Tagus.   The latter had its rise in Spanish
territory, but flowed through Portugal in its lower
course.   The Spanish government had never thought of
suggesting that its people had a right to the free navigation
of the Tagus.[1]   The cases were not analogous, because in
1763, when France divided her American possessions between England and Spain, she had made this arrangement
as a part of the general settlement.   The Spaniards were
willing to go a long way toward opening their ports to
American commerce if this servitude on the Mississippi
could be done away with.[2]   They disliked the republicanism of the Americans and did not wish to aid them
to build up their western trade and settlements.   If
they could not close the Mississippi trade to the westerners,

[1] " Lee Papers " in Harvard University Library, vii, 137.
[2] *Diplomatic Correspondence of the
United States, 1783–1789* (Washington,
7 vols., 1833–1834), vi, 79–267; W. C.
Ford's *The United States and Spain in
1790*, pp. 7–16; and the writings of Jay,
Madison, Jefferson, and Washington.
See also *American Historical Review*,
viii, 5–10; ix, 748; x, 817.

possibly the best thing might be to include their settlements within Spanish territory. Elusive intrigues were begun, but whether they amounted to anything is still uncertain.

The divergence in views between the dwellers east of the Alleghanies and those west of the mountains is most noticeable on this point. Washington thought that it would be for the best interest of the settlers in the mid Ohio Valley to bring their products to the seaboard through one of the communications which nature had provided between the Atlantic States and the western settlements. Whenever the latter should become populous and extend to the Mississippi, no power could deprive them of the use of that river; why, then, prematurely urge the matter, "if it is our interest to let it sleep"?[1] Henry Lee, to whom this letter was addressed, answered that Washington's reasoning was conformable to the prevalent doctrine in Congress. The Spaniards were willing to provide the United States with commercial facilities elsewhere if this right were given up; why not, then, he asked, "agree to the exclusion of the Mississippi?" Those who were engaged in commerce in New England, New York, and Philadelphia were entirely of Washington's mind. John Jay, who was then Secretary of Foreign Affairs, fell in with these ideas and began negotiations with Gardoqui on this basis.

Those who proposed to barter the right to freely navigate the Mississippi for the purpose of building up the commerce of a few northern seaports and the encouragement of the plans for improving the Potomac and the James and opening roads through the passes of the Alleghanies reckoned without the settlers in Kentucky and

---

[1] *Writings of Washington* (Ford ed.), xi, 41.

Tennessee. They were energetic and outspoken frontiersmen, ardent believers in their own rights, and jealous of eastern control. There were Virginians, too, who argued vigorously for the westerners. Especially, Jefferson could hardly find words to express his detestation of the pusillanimity of those who would sell the right to use the facilities that nature had given them for a convenient trade with the West Indies and the Mediterranean. The Kentuckians talked loudly of secession and so did the settlers of Tennessee. The Virginia Assembly replied to the former that they could separate whenever they saw fit, provided they assumed their share of Virginia's debts and general expenses. Upon this, the Kentuckians drew back, but the dangers of the situation so wrought upon Jay that he abandoned all thought of going on with the Spanish negotiation. The suggestion of secession aroused the fears of many people and made them more willing to consent to the establishment of a central government that would be strong enough to curb Kentuckians and Spaniards alike.

North of the Ohio, there were few settlers from the Atlantic seaboard. This very fact was an unfavorable comment on the existing confederation. The British still held the valuable posts on the Great Lakes. The Indians attacked the pioneers as they floated down the Ohio or explored the country. The dwellers in the old French towns had been harshly treated by the Virginians and neglected by the Congress. The Spaniards from south and west and the British from the north set on foot intrigue after intrigue, and the United States in Congress assembled was powerless. The future demanded a more perfect union; without it, the whole western country might be lost.

Helplessness was the keynote of the existing government. It was neither respected abroad nor obeyed at
home. Interstate jealousies and conflicts and intrastate
disorders were the rule of the hour. It remained to be
seen whether the delegates who assembled in the Federal
Convention at Philadelphia in June, 1787, could devise
something that would at once meet the needs of the day
and secure the approval of the people of the United States.

NOTES

I. General Bibliography. — George Bancroft brought together an immense mass of material on the years 1781 to 1789 in the text and appendix of his *History of the Formation of the Constitution of the United States*. This was published at New York in 1882 in two volumes as a separate work; it forms volume vi of the " Author's Last Revision " (New York, 1885). The most important portion of the original work was the long appendix of letters and papers illustrating the general theme; these are omitted from the " Last Revision." The text is written in a more restrained style than Bancroft's earlier volumes and is therefore more satisfying to the student, but in places it is uncritical. Practically no attention is paid to the influence of economic forces. The first volume of John Bach McMaster's *History of the People of the United States since the Revolution* (New York, 1888) covers the period from 1783 to 1790. It has to do with all the activities of humanity and is based on an untiring research in newspapers and pamphlets; but little time was spent on manuscript material. John Fiske's *Critical Period of American History, 1783–89* (Boston, 1888) is a pleasant exposition of the facts given in more detail by Bancroft and McMaster. F. S. Oliver's *Alexander Hamilton, an Essay on American Union* (London, 1907) is a moderate English view of the founding of the federal government.

II. The Shays Rebellion. — George Richards Minot's *History of the Insurrections, in Massachusetts, In the Year MDCCLXXXVI, and the Rebellion consequent thereon* Worcester, 1788) was written when the reaction consequent upon these disorders was strong. The volume, therefore, reflects the conservative view and is somewhat lacking in charity towards the insurgents. Since then no formal detailed account has been printed. Joseph Parker Warren, while a student, began a research on this theme which he used for his doctoral thesis. After attaining his degree, he continued his researches in this direction and was on the point of publication at the moment of his premature death in 1909. It is greatly to be wished that some one would take up this work where he left it and push it to completion. He contributed a few documents to the *American Historical Review* (ii, 693). The first of these is Shepard's report of the engagement at Springfield. This had already been printed in the *Papers and Proceedings* of the Connecticut Valley Historical Society (i, 86) in connection with the article " Springfield in the Insurrection of 1786 " by William L. Smith. Among recent papers on the subject are those by John Noble,[1] Dr S. A. Green,[2] the Rev. Grindall Reynolds,[3] and a remarkable disquisition by Jonathan Smith read before the Clinton (Mass.) Historical Society on September 14, 1903 entitled "Some Features of Shays' Rebellion."

[1] American Antiquarian Society's *Proceedings*, October, 1902.

[2] Massachusetts Historical Society's *Proceedings*, November, 1884.

[3] In his *Historical and Other Papers*, 195–244.

CHAPTER XVI

THE FEDERAL CONVENTION AND ITS WORK

MAY 14, 1787, was the day set for the opening of the Convention at Philadelphia to revise the Articles of Confederation, but few delegates were then on the ground. It was not until the 25th of the month that seven States were represented, and not until the 1st of June that the active debating began. Those who had been prompter in arriving than their colleagues, had passed their time in friendly discussion and had come near agreement on general points before Washington took the chair as president of the Convention. Otherwise it is difficult to account for the rapidity with which the delegates decided to propose a plan that contemplated the destruction of the existing federal organization and the establishment of a consolidated government that would be national[1] in aim and supreme in operation. In the future, should this scheme be adopted, the existing state organizations would become secondary; the individual citizen would be directly responsible to the general government; and the acts of the new legislative body would be supreme throughout the land. It is safe to say that had this outcome been anticipated, had the state legislatures foreseen that the movement, in which they were asked to take part, would end in the loss of state sovereignty and the establishment of a government,

---

[1] In 1826 Madison sought to explain away the use of the word "national" by stating that "the term was used, not in contradistinction to a limited, but to a *federal*, Government"; it was not regarded as equivalent to unlimited or consolidated. He goes on to say that the term "national" was used because there was no word that was applicable to "the new and unique System." *Documentary History of the Constitution*, v, 333.

federal only in name, not one State would have accepted the invitation of Congress and appointed delegates.[1] The scheme formulated at Philadelphia was so wise in itself and so masterfully advocated by its friends that, once before the voters, its ratification could not be prevented and the last stage in the American Revolution was peacefully accomplished. The delegates came together intent on remedying the defects of the Articles of Confederation and did it by replacing the existing framework from foundation up by a form of government that was new to America and to the world.

The adoption of the Ninth, Tenth, and Eleventh Amendments within ten years of Washington's inauguration went far toward revolutionizing the Constitution as it came from the Convention and as it was ratified by the States by placing in it many of the attributes of federal organization. The Ninth Amendment[2] prohibited, or seemed to prohibit, a "broad construction" of the organic law; the Tenth[3] expressly declared that undelegated powers were reserved to the States or to the people; and the Eleventh[4] forbade

---

[1] In his biography of *Daniel Webster* (p. 176, *American Statesmen* series) Henry Cabot Lodge asserted that in 1788 not a man in the country looked upon the new system as anything but experimental and that each and every state might withdraw at will. This statement has attracted much attention. Its accuracy has been denied by D. H. Chamberlain and Charles Francis Adams in Massachusetts Historical Society's *Proceedings*, Second Series, xvi, 151; xvii, 99; xx, 477. Mr. Adams's essay is also printed in his *Studies, Military and Diplomatic*, vi. Caleb William Loring's *Nullification, Secession, Webster's Argument, and the Kentucky and Virginia Resolutions considered in reference to the Constitution and historically* (New York, 1893) is an earlier argument against the accuracy of Lodge's dictum.

[2] [ARTICLE IX]
"The enumeration in the Constitution, of certain rights, shall not be construed to deny or disparage others retained by the people."

[3] [ARTICLE X]
"The powers not delegated to the United States by the Constitution, nor prohibited by it to the States, are reserved to the States respectively or to the people." (Articles IX and X appear to have been in force from Nov. 3, 1791).

[4] [ARTICLE XI]
"The Judicial power of the United States shall not be construed to extend to any suit in law or equity, commenced or prosecuted against one of the United States by Citizens of another State or by Citizens or Subjects of any Foreign

the suing of a State by private persons. "The people" had recalled their earlier determination and modified the organic law so that the question of its national character became a matter of judicial interpretation and legislative conflict.

In reading over the records of the debates of the Federal Convention, one is amazed at the slight attention paid to the history of early confederations, except to shun the weaknesses which the annals of those leagues plainly set forth.[1] The historical knowledge of Madison and his colleagues was great, and some of them had come to Philadelphia with synopses of the sins of former federations carefully drawn out on paper. They avoided these evil precedents and drew their inspiration from the history of their own time, from the experience of themselves and their fathers in America and in England, and from their reading of the political theorists, from Aristotle and Plato to Harrington and Locke.[2] The path to efficiency in gov-

State." (Proclaimed to be in force Jan. 8, 1798.) This change grew out of the decision of the Supreme Court in the case of Chisholm *vs.* Georgia. In delivering his opinion James Wilson, one of the associate justices, declared that the problem was, " Do the people of the United States form a nation?" His answer was in the affirmative, and the Eleventh Amendment was proposed by Congress and ratified by the States. After this time there certainly was ground for argument as to the character of the Constitution and the government established under it.

Burton Alva Konkle has an interesting memoir on *James Wilson and the Constitution* and presumably will elaborate the theme in his biography of Wilson soon to be published. Professor Albert Bushnell Hart contributed " A Wilson Bibliography" to the *James Wilson Memorial Volume.*

[1] Edward G. Bourne examined this subject most carefully in the American Historical Association's *Reports*, 1896, vol. i, p. 221. " If we recur to history and review the annals of mankind, I undertake to say that no instance can be produced by the most learned man of any confederate government that will justify a continuation of the present one." Madison in the Virginia Ratifying Convention, quoted by Bourne on p. 227.

[2] Professor Archibald C. Coolidge brought together many interesting facts in a stimulating essay on the *Theoretical and Foreign Elements in the Formation of the American Constitution* (Freiburg, 1892). See also James Harvey Robinson's " Original and Derived Features of the Constitution" in the *Annals* of the American Academy of Political and Social Science, i, 203–243.

There are references to the New England Confederation in the debates in the ratifying conventions (Elliot's *Debates*, ii, 30; iii, 132).

ernment lay clearly in the direction of the establishment
of a single political fabric in which the good points of the
state organizations could be repeated and the defects that
inexperience and idiosyncrasy had placed in them carefully
avoided.   The trouble in the realization of any such ideal
was that too rigid a plan would certainly fail of adoption
by the voters in the several States.   To humor them, concessions were made to the idea of federalism that made the
document susceptible of different interpretations, especially
after the adoption of the amendments that have just been
noted.   Had Madison, Hamilton, George Mason, or James
Wilson been perfectly free to formulate an ideal government
for a great nation in which the local political organizations
should be given no more important functions than those that
were associated with boroughs and counties, they, or any one
of them, could have produced a much better scheme than the
one that was adopted.   But History proceeds by compromise, and the annals of America have furnished no exception to this rule.

The delegates had not proceeded far in their deliberations before they were convinced of the undesirableness
of giving prominence to the word "national."   At first
they substituted for it the phrase " We, the people of the
States of New Hampshire, Massachusetts," etc.   This so
clearly presupposed a federal organization that later the
words " We the People of the United States " were used
to describe the parties to the instrument.   This phrase
might be interpreted in several ways; but the further
declaration that the Constitution and the laws and treaties
made under it "shall be the supreme law of the Land "
could have only one meaning.   Moreover, standing apart
from the legislative branch and the executive, they set a
Supreme Court with power to hear and determine all

2 K

cases in law and equity arising under the Constitution. These phrases made the national judiciary all-powerful, and there can be little question that the members of the Convention so intended.

How to secure the supremacy of the national government occasioned much debate. One proposition was that the national legislature should have the power to annul state laws ; but the exercise of this authority would lead to dangerous commotions. Many of the delegates were strongly attracted to the establishment of a Council of Revision like that of New York under its first constitution. It proved to be a matter of difficulty to devise any method of appointing the members of such a council, and, moreover, its decisions would necessarily take the form of the negative of state law. The framers of the Constitution fell back, therefore, upon the practice of colonial days whereby the Privy Council had declared colonial laws null and void because they were contrary to the constitution.[1] This had been done on appeal from colonial courts, or in answer to petitions that had been presented to the king as the fountain of justice.[2] They determined to propose the establishment of a national tribunal to decide as to the constitutionality of laws, State and national, and also to hear cases in which the representatives of foreign countries or of the States of the Union were particularly concerned. This mode of procedure would seem to be judicial, and the national gov-

[1] For a list of books on the origin of the Supreme Court, see Note II at end of chapter.

[2] On the general subject of appeals from colonial courts, see an excellent article by Harold D. Hazeltine in the *Reports* of the American Historical Association for 1894, p. 299; Chalmers's *Opinions of Eminent Lawyers* (London, 1814), i, 197, 353, etc.; Brinton Coxe's *Essay on Judicial Power and Unconstitutional Legislation* (Philadelphia, 1893) ; J. B. Thayer's " Origin and Scope of the American Doctrine of Constitutional Law " in the *Harvard Law Review* (Cambridge, 1893), vii, 129; and G. L. Sioussat's " English Statutes in Maryland " in *Johns Hopkins University Studies*, xxi, 481–494.

ernment would not directly annul a state law and thereby give incitement to civil strife.

The case that best illustrates the procedure of pre-Revolutionary days is that which is associated with the name of John Winthrop, son of Wait Still Winthrop, at one time chief justice of Massachusetts, and through him descended from John Winthrop, governor of Connecticut, and John Winthrop, founder of Massachusetts. Colonial conditions and Puritan ethics demanded different laws of inheritance from those that prevailed in England. There land usually passed to the eldest son. It was his business to take care of his younger brothers and his sisters until offices or husbands were provided for them. In America, in new settlements all the members of the family labored together to clear the land and work the farm. It seemed only right, therefore, that they should all participate in the ownership of the land when the father died without leaving a will providing for a specific division of the estate. Massachusetts, however, had for years provided that the eldest son should receive a double portion ; the other children sharing equally.[1] This law had been confirmed by the King in Council after the establishment of the government under the province charter. Seven years later, the colony of Connecticut passed a similar law, but this was not submitted to the king, because the Connecticut charter only required that its laws should be " not contrary to the laws of England."

After Judge Winthrop's death in 1717, his son John took possession of his lands in Connecticut and also of the personal estate. There was a sister living at Boston whose husband's name was Lechmere. For some reason Winthrop thought best to keep all the property in his hands, from time to time giving his sister money. This arrangement

[1] *Massachusetts Province Laws,* i, 44.

did not meet with the approbation of some of Lechmere's creditors, who caused Winthrop to be arrested, as he was leaving his sister's house in Roxbury, and thus precipitated a long and bitter fight. Winthrop had paid no attention to the Connecticut laws regulating the distribution of the estates of deceased persons. He lost suit after suit in the courts of that colony, and the property was placed in Lechmere's hands. Winthrop then went to England and petitioned the king for justice, claiming that the inheritance act of Connecticut was contrary to the laws of England. The Privy Council agreed with him and an Order in Council was issued annulling the Connecticut law (February 15, 1727).[1]

The next case arose in Massachusetts. Boston Common, July 3, 1728, was the scene of a duel between Henry Phillips and Benjamin Woodbridge, in which the latter was killed. The laws of that colony punished duelling with six months' imprisonment or less, a fine of not more than one hundred pounds, or corporal punishment, — "not extending to member or pillory," — or all three of them.[2] The successful duellist fled to France and died there without leaving a will. The property was divided according to the provisions of the Massachusetts law. His surviving brother

[1] The documents in the Winthrop case are printed at length in the *Collections* of the Massachusetts Historical Society, Sixth Series, v; *Colonial Records of Connecticut*, vii, ix, Appendix; Connecticut Historical Society's *Collections*, vol. iv, "The Talcott Papers." The latter citations refer to the case of Clark *vs.* Tousey. This also related to lands in Connecticut and was appealed to England. The Privy Council in 1745 recognized the injustice of their action as to land titles in that colony and decreed the validity of the Connecticut law. This decision was not to be retroactive and the Winthrop lands were not to be disturbed.

[2] Act of 1719 (*Massachusetts Province Laws*, ii, 135). This duel led to a revision of the law. In 1728, it was enacted (*ibid.*, ii, 516), that a person participating in a duel should sit on the gallows for one hour with a rope around his neck and suffer imprisonment for twelve months; that a Christian burial should be denied to the person killed in the duel who should be buried in a trench with a stake driven through his body. It is to be noted that the act of 1719 is the first colonial enactment on the subject of duelling.

laid claim to all his lands under the English practice. Being defeated in the Massachusetts courts, he appealed to England, and the Privy Council dismissed his case with costs — on the ground that the Massachusetts law had been confirmed by the crown.

Coming down to a later time, there is a case of especial interest that arose out of the commercial conditions prevailing in the last French and Indian War. It seems that the brig *Providence*, belonging to Obadiah, Nicholas, and John Brown, had been insured against perils of the sea, pirates, and British cruisers while on a voyage from Providence, her home port, to the Bight of Leogane with liberty to go to the south side of the island of San Domingo. She was provided with a " flag of truce " to enable her to enter the enemy's ports. The insurance was effected with David and William McMurtrie of Philadelphia at the rate of twenty-three per cent. She was captured while on the voyage by the British privateer, *Polly's Revenge*, and condemned by a prize court. The McMurtries refused to pay the insurance. The Browns sued them in Pennsylvania and got a decision in their favor. The McMurtries appealed to England, but notwithstanding the circumstances of the case,[1] the Privy Council confirmed the decision of the Pennsylvania court. The facts of trading with the enemy and of insuring against capture by the ships of one's own country are insignificant in comparison with the course of procedure, the residents in one colony suing the dwellers in another, and the matter being finally decided by the supreme judicial authority of the empire.

In the Committee of the Privy Council for Appeals we see a supreme court exercising effective legal control

---

[1] Minutes of more than twenty appealed cases decided between 1760 and 1765 are in the " Hardwicke Papers " in the British Museum (Transcripts in the Library of Congress); among them this one.

throughout the colonies, not by its own decree, indeed, but through orders in council. Its functions were clearly judicial, and were exercised only in cases that were brought before it.[1] It acted as a court of appeal from lower courts, and it reversed or advised the reversal of the decrees of colonial tribunals on the ground that the laws under which they had acted were contrary to the laws and customs of England or to some specific act of Parliament. It was the precedent for the Supreme Court of the newly modeled United States.

With rebellion the American colonists no longer recognized the authority of English courts or of the King in Council. With independence, they established courts of their own and throughout the period of statehood, the highest court of each of the thirteen settled these questions for its State. The form in which the matter came up for decision was as to an act of a state legislature. It was generally recognized that a constitution was superior to an act of the legislative body and that the judges in interpreting it were to be guided by the principles of the Common Law. The first case to arise was that of Josiah Phillips, who was attainted by the Virginia Assembly in May, 1778, for making war upon the people of that commonwealth. When his case came before the legal authorities, they disregarded the act of attainder[2] and tried, convicted, and sentenced him to death as a highway robber.

The next case in point of time arose in New Jersey. That State by its configuration offered peculiar facilities for running goods through the lines from the British store-

[1] For an interesting Rhode Island case, see Note III at end of the chapter.

[2] Professor St. George Tucker in his edition of Blackstone's *Commentaries* (Philadelphia, 1803, vol. i, Appendix, p. 293) states positively that the "court refused to pass the sentence" under the act of attainder. Professor W. P. Trent has an interesting paper in opposition to this dictum in the *American Historical Review*, i, 444, — with abundant references.

houses at New York. On October 8, 1778, the legislature passed a Seizure Act to put an end to this trade with the enemy. Under it cases might be tried by a jury of "six good and lawful Men of the County" or by the judge without any jury.[1] In due season Major Elisha Walton seized silks and other goods of "such a quantity and such a quality as could not be purchased in all the stores of New Jersey," alleging that they had been run through the lines. Two men appeared as claimants, John Holmes and Solomon Ketcham; but the goods were awarded to Walton. Even before the jury of six men had given its verdict, Holmes and Ketcham had applied to the supreme court of the State for relief. The case was argued in November, 1779. The principal reason put forward for the reversal of the decision of the lower court was that according to the "Laws of the Land" the jury should have consisted of twelve men and not of six. The justices of the supreme court were not at all anxious to become embroiled with the legislature and put off making any decision in the hope that the law might be changed. Finally, in 1780, as the Assembly had not done this, they ordered the judgment of the lower court to be reversed. Their opinions have never been found, but the position taken by the justices is clearly seen in a petition that was presented to the Assembly complaining that they had "set aside some of the laws as unconstitutional."[2]

---

[1] The form of the law was peculiar in that it provided for the trial of cases arising under it before a jury when demanded in accordance with an act that had been passed in February, 1775. It was this law that authorized the hearing of certain classes of cases before juries of six men instead of before the usual number. Peter Wilson's *Acts of New Jersey* (Trenton, 1784), Appendix, No. V; Samuel Allinson's *Acts of New Jersey* (Burlington, N. J., 1776), 470–472. This case has been most carefully described by Austin Scott in *American Historical Review*, iv, 456.

[2] Three months after this decision was rendered the legislature provided by law that a jury of twelve men should be impaneled whenever demanded by either party to a suit. Wilson's *Acts of New Jersey*, Appendix, No. viii. The case of Commonwealth *vs.* Caton, 1782,

The best known of the cases that came up in state courts before 1788 in which the judges refused to acknowledge the constitutionality of an act of the legislature was that of Trevett vs. Weeden in Rhode Island. For a long time this was looked upon as standing by itself largely because an account of it was printed in pamphlet form at an early date,[1] while the record of the other cases remained in manuscript. Otherwise it has no more importance from the point of view of the present discussion than the case just described or the North Carolina case that will be noted later. With the constantly increasing mass of paper money in Rhode Island a growing disinclination to accept it in payment was seen and led to the passage of a " Forcing Act " and, finally, to a law providing a fine of not less than six pounds nor more than thirty for any person who should refuse to receive paper money, — on conviction by a majority of the judges without the intervention of a jury. In due course one John Trevett, a cabinet-maker, appeared in the butcher shop of John Weeden at Newport and tendered him Rhode Island paper bills in payment for provisions. Weeden, who had received town aid only a few months before, refused to accept them and ere long found himself in court. The information alleged that Weeden "not regarding the Laws & Statutes of the said State but the same intending to break and make void and annul with Force & Arms in open Market, did then & there presumptuously daringly, and contemptuously refuse to take and receive of the aforesaid Trevett the Bills

in Virginia involved the authority of a resolve of the House of Delegates of that State and not an act of the legislature. In 1784, in New York, in the case of Rutgers vs. Waddington, Alexander Hamilton obtained a verdict contrary to the provisions of an act of the state assembly, but it does not appear that the question of the constitutionality of the law was directly involved.

[1] J. M. Varnum, The Case of Trevett against Weeden: . . . also The Case of the Judges of said Court (Providence, 1787).

of Credit." The case at once attracted keen interest, and the foremost lawyers in the State volunteered their services in Weeden's behalf. In answer to the complaint Weeden's counsel alleged that the law did not authorize the court " to impannel a Jury to try the facts charged in the Information, and so the same is unconstitutional and void." The court merely declared that the complaint did not come under the cognizance of the justices present and dismissed it.[1]

In Rhode Island the judges were appointed annually by the Assembly. Their refusal to enforce an act of that body aroused indignation among the politicians. The judges were summoned before the Assembly " to render their reasons for adjudging an Act of the General Assembly unconstitutional, and so void." Three of them attended and spoke at length. Judge Howell, the youngest of them, referring to the language of the summons, said that it was not warranted by the record, because the judges had not stated that the act was void. They had simply refused to take cognizance of the information. For one, he declared that the penal law was unconstitutional and furthermore asserted that judges could not be held answerable for their opinions unless they were charged with criminality. Another of the three, Judge Hazard, stated that he had favored the emission of paper currency, but that the opinion which he gave upon the trial against the law was dictated by the energy of truth. The members of the Assembly were evidently somewhat disturbed by the attitude of the justices. They debated the matter and then sought the opinion of William Channing, the attorney-

[1] Ms. records in the Newport County Court House, 1772–1779, pp. 281, 282. This was communicated to me by Mr. John T. Nightingale. Two other complaints by Trevett, " similar Informations & similar Please being made," were likewise dismissed.

general of the State.   He declared that the determination
of the judges was conformable to the principles of constitutional law ; but whether it was or not there would be a
fatal interruption of government if judges were to be removed from office for a mere matter of opinion, without
a charge of criminality.   The attorney-general and the
judges were not recalled, but none of them were reap-
pointed when their terms of service had expired.

The last case in this series arose in North Carolina and
turned upon the same point, the unconstitutionality of a
law of that State providing for the disposal of property by
the decree of a court without the intervention of a jury.
In this case[1] as in the others the judges were plainly
unwilling to antagonize the legislature, if it could be
avoided.   But in North Carolina, as in New Jersey, the
Assembly refused to repeal the law or postpone action,
and the judges thereupon declared it to be unconstitutional.   This case in its legal aspects resembles the others
very closely ; but, while they were accomplished facts,
the discussion of this matter was going on at the time
that the Federal Convention was in session at Philadelphia.   It attracted the attention of Richard Dobbs Spaight,
one of the delegates from North Carolina.   He wrote to
James Iredell, the leading counsel in opposition to the law,
that the judges by their decision united in their own persons
legislative and judicial power which no monarch in Europe
enjoyed and which " would be more despotic than the
Roman Decemvirate, and equally as insufferable."[2]   Iredell,
replied that a constitution was in the nature of a fundamental law and that the legislature was its creature.   It

[1] Bayard *vs.* Singleton, J. B. Thayer
gives the leading points of this case in
his *Cases on Constitutional Law*, Part i,
78.

[2] G. J. McRee's *Life and Correspondence of James Iredell* (New York,
1858), ii, 169.

was no part of the judge's business to serve as arbiters, but when a law is brought before them, they necessarily have to determine whether it is conformable to the constitution or not. If it is not in harmony with the organic law, it is unconstitutional, and so void.[1]

The establishment of a national government being once conceded, the provision for the Supreme Court followed as a matter of course.[2] It aroused little debate in the Convention itself, and the opponents of the new Constitution in the ratifying conventions did not base their opposition on this point. Patrick Henry, from his reputation and political ability, was their leader. He disliked the establishment of a new state in place of the existing thirteen. He approved of the Supreme Court, but thought that the grant of power might well be made more explicit. In the Virginia Ratifying Convention the question of the power of the Supreme Court to declare laws unconstitutional came up for debate, and John Marshall expressly stated that if Congress made a law " not warranted by any of the powers enumerated, it would be considered by the judges as an infringement of the Constitution which they are to guard. They would not

[1] The three New Jersey men who had borne foremost parts in the decision of the case of Holmes *vs.* Walton were members of the Convention : David Brearly who had given the decision of the court, William Patterson who had acted as counsel in opposing the law of 1778, and William Livingston who had secured its modification by the Assembly. William R. Davie of North Carolina, another member of the Convention, had been concerned in the case of Bayard *vs.* Singleton, and Alexander Hamilton had won a case in New York partly, perhaps, on this very ground. Elbridge Gerry of Massachusetts had not been directly concerned in any similar case; but he stated in the Convention that the judges in Massachusetts had declared laws of that State to be null and void (Elliot's *Debates*, v, 151). These men certainly knew what they were doing when they voted for the establishment of the Supreme Court of the United States.

Dean Trickett of the Dickinson School of Law holds that the Convention did not intend that the Supreme Court should declare acts of Congress null and void, because it gave the court no protection against an increase of its numbers by legislation (*North American Review*, August, 1907).

[2] Robert Ludlow Fowler discusses the question of the origin of this court in *American Law Review*, xxix, 711.

consider such a law as coming under their jurisdiction. They would declare it void." [1]   The framers took good care of the judges of the Supreme Court.   They provided for their appointment during good behavior with salaries that cannot be diminished.   Moreover, this court exists by virtue of the Constitution itself; it cannot be destroyed by act of Congress, but only by an amendment to the Constitution.   It is conceivable that a President and a Congress hostile to an existing set of judges might " swamp" the Supreme Court by the appointment of a sufficient number of justices to change a minority to a majority.   Nothing of the kind has ever been attempted. The Supreme Court slowly changing in personnel has outlived presidents and congresses both friendly and unfriendly.   As public opinion clears, as one judge after another leaves the bench and a successor takes his place, the mind of the court alters and the rules of reason and the mandates of " the law" are differently applied.   Always the court has gone on its way performing its gyroscopic function of keeping the ship of state steadily on her course.

The Convention provided the new government with ample means for meeting its expenditures, paying its debts, and protecting itself from attack.   This was accomplished by authorizing it to levy and collect taxes and duties that would be adequate to all its needs.   Some reservations were made as to the exercise of the power to levy money by direct taxation.   In the end it was decided that this

---

[1] Elliot's *Debates*, iii, 553. Writing to Madison from Paris on December 20, 1787, Jefferson gave his approval of the negative conferred on the President with one-third of either House; but stated that he "should have liked it better had the Judiciary been associated for that purpose, or invested with a similar and separate power." *Bulletin of Bureau of Rolls and Library of the Department of State*, No. 11, Part i, p. 412. For Hamilton's opinion, see *The Federalist*, No. lxxviii.

must be apportioned according to the rule prescribed for
representation. This qualification has made it almost
impossible for the central government to raise money by
direct taxes and has forced it to rely upon various forms
of indirect taxation which are more easy to collect but
are likely to prove insidious by reason of their inconspicu-
ousness. Arming the proposed government with ample
means and giving it the power to punish delinquents
through its own courts delivered the final stab at state
sovereignty and in its place established an efficient national
organization.

The new fabric, being in reality the organic law of a body
politic or state as the word is used by international lawyers and political theorists, it was natural that its framework should closely resemble that which had been worked
out in the constitutions of the several States that were now
to be merged into one political organization.[1]　The government, therefore, is divided into three branches, — executive,
legislative, and judicial. Each is in a measure independent
of the other two and endowed with strength to resist
encroachments. The Supreme Court can decline to recognize the validity of an act of Congress; the executive is
in control of the army and navy; and the legislative branch
by refusing to vote money can do something toward making
innocuous the action of both the executive and judicial.
The executive and legislative branches are bound together
more closely than political purists would prescribe, as the
President has a qualified veto on all legislative measures
passed by Congress; while, on the other hand, the Senate
sharing in appointments and in the exercise of the treaty-
making power possesses important executive functions.
In the distribution of these checks and balances the makers

[1] See tables at end of Chapter xiv.

of the Constitution achieved phenomenal success.   They
were guided by the treatise of Montesquieu on the " Esprit
de Lois," but otherwise they drew from their own experience in Congress and in the state governments.   In the
arrangement of detail, many differences appeared which
time and again threatened to wreck the whole movement.

One of the most objectionable. features of the existing
federal system was the equal vote in Congress enjoyed by
the smaller States at the expense of the larger ones.   In
1776 and 1777, when the Articles of Confederation were
under discussion, the instincts of self-preservation demanded
united action, and the objectors to this part of the plan
drew back when secession seemed imminent.   Now, they
were convinced that almost anything would be better than
continuing with the Confederation government.   Many
people outside of the Convention and some of those in it
were thinking and writing of the possibility of three confederations, if they could not have a new organization that
was acceptable to all.   The delegates from the larger
States declared that there was no object in forming another
government, if in that the smaller States were to hold the
larger by the throat as they did in the present one, while
enjoying the protection procured by the contributions of
the larger.   Franklin and other delegates from Virginia,
Pennsylvania, and Massachusetts argued earnestly for
representation in proportion to population.   Franklin
caused a resolution of the Continental Congress to be read
in which it was stated that the equal vote had been
adopted because proper statistics were not available.   The
discussion at once assumed a triangular form, the question
of the representation of slaves coming in to divide the
interests and the sympathies of the delegates from the
large and the small States.   Should representation be

apportioned according to free inhabitants of the several
States, or to the total population, and if representatives were
apportioned in one of these modes, should contributions be
in the same ratio? Elbridge Gerry of Massachusetts waxed
indignant on this point, and demanded to know why South
Carolina slaves should be represented when Massachusetts
horses were not. Representatives of the larger States became annoyed by the attitude of some of the delegates from
the smaller ones and suggested that if the latter did not
yield, they would form a confederacy by themselves which
the smaller States might join or not as they pleased. The
reply was that it would be just as well to be subjected to a
foreign power as to be under the dominion of the larger
States. The only way to maintain any kind of harmony in
the Convention was to postpone discussions on critical
matters whenever the debate became heated.

As soon as the determination was reached to establish a
legislative branch consisting of two houses, the door opened
for a compromise. Why would not an equitable arrangement be to have the representation in the House apportioned
according to the number of people living in each State,
while the Senate should be the representative of the States
in their corporative capacities. Another suggestion looked
to the apportioning representatives and direct taxes according to an artificial number that came to be called the
"federal ratio." This provided that the official numbering
of the States for these purposes "shall be determined by
adding to the whole number of free persons, including
those bound to service for a term of years and excluding
Indians not taxed, three-fifths of all other persons." [1]

---

[1] This arrangement affected the balance of parties in the national House of
Representatives. As a rule it produced
no vital effect on presidential elections.
In 1800, however, had the presidential
electors been apportioned according to
the free population Adams would have
had more votes than Jefferson and the

Friction between slave and free states was largely done away with by this arrangement.   The smaller States were placated by giving each State, regardless of its size, two senators to be chosen by the legislatures thereof.   At first each State was to have one vote in the Senate,[1] but suddenly toward the close of the proceedings, a draft of the proposed constitution appeared with the provision that each senator should have one vote, thereby destroying one-half of the significance of the Senate.[2]   The larger States had won something, but their delegates were still restless. Their susceptibilities were alleviated by providing that money bills should originate in the House.   As the Senate was permitted to amend these as well as other bills, the arrangement was largely nugatory.   For the time being, it served to make the delegates from the larger States feel that they had done their duty in protecting the rights of their constituents.

The establishment of the executive gave a good deal of trouble to the makers of the Constitution.   The States generally had single executive heads.   These were termed

---

fall of the Federalists would not have occurred at that time.   This subject will be examined in a later volume.   On April 18, 1783, Congress had asked the States to substitute this ratio for the land valuation provided in the Articles, *Journals of Congress*, viii, 189.

[1] Roger Sherman had suggested a dual method of legislating partly by States, partly by population, as far back as 1776.   See L. H. Boutell's " Roger Sherman in the Federal Convention " in American Historical Association's *Reports*, 1893, 231, and his *Life of Roger Sherman*, ch. viii.

[2] Charles C. Pinckney gave the following explanation of this change in the South Carolina House of Representatives.   He said that in the old Confederation, each State had an equal vote in Congress.   By the present Constitution each State would send two members to the Senate who would vote *per capita*. The old method was inconvenient. " But now that the senators vote individually, and not by states, each state will be anxious to keep a full representation in the Senate: . . . We shall thus have no delay, and business will be conducted in a fuller representation of the states than it hitherto has been.   All the members of the Convention, who had served in Congress, were so sensible of the advantage attending this mode of voting, that the measure was adopted unanimously.   For my own part, I think it infinitely preferable to the old method. So much for the manner of voting." Elliot's *Debates*, iv, 280.   The quoted matter, except the last sentence, is in Farrand's *Records*, iii, 252.

governors after the old colonial designation. Some of them shared their functions with the legislative branch or were guided and more or less controlled by an executive council. The Convention determined upon a single chief magistrate to be denominated the President, thereby continuing the distinction between the general government and the States that had insensibly grown up when the Continental Congress was presided over by men of commanding figure, like John Hancock and Henry Laurens. When it came to defining the power of the chief executive, the task proved to be by no means easy. Should he be given a council to advise him as to appointments, and how should the Secretary of State and other heads of departments be selected, and what should be their relations to their chief? The Constitution authorized him to require the opinion in writing of the heads of departments upon any subject relating to the duties of their office, but there is no suggestion that he must follow their advice. Before entering upon his duties, the President must take an oath to faithfully execute his office and to the best of his ability preserve, protect, and defend the Constitution of the United States. Whenever the Constitution is endangered by foes from without or from within, his power for the preservation of the government is that of an absolute monarch. Notwithstanding the autocratic power of the chief magistrate, provided he exerts it, there is not one word in the Constitution limiting the number of times that one man may be chosen to this high office. A wise custom begun by Washington and continued by Jefferson, Madison, Monroe, and Jackson has grown up limiting its duration to two terms or eight years in all.

After the principles had been agreed to, the whole matter was referred to a Committee of Detail which brought

2 L

some order out of the chaos of resolutions and amendments. After more debating, the instrument was handed
over to a Committee for Style and Arrangement. This
was composed of W. S. Johnson of North Carolina, Hamilton, Gouverneur Morris, Madison, and King. The actual
phrasing seems to have been left to Morris; but he sometimes followed suggestions made by persons who were
not members of the committee. The draft of the Constitution when it reappeared in the Convention was widely
different in many respects from the project that had been
committed to it. By changes in phraseology and arrangement and by the introduction here and there of phrases
like " impair the obligation of contracts " the friends of
strong government accomplished a large part of the purpose that had brought them to Philadelphia.

In all this time a few changes had been made that satisfied one or more delegates and brought them to vote for
the instrument as a whole. Some delegates, among them
George Mason, had greatly at heart the restriction of the
powers of the proposed Congress as to the regulation of
navigation and trade. He was also interested in other
constitutional projects that did not win the approbation
of a majority. In the end, therefore, he refused to sign
the Constitution as did Edmund Randolph and Elbridge
Gerry. Other members who did sign it were not enthusiastically in favor of it. Among these were Washington,
Franklin, and Hamilton. Franklin stated his convictions
in his usual happy phrases. He had lived long and had
come to doubt his own judgment and to pay more respect to the judgment of others. He had agreed to the
Constitution with all its faults because a " General Government " was necessary. He hoped that other members of the Convention who had objections to the in-

strument would with him doubt a little of their own in-
fallibility. Hamilton said that "no man's ideas were more
remote from the plan than his own were known to be,"
but the question being between anarchy and convulsion,
on the one side, and the chance of good on the other, he
hoped that every member would sign. Opposition to the
plan had been largely conciliated by the adoption of an
Article providing for future amendments. These might
be made by a convention called for the purpose, or they
might be proposed by the Congress and assented to by
three-fourths of the state legislatures. At the time, it
was expected that changes would be not infrequent, but
the process is so cumbersome that of two thousand amendments that have been proposed only fifteen have been
adopted [1] up to 1912.

The first ten amendments that were proposed by Congress in September, 1789, and declared in force in December, 1791, would have obviated many of the objections to
that instrument on the part of some of those who signed
their names to it as well as of many delegates to the
ratifying conventions. These were adopted so soon after
the organization of the new government that the Constitution has practically always included them. One of the
greatest objections that was made to it was that it contained no bill of rights. It was argued that this failure
to provide a guarantee of popular liberties was due to
the reactionary tendencies of the framers or to the fact
that they were aristocrats. The real reason why no such
feature w s incorporated in the document was the belief
that the United States courts would preserve the people
from executive and legislative tyranny by interpreting the

[1] Herman V. Ames's "Proposed *Report* of the American Historical Asso-
Amendments to the Constitution of the ciation for 1896.
United States" forming vol. ii of the

Constitution in the light of the Common Law and the rules of reason. The absence of such express provisions proved to be a stumbling-block to the general acceptance of the plan. In the administration of the government, it has turned out that the scope of its authority has depended mainly upon the interpretation of the instrument by the courts. The clause authorizing Congress " to make all Laws which shall be necessary and proper for carrying into Execution " the powers vested in the government or in any department thereof has been expounded in the most liberal manner possible, and has given the Constitution a fluidity that one would hardly expect it to have from the mere perusal of its phraseology.

The last clause of the Constitution declares that it was " Done in Convention, by the unanimous consent of the States present " and that the ratification of the conventions of nine States " shall be sufficient for the establishment of this Constitution between the States so ratifying the same." It was in this guise that it came before the United States in Congress assembled and was by them transmitted to the several States. It was a most revolutionary scheme because it proposed that nine of the existing thirteen States agreeing to it should secede [1] from the existing federal union, establish a new government for themselves, and leave the other States to shift for themselves as well as they might. The Articles of Confederation were indefinite on many points, but on this one point they were precise. No change was to be made in them without the consent of " the legislatures of every state." [2] Nevertheless, the dangers threatening society

[1] Mr. Samuel E. Morison informs me that S. A. Otis, one of the Massachusetts delegates in Congress, referred to the establishment of the new union as equivalent to a secession from the old.

[2] The Thirteenth Article of Confederation is as follows: " Every state shall abide by the determinations of the united states in congress assembled, on all questions which by this confedera⸠

were so great that the members of Congress pushed the
new scheme one step nearer completion, by transmitting
it to the States for ratification or rejection by conventions
to be chosen by the people.

Ratifying conventions were held in all the States except
Rhode Island, which remained persistently aloof. The
delegates to these conventions were usually chosen by
those persons in the several States who had the right
to vote for the members of the lower house of the state
legislature, and the apportionment was the same. In
New York, however, the Assembly interpreted the word
" people," which was used in the resolution of Congress,
transmitting the Constitution for state action to mean
something more than the qualified voters and gave all free
men the right to vote on this occasion. In some States,
there was a keen contest as to whether any convention
should be held. In Pennsylvania, party strife between
the conservatives and the radicals was very bitter. Those
who were opposed to the ratification of the new Constitution probably formed a majority of the qualified voters
in the State; but the call for the convention was rushed
through the Assembly before the opponents had a chance
to get together and organize. This bit of sharp practice
was unfortunate in that it aroused a more determined
opposition to ratification than slower measures would
have evoked.

Ordinarily, public opinion had been inclined to follow
the lead of Virginia and Massachusetts. Now, the
smaller States realized that they had gained much more

tion are submitted to them. AND the
Articles of this confederation shall be
inviolably observed by every state, and
the union shall be perpetual; nor shall
any alteration at any time hereafter
be made in any of them; unless such
alteration be agreed to in a congress of
the united states, and be afterwards confirmed by the legislatures of every state."

in the Federal Convention than they were likely to get in case another general convention were held, and hastened to ratify the Constitution. Delaware, New Jersey, Georgia, and Connecticut ratified in December, 1787, and January, 1788. With them, were Pennsylvania [1] which was the second State to ratify, and Massachusetts,[2] which fell into line in February. This gave six States in favor, with only three more needed to secure the setting up of the new government. Maryland ratified in April, and South Carolina followed in May. The conventions of New Hampshire, Virginia, and New York were then in session; favorable action by any one of them would settle the matter. New Hampshire ratified on the 21st of June, and Virginia followed on the 25th of that month before the news of the triumph of the Constitution was known at Richmond.

In Virginia, the contest was exceedingly bitter and prolonged. The opposition was led by Patrick Henry, who, besides being the foremost political orator of his time, was an adroit political manager. He was ably seconded by Richard Henry Lee, who wrote a series of letters [3] that

[1] The circumstances of the calling of the Pennsylvania Convention were characteristic — the motion being made in the Assembly before the Constitution had been officially laid before that body. The vote was made possible only by keeping two members of the minority on the floor of the house by physical means. The debates in the Convention are among the best. See J. B. McMaster and F. D. Stone, *Pennsylvania and the Federal Constitution, 1787–1788* (Philadelphia, 1888).

[2] *Debates and Proceedings in the Convention of the Commonwealth of Massachusetts, 1788* (Boston, 1856). This is the third edition of the debates of this convention and the most useful. See also S. B. Harding's "Federal Constitution in Massachusetts" (*Harvard Historical Studies*, No. ii); Dr. Belknap's "Minutes" in Massachusetts

Historical Society's *Proceedings*, for 1855–1858, p. 296; Essex Institute's *Collections*, xxxv, 81.

[3] *Observations leading to a Fair Examination of the System of Government proposed by the late Convention . . . in a number of Letters from the Federal Farmer to the Republican* (no place of publication, 1787); *An Additional Number of Letters from the Federal Farmer to the Republican . . . calculated to Illustrate and Support the Principles and Positions laid down in the preceding Letters* (no place, 1788).

The history of the Constitution in Virginia is admirably set forth in a series of letters printed in the *Proceedings* of the Massachusetts Historical Society for 1903. These were gathered by Mr. Worthington C. Ford mainly from the files in the State Department.

had a great vogue, and are still useful as containing an
admirable statement of the objections to the proposed organic law. Edmund Randolph and George Mason also
gave effective assistance. Henry's principal objection
comes out in the first speech that he made in the convention. The proposed government, he declared, would be an
" utter annihilation of the most solemn engagements of the
states — a proposal of establishing nine states into a confederacy, to the eventual exclusion of four states." He referred
to the awful magnitude of the dangers that must have been
borne in upon the minds of the members of the Federal
Convention to induce them to propose an entire alteration
of government. " I am sure," he said, " they were fully
impressed with the necessity of forming a great consolidated government, instead of a confederation. That this
is a consolidated government is demonstrably clear ; and
the danger of such a government is, to my mind, very
striking. . . . What right had they to say, *We, the people ?*
. . . Who authorized them to speak the language of,
We, the people, instead of, *We, the states ?* States are the
characteristics and the soul of a confederation. If the
states be not the agents of this compact, it must be one
great, consolidated, national government, of the people of
all the states." [1] Richard Henry Lee in his first " Letter "
asserted that the proposed plan appeared " to be partly
federal, but principally however, calculated ultimately to
make the states one consolidated government." He thought
that such a " compleat consolidating plan " deserved to be
carefully considered by every American because if it proved
to be impracticable its adoption would be a fatal error.
As to the details of this scheme, Lee thought that the general government, so far as the executive was concerned,

[1] Elliot's *Debates*, iii, 21, 22.

would " have a strong tendency to aristocracy, or the government of the few." The judicial department especially troubled him, for powers were improperly blended in the hands of the same men, — since the judges of the Supreme Court were to administer both law and equity. In the fourth "Letter," Lee turned to a new subject, observing that " when the people shall adopt the proposed constitution it will be their last and supreme act," since it will be adopted by the people of the United States and wherever this Constitution " shall be incompatible with the ancient customs, rights, the laws or the constitutions heretofore established in the United States, it will entirely abolish them and do them away — " and so would the laws of the new government.[1]

James Madison [2] and John Marshall spoke most effectively for the Constitution in the convention, but had not Washington come to their aid, their efforts might have been fruitless. A little earlier he had written to the governor of Maryland [3] that he favored the Constitution and that all reports to the contrary were false. The hesitation of Georgia filled him with anger ; he thought that the necessity of a general government was so urgent that its opponents must be wicked or insane.[4] The ratification by New Hampshire in June, 1788, gave life to the new Constitution, but the Union would have made a sorry figure had not New York joined those States which found shelter under the " New Roof," to repeat the phraseology of that day.

[1] R. H. Lee's *Observations . . . in . . . Letters from the Federal Farmer*, 8, 10, 19, 29.

[2] Answering Henry and other objectors, Madison said, " With respect to converting the confederation to a complete consolidation, I think no such consequence will follow from the Constitution." Elliot's *Debates*, iii, 34.

[3] *Writings of Washington* (Ford ed.), xi, 244. B. C. Steiner has two articles on the Constitution in Maryland in the *American Historical Review*, v.

[4] Washington to Henry Knox, January 10, 1788; to Samuel Powell, January 17, 1788 (" Sparks Mss.," No. 65, fo. 86, 88).

Nowhere had the contest been keener than in New York. That State was then divided between an agricultural interior and a small but rich and populous commercial district on tide water. The merchants and men of settled fortunes and the professional men living in New York City and the immediate neighborhood favored ratification; but when the convention met, their delegates found themselves confronted by a large majority. For some time it seemed almost impossible to make any headway against the opposition. In Alexander Hamilton and John Jay, the Constitution found its ablest defenders. With Madison, they had already written a series of expository papers that were gathered into one volume under the name of " The Federalist." [1] These still form the best commentary on the principles of government that underlie the American commonwealth. Hamilton's speeches in the New York rati fying convention do not ring so true as his papers in this series. His hearers knew that he looked upon the new instrument as a worthless fabric and was befriending it only because it was the one thing that stood between them and anarchy. Probably his arguments and those of Jay and Robert R. Livingston and of others who sided with them produced little effect upon the members of the majority, who were ably led by Melancthon Smith and John Lansing, Jr. The ratifications of New Hampshire and Virginia placed New York in a difficult position, for if she stayed out, she would have New England on the one side and the Delaware States on the other, and even with her remarkable position, she might and probably would lose a large part of her commerce. Massachusetts and some

[1] On the authorship of the different papers, see Edward G. Bourne in *American Historical Review*, ii, 443; Paul Leicester Ford in *ibid.*, ii, 675; and Lodge in the Introduction to his edition of *The Federalist* which forms a supplementary volume to his *Writings of Alexander Hamilton*.

other States had proposed amendments while ratifying the instrument as it stood. Would it not be well for New York to do the same, or why should not her ratification be conditional upon the adoption of amendments by the new government when it was organized? Hamilton consulted Madison as to the possibility of this being done and received from him a distinct statement of opinion that the Constitution must be ratified or rejected as it stood, and that a State which had once ratified could not constitutionally secede.[1] Suddenly, without any apparent reason, Smith and Lansing abandoned their attitude of unreconcilable opposition. They announced their willingness to ratify the Constitution with suggested amendments. Enough of their followers swung into line to carry the day. There were now eleven of the thirteen States within the Union, North Carolina and Rhode Island alone remaining aloof.

It has been said that if one should draw a line parallel to the seacoast and fifty miles inland from it, that one side would "pretty accurately"[2] represent the Federalist area whence came the friends of the Constitution and the other the more democratic portions of the community

[1] These letters are printed in John C. Hamilton's *Works of Alexander Hamilton* (i, 465). As the dates given to the letters do not correspond with the almanac, Mr. Gaillard Hunt most kindly searched the Hamilton Papers and the Madison Papers at Washington for them. Madison's letter is not there, and Hamilton's is without month or year. It is indorsed in Madison's writing; "A. Hamilton, 1788, special reservation of right to secede." Moreover, the reports of the debates of the New York ratifying convention do not bear out J. C. Hamilton's assertion that Madison's letter was read in the Convention and that a short time thereafter the Constitution was unconditionally ratified. There is so much doubt as to the genuineness of the text of

the letter as printed by J. C. Hamilton that it would be well to find some other basis for argument.

[2] These qualifying words are used by Professor E. P. Smith in his "Movement Towards a Second Constitutional Convention in 1788" in Jameson's *Essays in the Constitutional History of the United States*, 67. Professor Orin G. Libby, commenting upon this, declares that if this had been correct, the Constitution "would have been rejected in New Hampshire, Massachusetts, Virginia, and Georgia" ("Geographical Distribution of Vote on the Constitution" in the *Bulletin of the University of Wisconsin*, Economics and History Series, vol. i, No. 1, pp. 3, 49).

where its opponents dwelt. The favorers of the plan were the commercial classes, those who lived on settled incomes and the men of education ; these for the most part resided to the eastward of this line. Westward were the frontier settlements, the regions devoted mainly to agriculture and the homes of the more recent immigrants from Europe. There were exceptions to this rule as, for instance, the settlers in the Valley of Virginia and in western Maryland and Pennsylvania. The people of these sections favored the Constitution, and without their aid it would not have been ratified in 1788. The settlers in what is now West Virginia also generally favored the ratification of the Constitution, but those in the district that later became the State of Kentucky were opposed to it, not because they feared its aristocratic tendencies, but because they were convinced that the government which would be established under it would surrender to Spain the free navigation of the Mississippi in exchange for commercial privileges.

The ratification of the Constitution by nine States brought the question of the new government once more before the expiring Congress of the Confederation, as arrangements must be made for the election of the President and the members of the new Congress and place and time fixed for the inauguration. The debates lasted for several days and were quite animated ; but did not turn at all upon whether the old Congress should authorize the establishment of the new government in direct opposition to the provisions of the Articles of Confederation or should be faithful to their obligations to North Carolina and Rhode Island. The only question that interested them was whether New York, Philadelphia, or some more southern town should be the temporary capital of the new United

States. Finally, the argument of the expensiveness of a removal from New York prevailed, and it was decided to hold the elections on the first Wednesday in January, 1789, "and that the first Wednesday in March next be the time, and the present seat of Congress the place, for commencing proceedings under the said constitution."

NOTES

I. Bibliography. — Jonathan Elliot's *Debates, Resolutions, and other Proceedings in Convention, on the Adoption of the Federal Constitution as recommended by the General Convention at Philadelphia* (3 vols., Washington, 1827–1830), is the standard authority. A supplementary volume entitled *Journal and Debates of the Federal Convention, with the Constitution*, etc., was published in 1830 as volume iv. A "second edition" with considerable additions was printed at Washington in 1836. This second edition includes a fifth volume, published in 1845, with the following title: *Debates on the Adoption of the Federal Constitution . . . as reported by James Madison*. The whole set was reprinted at Philadelphia in 1861.[1] In 1894, the Department of State at Washington began the printing of the *Documentary History of the Constitution of the United States* (5 vols., Washington, 1894–1905) under the editorship of Andrew H. Allen, who was then in charge of the Bureau of Rolls and Library. At first progress was slow, owing to lack of appropriations, and changes in the original writing could only be shown by brackets, carets, italics, and other devices. The third volume contains Madison's "Debates" printed from the original manuscript with all the changes that had been made in the manuscript itself shown in type. Professor Max Farrand has printed in a consecutive text[2] Madison's notes as he originally wrote them, giving side by side the other versions of the doings of the Federal Convention, and has illustrated this matter by a volume of letters, most of which are also to be found in the later volumes of the *Documentary History*.

Madison's "Debates" are in the *Writings of James Madison*, edited by Gaillard Hunt (vols. iii and iv), and his speeches in the

[1] The bibliography of Elliot's *Debates* is given in P. L. Ford's *Pamphlets on the Constitution*, 392. In speaking of the second edition, Ford says that it, "in spite of its imperfections, is the great store house of American constitutional history." The title of the second edition is *The Debates in the several State Conventions, on the Adoption of the Federal Constitution, as recommended by the General Convention at Philadelphia, in 1787. Together with the Journal of the Federal Convention.*

[2] *The Records of the Federal Convention of 1787*, edited by Max Farrand (3 vols., New Haven, 1911). Professor Farrand has also written several articles on the formation of the Constitution. See especially "The Federal Constitution and the Defects of the Confederation" in *American Political Science Review*, ii, 532; "Compromises of the Constitution" in *American Historical Review*, ix; "George Washington in the Federal Convention" in *Yale Review*, November, 1907; and an article on the work of the Convention in *ibid.*, July, 1912.

Virginia Convention are in volume v. The "Debates" are also found in the Congress edition of Madison's works. A book with a distinct anti-Madison tone is Charles C. Nott's *The Mystery of the Pinckney Draught* (New York, 1908).

The collected writings of Washington, Jefferson, Madison, Hamilton, and other leading men are replete with matter illustrating the motives of the men who made the Constitution and the means by which they accomplished their object. The journals of the Congress of the Confederation as at present in print are peculiarly irritating; the student must go to the Congressional library at Washington.

II. **The Supreme Court.** — The origin of the Supreme Court has been traced back to the Federal Court of Appeals under the Articles of Confederation by Professor J. F. Jameson and by J. C. Bancroft Davis, for a long time reporter of the decisions of the Supreme Court. This theory leaves out of account the great difference in the authority and the functions of the two tribunals and proceeds upon the assumption that the new government, like its predecessor, was truly federal. The case that best illustrates the virtues and failings of the older court is that which arose over the sloop *Active* or the case of Olmsted *vs.* Houston, which is also interesting because of its dramatic qualities (*Pennsylvania Magazine of History*, xvi, 386). See Jameson's "The Predecessor of the Supreme Court" in his *Essays in the Constitutional History of the United States,* and his "Old Federal Court of Appeal" in American Historical Association's *Papers,* iii, 383; and Davis's "Appendix to the Reports of the Decisions of the Supreme Court of the United States" in *United States Reports,* vol. 131. The early cases that were decided are given in A. J. Dallas's *Cases in Several Courts of the United States.* See also H. L. Carson's *Supreme Court of the United States: its History* (Part I deals with the pre-convention history; Part II carries the story through the adoption of the Judiciary Act of 1789); Roger Foster's *Commentaries on the Constitution of the United States, Historical and Juridical,* vol. i, chs. i, ii (the treatment of this part is historical). St. George Tucker's edition of Blackstone's *Commentaries* (Philadelphia, 1803) is significant on account of the scholarship and the strict-constructionist views of the editor.[1] The same may be said

---

[1] These are given especially in the Appendix to the two parts of volume i. Of these Note D, "View of the Constitution of the United States" (Pt. i, pp. 140-377); Note E, "Of the Unwritten, or Common Law of England, and its Introduction into, and Authority within the United American States" (Pt. i, pp. 378-439); and Note H, "On the State of Slavery in Virginia" (Pt. ii, pp. 31-85).

of John Randolph Tucker's *Constitution of the United States* (Chicago, 1899). This is a critical discussion of the genesis, development, and interpretation of that instrument. It is edited by Henry St. George Tucker, the author's son, and like the father a professor in Washington and Lee University. The two works, therefore, state the opinions of three generations of Virginia jurists.

III. The Torrey Case. — Another instance of the working of the imperial judicial system arose over the claims of two clergymen to lands in Rhode Island which were fought out in the first half of the eighteenth century. The disputed lands were situated on Narragansett Bay to the northward of Point Judith and had been set apart by the early proprietors for the encouragement of clergymen "in their sentiments orthodox" who should be employed to preach God's word to the settlers. Two Congregational parsons successively enjoyed the use of these lands; the second of these was John Torrey. Into this community came an Episcopalian missionary, William McSparran. He was an energetic man who intended to have all his rights and was willing, nay anxious, to fight for them. He looked upon himself and not his Congregational neighbor as the orthodox person who was preaching to the settlers of the Narragansett country and therefore entitled to the use of the lands that had been appropriated by the Rev. Mr. Torrey. He instituted suits in the courts of the colony and was successful. Mr. Torrey appealed to the King in Council. On the report of the Lords of the Committee of Appeals an Order in Council was issued reversing the decisions of the Rhode Island courts and directing the appellant to be put in possession of the disputed lands. McSparran now discovered new evidence and began a new set of suits. These being decided against him in the colony, he appealed to England. By this time the contest had assumed a religious phase. New England Congregationalists rallied to the aid of their champion, and contributions poured in from all the churches to enable him to fight the case in England. Again Mr. Torrey was successful, the King in Council confirming the judgment of the Rhode Island Court.

The final Order in Council was issued in 1734. A copy is in the " Book of Land Evidences," No. 2, p. 674, at South Kingston, R.I. Other papers are preserved in the " Prince Collection " belonging to the Old South Church of Boston. See also Potter's *Early History of Narragansett* and Updike's *Narragansett Church.*

CHAPTER XVII

In 1760 at the opening of the momentous epoch covered in this volume, the population of the English colonies on the continent of North America was about one and one-half million souls. In thirty years of civil strife, war and readjustment, this number had increased to nearly four millions. Of this two million and a half increase in the total population, all but 110,000 was in the older settled region to the eastward of the Appalachian water parting. One hundred and ten thousand or one hundred and twenty-five thousand at the very utmost would represent all the people living in the western country in 1790, north of the Ohio as well as south of that river. Looking at the map facing this page, one is impressed with the filling up of the vacant spaces east of the mountains and with the extent of the area of settlement west of the Alleghanies in the fifteen years following Lexington and Concord; but, owing to the sparseness of population in this new country, the absolute number was small. It was indeed in future possibilities, rather than in present power, that this extension of civilization was remarkable. The time had come to formulate a policy of colonization fitted for a republican state, — an ideal system was shadowed forth in the ordinance that was adopted by the Congress of the Confederation in 1787, at the very time that the Federal Convention was busy with its task at Philadelphia in providing a government for the people of the old settled portions of the country.

The war had borne heavily upon the commercial towns of the seacoast. British armies had occupied the four largest of them at one time or another, and the commercial depression following on the treaty of peace had retarded their recovery. The largest city of that time was Philadelphia, but nowadays it would be regarded as out of the municipal category altogether and only deserving the name of town. In 1760, it had less than twenty thousand inhabitants in comparison with fifteen thousand each in Boston and New York, or fifty thousand in round numbers for the three. In 1790, the total of the three had risen to ninety-three thousand, Philadelphia then boasting of 42,444 inhabitants, a number that may be compared with the 44,885 of the city of Youngstown, Ohio, in the year 1900. The other cities in the United States in 1790 were Charleston, Baltimore, Salem, and Newport, which had a combined population of 44,499. The statisticians searching for a criterion of urban population, as opposed to rural, have been forced to count Salem and everything larger as in the first class, but even then the urban stands to the rural as only a little over three one hundredths of the whole.[1] On the other hand, the growth of New York and Philadelphia during this thirty-year period shadowed forth the position which they were to occupy in future years. Boston had remained practically stationary, but New York had doubled and Philadelphia had nearly trebled in size.

Turning now to the distribution of the people in the four sections into which the country may conveniently be

[1] See *A Century of Population Growth* published by the Bureau of the Census, S. N. D. North, Director (Washington, 1909). The figures in the text are given in round numbers which are quite sufficient in view of the speculative character of all estimates of population before the taking of the Third Census in 1810.

2 M

divided, we find that New England and the Middle States each contained about one million inhabitants. Of the other two million the four Southern States had eighteen hundred thousand and the western settlements put together a little over one hundred thousand. In 1790, one is able to differentiate the free and slave population with a somewhat greater degree of confidence than was possible in making a similar computation for the year 1760,[1] and reaches the conclusion that the white population of the Southern States was then about eleven hundred thousand in comparison with nearly two millions in the States north of Mason and Dixon line.

Since 1775, the occupation of the western country had gone steadily on, although few settlers as yet had directed their movements to the land north of the Ohio River. There were many obstacles to the rapid settlement of the back lands beyond the mountains. It was hard to get there from the Atlantic seaboard through the passes of the Alleghanies and then by wilderness roads or by boat to the new centers of colonization. When once the forest had yielded to the axe and a surplus of produce had been raised, it was difficult to get it to market. The journey through the mountains to the commercial towns of the East was long, costly, and hazardous. New Orleans, near the mouth of the Mississippi, was more easily reached, but the return trip from that point was tiresome by water and dangerous by land. In 1784, Washington traveled through the mountains to the Ohio Valley and returning wrote several interesting and important letters on the subject of the western lands. He declared that such was the rage for speculating in and forestalling lands that scarce a valuable spot within easy reach of the Ohio was left without a claimant. Men talked of fifty thousand acres

---

[1] For the figures for 1760, see the present work, vol. ii, 491.

or even five hundred thousand with as much facility as a gentleman formerly did of one thousand.[1] The squatters were not confining themselves to the southern side of the river, but in defiance of Congress had passed over and were arousing the suspicion and jealousy of the natives.

The Indians in the northwestern country disliked the coming of the Americans and were urged on by the British traders and by the British officials who still lived in the posts on the southern side of the boundary line as arranged in the Treaty of 1783. The retention of these posts also secured to the British the monopoly of the Indian trade and the traffic in furs, depriving the American pioneers of the most certain source of profit in the occupation of a new country, and also of the easiest means of securing a hold on the aborigines. The Virginia cession of her claims to lands northwest of the Ohio was completed in March, 1784. Following on this, the government of the Confederation made treaties with the Iroquois and with the Indians living in the southern part of what is now the State of Ohio. By these the country westward from Cuyahoga River was divided between the white men and the red, the Indians reserving the northern third and abandoning the southern two-thirds to the United States. The most important of these treaties was made at Fort McIntosh in 1786. Among the negotiators of this instrument were Doctor Arthur Lee and General Samuel H. Parsons. In 1787, Fort Harmar was built at the spot where the Muskingum flows into the Ohio, and troops marched over the country destroying the squatters' cabins. It had become very necessary to pass some effective legislation for the se-

---

[1] To Jacob Read, November 3, 1784. In the "Schedule of Property" comprehended in Washington's will are the following lots west of the mountains: Ohio River, 9744 acres; Great Kanawha, 23,341; Little Miami, 3051; Kentucky, 5000, or 41,136 acres in all exclusive of his lands in the settled parts of Virginia (Worthington C. Ford's *Wills of George Washington*, 121).

curity of land titles and for the political organization of this new region on republican lines.

Hitherto the mode of colonizing wild lands which had prevailed in the North and in the South had been widely different. According to English law and imperial practice, the title to American soil was in the king and in those to whom he had granted it, subject in each case to the conditions of the letters patent. English conceptions of landholding were still distinctly feudal, and American land grants had been based directly upon those ideals. As the king could not alienate the property of the crown, these patents were made on terms of a rental tenure. The proprietor not possessing them in fee simple could not sell them outright. There had grown up, therefore, the system of quitrent tenure by which the possessor of the soil paid rent annually and forever to king or proprietor. Outside of New England, the early proprietarial rights had been resumed by the crown, except in the case of Pennsylvania, Delaware, and Maryland. In some of the royal provinces, great estates were held in single hands and were leased to tenants. In Pennsylvania, the Penn family held large estates on a manorial tenure from themselves. In New York, the Livingstons, the Van Rensselaers, and others possessed enormous tracts either by grant from the Old Dutch governors or from their early English successors. In Virginia, there were the Fairfax estates that came down from the time of Charles II and in North Carolina, the great Granville property. Quitrents were not high, two shillings for each hundred acres being the ordinary amount. The objection to the system was that the rental had to be paid on unimproved land as well as on productive farms. To the proprietor of a rich plantation, it was a matter of small moment; but to the settler on the frontier, where hard money was scarce and the collector's office far away, the system was oppressive and had led to more than one insurrection. Quitrents paid to a royal official bore all the marks of taxes. Had they been levied according to the productive value of the land, and had the peculiar circumstances of different groups of settlers been intelligently considered, it is conceivable that this system might have developed into something closely resembling a single tax levied upon land, increasing in amount as land increased in value. As the system was administered, it was detested by the dwellers in the provinces where it prevailed, and at the Revolution not one proposition was made for its continuance.

In Virginia and to the southward, every newcomer had the right to take up land, so many acres per head. This system of head rights which began in Virginia led to the method of the indiscriminate location of new land. Any one possessing a right to take up fifty acres or more could go out to the back regions, pick out his lot, seek the proper office, get an order for its survey, and then upon performing certain conditions as to seating, get a title from the crown. With the French and Indian War, there came grants of lands to soldiers, and this system found imitation in the Revolution. There thus came into existence hundreds of thousands of military warrants, each one authorizing its holder to go out to the frontier and locate the lands that best suited his eye. Washington himself bought warrants of old soldiers and located enormous tracts of land. This system of "indiscriminate location," of picking out one's lands first and then having them surveyed, possessed the merit of elasticity. Its defect was in its indistinctness. No sooner had the original locator marked on tree and stake the limits of his tract and departed for the nearest land office to get a warrant of survey, than some other pioneer might come along and jump his claim. It also led to the establishment of isolated settlements and the preëmption of all the best spots for speculative purposes.

In New England, the land had originally been granted on a socage tenure. The Massachusetts Bay Company, with its general disregard of legal obligations to the home government, had granted its lands practically in fee simple or absolute ownership. This had made trouble for the grantees in the time of Andros, but in the Province Charter of 1691, the king had confirmed the existing grants. Moreover, he had authorized the provincial legislature to make new ones without submitting them to the home authorities for confirmation. In laying out the lands for occupancy, the Massachusetts authorities had proceeded on the principle of intensive settlement, — one township or group of townships being granted at a time.[1] A township was a large body of land which was surveyed and granted with definite boundaries. At first, these were given to actual settlers, but in later time, they were bestowed upon groups of promoters who were termed proprietors. They guaranteed prompt settlement by desirable colonists. Sometimes, one or more of the proprietors would himself take up his residence in the newly settled township. They sold their lands outright, reserving certain lots for themselves and for purposes of religion and education. The advantages of the New England system was that colonization proceeded in an

---

[1] Melville Egleston's *Land Systems of New England* (privately printed in 1880 and afterwards reprinted in the *Johns Hopkins Studies*, Fourth Series, xi, xii). On conditions of settlement and landholding in general in the colonies, see Amelia C. Ford's "Colonial Precedents of our National Land System" in *Bulletin* of the University of Wisconsin, No. 352.

orderly manner, each newly settled community being
within easy support of a stronger neighbor. It lacked
the elasticity of the southern plan, and where settlers
were many, surveyors few, and the coveted land remote
from the seat of government it was likely to be put aside
for the more convenient method. In the earlier time,
lands had been given to eligible colonizers without price,
a settled town being of more value than any amount of
money that could reasonably be exacted. But now, lands
were coming to have more value in the public mind and
were being put up for sale to intending settlers.

According to the revolutionary theory, the people of
each State themselves constituted the society upon which
the political organization was based. With independence,
therefore, the rights of the crown passed to the people, the
landholders ceasing to pay quitrents to the crown officials
and paying them to no one else. As to the waste lands,
those within the state limits were disposed of by the
States, and those outside of the state boundaries became
the subject of debate in Congress and in the press. Pelatiah Webster addressed himself to the solution of the
problem of the best use to be made of the back lands and
offered many helpful suggestions on this topic, as he did
on others that have been mentioned in preceding pages.
In 1781, he published at Philadelphia " An Essay on the
Extent and Value of our Western Unlocated Lands and
the Proper Method of disposing of them." [1]   History told
him that in all revolutions of government, all crown lands,
jewels, and everything else which had belonged to the
supreme power which lost ever passed to the supreme
power which gained. What were once crown lands,
therefore, belonged to the thirteen States. Some people

[1] *Political Essays* (Philadelphia, 1791), pp. 485–501.

had thought that the uncultivated lands should be sold or
mortgaged to foreign States for money. Webster ab-
horred " the very idea of *strangers* having their *paw on
any of our lands*." Besides, there was money enough in
the country as it was. On the contrary, he advised that
townships of six, eight, or ten miles square should be
surveyed contiguous to the settled country and the lands
sold at auction to the highest bidder for not less than one
Spanish dollar per acre, and that the purchaser should be
obliged to improve his purchase within two or three years
or forfeit the land. When the first tier of townships had
been sold, another tier might be surveyed and opened to
settlement. He thought that the western territory in
this way could be made to produce two hundred million
hard dollars. This method would obviate speculation and
would give every inhabitant of the original States an equal
chance of procuring lands for himself and his family.

David Howell of Rhode Island and one of her delegates
in Congress wrote many interesting letters upon various
subjects. In February, 1784, it seemed to him that " the
western world," meaning by that the back lands, opened
an amazing prospect as a national fund. " As a source of
future population and strength, it is a guaranty of our independence. As its inhabitants will be mostly cultivators
of the soil, republicanism looks to them as its guardians." [1]
Jefferson already had also turned the whole matter over
in his mind. The proposition to sell the waste lands
seemed to him to be most unwise, — the western settlers
would be liable for their proportion of the Continental
debt and ought not to be expected to pay more. Charging them for their lands " will disgust them, and cause an
avulsion of them from the common union. They will

[1] *Rhode Island in the Continental Congress*, 479.

settle the lands in spite of everybody." A settler would be worth annually to the public twenty times what he could have been charged for his farm.

In 1784, Jefferson was in Congress as a delegate from Virginia. By this time his own experience and the urgent needs of the government had convinced him that it was necessary to get as much money as possible from the western lands. As chairman of a committee, he reported a plan for their disposal and government. Ten States should be ultimately formed on the national domain northwest of the Ohio. These were to be bounded by parallels of latitude and meridians of longitude. Jefferson proposed that these should be named Sylvania, Michigania, Cherronesus, Assenisipia, Metropotamia, Illinoia, Saratoga, Washington, Polypotamia, Pelisipia. These names appeared in the report of the committee, but they were soon dropped, although they persisted for some time on the maps. Whenever a bit of this territory was offered for sale by Congress, the settlers were to establish a temporary government and adopt the constitution and laws of any one of the original States, subject to alteration by the territorial legislature. Whenever there were twenty thousand free inhabitants in any one of the proposed States, they might hold a convention, establish a permanent constitution, and send a delegate to Congress who might join in debate, but was not to vote. Whenever any of these States had as many free inhabitants as the least numerous of the original thirteen, it shall be admitted "by its delegates into the Congress . . . on an equal footing with the said original states." Certain conditions were enumerated in the ordinance as forming "a charter of compact" which shall stand as fundamental constitutions between the thirteen original States and each of the new ones not

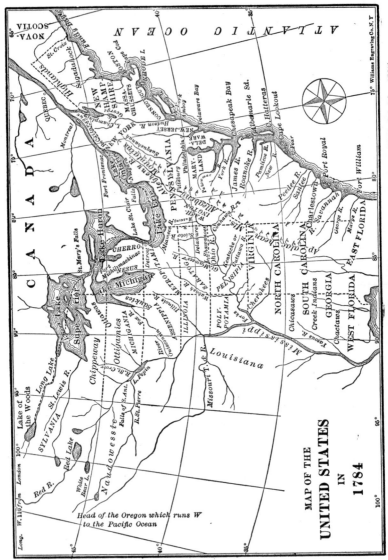

MAP OF THE
UNITED STATES
IN
1784

After a Map engraved by H. D. Pursell for F. Bailey's *Pocket Almanac* (Philadelphia, 1785)

to be altered except by join consent of Congress and the particular State involved. In Jefferson's report these conditions were five in number: (1) that the new State shall remain part of the United States; (2) shall be subject to the central government "in all those cases in which the original states shall be so subject"; (3) shall be liable for their portion of the federal debt; and (4) their government shall be republican in form. The fifth condition and the most memorable was that excluding slavery from the new States after the year 1800. This last provision shared the fate of the names and does not appear in the Ordinance as it was adopted on April 23, 1784. On the other hand two new conditions were inserted to restrain the proposed governments from taxing the national lands within their borders or interfering with the disposal of them by Congress.[1]

Jefferson was also a member of a committee that was charged with proposing means by which the western lands might be disposed of.[2] This particular matter was not finally acted upon by Congress until after his departure from Annapolis on his way to France as representative of the United States. His original plan was to divide the back lands into "hundreds of ten geographical miles square" to be marked by lines running due north

[1] The report is printed in P. L. Ford's *Writings of Jefferson*, iii, 429. Facing p. 428 is a facsimile of a printed copy of the report with the changes made in Congress noted upon it. The earlier report is given in facsimile of the original manuscript on pp. 408, 410, and 412 of the same volume. In a note to p. 430, Ford asserts that this document " ranks in historical importance of all those drawn by Jefferson " next to the Declaration of Independence and but for its supercession by the Ordinance of 1787, it would rank among all papers immediately after the Constitution.

Certainly it may at least be regarded as the first draft of the great Ordinance. Ford attributes the little reputation which this paper has gained to the jealousy of New England historians and to the fact that at a later time it was desirable to divert public attention in the South away from Jefferson's earlier pronunciamenta against negro slavery. The Ordinance, as adopted, is printed in *Journals of Congress* under the date, April 23, 1784, and also in broadside.

[2] Ford's *Writings of Jefferson*, iii, 475.

and south and by others crossing them at right angles. Each hundred should be divided into lots of one mile square which could be paid for in loan office certificates reduced to their specie value. The term "hundred" soon disappeared and a new committee reported a plan for the survey of certain ranges of townships which should be parceled out for the use of the soldiers or sold at public auction in the several States. Each township was to be divided into thirty-six lots of one mile square or six hundred and forty acres. Four of these lots were to be reserved for future sale by the United States, as was one-third part of all gold, silver, lead, and copper. In each township, lot number sixteen was to be devoted to the maintenance of public schools.[1] As Jefferson's Ordinance of 1784 was the basis on which the American plan of colonization was founded, so this Ordinance of 1785 is the forerunner of the land system of the next century. The fever of speculation and the anxiety of would-be emigrants to begin the work of clearing their farms put it out of the memory of Congress and of colonizers for the next few years.

The desire for large tracts of land in the western country upon which colonies might be established had enticed many men of influence and means into speculative ventures. Some of the promoters of these schemes had survived the war, and were in good standing as successful patriots. They came forward with propositions for the confirmation of their royal patents, but Congress did not take kindly to this idea. While the Continental Line was still encamped at Newburg on the Hudson, many of the

---

[1] The genesis and history of this ordinance is traced by Payson J. Treat in *The National Land System, 1785–1820* (New York, 1910). The Ordinance of 1785 was printed in broadside at Philadelphia at the time. It is also in *Journals of Congress* under date of May 20, 1785, and in the Appendix to Treat's book.

more prominent officers had planned to establish a military colony on the farther side of the Ohio.[1] They had presented their scheme to Washington who forwarded it to Congress with his heartiest commendations. The time was inopportune, the Virginia cession had not yet been made nor had the Treaty of Peace been concluded at Paris. This project was therefore laid aside. Late in 1785, James Monroe made a journey westward. He was impressed with the "miserably poor" character of the country, especially of the lands near Lake Michigan and Lake Erie and in the Illinois valley. Writing to Jefferson, he hazarded the conjecture that this whole region might never contain enough inhabitants to entitle them to admission to the confederacy as a State. As the number required was that of the inhabitants of the smallest of the original thirteen States, Monroe's appraisement of the capacity of the Old Northwest was not very high, to say the least. It is by no means impossible that these disparagements may have inclined the members of Congress to take a more lenient view of propositions that were brought before them by the Ohio Company of New England.

Rufus Putnam had been one of the promoters of the proposed military colony that has just been noticed. With Samuel Holden Parsons, Manasseh Cutler,[2] and Winthrop Sargent, Putnam set on foot the Ohio Company of Associates[3]

---

[1] *Life, Journals, . . . of Manasseh Cutler*, i, 152, and fol.

[2] See W. P. and J. P. Cutler's *Life, Journals, and Correspondence of Rev. Manasseh Cutler* (Cincinnati, 1888), i, 178–197, 230, 236, 292–305, 319–322. Something on this subject will also be found in ch. xxvi of C. S. Hall's *Life and Letters of Samuel H. Parsons*, and in W. H. Smith's *Life and Public Services of Arthur St. Clair. . . . With his Correspondence and other Papers* (2 vols.

Cincinnati, 1882). Of the compendious accounts Sidney Crawford's "Rufus Putnam" in American Antiquarian Society's *Proceedings* for October, 1898 and E. C. Dawes' *The Beginning of the Ohio Company* are useful.

[3] The Articles of Agreement, the Contract, and other papers were printed in a forty-five page pamphlet at New York in 1787, entitled *Articles of an Association by the name of the Ohio Company*.

and sold stock to subscribers. The surveyors of the lands directly west of Pennsylvania had noticed a particularly choice tract at the confluence of the Ohio and Muskingum rivers. Parsons went to New York to secure a grant of these lands from Congress, and, failing, the Company sent Cutler to try his hand on the job. He was a native of Connecticut, had served as chaplain in the Revolution, was now the settled minister at Ipswich Village in Massachusetts and was a man of high scientific attainments. He took not unkindly to the devious methods that were necessary in those days to put a contract through Congress, and the perusal of his journal inspires one with the thought that lobbying is by no means a modern art. Colonel Duer, Secretary of the Treasury Board, and other New Yorkers were intent on getting some million acres on the Scioto River, but they had no thought of paying for them. Cutler took them into his combination; but, at the last moment, he made two contracts putting the Ohio Company into one and the Scioto people into the other. On one occasion, Duer assured Cutler that he had "got the length" of Dr. Arthur Lee's foot; and had inspired that personage — who was on the Treasury Board — with the thought that the shrewd promoter was "an open, frank, honest New England man, which he considers as an uncommon animal." In the middle of the negotiations, Cutler became convinced that pushing Parsons for appointment as Governor of the new Northwest Territory was interfering with the success of the scheme. He therefore withdrew Parsons for that office and suggested the appointment of Arthur St. Clair, the President of Congress. When this became known, Cutler writes that matters went more smoothly. One thing is reasonably certain that the Company's agent used his remarkable powers to secure lands at a low rate for the Associates and not to inject any advanced ideas as to social development into the Ordinance of 1787. The Ohio Company obtained a right to take up about one and one-half million acres. For this they were to pay half a million dollars down with the contract, but not to receive a deed until another half million was paid. They were, however, to have the right of entry and occupancy and there were various conditions as to using military warrants for some of the payments. These figures sound very formidable and Cutler was amply justified in congratulating himself upon having signed the largest contract that had ever been made in America; but the dollars were those of Continental obligations then worth about eight cents in specie, while the acres were full sized as surveyed. Section sixteen in each township was reserved for educational purposes and another for religious uses. Three sections were retained by Congress for future disposition and two whole townships were set apart for a university.

While Manasseh Cutler was pushing to completion the contract for the sale of western lands to the Ohio Company and the members of the Federal Convention were formulat· ing the Constitution at Philadelphia, the Congress of the Confederation was revamping and strengthening the Ordinance of 1784 with a view to providing "a strong-toned government" for the security of property in the Northwest Territory "among uninformed and perhaps licentious people, as the greater part of those who go there are." [1] These are the words of Richard Henry Lee, who probably reflected the desire of Cutler and his associates for a more detailed organic law than the old ordinance and

---

[1] R. H. Lee to Washington, July 15, 1787, quoted by W. P. Cutler in an article in the *Magazine of American History* xxii, 484.

especially for some direct guarantee of property rights in the new territory.

The Ordinance of 1787 was adopted by Congress on July 13.[1] It provided a temporary government for the whole territory by officials to be appointed by Congress. These were a governor, secretary, and three judges. These possessed the usual powers of such officials. In addition, the governor and judges were to adopt such laws of the original States as may be necessary and best suited to the circumstances of the district. They were to report their action in this regard to Congress which might disapprove of any or all of these laws at its discretion. So soon as the district should contain five thousand free male inhabitants, a representative assembly was to be chosen by the freeholders. Their first duty after coming together was to nominate ten persons from whom Congress should appoint five to form a legislative council. The general assembly or legislature consisting of the governor, the legislative council, and the house of representatives had authority to make laws for the good government of the district, not repugnant to the provisions of the Ordinance; but the governor possessed an absolute veto on all legislative acts. The territory might be formed into districts and ultimately be divided into not less than three nor more than five States. Whenever any one of these divisions should contain sixty thousand free inhabitants, it "shall be admitted, by its delegates, into the Congress of the United States, on an equal footing with the original States, in all respects whatever; and shall be at liberty to form a permanent constitution and State government." The limitation on the power of the new States as compared with the original States was contained in the condition

[1] For bibliography see note at end of the chapter.

that the constitution and government so formed shall be republican and in conformity to the principles contained in these articles.

The principles just referred to are set forth in the second and fourteenth sections of the Ordinance. The provisions embodied in the latter section "shall be considered as articles of compact, between the original States and the people and States in the said territory, and forever remain unalterable, unless by common consent." The former of these two sections provided that the estates of proprietors within the territory who should die intestate, or without leaving a will, were to descend in equal parts to their children or other legal representative, saving to the widow a third part of all real and personal estate. This provision of the Ordinance marked out practically a new principle although it applied only to the property left by persons dying intestate. In England from time immemorial, the rule of primogeniture had prevailed, the eldest son taking the property and caring for his younger brothers and his sisters. In 1670 this rule has been relaxed by the passage of an act of Parliament authorizing the equal distribution of personal property among all the children. The New Englanders had broken away from this rule and had provided by law for the division of estates in equal parts with the exception that the eldest son had a double share. Elsewhere primogeniture prevailed as to the realty, but the colonists had generally adopted the law of 1670 as to personal estate. They had tried to extend it to include the real estate as well, but in this respect, as in many others, had been defeated by the royal veto. With the Revolution, they were able to realize their wishes in this matter as in others.

Social conditions in Virginia had long depended in great

2 N

measure upon the rule of primogeniture, the principal estates descending to the eldest son.   Prosperous planters
had taken care of the younger sons by bequeathing to them
plantations which they had acquired in their own lifetime.
Jefferson with his progressivism drafted a law that went
far beyond the practice of English law or of any other
American colony or State.   In his scheme which was
adopted by the Virginia Assembly in 1785, he reverted to
ideas that are associated with the Roman Law rather than
with the Common Law.   This famous enactment decreed
that in the future, the property of an intestate shall descend
and pass in parcenary or coheirship to his children or
their descendants if there were any, and if there were none
to his father and then to his mother, brothers, and sisters
and their descendants.   It is the provision for the ascent
of property in certain cases and the ranking of the mother
next to the father that the novelty of Jefferson's plan consists.   The members of Congress in 1787 did not proceed
along this line, but adopted what had come to be the general American practice, outside of New England.

Turning now to the fourteenth section, it is interesting
to notice that its articles duplicate in principle Jefferson's
Ordinance of 1784, as to the admission of the new
colonies to an equality with the original States, providing
for the perpetuation of republican principles, obedience
to the central government, and forbidding slavery.   The
new principles in the later Ordinance are those relating to
religion, education, and property.   They declare that no
person demeaning himself peaceably, " shall ever be mo-
lested on account of his mode of worship, or religious
sentiments, in the said territories," that education shall
forever be encouraged, and that no law ought ever to be
made " that shall, in any manner whatever, interfere with

or affect private contracts, or engagements, *bona fide*, and without fraud previously formed." It is noticeable that at about the same time the makers of the Constitution included within their work a clause forbidding the States, old as well as new, to pass any law "impairing the Obligation of Contracts." The authorship of nearly every important clause in the Constitution or in the Ordinance has been the subject of controversy [1] between the descendants and admirers of the great men of those days. In this case, it seems not impossible that Manasseh Cutler with his shrewd business sense, caused the insertion of this condition into both documents, although the actual wording of the phrase in the Constitution may reflect Wilson's Scottish training. Otherwise, the clauses in the "compact" mark the social advance of the Revolutionary era which may be said to have then reached its highest point.

As to the constitutional or legal status of the Ordinance of 1787 or of Jefferson's earlier ordinance, or, indeed, of the contract made by Congress with the Ohio Company, nothing can be said. It is clear that the Congress of the Confederation had no power to make any of them. The great Ordinance stands on a footing with the Declaration of 1776. It is a statement of principles, of ideals, which are to be lived up to and which, in a great measure, have been realized. There is even more doubt as to the standing of the compact clause of the Ordinance than as to the other parts of it. Granting that Congress had power to establish governments in the western country, it surely had no authority to prohibit the dwellers in the States

[1] See William F. Poole in the *Papers* of the American Historical Association, iii, 287; and G. B. Loring in *ibid.*, iii, 300. Nathan Dane's own statements are in his *General Abridgment*, vii, 389, and in a letter to Daniel Webster, dated March 26, 1830, and printed in Massachusetts Historical Society's *Proceedings, 1867–1869*, p. 475. See also *Jefferson's Writings* (Ford ed.), iii, 407, 429, and the note on the latter page.

to be established therein from doing this, that, or the other.   If the new States were to be on a footing of equal-ity with the older States, they had a right to settle ques tions of labor, education, and religion for themselves.

The contract between Cutler and Sargent and the Treas-ury Board was signed on October 27, 1787.   At once the Ohio associates bestirred themselves to take possession of their lands.   In April of the next year, Rufus Putnam, with a body of surveyors, mechanics, and laborers reached the junction of the Ohio and the Muskingum and began the effective settlement of that part of the Northwest Terri-tory which developed into the State of Ohio.   Within a few months, some families joined them.   Then came Gov-ernor St. Clair and the three judges, who held the first Court of Quarter Sessions in September, 1788.   The town, or city, they named Marietta for the French queen, who had befriended the American radicals in their time of need and was shortly to die under the guillotine as the enemy of radicalism in France.   The new settlement ran the gait of pioneer villages with the additional handicap of an un-enduring soil.   Its early prospects were great, its first life was vigorous.   Then came hard times throughout the coun-try and a disastrous Indian war in the Northwest Terri-tory.   In July, 1793, there were only two hundred and thirty men within the limits of the Company's purchase, besides the French settlers at Gallipolis.

Cutler and Sargent conveyed the right to one-half of the land included in their second contract to Colonel Duer in consideration of the advancement by him of enough money to make the first payment for the Ohio Company. These lands were to be located near the Scioto River.[1]

---

[1] The best account of the Scioto Purchase is by E. C. Dawes in the *Magazine of American History*, xxii, 470–482.

No money was paid down on the Scioto contract. Duer
sent Joel Barlow, the New Haven poet, to Paris to engage
the services of French officers who had served in America
in securing settlers and purchasers for these lands. At
Paris Barlow fell in with an Englishman, Playfair by
name, who strongly belied his patronymic. Between them,
they forgot that they could convey only the right to occupy and cultivate and not deeds of ownership. Barlow
reported, enthusiastically, and Duer drew on him for money
to complete the contract, in part at least. The draft came
back protested; Playfair disappeared with the funds that
had been collected; and the French immigrants looked in
vain to Duer for redress. In time Congress came to the
relief of these pioneers of civilization in the Northwest,
giving them deeds to their lands without requiring further
payments.

In this bare recital of ordinances and contracts, the settlers
themselves have been lost to sight. They were of typical
pioneer stock, the most enterprising and physically robust
in the communities whence they came. They took with
them their energy, their skill, and their love of freedom,
and also the religious ideals and thirst for knowledge that
was a mark of the time. There was a certain James Brown
who traveled from North Carolina to Tennessee in the
year 1788 by way of the Ohio and Tennessee rivers.[1] He
had with him his wife and sons, and on his boat were the
ordinary household furnishings of the time. He also had
farming tools, ammunition, and bales of goods which were
probably designed for sale in his new home. More interesting than these are the books that he took with him :
four Bibles, one large and " 3 skool Bibles," Dr. Watts's

---

[1] "The Amount of Articles taken by
the Cherrokee Indiens from James Brown
on the 9th May 1788 at Necojack
Town " (Ms. inclosed in the petition of
Joseph Brown presented to Congress in
1810).

"Psalms and Hymns," the works of Josephus, and of Thomas Boston, the Scotch Presbyterian, and Bailey's "Dictionary." The *Mayflower*, herself, on her Pilgrim trip to Plymouth had not a more typical assortment of household goods and writings of learned men ; but she had not, as had James Brown's periagua, four negro slaves together valued at nine hundred and thirty-three dollars and thirty-three and one-third cents.

NOTE

Bibliography. — Jay A. Barrett has traced the "Evolution of the Ordinance of 1787" in a paper with that title which was published by the University of Nebraska in 1891. This monograph is abundantly supplied with bibliographical notes, especially those on pp. 49, 81, and at the end is an alphabetical list of "Authorities." Possibly, the clearest account of the history of the adoption of the Ordinance is that by John M. Merriam in American Antiquarian Society's *Proceedings* for April, 1888. Edward Coles's paper which he read before the Historical Society of Pennsylvania in June, 1856, and which is printed in the *Publications* of that society, is a serviceable essay, although it was written so long ago.[1] The later history of the Ordinance is given in Walter C. Haight's "Ordinance of 1787" in Michigan Political Science Association's *Publications*, vol. ii, no. 8. Max Farrand in a few pages has set forth the origin of the public territory of the United States in his *Legislation of Congress for the Government of the Organized Territories of the United States* (Newark, N. J., 1896) which relates, however, mainly to the later period.

[1] Among the briefer accounts are William F. Poole's *Ordinance of 1787;* Frederick D. Stone's "Ordinance of 1787" (*Pennsylvania Magazine of History*, xiii, 309); and Sidney Crawford's "Rufus Putnam" in American Antiquarian Society's *Proceedings* for October, 1898. B. A. Hinsdale has given a comprehensive account of this whole subject in chs. xi–xvi of his *Old Northwest*. A detailed bibliography is in Winsor's *America,* vii, Appendix I.

CHAPTER XVIII

THE adoption of the Constitution and the passage of the Ordinance of 1787 marked the highest point in the political and social revolution of the eighteenth century. From the inauguration of Washington onward for a decade, the current paused to be set in motion again by the acquisition of Louisiana and the incitements to social change that marked the Jeffersonian epoch. It will be convenient in this place to pass in review some of the sociological topics that have already been noticed in the earlier periods, for American history deals above all with the interaction of human aspirations and economic forces. The immigrants came to a new land where the social restrictions of the Old World civilization were largely lacking. They would have destroyed the rest of these had not the imperial government and powerful proprietors stood in the way. Now, when the Americans were their own masters, it might be expected that they would have swept away the remains of inequality and have diffused education throughout the land. Social institutions, however, had already become somewhat crystallized, and political organization had already taken on a certain measure of fixedness of form. Ideals had been established in politics and society that were hard to modify, although some of them were out of harmony with the economic environment. Thus it happened that while religion was freed from its bonds and education

552

was placed within the reach of a larger portion of the population, white servitude and black slavery did not cease with the Declaration of Independence. The former was clearly opposed to the doctrines formulated in that instrument and disappeared within a generation ; the latter, through economic causes, became intensified in one section of the country.

In colonial days, two labor systems had existed almost side by side : white servitude and negro slavery. The people saw nothing out of the way in contract white labor. They had objected to the importation of convicts. That necessarily stopped with the war and the acknowledgment of the independence of the United States. The immigration of poor white persons began immediately after the proclamation of peace and continued for years. Philadelphia was again the center of the movement. In the summer of 1784, thousands of immigrants arrived at that city from England, Scotland, and Germany, and five thousand, or even more, from Ireland.[1] There were more applicants for passage at Cork than the ships could carry. The practice of selling one's services for a term of years was renewed. In 1794, Washington was negotiating for the purchase of an indentured servant at Philadelphia ; and as late as 1817, an advertisement in a paper, published in that city, shows that vessels were still bringing redemptioners to the Delaware. The length of time that it took to dispose of the few laborers brought by this ship shows that the demand for indentured servants had greatly diminished, but the decline of the contract labor system and the rise of the wage earner as an important factor in industry and household life belong to a later time.

[1] *Independent Chronicle*, August 19, 26, 1784.

At the beginning of the Revolutionary era, slaves were owned in every colony. In June, 1770, Dr. Joseph Warren of Boston purchased a negro boy of Joshua Green. He paid nothing down, but gave thirty pounds current money in two notes and agreed to pay ten pounds more within three months in case he found the slave worth so much money.[1] Legally, no person could be born a slave in Massachusetts ; but this requirement of the statute book had not been much regarded.[2] In 1766, the general agitation for freedom was marked by the first suits instituted by slaves unlawfully held in bondage, and in that year the voters of Boston instructed their representatives in the General Court to propose a law prohibiting the importation and purchasing of slaves.[3] Seven years later, in 1773, a committee of slaves petitioned the Massachusetts legislature to grant them that "ample relief which, as men, they have a natural right to, and purposing, as soon as able, to transport themselves to some part of the coast of Africa."[4] The fate of this petition is not known, but in the next year a bill was passed to prevent the importation of slaves into the province. This measure was vetoed by Hutchinson, and his action met with the approval of the home government, for, in 1776, Lord Dartmouth wrote that the colonists could not be allowed "to check or discourage a traffic so beneficial to the nation." Coming so soon after Lord Mansfield's decision in the Somerset case, this declaration by a leading member of the British government appears to be highly incongruous.

Negroes were held in bondage in England itself as well as in the English-American colonies. It was estimated

<hr>

[1] Massachusetts Historical Society's *Proceedings, 1875–1876*, p. 101.

[2] See the present work, vol. ii, 384.

[3] *Boston Town Records, 1758–1769*, pp. 183, 200.

[4] Massachusetts Historical Society's *Proceedings*, First Series, ii, 571.

that in 1770 there were no less than fifteen thousand of them in the home land. Some of these were personal attendants whom returning sugar planters, or members of their family, had taken to England; but there were undoubtedly many slaves owned there by persons who had never seen the plantations. The status of a slave in England was by no means certain. Several suits had been decided, usually in favor of the master; but Chief Justice Holt in the beginning of the century had given a decision in favor of the person held in bondage.[1] William Blackstone in his "Commentaries" declared that the spirit of liberty was so deeply implanted in the constitution and rooted in the soil that a slave, the moment he lands in England, "falls under the protection of the laws, and so far becomes a freeman; though the master's right to his service may probably still continue." His mind became unsettled on this point; in 1770, in getting out the fourth edition of his book, he changed the word "probably" to "possibly" so that the passage would read "though the master's right to his service may possibly still continue."[2] In December of the next year, James Somerset, a negro, was brought before Lord Chief Justice Mansfield on a writ of habeas corpus. Somerset had come to England with his master from Virginia, had run away, been retaken, and placed on a ship for exportation to Jamaica, there to be sold when this writ

---

[1] In 1729 Philip York, then Attorney-General and afterward Lord Chancellor Hardwicke, and Charles Talbot, Solicitor General and later Lord Chancellor, gave the following opinion: "We are of opinion, that a Slave by coming from the West-Indies to Great-Britain, or Ireland, either with or without his master, doth not become free; and that his master's property or right in him is not thereby determined or varied; and that baptism doth not bestow freedom on him, nor make any alteration in his temporal condition in these kingdoms: We are also of opinion, that the master may legally compel him to return again to the plantations." Granville Sharp's *Representation of the Injustice of Tolerating Slavery*, London, 1769, p. 2.

[2] *Commentaries on the Laws of England*, Third edition (Oxford, 1768), i, 127; *ibid.*, Fourth edition (Oxford, 1770), i, 127. See also Massachusetts Historical Society's *Proceedings*, 1863–64, p. 325.

was procured with a view to determining his status, —
which carried with it that of all others of his race in England.   Mansfield had no special predilection for negroes,
nor was he particularly sensitive as to the rights of man.   He
was an upholder of the Common Law.   He was cognizant
of the fact that thousands of slaves were held in bondage
in England and tried to induce their owners to secure the
passage of an act of Parliament which would secure to
them their property and relieve him of the necessity of
rendering a decision.   As this was not done, he finally
brought himself to declare that the state of slavery was
so odious that it could be supported by nothing but
positive law.   As there was no positive law, there was no
slavery.   He ordered Somerset's discharge and thus put an
end to human bondage, in England itself.   The relation of
this decision to slavery in the thirteen colonies was never
determined because the Revolutionary War began so soon
after its delivery.   As the English government for nearly
one hundred years had been annulling colonial laws by the
dozen on the pretence that they were contrary to the laws
and customs of England, it would seem that slavery must
have fallen dead throughout the length and breadth of the
British empire, although this does not appear to have been
the opinion of Lord Dartmouth.   Curiously enough, no
notice was taken of Mansfield's decision in America, although
it might well have set Virginia and South Carolina on fire.

Unquestionably, the leaders of public opinion in America
were becoming restive on the subject of negro slavery.
The slave owners themselves accounted for the inconsistency
of their views as to human rights and holding blacks in
bondage by saying that slaves were not members of the
political society ; but some of them had grave doubts as
to the rightfulness of their own actions.   In 1773, Patrick

Henry pitied the "unhappy lot" of the blacks and ab-
horred slavery itself.[1] Franklin, in the same year, expressed his satisfaction at the "disposition to abolish
slavery" which prevailed in North America.[2] Washington,
John Adams, and Jefferson likewise condemned the institution; but the Virginians were united in foreseeing the
difficulty of doing away with it. Probably, a majority of
the freeholders in Virginia and in North Carolina were
opposed to it, but in the condition of the representation,
there was no possibility of immediate abolition. The
colonists in general were bitterly hostile to the importation
of negroes.[3] As soon as they began to legislate for themselves without fear of the royal veto, they put an end to
it. In the American Association, every colony agreed to
stop importation for the time being. Jefferson included a
stirring condemnation of the traffic in the original draft of
the Declaration of Independence. In 1776, Jefferson with
George Wythe and others were appointed to revise the laws
of Virginia. Chapter fifty-one of the plan which they reported was in the form of a bill concerning slaves.[4] This
provided that slaves imported into the State should be set
free and that slaves already in the State might be emancipated by deed or by will. Jefferson also prepared an
amendment to this bill, to be introduced into the legislature

[1] W. W. Henry's *Patrick Henry*, i,
152.

[2] Sparks's *Franklin*, iii, 42. There
is much material on the general subject
in Mary S. Locke's *Anti-Slavery in
America, 1619–1808* and in George Liver-
more's *Historical Research respecting the
Opinions of the Founders of the Republic
on Negroes as Slaves* (Boston, 1862).
These papers, like nearly everything that
has been written on the subject of slavery,
give only one side of the subject; but
they give it very well.

[3] W. E. Burghardt Du Bois has
brought together much information on

this topic in his "Suppression of the
African Slave-trade to the United States
of America" (*Harvard Historical
Studies*, No. I). Presumably he would
think that the statement in the text is
too strong.

[4] All emancipated or manumitted
slaves were to leave the state within one
year from the date of their freedom, or
they shall be "out of the protection of
the laws"; see *Report of the Committee
of Revisors* (Richmond, 1784), p. 40.
This is reprinted in *Jefferson's Writings*
(Ford ed.), ii, 201.

whenever the bill itself might be debated. This provided
for the emancipation of all slaves born after the passage of
the act who should, however, remain with their parents
through the period of adolescence. They should then be
" colonized to such place as the circumstances of the time
should render most proper " [1] and an equal number of white
laborers should be imported. The time did not come during Jefferson's life to realize his hopes ; but something was
done by legislation to improve the status of the slave
in Virginia. In 1782, the assembly by law provided that
slaves could be freed by will or deed properly attested.[2]
Three years later (1785), they enacted that all slaves brought
into Virginia should be free after one year,[3] and in that,
year and the next, the laws as to the trial of slaves and
their giving witness were somewhat modified,[4] although
even then they were denied trial by jury and were still
limited in the matter of giving witness. In 1788 the laws
protecting masters whose servants died under correction
were repealed.[5]

In 1777, the Massachusetts House of Representatives
had on its table a bill for preventing the practice of holding persons in slavery within the limits of the State. In
June of that year a committee was appointed, probably
by the opponents of the measure, to write to Congress and
ascertain whether the emancipation of the Africans in
Massachusetts would be consistent with the union and
harmony of the United States. It does not appear that

[1] Jefferson's *Notes on the State of
Virginia* (ed. 1784), p. 251.
[2] Before 1782, slaves could be freed
for meritorious service, to be ascertained
by the governor and council, or for any
cause by act of the Assembly ; Hening's
Statutes of Virginia, vi, 112; ix, 320 ;
x, 115, 211, 372. The act of 1782 is in
ibid., xi, 39. Negroes who had served

in the Revolutionary forces and some
others who had performed faithful service were freed by special acts in 1783 and
later, *ibid.*, xi, 308, 362; xii, 380, 611, 613,
etc.
[3] *Ibid.*, xii, 182.
[4] *Ibid.*, xii, 182, 345.
[5] *Ibid.*, xii, 681.

this letter [1] was ever sent; certainly no reply to it was received. The Massachusetts constitution of 1780 contained the memorable words " All men are born free and equal." As the Revolution proceeded, emancipation of ·slaves in Massachusetts became frequent, and negroes who were not freed by their masters left them of their own accord and generally were not pursued, captured, and compelled to service. One negro, Quaco or Quork, had more value in his master's eyes, for ·fleeing, he was retaken, beaten, and imprisoned. A series of suits followed, the question at issue being what rights, if any, the alleged proprietor had in the negro. Twice the decision was rendered that he had none, and this put an end to any one being held as a slave within the limits of the Commonwealth (1783). From the papers that have come down, it is difficult to say whether this action was taken on the ground that slavery could not exist under the Common Law or whether it was based solely on the phrase noted above from the Massachusetts Bill of Rights.[2] However this may be, it is certain Massachusetts was the only State to report no slaves in the first census that was taken in 1790.

In Pennsylvania the Quakers had long been opposed to human slavery. In 1776, the yearly meeting declared all slaves held by Friends must be set free and threatened exclusion from the meeting for all who did not emancipate their negroes.[3] In 1780, the legislature of that State provided by law for the gradual emancipation of the slaves

---

[1] Massachusetts Historical Society's *Proceedings*, September, 1868, p. 332.

[2] For the history of this case see Emory Washburn's "Extinction of Slavery in Massachusetts" in Massachusetts Historical Society's *Proceedings* for May, 1857. Horace Gray printed the minutes of Chief Justice Cushing who presided at the final trial in *ibid.*, 1873–1875, p. 292, with some exceedingly valuable notes. The brief of Levi Lincoln, one of the counsel in the case is in *ibid.*, *Collections*, Fifth Series, iii, 438. Among the points noted is a question as to whether slavery is " in derogation of common law." Possibly this refers to Somerset's case. There is an interesting letter, written in 1795, in the same volume, p. 391.

[3] Sharpless, *Quaker Experiments*, 38

by declaring that no child thereafter born in Pennsylvania of slave parents shall be a slave.[1] These children, how‹ ever, were to occupy the position of servants until they reached the age of twenty-eight years; at which time all claims on their services were to cease. As Pennsylvania had already prohibited the importation of slaves, this law provided that eventually negro slavery would cease in the State; but the operation of any such plan was necessarily slow.

As the colored population increased, the people throughout the country showed more and more distrust of the free negroes. This was due in part to the habit of masters, in some places, of setting their slaves free when they were too old to work and thus forcing the town or county to maintain them in their old age; but in part it was due to other causes. This distrust is shown in legislation as in the Massachusetts law prohibiting the entrance of foreign free blacks into the Commonwealth.[2] New York, on the other hand, in 1788, encouraged manumission by ceasing to require bonds of the master that his freed slave should not become a public charge.[3] As the years go by, legislation against free blacks increases, but it is not until 1800 that the matter requires extended notice.

Before the Revolutionary epoch, religion had been closely connected with the government except in those colonies where the Quakers had impressed their ideas upon legislation. Even in them, the policy of the English government had made it necessary for many officers to take oaths or subscribe tests that were contrary to the scruples of Roman Catholics and Jews. Everywhere dissent was growing

[1] *Laws of Pennsylvania*, ii, 246; see also *ibid.*, iii, 268.

[2] *Acts and Laws of Massachusetts, 1786–87*, 626. By this law any free negro coming into the state and remaining for more than two months was liable to be whipped not exceeding ten lashes.

[3] See H. P. Johnston's "New York after the Revolution" in *Magazine of American History*, xxix, 315.

and toleration increasing. Jefferson is authority for the statement that in Virginia, two-thirds of the people were dissenters in 1776.[1] The Presbyterian clergy, and the Methodist and Baptist preachers had been indefatigable. Edmund Randolph, in his manuscript history of Virginia, says that they did not depend " upon the dead letter of written sermons, they understood the mechanism of haranguing." As to the regular clergy, they were planted on glebes with decent salaries " and a species of rank which was not wholly destitute of unction. . . . The dissenters, on the other hand, were fed and clothed, only as they merited the gratitude of their congregation." Whatever the cause, the Established Church had certainly grown weaker and the dissenting sects correspondingly stronger. The great men of the Old Dominion were all in favor of freedom of conscience and of worship, — Patrick Henry, James Madison, Thomas Jefferson, and Washington. The last named was a regular attendant at divine services. William White, Bishop of Pennsylvania, was rector of Christ Church, Philadelphia, during the war, and while Washington resided there in his presidency. He writes that Washington's behavior in church was always serious and attentive, but that he owes it to truth to declare that he never saw him kneeling during the service, although the pew that he occupied was within ten yards of the reading desk.[2] There can be no doubt that the days of strictness in religious observance had gone by in Virginia. It was found necessary to permit some regiments to have dissenting chaplains and in the famous Bill of

[1] Jefferson's *Notes on the State of Virginia* (ed. 1784) p. 289.

[2] Bird Wilson's *Memoir of William White, Bishop of Pennsylvania*, 189. For the struggle of the newly formed American Episcopal Church to obtain a regularly consecrated bishop, see the above memoir; W. S. Perry's *History of the American Episcopal Church*, ii, ch. iii; and E. E. Beardsley's *Life and Correspondence of the Right Reverend Samuel Seabury*.

Rights of 1776, the Convention declared that " religion or
the duty which we owe to our Creator, and the manner of
discharging it, can be directed only by reason and conviction;" all men, therefore, are entitled to freedom of conscience.[1] This was an expression of conviction, but the
actual repealing of laws compelling dissenters to conform
or suffer the consequences was left to later legislative
action. The penalties were done away with at an early
time, but it was not until 1785 that a positive enactment
was passed relieving men from the laws requiring the fre-
quenting or supporting of religious worship.[2] In the preceding year, 1784, dissenting clergymen had been authorized by law to perform the marriage ceremony and children of parents who had not been joined in wedlock by a
minister of the Established Church were declared to be
legitimate.

Side by side with the establishment of freedom of conscience proceeded the liberalizing of religious observance.
With the abrogation of the penal laws, the Episcopalian
parsons kept on living in their comfortable houses and
cultivating their glebes, but tithes no longer went to them.
They now had to be supported by their parishioners. In
1777, therefore, we find the leading men in several par-
ishes agreeing among themselves to support their rector.
In Albemarle County, Jefferson, Philip Mazzei, Samuel
Taliaferro, and seventeen others subscribed twenty-nine
pounds as the annual stipend of the Reverend Charles
Clay, " who early rejecting the tyrant and tyranny of
Britain proved his religion genuine by its harmony with
the liberties of mankind, . . . [and] ever addressed the God
of battles for victory to our arms, while others impiously

[1] As to the authorship of this clause
and the subject in general see Note at
end of the chapter

[2] Hening's *Statutes of Virginia*, xii,
84.

prayed that our enemies might vanquish and overcome us." The list of subscribers was headed by Jefferson, who gave six pounds, the largest of any single subscription.[1] Depriving the Episcopalian clergymen of public support did not satisfy the dissenters. They thought that all the church property should be sold for the benefit of the people as a whole. The Episcopalians desired to have their church incorporated by law and to have the State levy an assessment for religious purposes. Patrick Henry led in the fight for incorporation and for a general assessment, and Madison headed the forces against him. In 1785, an Incorporation Act was passed to be repealed two years later except in so far as it related to the glebes. No general assessment bill was ever passed, but in November, 1785, one was lost by only three votes.

The Massachusetts constitution of 1780 declared that it was " the right as well as the duty of all men in society " to worship the Supreme Being in the manner and season most agreeable to their consciences. Every denomination of Christians was equally under the protection of the law, but every town or parish must make suitable provision for the public teaching of religion. Every taxpayer was to contribute to the support of religion, but he might direct as to which minister in the town his contribution should be given, — if he did not do this, the money was to go to the support of the regular minister. This was merely continuing the existing practice and it was not until ten years of the next century had passed by that the compulsory payment of money for religious purposes was done away with. In New York the laws establishing religion in certain parts of the province were totally re-

[1] See three most interesting documents that Mr. W. C. Ford found among the autograph collections of the Massachusetts Historical Society and printed in their *Proceedings* for May, 1909, p. 341

pealed and in both New York and Massachusetts, the acts
of 1691 against Roman Catholic priests terminated by
reason of their being repugnant to the principles embodied
in the constitutions of those States.

The New York constitution contained some peculiar
provisions as to religion. Liberty of conscience and worship were guaranteed to every one provided that this
liberty should not be understood to justify practices that
were inconsistent with the peace and safety of the State.
No minister or priest could hold any civil or military
office. Quakers and others who scrupled bearing arms
were not to be compelled to do so, but they must pay
for this exemption such sums as the legislature might
from time to time direct. John Jay was a member of
the convention that made this constitution. With the
family traditions of the dragonnades fresh in recollection
he proposed to give the legislature power to deny toleration to any sect that it pleased. This being voted down,
he moved that no Roman Catholic should enjoy civil
rights or hold any land within the State, but this was
lost by a vote of 19 to 10. Jay and those who thought
with him succeeded, however, in securing the adoption
of a clause forbidding the naturalization of an immigrant
until he had renounced subjection to " every foreign king,
prince, potentate, and state in all matters ecclesiastical
as well as civil." [1] As only native-born citizens and
naturalized persons could exercise the franchise or hold
office under the constitution, this requirement excluded
from power all foreign-born Roman Catholics, and was
intended so to do.

Although freedom of conscience and of worship in reli-

[1] *Journals of the Provincial Congress . . . of New York*, i, 844, 845, 860. J. G. Shea printed a synopsis of anti-Catholic provisions of Revolutionary constitutions in his *Life of Archbishop Carroll*, ii, 157

gious matters had come to be the rule in the United
States, it by no means followed that religious disqualifi-
cations for office no longer existed. The makers of the
Massachusetts constitution of 1780 informed their constituents that while they did not conceive themselves to be
invested with power to set up one sect of Christians
above another, nevertheless they found themselves obliged
to provide for the exclusion from office of those " who
will not disclaim those Principles of Spiritual Jurisdiction
which Roman Catholics in some countries have held, and
which are subversive of a free Government established by
the People." The constitution of 1780, therefore, provided
that all persons chosen to any office under the government
should subscribe a declaration which contained, among
other things, the substance of the old declaration renounc-
ing the authority of all foreign princes and prelates.[1]
Officeholding was also confined to Protestants in New
Hampshire, North Carolina,[2] South Carolina,[3] and Georgia.[4]
The Rhode Islanders, on the other hand, in 1783, repealed
the law excluding Roman Catholics from the freedom of
the corporation which had stood on the statute book for
over a century.[5] In some States, Jews were likewise excluded from office by the requirement of belief in the
Christian religion as in New York and Maryland, and as
to some offices in Massachusetts. Ministers of whatever
religion were disqualified from office in New York [6] and
Maryland. In all the States, those who objected to taking
oaths, as the Quakers and Shakers and Mennonites, and,
at a later time, the Baptists were allowed to affirm. In

[1] See the present work, ii, 455.
[2] Iredell's *Laws of the State of North Carolina*, 280.
[3] Cooper's *Statutes of South Carolina*, i, 138, 139, 141.
[4] *Digest of the Laws of Georgia*, 7.
[5] Massachusetts Historical Society's *Collections*, Third Series, v, 244.
[6] *Journals of the Provincial Congress . . . of New York*, i, 897.

general, it may be said that although religion did not become entirely free and was still partially connected with the government in some States, it is practically true that religion was free in 1787, and that apart from the Roman Catholics and Jews no one was disqualified from office by reason of his religious convictions.

The Constitution of the United States as it came from the Federal Convention was silent on religious questions, as it was on many others. This attracted Patrick Henry's attention, and, partly at his suggestion, one of the amendments proposed by the Virginia ratifying convention was a statement as to freedom of religion in its widest sense. Leading men in other States agreed with Henry in this regard, and the first amendment to the Constitution expressed the general consensus of opinion that the federal government should make no law respecting an establishment of religion or prohibiting the free exercise thereof. One interpretation of this is contained in the treaty that was made with Tripoli in 1796 while Washington was President, and was confirmed by the Senate over which John Adams presided. The eleventh article of this instrument reads: "The Government of the United States is not in any sense founded on the Christian religion." Since treaties made by the President and confirmed by the Senate are the supreme law of the land, this pronouncement would seem to define the United States as the country of free religion.

Educational establishments, depending upon public grants and the income from invested funds, suffered severely during the war, and the supply of students and fees, where education was not free, also diminished. The confiscation of loyalist estates and the acquisition of the crown lands placed at the disposal of the States new funds which were

frequently used for educational purposes. Thus Massachusetts used some of the money obtained from the sale of
her lands in western New York for education, Connecticut
devoted all the proceeds of the sales of lands in the Western Reserve to the same purpose, and Pennsylvania gave
sixty thousand acres of wild lands for public schools. The
legislature of Georgia appropriated money derived from
the sale of wild lands and loyalist property for the establishment of academies in several counties and thereby
partly fulfilled the clause in the constitution of 1777 demanding the establishment and support at the general expense of a school in each county. In South Carolina,
also, the people were alive to the desirability of public
education as is shown by the presentment of the grand
jury of Georgetown in November, 1776: "2. We present
as a Grievance the want of Public Schools in the Interior
parts of the State."[1] It does not appear, however, that
very much was accomplished toward the enlargement of
general educational facilities in that State. In North
Carolina, this period was one of great activity in educational matters, no less than fourteen academies being
authorized by law.[2] Some of these were given lands,
others were permitted to raise money by lotteries, while
others seem to have depended upon private benefactions.

In the matter of higher education, this period was fruitful.
No less than three colleges were founded in South Carolina. In the case of one of these, land which had already
been granted for the establishment of a free school at
Charleston was now to be devoted to founding an institution for higher education at that place.[3] In the neigh-

---

[1] South Carolina manuscripts in the
Library of Congress.
[2] *North Carolina Records,* xxiv
(Laws, 1777-1788).

[3] Cooper's *Statutes of South Carolina,*
iv, 674 (act of 1785).

boring State of Georgia, also, steps were taken for the
founding of an institution of the higher grade to be known
as the University of Georgia. The act of the Assembly
bears date of 1785.[1] The preamble declares that education
is necessary to avoid confusions in a free government
where the people are the rulers. The governor, members
of the Council, Speaker of the House of Assembly, Chief
Justice of the State, and eleven citizens were to form the
" Senatus Academicus of the University of Georgia." The
officers of instruction and government were to be of
the Christian religion, and the property of the university
was exempted from taxation. A most interesting clause
provided that all schools supported by public money should
be considered as parts of the university and be under the
same regulations. It would seem, therefore, that the legislature in making these provisions had in mind the establishment of an educational system like that which was
later worked out in the newer States, west of the Alleghanies. In New York,[2] Pennsylvania,[3] and North Carolina,[4] the state governments also interested themselves in
enlarging the facilities for higher education. Everywhere,
indeed, as much progress was made as the resources of the
country permitted.

In no way was the growing enfranchisement of the mind
more clearly shown than in the case of medical education.
Ordinarily, one aspiring to the physician's place studied with
a practitioner, living in his house, performing the mechanical
parts of the business, as spreading plasters and making

---

[1] *Digest of the Laws of the State of Georgia*, 560.

[2] See acts of May and November, 1784, and of April, 1787, in *Laws of the State of New York*, i, 686; ii, 30, 524.

[3] In 1783, an act was passed for the establishment of Dickinson College in Cumberland County, Pennsylvania, and three years later 60,000 acres of public land were given to it. See *Laws of the Commonwealth of Pennsylvania*, ii, 413; iii, 158.

[4] *North Carolina Records*, xxv, 21, 24.

pills, and accompanying his chief on his daily rounds, thus gaining that knowledge which alone comes from actual contact with human suffering. Some physicians had more than one student. Oftentimes, the training thus gained was of great efficacy and was, occasionally, supplemented by attendance at the lectures and demonstrations in the institutions at Edinburgh and Vienna. The first school for preparation in medicine was the institution that later developed into the College of Physicians of Philadelphia.[1] Its beginnings go back to 1765 and are associated with the names of Morgan, Shippen, and Rush. After being a department of the College of Philadelphia, it became with that institution an integral portion of the University of Pennsylvania. From the beginning, excepting during the most trying years of the war, it prospered, partly on account of the clinical advantages which the Pennsylvania hospital furnished, but more particularly because of the intellectual vigor and enlightenment of those connected with it.

In Massachusetts, the movement to provide a school for the education of physicians came at a somewhat later time, and got its stimulus from the practice afforded in the camps and hospitals of the Revolutionary armies, and also in the facilities for dissection which they afforded. It had its origin in the founding of a medical professorship at Harvard and in the scientific activity of a Boston physician, Dr. John Warren, the younger brother of that more famous Joseph Warren who gave his life at Bunker Hill.[2] The ac-

[1] W. S. W. Ruschenberger's *An Account of the College of Physicians of Philadelphia.* Manasseh Cutler visited the establishment in 1787 and describes it in his journal under date of July 14 (*Life*, i, 279). See also *Catalogue of the Medical Graduates of the University of Pennsylvania; with an Historical Sketch* of the Origin, Progress, and Present State of the Medical Department (Philadelphia, 1836).

[2] Thomas F. Harrington's *Harvard Medical School, A History, Narrative and Documentary* (3 vols., New York, 1905).

tivity in medical circles also brought about the formation
of the Massachusetts Medical Society, whose business, in
part, it was to examine those who wished to practice
physic and give certificates of competence to those who
came up to its standard.   At one time it seemed as if there
would be friction between this society, and the proposed
Medical Institution of Harvard College ; but this was hap-
pily avoided.   The early years of this new medical school
were not very prosperous, owing, no doubt, to its unfortunate location in Cambridge where clinical facilities were
distinctly limited.

Secession from the British Empire enabled the American
people to carry out reforms in the treatment of poverty
that they had long desired to make, but had been unable
to accomplish, owing to the jealousy of the royal government of anything that looked like the protection of
colonial debtors against British creditors.   Possibly, the
two things that most readily come to mind when thinking
of the England of this period are the poor debtors confined
in noisome prisons with thieves, and other criminals, and
the mentally diseased who were exhibited in Bedlam like
so many wild beasts, or chained to the walls of outbuild-
ings connected with the almshouses.   The colonists were
no more merciful and enlightened in dealing with criminals
and maniacs than were the people in England.   The pages of
Henry Fielding, novelist and chairman of Westminster quarter sessions, contain no more gruesome description than
those which have been written of the old copper mine at
Simsbury, Connecticut, where prisoners labored and died almost in darkness, a hundred feet underground.[1]   Those were
the days before convicts were separated from the rest of

---

[1] Noah A. Phelps's *History of Simsbury, Granby and Canton*, chs. ix and
x ; and Richard H. Phelps's *History of*
the *Newgate of Connecticut at Simsbury*.

the community and housed and fed at public charge
They were marked by slitting the nose, slicing the ear, or
by branding and then turned loose to earn their food and
lodging as best they might, or they were transported beyond the home limits and sold to the highest bidders;
for punishment they were hanged, whipped, or pilloried.
Prisons in those days were places of detention for those
awaiting trial, not for those who were convicted.

Glimmerings of better days appear here and there. In
Pennsylvania, a few insane patients had been treated in
the hospital at Philadelphia which existed by virtue of
legislative enactment, although it was supported by private beneficence. In Virginia, in the winter of 1769–1770,
the Assembly provided for the establishment of a hospital
at Williamsburg "for the reception of idiots, lunatics, and
other persons of unsound mind." A committee was appointed, buildings were erected, and within a few years,
the establishment was in working order and is still in existence. It is the oldest institution for the care of the insane at public charge in the United States, if not in the
world.[1]

In the matter of the punishment of crime, there was little
betterment, and, indeed, the growing vigor of administration may have made the criminal's lot worse than it was
in the older time. In Massachusetts, in 1789, there occurred
an execution that arouses wonderment even to a student
well versed in the inhumanity of the eighteenth century.
The culprit was Rachel Wall. One evening she seized
hold of a girl on the public street, tore from her head her
bonnet, flung her down, took her shoes and buckles and

---

[1] The act is in Hening's *Statutes of
Virginia*, viii, 378. In 1873, Dr. Wilmer
of Williamsburg delivered a " Centennial
Address," which is printed in *Report of*
the *Eastern Lunatic Asylum of Virginia*
for 1873, pp. 18–31. See also L. G. Tyler's
Williamsburg, ch. xiv.

fled.   Possibly the fact that Rachel Wall was an old of-
fender may have influenced the jury, judges, and John
Hancock, the governor.   None of them seem to have had
the least doubt that the proper punishment for highway
robbery was death.   Rachel Wall was hanged and this
crime continued to be so treated in Massachusetts until
1804.[1]

Instances like the above were rare, probably because
highway robbery was not common, but volumes might be
filled with descriptions of punishments that would now
seem to be brutal in the extreme.   The topic is not a
promising one, but cannot be passed over in view of the
clause in the Eighth Amendment of the Constitution forbidding cruel and unusual punishments.   What seemed to our
Revolutionary forefathers as an ordinary everyday mode
of meeting crime to us would appear cruel and most unusual.   In the famous report of the Virginia law revisors
Jefferson suggested that robbery and burglary should be
punished by four years hard labor and reparation of double
the amount of the property taken.   Some of his suggestions, however, have a more rigorous sound.   The
poisoner was to suffer death by poisoning; the duellist
to be hanged, and if he were the challenger, his body after
death to be gibbeted.   Maiming and branding of criminals
clearly induced such practices on the part of private persons
against their enemies.   For these maimers Jefferson provided that the culprit should be disfigured in like sort with
his victim; if his own countenance lacked the part disfigured, he should suffer in some other of equal value to be
determined by a jury.   These suggestions are memorable
as showing how little way the foremost progressive of
his day had gone in some sociological directions.

[1] Massachusetts Historical Society's *Proceedings*, Second Series, xix, 178.

In the thirty years that have just been passed in review, the American people had seceded from the mother country, established republican forms of government within their thirteen States, and had gone far in the readjustment of economic life to their new conditions. They had devised a colonial system that harmonized with their political principles and was to succeed in the coming century beyond that of any other colonizing country of the earth. They had adopted a form of federal government that was new to the world, republican in essence and imperial in power. These were large achievements for a single generation. No wonder that they looked forward with hope to the coming years. Announcing the ratification of the Constitution by New Hampshire and Virginia, the " Pennsylvania Packet" on July 14, 1788, thus advertised the establishment of the new union : —

"SHIP NEWS—EXTRA

"Arrived safe in port, the ship 'Federal Constitution,' *Perpetual Union*, commander. In her came passengers *Flourishing Commerce, Public Faith, Confidence, Justice.*"

NOTE

I. Religion in Virginia. — Owing to the uncritical and filiopietistic assertions by Virginia writers and biographers, there has been much discussion as to the part played by the Old Dominion in bringing about religious liberty. The authorship of the famous sixteenth article in the Bill of Rights has been claimed for Henry;[1] it probably represented the necessity of conciliating the dissenters.[2] This declaration was in general terms and needed specific legislation to make it available. This was done in 1776, 1777, and 1779, but it was not until the passage of the act of 1785 that the precepts of the Bill of Rights were complied with. This law was drawn by Jefferson. It begins with the assertion that Almighty God hath created the mind free and that all attempts to influence it by punishments or by " civil incapacitations " are " a departure from the plan of the holy Author of our religion "; that civil rights had no more dependence on religion than on opinions in physic and geometry, and that to suffer the civil magistrate to intrude into the field of opinion destroys all religious liberty. For these reasons, " no man shall be compelled to frequent or support any religious worship, place, or minister whatsoever."

The doctrines embodied in this preamble aroused the indignation of " A Citizen of Philadelphia." He declared [3] that the act " seems calculated to destroy all religion, and to open the gates of scepticism and immorality to the people of that state." He thought the Assembly of Virginia must be deemed unacquainted with the nature of religion; " for who ever read of any in which the author of it did not endeavour to coerce the mind into an obedience to it."

---

[1] American Historical Association's *Papers*, ii, 23. Stillé's reply is in *ibid.*, iii, 205, and Henry's rejoinder in the same volume, p. 457. On this general subject see Philip Schaff's " Church and State in the United States " in *ibid.*, ii, 389.

[2] See Jefferson's *Notes on Virginia*, " Query xvii"; W. H. Foote's *Sketches of Virginia*, i, chs. xiv, xv; R. B. Semple's *The Baptists in Virginia* (Richmond, 1810), 32 ; C. F. James's *Documentary History of the Struggle*

for *Religious Liberty in Virginia;* W. T. Thom's " Struggle for Religious Freedom in Virginia : the Baptists " in *Johns Hopkins University Studies*, ser. 18, Nos. 10–12, pp. 54–81.

[3] *Considerations on an Act of the Legislature of Virginia, entitled, An Act for the Establishment of Religious Freedom* [J. Swanwick] (Philadelphia, 1786). The legislation may be easily followed in Hening's *Statutes of Virginia*, ix, xi. The act of 1785 is in the latter volume, p. 84.

This was printed in 1786. In 1887, Dr. Charles J. Stillé of Philadelphia denied that Virginia was the first State to separate religion and government and gave that honor to " Roger Williams and to Benjamin Franklin and his colleagues in the Pennsylvania Convention of 1776."

INDEX